Readings in
SOCIAL PSYCHOLOGY

Readings in _____
SOCIAL PSYCHOLOGY
General, Classic, and Contemporary Selections
FOURTH EDITION

WAYNE A. LESKO
Marymount University

ALLYN AND BACON
Boston ■ London ■ Toronto ■ Sydney ■ Tokyo ■ Singapore

Senior Editor: Carolyn O. Merrill
Editorial Assistant: Lara Zeises
Director of Field Marketing: Joyce Nilsen
Editorial-Production Administrator: Annette Joseph
Editorial-Production Service: Susan Freese, Communicáto, Ltd.
Electronic Composition: Cabot Computer Services
Composition Buyer: Linda Cox
Manufacturing Buyer: Megan Cochran
Cover Administrator: Jenny Hart
Cover Designer: Brian Gogolin

Library of Congress Cataloging-in-Publication Data

Readings in social psychology : general, classic, and contemporary
  selections / [compiled by] Wayne A. Lesko. — 4th ed.
      p. cm.
  Includes bibliographical references and index.
  ISBN 0-205-28720-4 (alk. paper)
  1. Social psychology. I. Lesko, Wayne A.
HM1033.R43 2000
302—dc21   99-20563
                                                       CIP

Printed in the United States of America

10 9 8 7 6 5 4 3   04 03 02 01 00

To my son, Matt

Brief Contents

Contents

Preface

THE TYPICAL SOCIAL psychology class ranges from sophomore through graduate levels, and the members may include majors who are required to take the course as well as nonmajors who have elected to do so. Regardless of the level or the audience, many instructors—myself included—feel that a collection of readings is a valuable means of promoting an understanding of the discipline.

Current collections of readings typically fall into two categories: professional articles from journals in the field or popular articles reprinted from such magazines as *Psychology Today*. The category of professional readings may include contemporary articles, classic articles, or a combination of the two. These articles provide excellent insight into the core of social psychology by describing not only the research outcomes but also the detailed methodology for how the results were obtained. Popular articles, on the other hand, lack the scientific rigor of journal articles but often present a broad overview of a number of findings pertaining to a particular topic. Clearly, both types of readings have advantages and disadvantages associated with them, depending on the particular level at which the course is taught.

In nearly two decades of teaching social psychology at both the undergraduate and graduate levels, I have found that students seem to respond best to a variety of reading formats. Popular articles are easy to understand and provide a good overview, while also generating critical thinking about an issue. Research articles provide insight into the methodological issues in social psychology and help the student develop a critical attitude in evaluating research contributions and conclusions. Classic research articles familiarize the student with early research that has had a lasting impact on social psychology, while contemporary works illustrate issues currently being studied and the methods used to investigate them.

Like the first three editions, this fourth edition of *Readings in Social Psychology: General, Classic, and Contemporary Selections* is designed to provide exactly that breadth of exposure to the different sources of information available in the field. In response to feedback from users of the last three editions of the book, as well as the need to update the selection of contemporary articles, more than half of the articles in this edition are new.

As in the previous editions, each chapter begins with an introduction to the topic, which is followed by three articles: one general (popular), one classic, and one contemporary. Each article begins with a short introduction that sets the stage, or provides a context for the article. Each article is followed by a set of Critical Thinking Questions, which ask the student to examine critically some part of the article presented, to speculate about generalizations and implications of the research, and, in some cases, to suggest new studies based on the information in the article. The classic articles are also followed by a list of Additional

Related Readings for students who may wish to examine more contemporary articles on the same topic.

The topical organization of *Readings in Social Psychology: General, Classic, and Contemporary Selections* (fourth edition) directly parallels that of Baron and Byrne's *Social Psychology: Understanding Human Interaction* (ninth edition). Even so, this edition of *Readings in Social Psychology* can be adapted readily for use with any other text or used in lieu of a text, depending on how the course is taught. Likewise, the book can be used with classes of varying levels, by structuring which articles will be emphasized and in how much detail they will be examined.

Finally, all articles are presented verbatim, in their entirety, since it is my firm belief that one valuable skill gained by students from reading research articles is the ability to abstract pertinent information from an original source. The only exception to this, necessitated by copyright ownership, is found in Table 1 of Article 14, which is an abbreviation of the Bem Sex Role Inventory.

A Note to the Reader, which follows this Preface, offers some suggestions on how to get the most out of this book. It is especially recommended for students who do not have an extensive background in reading research articles.

At this point, perhaps some notice is in order about several of the articles. Understandably, everything is representative of the time in which it was written, both in terms of the ideas presented and the language used. Some of the classic articles in this collection were written 30 or more years ago and are out of step with current language style. Moreover, some of the descriptions made and observations offered would be considered condescending and even offensive by today's standards. Please keep this in mind, and consider the context in which each of the articles was written.

ACKNOWLEDGMENTS

At Allyn and Bacon, I would like to thank Carolyn Merrill, Senior Editor, and Amy Goldmacher, former Editorial Assistant, for their guidance and help with the format of the book. I likewise wish to extend my gratitude to Sue Freese, of Communicáto, Ltd., for her excellent copyediting of this book. Thanks also go to Robert A. Baron, Rensselaer Polytechnic Institute, and Donn Byrne, State University of New York–Albany, who provided input about organization and content of the various editions.

I am especially indebted to my graduate and undergraduate students in social psychology at Marymount University, whose honest feedback on the contents of the first three editions helped me create a new, improved book of readings.

I also want to thank the various friends, colleagues, and graduate assistants who helped me and provided encouragement and advice over the many editions of this collection of readings. Without their input, this work would not have been possible.

Last but not least, I thank all of the authors and publishers of the articles contained in this book for their permission to reprint these materials. Their fine work in advancing the field of social psychology is what literally made this book possible.

W. L.

A Note to the Reader

AS YOU EMBARK on your study of social psychology, you will soon discover that the field is broad indeed. Many different topics will be encountered, but they all are related by the common thread that defines social psychology—namely, the study of individual behavior in social situations.

As a collection of readings, this book is designed to expose you to some of the most important areas of study within social psychology. Just as the topics found in the area of social psychology are diverse, so, too, are the ways in which social psychological knowledge is disseminated. If you are new to the field, most likely you have encountered one common source of information: articles in nonprofessional sources. For example, newspaper and magazine articles may present the information from some study in social psychology. Typically nontechnical pieces directed to the general public, these articles summarize a number of studies on a given topic and are fairly easy to comprehend. Each of the 14 chapters that comprise this book begins with such an article—what I have termed a *general* reading.

A second source of information is actually the backbone of social psychology: articles that appear in professional journals of the field. These articles are the primary means by which new ideas and the results of research are shared with the professional community. While they tend to be more technical and difficult to read compared to the general works, professional articles have the advantage of providing readers with sufficient detail to draw their own conclusions, rather than be forced to rely on someone else's interpretation of the information. Some of these articles represent research that has stood the test of time and are generally regarded as *classics* in the field; the second reading found in each chapter is such an article.

Finally, the last type of article found in each chapter is labeled *contemporary*. These articles are fairly recent examples of research currently being conducted in social psychology.

The format of each chapter is the same. Each opens with a brief introduction to the chapter topic; one general, one classic, and one contemporary article are then presented, in that order. Each article begins with an introduction written by me, which serves to focus your perspective before reading. Every article is then followed by Critical Thinking Questions. In some cases, these questions directly refer to information contained in the articles; in others, the questions are more speculative, asking you to go beyond the data presented. Finally, the classic articles contain Additional Related Readings. The references included here are either recent articles that address the same issues discussed in the classic article (a way of updating the current status of research on the topic) or a topic similar to the one discussed in the original. In either case, the interested student can use these references to find more information on the topic.

All of the articles in this collection are reprinted in their entirety. Not a word has been abridged or altered. (Again, the only exception is Table 1 of Article 14, which has been abbreviated due to a copyright restriction.) For the general articles, this should not be a problem for anyone. However, if this is the first time that you are reading journal articles from their primary sources, some assistance might be in order. First of all, do not allow yourself to be overwhelmed or intimidated. New students often are confused by some of the terminology that is used and are left totally dumbfounded by the detailed statistics that are usually part of such articles. Approached in the right way, these articles need not be intimidating and should be comprehensible to any reader willing to expend a little effort.

In reading a research article, I would like to make the following suggestions:

- Most articles begin with an Abstract or end with a Summary. If these are provided, begin by carefully reading them; they will give you an overview of why the study was conducted, what was done, and what the results were.

- Next, read the Introduction fairly carefully; this is where the authors describe previous research in the area and develop the logic for why they are conducting the experiment in the first place.

- The Methods section describes in detail the techniques used by the researchers to conduct their study; read this section thoroughly in order to understand exactly what was done.

- The next section, Results, is where the authors describe what was found in the study. This is often the most technically difficult part of the article; from your standpoint, you might want to skim over this part, focusing only on the sections that verbally describe what the results were. Do not worry about the detailed statistical analyses that are presented.

- Finally, you might want to read the Discussion section in some detail; here, the authors discuss the findings and implications of the study and perhaps suggest avenues for further study.

To summarize: Each article is fairly straightforward to comprehend, provided that you do not allow yourself to get too bogged down in the details and thus frustrated. The journey may seem difficult at times, but the end result—an appreciation and understanding of the complex issues of human social behavior—will be worth it. Enjoy!

W. L.

Readings in
SOCIAL PSYCHOLOGY

Chapter One

THE FIELD OF
SOCIAL PSYCHOLOGY

AN INTRODUCTION TO a course such as social psychology often includes a section on research methods. Nonmajors confronting this topic often wonder why they need to know about research methods when in all likelihood they will never actually conduct research. Whether you are majoring in psychology or not, familiarity with research methods will benefit you, for several reasons.

First, it will help you understand the studies that make up the knowledge base of social psychology. Familiarity with methodology will allow you to make informed decisions about the conclusions drawn by various studies. Second, and perhaps more important, some knowledge of research issues will allow you to be an intelligent consumer of research information. Results of studies often are reported to the general public in newspapers and magazines. Knowing something about the methods used to produce these results will better prepare you to decide whether the conclusions drawn are warranted. Finally, it is useful to fully appreciate why the results of experimental data are needed instead of just relying on common sense. Article 1, "Folk Wisdom: Was Your Grandmother Right?" shows how folk wisdom (i.e., common sense) often is contradictory and hence not very useful as a guideline for behavior.

Research is the basic underpinning of psychological science. Given the subject matter of social psychology, it is often difficult, if not impossible, to get unbiased results if subjects know what is being observed. For that reason, psychologists, in general, and social psychologists, in particular, often have relied on deception as a means of obtaining naive subjects. But what ethical issues are involved in the use of deception? And what if deception is so widely used that subjects expect to be deceived whenever they participate in a research study? What, if any, are the alternatives to the use of deception? These are some of the questions addressed in Article 2, "Human Use of Human Subjects."

Finally, Article 3 serves as a contemporary follow-up to the second article. "The Rise and Fall of Deception in Social Psychology and Personality Research, 1921 to 1994" reviews the extent to which research has employed deception over the years. It also provides some explanations as to why the use of deception was rare during the early years of social psychology research, dramatically increased during the 1960s and 1970s (the timeframe when Article 2 was published), and then began to decrease.

ARTICLE 1 _____

At the heart of all the articles you will read in this book is *research methodology*. Given a question you want to investigate, how do you go about actually collecting data?

There are a number of different ways of conducting social psychological research. One broad distinction is between *experimental methods* and *correlational (nonexperimental) methods*. Each method has potential advantages and disadvantages. One is not necessarily better than the other; it depends on what you are investigating.

Students encountering research methods literature for the first time are often surprised at the difficulty of designing and conducting a good piece of research. It is not as easy as it might seem on the surface. Numerous artifacts that can affect the outcome of a study need to be accounted for and controlled. An examination of the introductory chapters of most social psychology texts will give you a better understanding of some of these issues.

Sometimes, a study obtains results that are quite unexpected and surprises readers. Other times, however, readers may feel that the outcome of a study was totally expected—indeed, that it was just common sense. The reaction to such an article often is to question why it is even necessary to test the obvious.

The only problem with common sense is that it is often contradictory. For example, to whom are people most attracted: people like themselves or people different from themselves? Common sense would predict that "Birds of a feather flock together"; on the other hand, "Opposites attract." So which is it? As it turns out, common sense is not such a good predictor of actual behavior. The only way to know for sure is to go out and empirically test the concept.

The following article by Robert Epstein examines a number of common-sense ideas that have been passed down to us in light of what current research tells us about their validity. The article underscores the necessity of testing ideas empirically and why even supposedly obvious notions must be exposed to scientific scrutiny.

Folk Wisdom
Was Your Grandmother Right?
■ Robert Epstein

The table next to me at Fillipi's restaurant was a noisy one. Two men and two women in their 20s and 30s were arguing about a relationship issue. One of the men—call him Male #1—would soon be leaving the country for six months. Would the passion he shared with his beloved survive? The exchange went something like this:

Female #1 (probably the girlfriend): "When you really love someone, being apart makes you care even more. If someone is good to you, you sometimes take that for granted when the person is around every day. But when he's gone, all that good treatment is gone, too, and you realize just how much you had. You really start to yearn for him."

Male #2 (looking lustfully at Female #1, even though he seemed to be with the other woman): "That's right. The same thing happens when your parents die. You really start to miss and appreciate

Reprinted from *Psychology Today*, 1997 (November/December), 30, 46–50, 76. Reprinted with permission from *Psychology Today* magazine. Copyright © 1997 (Sussex Publishers, Inc.).

them. You even rewrite the past, forgetting the bad things and focusing on the good times and the kindness they showed you."

Female #1 (starting to look lovingly at Male #2): "Exactly. Everyone knows that absence makes the heart grow fonder."

Then Male #1, the one probably on his way to Thailand, spoke up. "Well, but . . ." He faltered, thinking hard about going on. All eyes were on him. He took a deep breath.

And then he said, slowly and deliberately, "But don't we also say, 'Out of sight, out of mind'?"

This was not good for anyone's digestion. Female #1's face turned the color of marinara sauce. Male #2 smiled mischievously, presumably imagining himself in bed with Female #1. Female #2 looked back and forth between her date and Female #1, also apparently imagining them in bed together. And Male #1, not wanting to face the carnage, lowered his eyes and tapped out a strange rhythm on the table top with his fork. Was he thinking about the classy Thai brothels he had read about on the Internet?

TRUTH OR POPPYCOCK?

"Absence makes the heart grow fonder" and "Out of sight, out of mind" are examples of folk wisdom—folk psychology, you might say. All cultures pass along wisdom of this sort—sometimes in the form of proverbs; sometimes through songs (remember Paul Simon's "Fifty Ways to Leave Your Lover"?), rhymes (Mother Goose), or stories (Aesop's fables); sometimes through laws and public information campaigns ("Stay alive, don't drink and drive"); and always through religion ("Do unto others as you would have them do unto you").

But folk wisdom is an unreliable, inconsistent kind of wisdom. For one thing, most proverbs coexist with their exact opposites, or at least with proverbs that give somewhat different advice. Does absence truly make the heart grow fonder, or are loved ones out of mind when they're out of sight? And isn't variety the spice of life? (If Male #1 had come up with *that* one, he might have been murdered on the spot.)

Do opposites attract, or do birds of a feather flock together? Should you love the one you're with, or would that be like changing horses in midstream? We all know that he who hesitates is lost, but doesn't haste make waste, and isn't patience a virtue, and don't fools rush in, and aren't you supposed to look before you leap?

And, sure, money is power, but aren't the best things in life supposed to be free? And since time is money, and money is power, and power corrupts, does that mean time also corrupts? Well, maybe so. After all, the Devil finds work for idle hands.

I've only covered a few well-known proverbs from the English-speaking world. Each culture passes along its own wisdom, which is not always meaningful to outsiders. In India, for example, people say, "Call on God, but row away from the docks," and Romanians advise, "Do not put your spoon into the pot that does not boil for you." In Bali they say, "Goodness shouts and evil whispers," while in Tibet the message is, "Goodness speaks in a whisper, but evil shouts."

You get the idea. Proverbs that relay wisdom about how we're supposed to live do not necessarily supply useful or reliable advice. In fact, proverbs are sometimes used merely to justify what we already do or believe, rather than as guidelines for action. What's more, we tend to *switch* proverbs to suit our current values and ideals. A young man might rationalize risky action by pointing out that "You only live once"; later in life—if he's still around—he'll probably tell you, "Better safe than sorry."

Is the situation hopeless? Can we glean any truths at all from the wisdom of the ages?

The behavioral sciences can help. Science is a set of methods for testing the validity of statements about the world—methods for getting as close to "truth" as we currently know how to get. Psychologists and other scientists have spent more than a century testing the validity of statements about human behavior, thinking, and emotions. How well does folk psychology stand up to scientific inquiry? What do we find when we test a statement like "Absence makes the heart grow fonder"? If, as I do, you sometimes rely on folk wisdom to guide your actions or teach your children, this is a question well worth considering.

Here's how five common proverbs measure up to behavioral research.

CONFESSION IS GOOD FOR THE SOUL

Psychologists don't study the soul, of course. But, says psychologist James W. Pennebaker, Ph.D., "If we define 'soul' loosely as who you are, how you feel about yourself, and how healthy you are, then confession is good for the soul." Pennebaker, a researcher at the University of Texas at Austin, is one of several behavioral scientists who have looked carefully at the results of "self-disclosure"—talking or writing about private feelings and concerns. His research suggests that for about two-thirds of us, self-disclosure has enormous emotional and physical benefits. Pennebaker's newly revised book, *Opening Up: The Healing Power of Expressing Emotion,* summarizes 15 years of compelling research on this subject.

Self-disclosure, as you might expect, can greatly reduce shame or guilt. In fact, studies of suspected criminals showed that they acted far more relaxed after confessing their crimes—despite the fact that punishment now awaited them. Self-disclosure may also provide the power behind talk therapy. "The fact that self-disclosure is beneficial," says Pennebaker, "may explain why all forms of psychotherapy seem to be helpful. Whether the therapy is behavioral or psychoanalytic, in the beginning the clients tell their stories."

Perhaps most intriguing are the physical effects of "confession." Pennebaker has found that self-disclosure may actually boost the immune system, spurring production of white blood cells that attack invading microorganisms, increasing production of antibodies, and heightening the body's response to vaccination.

But what about those other proverbs that advise us to keep our mouths shut? "Let sleeping dogs lie." "Least said is soonest mended." "Many have suffered by talking, few by silence." Can self-disclosure do harm? According to Pennebaker, self-disclosure is not likely to be beneficial when it's forced. University of Notre Dame psychologist Anita Kelly, Ph.D., has suggested, moreover, that revealing secrets may be harmful if the confidant is likely to be judgmental. And a 1989 study conducted by Maria Sauzier, M.D., of Harvard Medical School, showed that people often regret disclosures of child abuse. Sauzier found that nearly half of the parents whose children had disclosed sexual abuse (usually to the other parent or a therapist) felt that both the children and the families were harmed by the disclosures. And 19 percent of the adolescents who confessed that they had been abused regretted making the disclosures. In general, however, confession seems to be a surprisingly beneficial act.

ALL WORK AND NO PLAY MAKES JACK A DULL BOY

To me, the most frightening scene in the movie *The Shining* was the one in which actress Shelley Duvall, concerned that her husband (Jack Nicholson) was going crazy, approached the desk at which he had spent several months supposedly writing a novel. There she found hundreds of pages containing nothing but the sentence, "All work and no play makes Jack a dull boy" typed thousands of times on a manual typewriter. I've always wondered who did all that typing! And I've also wondered about the truth of the proverb. Once again, we're also faced with contradictory bits of folk wisdom that urge us to work until we drop: "Rest makes rusty." "Labor warms, sloth harms." "Labor is itself a pleasure."

Is too much work, without the balance of leisure activity ("play"), actually harmful? Research suggests that the answer is yes, with one possible exception: if you love your work—in other words, if you've been able to make your *avocation* your *vocation*—then work may provide you with some of the benefits of play.

In the 1940s, anthropologist Adam Curle pointed out that the distinction between work and leisure seems to be an unfortunate product of modern society. In many traditional cultures, he wrote, "there is not even a word for work." Work and play "are all of a piece," part of the integrated structure of daily living. But modern society has created the need for people to earn a living, an endeavor that can be difficult and can easily get out of hand. Hence, the modern pursuit of "leisure time" and "balance"—correctives for the desperate measures people take to pay their bills.

Study after study confirms the dangers of overwork. It may or may not make you a dull person, but it clearly dulls your mind. For example, recent research on fire fighters by Peter Knauth, Ph.D., shows that long work shifts increase reaction time and lower alertness. And studies with emergency room physicians show that overwork increases errors and impedes judgment. Indeed, a Hollywood cameraman, coming off an 18-hour work shift, made news recently when he lost control of his car and died in a crash.

Conversely, leisure activities have been shown in numerous studies by researchers Howard and Diane Tinsley, Virginia Lewis, and others, to relieve stress, improve mood, increase life satisfaction, and even boost the immune system.

Curiously, the hard-driven "type A" personalities among us are not necessarily Dull Jacks. According to a recent study of more than 300 college students by Robert A. Hicks, Ph.D., and his colleagues, type-A students claim to engage in considerably more leisure activities than their relaxed, type-B counterparts. Type As may simply live "more intensely" than type Bs, whether they're on the job or goofing off.

The distinction between work and play is, to some extent, arbitrary. But it's clear that if you spend too much time doing things you don't want to do, your performance, health, and sense of well-being will suffer.

BOYS WILL BE BOYS

The widely held (though politically incorrect) belief that boys are predisposed from birth to feel, learn, and perform differently from girls is strongly supported by research. For example, boys are, on average, considerably more aggressive than girls. They are left-handed more frequently than girls and tend to be better at math and at spatial rotation tasks. Girls, meanwhile, may perform certain kinds of memory tasks better. They also start talking earlier than boys, and, at the playground, they're more likely to imitate boys than boys are to imitate girls. And boys tend to listen more with their right ear, while girls tend to listen with both ears equally. These findings generally hold up cross-culturally, which suggests that they are at least somewhat independent of environmental influences. Upbringing plays an important role in gender differences, of course—even in the first days after birth, parents treat boy babies differently from girls—but converging evidence from psychology, neuroscience, and evolutionary biology suggests that many gender differences are actually programmed from birth, if not from conception.

Since the brain is the mechanism that generates behavior, where we find behavioral differences, we should also find neurological differences. Indeed, recent research suggests a host of differences between male and female brains. For example, although, on average, male brains are larger than female brains, the hemispheres of the brain seem to be better connected in females, which may help explain why females are more sensitive and emotional than males.

Behavior is also driven by hormones. Here, too, there are significant gender differences. From birth, testosterone levels are higher in males, which helps to account for males' aggressiveness. June Reinisch, Ph.D., then at Indiana University, studied boys and girls whose mothers had been exposed to antimiscarriage drugs that mimic testosterone. Not surprisingly, she found that these children of both sexes were considerably more aggressive than their counterparts with normal testosterone levels. But even among the exposed children, the boys were more aggressive than the girls.

So boys will indeed be boys (and, by implication, girls will be girls). But this is only true "on average." Male and female traits overlap considerably, which means that a particular male could be more emotional than most females and a particular female could be better at math than most males. To be fair, you have to go case by case.

EARLY TO BED, AND EARLY TO RISE, MAKES A MAN HEALTHY, WEALTHY, AND WISE

This proverb, often attributed to Ben Franklin, actually seems to have originated in the late 1400s, and Franklin may have lifted it from a collection of adages published in 1656. Historical trivia aside, research on sleep suggests that the proverb gives sound advice—but only because our culture is out-of-synch with the biology of nearly half the population.

Here's how it works: it's long been known that the body has natural rhythms. Those that occur on a 24-hour cycle are called "circadian" and include cycles of temperature change, wakefulness, and eating. For most people, these cycles are highly resistant to change. This much you probably have heard, but what you might not know is that there are two distinctly different circadian rhythm patterns. "Larks"—who show what researchers call "morningness" (honest!)—are people whose cycles peak early in the day. Not surprisingly, larks awaken early and start the day strong. "Owls"—people inclined toward "eveningness"—peak late in the day. In both cases, the peaks are associated with better performance on memory tasks, quicker reaction times, heightened alertness, and cheerful moods. Some people are extreme larks or owls, others are moderates, and a few fit neither category.

There's a problem here, especially if, like me, you're an extreme owl. The trouble is that many important human activities—business meetings, job interviews, weddings, classes, and so on—are conducted during daylight hours, when larks have a distinct advantage. Not surprisingly, owls spend much of their time griping about how out-of-synch they seem to be. A 1978 study of college students by Wilse B. Webb, Ph.D., and Michael H. Bonnet, Ph.D., of the University of Florida, paints a grim picture for people like me: "Larks reported waking up when they expected to, waking up feeling more rested, and waking up more easily than the owls." Larks also reported having "fewer worries" and getting "more adequate sleep," and they awakened feeling physically better than owls. The differences were even greater, moreover, when owls tried to adapt to the lark sleep pattern. What's more, these problems can impair not only owls' sense of restedness but also their bank account; a study of Navy personnel suggests that people who sleep well make considerably more money than people who sleep poorly.

The long and short of it is that if your biorhythms allow you easily to "go to bed with the lamb and rise with the lark" (another old proverb), you may indeed end up with more money, better health, and more life satisfaction—but only because your internal clock is more in-synch with the stock exchange.

SPARE THE ROD
AND SPOIL THE CHILD

A recent headline in my local newspaper proclaimed, "Spanking Backfires, Latest Study Says." I cringe when I see stories like this, because I believe they ultimately harm many children. People have come to confuse discipline with "abuse," which is quite a different beast. "Discipline"—whether in the form of "time outs," reprimands, or spankings—is absolutely necessary for parenting. Extensive research by psychologist Diana Baumrind, Ph.D., and others, has shown that permissive parenting produces children who can't handle independence and are unable to

behave in a socially responsible manner. A great many social problems that we face today may be the inadvertent product of a generation of well-meaning, misinformed, overly-permissive parents.

However, if all you provide is discipline, without affection and emotional support—the "authoritarian" parenting style—you can damage your children. Offspring of authoritarian parents tend to be hostile and defiant, and, like the victims of permissive parents, they too have trouble with independence.

The most effective parenting style involves both a high level of discipline and ample affection and support. That's the best approach for producing children who are self-reliant, socially responsible, and successful in their own relationships, research shows.

In the latest anti-spanking study, published in August by University of New Hampshire sociologist Murray Straus, Ph.D., children between the ages of 6 to 9 who were spanked more than three times a week displayed more misbehavior two years later. Doesn't this show that spanking causes misbehavior? Not at all. Correlational studies are difficult to interpret. Perhaps without those spankings, the kids would have been even worse off. It's also possible that many of these spankings were unnecessary or excessive, and that it was this inappropriate discipline that sparked the later misbehavior.

Conversely, at least eight studies with younger kids show that spanking can indeed improve behavior. The age of the child, in fact, is probably important. Children under the age of six seem to regard spanking as a parent's right. But older kids may view it as an act of aggression, and in such cases spanking's effects may not be so benign.

Punishment, verbal or physical, applied in moderation and with the right timing, is a powerful teaching tool. It should not be the first or the only tool that a parent uses, but it has its place.

TRUTH À LA CARTE

But what about the restaurant debate? Does absence make the heart grow fonder or not? Alas, not enough research has been conducted to shed much light on this question. We do know that "out of sight, out of mind" is true when we're fresh from the womb; young babies will behave as if a toy has vanished into thin air when the toy is moved out of sight. But our memories quickly improve. Research conducted by Julia Vormbrock, Ph.D., and others, shows that children grow more fond of their caregivers when they're separated from them—at least for a few days. After two weeks of separation, however, most children become "detached," reports Vormbrock.

Psychologist Robert Pelligrini, Ph.D., once asked 720 young adults about separation, and two-thirds said that "absence makes the heart grow fonder" seemed more true than "out of sight, out of mind." A poll, however, doesn't tell us much about the truth of the matter. To settle things, we'll need an experiment. Hmmm. First we'll need 100 couples, whom we'll give various tests of "fondness." Then we'll assign, at random, half of the couples to a Control Group and half to an Absence Group. Next we'll separate the partners in each couple in our Absence Group by, say, 1,000 miles for six months—somehow providing jobs, housing, and social support for every person we relocate. Finally, we'll readminister our fondness tests to all 100 couples. If we find significantly greater

---

RATING THE PROVERBS

HERE'S A QUICK RUNDOWN on how well some other common proverbs measure up to research findings:

★★★★★ LOOKS GOOD
★★★★ SOME EVIDENCE SUPPORTS IT
★★★ NOT CLEAR
★★ SOME EVIDENCE CASTS DOUBT
★ SCRAP HEAP

"ONCE BITTEN, TWICE SHY." Behind almost every dog or cat phobia, there's a bite or scratch. ★★★★★

"PRACTICE MAKES PERFECT." Even the brain-injured can often learn new material with sufficient repetition. ★★★★

"MISERY LOVES COMPANY." Depressed people often shun company, which unfortunately is part of the problem. ★★

"TWO HEADS ARE BETTER THAN ONE." Teams or groups typically produce better solutions than individuals do. ★★★★

"COLD HANDS, WARM HEART." Cold hands, poor circulation. See your physician. ★

"EVERY CLOUD HAS A SILVER LINING." Not really, but therapy techniques like cognitive restructuring can get you to think so, and that can get you through the day. ★★★

"OLD HABITS DIE HARD." When we fail at a task, we tend to resort to old behavior patterns, even those from childhood. ★★★★

"YOU CAN'T TEACH AN OLD DOG NEW TRICKS." You'll feel better, think more clearly, and may even live longer if you keep learning throughout life. ★★

"FAMILIARITY BREEDS CONTEMPT." People tend to like what's familiar. ★

"BLOOD WILL TELL." For better or worse, genes really do set limits on both physical characteristics and behavior. ★★★★

"A WOMAN'S PLACE IS IN THE HOME." Only when artificial barriers keep her there. ★

"WHEN THE CAT'S AWAY, THE MICE WILL PLAY." Kids and employees tend to slack off when their parents or supervisors are out of sight. ★★★★

"THERE'S NO ACCOUNTING FOR TASTES." Until you look at upbringing, biochemistry, evolutionary influences, and so on. ★★

levels of fondness in the separated couples than in the unseparated couples, we'll have strong support for the idea that absence makes the heart grow fonder.

Any volunteers? What? You would never subject yourself to such an absurd procedure? Well, fortunately, no one would ever conduct such research, either.

And that's the bottom line: the behavioral sciences can provide useful insights about how we should lead our lives, but there are limits to the kind of research that can be conducted with people. Folk wisdom may be flawed, but, in some instances, it's all we've got or will ever have. So don't put all you eggs in one basket.

CRITICAL THINKING QUESTIONS

1. A number of proverbs are rated in the box at the end of the article. Select one of the proverbs, and design a study that would test its validity.

2. Select one of the proverbs referred to in Question 1, and find a study that has been conducted on the topic. Summarize the results.

3. In addition to the folk wisdom mentioned in the article, what are other examples of common-sense ideas that contradict one another?

4. Many people rely on folk wisdom to guide their actions or explain certain situations. Is doing so ineffective or even dangerous? Or does folk wisdom (or common sense) still play a useful role in helping people manage their lives? Summarize the pros and cons of relying on folk wisdom as a guide to behavior.

ARTICLE 2 _____

Have you ever participated in a social psychology experiment? What were you thinking while you were participating? Were you accepting of the situation and the explanation you were given by the researcher, or were you trying to figure out the real purpose of the experiment? If you were doing the latter, you would be in good company, as many people have come to associate psychological research (and in particular, social psychology research) with the use of deception.

Deception has always been a staple in the research conducted in the field. But what exactly is *deception?* Is it simply another term for lying? In practice, deception in research can be located on a continuum from simply withholding from the subjects the true nature of the experiment to actively creating a cover story to try to keep the subjects from determining the actual purpose of the study. Deception is largely based on the assumption that if subjects knew the true nature of the experiment (the hypothesis being tested, that is), then they would not act naturally and hence contaminate the results.

This next classic article by Herbert C. Kelman explores the use of deception in social psychological experiments. After discussing some of the ethical issues involved in the use of deception, Kelman goes on to suggest how the use of deception should be handled, as well as alternatives to deception. In the years since the publication of this article in 1967, many changes in the ethical guidelines for the treatment of human subjects have been made. For example, it is now standard policy for institutions to have ethical review boards for the approval of any study involving human subjects. Nonetheless, deception in one form or another is still a common feature in social psychological research.

Human Use of Human Subjects
The Problem of Deception in Social Psychological Experiments[1]

■ Herbert C. Kelman

Though there is often good reason for deceiving Ss in social psychological experiments, widespread use of such procedures has serious (a) ethical implications (involving not only the possibility of harm to S, but also the quality of the E-S relationship), (b) methodological implications (relating to the decreasing naïveté of Ss), and (c) implications for the future of the discipline. To deal with these problems, it is necessary (a) to increase active awareness of the negative implications of deception and use it only when clearly justified, not as a matter of course; (b) to explore ways of counteracting and minimizing negative consequences of deception when it is used; and (c) to develop new experimental techniques that dispense with deception and rely on S's positive motivations.

In 1954, in the pages of the *American Psychologist,* Edgar Vinacke raised a series of questions about experiments—particularly in the area of small groups—in which "the psychologist conceals the true purpose and conditions of the experiment, or positively misinforms the subjects, or exposes them to painful, embarrassing, or worse, experiences, without the subjects' knowledge of what is going on [p. 155]." He summed up his concerns by asking, "What . . . is the proper

Reprinted from *Psychological Bulletin,* 1967, *67,* 1–11. Copyright © 1967 by the American Psychological Association. Reprinted with permission.

balance between the interests of science and the thoughtful treatment of the persons who, innocently, supply the data? [p. 155]." Little effort has been made in the intervening years to seek answers to the questions he raised. During these same years, however, the problem of deception in social psychological experiments has taken on increasingly serious proportions.[2]

The problem is actually broader, extending beyond the walls of the laboratory. It arises, for example, in various field studies in which investigators enroll as members of a group that has special interest for them so that they can observe its operations from the inside. The pervasiveness of the problem becomes even more apparent when we consider that deception is built into most of our measurement devices, since it is important to keep the respondent unaware of the personality or attitude dimension that we wish to explore. For the present purposes, however, primarily the problem of deception in the context of the social psychological experiment will be discussed.

The use of deception has become more and more extensive, and it is now a commonplace and almost standard feature of social psychological experiments. Deception has been turned into a game, often played with great skill and virtuosity. A considerable amount of the creativity and ingenuity of social psychologists is invested in the development of increasingly elaborate deception situations. Within a single experiment, deception may be built upon deception in a delicately complex structure. The literature now contains a fair number of studies in which second- or even third-order deception was employed.

One well-known experiment (Festinger & Carlsmith, 1959), for example, involved a whole progression of deceptions. After the subjects had gone through an experimental task, the investigator made it clear—through word and gesture—that the experiment was over and that he would now "like to explain what this has been all about so you'll have some idea of why you were doing this [p. 205]." This explanation was false, however, and was designed to serve as a basis for the true experimental manipulation. The manipulation itself involved asking subjects to serve as the experimenter's accomplices. The task of the "accomplice" was to tell the next "subject" that the experiment in which he had just participated (which was in fact a rather boring experience) had been interesting and enjoyable. He was also asked to be on call for

unspecified future occasions on which his services as accomplice might be needed because "the regular fellow couldn't make it, and we had a subject scheduled [p. 205]." These newly recruited "accomplices," of course, were the true subjects, while the "subjects" were the experimenter's true accomplices. For their presumed services as "accomplices," the true subjects were paid in advance—half of them receiving $1, and half $20. When they completed their service, however, the investigators added injury to insult by asking them to return their hard-earned cash. Thus, in this one study, in addition to receiving the usual misinformation about the purpose of the experiment, the subject was given feedback that was really an experimental manipulation, was asked to be an accomplice who was really a subject, and was given a $20 bill that was really a will-o'-the-wisp. One wonders how much further in this direction we can go. Where will it all end?

It is easy to view this problem with alarm, but it is much more difficult to formulate an unambiguous position on the problem. As a working experimental social psychologist, I cannot conceive the issue in absolutist terms. I am too well aware of the fact that there are good reasons for using deception in many experiments. There are many significant problems that probably cannot be investigated without the use of deception, at least not at the present level of development of our experimental methodology. Thus, we are always confronted with a conflict of values. If we regard the acquisition of scientific knowledge about human behavior as a positive value, and if an experiment using deception constitutes a significant contribution in such knowledge which could not very well be achieved by other means, then we cannot unequivocally rule out this experiment. The question for us is not simply whether it does or does not use deception, but whether the amount and type of deception are justified by the significance of the study and the unavailability of alternative (that is, deception-free) procedures.

I have expressed special concern about second-order deceptions, for example, the procedure of letting a person believe that he is acting as experimenter or as the experimenter's accomplice when he is in fact serving as the subject. Such a procedure undermines the relationship between experimenter and subject even further than simple misinformation about the purposes of the experiment; deception does not merely take place *within* the experiment, but encompasses the whole definition of the relationship between the parties involved. Deception that takes place while the person is within the role of subject for which he has contracted can, to some degree, be isolated, but deception about the very nature of the contract itself is more likely to suffuse the experimenter-subject relationship as a whole and to remove the possibility of mutual trust. Thus, I would be inclined to take a more absolutist stand with regard to such second-order deceptions—but even here the issue turns out to be more complicated. I am stopped short when I think, for example, of the ingenious studies on experimenter bias by Rosenthal and his associates (e.g., Rosenthal & Fode, 1963; Rosenthal, Persinger, Vikan-Kline, & Fode, 1963; Rosenthal, Persinger, Vikan-Kline, & Mulry, 1963). These experiments employed second-order deception in that subjects were led to believe that they were the experimenters. Since these were experiments about experiments, however, it is very hard to conceive of any alternative procedures that the investigators might have used. There is no question in my mind that these are significant studies; they provide fundamental inputs to present efforts at reexamining the social psychology of the experiment. These studies, then, help to underline even further the point that we are confronted with a conflict of values that cannot be resolved by fiat.

I hope it is clear from these remarks that my purpose in focusing on this problem is not to single out specific studies performed by some of my colleagues and to point a finger at them. Indeed, the finger points at me as well. I too have used deception, and have known the joys of applying my skills and ingenuity to the creation of elaborate experimental situations that the subjects would not be able to decode. I am now making active attempts to find alternatives to deception, but still I have not forsworn the use of deception under any and all circumstances. The questions I am raising, then, are addressed to myself as well as to my colleagues. They are questions with which all of us who are committed to social psychology must come to grips, lest we leave their resolution to others who have no understanding of what we are trying to accomplish.

What concerns me most is not so much that deception is used, but precisely that it is used without

question. It has now become standard operating procedure in the social psychologist's laboratory. I sometimes feel that we are training a generation of students who do not know that there is any other way of doing experiments in our field—who feel that deception is as much de rigueur as significance at the .05 level. Too often deception is used not as a last resort, but as a matter of course. Our attitude seems to be that if you can deceive, why tell the truth? It is this unquestioning acceptance, this routinization of deception, that really concerns me.

I would like to turn now to a review of the bases for my concern with the problem of deception, and then suggest some possible approaches for dealing with it.

IMPLICATIONS OF THE USE OF DECEPTION IN SOCIAL PSYCHOLOGICAL EXPERIMENTS

My concern about the use of deception is based on three considerations: the ethical implications of such procedures, their methodological implications, and their implications for the future of social psychology.

1. *Ethical implications.* Ethical problems of a rather obvious nature arise in the experiments in which deception has potentially harmful consequences for the subject. Take, for example, the brilliant experiment by Mulder and Stemerding (1963) on the effects of threat on attraction to the group and need for strong leadership. In this study—one of the very rare examples of an experiment conducted in a natural setting—independent food merchants in a number of Dutch towns were brought together for group meetings, in the course of which they were informed that a large organization was planning to open up a series of supermarkets in the Netherlands. In the High Threat condition, subjects were told that there was a high probability that their town would be selected as a site for such markets, and that the advent of these markets would cause a considerable drop in their business. On the advice of the executives of the shopkeepers' organizations, who had helped to arrange the group meetings, the investigators did not reveal the experimental manipulations to their subjects. I have been worried about these Dutch merchants ever since I heard about this study for the first time. Did some of them go out of business in anticipation of the heavy competition? Do some of them have

an anxiety reaction every time they see a bulldozer? Chances are that they soon forgot about this threat (unless, of course, supermarkets actually did move into town) and that it became just one of the many little moments of anxiety that must occur in every shopkeeper's life. Do we have a right, however, to add to life's little anxieties and to risk the possibility of more extensive anxiety purely for the purposes of our experiments, particularly since deception deprives the subject of the opportunity to choose whether or not he wishes to expose himself to the risks that might be entailed?

The studies by Bramel (1962, 1963) and Bergin (1962) provide examples of another type of potentially harmful effects arising from the use of deception. In the Bramel studies, male undergraduates were led to believe that they were homosexually aroused by photographs of men. In the Bergin study, subjects of both sexes were given discrepant information about their level of masculinity or femininity; in one experimental condition, this information was presumably based on an elaborate series of psychological tests in which the subjects had participated. In all of these studies, the deception was explained to the subject at the end of the experiment. One wonders, however, whether such explanation removes the possibility of harmful effects. For many persons in this age group, sexual identity is still a live and sensitive issue, and the self-doubts generated by the laboratory experience may take on a life of their own and linger on for some time to come.

Yet another illustration of potentially harmful effects of deception can be found in Milgram's (1963, 1965) studies of obedience. In these experiments, the subject was led to believe that he was participating in a learning study and was instructed to administer increasingly severe shocks to another person who after a while began to protest vehemently. In fact, of course, the victim was an accomplice of the experimenter and did not receive any shocks. Depending on the conditions, sizable proportions of the subjects obeyed the experimenter's instructions and continued to shock the other person up to the maximum level, which they believed to be extremely painful. Both obedient and defiant subjects exhibited a great deal of stress in this situation. The complexities of the issues surrounding the use of deception become quite apparent when one

reads the exchange between Baumrind (1964) and Milgram (1964) about the ethical implications of the obedience research. There is clearly room for disagreement, among honorable people, about the evaluation of this research from an ethical point of view. Yet, there is good reason to believe that at least some of the obedient subjects came away from this experience with a lower self-esteem, having to live with the realization that they were willing to yield to destructive authority to the point of inflicting extreme pain on a fellow human being. The fact that this may have provided, in Milgram's (1964) words, "an opportunity to learn something of importance about themselves, and more generally, about the conditions of human action [p. 850]" is beside the point. If this were a lesson from life, it would indeed constitute an instructive confrontation and provide a valuable insight. But do we, for the purpose of experimentation, have the right to provide such potentially disturbing insights to subjects who do not know that this is what they are coming for? A similar question can be raised about the Asch (1951) experiments on group pressure, although the stressfulness of the situation and the implications for the person's self-concept were less intense in that context.

While the present paper is specifically focused on social psychological experiments, the problem of deception and its possibly harmful effects arises in other areas of psychological experimentation as well. Dramatic illustrations are provided by two studies in which subjects were exposed, for experimental purposes, to extremely stressful conditions. In an experiment designed to study the establishment of a conditioned response in a situation that is traumatic but not painful, Campbell, Sanderson, and Laverty (1964) induced—through the use of a drug—a temporary interruption of respiration in their subjects. "This has no permanently harmful physical consequences but is nonetheless a severe stress which is not in itself painful . . . [p. 628]." The subjects' reports confirmed that this was a "horrific" experience for them. "All the subjects in the standard series said that they thought they were dying [p. 631]." Of course the subjects, "male alcoholic patients who volunteered for the experiment when they were told that it was connected with a possible therapy for alcoholism [p. 629]," were not warned in advance about the effect of the drug, since this information would have reduced the traumatic impact of the experience.[3] In a series of studies on the effects of psychological stress, Berkun, Bialek, Kern, and Yagi (1962) devised a number of ingenious experimental situations designed to convince the subject that his life was actually in danger. In one situation, the subjects, a group of Army recruits, were actually "passengers aboard an apparently stricken plane which was being forced to 'ditch' or crash-land [p. 4]." In another experiment, an isolated subject in a desolate area learned that a sudden emergency had arisen (accidental nuclear radiation in the area, or a sudden forest fire, or misdirected artillery shells—depending on the experimental condition) and that he could be rescued only if he reported his position over his radio transmitter, "which has quite suddenly failed [p. 7]." In yet another situation, the subject was led to believe that he was responsible for an explosion that seriously injured another soldier. As the authors pointed out, reactions in these situations are more likely to approximate reactions to combat experiences or to naturally occurring disasters than are reactions to various laboratory stresses, but is the experimenter justified in exposing his subjects to such extreme threats?

So far, I have been speaking of experiments in which deception has potentially harmful consequences. I am equally concerned, however, about the less obvious cases, in which there is little danger of harmful effects, at least in the conventional sense of the term. Serious ethical issues are raised by deception per se and the kind of use of human beings that it implies. In our other interhuman relationships, most of us would never think of doing the kinds of things that we do to our subjects—exposing others to lies and tricks, deliberately misleading them about the purposes of the interaction or withholding pertinent information, making promises or giving assurances that we intend to disregard. We would view such behavior as a violation of the respect to which all fellow humans are entitled and of the whole basis of our relationship with them. Yet we seem to forget that the experimenter-subject relationship—whatever else it is—is a *real* interhuman relationship, in which we have responsibility toward the subject as another human being whose dignity we must preserve. The discontinuity between the experimenter's behavior in

everyday life and his behavior in the laboratory is so marked that one wonders why there has been so little concern with this problem, and what mechanisms have allowed us to ignore it to such an extent. I am reminded, in this connection, of the intriguing phenomenon of the "holiness of sin," which characterizes certain messianic movements as well as other movements of the true-believer variety. Behavior that would normally be unacceptable actually takes on an aura of virtue in such movements through a redefinition of the situation in which the behavior takes place and thus of the context for evaluating it. A similar mechanism seems to be involved in our attitude toward the psychological experiment. We tend to regard it as a situation that is not quite real, that can be isolated from the rest of life like a play performed on stage, and to which, therefore, the usual criteria for ethical interpersonal conduct become irrelevant. Behavior is judged entirely in the context of the experiment's scientific contribution and, in this context, deception—which is normally unacceptable—can indeed be seen as a positive good.

The broader ethical problem brought into play by the very use of deception becomes even more important when we view it in the light of present historical forces. We are living in an age of mass societies in which the transformation of man into an object to be manipulated at will occurs "on a mass scale, in a systematic way, and under the aegis of specialized institutions deliberately assigned to this task [Kelman, 1965]." In institutionalizing the use of deception in psychological experiments, we are, then, contributing to a historical trend that threatens values most of us cherish.

2. *Methodological implications.* A second source of my concern about the use of deception is my increasing doubt about its adequacy as a methodology for social psychology.

A basic assumption in the use of deception is that a subject's awareness of the conditions that we are trying to create and of the phenomena that we wish to study would affect his behavior in such a way that we could not draw valid conclusions from it. For example, if we are interested in studying the effects of failure on conformity, we must create a situation in which the subjects actually feel that they have failed, and in which they can be kept unaware of our interest in observing conformity. In short, it is important to keep our subjects naïve about the purposes of the experiment so that they can respond to the experimental inductions spontaneously.

How long, however, will it be possible for us to find naïve subjects? Among college students, it is already very difficult. They may not know the exact purpose of the particular experiment in which they are participating, but at least they know, typically, that it is *not* what the experimenter says it is. Orne (1962) pointed out that the use of deception "on the part of psychologists is so widely known in the college population that even if a psychologist is honest with the subject, more often than not he will be distrusted." As one subject pithily put it, "'Psychologists always lie!'" Orne added that "This bit of paranoia has some support in reality [pp. 778–779]." There are, of course, other sources of human subjects that have not been tapped, and we could turn to them in our quest for naïveté. But even there it is only a matter of time. As word about psychological experiments gets around in whatever network we happen to be using, sophistication is bound to increase. I wonder, therefore, whether there is any future in the use of deception.

If the subject in a deception experiment knows what the experimenter is trying to conceal from him and what he is really after in the study, the value of the deception is obviously nullified. Generally, however, even the relatively sophisticated subject does not know the exact purpose of the experiment; he only has suspicions, which may approximate the true purpose of the experiment to a greater or lesser degree. Whether or not he knows the *true* purpose of the experiment, he is likely to make an effort to figure out its purpose, since he does not believe what the experimenter tells him, and therefore he is likely to operate in the situation in terms of his own hypothesis of what is involved. This may, in line with Orne's (1962) analysis, lead him to do what he thinks the experimenter wants him to do. Conversely, if he resents the experimenter's attempt to deceive him, he may try to throw a monkey wrench into the works; I would not be surprised if this kind of Schweikian game among subjects became a fairly well-established part of the culture of sophisticated campuses. Whichever course the subject uses, however, he is operating in terms of his own conception of the nature of the situation, rather than in terms of the conception that the experi-

menter is trying to induce. In short, the experimenter can no longer assume that the conditions that he is trying to create are the ones that actually define the situation for the subject. Thus, the use of deception, while it is designed to give the experimenter control over the subject's perceptions and motivations, may actually produce an unspecifiable mixture of intended and unintended stimuli that make it difficult to know just what the subject is responding to.

The tendency for subjects to react to unintended cues—to features of the situation that are not part of the experimenter's design—is by no means restricted to experiments that involve deception. This problem has concerned students of the interview situation for some time, and more recently it has been analyzed in detail in the writings and research of Riecken, Rosenthal, Orne, and Mills. Subjects enter the experiment with their own aims, including attainment of certain rewards, divination of the experimenter's true purposes, and favorable self-presentation (Riecken, 1962). They are therefore responsive to demand characteristics of the situation (Orne, 1962), to unintended communications of the experimenter's expectations (Rosenthal, 1963), and to the role of the experimenter within the social system that experimenter and subject jointly constitute (Mills, 1962). In any experiment, then, the subject goes beyond the description of the situation and the experimental manipulation introduced by the investigator, makes his own interpretation of the situation, and acts accordingly.

For several reasons, however, the use of deception especially encourages the subject to dismiss the stated purposes of the experiment and to search for alternative interpretations of his own. First, the continued use of deception establishes the reputation of psychologists as people who cannot be believed. Thus, the desire "to penetrate the experimenter's inscrutability and discover the rationale of the experiment [Riecken, 1962, p. 34]" becomes especially strong. Generally, these efforts are motivated by the subject's desire to meet the expectations of the experimenter and of the situation. They may also be motivated, however, as I have already mentioned, by a desire to outwit the experimenter and to beat him at his own game, in a spirit of genuine hostility or playful one-upmanship. Second, a situation involving the use of deception is inevitably highly ambiguous since a great deal of information relevant to understanding the structure of the situation must be withheld from the subject. Thus, the subject is especially motivated to try to figure things out and likely to develop idiosyncratic interpretations. Third, the use of deception, by its very nature, causes the experimenter to transmit contradictory messages to the subject. In his verbal instructions and explanations he says one thing about the purposes of the experiment; but in the experimental situation that he has created, in the manipulations that he has introduced, and probably in covert cues that he emits, he says another thing. This again makes it imperative for the subject to seek his own interpretation of the situation.

I would argue, then, that deception increases the subject's tendency to operate in terms of his private definition of the situation, differing (in random or systematic fashion) from the definition that the experimenter is trying to impose; moreover, it makes it more difficult to evaluate or minimize the effects of this tendency. Whether or not I am right in this judgment, it can, at the very least, be said that the use of deception does not resolve or reduce the unintended effects of the experiment as a social situation in which the subject pursues his private aims. Since the assumptions that the subject is naïve and that he sees the situation as the experimenter wishes him to see it are unwarranted, the use of deception no longer has any special obvious advantages over other experimental approaches. I am not suggesting that there may not be occasions when deception may still be the most effective procedure to use from a methodological point of view. But since it raises at least as many methodological problems as any other type of procedure does, we have every reason to explore alternative approaches and to extend our methodological inquiries to the question of the effects of using deception.

3. *Implications for the future of social psychology.* My third concern about the use of deception is based on its long-run implications for our discipline and combines both the ethical and methodological considerations that I have already raised. There is something disturbing about the idea of relying on massive deception as the basis for developing a field of inquiry. Can one really build a discipline on a foundation of such research?

From a long-range point of view, there is obviously something self-defeating about the use of deception.

As we continue to carry out research of this kind, our potential subjects become more and more sophisticated, and we become less and less able to meet the conditions that our experimental procedures require. Moreover, as we continue to carry out research of this kind, our potential subjects become increasingly distrustful of us, and our future relations with them are likely to be undermined. Thus, we are confronted with the anomalous circumstance that the more research we do, the more difficult and questionable it becomes.

The use of deception also involves a contradiction between our experimental procedures and our long-range aims as scientists and teachers. In order to be able to carry out our experiments, we are concerned with maintaining the naïveté of the population from which we hope to draw our subjects. We are all familiar with the experimenter's anxious concern that the introductory course might cover the autokinetic phenomenon, need achievement, or the Asch situation before he has had a chance to complete his experimental runs. This perfectly understandable desire to keep procedures secret goes counter to the traditional desire of the scientist and teacher to inform and enlighten the public. To be sure, experimenters are interested only in temporary secrecy, but it is not inconceivable that at some time in the future they might be using certain procedures on a regular basis with large segments of the population and thus prefer to keep the public permanently naïve. It is perhaps not too fanciful to imagine, for the long run, the possible emergence of a special class, in possession of secret knowledge—a possibility that is clearly antagonistic to the principle of open communication to which we, as scientists and intellectuals, are so fervently committed.

DEALING WITH THE PROBLEM OF DECEPTION IN SOCIAL PSYCHOLOGICAL EXPERIMENTS

If my concerns about the use of deception are justified, what are some of the ways in which we, as experimental social psychologists, can deal with them? I would like to suggest three steps that we can take: increase our active awareness of the problem, explore ways of counteracting and minimizing the negative effects of deception, and give careful attention to the development of new experimental techniques that dispense with the use of deception.

1. *Active awareness of the problem.* I have already stressed that I would not propose the complete elimination of deception under all circumstances, in view of the genuine conflict of values with which the experimenter is confronted. What is crucial, however, is that we always ask ourselves the question whether deception, in the given case, is necessary and justified. How we answer the question is less important than the fact that we ask it. What we must be wary of is the tendency to dismiss the question as irrelevant and to accept deception as a matter of course. Active awareness of the problem is thus in itself part of the solution, for it makes the use of deception a matter for discussion, deliberation, investigation, and choice. Active awareness means that, in any given case, we will try to balance the value of an experiment that uses deception against its questionable or potentially harmful effects. If we engage in this process honestly, we are likely to find that there are many occasions when we or our students can forego the use of deception—either because deception is not necessary (that is, alternative procedures that are equally good or better are available), because the importance of the study does not warrant the use of an ethically questionable procedure, or because the type of deception involved is too extreme (in terms of the possibility of harmful effects or of seriously undermining the experimenter-subject relationship).

2. *Counteracting and minimizing the negative effects of deception.* If we do use deception, it is essential that we find ways of counteracting and minimizing its negative effects. Sensitizing the apprentice researcher to this necessity is at least as fundamental as any other part of research training.

In those experiments in which deception carries the potential of harmful effects (in the more usual sense of the term), there is an obvious requirement to build protections into every phase of the process. Subjects must be selected in a way that will exclude individuals who are especially vulnerable; the potentially harmful manipulation (such as the induction of stress) must be kept at a moderate level of intensity; the experimenter must be sensitive to danger signals in the reactions of his subjects and be prepared to deal with crises when they arise; and, at the conclusion of the session, the experimenter must take time not only to reassure the subject, but also to help him work through his feelings about the experience to whatever degree may be required. In general, the principle that a subject ought not to leave the laboratory with greater anxiety or lower self-esteem than he came with is a good one to follow. I would go beyond it to argue that the subject should in some positive way be enriched by the experience, that is, he should come away from it with the feeling that he has learned something, understood something, or grown in some way. This, of course, adds special importance to the kind of feedback that is given to the subject at the end of the experimental session.

Postexperimental feedback is, of course, the primary way of counteracting negative effects in those experiments in which the issue is deception as such, rather than possible threats to the subject's well-being. If we do deceive the subject, then it is our obligation to give him a full and detailed explanation of what we have done and of our reasons for using this type of procedure. I do not want to be absolutist about this, but I would suggest it as a good rule of thumb to follow: Think very carefully before undertaking an experiment whose purposes you feel unable to reveal to the subjects even after they have completed the experimental session. It is, of course not enough to give the subject a perfunctory feedback, just to do one's duty. Postexperimental explanations should be worked out with as much detail as other aspects of the procedure and, in general, some thought ought to be given to ways of making them meaningful and instructive for the subject and helpful for rebuilding his relationship with the experimenter. I feel very strongly that to accomplish these purposes, we must keep the feedback itself inviolate and under no circumstance give the subject false feedback or pretend to be giving him feedback while we are in fact introducing another experimental manipulation. If we hope to maintain any kind of trust in our relationship with potential subjects, there must be no ambiguity that the statement "The experiment is over and I shall explain to you what it was all about" means precisely that and nothing else. If subjects have reason to suspect even that statement, then we have lost the whole basis for a decent human relationship with our subjects and all hope for future cooperation from them.

3. *Development of new experimental techniques.* My third and final suggestion is that we invest some of the creativity and ingenuity, now devoted to the construction of elaborate deceptions, in the search for alternative experimental techniques that do not rely on the use of deception. The kind of techniques that I have in mind would be based on the principle of eliciting the subject's positive motivations to contribute to the experimental enterprise. They would draw on the subject's active participation and involvement in the proceedings and encourage him to cooperate in making the experiment a success—not by giving the results he thinks the experimenter wants, but by conscientiously taking the roles and carrying out the tasks that the experimenter assigns to him. In short, the kind of techniques I have in mind would be designed to involve the subject as an active participant in a joint effort with the experimenter.

Perhaps the most promising source of alternative experimental approaches are procedures using some sort of role playing. I have been impressed, for example, with the role playing that I have observed in the context of the Inter-Nation Simulation (Guetzkow, Alger, Brody, Noel, & Snyder, 1963), a laboratory procedure involving a simulated world in which the subjects take the roles of decision-makers of various nations. This situation seems to create a high level of emotional involvement and to elicit motivations that have a real-life quality to them. Moreover, within this situation—which is highly complex and generally permits only gross experimental manipulations—it is possible to test specific theoretical hypotheses by using data based on repeated measurements as interaction between the simulated nations develops. Thus, a study carried out at the Western Behavioral Sciences Institute provided, as an extra, some interesting opportunities for testing hypotheses derived from balance theory, by the use of mutual ratings made by decision-makers of Nations A, B, and C, before and after A shifted from an alliance with B to an alliance with C.

A completely different type of role playing was used effectively by Rosenberg and Abelson (1960) in their studies of cognitive dilemmas. In my own research program, we have been exploring different kinds of role-playing procedures with varying degrees of success. In one study, the major manipulation consisted in informing subjects that the experiment to which they had just committed themselves would require them (depending on the condition) either to receive shocks from a fellow subject, or to administer shocks to a fellow subject. We used a regular deception procedure, but with a difference: We told the subjects before the session started that what was to follow was make-believe, but that we wanted them to react as if they really found themselves in this situation. I might mention that some subjects, not surprisingly, did not accept as true the information that this was all make-believe and wanted to know when they should show up for the shock experiment to which they had committed themselves. I have some questions about the effectiveness of this particular procedure. It did not do enough to create a high level of involvement, and it turned out to be very complex since it asked subjects to role-play subjects, not people. In this sense, it might have given us the worst of both worlds, but I still think it is worth some further exploration. In another experiment, we were interested in creating differently structured attitudes about an organization by feeding different kinds of information to two groups of subjects. These groups were then asked to take specific actions in support of the organization, and we measured attitude changes resulting from these actions. In the first part of the experiment, the subjects were clearly informed that the organization and the information that we were feeding to them were fictitious, and that we were simply trying to simulate the conditions under which attitudes about new organizations are typically formed. In the second part of the experiment, the subjects were told that we were interested in studying the effects of action in support of an organization on attitudes toward it, and they were asked (in groups of five) to role-play a strategy meeting of leaders of the fictitious organization. The results of this study were very encouraging. While there is obviously a great deal that we need to know about the meaning of this situation to the subjects, they did react differentially to the experimental manipulations and these reactions followed an orderly pattern, despite the fact that they knew it was all make-believe.

There are other types of procedures, in addition to role playing, that are worth exploring. For example, one might design field experiments in which, with the full cooperation of the subjects, specific experimental variations are introduced. The advantages of dealing with motivations at a real-life level of intensity might well outweigh the disadvantages of subjects' knowing the general purpose of the experiment. At the other extreme of ambitiousness, one might explore the effects of modifying standard experimental procedures slightly by informing the subject at the beginning of the experiment that he will not be receiving full information about what is going on, but asking him to suspend judgment until the experiment is over.

Whatever alternative approach we try, there is no doubt that it will have its own problems and complexities. Procedures effective for some purposes may be quite ineffective for others, and it may well turn out that for certain kinds of problems there is no adequate substitute for the use of deception. But there *are* alternative procedures that, for many purposes, may be as effective or even more effective than procedures built on deception. These approaches often involve a radically different set of assumptions about the role of the subject in the experiment: They require us to *use* the subject's motivation to cooperate rather than to bypass it; they may even call for increasing the sophistication of potential subjects, rather than maintaining their naïveté. My only plea is that we devote some of our energies to active exploration of these alternative approaches.

REFERENCES

Asch, S. E. Effects of group pressure upon the modification and distortion of judgments. In H. Guetzkow (Ed.), *Groups, leadership, and men.* Pittsburgh: Carnegie Press, 1951. Pp. 117–190.

Baumrind, D. Some thoughts on ethics of research: After reading Milgram's "Behavioral Study of Obedience." *American Psychologist,* 1964, **19**, 421–423.

Bergin, A. E. The effect of dissonant persuasive communications upon changes in a self-referring attitude. *Journal of Personality,* 1962, **30**, 423–438.

Berkun, M. M., Bialek, H. M., Kern, R. P., & Yagi, K. Experimental studies of psychological stress in man. *Psychological Monographs,* 1962, **76**(15, Whole No. 534).

Bramel, D. A dissonance theory approach to defensive projection. *Journal of Abnormal and Social Psychology,* 1962, **64**, 121–129.

Bramel, D. Selection of a target for defensive projection. *Journal of Abnormal and Social Psychology,* 1963, **66**, 318–324.

Campbell, D., Sanderson, R. E., & Laverty, S. G. Characteristics of a conditioned response in human subjects during extinction trials following a single traumatic conditioning trial. *Journal of Abnormal and Social Psychology,* 1964, **68**, 627–639.

Festinger, L., & Carlsmith, J. M. Cognitive consequences of forced compliance. *Journal of Abnormal and Social Psychology,* 1959, **58**, 203–210.

Guetzkow, H., Alger, C. F., Brody, R. A., Noel, R. C., & Snyder, R. C. *Simulation in international relations.* Englewood Cliffs, N.J.: Prentice-Hall, 1963.

Kelman, H. C. Manipulation of human behavior: An ethical dilemma for the social scientist. *Journal of Social Issues,* 1965, **21**(2), 31–46.

Milgram, S. Behavioral study of obedience. *Journal of Abnormal and Social Psychology,* 1963, **67**, 371–378.

Milgram, S. Issues in the study of obedience: A reply to Baumrind. *American Psychologist,* 1964, **19**, 848–852.

Milgram, S. Some conditions of obedience and disobedience to authority. *Human Relations,* 1965, **18**, 57–76.

Mills, T. M. A sleeper variable in small groups research: The experimenter. *Pacific Sociological Review,* 1962, **5**, 21–28.

Mulder, M., & Stemerding, A. Threat, attraction to group, and need for strong leadership. *Human Relations,* 1963, **16**, 317–334.

Orne, M. T. On the social psychology of the psychological experiment: With particular reference to demand characteristics and their implications. *American Psychologist,* 1962, **17**, 776–783.

Riecken, H. W. A program for research on experiments in social psychology. In N. F. Washburne (Ed.), *Decisions, values and groups.* Vol. 2. New York: Pergamon Press, 1962. Pp. 25–41.

Rosenberg, M. J., & Abelson, R. P. An analysis of cognitive balancing. In M. J. Rosenberg et al., *Attitude organization and change.* New Haven: Yale University Press, 1960. Pp. 112–163.

Rosenthal, R. On the social psychology of the psychological experiment: The experimenter's hypothesis as unintended determinant of experimental results. *American Scientist,* 1963, **51**, 268–283.

Rosenthal, R., & Fode, K. L. Psychology of the scientist: V. Three experiments in experimenter bias. *Psychological Reports,* 1963, **12**, 491–511. (Monogr. Suppl. 3-V12)

Rosenthal, R., Persinger, G. W., Vikan-Kline, L., & Fode, K. L. The effect of early data returns on data subsequently obtained by outcome-biased experimenters. *Sociometry*, 1963, **26**, 487–498.

Rosenthal, R., Persinger, G. W., Vikan-Kline, L., & Mulry, R. C. The role of the research assistant in the mediation of experimenter bias. *Journal of Personality,* 1963, **31**, 313–335.

Vinacke, W. E. Deceiving experimental subjects. *American Psychologist,* 1954, **9**, 155.

ENDNOTES

1. Paper read at the symposium on "Ethical and Methodological Problems in Social Psychological Experiments," held at the meetings of the American Psychological Association in Chicago, September 3, 1965. This paper is a product of a research program on social influence and behavior change supported by United States Public Health Service Research Grant MH-07280 from the National Institute of Mental Health.

2. In focusing on deception in *social* psychological experiments, I do not wish to give the impression that there is no serious problem elsewhere. Deception is widely used in most studies involving human subjects and gives rise to issues similar to those discussed in this paper. Some examples of the use of deception in other areas of psychological experimentation will be presented later in this paper.

3. The authors reported, however, that some of their other subjects were physicians familiar with the drug; "they did not suppose they were dying but, even though they knew in a general way what to expect, they too said that the experience was extremely harrowing [p. 632]." Thus, conceivably, the purposes of the experiment might have been achieved even if the subjects had been told to expect the temporary interruption of breathing.

CRITICAL THINKING QUESTIONS

1. Which of the studies mentioned in the article involves the greatest ethical issues? Why? Select one of the studies cited in this article, and suggest an alternative to the type of deception that was employed.

2. Should the use of deception be banned? Why or why not? If not, under what conditions should it be allowed? What impact would such a limitation have on social psychological research? Defend your position.

3. Who should determine what constitutes an ethically appropriate experiment? Professors? Students? Outside laypeople? Explain your answer. What would be the ideal composition of a board charged with reviewing research proposals? Why?

4. Obtain a copy of the current "American Psychological Association Guide for the Ethical Treatment of Human Subjects." Review these guidelines, considering how comprehensive they are. What criteria should be used in determining what is in the best interests of the subjects of an experiment?

5. What do you think of Kelman's position on "second-order" deception? Do you agree that it is of even greater concern than standard ("first-order") deception practices? Why or why not?

6. What do you think of Kelman's suggestions for the development of new experimental techniques as an alternative to deception? Find a research study that tried such a technique in lieu of deception. Alternatively, find a research study reported in this book of readings and suggest an alternative to the deception that was used. In either case, what might be lost and what might be gained by not deceiving subjects? Explain your answer.

ADDITIONAL RELATED READINGS

American Psychological Association. (1992). Ethical principles of psychologists and code of conduct. *American Psychologist, 47,* 1597–1611.

Thompson, A., & Fata, M. (1997). Relating the psychological literature to the American Psychological Association ethical standards. *Ethics and Behavior, 7,* 79–88.

ARTICLE 3 _____

Most of you taking a course in social psychology have likely already had at least a course in general or introductory psychology. If you have had such a course, you may recall that one of the chapters in your textbook was on social psychology. In that chapter, a classic and famous experiment by Stanley Milgram would have been discussed. (The original study by Milgram is found in Article 26 of this book.) Perhaps more so than any other social psychology experiment, this study by Milgram on obedience to authority is what many people remember from the social psychology chapter. Why? One reason is because of the shocking (no pun intended) results, which found that many people obeyed an experimenter to inflict harm on another person. But another reason for people's fascination with the Milgram study is the issue of how much deception it employed.

Is deception necessary? Some would argue that researchers would not be able to get unbiased results if subjects knew the true nature of the research. These individuals would argue that deception—at least, when properly used and the well-being of the subjects is kept in mind—is a valuable and necessary tool. Yet others would argue that deception—especially of the nature used by Milgram, for example—is never justified, since the potential harm to the subjects does not justify the end results of the experiment.

Has deception always been an integral part of social psychology research? According to the following article by Sandra D. Nicks, James H. Korn, and Tina Mainieri, the answer is no. The authors found that the use of deception in social psychology research peaked in the 1960s and 1970s (the time of the Milgram study, by the way). Before then, deception was seldom used, and since then, its use has declined. The authors explain these changes in deception practices in terms of changing theories and methodologies as well as evolving guidelines for the use of deception on human subjects. The article also is an excellent example of a method of inquiry called *content analysis,* which relies on already existing information for its data.

This article is best read in conjunction with the previous article (Article 2) on deception by Herbert Kelman. Keep in mind that Kelman's article was also published at the peak of using deception in social psychology research.

The Rise and Fall of Deception in Social Psychology and Personality Research, 1921 to 1994

■ Sandra D. Nicks, James H. Korn, and Tina Mainieri

The frequency of the use of deception in American psychological research was studied by reviewing articles from journals in personality and social psychology from 1921 to 1994. Deception was used rarely during the develop- *mental years of social psychology into the 1930s, then grew gradually and irregularly until the 1950s. Between the 1950s and 1970s the use of deception increased significantly. This increase is attributed to changes in*

From "The Rise and Fall of Deception in Social Psychology and Personality Research," by S. D. Nicks, J. H. Korn, and T. Mainieri, 1997, *Ethics and Behavior, 7*(1), 69–77. Copyright 1997 by Lawrence Erlbaum Associates, Inc. Reprinted with permission.

experimental methods, the popularity of realistic impact experiments, and the influence of cognitive dissonance theory. Since 1980 there appears to have been a decrease in the use of deception as compared to previous decades which is related to changes in theory, methods, ethical standards, and federal regulation of research.

The practice of deceiving research participants has become part of the standard methodology in psychological research, particularly in social psychology. If we accept the *Handbook of Social Psychology* (Lindzey, 1954) as the storehouse of knowledge and standards of research practice in this field, we see that deception in research was not discussed as an issue in the first edition in 1954. In 1968, however, the second edition of the handbook contained a chapter on experimentation written as a guide for researchers that contained explicit instructions on the use of deception (Aronson & Carlsmith, 1968). A revised version of this discussion appeared in the third edition (Aronson, Brewer, & Carlsmith, 1985).

Several surveys of the literature documented the increased use of deception through the 1970s. For example, Gross and Fleming (1982) studied the use of deception over a 20-year period and found a significant increase in its use from 1959 to 1969 with no significant decrease between 1969 to 1979. Adair, Duschenko, and Lindsay (1985) found similar results based on their own data and those of other investigators.

In a survey of four social psychology journals, Vitelli (1988) found that the use of deception had decreased between 1974 and 1985. He attributed this decline to an increase in the use of nonlaboratory methods such as surveys and questionnaires that are less likely to require the use of deception. In a more recent survey of the *Journal of Personality and Social Psychology* (JPSP), Sieber, Iannuzzo, and Rodriguez (1995) concluded that deception had decreased after the 1960s but had then increased again in the early 1990s.

Previous surveys have shown consistently that the use of deception gained in frequency during the 1960s and was at its peak during the 1970s. Those studies however, typically compared only 2 or 3 years (e.g., 1961 vs. 1971) and used different definitions of deception. The studies of Gross and Fleming (1982),

Vitelli (1988), and Sieber et al. (1995) included nonawareness of research participation as deception, whereas most other surveys only counted explicit misstatement of fact, that is, lies but not secrets. Our study sought to provide a more consistent picture by using one definition, examining several journals in social psychology and personality, and covering an extended period of time, starting in 1921 when the *Journal of Abnormal and Social Psychology* (JASP) began publication.

METHOD

We defined deception as an explicit misstatement of fact: stating a false purpose for an experiment, giving incorrect information about stimulus material, providing false feedback to participants about their or someone else's performance, or the use of confederates. We found that, in general, instances of the use of deception can be determined reliably, but that it is more difficult to classify particular kinds of deception. For that reason our analysis concerns only the combined frequency of all types of deception.

The purpose of the first phase of our research was to determine when deception began to be used. The first author read the method sections of all articles that reported empirical studies with human participants in JASP from its beginning in 1921 through 1948 and counted the number of articles in which deception was used. Later, the second author repeated this search for JASP articles from 1921 through 1933 to confirm that we had found all instances of the use of deception in the early years of this journal. This resulted in the discovery of one additional article that reported the use of deception. As an additional check on reliability the second author also searched all articles in JASP for 1935, 1940, and 1945. We agreed on the classification for 88 of 89 articles.

The rhetorical style of this period made this search more difficult than it was for later years. Authors often wrote narrative accounts of their research that mixed method with results and discussion. There was no section that began with a method heading, followed by subsections on participants and procedures. Sometimes it was difficult to determine what the experimenters told their participants, so that in a few cases we had to infer what was done or said from the context given in the articles.

In the second phase of this research, which covered the period from 1948 through 1994, six different raters reviewed articles. All raters used a standard scoring sheet on which they had recorded information from each article containing deception. In addition to the complete reference for the article, the critical information was a verbatim quotation that indicated how deception was used. Before gathering data each rater was required to demonstrate their understanding of the project by first correctly scoring a sample of articles. Early in this phase of our research we conducted occasional reliability checks that resulted in consistently high (over 95%) agreement on whether the article reported the use of deception. After 1950, when the format of journal articles had become standardized, it was much easier to determine whether deceptive methods had been used. The language concerning the use of deception almost always was specific; for example, "subjects were misinformed . . ." or "were led to believe . . . ," or it was stated explicitly that a confederate was used.

Raters reviewed sample volumes of JASP, its successor, JPSP, the *Journal of Personality* (JP), and the *Journal of Experimental Social Psychology* (JESP). We selected these journals as being representative of mainstream research in personality and social psychology. We began with JASP in 1948 because that was the date used in the earliest previous survey (Seeman, 1969) and then used 2 to 6 year intervals. We attempted to compare the use of deception in social psychological and personality research, but aban-doned this comparison because of the difficulty of placing many articles into one of these two categories. Neither the title of a journal nor the labeling of sections (as in JPSP) was found to be a reliable guide to the kinds of articles they included. For example, in some years JP published many articles that clearly would be categorized as social psychology. Also, many articles concern topics that are a combination of the two areas.

RESULTS

The first use of deception reported in JASP was by Hulsey Cason (1925) in his article, "Influence of Suggestion on Imagery in a Group Situation":

> The writer gave the above list of stimuli [which previously had been scaled so that all were equally effective] orally to the 50 members of his class in abnormal psychology with the suggestion that the first 6 stimuli in each group would not call out very vivid images, but that stimuli 7 to 12 were much more favorable for calling out clear images. An attempt was of course made to deceive the subjects. (p. 296)

Table 1 shows the percentage and number of articles using deception in JASP from 1921 to 1948. There is considerable variability in the data from year to year, with percentages ranging from 0 to 13.3 and the number of articles reporting deception ranging from 0 to 4.

Table 2 shows that for JASP and JPSP, the use of deception grew steadily from 1948 through 1968, remained above 50% in 1973 and 1979, declined in

TABLE 1 / Percentage and Number of Articles Using Deception in the *Journal of Abnormal and Social Psychology* from 1921 to 1948

Year	%	n	Year	%	n
1921–1924	0.0	(0)	1939	6.1	(2)
1925	7.7	(1)	1940	12.0	(3)
1926–1932	0.0	(0)	1941	13.3	(4)
1933	3.6	(1)	1942	7.1	(2)
1934	2.9	(1)	1943	0.0	(0)
1935	6.0	(2)	1944	12.9	(4)
1936	9.1	(3)	1945	3.2	(1)
1937	4.2	(1)	1946	12.5	(4)
1938	8.3	(2)	1947	5.7	(2)
			1948	12.5	(2)

the 1980s, and then increased slightly in 1989 and 1994. The pattern is about the same if we eliminate articles from JASP that dealt with abnormal psychology (the column headed JASP–SP in Table 2) to provide more consistency in the contents of the two versions of this journal.

Table 2 also includes the data from the other journals surveyed for this study. In JP there was a decrease in the use of deception between the years surveyed in the 1970s and 1980s. Similar to JPSP, JP demonstrated small increases in 1989 and 1994. The highest frequency of the use of deception was found for JESP. Only 1 of the 4 years we examined for that journal had a level of deception lower than 50%.

DISCUSSION

This study concerned the growth of the use of deception in social psychological and personality research primarily as represented by the major journals in these fields. We realize that our sample does not include all of the literature of social psychology at any time in the history of this field, but we conclude that the pattern that we found is representative of general research practices.

That pattern has three phases: (a) the development of experimental laboratory methods from the 1920s through the 1950s, when deception in research grew slowly and irregularly; (b) a period from the 1950s through the 1970s characterized by theory development and the popularity of realistic impact experiments; and (c) the 1980s, when changes in theory, method, and ethical standards were related to what appears to be a decline in the use of deception in research as compared with earlier decades.

During the early decades of its development as a discipline, social psychology consisted of a scattered array of topics and issues, with no distinguishing theories to bind the field. Although Gordon Allport (1935) stated that attitudes should be the central topic of social psychology, most work in the area of attitudes concerned their measurement (Smith, 1983) rather than their manipulation in the laboratory. Similarly, measurement had been the focus in the field of personality through the 1930s (Craik, 1986).

Most research in social psychology and personality during this period did not involve manipulation of independent variables. Instead, psychologists were concerned with recording social behavior through naturalistic observation and field studies, as well as with measurement of attitudes and opinions (Craik, 1986; Jones, 1985). Many studies labeled as experimental did not include such features as control groups or random assignment, although materials might be presented to participants in a laboratory setting. With infrequent manipulation of independent variables, the use of deceptive techniques in research was less likely than in later years when certain variables could only be manipulated by deceiving participants.

TABLE 2 / Percentage and Number of Articles Using Deception in Various Journals from 1948 to 1989

Year	JASP %	JASP n	JASP–SP %	JASP–SP n	JPSP %	JPSP n	JP %	JP n	JESP %	JESP n
1948	9.0	(2)	12.5	(2)						
1952	19.4	(12)	21.3	(10)						
1957	25.4	(36)	31.6	(36)						
1961	28.2	(59)	34.0	(54)						
1963	30.7	(57)	37.0	(51)						
1968					50.7	(99)	27.5	(11)		
1973					51.3	(102)	31.8	(14)		
1979					53.2	(88)	35.7	(15)	64.3	(27)
1983					41.3	(92)	17.4	(4)	67.6	(21)
1987					24.1	(56)	10.7	(3)	42.9	(12)
1989					29.9	(55)	11.1	(3)	65.5	(19)
1994					31.3	(54)	16.6	(4)	50.0	(11)

Kurt Lewin had the greatest impact on theory and method in social psychology, and it was his students in the 1930s and 1940s who began to carry out realistic laboratory experiments that used extensive deception. Lewin came to the United States in 1933, and the research program that he established contained the beginnings of the use of confederates, cover stories, and staged situations. In that same year, Saul Rosenzweig (1933) published an analysis of the experimental situation in which he specifically suggested the use of deception. Following publication of that paper, more studies began to appear that reported using deception, although the practice still was not common.

After World War Two the randomized experiment became the method of choice in experimental psychology and analysis of variance became the favored statistical technique (Rucci & Tweney, 1980). Social psychological studies that incorporated experimental manipulation increased from 30% in 1949 to 83% in 1959 (Christie, 1965). The use of deceptive techniques was an effective way for social psychologists to control many of the problematic extraneous variables that were involved in studying significant human problems. This approach to research design required the careful definition and manipulation of experimental variables, and in social psychology that often required considerable creativity.

Our data show that in 1968 over half of the articles in JPSP used some form of deception. In the same year a new edition of the *Handbook of Social Psychology* (Aronson & Carlsmith, 1968) appeared and included a chapter on experimentation that was presented as a guide that would help graduate students and others learn how to do laboratory research. The authors described the deception experiment as an important way of creating experimental realism, which they said was an essential component of social psychological research. This chapter made it clear not only that deception was an accepted research technique, but that it was an effective way to study important social problems (the relevance issue of the 1960s) and that those who used it effectively were admired for their creativity.

The use of deception in its more dramatic forms led to an extended debate concerning its ethical implications. This debate began with Diana Baumrind's critique of Milgram's study of obedience (Baumrind, 1964). There were strong arguments that deception is harmful to participants, the profession, and to society (e.g., Kelman, 1967). Others saw most deception as innocuous and argued that many important questions would be unanswered without its use (e.g., Christensen, 1988). The ethics of deception continues to be of interest (Fisher & Fyrberg, 1994).

Attempts to regulate ethical research practices increased during the 1970s. In 1973 the American Psychological Association revised their ethical principles to place greater constraints on the use of deception (American Psychological Association, 1973). The investigator was now charged with the responsibility of insuring that the use of deception was justified by the study's prospective value, to consider alternative procedures, and, if deception was used, to debrief participants as soon as possible. Deception was not prohibited, however, as long as the investigator considered these issues.

Also during the 1970s, federal regulation of research with humans began to have a more direct impact on psychologists. In 1971, social and behavioral research specifically were included in the federal policy on protection of human subjects. In 1974, regulations on grants administration stated that all research with humans must be reviewed by institutional boards, not only research that placed participants at risk (Faden & Beauchamp, 1986). However, the impact of these regulations and the American Psychological Association ethical standards on the use of deception was not seen immediately and did not seem to have an effect until the 1980s.

After 1979 there appears to have been a gradual decline in the use of deception from the levels of the 1960s and 1970s. We also found a decrease in the percentage of studies using deception in JPSP and JP, and the percentage was lower in 1987 than in 1983 for all three journals that we surveyed. Similar to Sieber et al. (1995), we found increases for these same journals in 1989 and 1994. However, these increases were small for JPSP and JP and did not show the use of deception to have returned to the frequency of the 1970s. The data for JESP was more variable than for the other two journals, showing a slight increase in 1979 from 1973, a reduction in 1987, an increase in 1989 and then another reduction in 1994. From these results it appears that the use of deception has decreased from the levels seen in the 1960s and 1970s, with some variability in the last two decades. This apparent decline in the use of deception in social psychology research since the 1970s is related to changes in theory and research practices, as well as the impact of imposing more rigid ethical standards.

One major change in theory between 1979 and 1994 was from the dominance of cognitive dissonance theory to that of attribution theories. Bagby, Parker, and Bury (1990) found that citations to Festinger in social psychological journals increased through the 1960s, peaked around 1972, and then gradually declined. In contrast, the rate of citations to Heider had peaked around 1975 with more than double the citations of Festinger and has only slightly declined since that period.

Jones (1985) discussed reasons for this shift in interest. First, it was easier to do attribution research that relied more on paper and pencil questionnaires than on elaborate scenarios with casts of confederates. Second, ethical standards changed accompanied by "the increasing pervasiveness of institutional monitoring of research practices" (p. 58). Partly because of the risk of rejection by institutional review boards, investigators became less willing to design experiments in which participants undergo manipulations that are psychologically uncomfortable.

Following the 1970s changes also were occurring in the types of methods used, with less emphasis being placed on randomized laboratory experiments and an increase in nonexperimental methods such as surveys and field studies (Adair et al., 1985; Vitelli, 1988; West, Newsom, & Fenaughty, 1992). We examined the articles for 2 years of JPSP and found an increase in the use of nonexperimental studies from 12% in 1973 to 23% in 1983.

In summary, we see that a combination of factors influenced the use of deception in research. Social psychologists developed a laboratory culture in which experimental realism and the impact experiment were valued. The leading theorists provided examples for acceptability in research methods, in terms of what was publishable and what was ethical. Deception also was fostered by the dominance of the randomized experimental design, which required manipulation of independent variables. Deceptive research practices

were limited, however, by the codifying of ethical standards in psychology and federal requirements for external review. As new theories and topics became popular in the 1980s, there was a reduction in the extent to which dramatic staged situations were used, and there probably has been some decline in the use of all types of deception. Perhaps, as this century comes to an end, the realism in research will be confined to the virtual reality of the computer screen.

ACKNOWLEDGMENTS

We thank John Chibnall, Andrew Pomerantz, and James Sweeney for assistance in data collection.

REFERENCES

Adair, J. G., Dushenko, T. W., & Lindsay, R. C. L. (1985). Ethical regulations and their impact on research practice. *American Psychologist, 40,* 59–72.

Allport, G. W. (1935). Attitudes. In C. Murchison (Ed.), *Handbook of social psychology* (pp. 798–844). Worchester, MA: Clark University Press.

American Psychological Association. (1973). *Ethical principles in the conduct of research with human participants.* Washington, DC: Author.

Aronson, E., Brewer, M., & Carlsmith, J. M. (1985). Experimentation in social psychology. In G. Lindzey & E. Aronson (Eds.), *The handbook of social psychology* (3rd ed., Vol. 1, pp. 441–486). New York: Random House.

Aronson, E., & Carlsmith, J. M. (1968). Experimentation in social psychology. In G. Lindzey & E. Aronson (Eds.), *The handbook of social psychology* (2nd ed., Vol. 2, pp. 1–79). Reading, MA: Addison-Wesley.

Bagby, R. M., Parker, J. D. A., & Bury, A. S. (1990). A comparative citation analysis of attribution theory and the theory of cognitive dissonance. *Personality and Social Psychology Bulletin, 16,* 274–283.

Baumrind, D. (1964). Some thoughts on ethics of research: After reading Milgram's "Behavioral study of obedience." *American Psychologist, 19,* 421–423.

Cason, H. (1925). Influence of suggestion on imagery in a group situation. *Journal of Abnormal and Social Psychology, 20,* 294–299.

Christensen, L. (1988). Deception in psychological research: When is its use justified? *Personality and Social Psychology Bulletin, 14,* 664–675.

Christie, R. (1965). Some implications of research trends in social psychology. In O. Klineberg & R. Christie (Eds.),

Perspectives in social psychology (pp. 141–152). New York: Holt, Rinehart, & Winston.

Craik, K. H. (1986). Personality research methods: An historical perspective. *Journal of Personality, 54,* 18–51.

Faden, R. R., & Beauchamp, T. L. (1986). *A history and theory of informed consent.* New York: Oxford University Press.

Fisher, C. B., & Fyrberg, D. (1994). Participant partners: College students weigh the costs and benefits of deceptive research. *American Psychologist, 49,* 417–427.

Gross, A. E., & Fleming, I. (1982). Twenty years of deception in social psychology. *Personality and Social Psychology Bulletin, 8,* 402–408.

Jones, E. E. (1985). Major developments in social psychology during the last past five decades. In G. Lindzey & E. Aronson (Eds.), *Handbook of social psychology* (3rd ed., Vol. 1, pp. 47–108). New York: Random House.

Kelman, H. (1967). Human use of human subjects: The problem of deception in social psychology. *Psychological Bulletin, 67,* 1–11.

Lindzey, G. (Ed.). (1954). *A handbook of social psychology* (Vols. 1–2). Cambridge, MA: Addison-Wesley.

Rosenzweig, S. (1933). The experimental situation as a psychological problem. *Psychological Review, 40,* 337–354.

Rucci, A. F., & Tweney, R. D. (1980). Analysis of variance and the "second discipline" of scientific psychology: A historical account. *Psychological Bulletin, 87,* 166–184.

Seeman, J. (1969). Deception in psychological research. *American Psychologist, 24,* 1025–1028.

Sieber, J. E., Iannuzzo, R., & Rodriguez, B. (1995). Deception methods in psychology: Have they changed in 23 years? *Ethics and Behavior, 5,* 67–85.

Smith, M. B. (1983). The shaping of American social psychology: A personal perspective from the periphery. *Personality and Social Psychology Bulletin, 9,* 165–180.

Vitelli, R. (1988). The crisis issue assessed: An empirical analysis. *Basic and Applied Social Psychology, 9,* 301–309.

West, S. G., Newsom, J. T., & Fenaughty, A. M. (1992). Publication trends in JPSP: Stability and change in topics, methods, and theories across two decades. *Personality and Social Psychology Bulletin, 18,* 473–484.

CRITICAL THINKING QUESTIONS

1. How would you define *deception?* Do you agree with the authors' operational definition of deception, or would you include other situations, such as nonawareness of participating in a research project? Why or why not? Develop a list of possible social psychology research deceptions, ranging from least to most questionable.

2. Find an article that uses deception, and criticize or defend its use. Could the study have been conducted in another way without using deception or at least with a different level or type of deception? Explain your answer.

3. Have you ever been the subject in an experiment that involved deception? If so, how did you feel afterward about your participation, once you had been debriefed and told the true nature of the study? If you personally have not been in such an experiment, ask some of your classmates if they have and how they felt about the experience.

4. Review the questions found in the previous article (Article 2) by Kelman. Would you answer any of them differently now, after reading the more recent information contained in Article 3? Explain your answer.

Chapter Two

SOCIAL PERCEPTION

How do we form impressions of other people? What information do we use in forming those impressions? How important are first impressions? How do we make judgments about why people act the way they do? These are some of the questions addressed by the readings in this chapter on social perception.

When we interact with another person, we are literally bombarded with information. What the person looks like, what he or she is saying, and how he or she is acting comprise but a fraction of the information available to us that we may use in forming an impression of the individual. One judgment we may make about another individual concerns his or her overall character. In other words, we want to know how honest, trustworthy, likeable, or good the person is. But exactly what are we looking for? And are some of us better than others at making accurate judgments?

A few years ago, a concept called *emotional intelligence* was proposed to explain the fact that some people seem to be more socially successful than others. Like its intelligence counterpart, emotional intelligence was viewed as a continuum of behaviors and characteristics associated with successful social outcomes, with some people being very low on this dimension and others very high. Article 4, "The EQ Factor," explores the development of this concept and discusses some of the controversy surrounding it and what can (or should) be done about developing emotional intelligence.

How long does it take for us to form an impression of a person? Is it almost immediate, or do we hold off on forming an impression until we really know more about the individual? Likewise, is all the information that is available about the other person equally relevant in forming our impressions, or are some factors more important than others? Research suggests that nonverbal cues are used to form initial impressions. Article 5, "The Warm-Cold Variable in First Impressions of Persons," examines some important additional factors influencing our judgments of other people. The article provides a fine example of the power of first impressions and the impact that they have on how we relate to others.

Finally, Article 6, "The Folk Concept of Intentionality," examines how people make judgments as to the underlying intentions behind others' actions. Specifically, the article presents a model that people may use in making such judgments. Given the implications of how we make attributions of responsibility, this conceptual and empirical article is most useful.

ARTICLE 4 _____

When we form an impression of another person, what factors influence our decision? His or her intelligence? Looks? Honesty? Empathy? The list could go on endlessly. In fact, an interaction of many factors ultimately leads to our judgment, and the factors that we find important or desirable are somewhat idiosyncratic, growing out of our own unique experiences and backgrounds. At the same time, there appear to be some universal characteristics that most people value. Who, for example, would prefer an untrustworthy friend to one who is trustworthy? People who possess more of these desirable characteristics may be better liked and more socially successful than others.

But what exactly are these desirable characteristics? For many years, people used the word *character* to describe the overall aspects of a person that might influence the perception of him or her as being good, likeable, trustworthy, and so on. What aspects are so influental, and do they cluster in some sort of group that might be called *social skills?* Recently, two researchers, Peter Salovey and John Mayer, coined the term *emotional intelligence* to describe the qualities that seem to enhance successful social behavior. This concept became wildly popular with publication of the best-selling book *Emotional Intelligence,* by Daniel Goleman, who also introduced the shortened term *EQ* to refer to the qualities. The basic notion is that just as IQ (i.e., intelligence quotient) may give some indiction of the overall level of a person's intellectual ability, EQ may give some insight into the level of social skills that an individual possesses.

The following article by Nancy Gibbs examines the origins of this concept of emotional intelligence and addresses some of controversy that still surrounds it.

The EQ Factor

■ Nancy Gibbs

It turns out that a scientist can see the future by watching four-year-olds interact with a marshmallow. The researcher invites the children, one by one, into a plain room and begins the gentle torment. You can have this marshmallow right now, he says. But if you wait while I run an errand, you can have two marshmallows when I get back. And then he leaves.

Some children grab for the treat the minute he's out the door. Some last a few minutes before they give in. But others are determined to wait. They cover their eyes; they put their heads down; they sing to themselves; they try to play games or even fall asleep. When the researcher returns he gives the children their hard-earned marshmallows. And then, science waits for them to grow up.

By the time the children reach high school, something remarkable has happened. A survey of the children's parents and teachers found that those who as four-year-olds had the fortitude to hold out for the second marshmallow generally grew up to be better adjusted, more popular, adventurous, confident and dependable teenagers. The children who gave in to temptation early on were more likely to be lonely, easily frustrated and stubborn. They buckled under stress and shied away from challenges. And when some of the students in the two groups took the Scholastic Aptitude Test, the kids who held out longer scored an average of 210 points higher.

When we think of brilliance we see Einstein, deep-eyed, woolly haired, a thinking machine with skin and mismatched socks. High achievers, we imagine, were wired for greatness from birth. But then you have to wonder why, over time, natural talent seems to ignite in some people and dim in others. This is where the

Reprinted from *Time,* October 2, 1995, pp. 60–66, 68. © 1995 Time Inc. Reprinted by permission.

marshmallows come in. It seems that the ability to delay gratification is a master skill, a triumph of the reasoning brain over the impulsive one. It is a sign, in short, of emotional intelligence. And it doesn't show up on an IQ test.

For most of this century, scientists have worshiped the hardware of the brain and the software of the mind; the messy powers of the heart were left to the poets. But cognitive theory could simply not explain the questions we wonder about most: why some people just seem to have a gift for living well; why the smartest kid in the class will probably not end up the richest; why we like some people virtually on sight and distrust others; why some people remain buoyant in the face of troubles that would sink a less resilient soul. What qualities of the mind or spirit, in short, determine who succeeds?

The phrase "emotional intelligence" was coined by Yale psychologist Peter Salovey and the University of New Hampshire's John Mayer five years ago to describe qualities like understanding one's own feelings, empathy for the feelings of others and "the regulation of emotion in a way that enhances living." Their notion is about to bound into the national conversation, handily shortened to EQ, thanks to a new book, *Emotional Intelligence* (Bantam; $23.95) by Daniel Goleman. Goleman, a Harvard psychology Ph.D. and a *New York Times* science writer with a gift for making even the chewiest scientific theories digestible to lay readers, has brought together a decade's worth of behavioral research into how the mind processes feelings. His goal, he announces on the cover, is to redefine what it means to be smart. His thesis: when it comes to predicting people's success, brainpower as measured by IQ and standardized achievement tests may actually matter less than the qualities of mind once thought of as "character" before the word began to sound quaint.

At first glance, there would seem to be little that's new here to any close reader of fortune cookies. There may be no less original idea than the notion that our hearts hold dominion over our heads. "I was so angry," we say, "I couldn't think straight." Neither is it surprising that "people skills" are useful, which amounts to saying, it's good to be nice. "It's so true it's trivial," says Dr. Paul McHugh, director of psychiatry at Johns Hopkins University School of Medicine. But

if it were that simple, the book would not be quite so interesting or its implications so controversial.

This is no abstract investigation. Goleman is looking for antidotes to restore "civility to our streets and caring to our communal life." He sees practical applications everywhere for how companies should decide whom to hire, how couples can increase the odds that their marriages will last, how parents should raise their children and how schools should teach them. When street gangs substitute for families and schoolyard insults end in stabbings, when more than half of marriages end in divorce, when the majority of the children murdered in this country are killed by parents and stepparents, many of whom say they were trying to discipline the child for behavior like blocking the TV or crying too much, it suggests a demand for remedial emotional education. While children are still young, Goleman argues, there is a "neurological window of opportunity" since the brain's prefrontal circuitry, which regulates how we act on what we feel, probably does not mature until mid-adolescence.

And it is here the arguments will break out. Goleman's highly popularized conclusions, says McHugh, "will chill any veteran scholar of psychotherapy and any neuroscientist who worries about how his research may come to be applied." While many researchers in this relatively new field are glad to see emotional issues finally taken seriously, they fear that a notion as handy as EQ invites misuse. Goleman admits the danger of suggesting that you can assign a numerical yardstick to a person's character as well as his intellect; Goleman never even uses the phrase EQ in his book. But he (begrudgingly) approved an "unscientific" EQ test in *USA Today* with choices like "I am aware of even subtle feelings as I have them," and "I can sense the pulse of a group or relationship and state unspoken feelings."

"You don't want to take an average of your emotional skill," argues Harvard psychology professor Jerome Kagan, a pioneer in child-development research. "That's what's wrong with the concept of intelligence for mental skills too. Some people handle anger well but can't handle fear. Some people can't take joy. So each emotion has to be viewed differently."

EQ is not the opposite of IQ. Some people are blessed with a lot of both, some with little of either.

What researchers have been trying to understand is how they complement each other; how one's ability to handle stress, for instance, affects the ability to concentrate and put intelligence to use. Among the ingredients for success, researchers now generally agree that IQ counts for about 20%; the rest depends on everything from class to luck to the neural pathways that have developed in the brain over millions of years of human evolution.

It is actually the neuroscientists and evolutionists who do the best job of explaining the reasons behind the most unreasonable behavior. In the past decade or so, scientists have learned enough about the brain to make judgments about where emotion comes from and why we need it. Primitive emotional responses held the keys to survival: fear drives the blood into the large muscles, making it easier to run; surprise triggers the eyebrows to rise, allowing the eyes to widen their view and gather more information about an unexpected event. Disgust wrinkles up the face and closes the nostrils to keep out foul smells.

Emotional life grows out of an area of the brain called the limbic system, specifically the amygdala, whence come delight and disgust and fear and anger. Millions of years ago, the neocortex was added on, enabling humans to plan, learn and remember. Lust grows from the limbic system; love, from the neocortex. Animals like reptiles that have no neocortex cannot experience anything like maternal love; this is why baby snakes have to hide to avoid being eaten by their parents. Humans, with their capacity for love, will protect their offspring, allowing the brains of the young time to develop. The more connections between limbic system and the neocortex, the more emotional responses are possible.

It was scientists like Joseph LeDoux of New York University who uncovered these cerebral pathways. LeDoux's parents owned a meat market. As a boy in Louisiana, he first learned about his future specialty by cutting up cows' brains for sweetbreads. "I found them the most interesting part of the cow's anatomy," he recalls. "They were visually pleasing—lots of folds, convolutions and patterns. The cerebellum was more interesting to look at than steak." The butchers' son became a neuroscientist, and it was he who discovered the short circuit in the brain that lets emotions drive action before the intellect gets a chance to intervene.

A hiker on a mountain path, for example, sees a long, curved shape in the grass out of the corner of his eye. He leaps out of the way before he realizes it is only a stick that looks like a snake. Then he calms down; his cortex gets the message a few milliseconds after his amygdala and "regulates" its primitive response.

Without these emotional reflexes, rarely conscious but often terribly powerful, we would scarcely be able to function. "Most decisions we make have a vast number of possible outcomes, and any attempt to analyze all of them would never end," says University of Iowa neurologist Antonio Damasio, author of *Descartes' Error: Emotion, Reason and the Human Brain.* "I'd ask you to lunch tomorrow, and when the appointed time arrived, you'd still be thinking about whether you should come." What tips the balance, Damasio contends, is our unconscious assigning of emotional values to some of those choices. Whether we experience a somatic response—a gut feeling of dread or a giddy sense of elation—emotions are helping to limit the field in any choice we have to make. If the prospect of lunch with a neurologist is unnerving or distasteful, Damasio suggests, the invitee will conveniently remember a previous engagement.

When Damasio worked with patients in whom the connection between emotional brain and neocortex had been severed because of damage to the brain, he discovered how central that hidden pathway is to how we live our lives. People who had lost that linkage were just as smart and quick to reason, but their lives often fell apart nonetheless. They could not make decisions because they didn't know how they felt about their choices. They couldn't react to warnings or anger in other people. If they made a mistake, like a bad investment, they felt no regret or shame and so were bound to repeat it.

If there is a cornerstone to emotional intelligence on which most other emotional skills depend, it is a sense of self-awareness, of being smart about what we feel. A person whose day starts badly at home may be grouchy all day at work without quite knowing why. Once an emotional response comes into awareness—or, physiologically, is processed through the neocortex—the chances of handling it appropriately improve. Scientists refer to "metamood," the ability to pull back and recognize that "what I'm feeling is anger," or sorrow, or shame.

Metamood is a difficult skill because emotions so often appear in disguise. A person in mourning may know he is sad, but he may not recognize that he is also angry at the person for dying—because this seems somehow inappropriate. A parent who yells at the child who ran into the street is expressing anger at disobedience, but the degree of anger may owe more to the fear the parent feels at what could have happened.

In Goleman's analysis, self-awareness is perhaps the most crucial ability because it allows us to exercise some self-control. The idea is not to repress feeling (the reaction that has made psychoanalysts rich) but rather to do what Aristotle considered the hard work of the will. "Anyone can become angry—that is easy," he wrote in the *Nicomachean Ethics*. "But to be angry with the right person, to the right degree, at the right time, for the right purpose, and in the right way—that is not easy."

Some impulses seem to be easier to control than others. Anger, not surprisingly, is one of the hardest, perhaps because of its evolutionary value in priming people to action. Researchers believe anger usually arises out of a sense of being trespassed against—the belief that one is being robbed of what is rightfully his. The body's first response is a surge of energy, the release of a cascade of neurotransmitters called catecholamines. If a person is already aroused or under stress, the threshold for release is lower, which helps explain why people's tempers shorten during a hard day.

Scientists are not only discovering where anger comes from; they are also exposing myths about how best to handle it. Popular wisdom argues for "letting it all hang out" and having a good cathartic rant. But Goleman cites studies showing that dwelling on anger actually increases its power; the body needs a chance to process the adrenaline through exercise, relaxation techniques, a well-timed intervention or even the old admonition to count to 10.

Anxiety serves a similar useful purpose, so long as it doesn't spin out of control. Worrying is a rehearsal for danger; the act of fretting focuses the mind on a problem so it can search efficiently for solutions. The danger comes when worrying blocks thinking, becoming an end in itself or a path to resignation instead of perseverance. Over-worrying about failing increases the likelihood of failure; a salesman so concerned about his falling sales that he can't bring himself to pick up the phone guarantees that his sales will fall even further.

But why are some people better able to "snap out of it" and get on with the task at hand? Again, given sufficient self-awareness, people develop coping mechanisms. Sadness and discouragement, for instance, are "low arousal" states, and the dispirited salesman who goes out for a run is triggering a high arousal state that is incompatible with staying blue. Relaxation works better for high energy moods like anger or anxiety. Either way, the idea is to shift to a state of arousal that breaks the destructive cycle of the dominant mood.

The idea of being able to predict which salesmen are most likely to prosper was not an abstraction for Metropolitan Life, which in the mid-'80s was hiring 5,000 salespeople a year and training them at a cost of more than $30,000 each. Half quit the first year, and four out of five within four years. The reason: selling life insurance involves having the door slammed in your face over and over again. Was it possible to identify which people would be better at handling frustration and take each refusal as a challenge rather than a setback?

The head of the company approached psychologist Martin Seligman at the University of Pennsylvania and invited him to test some of his theories about the importance of optimism in people's success. When optimists fail, he has found, they attribute the failure to something they can change, not some innate weakness that they are helpless to overcome. And that confidence in their power to effect change is self-reinforcing. Seligman tracked 15,000 new workers who had taken two tests. One was the company's regular screening exam, the other Seligman's test measuring their levels of optimism. Among the new hires was a group who flunked the screening test but scored as "superoptimists" on Seligman's exam. And sure enough, they did the best of all; they outsold the pessimists in the regular group by 21% in the first year and 57% in the second. For years after that, passing Seligman's test was one way to get hired as a MetLife salesperson.

Perhaps the most visible emotional skills, the ones we recognize most readily, are the "people skills" like

One Way to Test Your EQ

Unlike IQ, which is gauged by the famous Stanford-Binet tests, EQ does not lend itself to any single numerical measure. Nor should it, say experts. Emotional intelligence is by definition a complex, multifaceted quality representing such intangibles as self-awareness, empathy, persistence and social deftness.

Some aspects of emotional intelligence, however, can be quantified. Optimism, for example, is a handy measure of a person's self-worth. According to Martin Seligman, a University of Pennsylvania psychologist, how people respond to setbacks—optimistically or pessimistically—is a fairly accurate indicator of how well they will succeed in school, in sports and in certain kinds of work. To test his theory, Seligman devised a questionnaire to screen insurance salesmen at MetLife.

In Seligman's test, job applicants were asked to imagine a hypothetical event and then choose the response (A or B) that most closely resembled their own. Some samples from his questionnaire:

You forget your spouse's (boyfriend's/girlfriend's) birthday.
A. I'm not good at remembering birthdays.
B. I was preoccupied with other things.

You owe the library $10 for an overdue book.
A. When I am really involved in what I am reading, I often forget when its due.
B. I was so involved in writing the report, I forgot to return the book.

You lose your temper with a friend.
A. He or she is always nagging me.
B. He or she was in a hostile mood.

You are penalized for returning your income-tax forms late.
A. I always put off doing my taxes.
B. I was lazy about getting my taxes done this year.

You've been feeling run-down.
A. I never get a chance to relax.
B. I was exceptionally busy this week.

A friend says something that hurts your feelings.
A. She always blurts things out without thinking of others.
B. My friend was in a bad mood and took it out on me.

You fall down a great deal while skiing.
A. Skiing is difficult.
B. The trails were icy.

You gain weight over the holidays, and you can't lose it.
A. Diets don't work in the long run.
B. The diet I tried didn't work.

Seligman found that those insurance salesman who answered with more B's than A's were better able to overcome bad sales days, recovered more easily from rejection and were less likely to quit. People with an optimistic view of life tend to treat obstacles and setbacks as temporary (and therefore surmountable). Pessimists take them personally; what others see as fleeting, localized impediments, they view as pervasive and permanent.

The most dramatic proof of his theory, says Seligman, came at the 1988 Olympic Games in Seoul, South Korea, after U.S. swimmer Matt Biondi turned in two disappointing performances in his first two races. Before the Games, Biondi had been favored to win seven golds—as Mark Spitz had done 16 years earlier. After those first two races, most commentators thought Biondi would be unable to recover from his setback. Not Seligman. He had given some members of the U.S. swim team a version of his optimism test before the races; it showed that Biondi possessed an extraordinarily upbeat attitude. Rather than losing heart after turning in a bad time, as others might, Biondi tended to respond by swimming even faster. Sure enough, Biondi bounced right back, winning five gold medals in the next five races.

—By Alice Park

empathy, graciousness, the ability to read a social situation. Researchers believe that about 90% of emotional communication is nonverbal. Harvard psychologist Robert Rosenthal developed the PONS test (Profile of Nonverbal Sensitivity) to measure people's ability to read emotional cues. He shows subjects a film of a young woman expressing feelings—anger, love, jealousy, gratitude, seduction—edited so that one or another nonverbal cue is blanked out. In some instances the face is visible but not the body, or the woman's eyes are hidden, so that viewers have to judge the feeling by subtle cues. Once again, people with higher PONS scores tend to be more successful in their work and relationships; children who score well are more popular and successful in school, even [though] their IQs are quite average.

Like other emotional skills, empathy is an innate quality that can be shaped by experience. Infants as young as three months old exhibit empathy when they get upset at the sound of another baby crying. Even very young children learn by imitation; by watching how others act when they see someone in distress, these children acquire a repertoire of sensitive responses. If, on the other hand, the feelings they begin to express are not recognized and reinforced by the adults around them, they not only cease to express those feelings but they also become less able to recognize them in themselves or others.

Empathy too can be seen as a survival skill. Bert Cohler, a University of Chicago psychologist, and Fran Stott, dean of the Erikson Institute for Advanced Study in Child Development in Chicago, have found that children from psychically damaged families frequently become hypervigilant, developing an intense attunement to their parents' moods. One child they studied, Nicholas, had a horrible habit of approaching other kids in his nursery-school class as if he were going to kiss them, then would bite them instead. The scientists went back to study videos of Nicholas at 20 months interacting with his psychotic mother and found that she had responded to his every expression of anger or independence with compulsive kisses. The researchers dubbed them "kisses of death," and their true significance was obvious to Nicholas, who arched his back in horror at her approaching lips—and passed his own rage on to his classmates years later.

Empathy also acts as a buffer to cruelty, and it is a quality conspicuously lacking in child molesters and psychopaths. Goleman cites some chilling research into brutality by Robert Hare, a psychologist at the University of British Columbia. Hare found that psychopaths, when hooked up to electrodes and told they are going to receive a shock, show none of the visceral responses that fear of pain typically triggers: rapid heartbeat, sweating and so on. How could the threat of punishment deter such people from committing crimes?

It is easy to draw the obvious lesson from these test results. How much happier would we be, how much more successful as individuals and civil as a society, if we were more alert to the importance of emotional intelligence and more adept at teaching it? From kindergartens to business schools to corporations across the country, people are taking seriously the idea that a little more time spent on the "touchy-feely" skills so often derided may in fact pay rich dividends.

In the corporate world, according to personnel executives, IQ gets you hired, but EQ gets you promoted. Goleman likes to tell of a manager at AT&T's Bell Labs, a think tank for brilliant engineers in New Jersey, who was asked to rank his top performers. They weren't the ones with the highest IQs; they were the ones whose E-mail got answered. Those workers who were good collaborators and networkers and popular with colleagues were more likely to get the cooperation they needed to reach their goals than the socially awkward, lone-wolf geniuses.

When David Campbell and others at the Center for Creative Leadership studied "derailed executives," the rising stars who flamed out, the researchers found that these executives failed most often because of "an interpersonal flaw" rather than a technical inability. Interviews with top executives in the U.S. and Europe turned up nine so-called fatal flaws, many of them classic emotional failings, such as "poor working relations," being "authoritarian" or "too ambitious" and having "conflict with upper management."

At the center's executive-leadership seminars across the country, managers come to get emotionally retooled. "This isn't sensitivity training or Sunday-supplement stuff," says Campbell. "One thing they know when they get through is what other people

Square Pegs in the Oval Office?

If a high degree of emotional intelligence is a prerequisite for outstanding achievement, there ought to be no better place to find it than in the White House. It turns out, however, that not every man who reached the pinnacle of American leadership was a gleaming example of self-awareness, empathy, impulse control and all the other qualities that mark an elevated EQ.

Oliver Wendall Holmes, who knew intelligence when he saw it, judged Franklin Roosevelt "a second-class intellect, but a first-class temperament." Born and educated as an aristocrat, F.D.R. had polio and needed a wheelchair for most of his adult life. Yet, far from becoming a self-pitying wretch, he developed an unbridled optimism that served him and the country well during the Depression and World War II—this despite, or because of, what Princeton professor Fred Greenstein calls Roosevelt's "tendency toward deviousness and duplicity."

Even a first-class temperament, however, is not a sure predictor of a successful presidency. According to Duke University political scientist James David Barber, the most perfect blend of intellect and warmth of personality in a Chief Executive was the brilliant Thomas Jefferson, who "knew the importance of communication and empathy. He never lost the common touch." Richard Ellis, a professor of politics at Oregon's Willamette University who is skeptical of the whole EQ theory, cites two 19th century Presidents who did not fit the mold. "Martin Van Buren was well adjusted, balanced, empathetic and persuasive, but he was not very successful," says Ellis. "Andrew Jackson was less well adjusted, less balanced, less empathetic and was terrible at controlling his own impulses, but he transformed the presidency."

Lyndon Johnson as Senate majority leader was a brilliant practitioner of the art of political persuasion, yet failed utterly to transfer that gift to the White House. In fact, says Princeton's Greenstein, L.B.J. and Richard Nixon would be labeled "worst cases" on any EQ scale of Presidents. Each was touched with political genius, yet each met with disaster. "To some extent," says Greenstein, "this is a function of the extreme aspects of their psyches; they are the political versions of Van Gogh, who does unbelievable paintings and then cuts off his ear."

History professor William Leuchtenburg of the University of North Carolina at Chapel Hill suggests that the 20th century Presidents with perhaps the highest IQs—Wilson, Hoover and Carter—also had the most trouble connecting with their constituents. Woodrow Wilson, he says, "was very high strung [and] arrogant; he was not willing to strike any middle ground. Herbert Hoover was so locked into certain ideas that you could never convince him otherwise. Jimmy Carter is probably the most puzzling of the three. He didn't have a deficiency of temperament; in fact, he was too temperate. There was an excessive rationalization about Carter's approach."

That was never a problem for John Kennedy and Ronald Reagan. Nobody ever accused them of intellectual genius, yet both radiated qualities of leadership with an infectious confidence and openheartedness that endeared them to the nation. Whether President Clinton will be so endeared remains a puzzle. That he is a Rhodes scholar makes him certifiably brainy, but his emotional intelligence is shaky. He obviously has the knack for establishing rapport with people, but he often appears so eager to please that he looks weak. "As for controlling his impulses," says Willamette's Ellis, "Clinton is terrible."

—By Jesse Birnbaum. Reported by James Carney/Washington and Lisa H. Towle/Raleigh

think of them." And the executives have an incentive to listen. Says Karen Boylston, director of the center's team-leadership group: "Customers are telling businesses, 'I don't care if every member of your staff graduated with honors from Harvard, Stanford and Wharton. I will take my business and go where I am understood and treated with respect.'"

Nowhere is the discussion of emotional intelligence more pressing than in schools, where both the stakes and the opportunities seem greatest. Instead of constant crisis intervention, or declarations of war on drug abuse or teen pregnancy or violence, it is time, Goleman argues, for preventive medicine. "Five years ago, teachers didn't want to think about this," says principal Roberta Kirshbaum of P.S. 75 in New York City. "But when kids are getting killed in high school, we have to deal with it." Five years ago, Kirshbaum's school adopted an emotional literacy program, designed to help children learn to manage anger, frustration, loneliness. Since then, fights at lunchtime have decreased from two or three a day to almost none.

Educators can point to all sorts of data to support this new direction. Students who are depressed or angry literally cannot learn. Children who have trouble being accepted by their classmates are 2 to 8 times as likely to drop out. An inability to distinguish distressing feelings or handle frustration has been linked to eating disorders in girls.

Many school administrators are completely rethinking the weight they have been giving to traditional lessons and standardized tests. Peter Relic, president of the National Association of Independent Schools, would like to junk the SAT completely. "Yes, it may cost a heck of a lot more money to assess someone's EQ rather than using a machine-scored test to measure IQ," he says. "But if we don't, then we're saying that a test score is more important to us than who a child is as a human being. That means an immense loss in terms of human potential because we've defined success too narrowly."

This warm embrace by educators has left some scientists in a bind. On one hand, says Yale psychologist Salovey, "I love the idea that we want to teach people a richer understanding of their emotional life, to help them achieve their goals." But, he adds, "what I would oppose is training conformity to social expectations." The danger is that any campaign to hone emotional skills in children will end up teaching that there is a "right" emotional response for any given situation—laugh at parades, cry at funerals, sit still at church. "You can teach self-control," says Dr. Alvin Poussaint, professor of psychiatry at Harvard Medical School. "You can teach that it's better to talk out your anger and not use violence. But is it good emotional intelligence not to challenge authority?"

Some psychologists go further and challenge the very idea that emotional skills can or should be taught in any kind of formal, classroom way. Goleman's premise that children can be trained to analyze their feelings strikes Johns Hopkins' McHugh as an effort to reinvent the encounter group: "I consider that an abominable idea, an idea we have seen with adults. That failed, and now he wants to try it with children? Good grief!" He cites the description in Goleman's book of an experimental program at the Nueva Learning Center in San Francisco. In one scene, two fifth-grade boys start to argue over the rules of an exercise, and the teacher breaks in to ask them to talk about what they're feeling. "I appreciate the way you're being assertive in talking with Tucker," she says to one student. "You're not attacking." This strikes McHugh as pure folly. "The author is presuming that someone has the key to the right emotions to be taught to children. We don't even know the right emotions to be taught to adults. Do you really think a child of eight or nine really understands the difference between aggressiveness and assertiveness?"

The problem may be that there is an ingredient missing. Emotional skills, like intellectual ones, are morally neutral. Just as a genius could use his intellect either to cure cancer or engineer a deadly virus, someone with great empathic insight could use it to inspire colleagues or exploit them. Without a moral compass to guide people in how to employ their gifts, emotional intelligence can be used for good or evil. Columbia University psychologist Walter Mischel, who invented the marshmallow test and others like it, observes that the knack for delaying gratification that makes a child one marshmallow richer can help him become a better citizen or—just as easily—an even more brilliant criminal.

Given the passionate arguments that are raging over the state of moral instruction in this country, it is no wonder Goleman chose to focus more on neutral emotional skills than on the values that should govern their use. That's another book—and another debate.

—Reported by Sharon E. Epperson and Lawrence Mondi/New York, James L. Graff/Chicago and Lisa H. Towle/Raleigh

CRITICAL THINKING QUESTIONS

1. Think of a person you know whom you consider to be very socially successful. Does he or she seem to possess the qualities associated with emotional intelligence, as discussed in the article? Elaborate on how these (or other) qualities may have contributed to this person's social success.
2. Should emotional intelligence be taught to children? Why or why not? What issues would need to be considered? For instance, what emotional responses are deemed proper and should thus be taught? Defend your position.
3. Discuss the pros and cons of using an EQ test to screen potential employees for a job.
4. Besides those discussed in the article, what connections may exist between high emotional intelligence and successful behavior? Design a study that would test whether such a connection exists.
5. Would it be possible to teach a sort of remedial emotional intelligence to adults? Why or why not? Describe a study that could attempt to answer this question empirically.

ARTICLE 5 _____

A variety of sources of information may be available for use in forming an impression of a person. However, that does not mean that all of the information will be used or hold equal value. Some sources of information may carry more weight than others. For example, we may notice how the person acts, or we may have heard something about him or her from someone else. How do we use this information to develop an impression of the person?

Building on the classic work of S. E. Asch, Harold H. Kelley examines what can be called a *central organizing trait,* one that is important in influencing the impressions that we form. By examining the effect of changing just one adjective in describing a person (i.e., *warm* versus *cold*), the study demonstrates that this initial difference influenced how the subjects actually rated the person. Even more interesting is that these differences in initial impression carried over into how the subjects interacted with the person. The implication is that perhaps our initial impressions lead us to act in certain ways toward others, perhaps creating a self-fulfilling prophecy by giving us what we expected to see in the first place.

The Warm-Cold Variable in First Impressions of Persons
■ Harold H. Kelley

This experiment is one of several studies of first impressions (3), the purpose of the series being to investigate the stability of early judgments, their determinants, and the relation of such judgments to the behavior of the person making them. In interpreting the data from several nonexperimental studies on the stability of first impressions, it proved to be necessary to postulate inner-observer variables which contribute to the impression and which remain relatively constant through time. Also some evidence was obtained which directly demonstrated the existence of these variables and their nature. The present experiment was designed to determine the effects of one kind of inner-observer variable, specifically, *expectations* about the stimulus person which the observer brings to the exposure situation.

That prior information or labels attached to a stimulus person make a difference in observers' first impressions is almost too obvious to require demonstration. The expectations resulting from such preinformation may restrict, modify, or accentuate the impressions he will have. The crucial question is: What changes in perception will accompany a given expectation? Studies of stereotyping, for example, that of Katz and Braly (2), indicate that from an ethnic label such as "German" or "Negro," a number of perceptions follow which are culturally determined. The present study finds its main significance in relation to a study by Asch (1) which demonstrates that certain crucial labels can transform the entire impression of the person, leading to attributions which are related to the label on a broad cultural basis or even, perhaps, on an autochthonous basis.

Asch read to his subjects a list of adjectives which purportedly described a particular person. He then asked them to characterize that person. He found that the inclusion in the list of what he called *central* qualities, such as "warm" as opposed to "cold," produced a widespread change in the entire impression. This effect was not adequately explained by the halo effect since it did not extend indiscriminately in a positive or negative direction to all characteristics.

Reprinted from *Journal of Personality,* 1950, *18,* 431–439. Copyright © 1950 by Blackwell Publishers, Inc. Reprinted with permission.

Rather, it differentially transformed the other qualities, for example, by changing their relative importance in the total impression. Peripheral qualities (such as "polite" versus "blunt") did not produce effects as strong as those produced by the central qualities.[1]

The present study tested the effects of such central qualities upon the early impressions of *real* persons, the same qualities, "warm" vs. "cold," being used. They were introduced as preinformation about the stimulus person before his actual appearance; so presumably they operated as expectations rather than as part of the stimulus pattern during the exposure period. In addition, information was obtained about the effects of the expectations upon the observers' behavior toward the stimulus person. An earlier study in this series has indicated that the more incompatible the observer initially perceived the stimulus person to be, the less the observer initiated interaction with him thereafter. The second purpose of the present experiment, then, was to provide a better controlled study of this relationship.

No previous studies reported in the literature have dealt with the importance of first impressions for behavior. The most relevant data are found in the sociometric literature, where there are scattered studies of the relation between choices among children having some prior acquaintance and their interaction behavior. For an example, see the study by Newstetter, Feldstein, and Newcomb (8).

PROCEDURE

The experiment was performed in three sections of a psychology course (Economics 70) at the Massachusetts Institute of Technology.[2] The three sections provided 23, 16, and 16 subjects respectively. All 55 subjects were men, most of them in their third college year. In each class the stimulus person (also a male) was completely unknown to the subjects before the experimental period. One person served as stimulus person in two sections, and a second person took this role in the third section. In each case the stimulus person was introduced by the experimenter, who posed as a representative of the course instructors and who gave the following statement:

Your regular instructor is out of town today, and since we of Economics 70 are interested in the general problem of how various classes react to different instructors, we're going to have an instructor today you've never had before, Mr. ____. Then, at the end of the period, I want you to fill out some forms about him. In order to give you some idea of what he's like, we've had a person who knows him write up a little biographical note about him. I'll pass this out to you now and you can read it before he arrives. Please read these to yourselves and don't talk about this among yourselves until the class is over so that he won't get wind of what's going on.

Two kinds of these notes were distributed, the two being identical except that in one the stimulus person was described among other things as being "rather cold" whereas in the other form the phrase "very warm" was substituted. The content of the "rather cold" version is as follows:

Mr. ____ is a graduate student in the Department of Economics and Social Science here at M.I.T. He has had three semesters of teaching experience in psychology at another college. This is his first semester teaching Ec. 70. He is 26 years old, a veteran, and married. People who know him consider him to be a rather cold person, industrious, critical, practical, and determined.

The two types of preinformation were distributed randomly within each of the three classes and in such a manner that the students were not aware that two kinds of information were being given out. The stimulus person then appeared and led the class in a twenty-minute discussion. During this time the experimenter kept a record of how often each student participated in the discussion. Since the discussion was almost totally leader-centered, this participation record indicates the number of times each student initiated verbal interaction with the instructor. After the discussion period, the stimulus person left the room, and the experimenter gave the following instructions:

Now, I'd like to get your impression of Mr. ____. This is not a test of you and can in no way affect your grade in this course. This material will not be identi-

fied as belonging to particular persons and will be kept strictly confidential. It will be of most value to us if you are completely honest in your evaluation of Mr. _____. Also, please understand that what you put down will not be used against him or cause him to lose his job or anything like that. This is not a test of him but merely a study of how different classes react to different instructors.

The subjects then wrote free descriptions of the stimulus person and finally rated him on a set of 15 rating scales.

RESULTS AND DISCUSSION

1. Influence of warm-cold variable on first impressions. The differences in the ratings produced by the warm-cold variable were consistent from one section to another even where different stimulus persons were used. Consequently, the data from the three sections were combined by equating means (the S.D.'s were approximately equal) and the results for the total group are presented in Table 1. Also in this table is presented that part of Asch's data which refers to the qualities included in our rating scales. From this table it is quite clear that those given the "warm" preinformation consistently rated the stimulus person more favorably than those given the "cold" preinformation. Summarizing the statistically significant differences, the "warm" subjects rated the stimulus person as more considerate of others, more informal, more sociable, more popular, better natured, more humorous, and more humane. These findings are very similar to Asch's for the characteristics common to both studies. He found more frequent attribution to

TABLE 1 / Comparison of "Warm" and "Cold" Observers in Terms of Average Ratings Given Stimulus Persons

Item	Low End of Rating Scale	High End of Rating Scale	Average Rating		Level of Significance of Warm-Cold Difference	Asch's Data: Per Cent of Group Assigning Quality at Low End of Our Rating Scale*	
			Warm N = 27	Cold N = 28		Warm	Cold
1	Knows his stuff	Doesn't know his stuff	3.5	4.6			
2	Considerate of others	Self-centered	6.3	9.6	1%		
3†	Informal	Formal	6.3	9.6	1%		
4†	Modest	Proud	9.4	10.6			
5	Sociable	Unsociable	5.6	10.4	1%	91%	38%
6	Self-assured	Uncertain of himself	8.4	9.1			
7	High intelligence	Low intelligence	4.8	5.1			
8	Popular	Unpopular	4.0	7.4	1%	84%	28%
9†	Good natured	Irritable	9.4	12.0	5%	94%	17%
10	Generous	Ungenerous	8.2	9.6		91%	08%
11	Humorous	Humorless	8.3	11.7	1%	77%	13%
12	Important	Insignificant	6.5	8.6		88%	99%
13†	Humane	Ruthless	8.6	11.0	5%	86%	31%
14†	Submissive	Dominant	13.2	14.5			
15	Will go far	Will not get ahead	4.2	5.8			

*Given for all qualities common to Asch's list and this set of rating scales.
†These scales were reversed when presented to the subjects.

his hypothetical "warm" personalities of sociability, popularity, good naturedness, generosity, humorousness, and humaneness. So these data strongly support his finding that such a central quality as "warmth" can greatly influence the total impression of a personality. This effect is found to be operative in the perception of real persons.

This general favorableness in the perceptions of the "warm" observers as compared with the "cold" ones indicates that something like a halo effect may have been operating in these ratings. Although his data are not completely persuasive on this point, Asch was convinced that such a general effect was *not* operating in his study. Closer inspection of the present data makes it clear that the "warm-cold" effect cannot be explained altogether on the basis of simple halo effect. In Table 1 it is evident that the "warm-cold" variable produced differential effects from one rating scale to another. The size of this effect seems to depend upon the closeness of relation between the specific dimension of any given rating scale and the central quality of "warmth" or "coldness." Even though the rating of intelligence may be influenced by a halo effect, it is not influenced to the same degree to which considerateness is. It seems to make sense to view such strongly influenced items as considerateness, informality, good naturedness, and humaneness as dynamically more closely related to warmth and hence more perceived in terms of this relation than in terms of a general positive or negative feeling toward the stimulus person. If first impressions are normally made in terms of such general dimensions as "warmth" and "coldness," the power they give the observer in making predictions and specific evaluations about such disparate behavior characteristics as formality and considerateness is considerable (even though these predictions may be incorrect or misleading).

The free report impression data were analyzed for only one of the sections. In general, there were few sizable differences between the "warm" and "cold" observers. The "warm" observers attributed more nervousness, more sincerity, and more industriousness to the stimulus person. Although the frequencies of comparable qualities are very low because of the great variety of descriptions produced by the observers, there is considerable agreement with the rating scale data.

Two important phenomena are illustrated in these free description protocols, the first of them having been noted by Asch. *Firstly,* the characteristics of the stimulus person are interpreted in terms of the precognition of warmth or coldness. For example, a "warm" observer writes about a rather shy and retiring stimulus person as follows: "He makes friends slowly but they are lasting friendships when formed." In another instance, several "cold" observers described him as being, ". . . intolerant: would be angry if you disagree with his view. . ."; while several "warm" observers put the same thing this way: "Unyielding in principle, not easily influenced or swayed from his original attitude." *Secondly,* the preinformation about the stimulus person's warmth or coldness is evaluated and interpreted in the light of the direct behavioral data about him. For example, "He has a slight inferiority complex which leads to his coldness," and "His conscientiousness and industriousness might be mistaken for coldness." Examples of these two phenomena occurred rather infrequently, and there was no way to evaluate the relative strengths of these countertendencies. Certainly some such evaluation is necessary to determine the conditions under which behavior which is contrary to a stereotyped label resists distortion and leads to rejection of the label.

A comparison of the data from the two different stimulus persons is pertinent to the last point in so far as it indicates the interaction between the properties of the stimulus person and the label. The fact that the warm-cold variable generally produced differences in the same direction for the two stimulus persons, even though they are very different in personality, behavior, and mannerisms, indicates the strength of this variable. However, there were some exceptions to this tendency as well as marked differences in the *degree* to which the experimental variable was able to produce differences. For example, stimulus person A typically appears to be anything but lacking in self-esteem and on rating scale 4 he was generally at the "proud" end of the scale. Although the "warm" observers tended to rate him as they did the other stimulus person (i.e., more "modest"), the difference between the "warm" and "cold" means for stimulus person A is very small and not significant as it is for stimulus person B. Similarly, stimulus person B was seen as "unpopular" and "humorless," which agrees with his typical classroom behavior. Again the "warm" observers rated him more favorably on these items, but their ratings were not significantly different from those of the "cold" observers, as was true for the other stimulus person. Thus we see that the strength or compellingness of various qualities of the stimulus person must be reckoned with. The stimulus is not passive to the forces arising from the label but actively resists distortion and may severely limit the degree of influence exerted by the preinformation.[3]

2. *Influence of warm-cold variable on interaction with the stimulus person.* In the analysis of the frequency with which the various students took part in the discussion led by the stimulus person, a larger proportion of those given the "warm" preinformation participated than of those given the "cold" preinformation. Fifty-six per cent of the "warm" subjects entered the discussion, whereas only 32 per cent of the "cold" subjects did so. Thus the expectation of warmth not only produced more favorable early perceptions of the stimulus person but led to greater initiation of interaction with him. This relation is a low one, significant at between the 5 per cent and 10 percent level of confidence, but it is in line with the general principle that social perception serves to guide and steer the person's behavior in his social environment.

As would be expected from the foregoing findings, there was also a relation between the favorableness of the impression and whether or not the person participated in the discussion. Although any single item yielded only a small and insignificant relation to participation, when a number are combined the trend becomes clear cut. For example, when we combine the seven items which were influenced to a statistically significant degree by the warm-cold variable, the total score bears considerable relation to participation, the relationship being significant as well beyond the 1 per cent level. A larger proportion of those having favorable total impressions participated than of those having unfavorable impressions, the bi-serial correlation between these variables being .34. Although this relation may be interpreted in several ways, it seems most likely that the unfavorable perception led to a curtailment of interaction. Support for this comes from one of the other studies in this series (3). There it was found that those persons having unfavorable impressions of the instructor at the end of the first class meeting tended less often to initiate interactions with him in the succeeding four meetings than did those having favorable first impressions. There was also some tendency in the same study for those persons who interacted least with the instructor to change least in their judgments of him from the first to later impressions.

It will be noted that these relations lend some support to the autistic hostility hypothesis proposed by Newcomb (7). This hypothesis suggests that the possession of an initially hostile attitude toward a person leads to a restriction of communication and contact with him which in turn serves to preserve the hostile attitude by preventing the acquisition of data which could correct it. The present data indicate that a restriction of interaction is associated with unfavorable preinformation and an unfavorable perception. The data from the other study support this result and also indicate the correctness of the second part of the hypothesis, that restricted interaction reduces the likelihood of change in the attitude.

What makes these findings more significant is that they appear in the context of a discussion class where there are numerous *induced* and *own* forces to enter the discussion and to interact with the instructor. It seems likely that the effects predicted by Newcomb's hypothesis would be much more marked in a setting where such forces were not present.

SUMMARY

The warm-cold variable had been found by Asch to produce large differences in the impressions of personality formed from a list of adjectives. In this study the same variable was introduced in the form of expectations about a real person and was found to produce similar differences in first impressions of him in a classroom setting. In addition, the differences in first impressions produced by the different expectations were shown to influence the observers' behavior toward the stimulus person. Those observers given the favorable expectation (who, consequently, had a favorable impression of the stimulus person) tended to interact more with him than did those given the unfavorable expectation.

REFERENCES

1. Asch, S. E., Forming impressions of personality. *J. Abnorm. Soc. Psychol.,* 1946, *41,* 258–290.
2. Katz, D., and Braly, K. W. Verbal stereotypes and racial prejudice. In Newcomb, T. M. and Hartley, E. L. (eds.), *Readings in social psychology.* New York: Holt, 1947. Pp. 204–210.
3. Kelley, H. H. First impressions in interpersonal relations. Ph.D. thesis, Massachusetts Institute of Technology, Cambridge, Mass. Sept., 1948.
4. Krech, D., and Crutchfield, R. S. *Theory and problems of social psychology.* New York, McGraw-Hill, 1948.
5. Luchins, A. S. Forming impressions of personality: A critique. *J. Abnorm. Soc. Psychol.,* 1948, *43,* 318–325.
6. Mensch, I. N., and Wishner, J. Asch on "Forming impressions of personality": further evidence. *J. Personal.,* 1947, *16,* 188–191.
7. Newcomb, T. M. Autistic hostility and social reality. *Hum. Relations.,* 1947, *1,* 69–86.
8. Newsetter, W. I., Feldstein, M. H., and Newcomb, T. M. *Group adjustment: A study in experimental sociology.* Cleveland: Western Reserve University, 1938.

ENDNOTES

1. Since the present experiment was carried out, Mensch and Wishner (6) have repeated a number of Asch's experiments because of dissatisfaction with his sex and geographic distribution. Their data substantiate Asch's very closely. Also, Luchins (5) has criticized Asch's experiments for their artificial methodology, repeated some of them, and challenged some of the kinds of interpretations Asch made from his data. Luchins also briefly reports some tantalizing conclusions from a number of studies of first impressions of actual persons.

2. Professor Mason Haire, now of the University of California, provided valuable advice and help in executing the experiment.

3. We must raise an important question here: Would there be a tendency for "warm" observers to distort the perception in the favorable direction regardless of how much the stimulus deviated from the expectation? Future research should test the following hypothesis, which is suggested by Gestalt perception theory (4, pp. 95–98): If the stimulus differs but slightly from the expectation, the perception will tend to be *assimilated* to the expectation; however, if the difference between the stimulus and expectation is too great, the perception will occur by contrast to the expectation and will be distorted in the opposite direction.

CRITICAL THINKING QUESTIONS

1. Reread the information that was presented to the subjects to manipulate the warm-cold variable. The manipulation obviously produced a significant effect on the subjects' subsequent evaluations of the teacher. Do you feel that the manipulation was realistic? For example, how realistic is it to have a guest teacher described as "rather cold" in a brief biographical sketch? Could this particular manipulation have resulted in any experimental demand characteristics? Address the issue of the relative importance of experimental versus mundane realism as it pertains to this study.
2. How long lasting do you think first impressions are? For example, would they persist over the course of a semester or even longer? How could you test this?
3. What are the practical implications of this study? If you were working in a setting where you were interviewing and hiring applicants for a job, how could you use this information to help you make better, more accurate decisions?
4. The warm-cold information was provided by the instructor of the course, a person who presumably had high credibility. Do you think the credibility of the source of the information would affect how influenced the individuals were? How could you test this?

ADDITIONAL RELATED READINGS

Driscoll, D. M., & Gingrich, B. E. (1997). Effect of single-trait, social stereotype, and multi-trait expectancies on person impressions. *Journal of Social Behavior and Personality, 12,* 397–415.

Singh, R., Onglatco, M. L. U., Sriram, N., & Tay, A. B. G. (1997). The warm-cold variable in impression formation: Evidence for the positive-negative asymmetry. *British Journal of Social Psychology, 36,* 457–477.

ARTICLE 6 _____

As indicated in the two previous articles, we use a variety of information in forming our impressions of other people. In addition to observable characteristics, such as appearance, we place a lot of weight on people's actions. A critical factor in determining how to interpret an action may be what we see as the motivation behind it. For example, suppose someone says something that hurts our feelings. It may affect our perception of him or her very differently if we feel that the statement was deliberately meant to hurt or if it was unintentional. The issue, in other words, is *intention*.

How can we determine whether an act is intentional? Philosophers have argued the issues of intentionality for centuries, and court systems deal on a daily basis with the practical issue of determining the intentions behind given actions. After all, the difference between first-degree murder and manslaughter may hinge on the issue of premeditation, or intention.

Given the importance that we place on ascribing intention to other people's behavior (as well as our own), it is perhaps surprising that little empirical attention has been directed to understanding this concept. In an interesting series of studies, Bertram F. Malle and Joshua Knobe examine the concepts of *intention* and *intentionality* and propose a model for how people actually make judgments of intentionality.

The Folk Concept of Intentionality

■ Bertram F. Malle and Joshua Knobe

When perceiving, explaining, or criticizing human behavior, people distinguish between intentional and unintentional actions. To do so, they rely on a shared folk concept of intentionality. In contrast to past speculative models, this article provides an empirically based model of this concept. Study 1 demonstrates that people agree substantially in their judgments of intentionality, suggesting a shared underlying concept. Study 2 reveals that when asked to define directly the term intentional, people mention four components of intentionality: desire, belief, intention, and awareness. Study 3 confirms the importance of a fifth component, namely skill. In light of these findings, the authors propose a model of the folk concept of intentionality and provide a further test in Study 4. The discussion compares the proposed model to past ones and examines its implications for social perception, attribution, and cognitive development.

Judgments of intentionality set the course of social interactions. If considered intentional, a critical remark can be seen as a hurtful insult; a collision in the hallway, as a dangerous provocation; and a charming smile, as a hint of seduction. But if considered *unintentional*, that same remark may be excused; the same collision may lead to a new friendship; and the same smile might simply indicate a good mood.

The concept of intentionality thus permeates social behavior. The law relies on this concept as well, most notably in the distinction between intentional murder and manslaughter. Even the world of sports assigns more severe penalties for deliberate misdeeds, such as intentional fouling in basketball and intentional grounding in football. Juries, referees, and social agents alike distinguish between intentional and unintentional behavior; in doing so, they make use of a *folk concept of intentionality*. The present article explores this concept.

Psychology has traditionally studied intentionality as an objective fact about the mind (e.g., Fishbein &

Reprinted from *Journal of Experimental Social Psychology*, 1997, *33*, 101–121. Copyright © 1997 by Academic Press, Inc. Reprinted with permission.

Ajzen, 1975; Heckhausen, 1991; Libet, 1985; Ryan, 1970; Schneider & Shiffrin, 1977). But intentionality is also a social fact. Whether or not intentionality is truly an objective attribute of the mind, people certainly ascribe intentions to each other (Dennett, 1987; Heider, 1958; Shultz & Wells, 1985). Psychology must therefore examine this social role of intentionality—its significance as a shared folk concept that helps people understand each other and themselves.

Early attribution theorists emphasized the importance of intentionality in social perception (Heider, 1958; Jones & Davis, 1965; for a review see Maselli & Altrocchi, 1969), but they did not go further than speculating about this folk concept. More recent discussions of intentionality have also relied on speculative models (Fiske, 1989; Fleming & Darley, 1989; Shaver, 1985). Important empirical work in social and developmental psychology has explored the mediating role of perceived intention in helping behavior (e.g., Ickes & Kidd, 1976; Swap, 1991); aggression (e.g., Crick, 1995; Epstein & Taylor, 1967); relationship conflict (Hotaling, 1980; Fincham, Bradbury, & Grych, 1990); and judgments of responsibility, blame, or punishment (e.g., Armsby, 1971; Karniol, 1978; Piaget, 1932; Shaver, 1985; Shultz & Wright, 1985). This research has documented the ways in which judgments of intentionality influence other psychological processes, but it has not studied people's concept of intentionality itself. Research on children's theory of mind has begun to examine more directly when and how children acquire the concept of intention (e.g., Astington & Gopnik, 1991; Moses, 1993; Shultz, 1980; Wellman, 1990). Surprisingly, no corresponding research exists on the adult concept of intentionality, with the exception of informal interviews with five adults conducted by D'Andrade (1987). The present article therefore investigates the folk concept of intentionality and examines its implications for social perception, attribution, and development.

We first need to demonstrate that people show substantial agreement in judging behaviors for their intentionality. Only if such agreement exists are we justified to search for the folk concept that underlies those judgments.

STUDY 1

Participants rated a set of 20 behaviors for their intentionality. The behaviors were selected to range from clearly unintentional to clearly intentional. They were described verbally to minimize ambiguities arising from differential chunking, framing, and interpretation of the stimulus material. The format of verbal descriptions also simulates a natural communicative situation in which one person describes a behavior to a conversation partner, who then tries to infer that behavior's intentionality.

To determine whether people spontaneously use their own folk concept of intentionality when completing this rating task, some participants received a working definition of intentionality before making their judgments, while others did not receive such a definition. If people use their own folk concept, agreement should be high in either condition. In addition, we asked some participants to rate the behaviors from an observer perspective, and others, to rate them from an actor perspective. The shared folk concept of intentionality should produce equal agreement from either perspective.

Method

Participants and Procedure   Two samples were recruited for Study 1. Sample A consisted of 56 undergraduate students in an introductory psychology class at San Jose State University, who received course credit for their study participation. The questionnaire containing all instructions and measures was administered as part of a larger survey during a mass testing day at San Jose State University. The participants entered the laboratory at their leisure, received the survey booklets, and were tested in groups of 5 to 15. As each student finished the booklet, the experimenter thanked and debriefed that student.

Sample B consisted of 48 undergraduate students in an introductory psychology class at Stanford University, who received course credit for their study participation. The questionnaire containing all instructions and measures was administered at the end of an unrelated experiment (a computerized Stroop test) at Stanford University.

Material Both samples completed a questionnaire containing 20 verbally described behaviors (see Table 1). The behaviors were selected to cover a wide range of events, such as bodily states, emotions, actions, and accomplishments. Using our own folk knowledge, we attempted to select 10 intentional behaviors and 10 unintentional behaviors.

Participants rated the 20 behaviors from either of two perspectives. In the actor perspective ($n = 32$), they were instructed this way: "Please look at the 20 statements below. Each statement describes you doing something. Your task is to rate whether you would do that *intentionally.*" The behaviors were described as follows: "I asked somebody out for dinner"; "I am in a great mood today"; etc. In the observer perspective ($n = 72$), they were instructed this way: "Please look at 20 statements below. Each statement describes Anne doing something. Your task is to rate whether Anne does what she does *intentionally.*" The behaviors were described as follows: "Anne asked Mike out for dinner"; "Anne is in a great mood today"; etc.

About one-half of the participants in each sample received a working definition of intentionality before they rated the 20 behaviors. In the actor perspective, the definition read: "What do we mean by *intentional?* This means that you had a reason to do what you did and that you chose to do so." In the observer perspective, it read: "What do we mean by *intentional?* This means that the person had a *reason* to do what she did and that she *chose* to do so."

All participants rated how intentional they thought each behavior was, using an 8-point scale ranging from "not at all" (0) to "completely" (7) intentional.

Results

To begin with, we computed people's agreement across the 20 behaviors. In the whole sample, any two people showed an average intercorrelation of r (20) = .64, and any one person showed an average correlation of r (20) = .80 with the remaining group, resulting in a Cronbach α of 0.99. Agreement did not differ between the conditions with definition (.79) and without definition (.79), between actor perspective

TABLE 1 / People's Average Ratings of Intentionality for 20 Verbally Described Behaviors (Study 1)

	Mean	SD
Anne is sweating	1.37	1.61
Anne was yawning during the lecture	1.41	1.59
Anne was grinding her teeth during the test	2.00	1.63
Anne had a craving for cherries after dinner	2.23	1.72
Anne believed that she had the flu	2.69	1.99
Anne is in a great mood today	2.70	1.98
Anne is infatuated with Ben	3.20	1.95
Anne was worrying about the test results	3.69	1.91
Anne got admitted to Princeton	3.78	2.19
Anne interrupted her mother	4.58	1.94
Anne ignored Greg's arguments	5.22	1.73
Anne drove way above the speed limit	5.37	1.67
Anne applauded the musicians	5.77	1.49
Anne greeted her uncle politely	5.94	1.31
Anne refused the salesman's offer	6.22	1.28
Anne stole a pound of peaches	6.36	1.19
Anne asked Mike out for dinner	6.39	1.07
Anne invited Sue to have lunch with her	6.40	1.08
Anne watered her new plants	6.53	0.84

(.77) and observer perspective (.80), or between San Jose (.81) and Stanford (.78).

We also tested the stability of each of the 20 behaviors' average intentionality ratings across school, perspective, and definition. Using three sets of 20 pairwise *t* tests, we found no differences between schools, perspectives, or definition conditions. Not surprisingly, then, the two sets of 20 average ratings from each school were almost perfectly correlated, *r* = .98, and the same correlations were found for perspective and definition.

Discussion

People's substantial agreement in their differentiation among intentional and unintentional behaviors suggests the influence of a shared folk concept of intentionality. Most importantly, whether the instructions provided participants with a definition of intentionality had no effect on average agreement, suggesting that intentionality is not just a theoretical construct but a folk concept that people spontaneously use to classify behavior. People's high agreement in judgments of intentionality is comparable in size to their agreement in judgments of social desirability (e.g., Edwards, 1957). Both dimensions are deeply ingrained in our culture, so people have been reinforced many times for their stimulus differentiation along these central dimensions.

The results of Study 1 also show that actors and observers make the same distinctions among behaviors. In complex social situations, of course, knowledge and motivation differences between actors and observers may produce disagreement in judging particular behaviors (cf. Malle, 1996).

Having demonstrated that people agree substantially in their judgments of intentionality, we now examine the folk concept that underlies these judgments.

MODELS OF INTENTIONALITY

What might a definition of intentionality look like? A commonly cited model (e.g., Forguson, 1989) holds that to act intentionally one needs to have a desire (for an outcome) and appropriate beliefs (about how the act would lead to that outcome). Initial traces of this model can be found in Aristotle (1892/382 B.C.), but it was first elaborated by Hume (1978/1740). The two-way belief/desire model lies at the core of rational choice theory (Savage, 1954; von Neumann & Morgenstern, 1944) and led to well-known work in modern philosophy of action (e.g., Anscombe, 1957; Davidson, 1963; Goldman, 1970). But two-way models are incomplete. Suppose Anita fouls an opponent during a basketball game. Even if we know that Anita wants to win the game and believes that fouling her opponent would help her win, we still cannot be sure that she committed the foul intentionally. What is missing is Anita's specific intention, her *decision* to act on her desire and belief. To accommodate such cases, philosophers developed three-way models of intentional action, including beliefs, desires, and intentions (e.g., Brand, 1984; Bratman, 1987; Searle, 1983; Thalberg, 1984). Supporting this extension, researchers of children's developing theory of mind have suggested that children's concept of intentional action first includes the concept of desire and belief and later that of intention (Astington & Gopnik, 1991; Wellman, 1990). Similarly, D'Andrade (1987) has confirmed, in a small interview study, that people distinguish between desires and intentions.

Within social psychology, Heider's (1958) model of intentional action also recognizes *intention* as the central factor in personal causality, but it differs in several respects from the above tradition. In his model, *ability* and *trying* are the two personal factors determining intentional action, whereby trying further splits into the critical intention aspect (what a person is trying to do) and an exertion aspect (how hard the person is trying).[1] Heider was somewhat reluctant to draw a distinction between desire and intention (Heider, 1958, p. 110), but he did discuss desire as a precondition of trying (Heider, 1958, Chap. 5). He did not, however, assign a comparable role to beliefs.

Jones and Davis (1965) extended Heider's model by recognizing the importance of a *belief* component ("knowledge") in addition to ability. In their model, ascriptions of belief and ability are both necessary conditions for ascriptions of intention, while the role of desire remains unspecified.

In their conceptual definition of intentional action, Ossorio and Davis (1968) postulated *desire, knowledge,* and *skill,* as well as a conventionality condition—that the agent is "recognizably doing the sort of thing one would do in order to accomplish" one's goal (p. 358).

Shaver (1985), building on Heider, Jones, and the philosophical literature, suggested yet another way to define intentional action: An action is intentional if the agent has a *desire* for an outcome, *beliefs* about consequences of the action, and *beliefs about his or her ability* to perform the action. This definition does include the desire component but merges intention with intentional action and supplants ability with perceptions of ability.

These models disagree in what they identify as the necessary conditions for intentional action. The models also differ in what they are models of. Whereas Heider tried to explicate *people's* concept of intentional action, Jones and McGillis (1976) call the Jones and Davis (1965) model a "rational baseline model" that "does not summarize phenomenal experience" (p. 404). Ossorio and Davis (1968) went one step further, claiming that they explicated a conceptual truth that need not be (and cannot be) empirically validated. But it seems curious that different scholars have proposed different definitions for what should be a single conceptual truth. Detecting such a conceptual truth, moreover, would be an idle endeavor if ordinary people did not use the concept of intentionality in accordance with the definition.

Our paper therefore returns to Heider's (1958) goal of explicating people's folk concept of intentionality. Because neither Heider's nor any other model has been based on empirical data, we began our reconstruction of the folk concept of intentionality by asking people directly what it means to perform an action intentionally. We expected these direct definitions to be the first building block of our model.

STUDY 2

Method

Participants   The participants were 159 undergraduate students in introductory psychology classes at San Jose State University (*n* = 111) and Stanford University (*n* = 48), who received partial course credit for their participation.

Procedure and Materials   Participants in both samples completed a group-administered questionnaire that contained the following question: "When you say that somebody performed an action *intentionally,* what does this mean? Please explain." Participants wrote their answers on four empty lines printed below the question. The original answers were then transcribed and collected in a small booklet, which was used for coding the responses.

Coding of Definitions   First we excluded synonyms for the term "intentionally" (e.g., "on purpose," "purposefully," "deliberately"). After a training session, we classified synonyms with an agreement of 95%. An inspection of the remaining definitions revealed four main components: desire, belief, intention, and awareness. Abstracting from the clearest definitions, we then defined the following precise coding categories. To qualify for the desire category, a definition had to mention "the desire for an outcome or the outcome itself as a goal, purpose, or aim." To qualify for the belief category, a definition had to mention "beliefs or thoughts about the consequences of the act or the act itself *before* it takes place." To qualify for the intention category, a definition had to mention "the intention to perform the act, intending, meaning, deciding, choosing, or planning to perform the act. To qualify for the awareness category, a definition had to mention "awareness of the act *while* the person is performing it." In addition, we coded two infrequent categories: control ("mentioning personal causation or control") and external causes ("mentioning the absence of external influence such as chance").

We then independently coded the first two pages of the booklet (*n* = 44) into the six categories and agreed on 88% of the definitions. We discussed disagreements and adopted the following conventions to settle ambiguous cases: (*a*) The expression "with a reason" (four occurrences overall) was excluded because it was ambiguous; it could refer either to the desire or the belief component (see Malle, 1996). (*b*) References to "effort" (two occurrences overall) were coded in the intention category because effort is a symptom of intention, as pointed out by Heider (1958). (*c*) The term "premeditated" is defined in Webster's dictionary as "characterized by willful intent and a measure of belief" and was therefore coded both as intention and belief (seven occurrences over-all). We then coded the remaining eight pages of the booklet ($n = 115$), reaching perfect agreement on 95% of the definitions. Discussion settled 11 dis-agreements overall, and a total of 202 definitions was used for analysis.

Results

Twenty participants (13%) provided only synonyms. Of the remaining 139 participants, 54% mentioned exactly one component, 31% mentioned two or more. Table 2 displays how many of these participants mentioned any of the four dominant components, along with sample responses. (The distributions did not differ by school, so we collapsed across this fac-tor.)

The four dominant components (desire, belief, awareness, and intention) accounted for 96% of the definitions. The absence of external causes was men-tioned only six times; control was mentioned twice.

None of the participants mentioned all four com-ponents, presumably because the instructions to this study ("What does it mean that . . .") did not encour-age exhaustive definitions. However, those who men-tioned two or more components drew careful distinctions between them. They distinguished, for example, between intention and desire: "The person meant to act that way and was motivated to do so"; between belief and intention: "Someone gave thought to the action beforehand and chose to do it"; between intention and awareness: "They decided to do some-thing and then did it with full awareness of what they were doing"; and between belief and awareness: "This person thought about the action before he did it and was fully aware of performing the action while he was doing it."

Discussion

Study 2 suggests that the folk concept of intentional action includes (*a*) a desire for an outcome, (*b*) beliefs about the action leading to that outcome, (*c*) an inten-tion to perform that act, and (*d*) awareness of per-forming that act.

The desire and belief components map well onto the classic belief/desire model. In addition, partici-pants identified intention and awareness as two fur-ther components of intentionality.

The *intention* component links desire and belief to action. People appreciate that an intentional action does not derive from desire and belief alone but that its direct cause is an intention. The presence of an intention to act implies, however, both a desire for an outcome and a belief that the intended act will lead to that outcome. This hierarchical relation may explain why people more often mentioned an intention com-ponent than either a desire or a belief component. The hierarchical relation also highlights an important difference between intentions and desires: Intentions always have as their object an action, whereas desires can take any outcome as their object (even impossible states of the world). Anne may intend to buy a used car even though she wishes she had the money to buy a new one. Moreover, verbs of intention (to intend, plan, try) require an action verb in the infinitive that refers to the same agent as the one who has the intention. Ben may wish that his wife were less busy, but he cannot intend that she be less busy. According to people's folk conception, then, intentions are con-

TABLE 2 / The Four Explicit Components in People's Definitions of Intentionality (Study 2)

Component	Frequency (%)	Example
Desire	27	He did it in hopes of getting some result.
Belief	39	She thought about the act and its effect.
Intention	51	She made a decision to perform the action.
Awareness	23	He knows what he is doing.

trollable by the agent whereas desires are not (D'Andrade, 1987).

The *awareness* component specifies the agent's state of mind at the time of acting. Performing an intentional action thus requires at least minimal conscious awareness. This awareness, however, is more subtle and specific than mere conscious wakefulness: "Knowing what one is doing while doing it" (as one participant put it) is a self-reflective state in which the agent performs an act by consciously following the intention for *this* act (cf. Brand, 1984; Searle, 1983). The awareness component is crucial for identifying actions that conform to an intention but are not performed intentionally. Suppose that Ben forms an intention to call his mother. Then he recalls that he also needs to call his sister. So he picks up the phone to call his sister but dials the wrong number and ends up reaching his mother. Even though this behavior conforms to Ben's intention of calling his mother, Ben did not perform the behavior with the *awareness* of following his intention, so he did not call his mother intentionally.

None of the past models of intentionality predicted these particular definitions. First, Jones and Davis (1965) identified the belief and intention components but overlooked desire and awareness. Second, both Ossorio and Davis (1968) and Shaver (1985) identified desire and belief but overlooked intention and awareness. Finally, Heider's (1958) model of intentional action identified the intention and desire components but overlooked belief and awareness. In addition, Heider postulated exertion, along with intention, as an aspect of trying. Our participants, however, did not regard exertion as a necessary component of intentionality (only two people mentioned effort in their definitions). This should not be surprising, for Heider (1958) was correct that the degree of exertion during an action represents a *clue* to the action's intentionality (p. 114), but exertion is neither a necessary nor a sufficient condition for performing an action intentionally.

Interestingly, all previous models postulated an ability or skill component, whereas this component was absent from people's direct definitions. This absence therefore deserves careful attention. Consider Jerry, who is a novice at darts. He has never played darts before and is not particularly talented at games like this. Surprisingly, he hits triple 20 (a very difficult throw) on his first try. A friend dismisses the throw as a fluke, so Jerry tries again, this time missing badly. We can be confident that he *wanted* to hit triple 20; but would we say that he hit it *intentionally*?

Most people would not, as a pilot study shows: Although 77% of the participants agreed that Jerry *wanted* to hit triple 20 in his first flight, only 16% said that he hit it *intentionally*. In a second condition, however, in which Jerry hit triple 20 twice in a row, 55% of the participants now inferred that he hit it intentionally; χ^2 ($df = 1$, $N = 141$) = 22.7, $p < .001$.

Hitting triple 20 twice in a row apparently demonstrates skill, whereas hitting it once (and then missing) does not. Perhaps people only consider an action intentional if there is evidence of the actor's *skill*. Participants in Study 2 may have failed to mention skill in their definitions of intentionality because they only considered interpersonal behaviors, for which skill can be assumed. We therefore tested people's sensitivity to the presence or absence of skill in Study 3.

STUDY 3

In the darts study, Jerry had the *intention* to hit triple 20 (he tried to hit it), but he did not hit it *intentionally*. Judgments of *doing something intentionally* (i.e., judgments of intentionality) may therefore require evidence of skill in addition to evidence of intention. In Study 3 we independently manipulated the presence of desire, belief, and skill (while holding awareness constant) and asked the participants two questions: whether the actor *tried* to perform the particular action (judgment of intention) and whether he performed it *intentionally* (judgment of intentionality). We hypothesized that judgments of intention should depend on the presence or absence of desire and belief only. Since one can try without succeeding, skill should not influence these judgments. Judgments of intention should therefore be rare if either belief or desire is absent but considerably more frequent when both are present, regardless of skill. Judgments of *intentionality*, by contrast, should depend on the presence or absence not only of belief and desire but also of skill. Judgments of intentionality should therefore be rare when any of these three components is absent (holding awareness constant) but considerably more frequent if all components are present.

Method

Participants and Procedure   The participants were 132 undergraduate students in an introductory psychology class at Stanford University. They received class credit for completing a large survey that included a single-page questionnaire with all instructions and measures for this study.

Materials   The questionnaire, titled "Heads or Tails," contained a brief story followed by the dependent measures. The story opens with David sitting in a corner, waiting for his friends to decide what to do. He has been flipping a penny, trying to teach himself to make it land on the side he wants. Either "he has not been able to do better than chance" (skill absent) or "by now, he almost always succeeds" (skill present). His friends are trying to decide whether to see a movie. David either wants to see the movie (desire present) or does not want to see the movie (desire absent). Someone suggests flipping a coin to make a decision: "Let's just settle it quickly. We'll flip a coin: Tails, we go to the movie; heads, we hang out here." David either hears this suggestion (belief present) or does not hear it (belief absent). In either case, his friends ask him to flip the coin. He flips the coin and . . . it's tails.

We manipulated the critical information regarding desire, belief, and skill in four conditions: 1. Belief present, desire, and skill absent ("belief"). 2. Desire present, belief, and skill absent, ("desire"). 3. Belief and desire present, skill absent ("belief + desire"). 4. Belief, desire, and skill present ("belief + desire + skill"). Awareness was present in all four conditions.

After reading the story, participants answered the following questions (by checking a box for either Yes or No):

1. Do you think that David made the coin land on tails *intentionally?*
2. Do you think that David *tried* to make the coin land on tails?

One group of participants ($n = 87$) answered only one of the two questions, permitting a between-subject test. Another group ($n = 45$) answered both questions (counterbalanced across participants), permitting a within-subject test. Since the two tests produced identical results, we collapsed the data across this factor.

Results

Table 3 shows that attributions of *trying* (intention) were rare when either desire or belief was absent but frequent when both desire and belief were present (even when skill was absent). A two-way logit analysis (with adjacent difference contrasts for the condition factor) confirms that the desire condition and the belief condition did not differ from each other, that the desire + belief condition differed substantially from the desire condition ($p < .001$), and that the desire + belief + skill condition differed only marginally from the desire + belief condition ($z = 1.5$, $p < .10$). Attributions of *intentionality,* by contrast, were frequent only when all three components (including skill) were present. In a two-way logit analysis, none of the first three conditions differed from each other, but the desire + belief + skill condition differed signifi-

TABLE 3 / Percentage of "Yes" Responses for Trying to Get Tails and Getting Tails Intentionally with Manipulated Components of Intentionality (Study 3)

Components Present	Trying (%)	Intentionally (%)
Desire	21	0
Belief	31	0
Desire + belief	81	3
Desire + belief + skill	96	76

Note: The presence of awareness could be inferred.

cantly from the desire + belief condition ($p < .001$). These results held up in a three-way logit analysis as well, which introduced *question*—trying versus doing intentionally—as a factor. In the three-way interaction, the critical contrast between the desire + belief condition and the desire + belief + skill condition was significant ($z = 1.97$, $p < .05$).

Discussion

Study 3 thus suggests that people's judgments of intentionality are sensitive to skill information (Heider, 1958; Jones & Davis, 1965). For most social behaviors people may tacitly assume the actor's skill; but for dexterous or complex behaviors they require independent evidence of skill. Participants who provided definitions of intentionality in Study 2 focused on social behaviors, so they did not spontaneously mention skill. If one were to repeat Study 2 with explicit instructions for the participants to consider difficult behaviors from athletics, art, or science, the skill component might even appear in direct definitions of intentionality.

The skill component may lead to interesting actor–observer differences in judgments of intentionality. When an actor ascribes skill to himself (for bringing about a certain outcome), he holds a *self-efficacy belief* (Bandura, 1986). Actors' self-ascriptions of skill are thus indistinguishable from self-efficacy beliefs. Observers, however, can ascribe to the actor either a self-efficacy belief or skill itself (or both). Observers may acknowledge that the actor *thinks* she can bring about an outcome (has a self-efficacy belief), but they may not ascribe to her the actual skill of bringing it about. In judging intentionality, then, observers will often go beyond the actor's declared self-efficacy beliefs and look for evidence of actual skill.

The superstitious operator of a chance device, for instance, may acquire the *belief* that he can control the device's output, hence try to do so, and claim intentionality for this act. But a knowledgeable observer would not consider the person to be intentionally producing a certain outcome, because the person lacks the *skill* to turn an intention into an intentional action. Conversely, the frustrated subject in a learned helplessness experiment has lost her *belief* that she can

control the experimental device, hence does not even try to avoid shocks in the follow-up session, whereas a knowledgeable observer would ascribe to her the *skill* to control the device and would grant her intentionality if only she tried.

A MODEL OF THE FOLK CONCEPT OF INTENTIONALITY

In light of the findings of Studies 2 and 3, we now propose a model of the folk concept of intentionality, displayed in Fig. 1.

In people's folk concept of intentionality, performing an action intentionally requires the presence of five components: a desire for an outcome; beliefs about an action that leads to that outcome; an intention to perform the action; skill to perform the action; and awareness of fulfilling the intention while performing the action. For example, we are hereby intentionally writing a self-referential example to illustrate our model—that is, we wanted to provide a vivid illustration (desire); we thought that a self-referential example might be vivid (belief); we therefore decided to write such an example (intention); we had the skill to do so (skill); and we were aware of fulfilling our intention (awareness) while writing the example.

The model implies that desire and belief are necessary conditions for an intention. Study 3 confirmed this hypothesis, showing that people attributed an *intention* only if both belief and desire were present. The model also implies that, given an intention to act, skill and awareness are necessary conditions for acting *intentionally*. Study 3 confirmed the necessary role of skill. Study 4 now examines the role of awareness and thus provides a further test of the model.

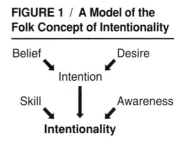

FIGURE 1 / A Model of the Folk Concept of Intentionality

STUDY 4

We hypothesized that awareness would function as a necessary component of intentionality, over and above the components already tested. In Study 4 we manipulated the presence of awareness in two brief stories and examined its impact (in addition to that of other components) on judgments of intentionality.

Method

Participants and Procedure   The participants were 225 undergraduate students in an introductory psychology class at Stanford University. They received class credit for completing a large survey that included a two-page questionnaire with all instructions and measures for this study.

Materials   The questionnaire was titled "Practical Reasoning Task." Participants were instructed to read several stories, ". . . each consisting of a few critical sentences. For each story, please read the sentences carefully and then answer the corresponding question." The variations of the two stories (with labels for identification) are described below.

The "trick story" consisted of three sentences. The first contained belief information (which was held constant), the second contained skill information, and the third contained awareness information (both of which were manipulated). Desire and intention could be inferred.

1. Jeremy once heard about a way to trick cashiers into giving back too much change. [belief]
2. (a) Jeremy is quite capable of performing this trick correctly. [skill] (b) Jeremy is incapable of performing this trick correctly. [no skill]
3. (a) Jeremy left the store, knowing that he received too much change. [awareness]. (b) Jeremy left the store, unaware that he received too much change. [no awareness]

After reading this story, all participants answered the following question (by checking a box for *Yes* or *No*): "Did Jeremy *intentionally* acquire too much change?" Participants were randomly assigned to the following information conditions: 1. Neither skill nor awareness present (control group). 2. Only skill present ("skill"). 3. Only awareness present ("awareness"). 4. Both skill and awareness present ("skill + awareness"). We hypothesized that Condition 4 would produce by far the highest frequency of intentionality judgments.

The "car story" consisted of three sentences. The first contained desire information, the second contained awareness information, the third contained belief information (all of which were manipulated). Skill and intention could be inferred.

1. (a) Frank hates George. [desire] (b) Frank likes George a lot. [no desire]
2. (a) Frank was aware of bumping into the blue BMW behind him. [awareness] (b) Frank wasn't aware of bumping into the blue BMW behind him. [no awareness]
3. (a) Frank knew that the blue BMW was George's car. [belief] (b) Frank didn't know that the blue BMW was George's car. [no belief]

All participants answered the question, "Did Frank *intentionally* bump into George's car?" Participants were randomly assigned to the following seven information conditions (omitting the condition in which none of the three components was present): 1. awareness only, 2. belief only, 3. desire only, 4. desire + awareness, 5. belief + awareness, 6. belief + desire, 7. belief + desire + awareness. We hypothesized that Condition 7 would produce by far the highest frequency of intentionality judgments.

Each participant received both stories. Conditions and order of stones were varied across participants.

Results and Discussion

Tables 4 and 5 display the results for the trick story and the car story, respectively. Both confirm the necessary role of awareness in judgments of intentionality. Attributions of intentionality are rare if awareness (or any other component of intentionality) is absent but frequent if all components are present.

To test this interpretation for significance, we computed two-way logit models, with condition as the independent variable and intentionality ascription (Yes vs No) as the dependent variable. We used difference contrasts to examine the impact of increasing

TABLE 4 / Percentage of "Yes" Responses for Acquiring Too Much Change Intentionally (Study 4)

Components Present	Intentionally (%)
Control group	5
Skill	7
Awareness	26
Skill + awareness	83

Note: The presence of belief was explicitly stated; the presence of desire and intention could be inferred.

TABLE 5 / Percentage of "Yes" Responses for Bumping into Somebody's Car Intentionally (Study 4)

Components Present	Intentionally (%)
Belief	3
Desire	26
Awareness	11
Desire + awareness	6
Belief + awareness	13
Belief + desire	18
Belief + desire + awareness	60

Note: The presence of skill and intention could be inferred.

numbers of components present. In the trick story, the skill condition and the control condition did not differ from each other; and together they differed somewhat from the awareness condition ($z = 3.2$, $p < .001$); but the greatest difference was between these three conditions and the awareness + skill condition, where all components of intentionality were present ($z = 8.5$, $p < .001$). In the car story, the first six conditions did not differ from each other, but together they differed from condition 7 ($z = 6.2$, $p < .001$), which was the only one that produced high rates of intentionality attributions.

Both stories produced less than perfect intentionality attributions (83% and 60%), probably because the vignettes were very concise and two components had to be inferred in each case. But these imperfect attribution rates also show that the vignettes were not so heavy-handed as to suggest only one correct judgment. Of course, to the theorist who has accepted the proposed model of intentionality the results may seem obvious. To the opposing theorist, however, who believes in unconsciously performed intentional actions (dispelling the awareness component), the results must be surprising, if not damaging.

GENERAL DISCUSSION

The present studies developed and tested a model of people's folk concept of intentionality. Naturally, these studies have limitations. The data have been collected on a student subject population and need to be replicated in community samples of varying ages and economic and ethnic backgrounds. Also, the vignette techniques, though particularly suitable for identifying conceptual relationships, need to be complemented by other methods, such as video-taped stimulus materials and codings of people's discussion about the intentionality of a given action. Finally, the explicated folk concept may hold only for people of Western cultures. Even if all cultures distinguished intentional from unintentional behavior, the specific conditions for ascribing intentionality might vary. Currently we have no empirical data to decide this issue (cf. Lillard, 1996).

Despite these limitations, the current studies suggest that people's folk concept of intentionality consists of five components (belief, desire, intention, awareness, and skill) that are hierarchically arranged, such that belief and desire are necessary conditions for attributions of *intention* and, given an intention, skill and awareness are necessary conditions for attributions of *intentionality*.

The present model has several strengths. First, it is empirically based. All five components were verified in judgment tasks, and four components were even identified in people's direct definitions of intentionality. Second, our model integrates past analyses of people's concept of intentionality (Heider, 1958; Jones & Davis, 1965; Ossorio & Davis, 1968; Shaver, 1985), which had disagreed about the particular subsets of components that define intentionality (e.g., belief and desire, belief and ability). The present model unites these past efforts by identifying all necessary components of intentionality as well as their interrelations.

Third, the present model clarifies inconsistencies in past models. For example, Heider's (1958) notion of "ability" seemed to subjectivize the skill component and confound it with the agent's perception of her skill (see also Shaver, 1985, p. 122). Many of Heider's (1958) examples of skill are indeed examples of the agent's perception of her skill: "Will I be able to do the task again?" (p. 84); "I can attain that goal" (p. 111). These subjective perceptions of skill (self-efficacy beliefs) are important from the actor's perspective, but they are not part of the folk concept of intentionality. What is part of this concept is the consideration of the agent's actual skill, as emphasized by Jones and Davis (1965). Perhaps these authors recognized the skill component because they analyzed judgments of intentionality from the observer perspective, where ascriptions of the agent's skill are clearly separated from ascriptions of mere self-efficacy beliefs.

Fourth, the present model clarifies a nagging terminological complexity—the relationship between *intention* (intending) on the one hand and *intentional action* on the other (cf. Bratman, 1987). Typically the concepts of intention and intentional action are treated as synonyms (e.g., Jones & Davis, 1965; Shaver, 1985; Shultz, 1988). Our data suggest, however, that people distinguish between attributions of *intention* (based on belief and desire information) and attributions of *doing something intentionally* (based on intention, skill, and awareness information). People thus apply the term *intention* to persons (who intend to do something) and the term *intentional* to actions (which are performed intentionally). When we speak of *intentionality,* then, we should speak of actions that were performed intentionally. In contrast, when we speak of an action that was *intended* (i.e., preceded by an intention), we should not automatically infer that such an action was performed intentionally; for if awareness or skill were missing, the action would be intended but not performed intentionally.

The folk distinction between intention and intentionality applies most readily to situations where a person has formed an intention but has not yet performed the intended action (Davidson, 1980). The more important test cases for this distinction, however, are those behaviors that were both intended by the agent and actually performed, but were performed accidentally rather than intentionally (because the agent was lacking awareness or skill). For example, John intended to hit the triple 20, ends up hitting it, but does so accidentally (because of luck, not skill). Therefore, a simple match between intention and outcome does not always suffice for an ascription of intentionality (e.g., "She intended to heal him, and now he is healed" does not rule out spontaneous healing). Such a matching rule is used by young children (Astington, 1991; Shultz & Wells, 1985), but for adults doing something intentionally requires more than the presence of an intention and its matching outcome. It also requires skill and awareness, two factors that bring about the outcome in the right (nonaccidental) way. For some social behaviors the presence of skill and awareness can be assumed, so judgments of intention and judgments of intentionality converge. But for other behaviors the presence of skill or awareness is questionable, so intentionality might be denied even if an intention is clearly evident.

This model of the folk concept of intentionality has several implications for social perception, attribution processes, and development, as discussed next.

Social Perception

Knowing the components of people's concept of intentionality, we may begin to investigate the cognitive process of *inferring* intentionality, its conditions of accuracy and bias, and methods of improving judgment sensitivity. For example, how can it happen that mere friendliness is misjudged as an intentional sexual overture? How do people recognize intentionally prolonged eye contact? How do they distinguish between intentional and accidental rudeness? We must also examine crucial individual differences. People may differ in their response thresholds of judging a behavior intentional, and different cultures may impose different social consequences for intentional behavior. Both personal and cultural miscommunication may stem from such subtle differences in judgments of intentionality.

Perceptions of intentionality also influence the evaluations of behavior: Actors receive more praise and more blame for actions that are considered intentional rather than unintentional (Shaver, 1985). Similarly, intentional acts of helping are more prone to be reciprocated than unintentional ones (e.g., Swap, 1991), and likewise for intentional acts of aggression (e.g., Taylor, Sahuntich, & Greenberg, 1979). A careful distinction between attributions of intention on the one hand and attributions of doing something intentionally on the other may lead to new hypotheses about the subtle logic of praise and blame. For example, people may distinguish between intentions and doing something intentionally more for positive behaviors than for negative behaviors because it is easy (and common) to have positive intentions but harder to fulfill them intentionally, whereas a person's negative intention is already deviant (and threatening to others) even before fulfilling it intentionally.

Attribution Processes

The concept of intentionality is essential to people's descriptions and explanations of behavior (Heider, 1958; Malle, 1996). Since Heider's book, however, most research on explanations omitted issues of intentionality (cf. Buss, 1978). One might suspect that, within attributional theories, the notion of controllability has taken the part of intentionality. But how exactly does controllability relate to intentionality?

Intentionality and Controllability   To examine the relation between these two concepts, we need to distinguish between two meanings of controllability. In one sense, controllability refers to types of *causes,* an attributional dimension introduced by Rosenbaum (1972) and Weiner (1979). A controllable cause of good grades would be effort; an uncontrollable cause would be test difficulty. But only among unintentional behaviors does the controllability of causes make a relevant distinction—Ben might regard the causes of his tiredness as controllable (hence he will sleep more) but the causes of his sadness as uncontrollable (making it worse). Intentional behaviors, in contrast, have by definition a controllable cause (i.e., an intention).

In this first sense, then, controllability and intentionality are distinct concepts because they apply to different objects—controllability applies to causes whereas intentionality applies to behaviors (Weiner, 1985). But the distinction between controllable and uncontrollable causes presupposes the distinction between intentional and unintentional behaviors, because only unintentional behaviors can have either controllable or uncontrollable causes.

Occasionally, controllability has been used in a second sense, referring to behaviors themselves (see Stratton *et al.,* 1986). Controllable behaviors are those that can be performed intentionally, whereas uncontrollable ones are those that can never be performed intentionally. Once a behavior is performed, however, people judge whether it was actually done intentionally, and their interest in explaining that behavior depends importantly on its intentionality (Malle & Knobe, in press).

Task Difficulty and Coercion   Heider's (1958) analysis of action also referred to environmental forces that hinder or facilitate action, namely task difficulty and coercion. Both of these factors *influence* certain components of people's judgments of intentionality, but they are not *necessary components* of the intentionality concept itself. Task difficulty is one of the clues that the perceiver may use to infer whether the actor has an intention or not. If an actor faces a difficult task, for example, perceivers may not expect the actor to try to accomplish it. More importantly, task difficulty can also be used to infer whether the actor has skill or not (Heider, 1958). But while skill is a necessary component of the folk concept of intentionality, task difficulty (or ease) is not. That is because performing even a very difficult task will be seen as intentional if the actor has the appropriate skill (along with the other four components); and performing even a very easy task will not be seen as intentional if the actor lacks the appropriate skill.

Similarly, perceived coercion influences judgments of intentionality. However, an analysis of this influence is complicated by an ambiguity in the term itself. Coercion sometimes means *physical coercion,* such as when A pushes B to the ground. In this case B's falling is unlikely to be seen as intentional because B had apparently no intention of falling to the ground. Perceived physical coercion thus often discourages the ascription of an intention and, in turn, of intentionality. More typically, coercion means *psychological coercion,* such as when C holds a gun to D's head and demands that D hand over his wallet. In this case D's handing over his wallet may well be seen as intentional: D decided to do it, however unwillingly, with the goal of saving his life. Shaver (1985) pointed out that coercion mitigates attributions of responsibility and blame but does not undermine an attribution of intentionality. We side with Shaver in arguing that (the absence of) coercion is not a necessary component of the concept of intentionality; but we hope for more research into the specific *effects* of perceived coercion on judgments of intentionality and responsibility.

Perceivers thus take task difficulty and coercion into account when they infer the actor's intention or skill; by implication, the two factors influence people's judgments of intentionality. But neither ease of task nor absence of coercion seems to be itself a necessary component of people's folk concept of intentionality.

Developmental Aspects

In an important sense, the adult concept of intentionality is the target toward which the child's concept of intentionality evolves. The present studies of the adult concept of intention and intentionality therefore generate research questions on children's acquisition of these concepts. For example, children initially use a simple desire psychology to make sense of other people's actions (Baldwin & Moses, 1994; Meltzoff, 1995; Tomasello, 1995; Wellman & Woolley, 1990; Wellman, 1991). This early desire concept, however, does not distinguish between desire and intention in the adult sense, so an important question is when children begin to make this distinction and what consequences it has for their judgments of action.

Furthermore, if children master the relationship between belief, desire, and intention, they must learn that a desired, foreseen, and intended act is not necessarily intentional. For one, the actor must fulfill her intention by having awareness of acting with the intention of doing so. This awareness is self-reflective, and it implies the capacity for subtle action identification processes (Wegner & Vallacher, 1986). Moreover, a desired, foreseen, and intended act can be a lucky strike—it takes skill to deserve an attribution of intentionality, even if the attribution of intention is beyond doubt. So another question is when children discover that both awareness and skill are important for making judgments of intentionality.

The process of internalizing the shared folk concept of intentionality may well reach into adolescence

(Kugelmass & Breznitz, 1968). In such a long-ranging learning process, many things can go wrong. An abusive childhood, for example, may seriously disturb a person's evolving ability to make accurate judgments of intentionality. These disturbances may have further social consequences, such as when an overreadiness to ascribe intentionality to potentially aggressive acts may result in retaliatory aggression on the part of the perceiver (Crick, 1995; Graham & Hudley, 1994).

CONCLUSION

Process distinctions such as that between "automatic" and "controlled" behavior (e.g., Schneider & Shiffrin, 1977; Uleman & Bargh, 1989) have helped illuminate objective mechanisms of cognition and action. But many *social consequences* of behavior depend on people's (not psychologists') distinctions and concepts. Folk concepts such as intentionality guide people's social behavior. If, as psychologists, we want to account for this behavior, we must understand its guiding folk concepts.

REFERENCES

Anscombe, G. E. M. (1957). *Intention.* Oxford: Basil Blackwell.

Aristotle (1892). *The Nicomachean ethics* (transl. by J. E. C. Welldon). London: Macmillan. (Originally published around 330 B.C.).

Armsby, R. E. (1971). A reexamination of the development of moral judgments in children. *Child Development, 42,* 1241–1248.

Astington, J. W. (1991). Intention in the child's theory of mind. In D. Frye & C. Moore (Eds.), *Children's theories of mind: Mental states and social understanding* (pp. 157–172). Hillsdale, NJ: Erlbaum.

Astington, J. W., & Gopnik, A. (1993). Developing understanding of desire and intention. In A. Whiten (Ed.), *Natural theories of mind* (pp. 39–50). Oxford: Basil Blackwell.

Baldwin, D. A., & Moses, L. J. (1994). Early understanding of referential intent and attentional focus: Evidence from language and emotion. In C. Lewis & P. Mitchell (Eds.), *Children's early understanding of mind: Origins and development* (pp. 133–156). Hove, England: Erlbaum.

Bandura, A. (1986). *Social foundations of thought and action. A social cognitive theory.* Englewood Cliffs, NJ: Prentice-Hall.

Bartsch, K., & Wellman, H. M. (1989). Young children's attribution of action to beliefs and desires. *Child Development, 60,* 946–964.

Brand, M. (1984). *Intending and acting: Toward a naturalized action theory.* Cambridge, MA: MIT Press.

Bratman, M. E. (1987). *Intention, plans, and practical reason.* Cambridge, MA: Harvard Univ. Press.

Buss, A. R. (1978). Causes and reasons in attribution theory: A conceptual critique. *Journal of Personality and Social Psychology, 36,* 1311–1321.

Crick, N. R. (1995). Relational aggression: The role of intent attributions, feelings of distress, and provocation type. *Development and Psychopathology, 7,* 313–322.

D'Andrade, R. (1987). A folk model of the mind. In D. Holland & N. Quinn (Eds.), *Cultural models in language and thought* (pp. 112–148). New York: Cambridge Univ. Press.

Davidson, D. (1963). Actions, reasons and causes. *Journal of Philosophy, 60,* 685–700.

Davidson, D. (1980). Intending. In *Essays on actions and events* (pp. 83–102). Oxford: Clarendon Press.

Dennett, D. C. (1987). *The intentional stance.* Cambridge, MA: MIT Press.

Edwards, A. L. (1957). *The social desirability variable in personality assessment and research.* New York: Dryden.

Epstein, S., & Taylor, S. P. (1967). Instigation to aggression as a function of degree of defeat and perceived aggressive intent of the opponent. *Journal of Personality, 35,* 265–289.

Fincham, F. D., Bradbury, T. N., & Grych, J. H. (1990). Conflict in close relationships: The role of interpersonal phenomena. In S. Graham & V. S. Folkes (Eds.), *Attribution theory: Applications to achievement, mental health, and interpersonal conflict* (pp. 161–184). Hillsdale, NJ: Erlbaum.

Fishbein, M., & Ajzen, I. (1975). *Belief, attitude, intention, and behavior: An introduction to theory and research.* Reading, MA: Addison-Wesley.

Fiske, S. T. (1989). Examining the role of intent: Toward understanding its role in stereotyping and prejudice. In J. S. Uleman & J. A. Bargh (Eds.), *Unintended thought: Limits of awareness, intention, and control* (pp. 253–283). New York: Guilford.

Fleming, J. H., & Darley, J. M. (1989). Perceiving choice and constraint: The effects of contextual and behavioral cues on attitude attribution. *Journal of Personality and Social Psychology, 56,* 27–40.

Forguson, L. (1989). *Common sense.* London: Routledge.

Goldman, A. (1970). *A theory of human action.* Englewood Cliffs, NJ: Prentice-Hall.

Graham, S., & Hudley, C. (1994). Attributions of aggressive and nonaggressive African-American male early adolescents: A study of construct accessibility. *Developmental Psychology, 30,* 365–373.

Heckhausen, H. (1991). *Motivation and action.* Berlin: Springer Verlag.

Heider, F. (1958). *The psychology of interpersonal relations.* New York: Wiley.

Hotaling, G. T. (1980). Attribution processes in husband–wife violence. In M. A. Straus & G. T. Hotaling (Eds.), *The social causes of husband–wife violence* (pp. 136–154). St. Paul: Univ. of Minnesota Press.

Hume, D. (1978). *A treatise of human nature.* L. A. Selby-Bigge & P. H. Nidditch (Eds.). New York: Oxford Univ. Press. (Originally published in 1740.)

Ickes, W. J., & Kidd, R. F. (1976). An attributional analysis of helping behavior. In J. H. Harvey, W. J. Ickes, & R. F. Kidds (Eds.), *New directions in attribution research* (Vol. 1, pp. 311–334). Hillsdale, NJ: Erlbaum.

Jones, E. E., & Davis, K. E. (1965). From acts to dispositions: The attribution process in person perception. In L. Berkowitz (Ed.), *Advances in experimental social psychology* (Vol. 2, pp. 371–388). Hillsdale, NJ: Erlbaum.

Jones, E. E., & McGillis, D. (1976). Correspondent inference and the attribution cube: A comparative reappraisal. In J. H. Harvey, W. J. Ickes, & R. F. Kidds (Eds.), *New directions in attribution research* (Vol. 1, pp. 389–420). Hillsdale, NJ: Erlbaum.

Karniol, R. (1978). Children's use of intention cues in evaluating behavior. *Psychological Bulletin, 85,* 76–85.

Kugelmass, S., & Breznitz, S. (1968). Intentionality in moral judgment: Adolescent development. *Child Development, 39,* 249–256.

Libet, B. (1985). Unconscious cerebral initiative and the role of conscious will in voluntary action. *Behavioral and Brain Sciences, 8,* 529–566.

Lillard, A. (1996). *Ethnopsychologies. Part I: Is "our" theory of mind universal?* Manuscript submitted for publication.

Locke, D., & Pennington, D. (1982). Reasons and other causes: Their role in attribution processes. *Journal of Personality and Social Psychology, 42,* 212–223.

Malle, B. F. (1996). *Intentionality in attribution: A theory of folk explanations of behavior.* Manuscript submitted for publication.

Malle, B. F., & Knobe, J. (in press). Which behaviors do people explain? A basic actor–observer asymmetry. *Journal of Personality and Social Psychology.*

Maselli, M. D., & Altrocchi, J. (1969). Attribution of intent. *Psychological Bulletin, 71,* 445–454.

Meltzoff, A. N. (1995). Understanding the intentions of others: Re-enactment of intended acts by 18-month-old children. *Developmental Psychology,* **31,** 1–16.

Moses, L. J. (1993). Young children's understanding of belief constraints on intention. *Cognitive Development,* **8,** 1–25.

Ossorio, P. G., & Davis, K. E. (1968). The self, intentionality, and reactions to evaluations of the self. In C. Gordon & K. J. Gergen (Eds.), *The self in social interaction.* New York: Wiley.

Piaget, J. (1932). *The moral judgment of the child.* New York: Harcourt, Brace.

Rosenbaum, R. M. (1972). *A dimensional analysis of the perceived causes of success and failure.* Unpublished doctoral dissertation, University of California, Los Angeles.

Ryan, T. A. (1970). *Intentional behavior. An approach to human motivation.* New York: Ronald Press.

Savage, L. J. (1954). *The foundation of statistics.* New York: Wiley.

Schneider, W., & Shiffrin, R. M. (1977). Controlled and automatic human information processing: Detection, search, and attention. *Psychological Review,* **84,** 1–66.

Searle, I. R. (1983). *Intentionality: An essay in the philosophy of mind.* Cambridge: Cambridge Univ. Press.

Shaver, K. G. (1985). *The attribution of blame.* New York: Springer-Verlag.

Shultz, T. R. (1980). Development of the concept of intention. In W. A. Collins (Ed.), *Development of cognition, affects, and social cognition. The Minnesota symposium on child psychology* (Vol. 13, pp. 131–164). Hillsdale, NJ: Erlbaum.

Shultz, T. R. (1988). Assessing intention: A computational model. In J. W. Astington, P. L. Harris, & D. R. Olson (Eds.), *Developing theories of mind* (pp. 341–367). New York: Cambridge Univ. Press.

Shultz, T. R., & Wells, D. (1985). Judging the intentionality of action-outcomes. *Developmental Psychology,* **21,** 83–89.

Shultz, T. R., & Wright, K. (1985). Concepts of negligence and intention in the assignment of moral responsibility. *Canadian Journal of Behavioural Science,* **17,** 97–108.

Stratton, P., Heard, D., Hanks, H. G. I., Munton, A. G., Brewin, C. R., & Davidson, C. (1986). Coding causal beliefs in natural discourse. *British Journal of Social Psychology,* **25,** 299–313.

Swap, W. C. (1991). When prosocial behavior becomes altruistic: An attributional analysis. *Current Psychology: Research and Reviews,* **10,** 49–64.

Taylor, S. P., Shuntich, R. J., & Greenberg, A. (1979). *Journal of Social Psychology,* **107,** 199–208.

Thalberg, I. (1984). Do our intentions cause our intentional actions? *American Philosophical Quarterly,* **21,** 249–260.

Tomasello, M. (1995). Joint attention as social cognition. In C. Moore & P. J. Dunham (Eds.), *Joint attention: Its origins and role in development* (pp. 103–130). Hillsdale, NJ: Erlbaum.

Uleman, J. S., & Bargh, J. A. (1989). *Unintended thought: Limits of awareness, intention, and control.* New York: Guilford.

von Neumann, J., & Morgenstern, O. (1944). *Theory of games and economic behavior.* Princeton: Princeton Univ. Press.

Wegner, D. M., & Vallacher, R. R. (1986). What do people think they're doing? Action identification and human behavior. *Psychological Review,* **94,** 3–15.

Weiner, B. (1979). A theory of motivation for some classroom experiences. *Journal of Educational Psychology,* **71,** 3–25.

Weiner, B. (1985). An attributional theory of achievement-related emotion and motivation. *Psychological Review,* **29,** 548–573.

Weiner, B. (1995). *Judgments of responsibility.* New York: Guilford.

Wellman, H. (1990). *Children's theories of mind.* Cambridge, MA: MIT Press.

Wellman, H. M. (1991). From desires to beliefs: Acquisition of a theory of mind. In A. Whiten (Ed.), *Natural theories of mind* (pp. 19–38). Oxford: Basil Blackwell.

Wellman, H. M., & Woolley, J. D. (1990). From simple desires to ordinary beliefs: The early development of everyday psychology. *Cognition,* **35,** 245–275.

ENDNOTE

1. Unfortunately, Heider's (1958) treatment of trying and intention is quite equivocal in the original text. Heider at times distinguishes intention from trying (p. 109) but at other times equates the two concepts (pp. 100, 110).

This article is partially based on the first author's doctoral dissertation completed at Stanford University. Portions of these results were previously presented in a paper given at the 1994 APS symposium "Studying folk psychology: Perceptions of intentionality in primates, children, and adults," in a poster for a 1995 "Theory of Mind conference" in Eugene, Oregon, and in an award address at the 1995 meeting of the Society of Experimental Social Psychology. We thank Laura Carstensen, Herbert Clark, Leonard Horowitz, Lara London, and Ronaldo Mendoza for commenting on earlier drafts of this paper.

CRITICAL THINKING QUESTIONS

1. The authors mention a number of limitations to their study, including the use of college students as subjects. Is there any reason to suspect that judgment of intentionality may be a function of an individual's age, economic condition, or ethnic background? Why or why not? Explain your answer.

2. How would you do a cross-cultural study to determine if the folk concept of intentionality is universal or culture specific? What inherent difficulties may be involved in conducting such a study?

3. The authors of the article speculate that "people may distinguish between intentions and doing something intentionally more for positive behaviors than for negative behaviors." Why might this be the case? Design a study to test this hypothesis.

4. Consider an incident in which someone said or did something that hurt or bothered you. In reviewing your judgment about the other person's action, how applicable are the five elements of intentionality, as described in the article? Are some elements missing from your judgment, or are other factors also operating? Explain your answers.

5. Design a longitudinal study to explore the development of the concept of *intentionality* from childhood to adulthood.

Chapter Three

SOCIAL COGNITION

THE WORLD AROUND us presents a complex array of information. Due simply to sheer volume, it is humanly impossible to pay attention to all the information available to us. So, given all of this information, how do we make sense of it? This chapter on social cognition examines some of the ways that people process information about themselves and others in order to make judgments.

A major interest of social psychologists is how people mentally process the information they receive. Decisions are not always based on a thorough analysis of the information at hand. Instead, people sometimes rely on mental shortcuts or intuition in reaching decisions. Common sense might suggest that thinking carefully about information in reaching decisions is better than making quick, intuitive judgments, at least for important matters. This view is challenged in Article 7, "Matters of Choice Muddled by Thought," which suggests that in some situations, at least, thinking too much might hinder effective decision making.

Social cognition also deals with how we make sense of ourselves. One interesting line of research has addressed the relationship between cognition and emotion. Specifically, do our mental processes influence what we feel, or do our feelings shape our mental processes? Article 8, "Cognitive, Social, and Physiological Determinants of Emotional State," is a classic investigation of the relationship between thought processes and emotion. The methods and findings of the study make interesting reading, but its implications are even more important: Is it possible to change the emotions we experience simply by changing the cognitive labels that we attach to them?

Finally, the last article in this chapter returns to the question of how we try to make sense of the world around us. Once we see the outcome of an event, what happens to our initial beliefs about the possibility that outcome would occur? This *hindsight bias,* or the tendency to distort prior beliefs in light of current knowledge, appears to be a fairly common social cognition process. This topic is explored in Article 9, "Hindsight Bias in Reaction to the Verdict in the O. J. Simpson Criminal Trial."

ARTICLE 7

Social cognition is concerned with the processes that people use to make sense of the social world. One finding from research in this area is that people tend to be *cognitive misers;* that is, all things being equal, people prefer to think as little as possible in reaching decisions. To help them achieve this goal, cognitive strategies, such as *heuristics* (mental shortcuts for understanding the world), are employed.

The use of such shortcuts may help an individual reach a decision more quickly and easily than if he or she carefully examines and thinks about the situation at hand. But at what cost? Common sense (and research) suggests that these mental shortcuts might not yield accurate outcomes. So, it would seem that if you want to make a good decision, you are better off spending the time to carefully think about the information at hand. However, this may not always be the case.

The next article, by Malcolm Gladwell, presents recent research indicating that, at least in some cases, thinking too much about a decision may actually hinder the quality of the outcome compared to the result produced when decision making is more intuitive and less thought out. Perhaps intuition does play a valuable role in decision making after all.

Matters of Choice Muddled by Thought
People Asked to Analyze Their Decisions
Tend to Act Differently, Often for the Worse

■ Malcolm Gladwell

This is the case against thinking too much.

In an experiment conducted recently at the University of Virginia, a large group of students was asked to select one of five art posters to take home. The options included impressionist paintings and pictures of animals. Half of the students, however, were first asked to analyze and write down the reasons for their choice.

The study found that those forced to explain their preferences in writing were much more likely to choose the animal posters than were their counterparts. When the researchers called all the students back three weeks later, the thinkers were far less happy with their posters than were those who chose without articulating their reasons. They wished they had chosen differently.

In the field of cognitive research, one of clinical psychology's hottest research areas, the poster experiment and dozens like it are fuel for a radical notion: The unexamined life may not be so bad after all. Thinking and analyzing and reasoning—the cornerstones of Western intellectual culture—may lead us not just to change our decisions but to change them for the worse.

"We're not talking about huge changes," said University of Virginia psychologist Timothy Wilson, who headed the poster study. "It's not like you ask a Democrat why they are a Democrat and they become a Republican. But the simple act of thinking about why you feel the way you do can change your mind about how you feel. That can be very consequential."

Consider the experiment published this month in the *Journal of Personality and Social Psychology* by Wilson and University of Pittsburgh researcher Jonathan Schooler. The two men chose five brands of strawberry jam that varied widely in quality. In a *Consumer*

Reports taste test, jam experts had ranked the five 1st, 11th, 24th, 32nd and 44th.

The experiment was set up like the poster trial. One group tasted each of the jams and ranked them immediately. Its ratings corresponded quite closely to those of the experts. The thinking group, however, was another story. Forced to write down their reasons for liking and disliking each brand, their preferences bore no resemblance to those of the experts or their peers in the control group.

In other words, it is not simply that thinking leads to decisions we may later regret. It also appears that thinking too much can lead to choices that, by an objective standard, can be called bad or wrong.

PICKING FROM A LINEUP

Schooler has another experiment that addresses this point more explicitly. He had two groups watch a videotape of a bank robbery. Afterward they were asked to pick the robber out from a police lineup. The intuitive group did well, choosing the correct perpetrator 65 percent of the time. The other group, however, asked to provide a detailed description of the robber immediately after viewing the tape, picked the right man in the police line only 35 to 40 percent of the time.

Psychologists in the field are quick to say that this does not mean all thinking is bad. Schooler, for example, says that if he changes the experiment to focus on something the bank robber said, the thinking group does far better. In this experiment, it appears the detrimental effects of thinking or verbalization are confined to visual memory of faces. In the case of the jam and poster experiments, it also appears that thinking impairs only people who are not experts. Asking a group of art historians to explain why they like Picasso over Vargas, for instance, does not appear to have any influence at all on their preferences.

What this does suggest, researchers say, is that there is some element of the way we feel that does not proceed from rational analysis or description. It may be the result of unconscious mental processing that cannot be translated into words.

Wilson argues that when people are forced to put their feelings into words, they inevitably come up with an incomplete or inadequate description. Asked to describe jam, they might come up with a reason that sounds logical but actually has nothing to do with their real preferences. By focusing on those reasons, they then talk themselves out of the way they really feel.

Schooler makes the same point about his bank-robber video. Visual memory is a form of non-verbal cognition. Trying to express the memory verbally, he says, somehow displaces the original, accurate image.

"Our society believes in the supremacy of language," Schooler says, "We have this tremendous emphasis on its value. But our research suggests that it is a two-edged sword. It has costs. What we are doing is finding out about those costs."

FIGURING OUT THE RULES

Another, more complicated explanation for this curious phenomenon involves what is referred to as implicit knowledge. Brooklyn College psychologist Arthur Reber has attempted to measure this unspoken intelligence in experiments with sequences of letters. Subjects sat down at a computer keyboard and strings of letters and numbers were flashed at them. They then had to reproduce sequence. This was done with 20 different sequences, with each repeated until all the subjects had correctly reproduced each one.

Reber then told everyone in the experiment that the letter sequences were formed according to a complex set of rules. (For example, the sequence pzr is never followed by a vowel.) But the subjects were not told what those rules were. A series of new sequences was then flashed on the screen and the subjects were asked to say whether they thought each sequence followed the (still unstated) rules of the first 20.

The experiment discovered several things. The first was that all people were very good at recognizing whether the new sequence fit the old rules, even when they had no conscious idea what the rules were. Second, the ability to analyze the new strings correctly had no substantial correlation with traditional measures of intelligence. High IQ people did the first memorization part of the experiment more quickly, but they were not any more successful at applying that new knowledge than chronic alcoholics or psychotics or the mentally retarded.

Finally, Reber found that when he asked people what they thought the rules were, their answers were useless. Some people insisted that certain sequences were legitimate even when they had previously—and properly—identified those sequences as grammatically incorrect during the test.

Reber concluded that we all have some reservoir of knowledge and innate mental abilities that help us solve problems and make decisions on a wide range of things that cannot be reached by language or traditional self-reflection.

Borrowing a phrase from philosopher Michael Polanyi, Reber calls this "tacit knowledge," a rich and powerful source of human feeling and behavior. Just don't think about it too much.

CRITICAL THINKING QUESTIONS

1. Based on the information in this article, in what situations might it be best for you to rely on intuition in making decisions? When might it be best to think carefully before making decisions? Why?

2. Many traditional measures of intelligence rely heavily on language skills and thus do not tap into the type of "tacit knowledge" referred to in the article. Is it possible to measure such knowledge? How?

3. Many people involved in intimate relationships feel that it is important from time to time to discuss the status of the relationship and their feelings for one another. Based on the information presented in this article, what may be some of the potential issues involved in doing this?

4. Design a study involving a real-life issue to test the hypothesis that thinking too much might hinder decision making in some situations.

ARTICLE 8 _____

How do you know what emotion you are experiencing? Ask that question of someone who has just learned that he or she has won the lottery, and the answer would undoubtedly be "thrilled," "excited," "overjoyed," or some such adjective to describe a very positive emotional state. Ask if it is actually anger that the winner is feeling, and he or she probably would look at you as if you were crazy. But how does that person *know* what emotion he or she is feeling?

The work that follows by Schachter and Singer is a classic study that addresses what determines a person's emotional state. Briefly, the authors' findings suggest that what we call *emotion* is partly due to some sort of physiological arousal. However, what we feel is also determined by the cognitive label that we attach to that physiological arousal. According to this approach, a person who experiences some sort of physiological arousal might subjectively experience one of two very different emotional states, either anger or euphoria, depending on how he or she labeled the experience. The article discusses the process as well as some of the conditions that result when this process occurs.

While reading the article, think of its implications: Is cognition a necessary part of emotion? Without it, what (if anything) would we feel? What about newborn children? Since their cognitive abilities are not yet fully developed, does that mean that they don't experience emotions?

Cognitive, Social, and Physiological Determinants of Emotional State[1]

■ Stanley Schachter and Jerome E. Singer

The problem of which cues, internal or external, permit a person to label and identify his own emotional state has been with us since the days that James (1890) first tendered his doctrine that "the bodily changes follow directly the perception of the exciting fact, and that our feeling of the same changes as they occur *is* the emotion" (p. 449). Since we are aware of a variety of feeling and emotion states, it should follow from James' proposition that the various emotions will be accompanied by a variety of differentiable bodily states. Following James' pronouncement, a formidable number of studies were undertaken in search of the physiological differentiators of the emotions. The results, in these early days, were almost uniformly negative. All of the emotional states experimentally manipulated were characterized by a general pattern of excitation of the sympathetic nervous system but

there appeared to be no clear-cut physiological discriminators of the various emotions. This pattern of results was so consistent from experiment to experiment that Cannon (1929) offered, as one of the crucial criticisms of the James-Lange theory, the fact that "the same visceral changes occur in very different emotional states and in non-emotional states" (p. 351).

More recent work, however, has given some indication that there may be differentiators. Ax (1953) and Schachter (1957) studied fear and anger. On a large number of indices both of these states were characterized by a similarly high level of autonomic activation but on several indices they did differ in the degree of activation. Wolf and Wolff (1947) studied a subject with a gastric fistula and were able to distinguish two patterns in the physiological responses of

Reprinted from *Psychological Review*, 1962, 69, 379–399.

the stomach wall. It should be noted, though, that for many months they studied their subject during and following a great variety of moods and emotions and were able to distinguish only two patterns.

Whether or not there are physiological distinctions among the various emotional states must be considered an open question. Recent work might be taken to indicate that such differences are at best rather subtle and that the variety of emotion, mood, and feeling states are by no means matched by an equal variety of visceral patterns.

This rather ambiguous situation has led Ruckmick (1936), Hunt, Cole, and Reis (1958), Schachter (1959) and others to suggest that cognitive factors may be major determinants of emotional states. Granted a general pattern of sympathetic excitation as characteristic of emotional states, granted that there may be some differences in pattern from state to state, it is suggested that one labels, interprets, and identifies this stirred-up state in terms of the characteristics of the precipitating situation and one's apperceptive mass. This suggests, then, that an emotional state may be considered a function of a state of physiological arousal[2] and of a cognition appropriate to this state of arousal. The cognition, in a sense, exerts a steering function. Cognitions arising from the immediate situation as interpreted by past experience provide the framework within which one understands and labels his feelings. It is the cognition which determines whether the state of physiological arousal will be labeled as "anger," "joy," "fear," or whatever.

In order to examine the implications of this formulation let us consider the fashion in which these two elements, a state of physiological arousal and cognitive factors, would interact in a variety of situations. In most emotion inducing situations, of course, the two factors are completely interrelated. Imagine a man walking alone down a dark alley; a figure with a gun suddenly appears. The perception-cognition "figure with a gun" in some fashion initiates a state of physiological arousal; this state of arousal is interpreted in terms of knowledge about dark alleys and guns and the state of arousal is labeled "fear." Similarly a student who unexpectedly learns that he has made Phi Beta Kappa may experience a state of arousal which he will label "joy."

Let us now consider circumstances in which these two elements, the physiological and the cognitive, are, to some extent, independent. First, is the state of physiological arousal alone sufficient to induce an emotion? Best evidence indicates that it is not. Marañon[3] (1924), in a fascinating study (which was replicated by Cantril & Hunt, 1932, and Landis & Hunt, 1932), injected 210 of his patients with the sympathomimetic agent adrenalin and then simply asked them to introspect. Seventy-one percent of his subjects simply reported their physical symptoms with no emotional overtones; 29% of the subjects responded in an apparently emotional fashion. Of these the great majority described their feelings in a fashion that Marañon labeled "cold" or "as if" emotions, that is, they made statements such as "I feel *as if* I were afraid" or "*as if* I were awaiting a great happiness." This is a sort of emotional "déjà vu" experience; these subjects are neither happy nor afraid, they feel "as if" they were. Finally a very few cases apparently reported a genuine emotional experience. However, in order to produce this reaction in most of these few cases, Marañon (1924) points out:

> One must suggest a memory with strong affective force but not so strong as to produce an emotion in the normal state. For example, in several cases we spoke to our patients before the injection of their sick children or dead parents and they responded calmly to this topic. The same topic presented later, during the adrenal commotion, was sufficient to trigger emotion. This adrenal commotion places the subject in a situation of "affective imminence." (pp. 307–308)

Apparently, then, to produce a genuinely emotional reaction to adrenalin, Marañon was forced to provide such subjects with an appropriate cognition.

Though Marañon (1924) is not explicit on his procedure, it is clear that his subjects knew that they were receiving an injection and in all likelihood knew that they were receiving adrenalin and probably had some order of familiarity with its effects. In short, though they underwent the pattern of sympathetic discharge common to strong emotional states, at the same time they had a completely appropriate cognition or explanation as to why they felt this way. This, we would suggest, is the reason so few of Marañon's subjects reported any emotional experience.

Consider now a person in a state of physiological arousal for which no immediately explanatory or appropriate cognitions are available. Such a state could result were one covertly to inject a subject with adrenalin or, unknown to him, feed the subject a sympathomimetic drug such as ephedrine. Under such conditions a subject would be aware of palpitations, tremor, face flushing, and most of the battery of symptoms associated with a discharge of the sympathetic nervous system. In contrast to Marañon's (1924) subjects he would, at the same time, be utterly unaware of why he felt this way. What would be the consequence of such a state?

Schachter (1959) has suggested that precisely such a state would lead to the arousal of "evaluative needs" (Festinger, 1954), that is, pressures would act on an individual in such a state to understand and label his bodily feelings. His bodily state grossly resembles the condition in which it has been at times of emotional excitement. How would he label his present feelings? It is suggested, of course, that he will label his feelings in terms of his knowledge of the immediate situation.[4] Should he at the time be with a beautiful woman, he might decide that he was wildly in love or sexually excited. Should he be at a gay party, he might, by comparing himself to others, decide that he was extremely happy and euphoric. Should he be arguing with his wife, he might explode in fury and hatred. Or, should the situation be completely inappropriate, he could decide that he was excited about something that had recently happened to him or, simply, that he was sick. In any case, it is our basic assumption that emotional states are a function of the interaction of such cognitive factors with a state of physiological arousal.

This line of thought, then, leads to the following propositions:

1. Given a state of physiological arousal for which an individual has no immediate explanation, he will "label" this state and describe his feelings in terms of the cognitions available to him. To the extent that cognitive factors are potent determiners of emotional states, it could be anticipated that precisely the same state of physiological arousal could be labeled "joy" or "fury" or "jealousy" or any of a great diversity of emotional labels depending on the cognitive aspects of the situation.

2. Given a state of physiological arousal for which an individual has a completely appropriate explanation (e.g., "I feel this way because I have just received an injection of adrenalin") no evaluative needs will arise and the individual is unlikely to label his feelings in terms of the alternative cognitions available.

Finally, consider a condition in which emotion inducing cognitions are present but there is no state of physiological arousal. For example, an individual might be completely aware that he is in great danger but for some reason (drug or surgical) remain in a state of physiological quiescence. Does he experience the emotion "fear"? Our formulation of emotion as a joint function of a state of physiological arousal and an appropriate cognition, would, of course, suggest that he does not, which leads to our final proposition.

3. Given the same cognitive circumstances, the individual will react emotionally or describe his feelings as emotions only to the extent that he experiences a state of physiological arousal.[5]

PROCEDURE

The experimental test of these propositions requires (a) the experimental manipulation of a state of physiological arousal, (b) the manipulation of the extent to which the subject has an appropriate or proper explanation of his bodily state, and (c) the creation of situations from which explanatory cognitions may be derived.

In order to satisfy the first two experimental requirements, the experiment was cast in the framework of a study of the effects of vitamin supplements on vision. As soon as a subject arrived, he was taken to a private room and told by the experimenter:

In this experiment we would like to make various tests of your vision. We are particularly interested in how certain vitamin compounds and vitamin supplements affect the visual skills. In particular, we want to find out how the vitamin compound called "Suproxin" affects your vision.

What we would like to do, then, if we can get your permission, is to give you a small injection of Suproxin. The injection itself is mild and harmless;

however, since some people do object to being injected we don't want to talk you into anything. Would you mind receiving a Suproxin injection?

If the subject agrees to the injection (and all but 1 of 185 subjects did) the experimenter continues with instructions we shall describe shortly, then leaves the room. In a few minutes a physician enters the room, briefly repeats the experimenter's instructions, takes the subject's pulse and then injects him with Suproxin.

Depending upon condition, the subject receives one of two forms of Suproxin—epinephrine or a placebo.

Epinephrine or adrenalin is a sympathomimetic drug whose effects, with minor exceptions, are almost a perfect mimicry of a discharge of the sympathetic nervous system. Shortly after injection systolic blood pressure increases markedly, heart rate increases somewhat, cutaneous blood flow decreases, while muscle and cerebral blood flow increase, blood sugar and lactic acid concentration increase, and respiration rate increases slightly. As far as the subject is concerned the major subjective symptoms are palpitation, tremor, and sometimes a feeling of flushing and accelerated breathing. With a subcutaneous injection (in the dosage administered to our subjects), such effects usually begin within 3–5 minutes of injection and last anywhere from 10 minutes to an hour. For most subjects these effects are dissipated within 15–20 minutes after injection.

Subjects receiving epinephrine received a subcutaneous injection of 1/2 cubic centimeter of a 1:1000 solution of Winthrop Laboratory's Suprarenin, a saline solution of epinephrine bitartrate.

Subjects in the placebo condition received a subcutaneous injection of 1/2 cubic centimeter of saline solution. This is, of course, completely neutral material with no side effects at all.

Manipulating an Appropriate Explanation

By "appropriate" we refer to the extent to which the subject has an authoritative, unequivocal explanation of his bodily condition. Thus, a subject who had been informed by the physician that as a direct consequence of the injection he would feel palpitations, tremor, etc. would be considered to have a completely appropriate explanation. A subject who had been informed only that the injection would have no side effects would have no appropriate explanation of his state. This dimension of appropriateness was manipulated in three experimental conditions which shall be called: Epinephrine Informed (Epi Inf), Epinephrine Ignorant (Epi Ign), and Epinephrine Misinformed (Epi Mis).

Immediately after the subject had agreed to the injection and before the physician entered the room, the experimenter's spiel in each of these conditions went as follows:

Epinephrine Informed. *I should also tell you that some of our subjects have experienced side effects from the Suproxin. These side effects are transitory, that is, they will only last for about 15 or 20 minutes. What will probably happen is that your hand will start to shake, your heart will start to pound, and your face may get warm and flushed. Again these are side effects lasting about 15 or 20 minutes.*

While the physician was giving the injection, she told the subject that the injection was mild and harmless and repeated this description of the symptoms that the subject could expect as a consequence of the shot. In this condition, then, subjects have a completely appropriate explanation of their bodily state. They know precisely what they will feel and why.

Epinephrine Ignorant In this condition, when the subject agreed to the injection, the experimenter said nothing more relevant to side effects and simply left the room. While the physician was giving the injection, she told the subject that the injection was mild and harmless and would have no side effects. In this condition, then, the subject has no experimentally provided explanation for his bodily state.

Epinephrine Misinformed. *I should also tell you that some of our subjects have experienced side effects from the Suproxin. These side effects are transitory, that is, they will only last for about 15 or 20 minutes. What will probably happen is that your feet will feel numb, you will have an itching sensation over parts of your body, and you may get a slight headache. Again these are side effects lasting 15 or 20 minutes.*

And again, the physician repeated these symptoms while injecting the subject.

None of these symptoms, of course, are consequences of an injection of epinephrine and, in effect, these instructions provide the subject with a completely inappropriate explanation of his bodily feelings. This condition was introduced as a control condition of sorts. It seemed possible that the description of side effects in the Epi Inf condition might turn the subject introspective, self-examining, possibly slightly troubled. Differences on the dependent variable between the Epi Inf and Epi Ign conditions might, then, be due to such factors rather than to differences in appropriateness. The false symptoms in the Epi Mis condition should similarly turn the subject introspective, etc., but the instructions in this condition do not provide an appropriate explanation of the subject's state.

Subjects in all of the above conditions were injected with epinephrine. Finally, there was a placebo condition in which subjects, who were injected with saline solution, were given precisely the same treatment as subjects in the Epi Ign condition.

Producing an Emotion Inducing Cognition

Our initial hypothesis has suggested that given a state of physiological arousal for which the individual has no adequate explanation, cognitive factors can lead the individual to describe his feelings with any of a diversity of emotional labels. In order to test this hypothesis, it was decided to manipulate emotional states which can be considered quite different—euphoria and anger.

There are, of course, many ways to induce such states. In our own program of research, we have concentrated on social determinants of emotional states and have been able to demonstrate in other studies that people do evaluate their own feelings by comparing themselves with others around them (Schachter 1959; Wrightsman 1960). In this experiment we have attempted again to manipulate emotional state by social means. In one set of conditions, the subject is placed together with a stooge who has been trained to act euphorically. In a second set of conditions the subject is with a stooge trained to act in an angry fashion.

Euphoria

Immediately[6] after the subject had been injected, the physician left the room and the experimenter returned with a stooge whom he introduced as another subject, then said:

> Both of you have had the Suproxin shot and you'll both be taking the same tests of vision. What I ask you to do now is just wait for 20 minutes. The reason for this is simply that we have to allow 20 minutes for the Suproxin to get from the injection site into the bloodstream. At the end of 20 minutes when we are certain that most of the Suproxin has been absorbed into the bloodstream, we'll begin the tests of vision.

The room in which this was said had been deliberately put into a state of mild disarray. As he was leaving, the experimenter apologetically added:

> The only other thing I should do is to apologize for the condition of the room. I just didn't have time to clean it up. So, if you need any scratch paper or rubber bands or pencils, help yourself. I'll be back in 20 minutes to begin the vision tests.

As soon as the experimenter had left, the stooge introduced himself again, made a series of standard icebreaker comments, and then launched his routine. For observation purposes, the stooge's act was broken into a series of standard units, demarcated by a change in activity or a standard comment. In sequence, the units of the stooge's routine were the following:

1. Stooge reaches for a piece of paper and starts doodling saying, "They said we could use this for scratch, didn't they?" He doodles a fish for some 30 seconds, then says:
2. "This scrap paper isn't even much good for doodling" and crumples paper and attempts to throw it into wastebasket in far corner of the room. He misses but this leads him into a "basketball game." He crumples up other sheets of paper, shoots a few baskets, says "Two points" occasionally. He gets up and does a jump shot saying, "The old jump shot is really on today."
3. If the subject has not joined in, the stooge throws a paper basketball to the subject saying, "Here, you try it."

4. Stooge continues his game saying, "The trouble with paper basketballs is that you don't really have any control."

5. Stooge continues basketball, then gives it up saying, "This is one of my good days. I feel like a kid again. I think I'll make a plane." He makes a paper airplane saying, "I guess I'll make one of the longer ones."

6. Stooge flies plane. Gets up and retrieves plane. Flies again, etc.

7. Stooge throws plane at subject.

8. Stooge, flying plane, says, "Even when I was a kid, I was never much good at this."

9. Stooge tears off part of plane saying, "Maybe this plane can't fly but at least it's good for something." He wads up paper and making a slingshot of a rubber band begins to shoot the paper.

10. Shooting, the stooge says, "They [paper ammunition] really go better if you make them long. They don't work right if you wad them up."

11. While shooting, stooge notices a sloppy pile of manila folders on a table. He builds a tower of these folders, then goes to the opposite end of the room to shoot at the tower.

12. He misses several times, then hits and cheers as the tower falls. He goes over to pick up the folders.

13. While picking up, he notices, behind a portable blackboard, a pair of hula hoops which have been covered with black tape with a few wires sticking out of the tape. He reaches for these, taking one for himself and putting the other aside but within reaching distance of the subject. The stooge tries the hula hoop, saying, "This isn't as easy as it looks."

14. Stooge twirls hoop wildly on arm, saying, "Hey, look at this—this is great."

15. Stooge replaces the hula hoop and sits down with his feet on the table. Shortly thereafter the experimenter returns to the room.

This routine was completely standard, though its pace, of course, varied depending upon the subject's reaction, the extent to which he entered into this bedlam and the extent to which he initiated activities of his own. The only variations from this standard routine were those forced by the subject. Should the subject originate some nonsense of his own and request the stooge to join in, he would do so. And, he would, of course, respond to any comments initiated by the subject.

Subjects in each of the three "appropriateness" conditions and in the placebo condition were submitted to this setup. The stooge, of course, never knew in which condition any particular subject fell.

Anger

Immediately after the injection, the experimenter brought a stooge into the subject's room, introduced the two and after explaining the necessity for a 20 minute delay for "the Suproxin to get from the injection site into the bloodstream" he continued, "We would like you to use these 20 minutes to answer these questionnaires." Then handing out the questionnaires, he concludes with, "I'll be back in 20 minutes to pick up the questionnaires and begin the tests of vision."

Before looking at the questionnaire, the stooge says to the subject,

> *I really wanted to come for an experiment today, but I think it's unfair for them to give you shots. At least, they should have told us about the shots when they called us; you hate to refuse, once you're here already.*

The questionnaires, five pages long, start off innocently requesting face sheet information and then grow increasingly personal and insulting. The stooge, sitting directly opposite the subject, paces his own answers so that at all times subject and stooge are working on the same question. At regular points in the questionnaire, the stooge makes a series of standardized comments about the questions. His comments start off innocently enough, grow increasingly querulous, and finally he ends up in a rage. In sequence, he makes the following comments.

1. Before answering any items, he leafs quickly through the questionnaire saying, "Boy, this is a long one."

2. Question 7 on the questionnaire requests, "List the foods that you would eat in a typical day." The stooge comments, "Oh for Pete's sake, what did I have for breakfast this morning?"

3. Question 9 asks, "Do you ever hear bells? _____ How often? _____" The stooge remarks, "Look at Question 9. How ridiculous can you get? I hear bells every time I change classes."

4. Question 13 requests, "List the childhood diseases you have had and the age at which you had them" to which the stooge remarks, "I get annoyed at this childhood disease question. I can't remember what childhood diseases I had, and especially at what age. Can you?"

5. Question 17 asks, "What is your father's average annual income?" and the stooge says, "This really irritates me. It's none of their business what my father makes. I'm leaving that blank."

6. Question 25 presents a long series of items such as "Does not bathe or wash regularly," "Seems to need psychiatric care," etc. and requests the respondent to write down for which member of his immediate family each item seems most applicable. The question specifically prohibits the answer "None" and each item must be answered. The stooge says, "I'll be damned if I'll fill out Number 25. 'Does not bathe or wash regularly'—that's a real insult." He then angrily crosses out the entire item.

7. Question 28 reads: "How many times each week do you have sexual intercourse?" 0–1 _____ 2–3 _____ 4–6 _____ 7 and over _____. The stooge bites out, "The hell with it! I don't have to tell them all this."

8. The stooge sits sullenly for a few moments then he rips up his questionnaire, crumples the pieces and hurls them to the floor, saying, "I'm not wasting any more time. I'm getting my books and leaving" and he stamps out of the room.

9. The questionnaire continues for eight more questions ending with: "With how many men (other than your father) has your mother had extramarital relationships?" 4 and under _____; 5–9 _____; 10 and over _____.

Subjects in the Epi Ign, Epi Inf and Placebo conditions were run through this "anger" inducing sequence. The stooge, again, did not know to which condition the subject had been assigned.

In summary, this is a seven condition experiment which, for two different emotional states, allows us (a) to evaluate the effects of "appropriateness" on emotional inducibility and (b) to begin to evaluate the effects of sympathetic activation on emotional inducibility. In schematic form the conditions are the following:

Euphoria	*Anger*
Epi Inf	Epi Inf
Epi Ign	Epi Ign
Epi Mis	Placebo
Placebo	

The Epi Mis condition was not run in the Anger sequence. This was originally conceived as a control condition and it was felt that its inclusion in the Euphoria conditions alone would suffice as a means of evaluating the possible artifactual effect of the Epi Inf instructions.

Measurement

Two types of measures of emotional state were obtained. Standardized observation through a one-way mirror was the technique used to assess the subject's behavior. To what extent did he act euphoric or angry? Such behavior can be considered in a way as a "semi-private" index of mood for as far as the subject was concerned, his emotional behavior could be known only to the other person in the room—presumably another student. The second type of measure was self-report in which, on a variety of scales, the subject indicated his mood of the moment. Such measures can be considered "public" indices of mood for they would, of course, be available to the experimenter and his associates.

Observation

Euphoria   For each of the first 14 units of the stooge's standardized routine an observer kept a running chronicle of what the subject did and said. For each unit the observer coded the subject's behavior in one or more of the following categories:

Category 1: Joins in activity.   If the subject entered into the stooge activities, e.g., if he made or flew airplanes, threw paper basketballs, hula hooped, etc., his behavior was coded in this category.

Category 2: Initiates new activity. A subject was so coded if he gave indications of creative euphoria, that is, if, on his own, he initiated behavior outside of the stooge's routine. Instances of such behavior would be the subject who threw open the window and, laughing, hurled paper basketballs at passersby; or, the subject who jumped on a table and spun one hula hoop on his leg and the other on his neck.

Categories 3 and 4: Ignores or watches stooge. Subjects who paid flatly no attention to the stooge or who, with or without comment, simply watched the stooge without joining in his activity were coded in these categories.

For any particular unit of behavior, the subject's behavior was coded in one or more of these categories. To test reliability of coding two observers independently coded two experimental sessions. The observers agreed completely on the coding of 88% of the units.

Anger   For each of the units of stooge behavior, an observer recorded the subject's responses and coded them according to the following category scheme:

Category 1: Agrees. In response to the stooge the subject makes a comment indicating that he agrees with the stooge's standardized comment or that he, too, is irked by a particular item on the questionnaire. For example, a subject who responded to the stooge's comment on the "father's income" question by saying, "I don't like that kind of personal question either" would be so coded (scored +2).

Category 2: Disagrees. In response to the stooge's comment, the subject makes a comment which indicates that he disagrees with the stooge's meaning or mood; e.g., in response to the stooge's comment on the "father's income" question, such a subject might say, "Take it easy, they probably have a good reason for wanting the information" (scored –2).

Category 3: Neutral. A noncommittal or irrelevant response to the stooge's remark (scored 0).

Category 4: Initiates agreement or disagreement. With no instigation by the stooge, a subject, so coded, would have volunteered a remark indicating that he felt the same way or, alternatively, quite differently than the stooge. Examples would be "Boy I hate

this kind of thing" or "I'm enjoying this" (scored +2 or –2).

Category 5: Watches. The subject makes no verbal response to the stooge's comment but simply looks directly at him (scored 0).

Category 6: Ignores. The subject makes no verbal response to the stooge's comment nor does he look at him; the subject, paying no attention at all to the stooge, simply works at his own questionnaire (scored –1).

A subject was scored in one or more of these categories for each unit of stooge behavior. To test reliability, two observers independently coded three experimental sessions. In order to get a behavioral index of anger, observation protocol was scored according to the values presented in parentheses after each of the above definitions of categories. In a unit-by-unit comparison, the two observers agreed completely on the scoring of 71% of the units jointly observed. The scores of the two observers differed by a value of 1 or less for 88% of the units coded and in not a single case did the two observers differ in the direction of their scoring of a unit.

Self-Report of Mood and Physical Condition

When the subject's session with the stooge was completed, the experimenter returned to the room, took pulses and said:

Before we proceed with the vision tests, there is one other kind of information which we must have. We have found, as you can probably imagine, that there are many things beside Suproxin that affect how well you see in our tests. How hungry you are, how tired you are, and even the mood you're in at the time—whether you feel happy or irritated at the time of testing will affect how well you see. To understand the data we collect on you, then, we must be able to figure out which effects are due to causes such as these and which are caused by Suproxin.

The only way we can get such information about your physical and emotional state is to have you tell us. I'll hand out these questionnaires and ask you to answer them as accurately as possible. Obviously our data on the vision tests will only be as accurate as your description of your mental and physical state.

In keeping with this spiel, the questionnaire that the experimenter passed out contained a number of mock questions about hunger, fatigue, etc., as well as questions of more immediate relevance to the experiment. To measure mood or emotional state the following two were the crucial questions:

1. How irritated, angry or annoyed would you say you feel at present?

I don't feel at all irritated or angry	I feel a little irritated and angry	I feel quite irritated and angry	I feel very irritated and angry	I feel extremely irritated and angry
(0)	(1)	(2)	(3)	(4)

2. How good or happy would you say you feel at present?

I don't feel at all happy or good	I feel a little happy and good	I feel quite happy and good	I feel very happy and good	I feel extremely happy and good
(0)	(1)	(2)	(3)	(4)

To measure the physical effects of epinephrine and determine whether or not the injection had been successful in producing the necessary bodily state, the following questions were asked:

1. Have you experienced any palpitation (consciousness of your own heart beat)?

Not at all	A slight amount	A moderate amount	An intense amount
(0)	(1)	(2)	(3)

2. Did you feel any tremor (involuntary shaking of the hands, arms or legs)?

Not at all	A slight amount	A moderate amount	An intense amount
(0)	(1)	(2)	(3)

To measure possible effects of the instructions in the Epi Mis condition, the following questions were asked:

1. Did you feel any numbness in your feet?
2. Did you feel any itching sensation?
3. Did you experience any feeling of headache?

To all three of these questions was attached a four-point scale running from "Not at all" to "An intense amount."

In addition to these scales, the subjects were asked to answer two open-end questions on other physical or emotional sensations they may have experienced during the experimental session. A final measure of bodily state was pulse rate which was taken by the physician or the experimenter at two times—immediately before the injection and immediately after the session with the stooge.

When the subjects had completed these questionnaires, the experimenter announced that the experiment was over, explained the deception and its necessity in detail, answered any questions, and swore the subjects to secrecy. Finally, the subjects answered a brief questionnaire about their experiences, if any, with adrenalin and their previous knowledge or suspicion of the experimental setup. There was no indication that any of the subjects had known about the experiment beforehand but 11 subjects were so extremely suspicious of some crucial feature of the experiment that their data were automatically discarded.

Subjects

The subjects were all male, college students taking classes in introductory psychology at the University of Minnesota. Some 90% of the students in these classes volunteer for a subject pool for which they receive two extra points on their final exam for every hour that they serve as experimental subjects. For this study the records of all potential subjects were cleared with the Student Health Service in order to insure that no harmful effects would result from the injections.

Evaluation of the Experimental Design

The ideal test of our propositions would require circumstances which our experiment is far from realizing. First, the proposition that: "A state of physiological arousal for which an individual has no immediate explanation will lead him to label this state in terms of the cognitions available to him" obviously requires conditions under which the subject does not and cannot have a proper explanation of his bodily state. Though we toyed with such fantasies as ventilating the experimental room with vaporized adrenalin, reality forced us to rely on the disguised injection of Suproxin—a technique which was far from ideal for no matter what the experimenter told them, some subjects would inevitably attribute their feelings to the injection. To the extent that subjects did so, differences between the several appropriateness conditions should be attenuated.

Second, the proposition that: "Given the same cognitive circumstances the individual will react emotionally only to the extent that he experiences a state of physiological arousal" requires for its ideal test the manipulation of states of physiological arousal and of physiological quiescence. Though there is no question that epinephrine effectively produces a state of arousal, there is also no question that a placebo does not prevent physiological arousal. To the extent that the experimental situation effectively produces sympathetic stimulation in placebo subjects, the proposition is difficult to test, for such a factor would attenuate differences between epinephrine and placebo subjects.

Both of these factors, then, can be expected to interfere with the test of our several propositions. In presenting the results of this study, we shall first present condition by condition results and then evaluate the effect of these two factors on experimental differences.

RESULTS

Effects of the Injections on Bodily State

Let us examine first the success of the injections at producing the bodily state required to examine the propositions at test. Does the injection of epinephrine produce symptoms of sympathetic discharge as compared with the placebo injection? Relevant data are presented in Table 1 where it can be immediately seen that on all items subjects who were in epinephrine conditions show considerably more evidence of sympathetic activation than do subjects in placebo conditions. In all epineprine conditions pulse rate increases significantly when compared with the decrease characteristic of the placebo conditions. On the scales it is clear that epinephrine subjects experience considerably more palpitation and tremor than do placebo subjects. In all possible comparisons on these symptoms, the mean scores of subjects in any of the epinephrine conditions are greater than the corresponding scores in the placebo conditions at better than the .001 level of significance. Examination of the absolute values of these scores makes it quite clear that subjects in epinephrine conditions were, indeed, in a state of physiological arousal, while most subjects in placebo conditions were in a relative state of physiological quiescence.

The epinephrine injection, of course, did not work with equal effectiveness for all subjects; indeed for a

TABLE 1 / Effects of the Injections on Bodily State

| Condition | N | Pulse | | Self-Rating of | | | | |
		Pre	Post	Palpitation	Tremor	Numbness	Itching	Headache
Euphoria								
Epi Inf	27	85.7	88.6	1.20	1.43	0	0.16	0.32
Epi Ign	26	84.6	85.6	1.83	1.76	0.15	0	0.55
Epi Mis	26	82.9	86.0	1.27	2.00	0.06	0.08	0.23
Placebo	26	80.4	77.1	0.29	0.21	0.09	0	0.27
Anger								
Epi Inf	23	85.9	92.4	1.26	1.41	0.17	0	0.11
Epi Ign	23	85.0	96.8	1.44	1.78	0	0.06	0.21
Placebo	23	84.5	79.6	0.59	0.24	0.14	0.06	0.06

few subjects it did not work at all. Such subjects reported almost no palpitation or tremor, showed no increase in pulse and described no other relevant physical symptoms. Since for such subjects the necessary experimental conditions were not established, they were automatically excluded from the data and all further tabular presentations will not include such subjects. Table 1, however, does include the data of these subjects. There were four such subjects in euphoria conditions and one of them in anger conditions.

In order to evaluate further data on Epi Mis subjects it is necessary to note the results of the "numbness," "itching," and "headache" scales also presented in Table 1. Clearly the subjects in the Epi Mis condition do not differ on these scales from subjects in any of the other experimental conditions.

Effects of the Manipulations on Emotional State

Euphoria   Self-report. The effects of the several manipulations on emotional state in the euphoria conditions are presented in Table 2. The scores recorded in this table are derived, for each subject, by subtracting the value of the point he checks on the irritation scale from the value of the point he checks on the happiness scale. Thus, if a subject were to check the point "I feel a little irritated and angry" on the irritation scale and the point "I feel very happy and good" on the happiness scale, his score would be +2. The higher the positive value, the happier and better the subject reports himself as feeling. Though we employ an index for expositional simplicity, it should be noted that the two components of the index each yield results completely consistent with those obtained by use of this index.

Let us examine first the effects of the appropriateness instructions. Comparison of the scores for the Epi Mis and Epi Inf conditions makes it immediately clear that the experimental differences are not due to artifacts resulting from the informed instructions. In both conditions the subject was warned to expect a variety of symptoms as a consequence of the injection. In the Epi Mis condition, where the symptoms were inappropriate to the subject's bodily state the self-report score is almost twice that in the Epi Inf condition where the symptoms were completely appropriate to the subject's bodily state. It is reasonable, then, to attribute differences between informed subjects and those in other conditions to differences in manipulated appropriateness rather than to artifacts such as introspectiveness or self-examination.

It is clear that, consistent with expectations, subjects were more susceptible to the stooge's mood and consequently more euphoric when they had no explanation of their own bodily states than when they did. The means of both the Epi Ign and Epi Mis conditions are considerably greater than the mean of the Epi Inf condition.

It is of interest to note that Epi Mis subjects are somewhat more euphoric than are Epi Ign subjects. This pattern repeats itself in other data shortly to be presented. We would attribute this difference to differences in the appropriateness dimension. Though, as in the Epi Ign condition, a subject is not provided with an explanation of his bodily state, it is, of course, possible that he will provide one for himself which is not derived from his interaction with the stooge. Most reasonably he could decide for himself that he feels this way because of the injection. To the extent that he does so he should be less susceptible to the stooge. It seems probable that he would be less likely to hit on such an explanation in the Epi Mis condition than in the Epi Ign condition for in the Epi Mis condition both the experimenter and the doctor have told him that the effects of the injection would be quite differ-

TABLE 2 / Self-Report of Emotional State in the Euphoria Conditions

Condition	N	Self-Report Scales	Comparison	p
Epi Inf	25	0.98	Epi Inf vs. Epi Mis	< .01
Epi Ign	25	1.78	Epi Inf vs. Epi Ign	.02
Epi Mis	25	1.90	Placebo vs. Epi Mis, Ign, or Inf	ns
Placebo	26	1.61		

All *p* values reported throughout paper are two-tailed.

ent from what he actually feels. The effect of such instructions is probably to make it more difficult for the subject himself to hit on the alternative explanation described above. There is some evidence to support this analysis. In open-end questions in which subjects described their own mood and state, 28% of the subjects in the Epi Ign condition made some connection between the injection and their bodily state compared with the 16% of subjects in the Epi Mis condition who did so. It could be considered, then, that these three conditions fall along a dimension of appropriateness, with the Epi Inf condition at one extreme and the Epi Mis condition at the other.

Comparing the placebo to the epinephrine conditions, we note a pattern which will repeat itself throughout the data. Placebo subjects are less euphoric than either Epi Mis or Epi Ign subjects but somewhat more euphoric than Epi Inf subjects. These differences are not, however, statistically significant. We shall consider the epinephrine-placebo comparisons in detail in a later section of this paper following the presentation of additional relevant data. For the moment, it is clear that, by self-report manipulating appropriateness has had a very strong effect on euphoria.

Behavior. Let us next examine the extent to which the subject's behavior was affected by the experimental manipulations. To the extent that his mood has been affected, one should expect that the subject will join in the stooge's whirl of manic activity and initiate similar activities of his own. The relevant data are presented in Table 3. The column labeled "Activity index" presents summary figures on the extent to which the subject joined in the stooge's activity. This is a weighted index which reflects both the nature of the activities in which the subject engaged and the amount of time he was active. The index was devised by assigning the following weights to the subject's activities: 5—hula hooping; 4—shooting with slingshot; 3—paper airplanes; 2—paper basketballs; 1—doodling; 0—does nothing. Pretest scaling on 15 college students ordered these activities with respect to the degree of euphoria they represented. Arbitrary weights were assigned so that the wilder the activity, the heavier the weight. These weights are multiplied by an estimate of the amount of time the subject spent in each activity and the summed products make up

TABLE 3 / Behavioral Indications of Emotional State in the Euphoria Conditions

Condition	N	Activity Index	Mean Number of Acts Initiated
Epi Inf	25	12.72	.20
Epi Ign	25	18.28	.56
Epi Mis	25	22.56	.84
Placebo	26	16.00	.54

p value			
Comparison		Activity Index	Initiates
Epi Inf vs. Epi Mis		.05	.03
Epi Inf vs. Ipi Ign		ns	.08
Plac vs. Epi Mis. Ign. or Inf		ns	ns

Tested by χ^2 comparison of the proportion of subjects in each condition initiating new acts.

the activity index for each subject. This index may be considered a measure of behavioral euphoria. It should be noted that the same between-condition relationships hold for the two components of this index as for the index itself.

The column labeled "Mean number of acts initiated" presents the data on the extent to which the subject deviates from the stooge's routine and initiates euphoric activities of his own.

On both behavioral indices, we find precisely the same pattern of relationships as those obtained with self-reports. Epi Mis subjects behave somewhat more euphorically than do Epi Ign subjects who in turn behave more euphorically than do Epi Inf subjects. On all measures, then, there is consistent evidence that a subject will take over the stooge's euphoric mood to the extent that he has no other explanation of his bodily state.

Again it should be noted that on these behavioral indices, Epi Ign and Epi Mis subjects are somewhat more euphoric than placebo subjects but not significantly so.

Anger Self-report. Before presenting data for the anger conditions, one point must be made about the anger manipulation. In the situation devised, anger, if manifested, is most likely to be directed at the experimenter and his annoyingly personal questionnaire. As we subsequently discovered, this was rather unfortunate, for the subjects, who had volunteered for the experiment for extra points on their final exam, simply refused to endanger these points by publicly blowing up, admitting their irritation to the experimenter's face or spoiling the questionnaire. Though as the reader will see, the subjects were quite willing to manifest anger when they were alone with the stooge, they hesitated to do so on material (self-ratings of mood and questionnaire) that the experimenter might see and only after the purposes of the experiment had been revealed were many of these subjects willing to admit to the experimenter that they had been irked or irritated.

This experimentally unfortunate situation pretty much forces us to rely on the behavioral indices derived from observation of the subject's presumably private interaction with the stooge. We do, however, present data on the self-report scales in Table 4. These figures are derived in the same way as the figures presented in Table 2 for the euphoria conditions, that is, the value checked on the irritation scale is subtracted from the value checked on the happiness scale. Though, for the reasons stated above, the absolute magnitude of these figures (all positive) is relatively meaningless, we can, of course, compare condition means within the set of anger conditions. With the happiness-irritation index employed, we should, of course, anticipate precisely the reverse results from those obtained in the euphoria conditions; that is, the

Epi Inf subjects in the anger conditions should again be less susceptible to the stooge's mood and should, therefore, describe themselves as in a somewhat happier frame of mind than subjects in the Epi Ign condition. This is the case; the Epi Inf subjects average 1.91 on the self-report scales while the Epi Ign subjects average 1.39.

Evaluating the effects of the injections, we note again that, as anticipated, Epi Ign subjects are somewhat less happy than Placebo subjects but, once more, this is not a significant difference.

Behavior. The subject's responses to the stooge, during the period when both were filling out their questionnaires, were systematically coded to provide a behavioral index of anger. The coding scheme and the numerical values attached to each of the categories have been described in the methodology section. To arrive at an "Anger index" the numerical value assigned to a subject's responses to the stooge is summed together for the several units of stooge behavior. In the coding scheme used, a positive value to this index indicates that the subject agrees with the stooge's comment and is growing angry. A negative value indicates that the subject either disagrees with the stooge or ignores him.

The relevant data are presented in Table 5. For this analysis, the stooge's routine has been divided into two phases—the first two units of his behavior (the "long" questionnaire and "What did I have for break-

TABLE 4 / Self-Report of Emotional State in the Anger Conditions

Condi-tion	N	Self-Report Scales	Comparison	p
Epi Inf	22	1.91	Epi Inf vs. Epi Ign	.08
Epi Ign	23	1.39	Placebo vs. Epi Ign or Inf	ns
Placebo	23	1.63		

TABLE 5 / Behavioral Indications of Emotional State in the Anger Conditions

Condition	N	Neutral Units	Anger Units
Epi Inf	22	+0.07	−0.18
Epi Ign	23	+0.30	+2.28
Placebo	22[a]	−0.09	+0.79

Comparison for Anger Units	p
Epi Inf vs. Epi Ign	< .01
Epi Ign vs. Placebo	< .05
Placebo vs. Epi Inf	ns

[a]For one subject in this condition the sound system went dead and the observer could not, of course, code his reactions.

fast?") are considered essentially neutral revealing nothing of the stooge's mood; all of the following units are considered "angry" units for they begin with an irritated remark about the "bells" question and end with the stooge's fury as he rips up his questionnaire and stomps out of the room. For the neutral units, agreement or disagreement with the stooge's remarks is, of course, meaningless as an index of mood and we should anticipate no difference between conditions. As can be seen in Table 5, this is the case.

For the angry units, we must, of course, anticipate that subjects in the Epi Ign condition will be angrier than subjects in the Epi Inf condition. This is indeed the case. The Anger index for the Epi Ign condition is positive and large, indicating that these subjects have become angry, while in the Epi Inf condition the Anger index is slightly negative in value indicating that these subjects have failed to catch the stooge's mood at all. It seems clear that providing the subject with an appropriate explanation of his bodily state greatly reduces his tendency to interpret his state in terms of the cognitions provided by the stooge's angry behavior.

Finally, on this behavioral index, it can be seen that subjects in the Epi Ign condition are significantly angrier than subjects in the Placebo condition. Behaviorally, at least, the injection of epinephrine appears to have led subjects to an angrier state than comparable subjects who received placebo shots.

Conformation of Data to Theoretical Expectations

Now that the basic data of this study have been presented, let us examine closely the extent to which they conform to theoretical expectations. If our hypotheses are correct and if this experimental design provided a perfect test for these hypotheses, it should be anticipated that in the euphoria conditions the degree of experimentally produced euphoria should vary in the following fashion:

Epi Mis ≥ Epi Ign > Epi Inf = Placebo

And in the anger conditions, anger should conform to the following pattern:

Epi Ign > Epi Inf = Placebo

In both sets of conditions, it is the case that emotional level in the Epi Mis and Epi Ign conditions is considerably greater than that achieved in the corresponding Epi Inf conditions. The results for the Placebo condition, however, are ambiguous for consistently the Placebo subjects fall between the Epi Ign and the Epi Inf subjects. This is a particularly troubling pattern for it makes it impossible to evaluate unequivocally the effects of the state of physiological arousal and indeed raises serious questions about our entire theoretical structure. Though the emotional level is consistently greater in the Epi Mis and Epi Ign conditions than in the Placebo condition, this difference is significant at acceptable probability levels only in the anger conditions.

In order to explore the problem further, let us examine the experimental factors identified earlier, which might have acted to restrain the emotional level in the Epi Ign and Epi Mis conditions. As was pointed out earlier, the ideal test of our first two hypotheses requires an experimental setup in which the subject has flatly no way of evaluating his state of physiological arousal other than by means of the experimentally provided cognitions. Had it been possible to physiologically produce a state of sympathetic activation by means other than injection, one could have approached this experimental ideal more closely than in the present setup. As it stands, however, there is always a reasonable alternative cognition available to the aroused subject—he feels the way he does because of the injection. To the extent that the subject seizes on such an explanation of his bodily state, we should expect that he will be uninfluenced by the stooge. Evidence presented in Table 6 for the anger condition

TABLE 6 / The Effects of Attributing Bodily State to the Injection on Anger in the Anger Epi Ign Condition

Condition	N	Anger Index	p
Self-informed subjects	3	−1.67	ns
Others	20	+2.88	ns
Self-informed vs. Others			.05

and in Table 7 for the euphoria conditions indicates that this is, indeed, the case.

As mentioned earlier, some of the Epi Ign and Epi Mis subjects in their answers to the open-end questions clearly attributed their physical state to the injection, e.g., "the shot gave me the shivers." In Tables 6 and 7 such subjects are labeled "Self-informed." In Table 6 it can be seen that the self-informed subjects are considerably less angry than are the remaining subjects; indeed, they are not angry at all. With these self-informed subjects eliminated the difference between the Epi Ign and the Placebo conditions is significant at the .01 level of significance.

Precisely the same pattern is evident in Table 7 for the euphoria conditions. In both the Epi Mis and the Epi Ign conditions, the self-informed subjects have considerably lower activity indices than do the remaining subjects. Eliminating self-informed subjects, comparison of both of these conditions with the Placebo condition yields a difference significant at the .03 level of significance. It should be noted, too, that the self-informed subjects have much the same score on the activity index as do the experimental Epi Inf subjects (Table 3).

It would appear, then, that the experimental procedure of injecting the subjects, by providing an alter-native cognition, has, to some extent, obscured the effects of epinephrine. When account is taken of this artifact, the evidence is good that the state of physiological arousal is a necessary component of an emotional experience for when self-informed subjects are removed, epinephrine subjects give consistent indications of greater emotionality than do placebo subjects.

Let us examine next the fact that consistently the emotional level, both reported and behavioral, in Placebo conditions is greater than that in the Epi Inf conditions. Theoretically, of course, it should be expected that the two conditions will be equally low, for by assuming that emotional state is a joint function of a state of physiological arousal and of the appropriateness of a cognition we are, in effect, assuming a multiplicative function, so that if either component is at zero, emotional level is at zero. As noted earlier this expectation should hold if we can be sure that there is no sympathetic activation in the Placebo conditions. This assumption, of course, is completely unrealistic for the injection of placebo does not prevent sympathetic activation. The experimental situations were fairly dramatic and certainly some of the placebo subjects gave indications of physiological arousal. If our general line of reasoning is correct, it should be anticipated that the emotional level of subjects who give indications of sympathetic activity will be greater than that of subjects who do not. The relevant evidence is presented in Tables 8 and 9.

As an index of sympathetic activation we shall use the most direct and unequivocal measure available—change in pulse rate. It can be seen in Table 1 that the predominant pattern in the Placebo condition is a

TABLE 7 / The Effects of Attributing Bodily State to the Injection on Euphoria in the Euphoria Epi Ign and Epi Mis Conditions

Epi Ign			
	N	Activity Index	*p*
Self-informed subjects	8	11.63	ns
Others	17	21.14	ns
Self-informed vs. Others			.05
Epi Mis			
	N	Activity Index	*p*
Self-informed subjects	5	12.40	ns
Others	20	25.10	ns
Self-informed vs. Others			.10

TABLE 8 / Sympathetic Activation and Euphoria in the Euphoria Placebo Condition

Subjects Whose:	*N*	Activity Index	*p*
Pulse decreased	14	10.67	ns
Pulse increased or remained same	12	23.17	ns
Pulse decrease vs. pulse increase or same			.02

TABLE 9 / Sympathetic Activation and Anger in Anger Placebo Condition

Subjects Whose:	N[a]	Activity Index	p
Pulse decreased	13	+0.15	ns
Pulse increased or remained same	8	+1.69	ns
Pulse decrease vs. pulse increase or same			.01

[a]N reduced by two cases owing to failure of sound system in one case and experimenter's failure to take pulse in another.

decrease in pulse rate. We shall assume, therefore, that those subjects whose pulse increases or remains the same give indications of sympathetic activity while those subjects whose pulse decreases do not. In Table 8, for the euphoria condition, it is immediately clear that subjects who give indications of sympathetic activity are considerably more euphoric than are subjects who show no sympathetic activity. This relationship is, of course, confounded by the fact that euphoric subjects are considerably more active than non-euphoric subjects—a factor which independent of mood could elevate pulse rate. However, no such factor operates in the anger condition where angry subjects are neither more active nor talkative than calm subjects. It can be seen in Table 9 that Placebo subjects who show signs of sympathetic activation give indications of considerably more anger than do subjects who show no such signs. Conforming to expectation, sympathetic activation accompanies an increase in emotional level.

It should be noted, too, that the emotional levels of subjects showing no signs of sympathetic activity are quite comparable to the emotional level of subjects in the parallel Epi Inf conditions (see Tables 3 and 5). The similarity of these sets of scores and their uniformly low level of indicated emotionality would certainly make it appear that both factors are essential to an emotional state. When either the level of sympathetic arousal is low or a completely appropriate cognition is available, the level of emotionality is low.

DISCUSSION

Let us summarize the major findings of this experiment and examine the extent to which they support the propositions offered in the introduction of this paper. It has been suggested, first, that given a state of physiological arousal for which an individual has no explanation, he will label this state in terms of the cognitions available to him. This implies, of course, that by manipulating the cognitions of an individual in such a state we can manipulate his feelings in diverse directions. Experimental results support this proposition for following the injection of epinephrine, those subjects who had no explanation for the bodily state thus produced, gave behavioral and self-report indications that they had been readily manipulable into the disparate feeling states of euphoria and anger.

From this first proposition, it must follow that given a state of physiological arousal for which the individual has a completely satisfactory explanation, he will not label this state in terms of the alternative cognitions available. Experimental evidence strongly supports this expectation. In those conditions in which subjects were injected with epinephrine and told precisely what they would feel and why, they proved relatively immune to any effects of the manipulated cognitions. In the anger condition, such subjects did not report or show anger; in the euphoria condition, such subjects reported themselves as far less happy than subjects with an identical bodily state but no adequate knowledge of why they felt they way they did.

Finally, it has been suggested that given constant cognitive circumstances, an individual will react emotionally only to the extent that he experiences a state of physiological arousal. Without taking account of experimental artifacts, the evidence in support of this proposition is consistent but tentative. When the effects of "self-informing" tendencies in epinephrine subjects and of "self-arousing" tendencies in placebo subjects are partialed out, the evidence strongly supports the proposition.

The pattern of data, then, falls neatly in line with theoretical expectations. However, the fact that we were forced, to some extent, to rely on internal analyses in order to partial out the effects of experimental artifacts inevitably makes our conclusions somewhat tentative. In order to further test these propositions on the interaction of cognitive and physiological determinants of emotional state, a series of additional experiments, published elsewhere, was designed to rule out or overcome the operation of these artifacts. In the first of these, Schachter and Wheeler (1962) extended the range of manipulated sympathetic activation by employing three experimental groups—epinephrine, placebo, and a group injected with the sympatholytic agent, chlorpromazine. Laughter at a slapstick movie was the dependent variable and the evidence is good that amusement is a direct function of manipulated sympathetic activation.

In order to make the epinephrine-placebo comparison under conditions which would rule out the operation of any self-informing tendency, two experiments were conducted on rats. In one of these Singer (1961) demonstrated that under fear inducing conditions, manipulated by the simultaneous presentation of a loud bell, a buzzer, and a bright flashing light, rats injected with epinephrine were considerably more frightened than rats injected with a placebo. Epinephrine-injected rats defecated, urinated, and trembled more than did placebo-injected rats. In nonfear control conditions, there were no differences between epinephrine and placebo groups, neither group giving any indication of fear. In another study, Latané and Schachter (1962) demonstrated that rats injected with epinephrine were notably more capable of avoidance learning than were rats injected with a placebo. Using a modified Miller-Mowrer shuttle-box, these investigators found that during an experimental period involving 200 massed trials, 15 rats injected with epinephrine avoided shock an average of 101.2 trials while 15 placebo-injected rats averaged only 37.3 avoidances.

Taken together, this body of studies does give strong support to the propositions which generated these experimental tests. Given a state of sympathetic activation, for which no immediately appropriate explanation is available, human subjects can be readily manipulated into states of euphoria, anger, and amusement. Varying the intensity of sympathetic activation serves to vary the intensity of a variety of emotional states in both rats and human subjects.

Let us examine the implications of these findings and of this line of thought for problems in the general area of the physiology of the emotions. We have noted in the introduction that the numerous studies on physiological differentiators of emotional states have, viewed en masse, yielded quite inconclusive results. Most, though not all, of these studies have indicated no differences among the various emotional states. Since as human beings, rather than as scientists, we have no difficulty identifying, labeling, and distinguishing among our feelings, the results of these studies have long seemed rather puzzling and paradoxical. Perhaps because of this, there has been a persistent tendency to discount such results as due to ignorance or methodological inadequacy and to pay far more attention to the very few studies which demonstrate *some* sort of physiological differences among emotional states than to the very many studies which indicate no differences at all. It is conceivable, however, that these results should be taken at face value and that emotional states may, indeed, be generally characterized by a high level of sympathetic activation with few if any physiological distinguishers among the many emotional states. If this is correct, the findings of the present study may help to resolve the problem. Obviously this study does *not* rule out the possibility of physiological differences among the emotional states. It is the case, however, that given precisely the same state of epinephrine-induced sympathetic activation, we have, by means of cognitive manipulations, been able to produce in our subjects the very disparate states of euphoria and anger. It may indeed be the case that cognitive factors are major determiners of the emotional labels we apply to a common state of sympathetic arousal.

Let us ask next whether our results are specific to the state of sympathetic activation or if they are generalizable to other states of physiological arousal. It is clear that from our experiments proper, it is impossible to answer the question for our studies have been concerned largely with the effects of an epinephrine created state of sympathetic arousal. We would suggest, however, that our conclusions are generalizable to almost any pronounced internal state for which no appropriate explanation is available. This suggestion receives some support from the experiences of Nowlis and Nowlis (1956) in their program of research on the effects of drugs on mood. In their work the Nowlises typically administer a drug to groups of four subjects who are physically in one another's presence and free to interact. The Nowlises describe some of their results with these groups as follows:

> At first we used the same drug for all 4 men. In those sessions seconal, when compared with placebo, increased the checking of such words as expansive, forceful, courageous, daring, elated, and impulsive. In our first statistical analysis we were confronted with the stubborn fact that when the same drug is given to all 4 men in a group, the N that has to be entered into the analysis is 1, not 4. This increases the cost of an already expensive experiment by a considerable factor, but it cannot be denied that the effects of these drugs may be and often are quite contagious. Our first attempted solution was to run tests on groups in which each man had a different drug during the same session, such as 1 on seconal, 1 on benzedrine, 1 on dramamine, and 1 on placebo. What does seconal do? Cooped up with, say, the egotistical benzedrine partner, the withdrawn, indifferent dramamine partner, and the slightly bored lactose man, the seconal subject reports that he is distractible, dizzy, drifting, glum, defiant, languid, sluggish, discouraged, dull, gloomy, lazy, and slow! This is not the report of mood that we got when all 4 men were on seconal. It thus appears that the moods of the partners do definitely influence the effect of seconal. (p. 350)

It is not completely clear from this description whether this "contagion" of mood is more marked in drug than in placebo groups, but should this be the case, these results would certainly support the suggestion that our findings are generalizable to internal states other than that produced by an injection of epinephrine.

Finally, let us consider the implications of our formulation and data for alternative conceptualizations of emotion. Perhaps the most popular current conception of emotion is in terms of "activation theory" in the sense employed by Lindsley (1951) and Woodworth and Schlosberg (1958). As we understand this theory, it suggests that emotional states should be considered as at one end of a continuum of activation which is defined in terms of degree of autonomic arousal and of electroencephalographic measures of activation. The results of the experiment described in this paper do, of course, suggest that such a formulation is not completely adequate. It is possible to have very high degrees of activation without a subject either appearing to be or describing himself as "emotional." Cognitive factors appear to be indispensable elements in any formulation of emotion.

SUMMARY

It is suggested that emotional states may be considered a function of a state of physiological arousal and of a cognition appropriate to this state of arousal. From this follows these propositions:

1. Given a state of physiological arousal for which an individual has no immediate explanation, he will label this state and describe his feelings in terms of the cognitions available to him. To the extent that cognitive factors are potent determiners of emotional states, it should be anticipated that precisely the same state of physiological arousal could be labeled "joy" or "fury" or "jealousy" or any of a great diversity of emotional labels depending on the cognitive aspects of the situation.

2. Given a state of physiological arousal for which an individual has a completely appropriate explanation, no evaluative needs will arise and the individual is unlikely to label his feelings in terms of the alternative cognitions available.

3. Given the same cognitive circumstances, the individual will react emotionally or describe his feelings as emotions only to the extent that he experiences a state of physiological arousal.

An experiment is described which, together with the results of other studies, supports these propositions.

REFERENCES

Ax, A. F. Physiological differentiation of emotional states. *Psychosom. Med.*, 1953, *15*, 435–442.

Cannon, W. B. *Bodily changes in pain, hunger, fear and rage.* (2nd ed.) New York: Appleton, 1929.

Cantril, H., & Hunt, W. A. Emotional effects produced by the injection of adrenalin. *Amer. J. Psychol.,* 1932, *44,* 300–307.

Festinger, L. A theory of social comparison processes. *Hum. Relat.,* 1954, *7,* 114–140.

Hunt, J. McV., Cole, M. W., & Reis, E. E. Situational cues distinguishing anger, fear, and sorrow. *Amer. J. Psychol.,* 1958, *71,* 136–151.

James, W. *The principles of psychology.* New York: Holt, 1890.

Landis, C., & Hunt, W. A. Adrenalin and emotion. *Psychol. Rev.,* 1932, *39,* 467–485.

Latané, B., & Schachter, S. Adrenalin and avoidance learning. *J. Comp. Physiol. Psychol.,* 1962, *65,* 369–372.

Lindsley, D. B. Emotion. In S. S. Stevens (Ed.), *Handbook of experimental psychology.* New York: Wiley, 1951. Pp. 473–516.

Marañon, G. Contribution à l'étude de l'action émotive de l'adrénaline. *Rev. Francaise Endocrinol.,* 1924, *2,* 301–325.

Nowlis, V., & Nowlis, H. H. The description and analysis of mood. *Ann. N. Y. Acad. Sci.,* 1956, *65,* 345–355.

Ruckmick, C. A. *The psychology of feeling and emotion.* New York: McGraw-Hill, 1936.

Schachter, J. Pain, fear, and anger in hypertensives and normotensives: A psychophysiologic study. *Psychosom. Med.,* 1957, *19,* 17–29.

Schachter, S. *The psychology of affiliation.* Stanford, CA: Stanford Univer. Press, 1959.

Schachter, S., & Wheeler, L. Epinephrine, chlorpromazine, and amusement. *J. Abnorm. Soc. Psychol.,* 1962, *65,* 121–128.

Singer, J. E. The effects of epinephrine, chlorpromazine and dibenzyline upon the fright responses of rats under stress and non-stress conditions. Unpublished doctoral dissertation, University of Minnesota, 1961.

Wolf, S., & Wolff, H. G. *Human gastric function.* New York: Oxford Univer. Press, 1947.

Woodworth, R. S., & Schlosberg, H. *Experimental psychology.* New York: Holt, 1958.

Wrightsman, L. S. Effects of waiting with others on changes in level of felt anxiety. *J. Abnorm. Soc. Psychol.,* 1960, *61,* 216–222.

ENDNOTES

1. This experiment is part of a program of research on cognitive and physiological determinants of emotional state which is being conducted at the Department of Social Psychology at Columbia University under PHS Research Grant M-2584 from the National Institute of Mental Health, United States Public Health Service. This experiment was conducted at the Laboratory for Research in Social Relations at the University of Minnesota.

The authors wish to thank Jean Carlin and Ruth Hase, the physicians in the study, and Bibb Latané and Leonard Weller who were the paid participants.

2. Though our experiments are concerned exclusively with the physiological changes produced by the injection of adrenalin, which appear to be primarily the result of sympathetic excitation, the term physiological arousal is used in preference to the more specific "excitation of the sympathetic nervous system" because there are indications, to be discussed later, that this formulation is applicable to a variety of bodily states.

3. Translated copies of Marañon's (1924) paper may be obtained by writing to the senior author.

4. This suggestion is not new for several psychologists have suggested that situational factors should be considered the chief differentiators of the emotions. Hunt, Cole, and Reis (1958) probably make this point most explicitly in their study distinguishing among fear, anger, and sorrow in terms of situational characteristics.

5. In his critique of the James-Lange theory of emotion, Cannon (1929) also makes the point that sympathectomized animals and patients do seem to manifest emotional behavior. This criticism is, of course, as applicable to the above proposition as it was to the James-Lange formulation. We shall discuss the issues involved in later papers.

6. It was, of course, imperative that the sequence with the stooge begin before the subject felt his first symptoms for otherwise the subject would be virtually forced to interpret his feelings in terms of events preceding the stooge's entrance. Pretests had indicated that, for most subjects, epinephrine-caused symptoms began within 3–5 minutes after injection. A deliberate attempt was made then to bring in the stooge within 1 minute after the subject's injection.

CRITICAL THINKING QUESTIONS

1. In order to conduct the experiment, the researchers deceived the subjects. What ethical issues are involved in this type of research? The obvious deception was not telling the subjects the true nature of the experiment. Does the use of injections of a drug that had a physiological impact on the subjects prompt additional ethical considerations? Explain your answer.

2. This study examines the effects of just one drug, epinephrine, which has excitatory effects on people. Would you expect a similar pattern of results for other classes of drugs? Why or why not? Which ones might be interesting to study?

3. What might the implications of this study be for people who use drugs in a social setting? Would the feelings that they associate with using drugs be due to how others around them responded? Explain your answer. How could you test this possibility?

4. Do you think it is possible to change the emotion you are experiencing by changing the label of the emotion? For example, if you were afraid of public speaking, could you change your emotion from a negative one (fear) to a positive one (excitement) by changing the label given to your physiological arousal? Have you had any personal experience with something like this that may have occurred or a situation when you were aware of how other people influenced how you interpreted the situation? Explain your answer.

ADDITIONAL RELATED READINGS

Lazarus, R. S. (1984). On the primacy of cognition. *American Psychologist, 39,* 124–129.
Zajonc, R. B. (1984). On the primacy of affect. *American Psychologist, 39,* 117–123.

ARTICLE 9 _____

Have you ever heard about the breakup of a married couple you know and thought, "I'm not surprised; I didn't think it would last." Or while observing a series of events unfold, have you ever known all along that things would turn out the way they did? If so, you may have experienced a very common social cognition effect known as *hindsight bias*.

Basically, hindsight bias is at work when someone erroneously believes that he or she knew all along what the outcome would be but confirms this belief only *after* the outcome is known. In short, the individual forgets or distorts what his or her beliefs were prior to learning the outcome. Part of this effect is due to selective remembering of the evidence, in which people focus primarily on the information that is congruent with the actual outcome and forget the inconsistent information. In a sense, we retroactively construct a series of causal links that explain the current outcome. What we may fail to realize, however, is that given a different outcome, we would have been just as likely to explain it, as well.

As is true of much research in the area of social cognition, research on hindsight bias usually is conducted in the laboratory using hypothetical situations. Occasionally, however, a real-life situation occurs that lends itself to testing the effect outside the lab. The following article by Fred B. Bryant and Jennifer Howard Brockway is based on a study that tested people's hindsight bias in reaction to a very high-profile legal case: the O. J. Simpson criminal trial. The article also discusses how this bias may develop over time and the potential impact of the mass media in influencing the development of hindsight bias.

Hindsight Bias in Reaction to the Verdict in the O. J. Simpson Criminal Trial

■ Fred B. Bryant and Jennifer Howard Brockway

Students estimated the chance that O. J. Simpson would be convicted or acquitted of murder and the likelihood of large-scale violence following conviction, at 3 points in time: 2 hr before the announcement of the not guilty verdict, 2 days after the verdict, and 1 week after the verdict. Within-subjects analyses revealed that estimates of the probability of conviction made 2 hr before the not guilty verdict were higher than estimates of prior probability made 2 days after the verdict. Supporting hypotheses, the tendency to recall a higher chance of conviction after the verdict was strongest among those who initially perceived acquittal to be least likely. Contrary to predictions, however, the perceived probability of acquittal did not significantly increase until 1 week after the verdict. Estimates of the prior likelihood of violence following a guilty verdict also increased immediately after the verdict and remained high 1 week later. Results are discussed in terms of the influence of mass media and cognitive processes on the development of hindsight bias over time.

Hindsight bias refers to people's tendency to view an event as more inevitable and foreseeable after the event has occurred (Fischhoff, 1975, 1977; Hawkins & Hastie, 1990; Leary, 1982). Knowing the outcome of an uncertain event makes that outcome seem to have been more likely in the first place (i.e., in hind-

From "Hindsight Bias in Reaction to the Verdict in the O. J. Simpson Criminal Trial," by F. B. Bryant and J. H. Brockway, 1997, *Basic and Applied Social Psychology, 7*(2), 225–241. Copyright 1997 by Lawrence Erlbaum Associates, Inc. Reprinted with permission.

sight), compared to likelihood estimates made before knowing the outcome (i.e., in foresight). This retrospective distortion presumably results from an automatic cognitive assimilation of new and old information (Fischhoff, 1977). After the outcome, people generate a plausible account of how the event could have been predicted (i.e., they assimilate the old knowledge to the new), making the outcome seem more inevitable in the reinterpreted situation (Nario & Branscombe, 1995; Ross, Lepper, Strack, & Steinmetz, 1977). Thus, people tend to recall the past in ways that confirm the present (cf. Loftus & Loftus, 1980).

Although considerable experimental research has examined hindsight bias in the laboratory, less empirical work has explored hindsight bias in reaction to naturally occurring, real-world events. Two notable exceptions include studies of hindsight bias in reaction to President Nixon's 1972 trip to China and the Soviet Union (Fischhoff & Beyeth, 1975) and in reaction to the 1980 presidential election (Leary, 1982). This study used a repeated measures survey design to examine hindsight bias in people's reactions to the not guilty verdict in the criminal trial of O. J. Simpson.

The unique prominence and dramatic nature of this event made it an ideal, naturally occurring stage for social research. Indeed, the trial has received some empirical attention, including efforts to understand how racial similarity influenced judgments of Simpson's guilt or innocence (Mixon, Foley, & Orme, 1995). A fortuitous circumstance was particularly advantageous for our purposes. The jury reached a verdict on a Friday after less than 4 hr of deliberation, but the judge decided to wait until the following Tuesday to announce the verdict publicly. A large portion of the general population was aware of the unfolding drama and, thus, was about to be exposed to the same uncertain outcome. This offered a rare opportunity for applied social research on hindsight bias.

RESEARCH OBJECTIVES

In this study, we tested the hypotheses that, after the not guilty verdict, retrospective estimates of the prior probability of conviction would decline and retro-spective estimates of the prior probability of acquittal would increase, relative to estimates of likelihood made before the announcement of the verdict. We reasoned that this hindsight bias could unfold in at least two ways. First, it might emerge shortly after the verdict's announcement and persist over time. This pattern is consistent with Fischhoff's (1977) notion of the assimilation process as "natural and immediate" (p. 356); and with Hawkins and Hastie's (1990) conclusion that "results hold across a range of time intervals (minutes to weeks) between initial . . . and second judgments" (p. 314). Alternatively, hindsight distortion might develop gradually over time, especially if outcomes are unexpected and difficult to explain (Nario & Branscombe, 1995).

We also examined whether the magnitude of hindsight bias varied as a function of people's initial beliefs about the likelihood of conviction or acquittal. There is evidence that hindsight distortion is strongest for events initially judged to be least plausible (Fischhoff, 1977; Wood, 1978). When people reconstruct the past to fit the present, more distortion is involved when assimilating those past possible outcomes that were viewed prospectively as least probable. Based on this reasoning and given the verdict, we hypothesized that the less likely people believed it was that O. J. would be acquitted, the stronger hindsight bias they would show. If O. J. had been convicted, those who saw conviction as least likely would be expected to show the strongest hindsight bias.

Finally, we investigated whether a negative consequence of the verdict that did *not* occur—specifically, large-scale violence in Los Angeles following Simpson's conviction—was seen, after the fact, as more likely or less likely. What kinds of changes over time should one expect to find in people's judgments about what might have resulted as a consequence of something that did not happen (i.e., violence following conviction)? A straightforward hindsight analysis suggests that violence, because it did not happen, should be seen as less likely when viewed retrospectively. Assuming that hindsight bias also makes O. J.'s conviction seem less probable after the fact, would postconviction violence seem all the more unlikely in retrospect? With these questions in mind, we examined temporal changes in the perceived likelihood of violence following conviction.

METHOD

Participants and Procedure

Participants were undergraduate students in an introductory statistics class at a private midwestern university who voluntarily completed three waves of a one-page paper-and-pencil survey. Of 30 participants included in the initial pretest, 3 (10%) were lost at the second wave (*n* = 27), and 4 more (13%) were lost at the third wave (*n* = 23); sex of the participants was unrelated to attrition. The final sample of 23 students included 17 women (74%) and 6 men (26%), with a mean age of 21.1 years (*SD* = 3.0). This final sample was predominantly (57%) White (*n* = 13), with 0 African Americans, 5 Asian Americans (22%), and 5 students of other ethnic backgrounds (22%).

Design and Procedure

Participants completed a set of one-page self-report measures at three different points in time: (a) *2 hr before* the announcement of the verdict (Time 1), (b) *2 days after* the announcement of the verdict (Time 2), and (c) *1 week after* the announcement of the verdict (Time 3). We used 2-day and 7-day posttest intervals because these times corresponded to regular meetings of the class in which participants met.[1] At each measurement, participants listed the last four digits of their social security number to link responses over time, and they were assured that their answers would remain confidential.

Dependent Measures

Time 1 Two hr before the verdict was announced, participants completed an initial self-report questionnaire. After furnishing information about their age, sex, and race, participants indicated whether or not they were aware of the O. J. Simpson criminal trial (100%), whether they believed Simpson was guilty (83%) or innocent (17%), and their confidence in this belief (79% vs. 60%, respectively), $t(21) = 1.7$, $p < .11$, two-tailed.

Respondents then made separate estimates of the chance that the jury would convict Simpson of first-degree murder, convict Simpson of second-degree murder, or find Simpson not guilty (0 = *absolutely no*

chance, 100 = *absolute certainty*). In light of evidence that people's estimates of the probability of each possible outcome do not necessarily sum to 1.00 (Kahneman & Tversky, 1979; Peterson & Beach, 1967; Tversky & Kahneman, 1988), we did not constrain these chance estimates to total 100%; instead, we allowed participants to make independent judgments of each possible outcome. This strategy gave respondents the freedom to express their subjective impressions as they perceived them (cf. Baron, 1988; von Winterfeldt & Edwards, 1986). Participants also used a 7-point Likert-type scale ranging from 1 (*not very likely*) to 7 (*very likely*) to estimate the likelihood, if Simpson were convicted of murder, of large-scale violence in the city of Los Angeles.

Time 2 Forty-eight hr after completing the first survey (i.e., 2 days postverdict), participants completed a second survey that initially checked their awareness of the verdict (100%) and whether they believed Simpson was guilty (83%) or innocent (17%). They were then asked, "Looking back on it all now, what was the chance that the jury would . . . ?": (a) convict O. J. Simpson of first-degree murder, (b) convict O. J. Simpson of second-degree murder, and (c) find O. J. Simpson not guilty (0 = *absolutely no chance*, 100 = *absolute certainty*). Once again, these chance estimates were not constrained to total 100%. Respondents also estimated the likelihood that large-scale violence would have occurred had Simpson been convicted. These estimates were indicated on a 7-point scale ranging from 1 (*not very likely*) to 7 (*very likely*).

Time 3 Exactly 1 week after completing the first survey questionnaire (i.e., 7 days postverdict), participants completed a third survey form containing the same measures as at Time 2, except for the item assessing awareness of the verdict.

RESULTS

Temporal Effects on the Perceived Probability of Conviction and Acquittal

To maximize statistical power, we tested hypotheses using repeated measures analyses of variance

(ANOVAs) to evaluate planned orthogonal within-subjects contrasts (cf. Rosenthal & Rosnow, 1985). Specifically, we evaluated the two plausible patterns of temporal change in people's perceived probabilities separately for each verdict.[2] The first within-subjects contrast (Contrast 1) hypothesized a sudden, stable shift to hindsight bias—that is, toward reduced probabilities for the verdicts that did not happen (orthogonal weights of 2, –1, –1, for ratings of first- and second-degree murder) and toward increased probabilities for the verdict that did happen (orthogonal weights of –2, 1, 1, for acquittal). The second within-subjects contrast (Contrast 2) hypothesized a gradual, linear trend toward hindsight bias—that is, toward reduced probabilities for the verdicts that did not happen (orthogonal weights of 1, 0, –1, for ratings of first- and second-degree murder) and toward increased probabilities for the verdict that did happen (orthogonal weights of –1, 0, 1, for acquittal).

Because these planned contrasts were hypothesized a priori, they were evaluated as one-tailed tests, thus providing increased power compared to omnibus repeated measures ANOVAs. Furthermore, planned contrasts do not require participants' probability estimates to meet the so-called sphericity assumption of homogeneity of covariance across time (Rosenthal & Rosnow, 1985), a necessary requirement of omnibus repeated measures ANOVAs that temporal data often violate (Winer, 1971). Indeed, participants' probability estimates met the sphericity assumption for both guilty verdicts ($ps > .10$ by Bartlett's test), but not for acquittal ($p < .05$).

First-Degree Murder   Whereas the test of Contrast 1 (i.e., sudden, stable increase) was only marginally significant for probability estimates of first-degree murder, $t(22) = 1.5$, $p < .07$, Hedges's corrected effect size (g) = .31, the test of Contrast 2 (i.e., gradual change) was highly significant, $t(22) = 3.1$, $p < .003$, $g = .62$. One-tailed pairwise t tests following up these effects revealed that the perceived chance of conviction for first-degree murder declined from Time 1 to Time 2, $t(22) = -2.4$, $p < .013$, and remained constant from Time 2 to Time 3, $t(22) = -0.2$, ns. In addition, the perceived chance of a first-degree murder conviction was lower at Time 3 than at Time 1, $t(22) = -3.1$, $p < .003$. These results suggest that hindsight bias con-

cerning a first-degree murder verdict emerged within 48 hr after O. J. Simpson's acquittal and was even more pronounced a week later.

Following the approach of Fischhoff and his associates (Fischhoff, 1975, 1977; Fischhoff & Beyeth, 1975), we also classified participants in terms of whether their probability estimates increased, decreased, or stayed the same between Times 1 and 3. We then performed a one-tailed sign test to evaluate the hypothesis that more participants showed decreases in the perceived chance of first-degree murder conviction than would be expected by chance. Confirming the a priori hypothesis, 13 (57%) of the 23 participants lowered their estimates of the chance of a first-degree murder conviction over the 1-week period, $p < .02$.

Second-Degree Murder   Both Contrast 1, $t(22) = 1.7$, $p = .05$, $g = .34$, and Contrast 2, $t(22) = 3.9$, $p < .001$, $g = .79$, were statistically significant for probability estimates of second-degree murder. Paralleling results for the first-degree murder verdict, one-tailed pairwise t tests revealed that the perceived chance of conviction for second-degree murder declined from Time 1 to Time 2, $t(22) = -3.2$, $p < .003$, and remained constant from Time 2 to Time 3, $t(22) = -1.2$, ns. In addition, the perceived chance of a second-degree murder conviction was lower at Time 3 than at Time 1, $t(22) = -3.9$, $p < .004$. Thus, estimates of both conviction verdicts show somewhat stronger evidence for Contrast 2 than for Contrast 1. These findings suggest that hindsight bias regarding the rejected verdict (i.e., lower estimates of the prior probability of conviction) generally occurred within 2 days after the not guilty verdict and grew even stronger a week later. Confirming the a priori hypothesis, 15 (65%) of the 23 participants lowered their estimates of the chance of a second-degree murder conviction over the 1-week period, $p < .02$, one-tailed sign test.

Acquittal   Contrary to results for the two conviction verdicts, the test of Contrast 1 (i.e., sudden, stable increase) was nonsignificant for probability estimates of acquittal, $t(22) = 1.1$, $p < .14$, $g = .22$. As found for the two conviction verdicts, however, the test of Contrast 2 (i.e., gradual change) was statistically significant for ratings of acquittal, $t(22) = 1.7$, $p < .05$, $g =$

.35. Contrary to predictions, participants did not increase their estimates of the prior probability of acquittal 2 days after the verdict, $t(22) = 0.5$, $p < .30$. Instead, higher estimates of the chance of acquittal were not evident until 1 week after the verdict, at which time the perceived probability of acquittal was higher than it had been both 2 hr before the verdict, $t(22) = 1.7$, $p < .05$, and 2 days after the verdict, $t(22) = 1.7$, $p < .05$. These results indicate that hindsight bias regarding the verdict (i.e., higher estimates of the prior probability of acquittal) did not emerge until 3 to 7 days after the verdict was announced. The means contributing to these effects for all three verdicts are displayed in Figure 1. Confirming the a priori hypothesis, 14 (61%) of the 23 participants raised their estimates of the chance of acquittal over the 1-week period, $p < .02$, one-tailed sign test.

Hindsight Bias and Initial Beliefs about Acquittal

To examine the impact of initial beliefs about the plausibility of acquittal on the magnitude of hindsight bias, we transformed pretest estimates of the chance of acquittal into the form of a priori odds and posttest estimates of the chances of acquittal into a posteriori odds. The ratio of a priori and a posteriori odds for acquittal provides an average likelihood ratio for the impact of the acquittal verdict at the posttest (cf. Fischhoff, 1975, p. 291). These likelihood ratios ranged from 0.0 to 4.0 at Time 2 ($M = 1.3$) and from 0.0 to 3.3 at Time 3 ($M = 1.5$). Thus, on average, the acquittal verdict increased the perceived likelihood of acquittal by about 30% at Time 2 and 50% at Time 3.

Confirming hypotheses, there was a significant negative correlation between the prior odds of acquittal and the likelihood ratios associated with acquittal at Time 2, $r(20) = -.61$, $p < .001$, $g = 1.48$, and Time 3, $r(20) = -.81$, $p < .0001$, $g = 2.66$.[3] In other words, the less likely participants initially thought it was that Simpson would be acquitted, the greater the verdict's impact at the posttest. These findings support the notion that hindsight distortion is strongest for events initially judged to be least plausible (Fischhoff, 1975; Wood, 1978).

FIGURE 1 / Estimates of the Chances of Conviction and Acquittal in the O. J. Simpson Criminal Trial, Over Time

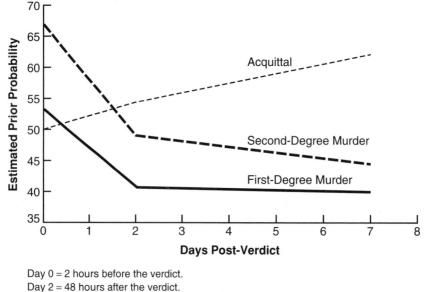

Day 0 = 2 hours before the verdict.
Day 2 = 48 hours after the verdict.
Day 7 = 1 week after the verdict.

Temporal Effects on the Perceived Likelihood of Postconviction Violence

Because it was difficult to make specific hypotheses about changes in the perceived likelihood of violence following conviction, we used omnibus repeated measures ANOVA to examine temporal changes in participants' estimates of the likelihood of postconviction violence. Because these data violated the sphericity assumption ($p < .05$, by Bartlett's test), we used the Greenhouse–Geisser (1959) correction procedure to adjust the degrees of freedom (adjustment $\varepsilon = .79$) to obtain more accurate F ratios (cf. Winer, 1971). Results revealed a significant main effect of time, $F(2, 42) = 4.3$, Greenhouse–Geisser $p < .05$, $g = .47$. Two-tailed pairwise t tests disclosed that the perceived likelihood of violence increased from Time 1 to Time 2, $t(22) = 3.5$, $p < .002$, and was then stable from Time 2 to Time 3, $t(22) = -0.9$, $p > .36$. Thus, although participants' estimates of a guilty verdict's likelihood *decreased* from Time 1 to Time 3, $t(22)s > -3.0$, $ps < .003$, their estimates of the likelihood of violence following a guilty verdict *increased* from Time 1 to Time 3, $t(22) = 2.0$, $p < .05$. Table 1 displays Pearson

product–moment correlation coefficients, means, and standard deviations for the repeated dependent measures.

DISCUSSION

Hindsight bias was evident in students' reactions to the not guilty verdict in the O. J. Simpson criminal trial. Lower estimates of the prior probability of conviction (the rejected verdict) emerged first, within 48 hr of the verdict's announcement. However, higher estimates of the prior probability of acquittal (the actual verdict) were not evident until 1 week after the verdict. In other words, hindsight distortion was only partial at first and required time to develop fully. Within 2 days after the verdict, what did not happen (i.e., conviction) seemed less likely; only later did the outcome (i.e., acquittal) seem more likely to have occurred. Evidently, a retrospective sense of the inevitable took longer to develop than did a retrospective sense of the implausible. It is unclear what we would have found had we forced people's chance estimates to total 100%, as is often done (e.g., Fischhoff, 1975;

TABLE 1 / Pearson Product–Moment Correlations, Means, and Standard Deviations for the Repeated Dependent Measures ($n = 23$)

Measures	1	2	3	4	5	6	7	8	9	10	11	12
Time 1, chances of:												
1. First-degree murder conviction												
2. Second-degree murder conviction	50											
3. Acquittal	−35	−32										
4. Postconviction violence	09	−09	−15									
Time 2, chances of:												
5. First-degree murder conviction	52	40	−09	−06								
6. Second-degree murder conviction	04	41	08	−01	39							
7. Acquittal	−24	−08	07	−03	−46	−61						
8. Postconviction violence	27	02	−15	75	07	16	−07					
Time 3, chances of:												
9. First-degree murder conviction	68	27	−05	−02	71	25	−47	05				
10. Second-degree murder conviction	16	40	−03	12	47	76	−55	23	38			
11. Acquittal	−32	−15	13	−24	−40	−45	69	−16	−63	−66		
12. Postconviction violence	40	39	−12	56	20	34	−09	78	03	30	−11	
M	53.3	67.0	50.0	3.9	40.4	48.9	54.4	4.8	39.8	44.3	62.2	4.6
SD	28.1	22.4	28.3	1.8	22.8	27.6	29.7	1.6	23.3	27.6	24.0	1.8

Note: Decimals have been omitted from correlation coefficients. $|rs| > .41$ are significantly different from zero at $p < .05$, two-tailed.

Leary, 1982). Obviously, future research should explore more systematically how remembered probabilities of once-future outcomes are shaped over time.

Several plausible explanations exist for the unexpected asymmetry in hindsight bias concerning conviction and acquittal.[4] Because participants knew the jury had reached a decision very quickly (i.e., after only a few hours of deliberation), perhaps this knowledge raised the perceived probability of acquittal at the pretest. However, retrospective self-reports contradict this interpretation. When asked 2 weeks afterward if they had been aware beforehand of the jury's quick verdict, 83% of the sample (19 of 23) reported they had been aware. But only 2 (11%) of these 19 respondents reported the quick verdict made acquittal seem more likely, and 74% (14) said the quick verdict made conviction seem more probable.

Another possible explanation for the delayed increase in probability estimates of acquittal involves the nearly unavoidable effects of exposure to mass media coverage following the Simpson verdict (cf. Slovic, Fischhoff, & Lichtenstein, 1980). Many news reports and media images immediately after the verdict portrayed people's astonishment in response to acquittal (e.g., Gottlieb, 1995). This social feedback may have served as a reminder of how unexpected the verdict was, thereby heightening memory for initial judgments and suppressing people's inclination to see what happened as more inevitable, until media coverage subsided (cf. Hell, Gigerenzer, Gauggel, Mall, & Mueller, 1988).

Given the extensive media reporting of the aftermath of the verdict, people's tendency to rely on the availability heuristic in judging probabilities may have strengthened their belief that acquittal was relatively unlikely (cf. Slovic et al., 1980). Availability bias refers to people's tendency to evaluate the likelihood of events based on how quickly associations and similar instances can be retrieved (Tversky & Kahneman, 1973). Indeed, the ease with which one could readily access or imagine an acquittal outcome was likely to have decreased amid the mass media's portrayal of people's surprised disbelief following the Simpson verdict. Similar interpretations have been offered to explain the effects of other large-scale, naturally occurring events, such as the national broadcast of the nuclear holocaust TV film *The Day After* (Schofield &

Pavelchak, 1985) and the self-disclosure of HIV infection by well-known basketball star Earvin "Magic" Johnson (Kalichman, Russell, Hunter, & Sarwer, 1993).

To explore this possible media effect, we analyzed archival data. As a measure of media news coverage, we examined transcript summaries of national television and radio broadcasts before and after the verdict. We selected the American Broadcasting Company (ABC TV) and the National Public Radio (NPR) network as indicators of national television and radio news coverage, respectively. These daily transcript summaries divided television and radio news and public affairs programming on the two national networks into 20-min segments and reported the number of segments that contained coverage of the O. J. Simpson trial for each program (*Video Index: O. J. Simpson Index,* 1996). From these transcript summaries, we coded the daily number of segments on ABC TV and NPR that included news coverage of the Simpson trial during the week before, the day of, and the week after the verdict. Because some segments may have been devoted entirely to the trial and others may only have mentioned it briefly, we conservatively scored each segment that included coverage of the Simpson case as lasting 10 min. This yielded a daily index of the number of minutes of news coverage that ABC TV and NPR devoted to the Simpson trial.

During the week before the verdict, a daily average of 47.9 min of television and 24.3 min of radio news coverage was broadcast concerning the trial. News coverage increased on the day of the verdict (ABC TV = 305 min; NPR = 180 min) and remained relatively high the following day (ABC TV = 165 min; NPR = 100 min). Two days after the verdict, however, news coverage of the Simpson case returned to baseline (ABC TV = 45 min; NPR = 40 min) and remained at or below baseline the following 5 days (ABC TV M = 21 min; NPR M = 25 min). These data suggest that media coverage of the Simpson trial increased immediately after the verdict and then quickly tapered off within 48 hr (see Figure 2). This finding supports the notion that probability estimates of acquittal did not shift until after media coverage waned.

Besides availability bias, causal attribution is another cognitive mechanism that may explain the delayed increase in probability estimates of acquittal.

FIGURE 2 / **Estimated Number of Minutes of National News Coverage of the O. J. Simpson Criminal Trial Broadcast on the American Broadcast Company Television and National Public Radio Networks, during the Week before, the Day of, and the Week after the Verdict**

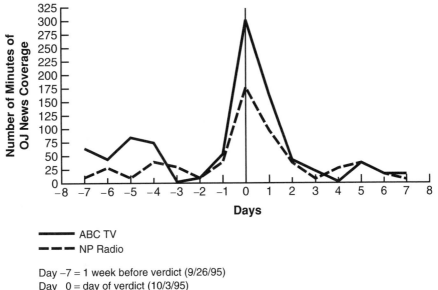

Day −7 = 1 week before verdict (9/26/95)
Day 0 = day of verdict (10/3/95)
Day 7 = 1 week after verdict (10/10/95)

Probability estimates of acquittal may have taken time to develop because participants initially found it difficult to explain the unexpected acquittal verdict. Students' pretest ratings suggest that 2 hr before the verdict was announced, they believed Simpson would be convicted of second-degree murder. Based on this fact, we can assume that (a) the preponderance of prior causal antecedents was perceived as leading to conviction (Nario & Branscombe, 1995); and (b) once antecedents were linked to conviction, the possibility of acquittal was inhibited or constrained as difficult to imagine (Hawkins & Hastie, 1990).

Furthermore, at both Times 1 and 2, nearly 9 out of 10 students (86%) believed that Simpson was guilty of murder (Fisher's exact p = .0087). This enduring belief in O. J.'s guilt, coupled with a shortage of prior causal antecedents predictive of acquittal, may have made it difficult to construct a plausible causal explanation for the unexpected verdict. As Nario and Branscombe (1995) argued:

Perceivers become convinced that an outcome "was inevitable" once it is explainable in terms of the

antecedents preceding it . . . exaggerated likelihood effects may depend both on the number of predictive antecedents available at encoding and the degree to which these antecedents are perceived as contributing to the causal explanation of the outcome at hand. (p. 1252)

Perhaps it took people several days to construct a plausible causal explanation for Simpson's acquittal, after which time hindsight bias concerning the inevitability of acquittal emerged. Why did probability estimates of conviction, in contrast, decrease immediately after the verdict? People simply may have discounted their initial estimates of conviction as too high and may have lowered them retrospectively (cf. Hawkins & Hastie, 1990). This reasoning suggests that the more difficult it is to explain an outcome, the greater will be the delay in the perceived inevitability of its occurrence.

There are, however, several potential methodological problems in interpreting our results. Although we argue that knowledge about the verdict is responsible for the temporal changes observed, our study did not include a control group of people who heard nothing about the verdict before providing posttest ratings. Indeed, it would have been difficult to find or construct a group of "untreated" controls among this student population (just as extensive publicity made it difficult initially to find jurors who were uninformed about the Simpson case). This leaves open the possibility that changes in probability estimates over time were simply the effects of regression toward the mean. People's probability estimates may have been especially high just before the verdict's announcement (at the pretest) and simply may have regressed to the mean at the second testing.[6]

Two pieces of evidence contradict the notion that the observed temporal changes are simply regression artifacts. First, the temporal profile of probability estimates does not match that expected of a simple regression effect. Regression to the mean would be expected to produce a sharp change between Times 1 and 2 because extreme scores regress toward their mean, and no change between Times 2 and 3 because scores fluctuate randomly about the mean (i.e., Contrast 1). Contrary to this expected pattern, however, temporal changes in students' probability estimates more clearly conformed to a linear model (i.e., Contrast 2).

A second piece of evidence that is inconsistent with a straightforward regression explanation is the asymmetry found in ratings of conviction and acquittal. If temporal changes in probability estimates are simply regression artifacts, all three verdicts should have shown the same sharp demarcation between Times 1 and 2. However, statistically significant differences between Times 1 and 2 emerged only for estimates of conviction and not for estimates of acquittal. Indeed, when acquittal ratings are reverse scored (so that conviction and acquittal ratings are coded in the same direction), the regression lines for conviction and acquittal are highly distinct at both Time 2 (first-degree murder: $\hat{y} = .42x + 18$; second-degree murder: $\hat{y} = .51x + 15$; acquittal: $\hat{y} = .07x + 43$) and Time 3 (first-degree murder: $\hat{y} = .56x + 10$; second-degree murder: $\hat{y} = .49x + 11$; acquittal: $\hat{y} = .11x + 33$). This suggests that regression artifacts alone do not explain these findings.

Another potential problem in interpreting results concerns the wording of the questions used to measure perceived probability retrospectively. At each posttest, we examined hindsight by asking students "Looking back on it all now, what was the chance that the jury would" convict or acquit O. J. Simpson of murder? However, it is unclear how participants interpreted this question. A more clearly worded alternative question might have been "What would you have said, before the verdict was announced, was the chance that . . . ?" Given the verdict, one might argue that the chance of conviction was less than earlier thought. It is critical to be sure that participants interpreted the hindsight question not as a report of the chance of conviction or acquittal at the earlier time, but as a retrospective report of their earlier belief about what the chance was (cf. Hawkins & Hastie, 1990).

To address the problem of question wording directly, we collected additional data. Students in a comparable group, sampled from the same class during the following semester (20 weeks postverdict), were asked (according to random assignment) one of two sets of questions about the three possible O. J. Simpson verdicts: (a) the original set of questions ("Looking back on it all now, what was the chance that the jury would . . . ?"), or (b) a more explicitly hindsight-focused alternative ("What would you have said, before the verdict was announced, was the chance that . . . ?"). Results revealed nonsignificant differences between the old ($n = 30$) and new ($n = 29$) measures for first-degree murder, $t(57) = -0.8$, $p < .41$; second-degree murder, $t(57) = 0.6$, $p < .57$; and acquittal, $t(57) = 1.0$, $p < .33$, all two-tailed. Although this evidence does not prove that these questions are equivalent, the findings suggest that the temporal changes observed in probability estimates for the O. J. Simpson verdict are true hindsight phenomena.

Another potential methodological problem concerns the effects of repeated testing. Across multiple testings, people simply may have pondered their probability estimates and changed them. Concerning this possibility, the independent group of 30 students who completed only the original measures (i.e., posttest only) provides evidence of what probability estimates would have been had participants not been tested repeatedly. Comparing participants' probability estimates at Time 3 ($n = 23$) with estimates of the 30 posttest-only participants revealed nonsignificant differences for first-degree murder, $t(51) = -0.3$, $p < .77$;

second-degree murder, $t(51) = 0.2$, $p < .82$; and acquittal, $t(51) = -0.1$, $p < .92$, all two-tailed. Furthermore, probability estimates made 20 weeks after the verdict were (a) significantly lower than original pretest estimates for both first-degree murder, $t(51) = -2.2$, $p < .05$, and second-degree murder, $t(51) = -3.2$, $p < .003$, both one-tailed; and (b) marginally higher than original pretest estimates for acquittal, $t(51) = 1.5$, $p < .07$, one-tailed. These findings not only rule out testing effects, but also document the existence of hindsight bias 5 months after the verdict.

Whereas hindsight effects were found for estimates of the probability of conviction and acquittal, estimates of the probability of large-scale violence if Simpson were convicted appear, at first glance, to show a reverse hindsight distortion (i.e., what did not occur is seen as more probable). Because neither conviction nor widespread violence occurred, we thought that both might be seen post hoc as having been less likely all along. But, students perceived postconviction violence as having been *more* likely from the outset. We offer two explanations for this apparent anomaly.

First, it is possible that participants had difficulty in answering this type of conditional probability question (Slovic & Fischhoff, 1977). Students may have found it confusing to consider the possible occurrence of two different outcomes (i.e., conviction and violence), neither of which happened. As Slovic and Fischhoff noted, "Before a firmer conclusion can be drawn about the conditionality hypothesis, further research is needed on how people make such hypothetical judgments about the way possible futures will appear should they come about" (p. 550).

However, there is another way of interpreting the reverse bias. The acquittal verdict was a cause for exuberant celebration among many Black Americans, who saw it as an unexpected victory over a "racist" legal system. The strength of their immediate emotional reaction was surprising to many, Whites and Blacks alike. As noted in the transcript summary from a town meeting broadcast on ABC World News Tonight on the evening of the verdict (*Video Index: O. J. Simpson Index,* 1996), "A strong racial undertow is apparent in reactions among Los Angeles residents to the verdict, with blacks elated and many whites stunned, and both groups expressing disbelief at the others' reaction" (p. 14). Media coverage of large numbers of people celebrating the not guilty verdict with great emotional intensity may have strengthened the belief that these same jubilant crowds would have channeled their joy into rage had O. J. been convicted. If this is so, students who raised the prior probability of postconviction violence may have been saying "I knew it all along" (cf. Hawkins & Hastie, 1990).

Our research conclusions are constrained by several important limitations. First, sample size was relatively small, and the asymmetry in conviction and acquittal ratings at Time 2 may be due to the variability of our small sample. Second, the absence of Black respondents made it impossible to analyze the effects of racial similarity on hindsight distortion (cf. Mixon et al., 1995). Third, we did not include a measure of participants' media exposure, which would have allowed us to test the media-influence interpretation more directly. Finally, because our results are based on a naturalistic event, they are limited in generalizability and replicability. Nevertheless, this study contributes to our understanding of how hindsight bias unfolds in reaction to real-world events.

ACKNOWLEDGMENTS

The authors thank Robert Russell, Michael Strube, Tricia Tenpenny, Linda Thomas, Scott Tindale, Kevin Weinfurt, Paul Yarnold, and the anonymous reviewers for helpful feedback on an earlier draft of this article. We also are grateful to Courtney Jamieson, Rebecca Larson, and Journal Graphics, Inc. for help in obtaining information about national news coverage.

REFERENCES

Baron, J. (1988). *Thinking and deciding.* Cambridge, England: Cambridge University Press.

Cook, T. D., & Campbell, D. T. (1979). *Quasi-experimentation: Design and analysis issues for field settings.* Chicago: Rand McNally.

Fischhoff, B. (1975). Hindsight ≠ foresight: The effect of outcome knowledge on judgments under uncertainty. *Journal of Experimental Psychology: Human Perception and Performance, 1,* 288–299.

Fischhoff, B. (1977). Perceived informativeness of facts. *Journal of Experimental Psychology: Human Perception and Performance, 3,* 349–358.

Fischhoff, B., & Beyeth, R. (1975). "I knew it would happen": Remembered probabilities of once-future things. *Organizational Behavior and Human Performance, 13,* 1–16.

Gottlieb, M. (1995, October 4). Jury clears Simpson in double murder: Racial split at end, as at the start—Spellbound nation divides on verdict. *The New York Times,* p. A1.

Greenhouse, S. W., & Geisser, S. (1959). On methods in the analysis of profile data. *Psychometrika, 24,* 95–112.

Hawkins, S. A., & Hastie, R. (1990). Hindsight: Biased judgments of past events after the outcomes are known. *Psychological Bulletin, 107,* 311–327.

Hell, W., Gigerenzer, G., Gauggel, S., Mall, M., & Mueller, M. (1988). Hindsight bias: An interaction of automatic and motivational factors? *Memory & Cognition, 16,* 533–538.

Kahneman, D., & Tversky, A. (1979). Prospect theory: An analysis of decision under risk. *Econometrika, 47,* 263–291.

Kalichman, S. C., Russell, R. L., Hunter, T. L., & Sarwer, D. B. (1993). Earvin "Magic" Johnson's HIV serostatus disclosure: Effects on men's perceptions of AIDS. *Journal of Consulting and Clinical Psychology, 61,* 887–891.

Leary, M. R. (1982). Hindsight distortion and the 1980 presidential election. *Personality and Social Psychology Bulletin, 8,* 257–263.

Loftus, E. F., & Loftus, G. (1980). On the performance of stored information in the human brain. *American Psychologist, 35,* 409–420.

Mixon, K. D., Foley, L. A., & Orme, K. (1995). The influence of racial similarity on the O. J. Simpson trial. *Journal of Social Behavior and Personality, 10,* 481–490.

Nario, M. R., & Branscombe, N. R. (1995). Comparison processes in hindsight and causal attribution. *Personality and Social Psychology Bulletin, 21,* 1244–1255.

Peterson, C. R., & Beach, L. R. (1967). Man as an intuitive statistician. *Psychological Bulletin, 68,* 29–46.

Rosenthal, R., & Rosnow, R. L. (1985). *Contrast analysis: Focused comparisons in the analysis of variance.* Cambridge, England: Cambridge University Press.

Ross, L., Lepper, M. R., Strack, F., & Steinmetz, J. (1977). Social explanation and social expectation: Effects of real and hypothetical explanations on subjective likelihood. *Journal of Personality and Social Psychology, 35,* 817–829.

Schofield, J. W., & Pavelchak, M. (1985). *The Day After:* The impact of a media event. *American Psychologist, 40,* 542–548.

Slovic, P., & Fischhoff, B. (1977). On the psychology of experimental surprises. *Journal of Experimental Psychology: Human Perception and Performance, 3,* 544–551.

Slovic, P., Fischhoff, B., & Lichtenstein, S. (1980). Facts versus fears: Understanding perceived risk. In D. Kahneman, P. Slovic, & A. Tversky (Eds.), *Judgment under uncertainty: Heuristics and biases* (pp. 463–489). Cambridge, England: Cambridge University Press.

Tversky, A., & Kahneman, D. (1973). Availability: A heuristic for judging frequency and probability. *Cognitive Psychology, 5,* 207–232.

Tversky, A., & Kahneman, D. (1988). Rational choice and the framing of decisions. In D. E. Bell, H. Raiffa, & A. Tversky (Eds.), *Decision making: Descriptive, normative, and prescriptive interactions* (pp. 167–192). Cambridge, England: Cambridge University Press.

Video index: O. J. Simpson index. (1996). Transcript. Denver, CO: Journal Graphics.

von Winterfeldt, D., & Edwards, W. (1986). *Decision analysis and behavioral research.* Cambridge, England: Cambridge University Press.

Weinfurt, K. P. (1996). Multivariate analysis of variance. In L. C. Grimm & P. R. Yarnold (Eds.), *Reading and understanding multivariate statistics* (pp. 245–276). Washington, DC: American Psychological Association.

Winer, B. J. (1971). *Statistical principles in experimental design* (2nd ed.). New York: McGraw-Hill.

Wood, G. (1978). The knew-it-all-along effect. *Journal of Experimental Psychology: Human Perception and Performance, 4,* 345–353.

ENDNOTES

1. Students completed the pretest measures on Tuesday, October 3, 1995, at 10:05 a.m. Central Time. The verdict was announced at 12:05 p.m. (Central), October 3.

2. To explore the possible effects of sex on probability estimates, we conducted a mixed-effects multivariate repeated measures ANOVA that included both a between-group factor (i.e., sex) and a doubly repeated within-subjects factor (i.e., chance estimates repeated across the three possible verdicts repeated at three times). The main effect of sex, $F(1, 21) = 0.4$, $p > .55$. and all three of its interactions terms, $Fs < 1.5$, $ps > .23$, were nonsignificant. Therefore, we excluded sex from subsequent analyses. We used individual repeated measures ANOVAs to test a priori contrasts for each verdict separately without an initial doubly repeated (verdicts within times) multivariate repeated measures ANOVA, because we did not necessarily expect all verdict ratings to reflect the same latent construct and because multivariate ANOVA protects the experimentwise alpha level only when the null hypothesis is true (Weinfurt, 1996).

3. Because one participant estimated a 0% chance of acquittal at the pretest (producing an invalid likelihood ratio for that individual), analyses of the likelihood ratio of posttest probability to pretest probability included only 22 valid cases for the acquittal verdict.

4. This type of asymmetry in hindsight distortion was reported at least once before in the literature, although it was of the opposite polarity. Studying reactions to President Nixon's 1972 trip to China and the Soviet Union, Fischhoff and Beyeth (1975) found that people raised the recalled probability of events that they believed had occurred during the trip more than they lowered the recalled probability of events that they believed had not occurred. Whereas subjects in Fischhoff and Beyeth's study were more certain about some events that occurred during Nixon's trip and less certain about others, participants in our study all knew the verdict in the Simpson trial with complete certainty.

5. News and public affairs programming on ABC TV during the study period included 10 regularly scheduled shows (*20/20, Day One, Good Morning America, Nightline, Primetime, World News Tonight, Turning Point, This Week With David Brinkley, World News Saturday,* and *World News Sunday*) and three special news broadcasts. News and public affairs programming on NPR included 4 regularly scheduled shows (*All Things Considered,*

Morning Edition, Weekend Edition—Saturday, and *Weekend Edition—Sunday*). The number of daily segments of Simpson news coverage on television and radio was strongly correlated, $r(13)=$ .92, $p < .0001$, one-tailed; and ABC TV ($M = 6.37$ segments) broadcast more coverage of the trial than did NPR ($M = 4.00$ segments), pairwise $t(14) = 2.2$, $p < .05$, two-tailed.

6. As a means of ruling out regression artifacts in field settings, Cook and Campbell (1979) suggested including at least two waves of pretest measures in pretest–posttest designs. If pretest scores are stable over time, regression is a less plausible explanation for observed pretest–posttest differences. Because of the timing of the verdict's announcement, however, we were unable to include more than one pretest in this study. On Friday, the public was told that a verdict had been reached but would not be announced until the following Tuesday. Although this provided a 4-day window of opportunity for pretesting, the class from which the study participants were sampled met only on Tuesdays and Thursdays.

CRITICAL THINKING QUESTIONS

1. The authors of the article acknowledge that one limitation of the study is that "the absence of Black respondents made it impossible to analyze the effects of racial similarity on hindsight distortion." Do you think that race would be an issue in hindsight bias? Or is hindsight bias a cognitive process that is independent of race? Find evidence from the area of social cognition that supports your position.

2. The study did not control for the effects of media exposure on hindsight bias. How could exposure to media accounts of the trial be controlled using the same or a similar experimental design?

3. Describe a situation in which you have seen someone you know display hindsight bias.

4. What potential problems may result from people's tendency to use hindsight bias? For example, might someone who is prone to hindsight bias also be overly (and perhaps falsely) confident to predict future outcomes? Why or why not?

5. Design a study to test hindsight bias in an election. Include the details of who would be tested, when they would be tested, what questions would be asked, and any variables that would need to be controlled in the study.

Chapter Four

ATTITUDES

THE STUDY OF attitudes is considered by many social psychologists to be the core issue in understanding human behavior. How we act in any given situation is the product of the attitudes that we have formed, which in turn are based on the experiences we have had.

Whether or not we believe that attitudes constitute the core of social psychology, the study of attitudes and attitude change has been prominent in social psychological research from the beginning. Part of this interest has been theoretically driven. How attitudes are formed and how they can be changed, as well as what factors make some attitudes so resistant to change, are but a few of the topics that theorists have studied. However, there is also a more pragmatic, applied reason for this interest in attitudes: Principles of attitude change and attitude measurement have a direct bearing on several major industries and even psychotherapy. For example, survey organizations and advertising agencies focus on attitudes, measuring what they are, how they change over time, as well as how best to change them. Likewise, a major goal of both therapy and health promotion might be viewed as modifying people's dysfunctional or health-endangering attitudes and behaviors. Theoretical research often has provided the foundation for the principles applied by clinicians, health professionals, and advertisers.

The readings in this chapter relate to various aspects of attitudes. Article 10, " Don't Even Think about It!" examines the issue of taboos as being a prime example of deeply held attitudes. How are taboos formed? Why are they maintained? How are they changed?

Article 11, "Cognitive Consequences of Forced Compliance," is a classic demonstration of a powerful theoretical model in social psychology known as *cognitive dissonance*. It is an excellent example of how common-sense predictions often are exactly opposite of what actually occurs.

Finally, Article 12, "Cognitive Reactions to Smoking Relapse: The Reciprocal Relation between Dissonance and Self-Esteem," provides a contemporary test of the cognitive dissonance hypothesis described in Article 11, which was first presented nearly 40 years ago. Article 12 suggests how the concept of dissonance may be used to help people quit smoking and how this effect may be vastly different among individuals, depending on their overall levels of self-esteem.

ARTICLE 10 _____

Obviously, attitudes are formed in a great variety of ways. Some are the result of direct experience. For instance, we meet someone from a certain country and, based on that limited experience, form an attitude (or stereotype) about people from that country. In other words, we generalize our experience to form an attitude. In many other cases, however, we do not experience the person, situation, or event directly but rather indirectly. These so-called *secondhand attitudes* are the result of information we received from someone else, such as our parents or friends. In fact, this kind of information is a major source of our beliefs.

The number of attitudes that people hold can be virtually limitless; however, some attitudes are held more strongly than others. The strength of these attitudes often can be seen most clearly by their absence. That is, what topics do we never discuss? What would we never admit, or what would we never do? In other words, what are our *taboos?* A taboo involves the three elements that comprise all attitudes: First, there is a *cognitive* or *belief* component, which is what we believe is or should be true. Additionally, there is an *affective* or *emotional* component to the taboo. We not only believe something to be true, we also feel very strongly about it. Just the idea of the taboo being violated may fill us with disgust. Finally, the taboo involves a *behavior tendency;* we strongly tend to avoid doing things that violate our taboo belief and affective components.

Many taboos are shared among pepole in a culture, while others are unique to individuals. Thus, most people in a given society tend to believe that it is acceptable to eat certain foods while other foods are off limits. Sometimes, taboos are more unique, such as beliefs that certain topics should never be mentioned to certain people. In all cases, taboos serve to set limits (sometimes, severe limits) on what we believe, feel, and do.

The following article by Michael Ventura examines the topic of taboos, including their origins and the impact that they have on our daily lives. After reading the article, you may agree with the author that we are not really as free as we would like to believe, despite the fact that freedom is a central concept in American culture.

Don't Even Think about It!

■ Michael Ventura

Taboos come in all sizes. Big taboos: when I was a kid in the Italian neighborhoods of Brooklyn, to insult someone's mother meant a brutal fight—the kind of fight no one interferes with until one of the combatants goes down and stays down. Little taboos: until the sixties, it was an insult to use someone's first name without asking or being offered permission. Personal taboos: Cyrano de Bergerac would not tolerate the mention of his enormous nose. Taboos peculiar to one city: in Brooklyn (again), when the Dodgers were still at Ebbets Field, if you rooted for the Yankees you kept it to yourself unless you wanted a brawl. Taboos, big or small, are always about having to respect somebody's (often irrational) boundary—or else.

There are taboos shared within one family: my father did not feel free to speak to us of his grandmother's suicide until his father died. Taboos within intellectual elites: try putting a serious metaphysical or spiritual slant on a "think-piece" (as we call them in the trade) written for the *New York Times,* the

Washington Post, or most big name magazines—it won't be printed. Taboos in the corporate and legal worlds: if you're male, you had best wear suits of somber colors, or you're not likely to be taken seriously; if you're female, you have to strike a very uneasy balance between the attractive and the prim, and even then you might not be taken seriously. Cultural taboos: in the Jim Crow days in the South, a black man who spoke with familiarity to a white woman might be beaten, driven out of town, or (as was not uncommon) lynched.

Unclassifiable taboos: in Afghanistan, as I write this, it is a sin—punishable by beatings and imprisonment—to fly a kite. Sexual taboos: there are few communities on this planet where two men can walk down a street holding hands without being harassed or even arrested; in Afghanistan (a great place for taboos these days) the Taliban would stone them to death. Gender taboos: how many American corporations (or institutions of any kind) promote women to power? National taboos: until the seventies, a divorced person could not run for major public office in America (it wasn't until 1981 that our first and only divorced president, Ronald Reagan, took office); today, no professed atheist would dare try for the presidency. And most readers of this article probably approve, as I do, of this comparatively recent taboo: even the most rabid bigot must avoid saying "nigger," "spic," or "kike" during, say, a job interview—and the most macho sexist must avoid words like "broad."

Notice that nearly all of our taboos, big and small, public and intimate, involve silence—keeping one's silence, or paying a price for not keeping it. Yet keeping silent has its own price: for then silence begins to fill the heart, until silence becomes the heart—a heart swelling with restraint until it bursts in frustration, anger, even madness.

The taboos hardest on the soul are those which fester in our intimacies—taboos known only to the people involved, taboos that can make us feel alone even with those to whom we're closest. One of the deep pains of marriage—one that also plagues brothers and sisters, parents and children, even close friends—is that as we grow more intimate, certain silences often become more necessary. We discover taboo areas, both in ourselves and in the other, that

cannot be transgressed without paying an awful price. If we speak of them, we may endanger the relationship; but if we do not speak, if we do not violate the taboo, the relationship may become static and tense, until the silence takes on a life of its own. Such silences are corrosive. They eat at the innards of intimacy until, often, the silence itself causes the very rupture or break-up that we've tried to avoid by keeping silent.

THE CANNIBAL IN US ALL

You may measure how many taboos constrict you, how many taboos you've surrendered to—at home, at parties, at work, with your lover or your family—by how much of yourself you must suppress. You may measure your life, in these realms, by what you cannot say, do, admit—cannot and must not, and for no better reason than that your actions or words would disrupt your established order. By this measure, most of us are living within as complex and strictured a system of taboos as the aborigines who gave us the word in the first place. You can see how fitting it is that the word "taboo" comes from a part of the world where cannibalism is said to be practiced to this day: the islands off eastern Australia—Polynesia, New Zealand, Melanesia. Until 1777, when Captain James Cook published an account of his first world voyage, Europe and colonial America had many taboos but no word that precisely meant taboo. Cook introduced this useful word to the West. Its instant popularity, quick assimilation into most European languages, and constant usage since, are testimony to how much of our lives the word describes. Before the word came to us, we'd ostracized, coerced, exiled, tormented, and murdered each other for myriad infractions (as we still do), but we never had a satisfying, precise word for our reasons.

We needed cannibals to give us a word to describe our behavior, so how "civilized" are we, really? We do things differently from those cannibals, on the surface, but is the nature of what we do all that different? We don't cook each other for ceremonial dinners, at least not physically (though therapists can testify that our ceremonial seasons, like Christmas and Thanksgiving, draw lots of business—something's cooking).

But we stockpile weapons that can cook the entire world, and we organize our national priorities around their "necessity," and it's a national political taboo to seriously cut spending for those planet-cookers. If that's "progress," it's lost on me. In China it's taboo to be a Christian, in Israel it's taboo to be a Moslem, in Syria it's taboo to be a Jew, in much of the United States it's still taboo to be an atheist, while in American academia it's taboo to be deeply religious. Our headlines are full of this stuff. So it's hardly surprising that a cannibal's word still describes much of our behavior.

I'm not denying the necessity of every society to set limits and invent taboos (some rational, some not) simply in order to get on with the day—and to try to contain the constant, crazy, never-to-be-escaped longings that blossom in our sleep and distract or compel us while awake. Such longings are why even a comparatively tiny desert tribe like the ancient Hebrews needed commandments and laws against coveting each other's wives, stealing, killing, committing incest. That tribe hadn't seen violent, sexy movies, hadn't listened to rock 'n' roll, hadn't been bombarded with ads featuring half-naked models, and hadn't watched too much TV. They didn't need to. Like us, they had their hearts, desires, and dreams to instruct them how to be very, very naughty. The taboo underlying all others is that we must not live by the dictates of our irrational hearts—as though we haven't forgiven each other, or ourselves, for having hearts.

If there's a taboo against something, it's usually because a considerable number of people desire to do it. The very taboos that we employ to protect us from each other and ourselves, are a map of our secret natures. When you know a culture's taboos (or an individual's, or a family's) you know its secrets—you know what it really wants.

FAVORITE TABOOS

It's hard to keep a human being from his or her desire, taboo or not. We've always been very clever, very resourceful, when it comes to sneaking around our taboos. The Aztecs killed virgins and called it religion. The Europeans enslaved blacks and called it econom-

ics. Americans tease each other sexually and call it fashion.

If we can't kill and screw and steal and betray to our heart's desire, and, in general, violate every taboo in sight—well, we can at least watch other people do it. Or read about it. Or listen to it. As we have done, since ancient times, through every form of religion and entertainment. The appeal of taboos and our inability to escape our longing for transgression (whether or not we ourselves transgress) are why so many people who call themselves honest and law-abiding spend so much time with movies, operas, soaps, garish trials, novels, songs, Biblical tales, tribal myths, folk stories, and Shakespeare—virtually all of which, both the great and the trivial, are about those who dare to violate taboos. It's a little unsettling when you think about it: the very stuff we say we most object to is the fundamental material of what we call culture.

That's one reason that fundamentalists of all religions are so hostile to the arts. But fundamentalists partake of taboos in the sneakiest fashion of all. Senator Jesse Helms led the fight against the National Endowment for the Arts because he couldn't get the (vastly overrated) homosexual art of Robert Mapplethorpe or the most extreme performance artists out of his mind—he didn't and doesn't want to. He, like all fundamentalists, will vigorously oppose such art and all it stands for until he dies, because his very opposition gives him permission to concentrate on taboo acts. The Taliban of Afghanistan will ride around in jeeps toting guns, searching out any woman who dares show an inch of facial skin or wear white socks (Taliban boys consider white socks provocative), and when they find such a woman they'll jail and beat her—because their so-called righteousness gives them permission to obsess on their taboos. Pat Robertson and his ilk will fuss and rage about any moral "deviation," any taboo violation they can find, because that's the only way they can give themselves permission to entertain the taboos. They get to not have their taboo cake, yet eat it too.

We are all guilty of this to some extent. Why else have outlaws from Antigone to Robin Hood to Jesse James to John Gotti become folk heroes? Oedipus killed his father and slept with his mother, and we've been performing that play for 2500 years because he is the ultimate violator of our deepest taboos. Aristotle said we watch such plays for "catharsis," to purge our desires and fears in a moment of revelation. Baloney. Ideas like "catharsis" are an intellectual game, to glossy-up our sins. What's closer to the truth is that we need Oedipus to stand in for us. We can't have changed much in 2500 years, if we still keep him alive in our hearts to enact our darkest taboos for us. Clearly, the very survival of Oedipus as an instantly recognizable name tells us that we still want to kill our fathers and screw our mothers (or vice versa).

A COUNTRY OF BROKEN TABOOS

Taboos are a special paradox for Americans. However much we may long for tradition and order, our longings are subverted by the inescapable fact that our country was founded upon a break with tradition and a challenge to order—which is to say, the United States was founded upon the violation of taboos. Specifically, this country was founded upon the violation of Europe's most suffocating taboo: its feudal suppression (still enforced in 1776, when America declared its independence) of the voices of the common people. We were the first nation on earth to write into law that any human being has the right to say anything, and that even the government is (theoretically) not allowed to silence you.

At the time, Europe was a continent of state-enforced religions, where royalty's word was law and all other words could be crushed by law. (Again: taboo was a matter of enforced silence.) We were the first nation to postulate verbal freedom for everyone. All our other freedoms depend upon verbal freedom; no matter how badly and how often we've failed that ideal, it still remains our ideal.

Once we broke Europe's verbal taboos, it was only a matter of time before other traditional taboos fell too. As the writer Albert Murray has put it, Americans could not afford piety in their new homeland: "You can't be over respectful of established forms; you're trying to get through the wilderness of Kentucky." Thus, from the moment the Pilgrims landed, our famous puritanism faced an inherent contradiction. How could we domesticate the wilderness of this continent; how could peasants and rejects and "commoners" form a strong and viable nation; how could we develop all the new social forms and technologies necessary to blend all the disparate peoples who came here—without violating those same Puritan taboos which are so ingrained, to this day, in our national character?

It can't be over-emphasized that America's fundamental stance against both the taboos of Europe and the taboos of our own Puritans, was our insistence upon freedom of speech. America led the attack against silence. And it is through that freedom, the freedom to break the silence, that we've destroyed so many other taboos. Especially during the last 40 years, we've broken the silence that surrounded ancient taboos of enormous significance. Incest, child abuse, wife-battering, homosexuality, and some (by no means all) forms of racial and gender oppression, are not merely spoken of, and spoken against, they're shouted about from the rooftops. Many breathe easier because of this inevitable result of free speech. In certain sections of our large cities, for the first time in modern history, gay people can live openly and without fear. The feminist movement has made previously forbidden or hidden behaviors both speakable and doable. The National Organization of Women can rail against the Promise Keepers all they want (and they have some good reasons), but when you get a million working-class guys crying and hugging in public, the stoic mask of the American male has definitely cracked. And I'm old enough to remember when it was shocking for women to speak about wanting a career. Now virtually all affluent young women are expected to want a career.

Fifty years ago, not one important world or national leader was black. Now there are more people of color in positions of influence than ever. Bad marriages can be dissolved without social stigma. Children born out of wedlock are not damned as "bastards" for something that wasn't their fault. And those of us who've experienced incest and abuse have finally found a voice, and through our voices we've achieved a certain amount of liberation from shame and pain.

These boons are rooted in our decidedly un-Puritan freedom of speech. But we left those Puritans behind a long time ago—for the breaking of silence is the fundamental political basis of our nation, and no taboo is safe when people have the right to speak.

KEEPER OF YOUR SILENCE

In the process, though, we've lost the sanctity of silence. We've lost the sense of dark but sacred power inherent in sex, in nature, even in crime. Perhaps that is the price of our new freedoms.

It's also true that by breaking the silence we've thrown ourselves into a state of confusion. The old taboos formed part of society's structure. Without them, that structure has undeniably weakened. We are faced with shoring up the weakened parts, inventing new ways of being together that have pattern and order—for we cannot live without some pattern and order—but aren't so restrictive. Without sexual taboos, for instance, what are the social boundaries between men and women? When are they breached? What is offensive? Nobody's sure. Everybody's making mistakes. This is so excruciating that many are nostalgic for some of the old taboos. But once a taboo is broken, then for good or ill it's very hard, perhaps impossible, to reinstate it.

But there is another, subtler confusion: yes, enormous taboos have fallen, but many taboos, equally important, remain. And, both as individuals and as a society, we're strained enough, confused enough, by the results of doing away with so many taboos in so short a time, that maybe we're not terribly eager for our remaining taboos to fall. We may sincerely desire that, but maybe we're tired, fed up, scared. Many people would rather our taboos remain intact for a couple of generations while we get our act together again, and perhaps they have a point. But the price of taboo remains what it's always been: silence and constriction.

What do we see, when we pass each other on the street, but many faces molded by the price paid for keeping the silences of the taboos that remain—spirits confined within their own, and their society's, silences? Even this brief essay on our public and intimate strictures is enough to demonstrate that we are still a primitive race, bounded by fear and prejudice,

with taboos looming in every direction—no matter how much we like to brag and/or bitch that modern life is liberating us from all the old boundaries. The word taboo still says much more about us than most prefer to admit.

What is the keeper of your silence? The answer to that question is your own guide to your personal taboos. How must you confine yourself in order to get through your day at the job, or to be acceptable in your social circle? The answer to that is your map of your society's taboos. What makes you most afraid to speak? What desire, what word, what possibility, freezes and fevers you at the same time, making any sincere communication out of the question? What makes you vanish into your secret? That's your taboo, baby. You're still in the room, maybe even still smiling, still talking, but not really—what's really happened is that you've vanished down some hole in yourself, and you'll stay there until you're sure the threat to your taboo is gone and it's safe to come out again. If, that is, you've ever come out in the first place. Some never have.

What utterance, what hint, what insinuation, can quiet a room of family or friends? What makes people change the subject? What makes those at a dinner party dismiss a remark as though it wasn't said, or dismiss a person as though he or she wasn't really there? We've all seen conversations suddenly go dead, and just as suddenly divert around a particular person or subject, leaving them behind in the dead space, because something has been said or implied that skirts a silently shared taboo. If that happens to you often, don't kid yourself that you're living in a "free" society. Because you're only as free as your freedom from taboos—not on some grand abstract level, but in your day-to-day life.

It is probably inherent in the human condition that there are no "last" taboos. Or perhaps it just feels that way because we have such a long way to go. But at least we can know where to look: right in front of our eyes, in the recesses of our speechlessness, in the depths of our silences. And there is nothing for it but to confront the keepers of our silence. Either that, or to submit to being lost, as most of us silently are, without admitting it to each other or to ourselves—lost in a maze of taboos.

In Search of the Last Taboo

There is no "last taboo," according to Michael Ventura. But there certainly are a lot of contenders, scattered like clues in a treasure hunt for the heart of our culture. Here, an assortment of last taboos "discovered" by the media in the past few years.

"What a great story: **Incest**. The last taboo!"—*Esquire,* on Kathryn Harrison's memoir *The Kiss.*

"'The very word is a room-emptier,' Tina Brown wrote in her editor's note when, in 1991, Gail Sheehy broke the silence with a story in *Vanity* Fair. . . . **Menopause** may be the last taboo."
—*Fort Lauderdale Sun-Sentinel*

"The last taboo for women is not, as Gail Sheehy would have it, menopause, but **facial hair.**"
—*New York Times*

"At a time when this is the last taboo, Moreton depicts **erections**."—*Sunday Telegraph,* describing sculptor Nicholas Moreton's work.

"Virtually no representations of **faith** are seen on television, it's the last taboo."—*Columbus Dispatch*

"Anything with **sex with underage kids** is the last taboo."—*Toronto Star*

"The last taboo: an openly **homosexual** actor playing a **heterosexual** lead."—*Boston Globe*

"With sexual mores gone the way of Madonna, **picking up the tab** has become the last taboo for women."—*Philadelphia Inquirer*

"Most Americans, if they think about **class** at all (it may be our last taboo subject), would surely describe themselves as middle class regardless of a petty detail like income."—*Los Angeles Times Syndicate*

"The Last Taboo Is **Age**: Why Are We Afraid of It?"—headline in the *Philadelphia Inquirer*

"Smash the last taboo! [Timothy] Leary says he's planning the first . . . **interactive suicide**."
—*Washington Post*

"**Money** is the last taboo."—Calgary *Herald*

"**Menstruation** may be the last taboo."—*Manchester Guardian Weekly*

"The real last taboo is that of **privacy and dignity**."—*Montreal Gazette*

"And then there's **bisexuality**, the last taboo among lesbians."—*Los Angeles Times*

"I think **personal smells** are one of the last taboos."—*The Observer*

"Television's last taboo, long after f-words and pumping bottoms became commonplace, was the **full-frontal vomit**. Now, even that last shred of inhibition has gone, and every drama . . . [has] a character heaving his guts all over the camera."—*The (London) Mail*

"**Tanning**. The last taboo. If you're tan, then your IQ must be lower than the SPF of the sunscreen you'd be using if you had any brains."—*Los Angeles Times*

CRITICAL THINKING QUESTIONS

1. What do you believe are the five strongest and most universally held taboos in your culture? What would be the sanctions for someone who violated these taboos? Why do these taboos remain so strong, and what function may each serve? Explain your answers.

2. Discuss two beliefs or behaviors that have been considered taboo in your lifetime but are not any longer. When and why did each of these taboos disappear? Is there any particular reason each disappeared when it did rather than, say, 50 years before? Explain your answers.

3. Name two current taboos that you do not believe will be considered taboos 20 years from now. What will it take to eliminate each of these taboos? In your opinion, what are the effects of eliminating taboos? Discuss the positive versus negative effects.

4. Do you hold any personal taboos (as opposed to cultural taboos)? For example, are there certain topics that you cannot discuss or things that you cannot do with certain people yet can with others? Discuss what you believe are the origins, functions, and impacts of these personal taboos on you and on the people affected by them.

ARTICLE 11 _____

Suppose someone asked you to publicly say something that contradicted your privately held beliefs and then offered you either a small reward (say, $1) or a large reward ($20) for doing so. Under which of those conditions would you be most likely to actually change your privately held belief to bring it more into the realm of what you just said? If you guessed that would be most likely to happen in the $20 condition, you would have guessed wrong.

A major theory in social psychology is known as *cognitive dissonance*. Briefly stated, this theory says that people feel a tension when they are aware of an inconsistency either between two attitudes or between an attitude and a behavior. Moreover, the theory asserts that such tension produces some type of change to reduce the state of dissonance. The resulting outcome often is counterintuitive to what common sense would predict. The exact conditions under which cognitive dissonance operates and how it is reduced have been investigated in many experiments over the years.

The following article by Leon Festinger and James M. Carlsmith is *the* classic study on dissonance theory. The hypothesis being tested is a simple yet powerful and nonobvious one. Aside from the outcomes, of particular interest is the elaborate design of the experiment. While reading the article, put yourself in the shoes of the subjects and try to imagine how their thinking might account for the obtained results.

Cognitive Consequences of Forced Compliance

■ Leon Festinger and James M. Carlsmith

What happens to a person's private opinion if he is forced to do or say something contrary to that opinion? Only recently has there been any experimental work related to this question. Two studies reported by Janis and King (1954; 1956) clearly showed that, at least under some conditions, the private opinion changes so as to bring it into closer correspondence with the overt behavior the person was forced to perform. Specifically, they showed that if a person is forced to improvise a speech supporting a point of view with which he disagrees, his private opinion moves toward the position advocated in the speech. The observed opinion change is greater than for persons who only hear the speech or for persons who read a prepared speech with emphasis solely on elocution and manner of delivery. The authors of these two studies explain their results mainly in terms of mental rehearsal and thinking up new arguments. In this way,

they propose, the person who is forced to improvise a speech convinces himself. They present some evidence, which is not altogether conclusive, in support of this explanation. We will have more to say concerning this explanation in discussing the results of our experiment.

Kelman (1953) tried to pursue the matter further. He reasoned that if the person is induced to make an overt statement contrary to his private opinion by the offer of some reward, then the greater the reward offered, the greater should be the subsequent opinion change. His data, however, did not support this idea. He found, rather, that a large reward produced less subsequent opinion change than did a smaller reward. Actually, this finding by Kelman is consistent with the theory we will outline below but, for a number of reasons, is not conclusive. One of the major weaknesses of the data is that not all subjects in the experi-

Reprinted from *Journal of Abnormal and Social Psychology*, 1959, 58, 203–210.

ment made an overt statement contrary to their private opinion in order to obtain the offered reward. What is more, as one might expect, the percentage of subjects who complied increased as the size of the offered reward increased. Thus, with self-selection of who did and who did not make the required overt statement and with varying percentages of subjects in the different conditions who did make the required statement, no interpretation of the data can be unequivocal.

Recently, Festinger (1957) proposed a theory concerning cognitive dissonance from which come a number of derivations about opinion change following forced compliance. Since these derivations are stated in detail by Festinger (1957, Ch. 4), we will here give only a brief outline of the reasoning.

Let us consider a person who privately holds opinion "X" but has, as a result of pressure brought to bear on him, publicly stated that he believes "not X."

1. This person has two cognitions which, psychologically, do not fit together: one of these is the knowledge that he believes "X," the other the knowledge that he has publicly stated that he believes "not X." If no factors other than his private opinion are considered, it would follow, at least in our culture, that if he believes "X" he would publicly state "X." Hence, his cognition of his private belief is dissonant with his cognition concerning his actual public statement.

2. Similarly, the knowledge that he has said "not X" is consonant with (does fit together with) those cognitive elements corresponding to the reasons, pressures, promises of rewards and/or threats of punishment which induced him to say "not X."

3. In evaluating the total magnitude of dissonance, one must take account of both dissonances and consonances. Let us think of the sum of all the dissonances involving some particular cognition as "D" and the sum of all the consonances as "C." Then we might think of the total magnitude of dissonance as being a function of "D" divided by "D" plus "C."

Let us then see what can be said about the total magnitude of dissonance in a person created by the knowledge that he said "not X" and really believes "X." With everything else held constant, this total magnitude of dissonance would decrease as the number and importance of the pressures which induced

him to say "not X" increased. Thus, if the overt behavior was brought about by, say, offers of reward or threats of punishment, the magnitude of dissonance is maximal if these promised rewards or threatened punishments were just barely sufficient to induce the person to say "not X." From this point on, as the promised rewards or threatened punishment become larger, the magnitude of dissonance becomes smaller.

4. One way in which the dissonance can be reduced is for the person to change his private opinion so as to bring it into correspondence with what he has said. One would consequently expect to observe such opinion change after a person has been forced or induced to say something contrary to his private opinion. Furthermore, since the pressure to reduce dissonance will be a function of the magnitude of the dissonance, the observed opinion change should be greatest when the pressure used to elicit the overt behavior is just sufficient to do it.

The present experiment was designed to test this derivation under controlled, laboratory conditions. In the experiment we varied the amount of reward used to force persons to make a statement contrary to their private views. The prediction [from 3 and 4 above] is that the larger the reward given to the subject, the smaller will be the subsequent opinion change.

PROCEDURE

Seventy-one male students in the introductory psychology course at Stanford University were used in the experiment. In this course, students are required to spend a certain number of hours as subjects (*Ss*) in experiments. They choose among the available experiments by signing their names on a sheet posted on the bulletin board which states the nature of the experiment. The present experiment was listed as a two-hour experiment dealing with "Measures of Performance."

During the first week of the course, when the requirement of serving in experiments was announced and explained to the students, the instructor also told them about a study that the psychology department was conducting. He explained that, since they were required to serve in experiments, the department was conducting a study to evaluate these experiments in order to be able to improve them in the future. They were told that a sample of students would be interviewed after having served as *Ss*. They were urged to cooperate in these interviews by being completely frank and honest. The importance of this announcement will become clear shortly. It enabled us to measure the opinions of our *Ss* in a context not directly connected with our experiment and in which we could reasonably expect frank and honest expressions of opinion.

When the *S* arrived for the experiment on "Measures of Performance" he had to wait for a few minutes in the secretary's office. The experimenter (*E*) then came in, introduced himself to the *S* and, together, they walked into the laboratory room where the *E* said:

This experiment usually takes a little over an hour but, of course, we had to schedule it for two hours. Since we have that extra time, the introductory psychology people asked if they could interview some of our subjects. [Offhand and conversationally.] Did they announce that in class? I gather that they're interviewing some people who have been in experiments. I don't know much about it. Anyhow, they may want to interview you when you're through here.

With no further introduction or explanation the *S* was shown the first task, which involved putting 12 spools onto a tray, emptying the tray, refilling it with spools, and so on. He was told to use one hand and to work at his own speed. He did this for one-half hour. The *E* then removed the tray and spools and placed in front of the *S* a board containing 48 square pegs. His task was to turn each peg a quarter turn clockwise, then another quarter turn, and so on. He was told again to use one hand and to work at his own speed. The *S* worked at this task for another half hour.

While the *S* was working on these tasks, the *E* sat, with a stop watch in his hand, busily making notations on a sheet of paper. He did so in order to make it convincing that this was what the *E* was interested in and that these tasks, and how the *S* worked on them, was the total experiment. From our point of view the

experiment had hardly started. The hour which the *S* spent working on the repetitive, monotonous tasks was intended to provide, for each *S* uniformly, an experience about which he would have a somewhat negative opinion.

After the half hour on the second task was over, the *E* conspicuously set the stop watch back to zero, put it away, pushed his chair back, lit a cigarette, and said:

O.K. Well, that's all we have in the experiment itself. I'd like to explain what this has been all about so you'll have some idea of why you were doing this. [E pauses.] Well, the way the experiment is set up is this. There are actually two groups in the experiment. In one, the group you were in, we bring the subject in and give him essentially no introduction to the experiment. That is, all we tell him is what he needs to know in order to do the tasks, and he has no idea of what the experiment is all about, or what it's going to be like, or anything like that. But in the other group, we have a student that we've hired that works for us regularly, and what I do is take him into the next room where the subject is waiting—the same room you were waiting in before—and I introduce him as if he had just finished being a subject in the experiment. That is, I say: "This is so-and-so, who's just finished the experiment and I've asked him to tell you a little of what it's about before you start." The fellow who works for us then, in conversation with the next subject, makes these points: [The E then produced a sheet headed "For Group B" which had written on it: It was very enjoyable, I had a lot of fun, I enjoyed myself, it was very interesting, it was intriguing, it was exciting. The E showed this to the S and then proceeded with his false explanation of the purpose of the experiment.] Now, of course, we have this student do this, because if the experimenter does it, it doesn't look as realistic, and what we're interested in doing is comparing how these two groups do on the experiment—the one with this previous expectation about the experiment, and the other, like yourself, with essentially none.

Up to this point the procedure was identical for *Ss* in all conditions. From this point on they diverged somewhat. Three conditions were run, Control, One Dollar, and Twenty Dollars, as follows:

Control Condition

The *E* continued:

> Is that fairly clear? [Pause.] Look, that fellow [looks at watch] I was telling you about from the introductory psychology class said he would get here a couple of minutes from now. Would you mind waiting to see if he wants to talk to you? Fine. Why don't we go into the other room to wait? [The E left the S in the secretary's office for four minutes. He then returned and said:] O.K. Let's check and see if he does want to talk to you.

One and Twenty Dollar Conditions

The *E* continued:

> Is that fairly clear how it is set up and what we're trying to do? [Pause.] Now, I also have a sort of strange thing to ask you. The thing is this. [Long pause, some confusion and uncertainty in the following, with a degree of embarrassment on the part of the E. The manner of the E contrasted strongly with the preceding unhesitant and assured false explanation of the experiment. The point was to make it seem to the S that this was the first time the E had done this and that he felt unsure of himself.] The fellow who normally does this for us couldn't do it today—he just phoned in, and something or other came up for him—so we've been looking around for someone that we could hire to do it for us. You see, we've got another subject waiting [looks at watch] who is supposed to be in that other condition. Now Professor _____, who is in charge of this experiment, suggested that perhaps we could take a chance on your doing it for us. I'll tell you what we had in mind: the thing is, if you could do it for us now, then of course you would know how to do it, and if something like this should ever come up again, that is, the regular fellow couldn't make it, and we had a subject scheduled, it would be very reassuring to us to know that we had somebody else we could call on who knew how to do it. So, if you would be willing to do this for us, we'd like to hire you to do it now and then be on call in the future, if something like this should ever happen again. We can pay you a dollar (twenty dollars) for doing this for us, that is, for

doing it now and then being on call. Do you think you could do that for us?

If the *S* hesitated, the *E* said things like, "It will only take a few minutes," "The regular person is pretty reliable; this is the first time he has missed," or "If we needed you we could phone you a day or two in advance; if you couldn't make it, of course, we wouldn't expect you to come." After the *S* agreed to do it, the *E* gave him the previously mentioned sheet of paper headed "For Group B" and asked him to read it through again. The *E* then paid the *S* one dollar (twenty dollars), made out a hand-written receipt form, and asked the *S* to sign it. He then said:

> O.K., the way we'll do it is this. As I said, the next subject should be here by now. I think the next one is a girl. I'll take you into the next room and introduce you to her, saying that you've just finished the experiment and that we've asked you to tell her a little about it. And what we want you to do is just sit down and get into a conversation with her and try to get across the points on that sheet of paper. I'll leave you alone and come back after a couple of minutes. O.K.?

The *E* then took the *S* into the secretary's office where he had previously waited and where the next *S* was waiting. (The secretary had left the office.) He introduced the girl and the *S* to one another saying that the *S* had just finished the experiment and would tell her something about it. He then left saying he would return in a couple of minutes. The girl, an undergraduate hired for this role, said little until the *S* made some positive remarks about the experiment and then said that she was surprised because a friend of hers had taken the experiment the week before and had told her that it was boring and that she ought to try to get out of it. Most Ss responded by saying something like "Oh, no, it's really very interesting. I'm sure you'll enjoy it." The girl listened quietly after this, accepting and agreeing to everything the *S* told her. The discussion between the *S* and the girl was recorded on a hidden tape recorder.

After two minutes the *E* returned, asked the girl to go into the experimental room, thanked the *S* for talking to the girl, wrote down his phone number to continue the fiction that we might call on him again in the future and then said: "Look, could we check and see if that fellow from introductory psychology wants to talk to you?"

From this point on, the procedure for all three conditions was once more identical. As the *E* and the *S* started to walk to the office where the interviewer was, the *E* said: "Thanks very much for working on those tasks for us. I hope you did enjoy it. Most of our subjects tell us afterward that they found it quite interesting. You get a chance to see how you react to the tasks and so forth." This short persuasive communication was made in all conditions in exactly the same way. The reason for doing it, theoretically, was to make it easier for anyone who wanted to persuade himself that the tasks had been, indeed, enjoyable.

When they arrived at the interviewer's office, the *E* asked the interviewer whether or not he wanted to talk to the *S*. The interviewer said yes, the *E* shook hands with the *S,* said good-bye, and left. The interviewer, of course, was always kept in complete ignorance of which condition the *S* was in. The interview consisted of four questions, on each of which the *S* was first encouraged to talk about the matter and was then asked to rate his opinion or reaction on an 11-point scale. The questions are as follows:

1. Were the tasks interesting and enjoyable? In what way? In what way were they not? Would you rate how you feel about them on a scale from −5 to +5 where −5 means they were extremely dull and boring, +5 means they were extremely interesting and enjoyable, and zero means they were neutral, neither interesting nor uninteresting.

2. Did the experiment give you an opportunity to learn about your own ability to perform these tasks? In what way? In what way not? Would you rate how you feel about this on a scale from 0 to 10 where 0 means you learned nothing and 10 means you learned a great deal.

3. From what you know about the experiment and the tasks involved in it, would you say the experiment was measuring anything important? That is, do you think the results may have scientific value? In what way? In what way not? Would you rate your opinion on this matter on a scale from 0 to 10 where 0 means the results have no scientific value or impor-

tance and 10 means they have a great deal of value and importance.

4. Would you have any desire to participate in another similar experiment? Why? Why not? Would you rate your desire to participate in a similar experiment again on a scale from −5 to +5, where −5 means you would definitely dislike to participate, +5 means you would definitely like to participate, and 0 means you have no particular feeling about it one way or the other.

As may be seen, the questions varied in how directly relevant they were to what the *S* had told the girl. This point will be discussed further in connection with the results.

At the close of the interview the *S* was asked what he thought the experiment was about and, following this, was asked directly whether or not he was suspicious of anything and, if so, what he was suspicious of. When the interview was over, the interviewer brought the *S* back to the experimental room where the *E* was waiting together with the girl who had posed as the waiting *S*. (In the control condition, of course, the girl was not there.) The true purpose of the experiment was then explained to the *S* in detail, and the reasons for each of the various steps in the experiment were explained carefully in relation to the true purpose. All experimental *S*s in both One Dollar and Twenty Dollar conditions were asked, after this explanation, to return the money they had been given. All *S*s, without exception, were quite willing to return the money.

The data from 11 of the 71 *S*s in the experiment had to be discarded for the following reasons:

1. Five *S*s (three in the One Dollar and two in the Twenty Dollar condition) indicated in the interview that they were suspicious about having been paid to tell the girl the experiment was fun and suspected that that was the real purpose of the experiment.
2. Two *S*s (both in the One Dollar condition) told the girl that they had been hired, that the experiment was really boring but they were supposed to say it was fun.
3. Three *S*s (one in the One Dollar and two in the Twenty Dollar condition) refused to take the money and refused to be hired.

4. One *S* (in the One Dollar condition), immediately after having talked to the girl, demanded her phone number saying he would call her and explain things, and also told the *E* he wanted to wait until she was finished so he could tell her about it.

These 11 *Ss* were, of course, run through the total experiment anyhow and the experiment was explained to them afterwards. Their data, however, are not included in the analysis.

Summary of Design

There remain, for analysis, 20 *Ss* in each of the three conditions. Let us review these briefly: 1. *Control condition.* These *Ss* were treated identically in all respects to the *Ss* in the experimental conditions, except that they were never asked to, and never did, tell the waiting girl that the experimental tasks were enjoyable and lots of fun. 2. *One Dollar condition.* These *Ss* were hired for one dollar to tell a waiting *S* that tasks, which were really rather dull and boring, were interesting, enjoyable, and lots of fun. 3. *Twenty Dollar condition.* These *Ss* were hired for twenty dollars to do the same thing.

RESULTS

The major results of the experiment are summarized in Table 1 which lists, separately for each of the three experimental conditions, the average rating which the *Ss* gave at the end of each question on the interview. We will discuss each of the questions on the interview separately, because they were intended to measure different things. One other point before we proceed to examine the data. In all the comparisons, the Control condition should be regarded as a baseline from which to evaluate the results in the other two conditions. The Control condition gives us, essentially, the reactions of *Ss* to the tasks and their opinions about the experiment as falsely explained to them, without the experimental introduction of dissonance. The data from the other conditions may be viewed, in a sense, as changes from this baseline.

How Enjoyable the Tasks Were

The average ratings on this question, presented in the first row of figures in Table 1, are the results most important to the experiment. These results are the ones most directly relevant to the specific dissonance which was experimentally created. It will be recalled that the tasks were purposely arranged to be rather boring and monotonous. And, indeed, in the Control condition the average rating was −.45, somewhat on the negative side of the neutral point.

In the other two conditions, however, the *Ss* told someone that these tasks were interesting and enjoyable. The resulting dissonance could, of course, most directly be reduced by persuading themselves that the tasks were, indeed, interesting and enjoyable. In the One Dollar condition, since the magnitude of dissonance was high, the pressure to reduce this dissonance would also be high. In this condition, the average rating was +1.35, considerably on the positive side and significantly different from the Control condition at the .02 level[1] (*t* = 2.48).

In the Twenty Dollar condition, where less dissonance was created experimentally because of the greater importance of the consonant relations, there is

TABLE 1 / Average Ratings on Interview Questions for Each Condition

	Experimental Condition		
Question on Interview	Control (*N* = 20)	One Dollar (*N* = 20)	Twenty Dollars (*N* = 20)
How enjoyable tasks were (rated from −5 to +5)	−.45	+1.35	−.05
How much they learned (rated from 0 to 10)	3.08	2.80	3.15
Scientific importance (rated from 0 to 10)	5.60	6.45	5.18
Participate in similar exp. (rated from −5 to +5)	−.62	+1.20	−.25

correspondingly less evidence of dissonance reduction. The average rating in this condition is only –.05, slightly and not significantly higher than the Control condition. The difference between the One Dollar and Twenty Dollar conditions is significant at the .03 level ($t = 2.22$). In short, when an S was induced, by offer of reward, to say something contrary to his private opinion, this private opinion tended to change so as to correspond more closely with what he had said. The greater the reward offered (beyond what was necessary to elicit the behavior) the smaller was the effect.

Desire to Participate in a Similar Experiment

The results from this question are shown in the last row of Table 1. This question is less directly related to the dissonance that was experimentally created for the Ss. Certainly, the more interesting and enjoyable they felt the tasks were, the greater would be their desire to participate in a similar experiment. But other factors would enter also. Hence, one would expect the results on this question to be very similar to the results on "how enjoyable the tasks were" but weaker. Actually, the results, as may be seen in the table, are in exactly the same direction, and the magnitude of the mean differences is fully as large as on the first question. The variability is greater, however, and the differences do not yield high levels of statistical significance. The difference between the One Dollar condition (+1.20) and the Control condition (–.62) is significant at the .08 level ($t = 1.78$). The difference between the One Dollar condition and the Twenty Dollar condition (–.25) reaches only the .15 level of significance ($t = 1.46$).

The Scientific Importance of the Experiment

This question was included because there was a chance that differences might emerge. There are, after all, other ways in which the experimentally created dissonance could be reduced. For example, one way would be for the S to magnify for himself the value of the reward he obtained. This, however, was unlikely in this experiment because money was used for the reward and it is undoubtedly difficult to convince

oneself that one dollar is more than it really is. There is another possible way, however. The Ss were given a very good reason, in addition to being paid, for saying what they did to the waiting girl. The Ss were told it was necessary for the experiment. The dissonance could, consequently, be reduced by magnifying the importance of this cognition. The more scientifically important they considered the experiment to be, the less was the total magnitude of dissonance. It is possible, then, that the results on this question, shown in the third row of figures in Table 1, might reflect dissonance reduction.

The results are weakly in line with what one would expect if the dissonance were somewhat reduced in this manner. The One Dollar condition is higher than the other two. The difference between the One and Twenty Dollar conditions reaches the .08 level of significance on a two-tailed test ($t = 1.79$). The difference between the One Dollar and Control conditions is not impressive at all ($t = 1.21$). The result that the Twenty Dollar condition is actually lower than the Control condition is undoubtedly a matter of chance ($t = 0.58$).

How Much They Learned from the Experiment

The results on this question are shown in the second row of figures in Table 1. The question was included because, as far as we could see, it had nothing to do with the dissonance that was experimentally created and could not be used for dissonance reduction. One would then expect no differences at all among the three conditions. We felt it was important to show that the effect was not a completely general one but was specific to the content of the dissonance which was created. As can be readily seen in Table 1, there are only negligible differences among conditions. The highest t value for any of these differences is only 0.48.

DISCUSSION OF A POSSIBLE ALTERNATIVE EXPLANATION

We mentioned in the introduction that Janis and King (1954; 1956) in explaining their findings, proposed an explanation in terms of the self-convincing effect of mental rehearsal and thinking up new arguments by the person who had to improvise a speech. Kelman (1953), in the previously mentioned study, in attempting to explain the unexpected finding that the persons who complied in the moderate reward condition changed their opinion more than in the high reward condition, also proposed the same kind of explanation. If the results of our experiment are to be taken as strong corroboration of the theory of cognitive dissonance, this possible alternative explanation must be dealt with.

Specifically, as applied to our results, this alternative explanation would maintain that perhaps, for some reason, the *S*s in the One Dollar condition worked harder at telling the waiting girl that the tasks were fun and enjoyable. That is, in the One Dollar condition they may have rehearsed it more mentally, thought up more ways of saying it, may have said it more convincingly, and so on. Why this might have been the case is, of course, not immediately apparent. One might expect that, in the Twenty Dollar condition, having been paid more, they would try to do a better job of it than in the One Dollar condition. But nevertheless, the possibility exists that the *S*s in the One Dollar condition may have improvised more.

Because of the desirability of investigating this possible alternative explanation, we recorded on a tape recorder the conversation between each *S* and the girl. These recordings were transcribed and then rated, by two independent raters, on five dimensions. The ratings were, of course done in ignorance of which condition each *S* was in. The reliabilities of these ratings, that is, the correlations between the two independent raters, ranged from .61 to .88, with an average reliability of .71. The five ratings were:

1. The content of what the *S* said *before* the girl made the remark that her friend told her it was boring. The stronger the *S*'s positive statements about the tasks, and the more ways in which he said they were interesting and enjoyable, the higher the rating.
2. The content of what the *S* said *after* the girl made the above-mentioned remark. This was rated in the same way as for the content before the remark.
3. A similar rating of the overall content of what the *S* said.

4. A rating of how persuasive and convincing the *S* was in what he said and the way in which he said it.
5. A rating of the amount of time in the discussion that the *S* spent discussing the tasks as opposed to going off into irrelevant things.

The mean ratings for the One Dollar and Twenty Dollar conditions, averaging the ratings of the two independent raters, are presented in Table 2. It is clear from examining the table that, in all cases, the Twenty Dollar condition is slightly higher. The differences are small, however, and only on the rating of "amount of time" does the difference between the two conditions even approach significance. We are certainly justified in concluding that the *S*s in the One Dollar condition did not improvise more nor act more convincingly. Hence, the alternative explanation discussed above cannot account for the findings.

SUMMARY

Recently, Festinger (1957) has proposed a theory concerning cognitive dissonance. Two derivations from this theory are tested here. These are:

TABLE 2 / Average Ratings of Discussion between Subject and Girl

	Condition		
Dimensions Rated	One Dollar	Twenty Dollars	Value of *t*
Content before remark by girl (rated from 0 to 5)	2.26	2.62	1.08
Content after remark by girl (rated from 0 to 5)	1.63	1.75	0.11
Over-all content (rated from 0 to 5)	1.89	2.19	1.08
Persuasiveness and conviction (rated from 0 to 10)	4.79	5.50	0.99
Time spent on topic (rated from 0 to 10)	6.74	8.19	1.80

1. If a person is induced to do or say something which is contrary to his private opinion, there will be a tendency for him to change his opinion so as to bring it into correspondence with what he has done or said.
2. The larger the pressure used to elicit the overt behavior (beyond the minimum needed to elicit it) the weaker will be the above-mentioned tendency.

A laboratory experiment was designed to test these derivations. Subjects were subjected to a boring experience and then paid to tell someone that the experience had been interesting and enjoyable. The amount of money paid the subject was varied. The private opinions of the subjects concerning the experiences were then determined.

The results strongly corroborate the theory that was tested.

REFERENCES

Festinger, L. *A theory of cognitive dissonance.* Evanston, Ill.: Row Peterson, 1957.

Janis, I. L., & King, B. T. The influence of role-playing on opinion change. *Journal of Abnormal and Social Psychology,* 1954, *49,* 211–218.

Kelman, H. Attitude change as a function of response restriction. *Human Relations,* 1953, *6,* 185–214.

King, B. T., & Janis, I. L. Comparison of the effectiveness of improvised versus non-improvised role-playing in producing opinion changes. *Human Relations,* 1956, *9,* 177–186.

ENDNOTE

1. All statistical tests referred to in this paper are two-tailed.

CRITICAL THINKING QUESTIONS

1. Using the concept of dissonance theory, select an attitude or belief that you might want to change and design a procedure that could be effective in producing change in the desired direction.
2. This study was cited in Article 2 as an example of some of the ethical issues in social psychological research. What do you see as the ethical issues present in this experiment? Do you see any alternative to deception in this type of study? Why or why not?
3. Based on personal experience, have you ever suspected that cognitive dissonance was operating in some change that came about in your own attitudes? Elaborate on how that may have occurred.
4. Festinger and Carlsmith discuss a possible alternative explanation for the obtained results. What is your position on this alternative explanation? Discuss any other possible explanations for the findings of the study.
5. Might cognitive dissonance be operating in many real-life situations? For example, consider the initiation process (known as *hazing*) used in some social groups, such as fraternities, or the procedures used in the military as part of basic training. How might cognitive dissonance be operating in these or other situations to account for the outcomes of the experience?

ADDITIONAL RELATED READINGS

Heine, S. J., & Lehman, D. R. (1997). Culture, dissonance, and self-affirmation. *Personality and Social Psychology Bulletin, 23,* 389–400.

Petty, R. E., Wegener, D. T., & Fabrigar, L. R. (1997). Attitudes and attitude change. *Annual Review of Psychology, 48,* 609–647.

ARTICLE 12 _____

In the years since publication of Festinger and Carlsmith's classic study (Article 11), many experiments have been done to test dissonance theory and to elaborate on the conditions necessary for its operation. As it turns out, there are many different causes of dissonance. For example, dissonance may be aroused when a great deal of effort is involved in a given activity, as if a person needed to justify his or her expending so much effort to obtain a certain goal; this is sort of a "suffering leads to liking" effect. Dissonance will also likely be aroused when an individual has the freedom of choice to do (or not do) something. There is little reason to experience dissonance when you are forced to do something. You know why you did it: Someone *made* you do it. Finally, issues such as self-esteem may have an impact on the arousal (and subsequent reduction) of cognitive dissonance. People with higher levels of self-esteem may actually be *more* likely to engage in dissonance reduction than those with low levels of self-esteem when they see their behavior as being inconsistent with their beliefs.

Just as there are many causes of dissonance, so, too, there are multiple ways in which dissonance can be reduced once it has been aroused. For example, an individual could rationalize that there really is no inconsistency by reducing the cognition that led to the feelings of inconsistency in the first place. In other words, people can change how they think about a certain behavior, rather than change the behavior itself.

The following article by Frederick X. Gibbons, Tami J. Eggleston, and Alida C. Benthin examines the relationship between cognitive dissonance and self-esteem and success in quitting smoking. This article is an excellent example of a contemporary application of dissonance theory as well as an illustration of how this theory has practical applications to real-world problems.

Cognitive Reactions to Smoking Relapse
The Reciprocal Relation between Dissonance and Self-Esteem

■ Frederick X. Gibbons, Tami J. Eggleston, and Alida C. Benthin

Perceptions of health risk associated with smoking, commitment to quitting, and self-concept were assessed among smokers before, during, and after their participation in cessation clinics. Consistent with expectations derived from cognitive dissonance theory, results indicated that relapsers' perception of risk declined after they resumed smoking, although the decline was significant only for relapsers with high self-esteem; high self-esteem relapsers experienced a significantly greater decline in commitment to quitting than did low self-esteem relapsers; and decline in risk perception among relapsers was associated with maintenance of self-esteem. The implications of these results for dissonance theory and the study of smoking relapse and cessation are discussed.

When asked if they would like to quit, most people who smoke indicate that they would (U.S. Department of Health and Human Services [USDHHS], 1987), and eventually many of them do (up to 50%; USDHHS, 1989). However, before succeeding in quitting, they are likely to experience a number of failed attempts (three or more on average, Carmody,

1993). The frequency of smoking relapse has led researchers to invest considerable time in trying to figure out why so many smokers who have been able to quit have so much trouble maintaining abstinence (Brownell, Marlatt, Lichtenstein, & Wilson, 1986; Fisher, Haire-Joshu, Morgan, Rehberg, & Rost, 1990; Mermelstein, Karnatz, & Reichmann, 1992; Sutton, 1989; Wilson, 1992). In an effort to address this question, in the current study we focused on the impact of relapse on smokers' cognitions.

RISK PERCEPTIONS

When asked why they want to quit, the vast majority of smokers cite concern about the impact that smoking has on their health as the primary reason (Gibbons, McGovern, & Lando, 1991; Klesges, Brown, et al., 1988; Lando, 1989). Although it may not have been true as recently as 15 years ago (Mattson, Pollack, & Cullen, 1987), today most smokers claim to be well aware of the risks associated with their habit (Fisher et al., 1990; Greening & Dollinger, 1991). The extensive literature on risk perception that has accumulated during this period suggests that smokers recognize that their chances of developing smoking-related illnesses, such as emphysema and lung cancer, are elevated. Nonetheless, relative to nonsmokers, they still see less risk inherent in the behavior (Benthin, Slovic, & Severson, 1993; Klesges, Somes, et al., 1988; Lebovits & Strain, 1990; Lee, 1989; Viscusi, 1992).

Perceptions of risk or perceived vulnerability have been linked theoretically and empirically with a number of other health-relevant behaviors (see Janz & Becker, 1984). For example, the health belief model (Becker, 1974; Becker & Rosenstock, 1987), which is typical of most theories in the area (e.g., precaution adoption [Weinstein, 1988] and protection motivation theory [Rogers, 1983]), maintains that perceived vulnerability to negative outcomes is a determining factor in the decision to engage in virtually all health-promoting and health-harming behaviors, including smoking and smoking cessation (Flay et al., 1994; Pederson, Wanklin, & Baskerville, 1984). In particular, perceptions of health risk have been shown to be negatively related to intention to start smoking among adolescents (Flay et al., 1994; Leventhal, Glynn, & Fleming, 1987). Among current smokers,

risk perceptions are positively associated with intention to quit (Eiser, Sutton, & Wober, 1978; Klesges, Somes, et al., 1988; Prochaska, DiClemente, Velicer, Ginpil, & Norcross, 1985), with joining a cessation group (Boney-McCoy et al., 1992; Klesges, Brown, et al., 1988), with likelihood of initial quitting (Ho, 1989), and with number of previous quit attempts (Mullen, Hersey, & Iverson, 1987). The same is true with regard to perception of the benefits associated with smoking cessation. The greater the perceived benefits, the greater the intention to stop smoking (Sutton, 1987; Velicer, DiClemente, & Prochaska, 1985). Almost all of this research has examined the relation between risk perception and smoking intention, however. Regarding actual smoking behavior, including abstinence, it has been suggested that current perceptions of smoking risk and the benefits of quitting may be related to the ability to maintain abstinence among those who have already quit, but to date that relation has not been examined empirically (Mermelstein et al., 1992).

The Cognitive Impact of Relapse

Given the importance of risk perception and the high failure rate of cessation attempts, determining the effect that resumption of smoking has on risk perception is of considerable interest. More generally, the cognitive impact that smoking resumption has on the relapsed smoker may very well contribute to both the likelihood and the success of subsequent quit attempts and therefore appears to be an important consideration (Brownell et al., 1986; Mermelstein et al., 1992). And yet this topic has received relatively little empirical attention (Marlatt & Gordon's 1985 work on the impact of relapse on self-perception—the "abstinence violation effect"—is an important exception).

Change in Risk Perception

One study has examined this issue directly. Gibbons, McGovern, et al. (1991) assessed health risk perceptions among smokers before, during, and after a quit attempt. Results indicated that risk perceptions, which were quite high at the time these smokers started the quit program, declined significantly among those who relapsed. In a related study,

Gerrard, Gibbons, Benthin, and Hessling (1996) found that adolescents who increased their health risk behavior over time (i.e., smoking, drinking, and reckless driving) reported a corresponding increase in perceived health risk but a significant decline in how much concern about health was likely to influence their smoking behavior. In other words, they realized that what they were doing was risky, but they decided not to let this awareness influence their behavior. Because risk perception is associated with intention to quit, a decline in either risk perception or concern about risk among smokers would presumably be associated with a decline in commitment to quitting. In fact, this is what Gibbons, McGovern, et al. suggested, although they did not collect the data needed to test this hypothesis.

RISK PERCEPTIONS AND COGNITIVE DISSONANCE

Realizing that one's behavior is endangering one's health is certainly likely to arouse cognitive dissonance, which is why both Gibbons, McGovern, et al. (1991) and Gerrard et al. (1996) suggested that dissonance reduction may have been responsible for the changes in cognitions evidenced in their studies. In fact, there is a long history in social psychology, dating back to Festinger's (1957) original statement of the theory, of using smoking behavior as a means of illustrating the dissonance reduction process (this is still the case in many current textbooks). Festinger suggested that one way smokers reduce the dissonance produced by the realization that they are engaging in an "unwise" behavior is to "change his knowledge" about that behavior. Smokers may question the validity of the research linking smoking with disease, for example, or perhaps minimize their personal risk. In fact, several studies have demonstrated such skepticism about risk among smokers (Feather, 1962; Johnson, 1968; Pervin & Yatko, 1965). Those studies were conducted before the 1964 Surgeon General's report (U.S. Surgeon General's Advisory Committee on Smoking and Health, 1964) had a real impact on public awareness, however, and so denial of risk was still a reasonable option. Today, the evidence linking illness and smoking is even more compelling and much more widely accepted (USDHHS, 1990; Viscusi, 1992). Nonetheless, results of the Gibbons,

McGovern, et al. (1991) study suggest that altering their estimates of personal smoking danger may still be a method of dissonance reduction used by smokers.

Dissonance and Ego Threat

Another method of dealing with smoking-induced dissonance was suggested by Steele (1988; Steele, Spencer, & Lynch, 1993). He asserted that smokers may cope with the ego threat posed by awareness of smoking danger (specifically, "its implication that one is foolish or unable to control behavior," Steele, 1988, p. 262) by affirming or reaffirming their self-worth on some other dimension, such as personality. Although this certainly does not eliminate the cognitive inconsistency, it mitigates its impact on self-esteem. According to this perspective, cognitive dissonance poses a threat to self-esteem, which prompts some kind of response. The response—either reduction of the dissonance or self-affirmation—should, theoretically, serve an ego-protective function (cf. Tesser & Cornell, 1991).

Dissonance and Self-Esteem

Steele (1988) suggested that self-esteem not only affects dissonance reduction but is affected by it, as well. Specifically, he argued that a dissonance-provoking act should elicit more efforts at rationalization among low self-esteem persons than among high self-esteem persons, because they have fewer "worth-conferring self-aspects" or favorable alternative dimensions to rely on for self-affirmation. In contrast, high self-esteem persons, by definition, have a greater number of positive self-dimensions to consider when one dimension is threatened and thus should be less responsive to a particular threat to their self-image. As Steele et al. (1993) acknowledged, however, there is some disagreement on the question of how self-esteem is related to dissonance reduction. In particular, Aronson (1969, 1994) has maintained for some time that low self-esteem persons are less likely than high self-esteem persons to react to dissonance. His reasoning is that persons with low self-esteem are more accustomed to, and therefore less disturbed by, internal inconsistencies.

This latter perspective is generally congruent with another body of literature regarding self-esteem that indicates that, relative to people with high self-esteem, people with low self-esteem are more willing to accept information that suggests they have performed poorly or somehow been negligent (Brockner, 1979; Shrauger & Kelly, 1988), less self-serving in their attributions for failure (Bradley, 1978), more likely to acknowledge the riskiness of their own behavior (Smith, Gerrard, & Gibbons, in press), and more willing to change their attitudes and their behavior when confronted with information that suggests their behavior has been inappropriate or ineffective (Cohen, 1959; Knight & Nadel, 1986). Sometimes this lack of intransigence can be beneficial. Regarding health behavior, for example, students with low self-esteem have been shown to be more willing than high self-esteem students to change their attitudes toward birth control after learning that those attitudes could put them at risk for unplanned pregnancy (Gerrard, Kurylo, & Reis, 1991).

In short, when the inconsistency between attitude and behavior is attributable to the latter's being clearly inappropriate or unwise and therefore threatens self-esteem, low self-esteem persons appear to be less likely, and high self-esteem people more likely, to respond in a defensive manner. As Baumeister, Heatherton, and Tice (1993) suggested, ego threat causes high self-esteem people to "develop an overriding concern with maximizing their esteem, and this overriding concern appears sufficient to influence their behavioral judgment—and not always in optimal or adaptive ways" (p. 143). One implication of this reasoning is that the type of defensiveness demonstrated by the relapsers in the Gibbons, McGovern, et al. (1991) study, in terms of reduced risk perception, may be more pronounced among those with high self-esteem. If that is the case, it would suggest that this change in risk perception may serve an esteem-protective function.

OVERVIEW OF THE CURRENT STUDY

In the current study we had two distinct but related goals. One was to use dissonance theory to investigate further the cognitive changes that have been demonstrated to occur after smoking relapse (Gibbons, McGovern, et al., 1991). The second was the reverse of the first: to use smoking relapse as a means of investigating reactions to cognitive dissonance, specifically, the nature of the apparent reciprocal relation between dissonance reduction and self-esteem. We addressed the following specific questions:

1. Does self-esteem moderate the decline in health risk perception that accompanies relapse? In particular, is the decline greater among high self-esteem relapsers, as the defensiveness literature (see Baumeister, 1993) would suggest? Greater decline among high self-esteem relapsers would provide further support for the contention that the decline is evidence of dissonance reduction.

2. Is decline in risk perception a reaction to relapse or a precursor of it? If the decline is an indication of dissonance reduction, as expected (cf. Gibbons, McGovern, et al., 1991), it should occur after the relapse.

3. Does the dissonance reduction reflected in the (anticipated) reduction in risk perception among high self-esteem relapsers include a decline in their commitment to quitting?

4. Researchers have argued that dissonance reduction can reduce the "self-image distress" associated with the recognition of dissonance (Steele, 1988; Steele et al., 1993), just as self-affirmation can reduce the need for dissonance reduction (Tesser & Cornell, 1991). Thus our final hypothesis was that risk perception decline would have a self-esteem maintenance effect for relapsed smokers.

We tested these hypotheses with a sample of adult smokers who had joined cessation clinics. We assessed risk perception and commitment to quitting at the beginning and end of the clinics and 6 and 12 months after them. In addition, we assessed self-concept at the beginning of the clinics and 6 months after them. We compared high and low self-esteem abstainers and relapsers (i.e., smoking status at the 6-month follow-up) on each dimension.

METHOD

Participants

Participants had responded to newspaper ads placed by the American Lung Association of Iowa for stop-smoking clinics. All cessation groups were initiated and led by local lay facilitators, most of whom were former smokers and group participants. Packets were distributed in 52 groups to a total of about 270 people. About 5% declined to participate, and 2% returned questionnaires with too many missing responses to be usable, leaving a Time 1 *N* of 250. Of this initial group, 200 returned questionnaires at the 6-month follow-up. Of these 200 participants, 2 provided unusable data and 24 more had dropped out of the clinic shortly after the first session. We collected data from these 26 people but did not include them in the final analyses because their situations were not comparable to those of the others. The remaining 50 non-responders were fairly evenly divided into those who could not be contacted (wrong addresses, typically) and those who chose not to return the questionnaire. This return rate of 80% is considered good for follow-up surveys through the mail (Dillman, 1991).

The final sample of 174 participants had the following characteristics: Thirty-nine percent of them were male; they had a mean age of 42; they had been smoking for 24 years, with a current average of 27 cigarettes per day; and 95% of them had at least a high school diploma, with 63% having at least some college experience. More than 90% of the participants were White. These means are typical of cessation clinic participants, who tend to be better educated and to smoke more than smokers in the general population (McGovern, Lando, Roski, Pirie, & Sprafka, 1994).

Procedure

The Groups   The smoking cessation program was administered by the American Lung Association and followed a procedure developed by Lando (1993). The introductory session was followed by 12–15 sessions over an 8-week period, with all participants agreeing to quit together at the 6th session (in fact, 5% relapsed within 24 hr of the quit date). Each session lasted about an hour. Discussion focused on experiences (e.g., problems and successes) that participants had in their efforts to quit. The topic of health risk came up on occasion, but it was not broached by the facilitator and there was no formal discussion of any specific illnesses or health dangers; thus, no infor-

mation directly pertinent to the questions addressed in the study was provided in the groups.

Data Collection   During the first session, the facilitator asked all members if they would be willing to participate in a study concerning health and other issues related to smoking, in return for some payment—anywhere from $3 to $30 depending on how many questionnaires they returned. We collected data for the current study during the first and final group sessions (T1 and T2) and then by mail 6 months after the group quit date. In addition, we sent 12-month follow-up questionnaires to the 174 participants who had provided usable data at the 6-month follow-up, and of these participants 137 (79%) responded. The number of participants at each of the four waves is presented in Table 1.

Measures

In addition to the background information mentioned above, we elicited from participants the number of times they had made a serious effort to quit smoking, the two main reasons they wanted to quit smoking, whether they currently had or previously had had any serious illnesses (e.g., heart disease), and the names and phone numbers of two people whom we could call in the future to verify their smoking status.

Primary Dependent Measures   We measured self-esteem at T1 using the Rosenberg (1965) Self-Esteem Scale, a widely used and well-validated instrument. In addition, participants evaluated themselves on 11 adjectives (*smart, friendly, self-centered, attractive, honest, considerate, moody, dependent, irrational, weak,* and *reliable*), each followed by a 125-mm line with the anchors *not at all* and *very*. We reverse-scored the 5 negative adjectives, added them to the 6 positive adjectives, and divided the total by 11 to form a self-concept index (on a 125-point scale).[1] We assessed perceived smoking risk by asking participants to estimate on a scale from 0 to 100% the likelihood that they would develop each of four diseases if they stopped smoking permanently (i.e., nonsmoking risk, an indication of the perceived health benefit of quitting) and if they continued to smoke (i.e., the perceived health risk of smoking). The illnesses were heart disease, lung cancer, a heart attack, and arthritis. We included arthritis to determine whether participants would make a distinction between illnesses that were related to smoking and those that were not. They did not (results were stronger on the first three items but not significantly so), and so we averaged responses to the four items for both smoking and nonsmoking risk. Finally, we asked participants to indicate how committed they were to quitting on a 125-mm line from *not at all* to *very.* We administered the Rosenberg scale only at T1; all other measures were presented at each period of data collection. Other measures, intended for a different study (Gibbons & Eggleston, 1996), included perceptions of the typical smoker (Gibbons, Gerrard, et al., 1991) and measures of self-efficacy and social comparison.

Abstinence At the 6-month follow-up, we asked participants whether they were smoking on that date (i.e., point prevalence) and if so, how many cigarettes and how long they had refrained from smoking after quitting. We asked those who were currently abstaining whether they had ever smoked during the 6-month period and, if so, how long. The same abstinence questions were asked at the 12-month follow-up. We also conducted analyses in which we reclassified abstainers as relapsers if they had smoked at any time in the previous 6 months. This did not alter the pattern of results. Analyses examining time to relapse (i.e., length of abstinence) are reported in the Results section.

Reliability Alpha for the Rosenberg scale at T1 was .83. In each of the three waves of data collection, alphas for the primary measures were as follows: For the smoking risk indexes, all $\alpha s > .78$; for the nonsmoking risk indexes, all $\alpha s > .72$; and for the self-concept indexes, all $\alpha s > .61$. Correlations of the same indexes across (consecutive) time periods were all greater than .49 (all $ps < .001$). These correlations would have been attenuated somewhat by the (predicted) change in perceptions over time. In addition, smoking risk and nonsmoking risk (health benefit) were highly correlated ($r = .59$ at T1, .56 at 6-month follow-up, and .55 at 12-month follow-up, all $ps < .001$), and they did covary over time (i.e., change in smoking risk over time was correlated with change in nonsmoking risk; all $rs > .53$, all $ps < .001$). Given the high correlations, for the purposes of data reduction, we subtracted nonsmoking risk from smoking risk to form a single index of risk perception (all $\alpha s \geq .70$). Although we conducted analyses on all three indexes, we report only the results from the risk perception index, except in instances where results on the smoking and nonsmoking risk indexes differed.

Attrition To check on the representativeness and comparability of the various subsamples, we conducted a series of group comparisons. We compared those who did respond at the 6-month follow-up with those (from T1) who did not, those who responded at the 12-month follow-up with those (from T1) who did not, and those who responded at both the 6-month and 12-month follow-ups with those who re-

TABLE 1 / Number of Participants Who Provided Usable Data at Each Time Period

Time Period	Total	Relapsers	Abstainers
Time 1	250	—	—
Time 2 (final session)	143[a]	26	102
6-month follow-up	174	104	70
12-month follow-up	137	79	58

Note: The final session *N* is relatively low because a number of participants (mostly relapsers) had stopped attending the group sessions.
[a]One hundred twenty-eight participants indicated their abstinence status (15 did not).

TABLE 2 / Change in Perceived Risk as a Function of Self-Esteem and Smoking Status at the 6- and 12-Month Follow-Ups

	Smoking Status at 6-Month Follow-Up			
	Relapsers		Abstainers	
Time	Low Self-Esteem	High Self-Esteem	Low Self-Esteem	High Self-Esteem
Time 1				
M	23.6	29.8	31.8	33.5
SD	14.6	17.3	15.6	16.7
6-month follow-up				
M	20.6	17.2*	28.4	33.7
SD	17.7	14.4	18.6	17.5
n	29	67	26	41
Time 1				
M	23.3	31.9	32.8	33.6
SD	13.9	18.5	16.1	16.8
6-month follow-up				
M	19.9	18.1*	28.1	33.3
SD	18.1	13.2	18.8	16.5
12-month follow-up				
M	23.2	17.8*	27.6	29.6
SD	16.5	15.6	14.6	15.2
n	19	42	23	31

Note: Perceived risk = smoking risk − nonsmoking risk. A higher score means greater perceived smoking risk. Because not all participants responded at the 12-month follow-up, the bottom half of the table presents data from a subset of the 6-month follow-up group presented in the top half of the table.
*Significant decline from Time 1 ($p < .001$).

sponded only at the 6-month follow-up. These analyses compared participants on every T1 measure (age, sex, smoking habits, risk perceptions, self-esteem, etc.). The only significant difference reflected the fact that those who dropped out between the 6- and 12-month follow-ups were younger than those who stayed in the study ($p = .01$). Thus, there was no evidence to suggest that those who did respond were different (at least on our measures) from those who did not. Also, the sample size for each analysis was less than the total sample size for that time period because of individual subjects having missing data. For example, of the 137 participants who responded at the 12-month follow-up, 117 had answered the risk and benefit questions at the 6- and 12-month follow-ups—a total of 16 items—plus the self-esteem scale at T1 and therefore were included in that analysis (see Table 2). When participants had only one missing variable on an index (e.g., self-esteem), we assigned a

mean value to that variable and included their data in the analyses.

RESULTS

Overview

We present the results in four sections according to dependent measure: perception of risk, change in perception of risk, change in commitment to quitting, and change in self-concept. We conducted initial analyses with three levels of self-esteem (i.e., a three-way split of the Rosenberg scale). Because the results of those analyses indicated that the means for the high and medium self-esteem participants were virtually identical and equally distinct from the means for the low self-esteem group, we combined the medium and high groups. We refer to these participants as the high self-esteem group, but it should be kept in mind that we are actually referring to the top two thirds of the self-esteem distribution. The primary analyses were repeated measures analyses of variance (ANOVAs) involving T1 and 6-month follow-up perceptions, followed in some cases by paired *t* tests. Smoking status refers to whether participants were smoking at the 6-month follow-up. As can be seen in Table 1, attendance at the final session (T2) was relatively low and somewhat unbalanced, because relapsers were more likely than abstainers to have dropped out of the group by that time. Nonetheless, we report secondary analyses, involving T2 and 12-month follow-up data, when they are informative and justified by sample size.

We repeated all of the primary analyses as covariance analyses, using the prior measure (e.g., T1) as a covariate in the analysis of the later measure (e.g., 6-month follow-up). In each case, the effects remained significant and the pattern unchanged (thus significant effects presented here were not due to mean differences at T1). For simplicity's sake, we report only the repeated measures analyses. Similarly, we repeated the primary analyses using all of the relevant background and demographic measures as covariates (e.g., age and education level), and again the results remained essentially unchanged. Finally, we included gender as a factor in all analyses; however, because it did not produce any significant effects, we do not report those analyses here.

Abstinence

Of the 174 participants who responded at the 6-month follow-up, 70 (40%) claimed that they were not smoking cigarettes at that time. That figure is somewhat high (see Mermelstein et al., 1992), but not atypical of the Lando method (Lando, 1993). The number (58, or 42%) of respondents who reported abstinence at 12 months was also high, suggesting that relapsers may have been somewhat less likely to have returned our questionnaires. To check on their abstinence claims, we contacted persons listed by the participants (at T1) as being knowledgeable about their smoking status ("significant other verification," Ossip-Klein et al., 1991). We were able to contact verifiers for 50 of the 70 abstainers after the 6-month follow-up. We could not reach the other 20 because

we had the wrong phone number, they had moved, and so on. Of the 50 contact persons we reached, 46 verified the participant's claim and 3 others said they were fairly certain the participant was not smoking. Only one person disputed the participant's claim of abstinence. One factor that may have contributed to this apparent high percentage of accurate self-reporting is the fact that our study and questionnaires were clearly independent of the cessation clinic. However, efforts by previous researchers to verify abstinence claims with biochemical tests (e.g., saliva cotinine) have suggested that 95–100% of the claims are typically verified (see a review by Velicer, Prochaska, Rossi, & Snow, 1992). Thus, although it is quite possible that some of the participants in this study who claimed to be abstinent were not, that number was most likely very small.

Health Risk

Health Concern As in previous studies, concern about health was listed as a primary reason for quitting by almost the entire sample (89%).

T1 and 6-Month Follow-Up Analyses Means for the T1 risk index are presented in Table 2. In absolute terms, participants' risk perceptions were higher than is medically true (Lee, 1989; Viscusi, 1992); this was the case for both smoking and non-smoking risk (Centers for Disease Control and Prevention, 1993; Kristiansen, Harding, & Eiser, 1983).[2] These high perceptions are typical of smokers entering cessation clinics, however (Gibbons, McGovern, et al., 1991; Klesges, Brown, et al., 1988). A Self-Esteem × (eventual) Smoking Status ANOVA on these T1 risk indexes indicated that abstainers had higher risk perceptions at that time ($p = .03$).[3] Self-esteem was not a factor in T1 perceptions, however; it showed no main effect ($p > .13$) and did not correlate with T1 risk perception among relapsers or abstainers (all $ps > .12$). A repeated measures analysis of perceived risk at T1 and 6-month follow-up (see top half of Table 2) revealed a Smoking Status × Time interaction consistent with that found by Gibbons, McGovern, et al. (1991), $F(1, 159) = 4.80$, $p = .03$, in that relapsers lowered their risk perceptions considerably ($p < .001$), whereas abstainers' perceptions did not change significantly (*t*(159) < 1.00). In addition, this interaction was moderated by self-esteem, as indicated by a significant Smoking Status × Self-Esteem × Time interaction, *F*(1, 159) = 5.82, *p* = .02. The pattern of this interaction was as expected: Relapsers with low self-esteem did not lower their perceived risk significantly (*M* = –3.0), *t*(159) < 1.0, *p* > .35, whereas relapsers with high self-esteem reported a substantial drop (*M* = –12.6), *t*(159) = 6.21, *p* < .001 (see Figure 1). The difference in risk perception change among the relapsers was independent of their actual consumption: The number of cigarettes smoked per day did not correlate with self-esteem at either T1 or 6-month follow-up, and change in risk perception did not correlate with change in actual consumption (all *r*s < .07).

We also conducted regression analyses on these dependent measures. The results were very compa-

FIGURE 1 / Change in Perceived Risk from Smoking from Time 1 to 6-Month Follow-Up as a Function of Self-Esteem (SE) and Smoking Status

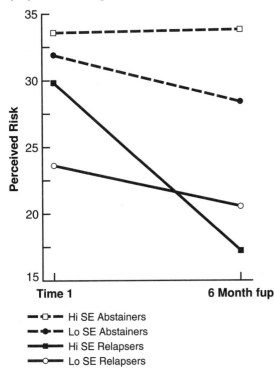

rable to those presented here, although they were somewhat weaker, largely because there were no significant differences between the high and medium self-esteem persons (i.e., the relation between self-esteem and risk perception change was not linear). Finally, the change pattern was similar across the four diseases, but, as might be expected, it was weakest on arthritis and heart attack, stronger on heart disease, and strongest on lung cancer. Generally speaking, the more closely the disease was actually linked to smoking, the more high self-esteem relapsers lowered their perception of its likelihood.

Change between 6- and 12-Month Follow-Up Repeated measures ANOVAs conducted on the three waves of data (see bottom half of Table 2) also revealed a Smoking Status × Self-Esteem × Time interaction, *F*(2, 222) = 4.41, *p* = .01. Focusing on just the change from 6-month follow-up to 12-month follow-up, high self-esteem relapsers' perceptions stayed about the same (*M* = –.03), whereas low self-esteem relapsers' perceptions increased slightly to a level comparable to where they were at T1. Once again, there were no significant changes in the abstainers' perceptions.

Risk versus Benefit Although the patterns of responses on the smoking and nonsmoking risk indexes were very similar, separate analyses of the two did provide two additional pieces of information: (a) The pattern was somewhat stronger for perceptions of smoking risk, because the high self-esteem relapsers reported the greatest decline on this index; (b) however, that same group was the only one to report an increase (albeit slight) in nonsmoking risk (i.e., a decline in the perceived benefit of stopping smoking). In short, changes in both perceived risk and perceived benefit contributed to the overall effect.

Change in Risk Perception as a Function of Smoking Status Change

Smoking Status at T2 In an attempt to determine when the change in risk perception occurred, we conducted two additional sets of analyses including the T2 (final group session) data. The first analysis categorized participants according to their T2 smoking status (20% of the sample had already relapsed by T2). A Smoking Status × Self-Esteem × Time repeated measures ANOVA on the T1/T2 responses revealed no effects, because the high self-esteem participants who had relapsed by T2 had not yet lowered their risk perception, which should have happened if the decline preceded the relapse. Their perceptions did drop subsequently (by the 6-month follow-up), but not significantly ($p = .09$). As can be seen in Table 3, there was a significant decline in risk perception among the low self-esteem abstainers by the 6-month follow-up, $t(224) = 2.05, p = .04$. This change was not anticipated, and we do not discuss it further.

T2 to 6-Month Follow-Up   The second analysis categorized participants into three groups as a function of change in status from T2 to 6-month follow-up (continued relapse, change from abstinence to relapse, and continued abstinence; see Table 3). This analysis revealed a main effect of time, with risk perceptions declining at each period, $F(2, 224) = 7.28, p < .001$. There were no other significant main effects. There was a significant Smoking Status × Time (T1, T2, and

6-month follow-up) interaction, however, $F(4, 224) = 2.46, p = .05$, which in turn was qualified by a Smoking Status × Self-Esteem × Time interaction, $F(4, 224) = 3.27, p = .01$. As can be seen in Table 3, high self-esteem participants who relapsed between T2 and the 6-month follow-up did report a significant drop in risk perception by the follow-up ($M = -17.4$), $t(224) = 5.49, p < .001$. With the exception of a tendency for continued relapsers to report some decline (mentioned above), there were no other significant changes in risk perception from T2 to the 6-month follow-up. Finally, neither T2 risk perception nor change in risk perception from T1 to T2 predicted 6-month smoking status (all $ps > .30$). In sum, there was no evidence that decline in risk perception preceded or predicted relapse; instead, the pattern was consistent with the idea that decline follows relapse (Gibbons, McGovern, et al., 1991).

Time to Relapse   As can be seen in Table 3, one reason there was not a significant decline at T2 among participants with high self-esteem who had relapsed by that time was that their original (T1) perceptions

TABLE 3 / Change in Perceived Risk as a Function of Self-Esteem and Change in Smoking Status from Time 2 (T2) to 6-Month Follow-Up

| | Smoking Status from T2 to 6-Month Follow-Up | | | | | |
| | Continued Relapse[a] | | Abstinence to Relapse[b] | | Continued Abstinence[c] | |
Time	Low Self-Esteem	High Self-Esteem	Low Self-Esteem	High Self-Esteem	Low Self-Esteem	High Self-Esteem
Time 1 (T1)						
M	24.4	25.5	23.8	39.9	32.2	31.3
SD	14.7	15.5	15.1	15.1	15.8	12.4
T2						
M	30.4	25.8	20.2	37.6	25.5*	33.1
SD	12.7	14.9	16.6	18.6	14.4	17.4
6-month follow-up						
M	24.5	19.5	20.8	20.2**	26.6	31.2
SD	20.6	14.5	17.2	13.9	18.4	17.6
n	7	19	12	24	23	33

Note: T2 was the final group session.
[a]Relapsed at T2 and at 6-month follow-up.
[b]Abstinent at T2 but relapsed at 6-month follow-up.
[c]Abstinent at both T2 and 6-month follow-up.
*Significant decline from T1 ($p \leq 05$).
**Significant decline from T1 and T2 ($p \leq .001$).

were relatively low ($M = 25.5$). This implies a relation, among relapsers, between initial risk perception and how long they maintained abstinence. In fact, the correlation between initial risk perception and time to relapse (i.e., how long they abstained) was significant ($r = .32$ for all relapsers and .41 for high self-esteem relapsers; both $ps < .001$). Moreover, the correlation between time to relapse and change in risk perception from T1 to the 6-month follow-up was $-.25$ ($-.37$ for high self-esteem relapsers; $p = .01$ and .002, respectively). Thus, the more risk the relapsers perceived at T1, the longer they stayed abstinent, and, ironically, the longer they stayed abstinent, the more their risk perceptions eventually declined.

Commitment to Quit

Analyses conducted on the commitment to quit question with all participants at T1 revealed no differences as a function of self-esteem or eventual smoking status (all $ps > .25$). We then performed Self-Esteem × Time repeated measures ANOVAs on the commitment question at T1 and the 6-month follow-up for just the relapsers (the wording of the question for the relapsers at the 6-month follow-up was actually commitment to "making another quit attempt"). As can be seen in Table 4, the pattern of responses was similar to that on the risk perception measure. Once again, the Self-Esteem × Time interaction was significant, $F(1, 100) = 4.86$, $p = .03$, reflecting the fact that whereas both low and high self-esteem participants declined in commitment ($p = .002$ and $p < .0001$, respectively), the high self-esteem relapsers reported significantly greater decline than did the low self-esteem relapsers. When we included 12-month follow-up data (also in Table 4), the Self-Esteem × Time interaction remained significant, $F(2, 128) = 3.34$, $p = .04$. Participants with low self-esteem remained at the same level at 12-month follow-up (the T1 to 6-month follow-up drop was no longer significant, in part because including the 12-month responses reduced the sample size), whereas participants with high self-esteem reported a slight increase in commitment by that time.

The similarity between the response patterns for the risk perception and commitment variables suggested that a relation existed between them, and, in fact, correlational analyses provided evidence of that.

At T1, the correlation between the two was .31 for all participants and .39 for relapsers (both $ps < .001$). In addition, as risk perception declined over time, so did commitment ($r = .20$, $p = .05$).

Self-Concept

To determine what impact change in risk perception had on self-concept, we conducted repeated measures analyses on the self-concept indexes. For this analysis, we divided participants into those who lowered their perceptions of risk from T1 to the 6-month follow-up and those who did not (i.e., dissonance "reducers" vs. "nonreducers"). We then performed a Smoking Status × Risk Perception Change ANOVA on the self-concept measure, first at T1, followed by a repeated measures ANOVA on the T1 to the 6-month follow-up responses.

TABLE 4 / Change in Commitment to Quitting among Relapsers as a Function of Self-Esteem

	Self-Esteem	
Time	Low	High
T1 to 6-Month Follow-Up		
Time 1 (T1)		
M	100.3	104.1
SD	24.7	23.2
6-month follow-up		
M	81.7*	70.0**
SD	26.9	33.6
n	32	70
T1 to 12-Month Follow-Up		
T1		
M	97.0	106.2
SD	25.2	22.7
6-month follow-up		
M	83.8	70.4**
SD	26.2	33.1
12-month follow-up		
M	83.2	74.8**
SD	22.9	33.7
n	21	45

Note: Scale = 0–125; the higher the score, the stronger the commitment.
*Significant decline from T1 with $p < .01$.
**Significant decline from T1 with $p < .001$.

The first analysis indicated that self-concept did not vary at T1 as a function of eventual smoking status or change in risk perception (all $ps > .25$). The second analysis (see Table 5) revealed a Smoking Status × Change × Time interaction, indicating that change in self-concept varied as a function of smoking status and change in risk perception, as expected $F(1, 160) = 9.92$, $p = .002$. Among the relapsers, those whose perception of smoking risk declined reported no change in self-concept ($M = .8$), despite having failed at their attempt to quit smoking. Those relapsers whose risk perception did not lower (35% of the group) did report a significant decline in self-concept during that time period, however ($M = -4.4$), $t(160) = 2.28$, $p = .02$. The exact opposite pattern occurred among the abstainers, although the changes were not significant. Specifically, abstainers who decided smoking was not as dangerous as they first thought reported a marginal drop in self-concept ($p = .08$), whereas those whose perception of risk increased and who continued to abstain reported a nonsignificant ($p = .14$) increase in self-concept.

With one exception, this pattern did not vary as a function of T1 self-esteem, and the Smoking Status × Self-Esteem × Risk Perception Change ANOVA was not significant ($p > .50$). The exception was the fact that the decline in self-concept reported by the relapsers whose risk perception did not decline (see Table 5) was significant for the high self-esteem people in that group ($M = -6.45$, $p = .01$) but not for the low self-esteem people ($M = -1.52$, $p > .60$). Finally, consistent with the results of the ANOVA, correlational analyses indicated that change in self-concept correlated with change in nonsmoking risk among the abstainers ($r = -.39$, $p < .001$) and with change in smoking risk among the relapsers ($r = -.31$, $p = .002$). Thus, the more benefit the abstainers saw to abstaining over time, the better they felt about themselves at 6-month follow-up, whereas the more the relapsers lowered their risk perceptions, the better they felt about themselves. Unexpectedly, increase in nonsmoking risk also correlated with increase in self-concept, but only among low self-esteem relapsers ($r = .55$, $p < .001$).

Once again, we conducted regression analyses, this time using T1 self-concept, smoking status, change in risk perception, and the interaction of status and risk perception change to predict self-concept at the 6-month follow-up. We performed these analyses first on all participants and then separately (without smoking status) on the abstainers and relapsers. In other words, regression analyses were intended to replicate the ANOVA analyses, and they did; in each case, the results were the same as the ANOVA results presented here. In sum, change in risk perception appeared to have differential and interpretable effects on the self-concepts of abstainers and relapsers.

TABLE 5 / Change in Self-Concept as a Function of Change in Risk Perception from Time 1 (T1) to 6-Month Follow-Up

| Time | Smoking Status at 6-Month Follow-Up | | | |
| | Relapsers | | Abstainers | |
	Decrease in Risk Perception	No Decrease in Risk Perception	Decrease in Risk Perception	No Decrease in Risk Perception
T1				
M	82.5	84.8	84.9	83.8
SD	12.1	11.3	12.7	8.7
6-month follow-up				
M	83.3	80.4*	81.3	86.6
SD	11.2	11.7	11.8	9.9
n	64	34	31	35

Note: Scale = 0–125; the higher the score, the more favorable the self-concept.
*Significant change in self-concept ($p = .02$).

DISCUSSION

As many social psychology texts suggest, anyone who smokes cigarettes is likely to experience some dissonance if he or she is at all aware of the health risks associated with the behavior. The responses of the smokers in the current study indicate clearly that they were well aware of those risks. In fact, concern about health was listed as the primary reason for joining the cessation groups. Their perception of health risk, in turn, correlated with initial commitment to quitting and was inflated in comparison with actual risk (Viscusi, 1992). Given the important role that risk perceptions apparently played in prompting the decision to quit, we assume that the experience of dissonance was particularly intense for the relapsers in this study. Moreover, their method of reducing this dissonance appears to have followed classic textbook process. They could not alter their behavior or their awareness of their behavior, so they changed their attitude toward the behavior instead.

Dissonance and Self-Esteem: A Reciprocal Relation

The Effect of Self-Esteem on Dissonance Reduction

The fact that these changes in cognitions were more pronounced among persons with high or moderate levels of self-esteem than among persons whose self-esteem was low is consistent with Aronson's (1969) perspective on dissonance effects and with research on the defensive tendencies of people with high self-esteem. This pattern does not appear to be consistent with Steele's argument (1988; Steele et al., 1993) that people with high self-esteem feel less need to reduce dissonance through self-justification than do people with low self-esteem because they have other positive self-dimensions to turn to (i.e., they can self-affirm) when one dimension is threatened. His reasoning is compelling and was supported empirically by Steele et al. (1993). The dissonance that prompted the self-justification in their study was relatively mild, however (rationalizing a choice of one product over another), and it did not involve threat. Our results suggest that when the dissonance is produced by a realization that one has engaged in behavior that is clearly unsuccessful and unwise, that is, when the threat to self-esteem is sufficient, high self-esteem

persons—who may very well have a higher threshold for such an admission—will react more than will low self-esteem persons (Brockner & Elkind, 1985), and that reaction entails more defensiveness and, in some instances, more dissonance reduction. One reason for this may be that severe threat tends to interfere with self-affirmation. Specifically, when the threat is severe, as was undoubtedly the case in the current study, it remains salient, making it difficult to switch attention to other self-dimensions. It is quite possible that if we had reminded the relapsers with high and moderate self-esteem of their self-esteem before asking them the risk questions (cf. Steele et al., 1993), or if we had encouraged them to self-affirm beforehand, they may not have lowered their risk perceptions or their commitment to quitting as much. This is an empirical question that also has implications for intervention (see below).

Our results are also generally consistent with a growing body of literature suggesting that the defensiveness of high self-esteem people can get them into some trouble (Baumeister et al., 1993). It may result in lower outcomes, for example, because they are unwilling to abandon a strategy that has proven ineffective (Knight & Nadel, 1986). It may also have a harmful effect on their health. In particular, they may be at greater risk of pregnancy because they are unwilling to admit that their previous sexual behavior has been risky (Gerrard et al., 1991; Smith et al., in press), or at greater risk for developing smoking-related illness because they rationalize (especially after relapse) that smoking is not all that dangerous. There is even evidence that because they are more willing to take risks (Baumeister, Tice, & Hutton, 1989), high self-esteem persons are more likely to choose to engage in behaviors that put their health in jeopardy, such as riding motorcycles or driving after drinking (Pelham, 1992).

The Effect of Dissonance Reduction on Self-Esteem

The experience of dissonance is generally aversive and often threatening to the self-concept (Steele, 1988). This being the case, there is every reason to expect that the type of dissonance associated with smoking relapse would have a noticeable impact on self-esteem. This was not true in the current study, however, for most of the smokers who relapsed. One group who did report a decline were the relapsers who increased their perceptions of risk. What this suggests is that lowering risk perception, which is typical of most relapsers, reduces the dissonance associated with the relapse, thereby protecting self-esteem. More generally, this type of dissonance reduction, like self-affirmation, apparently can serve a self-protective function. Once again, however, the long-term consequences of this protection may prove unhealthy.

Risk Perception and Commitment

Timing of the Perception Change   As in the Gibbons, McGovern, et al. (1991) study, risk perception declined among smokers who relapsed in the current study. Although we could not determine exactly when the decline took place (that would have required assessing smokers' risk perceptions shortly *before* they relapsed and again afterwards, which is very difficult to do), the pattern once again was consistent with the belief that it occurs after relapse. First, and most important, there was no evidence in the T2 data that either participants who had already relapsed or those who were about to relapse (between T2 and the 6-month follow-up) had lowered their risk perception by that time. Second, neither T2 perception nor change in perception from T1 to T2 predicted eventual smoking status. On the other hand, there was significant change among high self-esteem relapsers by the 6-month follow-up, and that was true whether they had relapsed before the final session or between the final session and the follow-up.

Commitment   Gibbons, McGovern, et al. (1991) also hypothesized that a decline in risk perception after relapse is accompanied by a decline in commitment to quitting. The hypothesis is a logical derivation of the literature linking risk perception with commitment, but the question had never been examined longitudinally. The current results support the hypothesis, in that commitment did decline significantly for all relapsers, but it declined much (i.e., significantly) more so for those who were high in self-esteem. Also, the correlation between risk perception and commitment was strong at T1 ($r = .31$); however, although the two did decline together, that correla-

tion was weaker at the 6-month follow-up ($r = .20$, $p < .05$) than it had been at T1. Similarly, risk perception was strongly related to "hold-out time" among relapsers ($r = .32$), and it was a significant but modest predictor of eventual outcome ($p = .05$; Avis, Smith, & McKinlay, 1989). This pattern of relations is complex, but an explanation can be offered.

When smokers decide to quit, their risk perception is high and is an important motivating factor. Those with relatively benign perceptions of smoking risk are likely to relapse early, whereas those who are more convinced of its perniciousness hold out longer. Some of the latter group eventually relapse (for a variety of reasons that we did not tap into in this study), and their risk perceptions on average then decline. On the other hand, as abstainers perceive more and more psychological distance between themselves and the behavior (as well as those who do it; Gibbons, Gerrard, et al., 1991), risk perception becomes less of an issue for them, to the point where it is only weakly related to maintenance. The overall result is a decline over time in the relation between risk perception and the desire to avoid smoking.

Implications for Smoking Cessation

Risk Perception and Relapse   One possibility raised by these data is that the decline in risk perception among high self-esteem relapsers, which appeared to have stabilized from the 6- to 12-month follow-up, was an indication that their interest in quitting was permanently dampened. There are two reasons why we do not believe this was the case and, in turn, why we do believe these data allow some optimism. First, there was evidence of a slight increase in commitment from the 6-month to the 12-month follow-up among the relapsers with high self-esteem. Second, the correlation between the number of previous quit attempts and risk perception at T1 was positive for all participants ($r = .20$, $p = .009$) and was especially strong among the relapsers ($r = .36$, $p < .001$). Thus, the more failed quit attempts a smoker had experienced, the higher his or her initial perception of smoking risk. If the decline in risk perception after each relapse were cumulative, a negative correlation would have been expected. Instead, what the correlation suggests is that risk perception eventually rebounds after relapse (cf. Weinstein, 1988); in fact, the positive correlation suggests it may rebound to a level even higher than it was before. When risk perception reaches a certain threshold again, the individual may then attempt to quit again.

Relapse Prevention   There are several suggestions raised by the current data that are relevant to interventions aimed at relapse prevention. First, allowing high self-esteem relapsers in cessation clinics to self-affirm shortly after relapse on some other dimension (e.g., to describe publicly some aspect of themselves that they consider to be particularly worthwhile) may serve to counter the need for the dissonance reduction evident in the decline in risk perception and commitment to quitting (Boney-McCoy, Gibbons, & Gerrard, 1996; Steele, 1988; Tesser & Cornell, 1991). The utility of this idea might be tested in a clinical trial. Second, public commitment significantly increases both the amount of and reactions to dissonance (Pervin & Yatko, 1965; Wicklund & Brehm, 1976). One potential drawback of being in a cessation group, then, is that it may lead to an even greater desire to lower one's risk perceptions—that is, reduce dissonance—after relapse. In contrast, it is possible that people trying to quit smoking on their own do not change their perceptions nearly as much, because they have not made a public commitment to quitting and therefore have not experienced as much dissonance. It should be kept in mind, however, that treatment programs do tend to be more successful than self-quit attempts (Curry, 1993; Lando, 1989); thus the "risk" associated with being in a group may not be a concern.

Timing   The current results support the contention of Mermelstein et al. (1992) that interventions intended to reduce the likelihood of relapse should include review of health risk information. These researchers raised the question of whether it is better to recycle relapsers back into cessation programs shortly after they have resumed smoking or to wait until they have had time to recover from the failure experience. Our data on this point are mixed. On one hand, there is some evidence that risk perceptions and commitment to quitting may come around on their own after relapse, and it is possible that reminding high self-esteem relapsers of their failure shortly after it happens may backfire and actually reduce interest in subsequent attempts. On the other hand, risk perceptions do appear to have some motivating value, and, of course, the longer a smoker waits to initiate another quit attempt, the more health damage is likely to occur in the interim. In short, although the current results are informative, the timing question remains open to debate.

Limitations of the Study

Several limitations of this study need to be reviewed. First, although response rates at the 6- and 12-month follow-ups were high, the possibility remains that those who chose to respond differed from nonresponders in terms of how much their risk perceptions had changed by the time they responded, even though all analyses indicated that their perceptions had not differed initially at T1. Second, our sample reflected the ethnic composition of the state from which it came (Iowa is more than 95% White). We have no reason to expect that a sample with a greater percentage of minorities would respond differently, but we also have no way of knowing at this point. Also, it is possible that the cognitive reactions to relapse that we identified may differ among people who try to quit on their own. For example, not having made a public commitment to quitting, they may experience less need to alter their risk perceptions. (It should be kept in mind, however, that most of the response that we detected in this study occurred well after the cessation groups had ended.) In short, as in most studies of smoking relapsers, the representativeness of the current sample is an issue to be considered. A third limitation is that we did not use biochemical verification of smoking status, and we were not able to check on all those who claimed abstinence. If previous research is any indication (Velicer et al., 1992), few of our abstainers were lying about their status. Still, the possibility that the abstainer group actually included some relapsers does exist. The low probabilities of both false reporting and the likelihood that false reporting produced a systematic bias in the pattern of results lead us to conclude that whereas the possibility of inaccurate categorization warrants some caution in data interpretation, it is not a major concern.

Conclusion

Risk perception, like commitment to quitting after smoking resumption, does decline among smoking relapsers, but much more so among those with moderate or high self-esteem than among those with low self-esteem. The decline in risk perception is apparently evidence of a dissonance reduction process. Moreover, it is a type of dissonance reduction that has some esteem-protecting benefits for the relapser. This suggests that relapse prevention interventions should take into account both change in risk perception and the function it can serve for those who relapse.

REFERENCES

Aronson, E. (1969). The theory of cognitive dissonance: A current perspective. In L. Berkowitz (Ed.), *Advances in experimental social psychology* (Vol. 4, pp. 1–34). San Diego, CA: Academic Press.

Aronson, E. (1994). *The social animal* (7th ed.). New York: W. H. Freeman.

Avis, N. E., Smith, K. W., & McKinlay, J. B. (1989). Accuracy of perceptions of heart attack risk: What influences perceptions and can they be changed? *American Journal of Public Health, 79,* 1608–1612.

Baumeister, R. E (1993). *Self-esteem: The puzzle of low self-regard.* New York: Plenum.

Baumeister, R. E., Heatherton, T. F., & Tice, D. M. (1993). When ego threats lead to self-regulation failure: Negative consequences of high self-esteem. *Journal of Personality and Social Psychology, 64,* 141–156.

Baumeister, R. E., Tice, D. M., & Hutton, D. G. (1989). Self-presentational motivations and personality differences in self-esteem. *Journal of Personality, 57,* 547–579.

Becker, M. H. (1974). The health belief model and personal health behavior. *Health Education Monographs, 2,* 324–473.

Becker, M. H., & Rosenstock, I. M. (1987). Comparing social learning theory and the health belief model. In W. B. Ward (Ed.), *Advances in health education and promotion* (Vol. 2, pp. 245–249). Greenwich, CT: JAI Press.

Benthin, A., Slovic, P., & Severson, H. (1993). A psychometric study of adolescent risk perception. *Journal of Adolescence, 16,* 153–168.

Boney-McCoy, S., Gibbons, F. X., & Gerrard, M. (1996). *Compensatory self-enhancement as a reaction to the consideration of health risk among persons with high self-esteem.* Manuscript submitted for publication.

Boney-McCoy, S., Gibbons, F. X., Reis, T. J., Gerrard, M.,

Luus, E., & Sufka, A. V. W. (1992). Perceptions of smoking risk as a function of smoking status. *Journal of Behavioral Medicine, 15,* 469–488.

Bradley, G. W. (1978). Self-serving biases in the attribution process: A reexamination of the fact or fiction question. *Journal of Personality and Social Psychology, 36,* 56–71.

Brockner, J. (1979). The effects of self-esteem, success-failure, and self-consciousness on task performance. *Journal of Personality and Social Psychology, 37,* 1732–1741.

Brockner, J., & Elkind, M. (1985). Self-esteem and reactance: Further evidence of attitudinal and moral consequences. *Journal of Experimental Social Psychology, 21,* 346–361.

Brownell, K., Marlatt, G. A., Lichtenstein, E., & Wilson, G. T. (1986). Understanding and preventing relapse. *American Psychologist, 41,* 765–782.

Carmody, T. P. (1993). Nicotine dependence: Psychosocial approaches to the prevention of smoking relapse. *Psychology of Addictive Behaviors, 7,* 96–102.

Centers for Disease Control and Prevention. (1993). Cigarette smoking-attributable mortality and years of potential life lost—United States, 1990. *Morbidity and Mortality Weekly Report, 42,* 645–649.

Cohen, A. R. (1959). Some implications of self-esteem for social influence. In C. I. Hovland & I. L. Janis (Eds.), *Personality and persuasibility* (pp. 102–120). New Haven, CT: Yale University Press.

Curry, S. J. (1993). Self-help interventions for smoking cessation. Special Section: Clinical research in smoking cessation. *Journal of Consulting and Clinical Psychology, 61,* 790–803.

Dillman, D. A. (1991). The design and administration of mail surveys. *Annual Review of Sociology, 17,* 225–249.

Eiser, J. R., Sutton, S. R., & Wober, M. (1978). "Consonant" and "dissonant" smokers and the self-attribution of addiction. *Addictive Behaviors, 3,* 99–106.

Feather, N. T. (1962). Cigarette smoking and lung cancer: A study of cognitive dissonance. *Australian Journal of Psychology, 14,* 55–64.

Festinger, L. A. (1957). *A theory of cognitive dissonance.* Evanston, IL: Row, Peterson.

Fisher, E. B., Haire-Joshu, D., Morgan, G. D., Rehberg, H., & Rost, K. (1990). State of the art: Smoking and smoking cessation. *American Review of Respiratory Diseases, 142,* 702–720.

Flay, B. R., Hu, F. B., Siddiqui, O., Day, L. E., Hedeker, D., Petraitis, J., Richardson, J., & Sussman, S. (1994). Differential influence of parental smoking and friends' smoking on adolescent initiation and escalation of smoking. *Journal of Social Behavior, 35,* 248–265.

Gerrard, M., Gibbons, F. X., Benthin, A. C., & Hessling, R. M. (1996). A longitudinal study of the reciprocal nature of risk behaviors and cognitions in adolescents: What you do shapes what you think and vice versa. *Health Psychology, 15,* 344–354.

Gerrard, M., Kurylo, M., & Reis, T. (1991). Self-esteem, erotophobia, and retention of contraceptive and AIDS information in the classroom. *Journal of Applied Social Psychology, 21,* 368–379.

Gibbons, F. X., & Eggleston, T. J. (1996). Smoker networks and the "typical smoker": A prospective analysis of smoking cessation. *Health Psychology, 15,* 469–476.

Gibbons, F. X., Gerrard, M., Lando, H. A., & McGovern, P. G. (1991). Social comparison and smoking cessation: The role of the "typical smoker." *Journal of Experimental Social Psychology, 27,* 239–258.

Gibbons, F. X., McGovern, P. G., & Lando, H. A. (1991). Relapse and risk perception among members of a smoking cessation clinic. *Health Psychology, 10,* 42–45.

Greening, L., & Dollinger, S. J. (1991). Adolescent smoking and perceived vulnerability to smoking-related causes of death. *Journal of Pediatric Psychology, 16,* 687–699.

Heatherton, T. F., & Polivy, J. (1991). Development and validation of a scale for measuring state self-esteem. *Journal of Personality and Social Psychology, 60,* 895–910.

Ho, R. (1989). Why do people smoke? Motives for the maintenance of smoking behavior and its possible cessation. *Australian Psychologist, 24,* 385–400.

Janz, N. K., & Becker, M. H. (1984). The health belief model: A decade later. *Health Education Quarterly, 11,* 1–47.

Johnson, R. E. (1968). Smoking and the reduction of cognitive dissonance. *Journal of Personality and Social Psychology, 9,* 260–265.

Klesges, R. C., Brown, K., Pascale, R. W., Murphy, M., Williams, E., & Cigrang, J. A. (1988). Factors associated with participation, attrition, and outcome in a smoking cessation program at the workplace. *Health Psychology, 7,* 575–589.

Klesges, R. C., Somes, G., Pascale, R. W., Klesges, L. M., Murphy, M., Brown, K., & Williams, E. (1988). Knowledge and beliefs regarding the consequences of cigarette smoking and their relationships to smoking status in a biracial sample. *Health Psychology, 7,* 387–401.

Knight, P. A., & Nadel, J. I. (1986). Humility revisited: Self-esteem, information search, and policy consistency. *Organizational Behavior and Human Decision Processes, 38,* 196–206.

Kristiansen, C. M., Harding, C. M., & Eiser, J. R. (1983). Beliefs about the relationship between smoking and causes of death. *Basic and Applied Social Psychology, 4,* 253–261.

Lando, H. A. (1989). Treatment outcome evaluation methodology in smoking cessation: Strengths and key issues. *Advances in Behavior Research Therapy, 11,* 201–214.

Lando, H. A. (1993). Formal quit smoking treatments. In C. T. Orleans & J. Slade (Eds.), *Nicotine addiction: Principles and management* (pp. 221–224). New York: Oxford University Press.

Lebovits, A. H., & Strain, J. J. (1990). The asbestos worker who smokes: Adding insult to injury. *Health Psychology, 9,* 405–417.

Lee, C. (1989). Perceptions of immunity to disease in adult smokers. *Journal of Behavioral Medicine, 12,* 267–277.

Leventhal, H., Glynn, K., & Fleming, R. (1987). Is the smoking decision an informed 'choice'? *Psychological Bulletin, 88,* 370–405.

Marlatt, G. A., & Gordon, J. R. (Eds.). (1985). *Relapse prevention: Maintenance strategies in addictive behavior change.* New York: Guilford Press.

Mattson, M. E., Pollack, E. S., & Cullen, J. W. (1987). What are the odds that smoking will kill you? *American Journal of Public Health, 77,* 425–431.

Mermelstein, R. J., Karnatz, T., & Reichmann, S. (1992). Smoking. In P. H. Wilson (Ed.), *Principles and practice of relapse prevention* (pp. 43–68). New York: Guilford Press.

McGovern, P. G., Lando, H. A., Roski, J., Pirie, P. L., & Sprafka, J. M. (1994). A comparison of smoking cessation clinic participants with smokers in the general population. *Tobacco Control, 3,* 329–333.

Mullen, P. D., Hersey, J. C., & Iverson, D. C. (1987). Health behavior models compared. *Social Science and Medicine, 24,* 973–981.

Ossip-Klein, D. J., Giovino, G. A., Megahed, N., Black, P. M., Emont, S. L., Stiggins, J., Schulman, E., & Moore, L. (1991). Effects of a smokers' hotline: Results of a 10-county self-help trial. *Journal of Consulting and Clinical Psychology, 59,* 325–332.

Pederson, L. L., Wanklin, J. M., & Baskerville, J. C. (1984). The role of health beliefs in compliance with physician advice to quit smoking. *Social Science and Medicine, 19,* 573–580.

Pelham, B. P. (1992). *On the limits of illusions: Exploring the costs and hazards of high self-regard.* Unpublished manuscript.

Pervin, L. A., & Yatko, R. J. (1965). Cigarette smoking and alternative methods of reducing dissonance. *Journal of Personality and Social Psychology, 2,* 30–36.

Prochaska, J. O., DiClemente, C. C., Velicer, W. F., Ginpil, S., & Norcross, J. C. (1985). Predicting change in smoking status for self-changers. *Addictive Behaviors, 10,* 395–406.

Rogers, R. W. (1983). Cognitive and physiological processes in fear appeals and attitude change: A revised theory of protection motivation. In J. T. Cacioppo & R. E. Petty (Eds.), *Social psychophysiology* (pp. 153–176). New York: Guilford Press.

Rosenberg, M. (1965). *Society and the adolescent self-image.* Princeton, NJ: Princeton University Press.

Shrauger, J. S., & Kelly, R. J. (1988). Global self-evaluation and changes in self-description as a function of information discrepancy and favorability. *Journal of Personality, 56,* 709–728.

Smith, G. E., Gerrard, M., & Gibbons, F. X. (in press). Self-esteem and the relation between risk behavior and perceived vulnerability. *Health Psychology.*

Steele, C. M. (1988). The psychology of self-affirmation: Sustaining the integrity of the self. In M. P. Zanna (Ed.), *Advances in experimental social psychology* (Vol. 21, pp. 261–302). San Diego, CA: Academic Press.

Steele, C. M., Spencer, S. J., & Lynch, M. (1993). Self-image resilience and dissonance: The role of affirmational resources. *Journal of Personality and Social Psychology, 64,* 885–896.

Sutton, S. (1987). Social-psychological approaches to understanding addictive behaviours: Attitude-behaviour and decision-making models. *British Journal of Addiction, 82,* 355–370.

Sutton, S. (1989). Relapse following smoking cessation: A critical review of current theory and research. In M. Gossop (Ed.), *Relapse and addictive behavior* (pp. 41–72). London: Tavistock/Routledge.

Tesser, A., & Cornell, D. P. (1991). On the confluence of self processes. *Journal of Experimental Social Psychology, 27,* 501–526.

U.S. Department of Health and Human Services, Public Health Service, Centers for Disease Control, Office of Smoking and Health. (1987). *The health general.* Rockville, MD: Author.

U.S. Department of Health and Human Services. (1989). *Reducing the health consequences of smoking. A report of the Surgeon General* (DHHS Publication No. CDC 89-8411). Washington, DC: U.S. Government Printing Office.

U.S. Department of Health and Human Services, Public Health Service, Centers for Disease Control. (1990). *The health benefits of smoking cessation* (DHHS Publication No. CDC 90-8416). Washington, DC: Author.

U.S. Surgeon General's Advisory Committee on Smoking and Health. (1964). *Smoking and health; report.* Princeton, NJ: Van Nostrand.

Velicer, W. F., DiClemente, C. C., & Prochaska, J. O. (1985). Decisional balance measure for assessing and predicting smoking status. *Journal of Personality and Social Psychology, 48,* 1279–1289.

Velicer, W. F., Prochaska, J. O., Rossi, J. S., & Snow, M. G. (1992). Assessing outcome in smoking cessation studies. *Psychological Bulletin, 111,* 23–41.

Viscusi, K. W. (1992). *Smoking: Making the risky decision.* New York: Oxford University Press.

Weinstein, N. D. (1988). The precaution adoption process. *Health Psychology, 7,* 355–386.

Wicklund, R. A., & Brehm, J. W. (1976). *Perspectives on cognitive dissonance.* Hillsdale, NJ: Erlbaum.

Wilson, P. H. (Ed.). (1992). *Principles and practice of relapse prevention.* New York: Guilford Press.

This research was supported by National Institute on Drug Abuse Grant DA07534A and American Heart Association Grant IA-92-GS-36.

We thank Hart Blanton, Sue Boney-McCoy, Meg Gerrard, and Harry Lando for their comments on the manuscript.

ENDNOTES

1. The purpose of this scale was to assess change in self-esteem. We used this scale because it was needed for another study (Gibbons & Eggleston, 1996) and we wanted to minimize the burden placed on participants. Also, this self-measure is likely to be more variable (i.e., sensitive to change) than is the trait Rosenberg Self-Esteem Scale, which has been shown not to be a good measure of esteem change (Heatherton & Polivy, 1991). In fact, the self-description index correlated with the Rosenberg scale ($r = .40, p < .001$). Given that it is not a standardized self-esteem scale, however, we refer to it generically as a "self-concept" measure.

2. An accurate assessment of risk would have been very difficult to calculate (Mattson et al., 1987), in part because summary statistics (e.g., actuarial data) report mortality rates for these diseases, but seldom morbidity rates, and it was only the latter that were relevant here. On average, the participants estimated that if they continued smoking, they had a 74% chance of contracting each of the three primary illnesses (heart disease, heart attack, and lung cancer), and that is clearly an overestimation.

3. This suggests that T1 risk perception was related to smoking status, and in fact a logistic regression indicated that was the case. Specifically, when we entered self-esteem and T1 risk perception and their interaction term into the equation, risk perception was the only significant predictor ($\beta = .34$, Wald = 3.78, $p = .05$). However, when we added T1 confidence in ability to quit to the equation, risk perception dropped down to marginal significance ($p = .16$). T1 risk perception (but not self-esteem) was also a marginally significant predictor of 12-month follow-up status ($p = .10$).

CRITICAL THINKING QUESTIONS

1. The authors suggest that allowing people with high self-esteem to self-affirm on some dimension shortly after relapse from quitting smoking may serve to counter the need for dissonance reduction and hence reduce relapse behavior. Design a study that would test this hypothesis.

2. The authors acknowledge that people who try to quit smoking on their own may not experience as much dissonance reduction (due to their lack of public commitment) as people who enroll in smoking-cessation programs. Design a study to test the possibility that public commitment is an important variable in successful smoking cessation.

3. Do you agree with the authors' contention that although their population was mostly white, there is no reason to suspect that minorities would react differently to the same experimental measures? In other words, do all people, regardless of background, face the same issues when trying to stop smoking? Or may group-specific factors also be involved in successful smoking cessation? Explain your answers.

4. Can the concepts and/or methodology of this article be applied to other behaviors with dire health consequences? For example, could a program be developed using these ideas to help change risky sexual practices? If so, how? If not, why? Select another health-related behavior that could be changed using dissonance, and outline a study to test your hypothesis.

Chapter Five

SOCIAL IDENTITY
Self and Gender

THE MAJORITY OF readings that you will encounter in this book focus on what might be called *situational variables:* particular circumstances that elicit predictable patterns of behavior in people. But do all people respond the same way in identical situations? Of course not. We each bring to every situation a set of experiences and characteristics that may influence how we act. Certainly, each of us has had unique life experiences that may be influential; biological dispositions, perhaps present from birth, may also play a role in determining behavior. Another influential factor is the personality of the individual.

But what is *personality?* Many theories have been developed to try to explain what this concept means. Some are *global theories* of personality, which attempt a total comprehensive portrait of an individual (e.g., Freud's), while others are *microtheories,* focusing on narrower, more particular dimensions of personality. Certainly, one major part of personality is *social identity*—the part of personality that is our internalized representation of how we view ourselves as being part of our social world. Two major parts of social identity—the *self* and *gender identity*—are addressed in the readings in this chapter.

Article 13, "The Many Me's of the Self-Monitor," looks at the sense of self that each of us has and asks whether that is comprised of a single sense of self or perhaps a number of selves, depending on the situation.

Article 14, "The Measurement of Psychological Androgyny," is a classic article that challenged the common-sense wisdom that the most appropriate gender-typed behavior is for a male to be masculine and a female, feminine. Perhaps masculinity and femininity are not mutually exclusive ends of a continuum after all.

Finally, the contemporary reading found in Article 15, "The Influence of Societal Factors on Female Body Image," concerns issues of both self-concept and gender. Specifically, consider the pervasive Western value that regards thinness as the physical ideal, especially for women. What impact does this have on body image and body satisfaction in women? The results of this study may help explain why the prevalence of eating disorders in women continues to increase.

ARTICLE 13 _____

Think about who you are. Do you have a stable sense of self, of knowing what you feel, believe, and want? Or do you have many selves, depending on when and in what situation you try to answer this question?

Now think about your behavior. Do you act consistently across many different situations? Or does your behavior depend on the specific situation in which you find yourself?

These questions are indeed intriguing. At one extreme may be individuals who consistently act the same way in every situation, even when doing so might not be appropriate. At the other extreme are people who modify their behavior to fit each situation, showing little consistency across contexts. These are the two extremes on a continuum of what is known as *self-monitoring*.

Self-monitoring refers to the extent to which an individual is aware of and able to control the impressions that he or she conveys to others. A high self-monitoring individual is very attuned to the situation and modifies his or her behavior according to the demands of the context. A low self-monitoring individual tends to behave more in accordance with internal dispositions than with the demands of the situation.

What are the consequences of these two styles of behaving? Does a high self-monitoring person actually have many different selves, while a low self-monitoring person has but a single self? The relationship between self-monitoring and the sense of self is but one of the issues addressed in the following article by Mark Snyder.

The Many Me's
of the Self-Monitor

■ Mark Snyder

The image of myself which I try to create in my own mind in order that I may love myself is very different from the image which I try to create in the minds of others in order that they may love me. —*W. H. Auden*

The concept of the self is one of the oldest and most enduring in psychological considerations of human nature. We generally assume that people are fairly consistent and stable beings: that a person who is generous in one situation is also likely to be generous in other situations, that one who is honest is honest most of the time, that a person who takes a liberal stance today will favor the liberal viewpoint tomorrow.

It's not always so: each of us, it appears, may have not one but many selves. Moreover, much as we might like to believe that the self is an integral feature of personal identity, it appears that, to a greater extent, the self is a product of the individual's relationships with other people. Conventional wisdom to the contrary, there may be striking gaps and contradictions—as Auden suggests—between the public appearances and private realities of the self.

Psychologists refer to the strategies and techniques that people use to control the impressions they convey to others as "impression management." One of my own research interests has been to understand why some individuals are better at impression management than others. For it is clear that some people are particularly sensitive to the ways they express and present themselves in social situations—at parties, job interviews, professional meetings, in confrontations of all kinds where one might choose to create and maintain an appearance, with or without a specific purpose in mind. Indeed, I have found that such people have developed the ability to carefully monitor their own performances and to skillfully adjust their performances when signals from others tell them that they are not having the desired effect. I call such persons "high self-monitoring individuals," and I have developed a 25-item measure—the Self-Monitoring Scale—that has proved its ability to distinguish high self-monitoring individuals from low self-monitoring individuals (see box [p. 135]). Unlike the high self-monitoring individuals, low self-monitoring individuals are not so concerned about taking in such information; instead, they tend to express what they feel, rather than mold and tailor their behavior to fit the situation.

My work on self-monitoring and impression management grew out of a long-standing fascination with explorations of reality and illusion in literature and in the theater. I was struck by the contrast between the way things often appear to be and the reality that lurks beneath the surface—on the stage, in novels, and in people's actual lives. I wanted to know how this world of appearances in social relationships was built and maintained, as well as what its effects were on the individual personality. But I was also interested in exploring the older, more philosophical question of whether, beneath the various images of self that people project to others, there is a "real me." If we are all actors in many social situations, do we then retain in any sense an essential self, or are we really a variety of selves?

SKILLED IMPRESSION MANAGERS

There are striking and important differences in the extent to which people can and do control their self-presentation in social situations: some people engage in impression management more often—and with greater skill—than others. Professional actors, as well as many trial lawyers, are among the best at it. So are successful salespeople, confidence artists, and politicians. The onetime mayor of New York, Fiorello LaGuardia, was particularly skilled at adopting the expressive mannerisms of a variety of ethnic groups. In fact, he was so good at it that in watching silent films of his campaign speeches, it is easy to guess whose vote he was soliciting.

Of course, such highly skilled performances are the exception rather than the rule. And people differ in the extent to which they can and do exercise control over their self-presentations. It is high self-monitoring individuals among us who are particularly talented in this regard. When asked to describe high self-monitoring individuals, their friends say that they are good at learning which behavior is appropriate in social situations, have good self-control of their emotional expression, and can effectively use this ability to create the impression they want. They are particularly skilled at intentionally expressing and accurately communicating a wide variety of emotions both vocally and facially. As studies by Richard Lippa of California State University at Fullerton have shown, they are usually such polished actors that they can effectively adopt the mannerisms of a reserved, withdrawn, and introverted individual and then do an abrupt about-face and portray, just as convincingly, a friendly, outgoing, and extroverted personality.

High self-monitoring individuals are also quite likely to seek out information about appropriate patterns of self-presentation. They invest considerable effort in attempting to "read" and understand others. In an experiment I conducted with Tom Monson (then one of my graduate students), various cues were given to students involved in group discussions as to what was socially appropriate behavior in the situation. For example, some of them thought that their taped discussions would be played back to fellow students; in those circumstances, I assumed they would want their opinions to appear as autonomous as possible. Others believed that their discussions were completely private; there, I assumed they would be most concerned with maintaining harmony and agreement in the group. High self-monitoring individuals were keenly attentive to these differences; they conformed with the group when conformity was the most appropriate behavior and did not conform when they knew that the norms of the larger student audience would favor autonomy in the face of social pressure. Low self-monitoring individuals were virtually unaffected by the differences in social setting: presumably, their self-presentations were more accurate reflections of their personal attitudes and dispositions.

Monitor Your Self

On the scale I have developed to measure self-monitoring, actors are usually high scorers, as are many obese people, who tend to be very sensitive about the way they appear to others. For much the same reason, politicians and trial lawyers would almost certainly be high scorers. Recent immigrants eager to assimilate, black freshmen in a predominantly white college, and military personnel stationed abroad are also likely to score high on the scale.

The Self-Monitoring Scale measures how concerned people are with the impression they are making on others, as well as their ability to control and modify their behavior to fit the situation. I believe that it defines a distinct domain of personality that is quite different from the traits probed by other standard scales.

Several studies show that skill at self-monitoring is not associated with exceptional intelligence or with a particular social class. Nor is it related, among other things, to being highly anxious or extremely self-conscious, to being an extrovert, or to having a strong need for approval. They may be somewhat power-oriented or Machiavellian, but high self-monitoring individuals do not necessarily have high scores on the "Mach" scale, a measure of Machiavellianism developed by Richard Christie of Columbia University. (Two items from the scale: "The best way to handle people is to tell them what they want" and "Anyone who completely trusts anyone else is asking for trouble.") The steely-eyes Machiavellians are more manipulative, detached, and amoral than high self-monitoring individuals.

The Self-Monitoring Scale describes a unique trait and has proved to be both statistically valid and reliable, in tests on various samples.

[Below] is a 10-item abbreviated version of the Self-Monitoring Scale that will give readers some idea of whether they are low or high self-monitoring individuals. If you would like to test your self-monitoring tendencies, follow the instructions and then consult the scoring key.

—M. S.

These statements concern personal reactions to a number of different situations. No two statements are exactly alike, so consider each statement carefully before answering. If a statement is true, or mostly true, as applied to you, circle the T. If a statement is false, or not usually true, as applied to you, circle the F.

1. I find it hard to imitate the behavior of other people. T F
2. I guess I put on a show to impress or entertain people. T F
3. I would probably make a good actor. T F
4. I sometimes appear to others to be experiencing deeper emotions than I actually am. T F
5. In a group of people I am rarely the center of attention. T F
6. In different situations and with different people, I often act like very different persons. T F
7. I can only argue for ideas I already believe. T F
8. In order to get along and be liked, I tend to be what people expect me to be rather than anything else. T F
9. I may deceive people by being friendly when I really dislike them. T F
10. I'm not always the person I appear to be. T F

SCORING: Give yourself one point for each of questions 1, 5 and 7 that you answered F. Give yourself one point for each of the remaining questions that you answered T. Add up your points. If you are a good judge of yourself and scored 7 or above, you are probably a high self-monitoring individual; 3 or below, you are probably a low self-monitoring individual.

Thus, as we might have guessed, people who are most skilled in the arts of impression management are also most likely to practice it.

Although high self-monitoring individuals are well skilled in the arts of impression management, we should not automatically assume that they necessarily use these skills for deceptive or manipulative purposes. Indeed, in their relationships with friends and acquaintances, high self-monitoring individuals are eager to use their self-monitoring abilities to promote smooth social interactions.

We can find some clues to this motive in the way high self-monitoring individuals tend to react to, and cope with, unfamiliar and unstructured social settings. In a study done at the University of Wisconsin, psychologists William Ickes and Richard Barnes arranged for pairs of strangers to spend time together in a waiting room, ostensibly to wait for an experiment to begin. The researchers then recorded the verbal and nonverbal behavior of each pair over a five-minute period, using video and audio tapes. All possible pairings of same-sex undergraduates at high, moderate, and low levels of self-monitoring were represented. Researchers scrutinized the tapes for evidence of the impact of self-monitoring on spontaneous encounters between strangers.

In these meetings, as in so many other aspects of their lives, high self-monitoring individuals suffered little or no shyness. Soon after meeting the other person, they took an active and controlling role in the conversation. They were inclined to talk first and to initiate subsequent conversational sequences. They also felt, and were seen by their partners to have, a greater need to talk. Their partners also viewed them as having been the more directive member of the pair. It was as if high self-monitoring individuals were particularly concerned about managing their behavior in order to create, encourage, and maintain a smooth flow of conversation. Perhaps this quality may help self-monitoring people to emerge as leaders in groups, organizations, and institutions.

DETECTING IMPRESSION MANAGEMENT IN OTHERS

High self-monitoring individuals are also adept at detecting impression management in others. To demonstrate this finely tuned ability, three communications researchers at the University of Minnesota made use of videotaped excerpts from the television program "To Tell the Truth." On this program, one of the three guest contestants (all male in the excerpts chosen for the study) is the "real Mr. X." The other two who claim to be the real Mr. X are, of course, lying. Participants in the study watched each excerpt and then tried to identify the real Mr. X. High self-monitoring individuals were much more accurate than their low self-monitoring counterparts in cor-

---

William James on the Roles We Play

A man has as many social selves as there are individuals who recognize him and carry an image of him in their mind. . . . But as the individuals who carry the images form naturally into classes, we may practically say that he has as many different social selves as there are distinct *groups* of persons about whose opinions he cares. He generally shows a different side of himself to each of these different groups. Many a youth who is demure enough before his parents and teachers swears and swaggers like a pirate among his "tough" young friends. We do not show ourselves to our children as to our club companions, to our masters and employers as to our intimate friends. From this there results what practically is a division of the man into several selves; and this may be a discordant splitting, as where one is afraid to let one set of his acquaintances know him as he is elsewhere; or it may be a perfectly harmonious division of labor, as where one tender to his children is stern to the soldiers or prisoners under his command.

—William James
The Principles of Psychology, 1890

rectly identifying the real Mr. X and in seeing through the deception of the other two contestants.

Not only are high self-monitoring individuals able to see beyond the masks of deception successfully but they are also keenly attentive to the actions of other people as clues to their underlying intentions. E. E. Jones and Roy Baumeister of Princeton University had college students watch a videotaped discussion between two men who either agreed or disagreed with each other. The observers were aware that one man (the target person) had been instructed either to gain the affection or to win the respect of the other. Low self-monitoring observers tended to accept behavior at face value. They found themselves attracted to the agreeable person, whether or not he was attempting to ingratiate himself with his discussion partner. In contrast, high self-monitoring observers were acutely sensitive to the motivational context within which the target person operated. They liked the target better if he was disagreeable when trying to ingratiate himself. But when he sought respect, they were more attracted to him if he chose to be agreeable. Jones and Baumeister suggest that high self-monitoring observers regarded agreeableness as too blatant a ploy in gaining affection and autonomy as an equally obvious route to respect. Perhaps the high self-monitoring individuals felt that they themselves would have acted with greater subtlety and finesse.

Even more intriguing is Jones's and Baumeister's speculation—and I share their view—that high self-monitoring individuals prefer to live in a stable, predictable social environment populated by people whose actions consistently and accurately reflect their true attitudes and feelings. In such a world, the consistency and predictability of the actions of others would be of great benefit to those who tailor and manage their own self-presentation in social situations. From this perspective, it becomes quite understandable that high self-monitoring individuals may be especially fond of those who avoid strategic posturing. Furthermore, they actually may prefer as friends those comparatively low in self-monitoring.

How can we know when strangers and casual acquaintances are engaged in self-monitoring? Are there some channels of expression and communication that are more revealing than others about a person's true,

inner "self," even when he or she is practicing impression management?

Both scientific and everyday observers of human behavior have suggested that nonverbal behavior—facial expressions, tone of voice, and body movements—reveals meaningful information about a person's attitudes, feelings, and motives. Often, people who engage in self-monitoring for deceptive purposes are less skilled at controlling their body's expressive movements. Accordingly, the body may be a more revealing source of information than the face for detecting those who engage in self-monitoring and impression management.

More than one experiment shows how nonverbal behavior can betray the true attitude of those attempting impression management. Shirley Weitz of the New School for Social Research reasoned that on college campuses where there are strong normative pressures supporting a tolerant and liberal value system, all students would avoid saying anything that would indicate racial prejudice—whether or not their private attitudes supported such behavior. In fact, she found that among "liberal" white males at Harvard University, the most prejudiced students (as determined by behavioral measures of actual attempts to avoid interaction with blacks) bent over backwards to *verbally* express liking and friendship for a black in a simulated interracial encounter. However, their *nonverbal* behaviors gave them away. Although the prejudiced students made every effort to say kind and favorable things, they continued to do so in a cool and distant tone of voice. It was as if they knew the words but not the music: they knew *what* to say, but not *how* to say it.

Another way that prejudice can be revealed is in the physical distance people maintain between themselves and the target of their prejudice. To demonstrate this phenomenon, psychologist Stephen Morin arranged for college students to be interviewed about their attitudes toward homosexuality. Half the interviewers wore "Gay and Proud" buttons and mentioned their association with the Association of Gay Psychologists. The rest wore no buttons and simply mentioned that they were graduate students working on theses. Without the students' knowledge, the distance they placed their chairs from the interviewer was measured while the interviews were going on. The measure of social distance proved to be highly revealing. When the student and the interviewer were of the same sex, students tended to establish almost a foot more distance between themselves and the apparently gay interviewers. They placed their chairs an average of 32 inches away from apparently gay interviewers, but only 22 inches away from apparently nongay interviewers. Interestingly, most of the students expressed tolerant, and at times favorable, attitudes toward gay people in general. However, the distances they chose to put between themselves and the interviewers they thought gay betrayed underlying negative attitudes.

IMPRESSION MANAGERS' DILEMMAS

The well-developed skills of high self-monitoring individuals ought to give them the flexibility to cope quickly and effectively with a diversity of social roles. They can choose with skill and grace the self-presentation appropriate to each of a wide variety of social situations. But what happens when the impression manager must effectively present a true and honest image to other people?

Consider the case of a woman on trial for a crime that she did not commit. Her task on the witness stand is to carefully present herself so that everything she does and says communicates to the jurors clearly and unambiguously her true innocence, so that they will vote for her acquittal. Chances are good, however, that members of the jury are somewhat skeptical of the defendant's claims of innocence. After all, they might reason to themselves, the district attorney would not have brought this case to trial were the state's case against her not a convincing one.

The defendant must carefully manage her verbal and nonverbal behaviors so as to ensure that even a skeptical jury forms a true impression of her innocence. In particular, she must avoid the pitfalls of an image that suggests that "she doth protest her innocence too much and therefore must be guilty." To the extent that our defendant skillfully practices the art of impression management, she will succeed in presenting herself to the jurors as the honest person that she truly is.

It often can take as much work to present a truthful image as to present a deceptive one. In fact, in this case, just being honest may not be enough when facing skeptical jurors who may bend over backwards to interpret any and all of the defendant's behavior—nervousness, for example—as a sign of guilt.

The message from research on impression management is a clear one. Some people are quite flexible in their self-presentation. What effects do these shifts in public appearance have on the more private realities of self-concept? In some circumstances, we are persuaded by our own appearances: we become the persons we appear to be. This phenomenon is particularly likely to occur when the image we present wins the approval and favor of those around us.

In an experiment conducted at Duke University by psychologists E. E. Jones, Kenneth Gergen, and Keith Davis, participants who had been instructed to win the approval of an interviewer presented very flattering images of themselves. Half the participants (chosen at random) then received favorable reactions from their interviewers; the rest did not. All the participants later were asked to estimate how accurately and honestly their self-descriptions had mirrored their true personalities.

Those who had won the favor of their interviewers considered their self-presentations to have been the most honest of all. One interpretation of this finding is that those people were operating with rather pragmatic definitions of self-concept: that which produced the most positive results was considered to be an accurate reflection of the inner self.

The reactions of other people can make it all the more likely that we become what we claim to be. Other people may accept our self-presentations at face value; they may then treat us as if we really were the way we pretend to be. For example, if I act as if I like Chris, chances are Chris will like me. Chris will probably treat me in a variety of friendly ways. As a result of Chris's friendliness, I may come to like Chris, even though I did not in the first place. The result, in this case, may be beneficial to both parties. In other circumstances, however, the skilled impression manager may pay an emotional price.

High self-monitoring orientation may be purchased at the cost of having one's actions reflect and communicate very little about one's private attitudes, feelings, and dispositions. In fact, as I have seen time and again in my research with my former graduate students Beth Tanke and Bill Swann, correspondence between private attitudes and public behavior is often minimal for high self-monitoring individuals. Evidently, the words and deeds of high self-monitoring individuals may reveal precious little information about their true inner feelings and attitudes.

Yet, it is almost a canon of modern psychology that a person's ability to reveal a "true self" to intimates is essential to emotional health. Sidney Jourard, one of the first psychologists to hold that view, believed that only through self-disclosure could we achieve self-discovery and self-knowledge: "Through my self-disclosure, I let others know my soul. They can know it, really know it, only as I make it known. In fact, I am beginning to suspect that I can't even know *my own soul* except as I disclose it. I suspect that I will know myself 'for real' at the exact moment that I have succeeded in making it known through my disclosure to another person."

Only low self-monitoring individuals may be willing or able to live their lives according to Jourard's prescriptions. By contrast, high self-monitoring individuals seem to embody Erving Goffman's view of human nature. For him, the world of appearances appears to be all, and the "soul" is illusory. Goffman defines social interactions as a theatrical performance in which each individual acts out a "line." A line is a set of carefully chosen verbal and nonverbal acts that express one's self. Each of us, in Goffman's view, seems to be merely the sum of our various performances.

What does this imply for the sense of self and identity associated with low and high self-monitoring individuals?

I believe that high self-monitoring individuals and low self-monitoring individuals have very different ideas about what constitutes a self and that their notions are quite well-suited to how they live. High self-monitoring individuals regard themselves as rather flexible and adaptive people who tailor their social behavior shrewdly and pragmatically to fit appropriate conditions. They believe that a person is whoever he appears to be in any particular situation: "I am me, the me I am right now." This self-image fits well with the way high self-monitoring individuals present themselves to the world. It allows them to act in ways that are consistent with how they believe they should act.

By contrast, low self-monitoring individuals have a firmer, more single-minded idea of what a self should be. They value and strive for congruence between "who they are" and "what they do" and regard their actions as faithful reflections of how they feel and think. For them, a self is a single identity that must not be compromised for other people or in certain situations. Indeed, this view of the self parallels the low self-monitoring individual's consistent and stable self-presentation.

What is important in understanding oneself and others, then, is not the elusive question of whether there is a quintessential self, but rather, understanding how different people define those attributes of their behavior and experience that they regard as "me." Theory and research on self-monitoring have attempted to chart the processes by which beliefs about the self are actively translated into patterns of social behavior that reflect self-conceptions. From this perspective, the processes of self-monitoring are the processes of self—a system of operating rules that translate self-knowledge into social behavior.

CRITICAL THINKING QUESTIONS

1. Self-monitoring can be measured along a continuum. What are the advantages and disadvantages for someone who scores very high on this dimension (i.e., a high self-monitoring individual)? Very low (i.e., a low self-monitoring individual)?

2. How might high versus low self-monitoring individuals act differently in an intimate situation such as dating? Give examples to support your answer.

3. How do you think differences in self-monitoring develop? In other words, why might some people be attuned to external factors while others are not? In your opinion, what level of self-monitoring might be best overall for healthy functioning? Explain your answers.

4. Article 11 dealt with the concept of cognitive dissonance. Based on your understanding of the concept, do you think that dissonance arousal in a given situation may affect the level of self-monitoring used by the person? How so?

ARTICLE 14 _____

Let's do a quick exercise. Make a list of words or adjectives that you would use to describe someone that you think of as being feminine. Make another list of masculine descriptors. Next, compare the lists. Does one set of characteristics seem better than the other or just different? Could it be that the different stereotypical characteristics associated with masculinity and femininity might each be important, depending on the situation?

Masculine characteristics are generally considered *instrumental,* meaning that they are useful in task- or goal-oriented situations. Feminine characteristics tend to be more *expressive,* meaning that they focus more on the affective concern of the welfare of others. Typically, American society socializes its members to believe that males should act masculine and females, feminine and that each gender should suppress the characteristics of its opposite.

The following classic article by Sandra L. Bem postulates that when males are only allowed to act masculine and females are only allowed to act feminine, each gender is, in a sense, limited in what it can do. Masculine males are thus good in situations that call for instrumental, get-the-job-done traits, whereas feminine females are good in settings where concern for the feelings of others is important. But what about the person of either gender who has both masculine *and* feminine characteristics? Might he or she not be more adaptive and flexible to a greater variety of human experiences? In short, might not this person be better adjusted than the more rigidly defined masculine males and feminine females? Besides attempting to answer these questions, Bem's article is also a good example of how an instrument designed to measure a dimension of behavior characteristics is developed.

The Measurement of Psychological Androgyny[1]

■ Sandra L. Bem

This article describes the development of a new sex-role inventory that treats masculinity and femininity as two independent dimensions, thereby making it possible to characterize a person as masculine, feminine, or "androgynous" as a function of the difference between his or her endorsement of masculine and feminine personality characteristics. Normative data are presented, as well as the results of various psychometric analyses. The major findings of conceptual interest are: (a) the dimensions of masculinity and femininity are empirically as well as logically independent; (b) the concept of psychological androgyny is a reliable one; and (c) highly sex-typed scores do not reflect a general tendency to respond in a socially desirable direction, but rather a specific tendency to describe oneself in accordance with sex-typed standards of desirable behavior for men and women.

Both in psychology and in society at large, masculinity and femininity have long been conceptualized as bipolar ends of a single continuum; accordingly, a person has had to be either masculine or feminine, but not both. This sex-role dichotomy has served to obscure two very plausible hypotheses: first, that many individuals might be "androgynous"; that is, they might be *both* masculine and feminine, *both* assertive and yielding, *both* instrumental and expressive—depending on the situational appropriateness of these various behaviors; and conversely, that strongly sex-

Reprinted from *Journal of Consulting and Clinical Psychology,* 1974, *42,* 155–162. Copyright © 1974 by the American Psychological Association. Reprinted by permission.

typed individuals might be seriously limited in the range of behaviors available to them as they move from situation to situation. According to both Kagan (1964) and Kohlberg (1966), the highly sex-typed individual is motivated to keep his behavior consistent with an internalized sex-role standard, a goal that he presumably accomplishes by suppressing any behavior that might be considered undesirable or inappropriate for his sex. Thus, whereas a narrowly masculine self-concept might inhibit behaviors that are stereotyped as feminine, and a narrowly feminine self-concept might inhibit behaviors that are stereotyped as masculine, a mixed, or androgynous, self-concept might allow an individual to freely engage in both "masculine" and "feminine" behaviors.

The current research program is seeking to explore these various hypotheses, as well as to provide construct validation for the concept of androgyny (Bem, 1974). Before the research could be initiated, however, it was first necessary to develop a new type of sex-role inventory, one that would not automatically build in an inverse relationship between masculinity and femininity. This article describes that inventory.

The Bem Sex-Role Inventory (BSRI) contains a number of features that distinguish it from other, commonly used, masculinity-femininity scales, for example, the Masculinity-Femininity scale of the California Psychological Inventory (Gough, 1957). First, it includes both a Masculinity scale and a Femininity scale, each of which contains 20 personality characteristics. These characteristics are listed in the first and second columns of Table 1, respectively. Second, because the BSRI was founded on a conception of the sex-typed person as someone who has internalized society's sex-typed standards of desirable behavior for men and women, these personality characteristics were selected as masculine or feminine on the basis of sex-typed social desirability and not on the basis of differential endorsement by males and females as most other inventories have done. That is, a characteristic qualified as masculine if it was judged to be more desirable in American society for a man than for a woman, and it qualified as feminine if it was judged to be more desirable for a woman than for a man. Third, the BSRI characterizes a person as masculine, feminine, or androgynous as a function of the difference between his or her endorsement of masculine and feminine personality characteristics. A person is thus sex typed, whether masculine or feminine, to the extent that this difference score is high, the androgynous, to the extent that this difference score is low. Finally, the BSRI also includes a Social Desirability scale that is completely neutral with respect to sex. This scale now serves primarily to provide a neutral context for the Masculinity and Femininity scales, but it was utilized during the development of the BSRI to insure that the inventory would not simply be tapping a general tendency to endorse socially desirable traits. The 20 characteristics that make up this scale are listed in the third column of Table 1.

ITEM SELECTION

Both historically and cross-culturally, masculinity and femininity seem to have represented two complementary domains of *positive* traits and behaviors (Barry,

TABLE 1 / Sample of Items on the Masculinity, Femininity, and Social Desirability Scales of the BSRI

Masculine Items	Feminine Items	Neutral Items
Aggressive	Tender	Friendly
Competitive	Affectionate	Conscientious

Note: This table includes only a few samples of the items found in the BSRI. For the full list of items in each category, see the original source.

Source: Reproduced by special permission of the Publisher, MIND GARDEN, Inc., 1690 Woodside Road #202, Redwood City, CA 94061 (650) 261-3500 from the **Bem Sex Role Inventory** by Sandra Bem. Copyright 1978 by Consulting Psychologists Press, Inc. All rights reserved. Further reproduction is prohibited without the Distributor's written consent.

Bacon, & Child, 1957; Erikson, 1964; Parsons & Bales, 1955). In general, masculinity has been associated with an instrumental orientation, a cognitive focus on "getting the job done"; and femininity has been associated with an expressive orientation, an affective concern for the welfare of others.

Accordingly, as a preliminary to item selection for the Masculinity and Femininity scales, a list was compiled of approximately 200 personality characteristics that seemed to the author and several students to be both positive in value and either masculine or feminine in tone. This list served as the pool from which the masculine and feminine characteristics were ultimately chosen. As a preliminary to item selection for the Social Desirability scale, an additional list was compiled of 200 characteristics that seemed to be neither masculine nor feminine in tone. Of these "neutral" characteristics, half were positive in value and half were negative.

Because the BSRI was designed to measure the extent to which a person divorces himself from those characteristics that might be considered more "appropriate" for the opposite sex, the final items were selected for the Masculinity and Femininity scales if they were judged to be more desirable in American society for one sex than for the other. Specifically, judges were asked to utilize a 7-point scale, ranging from 1 ("Not at all desirable") to 7 ("Extremely desirable"), in order to rate the desirability in American society of each of the approximately 400 personality characteristics mentioned above. (E.g., "In American society, how desirable is it for a man to be truthful?" "In American society, how desirable is it for a woman to be sincere?") Each individual judge was asked to rate the desirability of all 400 personality characteristics either "for a man" or "for a woman." No judge was asked to rate both. The judges consisted of 40 Stanford undergraduates who filled out the questionnaire during the winter of 1972 and an additional 60 who did so the following summer. In both samples, half of the judges were male and half were female.

A personality characteristic qualified as masculine if it was independently judged by both males and females in both samples to be significantly more desirable for a man than for a woman ($p < .05$).[2] Similarly, a personality characteristic qualified as feminine if it was independently judged by both males and females in both samples to be significantly more desirable for a woman than for a man ($p < .05$). Of those characteristics that satisfied these criteria, 20 were selected for the Masculinity scale and 20 were selected for the Femininity scale (see the first and second columns of Table 1, respectively).

A personality characteristic qualified as neutral with respect to sex and hence eligible for the Social Desirability scale (a) if it was independently judged by both males and females to be no more desirable for one sex than for the other ($t < 1.2, p > .2$) and (b) if male and female judges did not differ significantly in their overall desirability judgments of that trait ($t < 1.2, p > .2$). Of those items that satisfied these several criteria, 10 positive and 10 negative personality characteristics were selected for the BSRI Social Desirability scale in accordance with Edwards' (1964) finding that an item must be quite positive or quite negative in tone if it is to evoke a social desirability response set. (The 20 neutral characteristics are shown in the third column of Table 1.)

After all of the individual items had been selected, mean desirability scores were computed for the masculine, feminine, and neutral items for each of the 100 judges. As shown in Table 2, for both males and females, the mean desirability of the masculine and feminine items was significantly higher for the "appropriate" sex than for the "inappropriate" sex, whereas the mean desirability of the neutral items was no higher for one sex than for the other. These results are, of course, a direct consequence of the criteria used for item selection.

Table 3 separates out the desirability ratings of the masculine and feminine items for male and female judges rating their *own* sex. These own-sex ratings seem to best represent the desirability of these various items as perceived by men and women when they are asked to describe *themselves* on the inventory. That is, the left-hand column of Table 3 represents the phenomenology of male subjects taking the test and the right-hand column represents the phenomenology of female subjects taking the test. As can be seen in Table 3, not only are "sex-appropriate" characteristics more desirable for both males and females than "sex-inappropriate" characteristics, but the phenomenologies of male and female subjects are almost perfectly symmetric: that is, men and women are nearly equal in

TABLE 2 / Mean Social Desirability Ratings of the Masculine, Feminine, and Neutral Items

Item	Male Judges			Female Judges		
	Masculine Item	Feminine Item	Neutral Item	Masculine Item	Feminine Item	Neutral Item
For a man	5.59	3.63	4.00	5.83	3.74	3.94
For a woman	2.90	5.61	4.08	3.46	5.55	3.98
Difference	2.69	1.98	.08	2.37	1.81	.04
t	14.41*	12.13*	.17	10.22*	8.28*	.09

*$p < .001$.

their perceptions of the desirability of sex-appropriate characteristics, sex-inappropriate characteristics, and the difference between them ($t < 1$ in all three comparisons).

SCORING

The BSRI asks a person to indicate on a 7-point scale how well each of the 60 masculine, feminine, and neutral personality characteristics describes himself. The scale ranges from 1 ("Never or almost never true") to 7 ("Always or almost always true") and is labeled at each point. On the basis of his responses, each person receives three major scores: a Masculinity score, a Femininity score and, most important, an Androgyny score. In addition, a Social Desirability score can also be computed.

The Masculinity and Femininity scores indicate the extent to which a person endorses masculine and feminine personality characteristics as self-descriptive.

TABLE 3 / Mean Social Desirability Ratings of the Masculine and Feminine Items for One's Own Sex

Item	Male Judges for a Man	Female Judges for a Woman
Masculine	5.59	3.46
Feminine	3.63	5.55
Difference	1.96	2.09
t	11.94*	8.88*

*$p < .001$.

Masculinity equals the mean self-rating for all endorsed masculine items, and Femininity equals the mean self-rating for all endorsed feminine items. Both can range from 1 to 7. It will be recalled that these two scores are logically independent. That is, the structure of the test does not constrain them in any way, and they are free to vary independently.

The Androgyny score reflects the relative amounts of masculinity and femininity that the person includes in his or her self-description, and, as such, it best characterizes the nature of the person's total sex role. Specifically, the Androgyny score is defined as Student's t ratio for the difference between a person's masculine and feminine self-endorsement; that is, the Androgyny score is the difference between an individual's masculinity and femininity normalized with respect to the standard deviations of his or her masculinity and femininity scores. The use of a t ratio as the index of androgyny—rather than a simple difference score—has two conceptual advantages: first, it allows us to ask whether a person's endorsement of masculine attributes differs significantly from his or her endorsement of feminine attributes and, if it does ($|t| \geq 2.025$, $df = 38$, $p < .05$), to classify that person as significantly sex typed; and second, it allows us to compare different populations in terms of the percentage of significantly sex-typed individuals present within each.[3]

It should be noted that the greater the absolute value of the Androgyny score, the more the person is sex typed or sex reversed, with high positive scores indicating femininity and high negative scores indicating masculinity. A "masculine" sex role thus represents not only the endorsement of masculine attributes but the simultaneous rejection of feminine attributes. Similarly, a "feminine" sex role represents not only the endorsement of feminine attributes but the simultaneous rejection of masculine attributes. In contrast, the closer the Androgyny score is to zero, the more the person is androgynous. An "androgynous" sex role thus represents the equal endorsement of both masculine and feminine attributes.

The Social Desirability score indicates the extent to which a person describes himself in a socially desirable direction on items that are neutral with respect to sex. It is scored by reversing the self-endorsement ratings for the 10 undesirable items and then calculating the subject's mean endorsement score across all 20 neutral personality characteristics. The Social Desirability score can thus range from 1 to 7, with 1 indicating a strong tendency to describe oneself in a socially undesirable direction and 7 indicating a strong tendency to describe oneself in a socially desirable direction.

PSYCHOMETRIC ANALYSES

Subjects

During the winter and spring of 1973, the BSRI was administered to 444 male and 279 female students in introductory psychology at Stanford University. It was also administered to an additional 117 male and 77 female paid volunteers at Foothill Junior College. The data that these students provided represent the normative data for the BSRI, and, unless explicitly noted, they serve as the basis for all of the analyses that follow.

Internal Consistency

In order to estimate the internal consistency of the BSRI, coefficient alpha was computed separately for the Masculinity, Femininity and Social Desirability scores of the subjects in each of the two normative samples. (Nunnally, 1967). The results showed all three scores to be highly reliable, both in the Stanford sample (Masculinity α = .86; Femininity α = .80; Social Desirability α = .75) and in the Foothill sample (Masculinity α = .86; Femininity α = .82; Social Desirability α = .70). Because the reliability of the

Androgyny t ratio could not be calculated directly, coefficient alpha was computed for the highly correlated Androgyny difference score, Femininity-Masculinity, using the formula provided by Nunnally (1967) for linear combinations. The reliability of the Androgyny difference score was .85 for the Stanford sample and .86 for the Foothill sample.

Relationship between Masculinity and Femininity

As indicated earlier, the Masculinity and Femininity scores of the BSRI are logically independent. That is, the structure of the test does not constrain them in any way, and they are free to vary independently. The results from the two normative samples reveal them to be empirically independent as well (Stanford male r = .11, female r = −.14; Foothill male r = −.02, female r = −.07). This finding vindicates the decision to design an inventory that would not artifactually force a negative correlation between masculinity and femininity.

Social Desirability Response Set

It will be recalled that a person is sex typed on the BSRI to the extent that his or her Androgyny score reflects the greater endorsement of "sex-appropriate" characteristics than of "sex-inappropriate" characteristics. However, because of the fact that the masculine and feminine items are all relatively desirable, even for the "inappropriate" sex, it is important to verify that the Androgyny score is not simply tapping a social desirability response set.

Accordingly, product-moment correlations were computed between the Social Desirability score and the Masculinity, Femininity, and Androgyny scores for the Stanford and Foothill samples separately. They were also computed between the Social Desirability score and the absolute value of the Androgyny score. These correlations are displayed in Table 4. As expected, both Masculinity and Femininity were correlated with Social Desirability. In contrast, the near-zero correlations between Androgyny and Social Desirability confirm that the Androgyny score is not measuring a general tendency to respond in a socially desirable direction. Rather, it is measuring a very specific tendency to describe oneself in accordance

TABLE 4 / Correlation of Masculinity, Femininity, and Androgyny with Social Desirability

Sample	Masculinity with Social Desirability		Femininity with Social Desirability		Androgyny with Social Desirability		|Androgyny| with Social Desirability	
	Males	Females	Males	Females	Males	Females	Males	Females
Stanford	.42	.19	.28	.26	.12	.03	.08	−.10
Foothill	.23	.19	.15	.15	−.07	.06	−.12	−.09
Stanford and Foothill combined	.38	.19	.28	.22	.08	.04	.03	−.10

with sex-typed standards of desirable behavior for men and women.

Test-Retest Reliability

The BSRI was administered for a second time to 28 males and 28 females from the Stanford normative sample. The second administration took place approximately four weeks after the first. During this second administration, subjects were told that we were interested in how their responses on the test might vary over time, and they were explicitly instructed not to try to remember how they had responded previously. Product-moment correlations were computed between the first and second administrations for the Masculinity, Femininity, Androgyny, and Social Desirability scores. All four scores proved to be highly reliable over the four-week interval (Masculinity $r = .90$; Femininity $r = .90$; Androgyny $r = .93$; Social Desirability $r = .89$).

Correlations with Other Measures of Masculinity-Femininity

During the second administration of the BSRI, subjects were also asked to fill out the Masculinity-Femininity scales of the California Psychological Inventory and the Guilford-Zimmerman Temperament Survey, both of which have been utilized rather frequently in previous research on sex roles. Table 5 presents the correlations between these two scales and the Masculinity, Femininity, and Androgyny scales of the BSRI. As can be seen in the table, the Guilford-Zimmerman scale is not at all correlated with any of the three scales of the BSRI, whereas the California Psychological Inventory is moderately correlated with all three. It is

not clear why the BSRI should be more highly correlated with the CPI than with the Guilford-Zimmerman scale, but the fact that none of the correlations is particularly high indicates that the BSRI is measuring an aspect of sex roles which is not directly tapped by either of these two scales.

NORMS

Table 6 presents the mean Masculinity, Femininity, and Social Desirability scores separately by sex for both the Stanford and the Foothill normative samples. It also presents means for both the Androgyny t ratio and the Androgyny difference score. As can be seen in the table, males scored significantly higher than females on the Masculinity scale, and females scored significantly higher than males on the Femininity scale in both samples. On the two measures of androgyny, males scored on the masculine side of zero and females scored on the feminine side of

TABLE 5 / Correlation of the Masculinity-Femininity Scales of the California Psychological Inventory (CPI) and Guilford-Zimmerman Scale with the Masculinity, Femininity, and Androgyny Scales of the BSRI

Scale	CPI		Guilford-Zimmerman	
	Males	Females	Males	Females
BSRI Masculinity	−.42	−.25	.11	.15
BSRI Femininity	.27	.25	.04	−.06
BSRI Androgyny	.50	.30	−.04	−.06

Note: The CPI scale is keyed in the feminine direction, whereas the Guilford-Zimmerman scale is keyed in the masculine direction.

TABLE 6 / Sex Differences on the BSRI

Scale Score	Stanford University			Foothill Junior College		
	Males (*n* = 444)	Females (*n* = 279)	*t*	Males (*n* = 117)	Females (*n* = 77)	*t*
Masculinity						
M	4.97	4.57		4.96	4.55	
SD	.67	.69	7.62*	.71	.75	3.86*
Femininity						
M	4.44	5.01		4.62	5.08	
SD	.55	.52	13.88*	.64	.58	5.02*
Social Desirability						
M	4.91	5.08		4.88	4.89	
SD	.50	.50	4.40*	.50	.53	ns
Androgyny t Ratio						
M	−1.28	1.10		−.80	1.23	
SD	1.99	2.29	14.33*	2.23	2.42	5.98*
Androgyny Difference Score						
M	−0.53	.43		−.34	.53	
SD	.82	.93	14.28*	.97	.97	6.08*

*$p < .001$.

zero. This difference is significant in both samples and for both measures. On the Social Desirability scale, females scored significantly higher than males at Stanford but not at Foothill. It should be noted that the size of this sex difference is quite small, however, even in the Stanford sample.

Table 7 presents the percentage of subjects within each of the two normative samples who qualified as masculine, feminine, or androgynous as a function of the Androgyny *t* ratio. Subjects are classified as sex typed, whether masculine or feminine, if the androgyny *t* ratio reaches statistical significance ($|t| \geq 2.025$, *df* = 38, $p < .05$), and they are classified as androgynous if the absolute value of the *t* ratio is less than or equal to one. Table 7 also indicates the percentage of subjects who fall between these various cutoff points. It should be noted that these cut-off points are somewhat arbitrary and that other investigators should feel free to adjust them in accordance with the characteristics of their particular subject populations.

CONCLUDING COMMENT

It is hoped that the development of the BSRI will encourage investigators in the areas of sex differences and sex roles to question the traditional assumption that it is the sex-typed individual who typifies mental health and to begin focusing on the behavioral and societal consequences of more flexible sex-role self-concepts. In a society where rigid sex-role differentiation has already outlived its utility, perhaps the androgynous person will come to define a more human standard of psychological health.

REFERENCES

Barry, H., Bacon, M. K., & Child, I. L. A cross-cultural survey of some sex differences in socialization. *Journal of Abnormal and Social Psychology,* 1957, *55,* 327–332.

Bem, S. L. Sex-role adaptability: One consequence of psychological androgyny. *Journal of Personality and Social Psychology,* 1974, in press.

TABLE 7 / Percentage of Subjects in the Normative Samples Classified as Masculine, Feminine, or Androgynous

Item	Stanford University		Foothill Junior College	
	Males (*n* = 444)	Females (*n* = 279)	Males (*n* = 117)	Females (*n* = 77)
% feminine (*t* ≥ 2.025)	6	34	9	40
% near feminine (1 < *t* < 2.025)	5	20	9	8
% androgynous (−1 ≤ *t* ≤ +1)	34	27	44	38
% near masculine (−2.025 < *t* < −1)	19	12	17	7
% masculine (*t* ≤ −2.025)	36	8	22	8

Edwards, A. L. The measurement of human motives by means of personality scales. In D. Levine (Ed.), *Nebraska symposium on motivation: 1964.* Lincoln: University of Nebraska Press, 1964.

Erikson, E. H. Inner and outer space: Reflections on womanhood. In R. J. Lifton (Ed.), *The woman in America.* Boston: Houghton Mifflin, 1964.

Gough, H. G. *Manual for the California Psychological Inventory.* Palo Alto, Calif.: Consulting Psychologists Press, 1957.

Kagan, J. Acquisition and significance of sex-typing and sex-role identity. In M. L. Hoffman & L. W. Hoffman (Eds.), *Review of child development research.* Vol. 1. New York: Russell Sage Foundation, 1964.

Kohlberg, L. A cognitive-developmental analysis of children's sex-role concepts and attitudes. In E. E. Maccoby (Ed.), *The development of sex differences.* Stanford, Calif.: Stanford University Press, 1966.

Nunnally, J. C. *Psychometric theory.* New York: McGraw-Hill, 1967.

Parsons, T., & Bales, R. F. *Family, socialization, and interaction process.* New York: Free Press of Glencoe, 1955.

ENDNOTES

1. This research was supported by IROIMH 21735 from the National Institute of Mental Health. The author is grateful to Carol Korula, Karen Rook, Jenny Jacobs, and Odile van Embden for their help in analyzing the data.

2. All significance levels in this article are based on two-tailed *t* tests.

3. A Statistical Package for the Social Sciences (SPSS) computer program for calculating individual *t* ratios is available on request from the author. In the absence of computer facilities, one can utilize the simple Androgyny difference score, Femininity-Masculinity, as the index of androgyny. Empirically, the two indices are virtually identical (*r* = .98), and one can approximate the *t*-ratio value by multiplying the Androgyny difference score by 2.322. This conversion factor was derived empirically from our combined normative sample of 917 students at two different colleges.

CRITICAL THINKING QUESTIONS

1. Examine the sample items in Table 1 that are categorized as masculine, feminine, or neutral. Since this article was written in 1974, these items were selected more than two decades ago. Do you think that these items are still applicable today, or are some of them dated and perhaps even controversial? Have notions of masculinity and femininity changed over time? Explain.

2. The BSRI (Bem Self-Role Inventory) is a self-report instrument. Do you think the way someone describes his or her characteristics on paper is necessarily an accurate portrayal of the way he or she really acts? In what way? How could you test this possibility?

3. What do you think of the concept of *androgyny?* Would society be better off if more people were androgynous rather than being either masculine *or* feminine? Why or why not?

4. Based on the information in the article, describe specific situations where an androgynous individual might be better suited than either a masculine or feminine individual. In what, if any, situations would someone only capable of masculine behaviors be more appropriate? What about someone only capable of feminine behaviors? Explain your answers.

5. After reading the article, you should have a good grasp of the concept of androgyny. If you explained this concept to others, do you think that most people would agree that they would be better off if they were androgynous rather than either masculine or feminine? Why or why not?

ADDITIONAL RELATED READINGS

Burn, S. M., O'Neil, A. K., & Nederend, S. (1996). Childhood tomboyish and adult androgyny. *Sex Roles, 34,* 419–428.

Green, B. L., & Kenrick, D. T. (1994). The attractiveness of gender-typed traits at different relationship levels: Androgynous characteristics may be desirable after all. *Personality and Social Psychology Bulletin, 20,* 244–253.

ARTICLE 15 _____

A person's self-concept obviously is embedded in experience, to a large extent. How we view ourselves and the judgments we make about our own self-perceptions are influenced by many factors, ranging from direct experience to more general cultural factors as to what we believe should be valued. Furthermore, these cultural beliefs as to what should be valued may not be static but may change over time. Consider physical attractiveness, for instance, a topic that is more fully explored in Chapter 7. Cultural norms as to what is considered attractive are not necessarily the same today as they were 20 years ago. These norms are conveyed in many ways but are especially promulgated in the mass media. After all, everyone in American culture is exposed to a vast number of images—whether in photographs, on television, or in the movies—that all convey messages as to what constitutes physical attractiveness.

What impact might these messages about attractiveness have on our self-concepts? Do we compare ourselves to these media images and then judge our own attractiveness as a result? Or are these images more benign, having little impact on our own self-concepts? There has been speculation for some time that women's self-concepts, especially with regard to body satisfaction, are strongly influenced by media portrayals of female attractiveness. It even has been suggested that the high incidence of eating disorders, such as anorexia and bulimia, may be linked to the media's persistent focus on thinness, which is portrayed as the ideal in Western society.

Does this constant exposure to images of thinness have a major impact on women's self-concepts? The following article by Sheryl A. Monteath and Marita P. McCabe identifies factors that may be associated with female body image.

The Influence of Societal Factors on Female Body Image

■ Sheryl A. Monteath and Marita P. McCabe

ABSTRACT. This study was designed to identify factors associated with the perceptual and attitudinal components of female body image. The influence of society and factors thought to mediate the relationship between body image and society (field dependence, locus of control, and self-esteem) were investigated. Age and body mass index (BMI) were also included as independent variables. A total of 101 female university students in Australia ranging in age from 18 to 55 years (M = 24.11) participated in the study. A video camera apparatus (VCA) was used to assess perceptual distortion of body size. The VCA, the Body Esteem Scale, and the Appearance Evaluation subscale of the Multidimensional Body Self Relations Questionnaire were used to assess body satisfaction. On average, women underestimated their body sizes by 4%, and they typically wanted to be smaller than their actual body sizes. About two fifths of the women expressed moderate to strong negative feelings about both individual body parts and their bodies as a whole. Multiple regression analyses revealed that perceptual distortion of body size could not be predicted from the independent variables. Body satisfaction was best explained by societal factors, self-esteem, and BMI.

Reprinted from *The Journal of Social Psychology, 137,* 708–727, 1997. Reprinted with permission of the Helen Dwight Reid Educational Foundation. Published by Heldref Publications, 1319 Eighteenth St., N.W., Washington, D.C. 20036-1802. Copyright © 1997.

Our aim in the present study was to investigate factors that may affect a woman's perception of and attitudes toward her body. Body image involves both a perceptual and an attitudinal component. A disturbance in the perceptual component of body image typically is reflected in distorted perceptions of body size, shape, or appearance, whereas a disturbance in the attitudinal component usually results in dissatisfaction with body appearance or functional capacity.

Some researchers have suggested that perceptual distortion of body size is a characteristic unique to individuals with eating disorders. Garner, Garfinkel, Stancer, and Moldofsky (1976) compared obese and anorexic female patients with three non-eating-disordered control groups. The eating-disordered groups demonstrated more perceptual disturbances in body size. In contrast, Fernandez, Probst, Meerman, and Vandereycken (1993) found no differences in body size estimation between eating-disordered and non-eating-disordered women. The findings revealed that some participants overestimated, some underestimated, and others correctly perceived their body sizes.

Some studies of non-eating-disordered women have suggested that women show an overall tendency to underestimate the sizes of their bodies, whereas others have found that overestimation is the norm. Gardner and Tockerman (1993) found that, on average, females using a video camera apparatus (VCA) underestimated their body sizes. Those results differ from the findings of McCaulay, Mintz, and Glenn (1988), who found that 55% of female undergraduates perceived themselves to be overweight, whereas only 6% actually fell within that weight category.

These different findings can perhaps be explained in terms of the definitions of perceptual distortion. McCaulay et al. (1988) focused on the perception of body weight, which is perhaps different from the perception of body size. The varied research findings may also be due to the fact that some researchers employed methods that measure perception of the body as a whole, whereas others assessed perception of the body on a part-by-part basis. Some researchers have suggested that estimates based on the judgments of a whole-body gestalt may be more valid than estimates derived from judgments of individual body parts (Cash & Brown, 1987; Gardner & Tockerman,

1993; Keeton, Cash, & Brown, 1990), because estimates based on individual body parts almost always overestimate body size, are unrelated to verbally reported beliefs about one's size normativeness, tend to be idiosyncratic, and are largely independent of objective reality (Keeton et al., 1990).

Many researchers have suggested that perceptual distortion of body size also varies as a function of body weight. Some studies have suggested that people distort their body sizes to bring them closer to normalcy (Gray, 1977; Gustavson et al., 1990), whereas other studies have revealed a tendency for both overweight and underweight individuals to overestimate their sizes (Cash & Green, 1986; Collins, McCabe, Jupp, & Sutton, 1983).

The inconsistent research findings may have resulted from not only the variety of methods used but also from the difference in samples. Gustavson et al. (1990) and Gray (1977) used a sample composed of both males and females, whereas Cash and Green (1986) and Collins et al. (1983) used females only. Results may differ when a combined sample of men and women is used rather than a sample consisting only of women.

Clearly, research in the area of perceptual size distortion is plagued with contradictions and inconsistencies. It is unclear whether people in nonclinical samples show a general tendency to overestimate, underestimate, or accurately perceive their body sizes. The variability in findings may result from the wide range of techniques and definitions that have been employed to explore the perceptual component of body image.

Body dissatisfaction is currently common among women in Western societies. Rodin, Silberstein, and Striegel-Moore (1984) suggested that, for many, feeling fat is an everyday part of life; consequently, many women turn to chronic dieting as a solution.

One way that body satisfaction can be operationalized is through an assessment of the difference between an individual's perceived and ideal body size. Fallon and Rozin (1985) used this technique to investigate body satisfaction in a sample of males and females who completed the Stunkard Body Shapes Figure Scale (SBSFS). Participants selected the figure that best represented their current and ideal body sizes. A significant discrepancy existed between females' perceived actual and ideal body sizes. Typically, they expressed a desire to be thinner.

Lamb, Jackson, Cassiday, and Priest (1993) demonstrated that females in two different generations expressed a desire to be thinner, and the younger women desired much thinner bodies than the older generation did. Self-report questionnaires have indicated that women are not uniformly dissatisfied with the appearance of their bodies but are consistently dissatisfied with specific body areas. Cash, Winstead, and Janda (1986) revealed that these areas of dissatisfaction included the middle and lower sections of the body—areas commonly affected by weight gain. A considerable amount of research has suggested that body satisfaction is also influenced by body weight (Cash & Green, 1986; Toro, Castro, Garcia, Perez, & Cuesta, 1989). Cash and Green (1986) found that overweight women were significantly more dissatisfied with the appearance of their bodies than women from other weight categories were.

Self-report questionnaires and methods that assess the difference between actual and ideal body sizes appear to measure different aspects of body satisfaction. Actual versus ideal scores indicate satisfaction with overall body size. In contrast, self-report questionnaires identify specific areas of concern and tap into attitudes toward the body as well as satisfaction with the different parts of the body. Therefore, it may be advantageous to include multiple measures of body satisfaction to allow a more comprehensive understanding of the different components of body image.

Social factors are believed to be important in the development of a woman's body attitudes and perceptions. Research suggests that the Western female body ideal is ectomorphic or thin (Butler & Ryckman, 1993; Cohn & Adler, 1992; Garner & Garfinkel, 1980; Garner, Garfinkel, Schwartz, & Thompson, 1980; Lamb et al., 1993; Martinelli-Hall & Havassy, 1981; Mintz & Betz, 1988; Mishkind, Rodin, Silberstein, & Striegel-Moore, 1986; Myers & Biocca, 1992; Rodin et al., 1984; Toro et al., 1989). Garner et al. (1980) reported that concepts of feminine beauty have varied throughout history in Western societies and that over the past century, the idealized female shape has changed from voluptuous and curved to angular and lean.

One way that societal body ideals are conveyed to the public is through stereotypes related to appearance. In Western society, an extremely negative stereotype of overweight people exists. Larkin and Pines (1979) provided evidence for such a stereotype by asking their participants to read and evaluate written descriptions of individuals who differed only in terms of sex and weight. They rated overweight people more negatively than they rated people of average weight. These findings suggest that a negative overweight stereotype exists.

In contrast to this perception—that fat is synonymous with bad—is the stereotype that equates beauty with goodness. Dion, Berscheid, and Walster (1972) investigated this stereotype by asking participants to evaluate photographs of attractive, neutral, and unattractive individuals. Attractive individuals were assigned more positive personality traits and, perhaps accurately, were assumed to lead more happy, successful lives. This study provided evidence for the existence of a beauty stereotype in Western societies and suggested that its influence pervades many aspects of life. However, Eagly, Ashmore, Makhijani, and Longo (1991) cautioned that the physical attractiveness stereotype may not be as general as Dion et al. (1972) indicated. Eagly et al. suggested that the stereotype is strongest when ratings are associated with social competence.

Stereotypes are influential, especially when they are the only information that an observer has about a particular person. Women quickly learn that their social opportunities are affected by their beauty, and consequently their sense of their own attractiveness may become an integral part of women's self-concepts (Mazur, 1986).

According to empirical studies, the media in Western countries have portrayed a steadily thinning female body ideal (Stice & Shaw, 1994). In addition, a content analysis of popular magazines revealed that women's magazines contained 10.5 times as many articles as men's magazines relating to body weight (Andersen & DiDomenico, 1992). Researchers believe that these media messages promoting thinness are internalized by women from Western countries and that as a result, being slender becomes a goal that they strive to achieve (Myers & Biocca, 1992).

The evidence suggests that in Western countries, societal considerations affect both perceptual and attitudinal components of body image. Women whose bodies are consistent with the current societal ideal are much more likely to have healthy body images than are women whose bodies deviate from the ideal.

It has been suggested that field-dependent people are more influenced by societal ideals than are field-independent people. Gendebien and Smith (1992) compared levels of body size distortion and body satisfaction in field-independent and field-dependent individuals. Field-dependent women overestimated their sizes more than field-independent women did. Field-dependent women also distorted in an unfavorable direction those parts of the body that were most relevant to the current societal body ideal. In particular, the stomach, hips, and thighs emerged as the greatest areas of concern. No relationship was found between field dependence and the attitudinal component of body image. However, the scale Gendebien and Smith employed measured satisfaction with the whole body rather than with each body part. Field-dependent women may express dissatisfaction with areas of the body that are stressed by the societal ideal, rather than with the body as a whole (Thomas & Freeman, 1990).

A relationship between locus of control and the perceptual component of body image disturbance has also been found. Females with an external locus of control tend to overestimate their body sizes to a greater degree than those who have an internal locus of control (Garner et al., 1976; Mable, Balance, & Galgan, 1986). In addition, a relationship exists between the attitudinal component of body image and locus of control. In particular, women exhibiting external locus of control experience greater dissatisfaction with the appearance of their bodies than do women with internal locus of control (Adame & Johnson, 1989; Garner et al., 1976; Mable et al., 1986). This finding may indicate that women possessing an external locus of control feel powerless to alter the appearance of their bodies and thus experience distorted perceptions of and negative feelings about their bodies. In contrast, women with an internal locus of control perhaps believe that the appearance of their bodies is within their control. Their feelings of

empowerment may result in more positive views of their bodies.

Self-esteem may also mediate the relationship between societal factors and body image disturbance. A considerable amount of empirical research has shown that a relationship exists between self-esteem and the attitudinal component of body image (Mable et al., 1986; McAllister & Caltabiano, 1994; Mishkind et al., 1986; Thompson, Fabian, Moulton, Dunn, & Altabe, 1991; Vann Rackley, Warren, & Bird, 1988). Mable et al. (1986) found a consistent association between low self-esteem and low body satisfaction. No relationship, however, was found between self-esteem and perceptual distortion.

Consistent with these findings are those of Mintz and Betz (1986), who found that for both men and women, body satisfaction correlated positively with social self-esteem. This relationship was found to be significantly stronger for women and also for those who were slightly underweight. No differences were found between men and women who were of normal weight. However, the relationship that emerged may have been confounded with body weight. Underweight women were perhaps more likely to feel better about themselves and also to have more positive feelings about their bodies. Therefore, weight may have been responsible for the observed relationship between self-esteem and body satisfaction.

In the current study, we examined the relationship between societal factors and body image in a nonclinical sample of Australian women. We expected that

1. societal factors would be associated with perceptual distortion and body dissatisfaction;
2. field dependence would be associated with greater levels of perceptual distortion and greater dissatisfaction with the areas of the body that are stressed by the societal ideal;
3. an external locus of control would be related to greater levels of perceptual distortion and greater degrees of body dissatisfaction; and
4. no association would exist between self-esteem and perceptual distortion, but women with low self-esteem would demonstrate higher levels of body dissatisfaction.

METHOD

Participants

Participants were 101 female university students from Melbourne, Australia. Volunteer participants were recruited through a Research Participation Participant Pool that operated within the School of Psychology. Students were required to choose from a range of experiments to obtain course credit. Additional participants were recruited through advertising around the university campus. Participants ranged in age from 18 to 55 years ($M = 24.11$).

Materials

Video Camera Apparatus   We used a video camera apparatus (VCA) based on that used by Collins et al. (1983) to measure perceptual distortion of body size, satisfaction with body size, and perception of the societal body ideal. The apparatus consisted of a Sony Trinitron color television monitor and a Panasonic VHS video camera. The impulses received by the video camera were fed into the monitor so that an image could be observed on the screen. The frame size control of the monitor was disconnected, and an external control knob was fitted. Rotation of the external control knob allowed the image on the screen to be varied along the horizontal plane. The image could be adjusted from overweight (up to 74% larger than actual size), to normal weight, to underweight (up to 26% smaller than actual size) without distorting the height of the image.

Each participant was asked to adjust the image on the screen to represent her perceived body size. This adjustment measured perceptual distortion of body size. Perceived body size was divided by actual body size and multiplied by 100 to obtain a percentage score indicating the degree of overestimation or underestimation.

We also used the VCA to measure body satisfaction by subtracting each participant's perceived actual body size from her ideal body size. Negative scores indicated a desire to be thinner, and positive scores indicated a desire to be larger. Past research supports the validity of using the VCA as a measure of body satisfaction (Freeman, Thomas, Solyom, & Hunter, 1984).

Finally, we used the VCA to measure each participant's perception of the societal body ideal by asking her to adjust the image on the screen to represent the societal ideal. We calculated deviation from the societal ideal by subtracting actual body size from perception of the societal ideal. Negative scores indicated that the participant perceived the societal ideal to be smaller than actual body size, and positive scores indicated that the participant perceived the societal ideal to be larger than actual size.

Stunkard Body Shapes Figure Scale   We included the Stunkard Body Shapes Figure Scale (SBSFS; Stunkard, Sorenson, & Schlusinger, 1980) to provide a paper-and-pencil measure of the perceptual component of body image; the scale also served as a validity check for the VCA. The SBSFS consists of a row of nine female body silhouettes that range from thin to obese. Respondents were asked to select the images closest to their own body shapes and sizes.

The SBSFS also provided a paper-and-pencil measure of body satisfaction and perception of the societal body ideal. We measured body satisfaction by subtracting perceived actual size from ideal body size. We calculated deviation from the societal ideal by subtracting perceived actual body size from the perceived societal ideal. This calculation provided body satisfaction scores and societal deviation scores that could range from −8 to +8.

Body Esteem Scale   The Body Esteem Scale (BES; Franzoi & Shields, 1984) is a self-report measure of body satisfaction. Although it is based on the Body Cathexis Scale (Secord & Jourard, 1953), body image is not assumed to be unidimensional in the BES. The scale can be broken down into three female subscales that represent different aspects of body esteem: Sexual Attractiveness, Weight Concern, and Physical Condition.

Respondents rate 35 individual body parts and processes on a 5-point Likert-type scale ranging from *strong negative feelings* (1) to *strong positive feelings* (5). A BES score is obtained by adding the responses to each item. The total BES score can range from 35 to 175. Higher scores indicate higher body esteem.

We included a modified version of the BES to measure the participant's awareness of the societal ideal. In the modified version, participants were asked to rate each body part according to how they believe society sees their bodies. Responses to the modified BES were scored in the same manner as the original BES.

Appearance Evaluation Subscale of the Multidimensional Body Self Relations Questionnaire

The Appearance Evaluation subscale (AES; Cash, 1994) is a 7-item scale that we included to provide an additional measure of body satisfaction. Unlike the BES, the AES assesses satisfaction with the body as a whole, rather than on a part-by-part basis. Respondents rate their levels of agreement with the statements on a 5-point Likert-type scale, ranging from *definitely disagree* (1) to *definitely agree* (5). After negatively worded items are reverse coded, the scale can be scored by summing each response. This process yields an AES score that ranges from 7 to 35. Higher scores indicate greater satisfaction with appearance.

The Rod and Frame Test

We used the Rod and Frame Test (RFT; Witkin & Asch, 1948) to measure field dependence. The apparatus consists of a rod with an adjustable slant that is enclosed within a square frame. The frame can be tilted clockwise or counterclockwise. Participants are asked to adjust the rod slant so that it is vertical in relation to gravity. Judgments of field-dependent individuals tend to be influenced by the tilted frame, whereas field-independent individuals are not influenced by the tilt of the frame.

Rotter's Internal–External Locus of Control Scale

We used Rotter's (1966) IE Locus of Control Scale to measure locus of control. The scale consists of 23 question pairs in a forced-choice format and an additional 6 filler questions; it is scored by summing the external responses across all items, yielding a locus of control score that can range from 0 to 23. Higher scores indicate an external locus of control, and lower scores suggest an internal locus of control.

Rosenberg's Self-Esteem Scale

We used Rosenberg's (1965) Self-Esteem Scale to measure self-esteem. Composed of 10 items, the scale is designed to measure self-acceptance. Respondents rate their agreement with each item on a 4-point scale ranging from *strongly agree* (1) to *strongly disagree* (4). After negatively worded items are reverse coded, the scale is scored by summing the responses to all items, yielding a self-esteem score that can range from 10 to 40. Higher scores indicate higher self-esteem.

Additional Materials

In addition to the above materials, we used scales and a tape measure to measure height and weight and then calculated body mass index (BMI), a measure of body fat, according to the following equation:

$$BMI = \frac{\text{weight (kg)}}{\text{height}^2 \text{(m)}^2}.$$

Procedure

Testing occurred after the participant understood what was expected of her and had signed a consent form. Participants were assured of anonymity and confidentiality.

First, each participant changed into clothing that sufficiently revealed her body shape (private changing facilities were provided). Then the participant was positioned at a standard distance from the VCA so that a full-length view of her body (from neck to feet) could be observed on the television screen. She was given the control knob and was instructed to alter the image on the screen in response to the following instructions:

1. Adjust the image on the screen until it represents how you think your body looks.
2. Adjust the image on the screen until it represents how you would like your body to look.
3. Adjust the image on the screen until it represents how you believe society expects your body to look.

The participant was also asked whether she focused on her whole body or a specific body part while making the adjustments.

Once all of the adjustments had been made, the participant changed back into her regular clothing and completed the RFT. Four adjustments to the rod were made when the frame was rotated to the left 28°. The frame was then rotated to the right 28°, and another four adjustments were made. A field-dependence score was obtained by averaging the eight adjustments.

After completing the RFT, each participant completed a self-report questionnaire in private. The questionnaire contained the BES, the AES, Rotter's IE Scale, Rosenberg's Self-Esteem Scale, and the SBSFS. We included an additional two questions at the start of the questionnaire to assess the importance of societal influences during the VCA adjustments. A 5-point scale ranging from 1 (*not at all important*) to 5 (*could not be more important*) was used to rate importance.

RESULTS

Perceptual Distortion of Body Size

Using the VCA, the women, on average, underestimated their body sizes. Underestimation was not characteristic of the entire sample: 56% of the sample underestimated their body sizes, 25% correctly estimated their body sizes, and the remaining 15% overestimated their body sizes.

Body Satisfaction

Using the VCA, women expressed a strong desire to be smaller than their current sizes. Examination of frequencies revealed that 94% of the sample expressed a desire to be smaller than their perceived actual sizes, 5% were content with their current sizes, and only 1% of the sample expressed a desire to be larger. A similar pattern of responses occurred when participants were asked to select their ideal figures by using the SBSFS, providing support for the validity of the VCA as a measure of body satisfaction.

Responses to the BES indicated that 44% of the sample expressed moderate to strong negative feelings about different parts of their bodies. Similarly, 39% expressed moderate to strong negative feelings about their bodies as a whole (measured by the AES). Examination of the BES subscales indicated that satisfaction with the body was not equivalent across body regions. We found that 18% of the sample expressed moderate to strong negative feelings on the Sexual Attractiveness subscale, 71% expressed moderate to strong negative feelings on the Weight Concern

subscale, and 33% expressed moderate to strong negative feelings on the Physical Condition subscale. Clearly, items on the Weight Concern subscale generated the most dissatisfaction.

Societal Factors

Nearly all of the women (96%) perceived themselves to be larger than the societal ideal according to the VCA. A similar pattern of responses emerged when they were asked to select the figure that represented the societal ideal on the SBSFS, providing support for the validity of the VCA as a measure of the societal ideal.

A standard multiple regression analysis was conducted to test Hypotheses 1, 2, 3, and 4 and identify the factors that influence perceptual distortion of body size (Table 1).

The multiple regression coefficient did not differ significantly from 0, $F(7, 93) = 1.64$, $p > .05$, indicating that perceptual distortion of body size was not explained by the current independent variables.

These findings support the prediction that perceptual distortions would occur across all weight and age categories. In addition, the prediction that self-esteem would be unrelated to perceptual distortion of body size was supported. No support was found for the rest of the predictions associated with perceptual distortion of body size.

To test Hypotheses 1, 3, and 4, we conducted a standard multiple regression on body satisfaction as measured by the VCA. The multiple regression coefficient differed significantly from 0, $F(7, 93) = 7.22$, $p < .001$ (Table 1). BMI, self-esteem, and deviation from the societal ideal were all significant predictors of satisfaction with body size. BMI predicted 7%, self-esteem predicted 6%, and deviation from the societal ideal predicted 3% of the variance. Locus of control, field dependence, and age did not contribute to the explained variance.

In combination, the independent variables included in the multiple regression analysis contributed a further 0.19 (19%) in shared variability. Overall, 35% (30% adjusted) of the variability in body satisfaction (VCA) was predicted by importance of societal factors, locus of control, BMI, field dependence, self-esteem, deviation from the societal ideal, and age.

TABLE 1 / Predictions of Perceptual Distortion in Body Size, Satisfaction with Body Size, Satisfaction Measured by the BES, and Body Satisfaction Measured by the AES

Variable	B	sr²	F	Sig. F
Prediction of Perceptual Distortion of Body Size				
Importance of societal factors	.22	.00	.14	.712
BMI	−.60	.08	7.90	.006
Field dependence	1.98	.01	.86	.355
Self-esteem	.02	.00	.03	.872
Deviation from societal ideal (VCA)	.10	.02	2.52	.115
Locus of control	−.13	.00	.54	.462
Age	−25.87	.00	.17	.683
Constant	42.59		.53	.467
Prediction of Satisfaction as Measured by the VCA				
Importance of societal factors	1.18	.02	2.33	.130
Locus of control	−.34	.02	2.48	.119
BMI	.87	.07	10.73	.001
Field dependence	−2.71	.01	1.03	.314
Self-esteem	−.47	.06	8.35	.005
Deviation from societal ideal (VCA)	−.19	.03	4.96	.028
Age	151.12	.02	3.38	.069
Constant	−139.29		3.30	.072
Prediction of Satisfaction as Measured by the BES				
Deviation from societal ideal (SBSFS)	−2.04	.01	4.47	.037
Locus of control	−.13	.00	.24	.628
Field dependence	2.44	.00	.53	.468
Self-esteem	1.12	.05	23.61	.000
Age	−200.54	.01	4.12	.045
BES, rated by society	.62	.22	99.98	.000
BMI	.52	.00	1.95	.166
Constant	192.35		4.54	.036
Prediction of Satisfaction as Measured by the AES				
Deviation from societal ideal (SBSFS)	−.74	.01	3.64	.060
Locus of control	.03	.00	.08	.782
Field dependence	.20	.00	.02	.883
Self-esteem	.40	.07	18.51	.000
Age	7.94	.00	.04	.841
BES, rated by society	.10	.07	17.41	.000
BMI	−.32	.02	4.67	.033
Constant	−.13		.00	.997

Note: BES = Body Esteem Scale. AES = Appearance Evaluation subscale. BMI = body mass index. VCA = video camera apparatus. SBSFS = Stunkard Body Shapes Figure Scale.

To test Hypotheses 1, 2, 3, and 4, we conducted a multiple regression on body satisfaction as measured by the BES. The multiple regression coefficient differed significantly from 0, $F(7, 93) = 51.33$, $p < .001$ (Table 1). Deviation from the societal ideal, self-esteem, age, and BES rated by society were all significant predictors of body satisfaction. The squared semipartial correlation for deviation from the societal ideal was .01, indicating that 1% of the variance was accounted for by this variable. Self-esteem accounted for 5% of the variance, age accounted for 1% of the variance, and the BES rated by society contributed a further 22% in variance. Locus of control, BMI, and field dependence did not contribute to explained variance.

In combination, the independent variables included in the multiple regression analysis accounted for another 0.50 (50%) of the variance. Overall, 79% (77% adjusted) of the variability in BES scores was predicted by deviation from the societal ideal, locus of control, field dependence, self-esteem, age, BES rated by society, and BMI.

To test Hypotheses 1, 3, and 4, we conducted a multiple regression on body satisfaction as measured by the AES. The multiple regression coefficient differed significantly from 0, $F(7, 93) = 22.69$, $p < .001$ (Table 1). Self-esteem, BES rated by society, and BMI were each significant predictors of AES scores. The squared semipartial correlations for self-esteem and BES rated by society were both .07, indicating that these two variables each explained 7% of the variance. BMI explained 2% of the variance. Deviation from the societal ideal, locus of control, field dependence, and age did not contribute to the explained variance.

In combination, the independent variables included in the multiple regression analysis accounted for another 0.47 (47%) of the variance. Overall, 63% (60% adjusted) of the variability in body satisfaction was predicted by deviation from the societal ideal, locus of control, field dependence, self-esteem, age, BES rated by society, and BMI.

Hierarchical Multiple Regression Analyses

Using SPSS regression, we performed two hierarchical regressions to determine whether attitudinal measures enhanced the prediction of body size distortion beyond that afforded by the measures used in the preceding analysis. Two blocks of predictor variables were used. The first block consisted of attitudinal measures of body satisfaction: the BES and AES scores. The second block of predictor variables consisted of age, deviation from the societal ideal, locus of control, importance of societal factors, field dependence, BMI, and self-esteem.

The results of the hierarchical regression at each step of the analysis are shown in Table 2. The multiple regression coefficient was significantly different from 0 after Step 1 but not after Step 2. After Step 1, with the AES and BES scores entered into the equation, $R = .27$, $F(2, 98) = 3.74$, $p < .05$. Therefore, 7% (5% adjusted) of the variance in perceptual distortion of body size was explained by body attitudes. Inspection of the partial correlations revealed that AES scores predicted 4% of the variance.

After Step 2, with the addition of age, deviation from the societal ideal, locus of control, importance of societal factors, field dependence, BMI, and self-esteem, the regression analysis was no longer significant, $R = .40$, $F(9, 91) = 1.92$, $p > .05$. The change in R^2 was also not significant; R^2 change = .09, F change $(9, 91) = 1.37$, $p > .05$.

We used a hierarchical regression to determine whether attitudinal measures of body satisfaction enhanced the prediction of satisfaction with body size (VCA) beyond that afforded by the measures used in the previous analysis. Two blocks of predictors were employed in the analysis. The first block consisted of attitudinal measures of body satisfaction (BES and AES scores), and the second consisted of age, deviation from societal ideal, locus of control, importance of societal factors, field dependence, BMI, and self-esteem.

The results of the hierarchical regression at each step of the analysis are displayed in Table 3. Multiple R was found to be significantly different from 0 at each step of the analysis. After Step 1, with body attitudes entered into the equation, $R = .50$, $F(2, 98) = 16.63$, $p < .001$; a total of 25% (24% adjusted) of the variance in satisfaction with body size was accounted for by attitudinal measures. Inspection of the partial correlations revealed that the AES score was a significant predictor of satisfaction with body size. AES scores explained 3% of the variance. Combined, AES and BES scores accounted for 22% of the variance.

After Step 2, with age, deviation from societal ideal, locus of control, importance of societal factors, field dependence, BMI, and self-esteem entered into the analysis, $R = .65$, $F(9, 91) = 7.33$, $p < .001$. After Step 2, 42% (36% adjusted) of the variance in satisfaction with body size had been accounted for. This increase in R^2 from Step 1 to Step 2 was significant,

TABLE 2 / Prediction of Distortion of Body Size (with Attitudinal Measures Entered First)

Variable	B	sr^2	F	Sig. F
Step 1				
AES	.32	.04	4.04	.047
BES	−.02	.00	.15	.695
Constant	2.02		.36	.548
Step 2				
AES	.31	.03	3.23	.075
BES	.00	.00	.00	.952
Age	−31.89	.00	.26	.611
Deviation from societal ideal (VCA)	.12	.03	3.47	.066
Locus of control	−.15	.01	.81	.370
Importance of societal factors	.30	.00	.25	.618
Field dependence	1.63	.01	.60	.441
BMI	−.38	.02	2.76	.100
Self-esteem	−.19	.01	1.29	.259
Constant	42.55		.54	.463

Note: AES = Appearance Evaluation subscale. BES = Body Esteem Scale. VCA = video camera apparatus. BMI = body mass index.

R^2 change = .17, F change $(9, 91) = 3.74, p < .01$; the addition of these variables explained a further 17% of the variance in body size satisfaction over that afforded by attitudinal measures alone. Inspection of the partial correlations revealed that BMI significantly contributed 3% of the variance.

DISCUSSION

Although the majority of women in the current study underestimated their body sizes, underestimation was not characteristic of the entire sample. Indeed, some of the women overestimated their sizes, and others

TABLE 3 / Prediction of Satisfaction with Body Size (with Attitudinal Measures Entered First)

Variable	B	sr^2	F	Sig. F
Step 1				
AES	−.44	.03	4.51	.036
BES	−.11	.02	2.98	.087
Constant	35.54		64.72	.000
Step 2				
AES	−.19	.00	.75	.388
BES	−.12	.02	3.94	.050
Age	135.88	.02	2.96	.089
Deviation from societal ideal (VCA)	.15	.02	3.65	.059
Locus of control	−.32	.01	2.38	.126
Importance of societal factors	.92	.01	1.53	.220
Field dependence	−1.76	.00	.47	.496
BMI	.60	.03	4.64	.034
Self-esteem	−.06	.00	.10	.754
Constant	−113.37		2.35	.128

Note: AES = Appearance Evaluation subscale. BES = Body Esteem Scale. VCA = video camera apparatus. BMI = body mass index.

correctly perceived the size of their bodies. Fernandez et al. (1993), using a VCA to assess the perceptual component of body image, reported similar variability in the direction of body size distortion.

The degree to which a woman perceptually distorted her body size generally could not be predicted from the variables used in the current analyses, except for body attitudes, which predicted a small amount of the variance in perceptual distortion of body size. Although factors such as society, field dependence, locus of control, and self-esteem did not predict perceptual distortions, a woman's feelings about her body were of some importance. It remains unclear what other factors are important predictors of perceptual size distortion.

Age did not uniquely predict or correlate significantly with perceptual distortion. This finding may indicate that perceptual distortion of body size occurs for all ages. However, the distribution of ages in the current investigation was strongly positively skewed; a large proportion of the women in the sample were in their 20s.

The participants' perceived deviations of their bodies from the societal ideal were not associated with perceptual distortion of body size. The importance that participants attached to societal factors also did not predict or correlate with perceptual distortion. These findings suggest that societal factors are not important to the prediction of perceptual distortion of body size. In addition, the factors expected to mediate the relationship between societal influences and the perceptual component of body image (field dependence and locus of control) were also unrelated to perceptual size distortion.

These unexpected findings are inconsistent with the findings of past research in the area of perceptual distortion and are perhaps a result of the method employed in the current analysis. Past researchers who have investigated the contribution of field dependence (Gendebien & Smith, 1992) and locus of control (Garner et al., 1976; Mable et al., 1986) to the understanding of the perceptual component of body image have used mostly methods that result in overestimation of body size (i.e., methods that assess perceptual distortion on a part-by-part basis). It may be that field dependence and locus of control are related only to perceptual distortions of body parts and not to distortion of the whole body. In fact, Garner et al. (1976) found that locus of control was related only to the part-by-part measure and not to the holistic measure of perceptual size distortion. Further research is required to investigate what the various measures of perceptual size distortion are actually measuring.

The results of the VCA revealed that an overwhelming proportion (94%) of the sample expressed a desire to be thinner. These findings are consistent with past research (Fallon & Rozin, 1985; Lamb et al., 1993) and suggest that dissatisfaction with the size of one's body is common among a sample of non-eating-disordered Australian women.

A high proportion of women also expressed moderate to strong negative attitudes toward their individual body parts and their whole bodies. Slightly more expressed dissatisfaction with individual parts of their bodies than with their whole bodies, perhaps indicating that women in Western societies are more dissatisfied with specific parts of the body than with the entire body. Indeed, when the BES was broken down into its three main subscales, it became clear that areas primarily associated with weight gain generated the most dissatisfaction in women. Those body areas, which include the stomach, buttocks, hips, legs, waist, and thighs, are the areas that are most often stressed by the current Western societal ideal.

Much more variance was accounted for with the self-report measures than was accounted for with the VCA. This finding may be due to the fact that the VCA can assess satisfaction with overall body size only. Although use of a video image of the actual participant is clearly advantageous, the VCA is limited because it cannot differentially alter specific parts of the body. Consequently, the VCA may not provide an accurate assessment of body satisfaction for women who are unhappy with particular parts of their body. Perhaps self-report questionnaires provide a more comprehensive understanding of the factors relating to body satisfaction than the VCA does, because questionnaires allow participants to evaluate specific parts of the body separately. In addition, factors other than body size (i.e., shape or appearance) may be taken into consideration.

BMI correlated with all three measures of body satisfaction. It was also a predictor of satisfaction as measured by the VCA and the AES. In particular, increasing BMI was associated with a higher level of body dissatisfaction. This finding is consistent with past research investigating the relationship between body mass and body satisfaction (Cash & Green, 1986; Toro et al., 1989). Clearly, being thin is an important predictor of a woman's attitudes toward her body.

The finding that BMI predicted satisfaction as measured by the VCA and the AES but not by the BES suggests that BMI influences a woman's satisfaction with her body as a whole but not specific body parts. Women in the normal weight range showed just as much dissatisfaction with specific body parts as larger women, suggesting that it is not only body weight or size that women consider when they form their body attitudes.

The relationship between age and body satisfaction was not clear in the present investigation. Older women were more satisfied with individual body parts than younger women were, but there were no differences between the groups in satisfaction with the body as a whole.

The influence of society on a woman's level of body satisfaction was measured with four separate techniques. The VCA and the SBSFS were used to assess perceived deviation from the societal ideal. The BES rated by society provided a measure of society's feelings about one's body, and, finally, the participant was directly asked how important societal factors were for her.

The results of the VCA revealed that the perceived societal ideal for women was even thinner than their own personal body ideals. The women perceived that Western society sets an extreme ideal of thinness, and many women were highly influenced by this ideal. They did recognize, however, that the ideal is extreme, and as a consequence, their own ideal was about halfway between their actual body sizes and the societal ideal. Larger deviations from the societal ideal were associated with higher levels of body dissatisfaction. This finding suggests that societal expectations are influential and greatly affect how women feel about their bodies.

The results of the BES indicated that the women believed that Western society would rate their bodies more negatively than they would rate them themselves. In addition, the BES rated by society was also found to be a unique predictor of self-reported body attitudes. In particular, unfavorable BES ratings by society were associated with greater levels of body dissatisfaction. This finding suggests that a woman's feelings about her own body are highly influenced by the way in which she believes society views her body.

In combination, the findings of the current investigation suggest that the thin Western societal ideal has a negative effect on women's body attitudes. Although women are aware of these societal influences, most are unable to ignore the overwhelming pressure to be thin. The societal ideal of thinness becomes a goal that most women desire.

There were mixed results with respect to the role of mediating factors on body satisfaction. Field dependence was not associated with any of the measures we used to assess the attitudinal component of body image. Past research has shown that field-dependent individuals tend to focus on body parts that are emphasized by the Western societal ideal (Gendebien & Smith, 1992). Indeed, when the BES was broken down into its three main subscales, field dependence approached significance as a unique predictor of the Weight Concern subscale. Therefore, a trend for field dependence to be associated with greater dissatisfaction with areas of the body that are stressed by the societal ideal was evidenced.

Although past researchers have found a relationship between locus of control and a woman's level of body satisfaction (Garner et al., 1976; Mable et al., 1986), the relationship was unclear in the present investigation.

Locus of control was somewhat related to a woman's feelings about her individual body parts, but not feelings about her body as a whole. However, this relationship was not particularly strong, and therefore the findings should be interpreted with caution.

Consistent with past research, self-esteem was related to all three aspects of body satisfaction. This finding supports the contention that self-esteem mediates the relationship between societal factors and body satisfaction.

Although body image is composed of perceptions and attitudes, attitudes had the most pervasive influence on a woman's body image. Indeed, a woman's self-reported body attitudes predicted both perceptual distortion and satisfaction with body size. This finding is important because it suggests that negative body attitudes are the cause of the high levels of body image disturbance among women in Western societies. Perceptual distortions of body size were not as influential.

The importance of societal factors to the attitudinal component of body image suggests that societal attitudes must change if the current levels of female body image disturbance are to be reduced. Societal ideals and stereotypes are most often conveyed to the public through the media. If the media included in their images women of all shapes and sides, such changes might promote more positive attitudes toward women whose bodies are not consistent with the current Western societal ideal. As a result, such changes might consequently have a positive impact on women's body attitudes and their overall body images.

The following limitations were associated with the present investigation:

■ Although the VCA offered the important advantage of using an actual image of the participant, it could not differentially alter specific regions of the body. Past research has suggested that women tend to distort and experience negative attitudes toward specific areas of the body rather than their body as a whole. The VCA, in its current form, is insensitive to such differential body perceptions and attitudes. Future efforts should be directed toward the development of measures that retain the use of an image of the participant but alter specific regions of the body, rather than the body as a whole.

■ The current study focused only on female body image. Future research should be directed toward the study of body perceptions and attitudes in males.

■ Enlisting university students as participants may have limited the generalizability of the findings.

■ The nature of the present research may also have resulted in an unavoidably biased sample. The fact that participants were required to stand in front of a video camera in addition to having their weight recorded may have discouraged participants who were more likely to have distorted body perceptions and negative body attitudes.

REFERENCES

Adame, D. D., & Johnson, T. C. (1989). Physical fitness, body image, and locus of control in college freshman men and women. *Perceptual and Motor Skills, 68,* 400–402.

Andersen, A. E., & DiDomenico, L. (1992). Diet vs. shape content of popular male and female magazines: A dose response relationship to the incidence of eating disorders? *International Journal of Eating Disorders, 11,* 283–287.

Butler, J. C., & Ryckman, R. M. (1993). Perceived and ideal physiques in male and female university students. *The Journal of Social Psychology, 133,* 751–752.

Cash, T. F. (1994). *The Multidimensional Body-Self Relations Questionnaire.* [Unpublished user's manual]. (Available from T. F. Cash, Old Dominion University, Norfolk, VA)

Cash, T. F., & Brown, T. A. (1987). Body image in anorexia nervosa and bulimia nervosa: A review of the literature. *Behavior Modification, 11,* 487–521.

Cash, T. F., & Green, G. K. (1986). Body weight and body image among college women: Perception, cognition and affect. *Journal of Personality Assessment, 50,* 290–301.

Cash, T. F., Winstead, B. A., & Janda, L. H. (1986, April). Body image survey report: The great American shape-up. *Psychology Today, 20,* 30–44.

Cohn, L. D., & Adler, N. E. (1992). Female and male perceptions of ideal body shapes: Distorted views among Caucasian college students. *Psychology of Women Quarterly, 16,* 69–79.

Collins, J. K., McCabe, M. P., Jupp, J. J., & Sutton, J. E. (1983). Body percept change in obese females after weight reduction therapy. *Journal of Clinical Psychology, 39,* 507–511.

Dion, K., Berscheid, E., & Walster, E. (1972). What is beautiful is good. *Journal of Personality and Social Psychology, 24,* 285–290.

Eagly, A. H., Ashmore, R. D., Makhijani, M. G., & Longo, L. C. (1991). What is beautiful is good, but . . . : A meta-analytic review of research conducted on the physical attractiveness stereotype. *Psychological Bulletin, 110,* 109–128.

Fallon, A. E., & Rozin, P. (1985). Sex differences in perceptions of desirable body shape. *Journal of Abnormal Psychology, 94,* 102–105.

Fernandez, F., Probst, M., Meerman, R., & Vandereycken, W. (1993). Body size estimation and body dissatisfaction in eating disorder patients and normal controls. *International Journal of Eating Disorders, 16,* 307–310.

Franzoi, S. L., & Shields, S. A. (1984). The Body Esteem Scale: Multidimensional structure and sex differences in a college population. *Journal of Personality Assessment, 48,* 173–178.

Freeman, R. J., Thomas, C. D., Solyom, L., & Hunter, M. A. (1984). A modified video camera for measuring body image distortion: Technical description and reliability. *Psychological Medicine, 14,* 411–416.

Gardner, R. M., & Tockerman, Y. R. (1993). Body dissatisfaction as a predictor of body size distortion: A multidimensional analysis of body image. *Genetic, Social, and General Psychology Monographs, 119,* 125–145.

Garner, D. M., & Garfinkel, P. E. (1980). Socio-cultural factors in the development of anorexia nervosa. *Psychological Medicine, 10,* 647–656.

Garner, D. M., Garfinkel, P. E., Schwartz, D., & Thompson, M. (1980). Cultural expectations of thinness in women. *Psychological Reports, 47,* 483–491.

Garner, D. M., Garfinkel, R. E., Stancer, H. C., & Moldofsky, H. (1976). Body image disturbances in anorexia nervosa and obesity. *Psychosomatic Medicine, 38,* 327–336.

Gendebien, M. L., & Smith, M. O. (1992). Field dependence and perceptual, cognitive, and affective measures of body image in asymptomatic college students. *Personality and Individual Differences, 13,* 937–943.

Gray, S. H. (1977). Social aspects of body image: Perception of normalcy of weight and affect of college undergraduates. *Perceptual and Motor Skills, 45,* 1035–1040.

Gustavson, C. R., Gustavson, J. C., Pumariega, A. J., Reinarz, D. E., Dameron, R., Gustavson, A. R., Pappas, T., & McCaul, K. (1990). Body-image distortion among male and female college and high school students, and eating-disordered patients. *Perceptual and Motor Skills, 71,* 1003–1010.

Keeton, W. P., Cash, T. F., & Brown, T. A. (1990). Body image or body images? Comparative, multidimensional assessment among college students. *Journal of Personality Assessment, 54,* 213–230.

Lamb, C. S., Jackson, L. A., Cassiday, P. B., & Priest, D. J. (1993). Body figure preferences of men and women: A comparison of two generations. *Sex Roles, 28,* 345–358.

Larkin, J. C., & Pines, H. A. (1979). No fat persons need apply: Experimental studies of the overweight stereotype and hiring preference. *Sociology of Work and Occupations, 6,* 312–327.

Mable, H. M., Balance, D. G., & Galgan, R. J. (1986). Body-image distortion and dissatisfaction in university students. *Perceptual and Motor Skills, 63,* 907–911.

Martinelli-Hall, S., & Havassy, B. (1981). The obese woman: Causes, correlates and treatment. *Professional Psychology, 12,* 163–170.

Mazur, A. (1986). U.S. trends in feminine beauty and overadaptation. *The Journal of Sex Research, 22,* 281–303.

McAllister, R., & Caltabiano, M. L. (1994). Self-esteem, body-image and weight in noneating-disordered women. *Psychological Reports, 75,* 1339–1343.

McCaulay, M., Mintz, L., & Glenn, A. A. (1988). Body image, self-esteem, and depression-proneness: Closing the gender gap. *Sex Roles, 18,* 381–391.

Mintz, L. B., & Betz, N. E. (1986). Sex differences in the nature, realism, and correlates of body image. *Sex Roles, 15,* 185–195.

Mintz, L. B., & Betz, N. E. (1988). Prevalence and correlates of eating disordered behaviours among undergraduate women. *Journal of Counseling Psychology, 35,* 463–471.

Mishkind, M. E., Rodin, J., Silberstein, L. R., & Striegel-Moore, R. H. (1986). The embodiment of masculinity: Cultural, psychological and behavioral dimensions. *American Behavioral Scientist, 29,* 545–562.

Myers, P. N., & Biocca, F. A. (1992). The elastic body image: The effect of television advertising and programming on body image distortions in young women. *Journal of Communication, 42,* 108–134.

Rodin, J., Silberstein, L., & Striegel-Moore, R. (1984). Women and weight: A normative discontent. *Nebraska Symposium on Motivation,* 267–307.

Rosenberg, M. (1965). *Society and the adolescent self image.* Princeton, NJ: Princeton University Press.

Rotter, J. B. (1966). Generalised expectancies for internal versus external control of reinforcement. *Psychological Monographs, 80,* 1–28.

Secord, P. E., & Jourard, S. M. (1953). The appraisal of body-cathexis: Body-cathexis and the self. *Journal of Consulting Psychology, 17,* 343–347.

Stice, E., & Shaw, H. E. (1994). Adverse effects of the media portrayed thin-ideal on women and linkages to bulimic symptomatology. *Journal of Social and Clinical Psychology, 13,* 288–308.

Stunkard, A., Sorenson, T., & Schlusinger, F. (1980). Use of the Danish Adoption Register for the study of obesity and thinness. In S. Kety (Ed.), *The genetics of neurological and psychiatric disorders* (pp. 115–120). New York: Raven Press.

Thomas, C. D., & Freeman, R. J. (1990). The Body Esteem Scale: Construct validity of the female subscales. *Journal of Personality Assessment, 54,* 204–212.

Thompson, J. K., Fabian, L. J., Moulton, D. O., Dunn, M. E., & Altabe, M. A. (1991). Development and validation of the physical appearance related teasing scale. *Journal of Personality Assessment, 56,* 513–521.

Toro, J., Castro, J., Garcia, M., Perez, P., & Cuesta, L. (1989). Eating attitudes, sociodemographic factors and body shape evaluation in adolescence. *British Journal of Medical Psychology, 62,* 61–70.

Vann Rackley, J., Warren, S. A., & Bird, G. W. (1988). Determinants of body image in women at middle life. *Psychological Reports, 62,* 9–10.

Witkin, H. A., & Asch, S. E. (1948). Studies in space orientation, IV. Further experiments on perception of the upright with displaced visual fields. *Journal of Experimental Psychology, 38,* 762–782.

CRITICAL THINKING QUESTIONS

1. For the subjects involved in the study, "the perceived societal ideal for women was even thinner than their own personal body ideals." How do you account for this finding? Why didn't the women adopt the societal ideal for their own personal ideal?

2. The subjects in this study primarily were traditional-aged college students. Do you think the same results would be obtained if the subjects were 30-, 40-, or 50-year-old women? Why or why not? Propose a study that would test this hypothesis.

3. Do you think that men are affected by societal images in the same ways that women are? In other words, do societal stereotypes of male attractiveness affect men's self-concepts or body images? Or might other societal stereotypes have greater impacts on men? For example, could societal expectations of male success affect men's self-esteem? How could this possibility be tested?

4. The article states, "The importance of societal factors to the attitudinal component of body image suggests that societal attitudes must change if the current levels of female body image disturbance are to be reduced." Is it possible to change such societal factors? Or could women be made more immune to these influences, perhaps starting in childhood? Explain your answers.

5. The article concludes with a list of four possible limitations of the study. Select and discuss any one of them, and then design a study that could overcome that limitation.

Chapter Six

PREJUDICE
AND DISCRIMINATION

PREJUDICE. THINK OF the implications of that word. It is so negative that even people who are highly prejudiced often are reluctant to use that term to describe themselves. Instead, prejudiced people may say that their opinions about members of certain groups are accurate and well founded, perhaps even that these groups deserve disdain.

Although the words *prejudice* and *discrimination* are often used interchangeably, they actually refer to two different things. *Prejudice* is an attitude, a set of beliefs about a member of a group based just on membership in that group. *Discrimination,* on the other hand, is a behavior, the differential treatment of a person based on membership in a particular group. You do not need to look far for the results of prejudiced attitudes and discriminatory behaviors: History is full of suffering that has been inflicted on people due solely to their membership in particular groups.

Psychological research on prejudice and discrimination has studied various topics, including what causes them, what consequences they have, and how they can be reduced. Article 16, "Breaking the Prejudice Habit," presents evidence that even though people's responses to others may be based on cultural stereotypes, they also can learn to overcome these generalizations. The article presents an optimistic view that prejudice may not be an inevitable part of the human condition.

Article 17, "Experiments in Group Conflict," demonstrates the development as well as the eventual elimination of prejudice in a group of boys. This classic article clearly addresses some of the factors that may contribute to the development of prejudice and demonstrates at least one way that it may be reduced.

Article 18, "Feedback to Minorities: Evidence of a Positive Bias," examines an aspect of prejudice that may not readily be apparent: namely, the possibility that prejudice may sometimes result in *more* positive evaluations of the targets of the prejudice. While positive evaluations and feedback are usually thought of as desirable, they can have negative effects if the positive feedback was not genuinely deserved. This, in turn, may have serious consequences for minorities who may be the recipients of undeserved positive evaluations.

ARTICLE 16 _____

Just about anyone, by virtue of membership in a particular group, can be a target of prejudice and discrimination. The standard scenario is that a person is prejudged and reacted to not as an individual but as a member of some group, such that the general characteristics of the group are automatically attributed to the individual. This process is known as *stereotyping*.

Stereotypes are an everyday fact of life. Although we may hope that we judge every person as an individual, the cognitive strategies we use to make sense of our world, as discussed in Chapter 3, suggest otherwise. In particular, when confronted with a member of an identifiable group, we may rely on a stereotype as a sort of decision-making shortcut, rather than consider the person on his or her own merits. How we feel about the person and how we treat him or her will be based on the stereotype, not the individual. As such, stereotypes frequently underlie prejudiced attitudes and discriminatory behaviors.

Prejudice can be expressed in many forms. At one extreme are legalized forms of discrimination, such as the so-called Jim Crow laws of the past, which institutionalized discrimination against African Americans, and current laws that restrict women from combat roles in the U.S. military. At the other extreme are subtle types of differential treatment, such as how people are addressed or even how much eye contact they receive. While subtle, these types of behaviors may have a huge impact on the people against whom they are directed.

The following article by Patricia G. Devine looks at the conditions under which stereotypes may influence prejudice as well as those under which stereotypes may be ignored and nonprejudiced attitudes prevail. Devine's research presents the optimistic message that prejudice is a habit that can be broken.

Breaking the Prejudice Habit

■ Patricia G. Devine

Legal scholars, politicians, legislators, social scientists, and lay people alike have puzzled over the paradox of racism in a nation founded on the fundamental principle of human equality. Legislators responded with landmark legal decisions (e.g., Supreme Court ruling on school desegregation and the Civil Rights laws) that made overt discrimination based on race illegal. In the wake of the legislative changes, social scientists examined the extent to which shifts in whites' attitudes kept pace with the legal changes. The literature, however, reveals conflicting findings. Whereas overt expressions of prejudice on surveys declined (i.e., verbal reports), more subtle indicators (i.e., nonverbal measures) continue to reveal prejudice even among those who say they renounced prejudice. A central challenge presented to contemporary prejudice researchers is to explain the disparity between verbal reports and the more subtle measures.

Some reject the optimistic conclusion suggested by survey research and argue that prejudice in America is not declining; it is only changing form—becoming more subtle and disguised. By this argument, most (if not all) Americans are assumed to be racist, with only the *type* of racism differing between people. Such conclusions are based on the belief that *any* response that results in differential treatment between groups is taken as evidence of prejudice. However, this definition fails to consider *intent* or motive and is based on the assumption that nonthoughtful (e.g., nonverbal) responses are, by definition, more trustworthy than thoughtful responses. Indeed, nonverbal measures are assumed to be good indicators of prejudice precisely because they do not typically involve careful thought and people do not control them in the same way that they can control their verbally reported attitudes.

Rather than dismiss either response as necessarily untrustworthy, my colleagues and I have tried to understand the origin of both thoughtful and nonthoughtful responses. By directly addressing the disparity between thoughtful and nonthoughtful responses, our approach offers a more optimistic analysis regarding prospects for prejudice reduction than the extant formulations. To foreshadow, our program of research has been devoted to understanding (a) how and why those who truly renounce prejudice may continue to experience prejudice-like thoughts and feelings and (b) the nature of the rather formidable challenges and obstacles that must be overcome before one can succeed in reducing the disparity between thoughtful and nonthoughtful responses.

AUTOMATIC AND CONTROLLED PROCESSES IN PREJUDICE

The distinction between automatic and controlled cognitive processes has been central to our analysis in prejudice reduction. Automatic processes occur unintentionally, spontaneously, and unconsciously. We have evidence that both low- and high-prejudiced people are vulnerable to automatic stereotype activation. Once the stereotype is well-learned, its influence is hard to avoid because it so easily comes to mind. Controlled processes, in contrast, are under the intentional control of the individual. An important aspect of such processes is that their initiation and use requires time and sufficient cognitive *capacity*. Nonprejudiced responses require inhibiting the spontaneously activated stereotypes and deliberately activating personal beliefs to serve as the basis for responses. Without sufficient time or cognitive capacity, responses may well be stereotype-based and, therefore, appear prejudiced.

The important implication of the automatic/controlled process distinction is that if one looks only at nonthoughtful, automatic responses, one may well conclude that all white Americans are prejudiced. We have found important differences between low- and high-prejudiced people based on the personal beliefs that each hold, despite similar knowledge of and vul-

nerability to the activation of cultural stereotypes. Furthermore, low-prejudiced people have established and internalized nonprejudiced personal standards for how to treat members of stereotyped groups. When given sufficient time, low-prejudiced people censor responses based on the stereotype and, instead, respond based on their beliefs. High-prejudiced people, in contrast, do not reject the stereotype and are not personally motivated to overcome its effect on their behavior.

A strength of this approach is that it delineates the role of both thoughtful and nonthoughtful processes in response to stereotyped group members. Eliminating prejudice requires overcoming a lifetime of socialization experiences, which, unfortunately, promote prejudice. We have likened reducing prejudice to the breaking of a habit in that people must first make a decision to eliminate the habit and then *learn* to inhibit the habitual (prejudiced) responses. Thus, the change from being prejudiced to nonprejudiced is not viewed as an all or none event, but as a process during which the low-prejudiced person is especially vulnerable to conflict between his or her enduring negative responses and endorsed nonprejudiced beliefs. For those who renounce prejudice, overcoming the "prejudice habit" presents a formidable task that is likely to entail a great deal of internal conflict over a protracted period of time.

PREJUDICE WITH AND WITHOUT COMPUNCTION

In subsequent work, we examined the nature and consequences of the internal conflict associated with prejudice reduction. Specifically, we have focused on the challenges faced by those individuals who have internalized nonprejudiced personal standards and are trying to control their prejudiced responses, but sometimes fail. We have shown that people high and low in prejudice (as assessed by a self-report technique) have qualitatively different affective reactions to the conflict between their verbal reports concerning how they *should* respond in situations involving contact with members of stereotyped groups and how they say they actually *would* respond. Low-prejudiced people, for example, believe that they should not feel uncomfortable sitting next to an African American on a bus. High-prejudiced people disagree, indicating that it's acceptable to feel uncomfortable in this situation. When actual responses violate personal standards, low-prejudiced people experience guilt or "prejudice with compunction," but high-prejudiced individuals do not. For low-prejudiced people, the coexistence of such conflicting reactions threatens their nonprejudiced self-concepts. Moreover, these guilt feelings play a functional role in helping people to "break the prejudice habit." That is, violations combined with guilt have been shown to help low-prejudiced people to use controlled processes to inhibit the prejudiced responses and to replace them with responses that are based on their personal beliefs.

INTERPERSONAL DYNAMICS OF INTERGROUP CONTACT

Until recently, our research has focused rather exclusively on the nature of internal conflict associated with prejudice reduction efforts. However, many of the challenges associated with prejudice reduction are played out in the interpersonal arena, and we believe it's important to explore the relevance of our work to issues of intergroup tension. Thus, one of our current lines of research is devoted to exploring the nature of the challenges created by the intergroup contact when people's standards are "put on the line."

In interpersonal intergroup contact situations, we have found that although low-prejudiced people are highly motivated to respond without prejudice, there are few guidelines for "how to do the intergroup thing well." As a result, many experience doubt and uncertainty about how to express their nonprejudiced attitudes in intergroup situations. Thus, for low-prejudiced people, their high motivation to respond without prejudice may actually interfere with their efforts to convey accurately their nonprejudiced intentions. Under these circumstances, they become socially anxious; this anxiety disrupts the typically smooth and coordinated aspects of social interaction. Their interaction styles become awkward and strained resulting in nonverbal behaviors such as decreased eye contact and awkward speech patterns. These are exactly the types of subtle responses that have typically been interpreted as signs of prejudice or antipathy. Indeed, it is not possible to distinguish between the type of tension that arises out of antipathy toward the group or social anxiety based on these signs alone.

We argue that it may be important to acknowledge that there are qualitatively distinct forms of intergroup tension experienced by majority group members, which are systematically related to their self-reported level of prejudice. For some, the tension can arise out of antipathy, as was always thought in the prejudice literature, but for others, the tension arises out of anxiety over trying to do the intergroup thing well. Functionally then, we have different starting points for trying to reduce intergroup tension. Strategies for attempting to reduce intergroup tension differ when the problem is conceived as one of improving skills rather than one of changing negative attitudes.

CONCLUSION

To sum up, although it is not easy and clearly requires effort, time, and practice, prejudice appears to be a habit that can be broken. In contrast to the prevailing, pessimistic opinion that little progress is being made toward the alleviation of prejudice, our program of research suggests that many people appear to be embroiled in the difficult or arduous process of overcoming their prejudices. During this process, low-prejudiced people are confronted with rather formidable challenges from within, as people battle their spontaneous reactions, and from the interpersonal settings in which people's standards are put on the line. We are sanguine that by developing a realistic analysis of the practical challenges faced by those who renounce prejudice, we may be able to identify strategies that may facilitate their prejudice reduction efforts.

It is important to recognize that we are not claiming to have solved the problem of intergroup prejudice, nor are we suggesting that prejudice has disappeared. The past several years have witnessed a disturbing increase in the incidence of hate crimes against minorities. And a sizable proportion of white Americans continue to embrace old-fashioned forms of bigotry. Nevertheless, we hope that by developing an understanding of the challenges associated with breaking the prejudice habit, we may gain insight into the reasons low-prejudiced people establish and internalize nonprejudiced standards. Armed with this knowledge, we may be able to encourage high-prejudiced people to renounce prejudice. And when they do, we will be in a better position to understand their challenges and, perhaps, to assist them in their efforts.

CRITICAL THINKING QUESTIONS

1. Using the findings and implications reported in the article, design a program to teach children to overcome their reliance on stereotypes in making judgments about people.
2. Many studies on prejudice involve asking subjects about their attitudes toward particular groups. What do the findings of this article suggest about such techniques? Which is more likely to be activated in such a research setting, automatic or controlled processes? Explain your answers.
3. Design a study to teach low-prejudiced people to reduce or control their social anxiety when dealing with others about whom they have negative stereotypes.
4. Based on your own observations, has the overall level of prejudice in the United States decreased over the years? Or has the level remained the same, but how and where prejudice is expressed have changed? Give examples to support your position.
5. Being a member of a minority involves more than belonging to a numerically smaller group. It also involves the status and access to power and resources that a given group has. Using this criterion, women would be considered a minority group in American society. Apply the issues addressed in this article to how women are treated by men in our society.

ARTICLE 17 _____

In social psychology, the majority of research on prejudice and discrimination has focused on the patterns of attitudes that people have, the way they treat people differently depending on those attitudes, and the methods for trying to reduce or eliminate prejudiced attitudes and discriminatory behaviors. Not nearly as much effort has been directed to examining how prejudices are acquired in the first place.

The search for the origins of prejudice has taken many different routes. Some efforts have examined the historical origins of prejudice, considering factors such as the conditions of contact between the groups. Other approaches have looked at sociocultural and situational causes, such as conflict between groups and the socialization of children. Yet another factor that may cause prejudice is personality. Whether particular patterns of personality are more likely to be associated with prejudice is something that has been extensively examined.

The classic study that follows is an attempt to demonstrate the creation of prejudice in groups of boys. Muzafer Sherif's article is of interest for several reasons. It includes the manipulation of a situation that led to creating prejudice in boys where no prejudice had existed before; it also examines a method for eliminating the prejudice that had been created. Another interesting feature of the study is the naturalistic setting in which it was conducted.

Experiments in Group Conflict

■ Muzafer Sherif

Conflict between groups—whether between boys' gangs, social classes, "races" or nations—has no simple cause, nor is mankind yet in sight of a cure. It is often rooted deep in personal, social, economic, religious and historical forces. Nevertheless, it is possible to identify certain general factors which have a crucial influence on the attitude of any group toward others. Social scientists have long sought to bring these factors to light by studying what might be called the "natural history" of groups and group relations. Intergroup conflict and harmony is not a subject that lends itself easily to laboratory experiments. But in recent years there has been a beginning of attempts to investigate the problem under controlled yet life-like conditions, and I shall report here the results of a program of experimental studies of groups which I started in 1948. Among the persons working with me were Marvin B. Sussman, Robert Huntington, O. J. Harvey, B. Jack White, William R. Hood and Carolyn W. Sherif. The experiments were conducted in 1949, 1953 and 1954; this article gives a composite of the findings.

We wanted to conduct our study with groups of the informal type, where group organization and attitudes would evolve naturally and spontaneously, without formal direction or external pressures. For this purpose we conceived that an isolated summer camp would make a good experimental setting, and that decision led us to choose as subjects boys about eleven or twelve years old who would find camping natural and fascinating. Since our aim was to study the development of group relations among these boys under carefully controlled conditions, with as little interference as possible from personal neuroses, background influences or prior experiences, we selected normal boys of homogeneous background who did not know one another before they came to the camp.

They were picked by a long and thorough procedure. We interviewed each boy's family, teachers and school officials, studied his school and medical records, obtained his scores on personality tests and observed him in his classes and at play with his schoolmates. With all this information we were able to assure ourselves that the boys chosen were of like kind and background; all were healthy, socially well-adjusted, somewhat above average in intelligence and from stable, white, Protestant, middle-class homes.

None of the boys was aware that he was part of an experiment on group relations. The investigators appeared as a regular camp staff—camp directors, counselors and so on. The boys met one another for the first time in buses that took them to the camp, and so far as they knew it was a normal summer of camping. To keep the situation as lifelike as possible, we conducted all our experiments within the framework of regular camp activities and games. We set up projects which were so interesting and attractive that the boys plunged into them enthusiastically without suspecting that they might be test situations. Unobtrusively we made records of their behavior, even using "candid" cameras and microphones when feasible.

We began by observing how the boys became a coherent group. The first of our camps was conducted in the hills of northern Connecticut in the summer of 1949. When the boys arrived, they were all housed at first in one large bunkhouse. As was to be expected, they quickly formed particular friendships and chose buddies. We had deliberately put all the boys together in this expectation, because we wanted to see what would happen later after the boys were separated into different groups. Our object was to reduce the factor of personal attraction in the formation of groups. In a few days we divided the boys into two groups and put them in different cabins. Before doing so, we asked each boy informally who his best friends were, and then took pains to place the "best friends" in different groups as far as possible. (The pain of separation was assuaged by allowing each group to go at once on a hike and campout.)

As everyone knows, a group of strangers brought together in some common activity soon acquires an informal and spontaneous kind of organization. It comes to look upon some members as leaders, divides up duties, adopts unwritten norms of behavior, develops an *esprit de corps*. Our boys followed this pattern as they shared a series of experiences. In each group the boys pooled their efforts, organized duties and

divided up tasks in work and play. Different individuals assumed different responsibilities. One boy excelled in cooking. Another led in athletics. Others, though not outstanding in any one skill, could be counted on to pitch in and do their level best in anything the group attempted. One or two seemed to disrupt activities, to start teasing at the wrong moment or offer useless suggestions. A few boys consistently had good suggestions and showed ability to coordinate the efforts of others in carrying them through. Within a few days one person had proved himself more resourceful and skillful than the rest. Thus, rather quickly, a leader and lieutenants emerged. Some boys sifted toward the bottom of the heap, while others jockeyed for higher positions.

We watched these developments closely and rated the boys' relative positions in the group, not only on the basis of our own observations but also by informal sounding of the boys' opinions as to who got things started, who got things done, who could be counted on to support group activities.

As the group became an organization, the boys coined nicknames. The big, blond, hardy leader of one group was dubbed "Baby Face" by his admiring followers. A boy with a rather long head became "Lemon Head." Each group developed its own jargon, special jokes, secrets and special ways of performing tasks. One group, after killing a snake near a place where it had gone to swim, named the place "Moccasin Creek" and thereafter preferred this swimming hole to any other, though there were better ones nearby.

Wayward members who failed to do things "right" or who did not contribute their bit to the common effort found themselves receiving the "silent treatment," ridicule or even threats. Each group selected symbols and a name, and they had these put on their caps and T-shirts. The 1954 camp was conducted in Oklahoma, near a famous hideaway of Jesse James called Robber's Cave. The two groups of boys at this camp named themselves the Rattlers and the Eagles.

Our conclusions on every phase of the study were based on a variety of observations, rather than on any single method. For example, we devised a game to test the boys' evaluations of one another. Before an important baseball game, we set up a target board for the boys to throw at, on the pretense of making practice for the game more interesting. There were no marks on the front of the board for the boys to judge objectively how close the ball came to a bull's-eye, but, unknown to them, the board was wired to flashing lights behind so that an observer could see exactly where the balls hit. We found that the boys consistently overestimated the performances by the most highly regarded members of their group and underestimated the scores of those of low social standing.

The attitudes of group members were even more dramatically illustrated during a cook-out in the woods. The staff supplied the boys with unprepared food and let them cook it themselves. One boy promptly started to build a fire, asking for help in getting wood. Another attacked the raw hamburger to make patties. Others prepared a place to put buns, relishes and the like. Two mixed soft drinks from flavoring and sugar. One boy who stood around without helping was told by others to "get to it." Shortly the fire was blazing and the cook had hamburgers sizzling. Two boys distributed them as rapidly as they became edible. Soon it was time for the watermelon. A low-ranking member of the group took a knife and started toward the melon. Some of the boys protested. The most highly regarded boy in the group took over the knife, saying, "You guys who yell the loudest get yours last."

When the two groups in the camp had developed group organization and spirit, we proceeded to the experimental studies of intergroup relations. The groups had had no previous encounters; indeed, in the 1954 camp at Robber's Cave the two groups came in separate buses and were kept apart while each acquired a group feeling.

Our working hypothesis was that when two groups have conflicting aims—i.e., when one can achieve its ends only at the expense of the other—their members will become hostile to each other even though the groups are composed of normal well-adjusted individuals. There is a corollary to this assumption which we shall consider later. To produce friction between the groups of boys we arranged a tournament of games: baseball, touch football, a tug-of-war, a treasure hunt and so on. The tournament started in a spirit of good sportsmanship. But as it progressed good feeling soon evaporated. The members of each

group began to call their rivals "stinkers," "sneaks" and "cheaters." They refused to have anything more to do with individuals in the opposing group. The boys in the 1949 camp turned against buddies whom they had chosen as "best friends" when they first arrived at the camp. A large proportion of the boys in each group gave negative ratings to all the boys in the other. The rival groups made threatening posters and planned raids, collecting secret hoards of green apples for ammunition. In the Robber's Cave camp the Eagles, after a defeat in a tournament game, burned a banner left behind by the Rattlers; the next morning the Rattlers seized the Eagles' flag when they arrived on the athletic field. From that time on name-calling, scuffles, and raids were the rule of the day.

Within each group, of course, solidarity increased. There were changes: one group deposed its leader because he could not "take it" in the contests with the

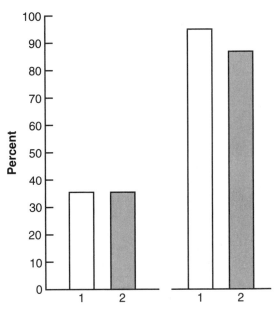

FIGURE 1 / **Friendship choices of campers for others in their own cabin are shown for Red Devils (*white*) and Bulldogs (*gray*). At first a low percentage of friendships were in the cabin group (*left*). After five days, most friendship choices were within the group (*right*).**

adversary; another group overnight made something of a hero of a big boy who had previously been regarded as a bully. But morale and cooperativeness within the group became stronger. It is noteworthy that this heightening of cooperativeness and generally democratic behavior did not carry over to the group's relations with other groups.

We now turned to the other side of the problem. How can two groups in conflict be brought into harmony? We first undertook to test the theory that pleasant social contacts between members of conflicting groups will reduce friction between them. In the 1954 camp we brought the hostile Rattlers and Eagles together for social events: going to the movies, eating in the same dining room and so on. But far from reducing conflict, these situations only served as opportunities for the rival groups to berate and attack each other. In the dining-hall line they shoved each other aside, and the group that lost the contest for the head of the line shouted "Ladies first!" at the winner. They threw paper, food and vile names at each other at the tables. An Eagle bumped by a Rattler was admonished by his fellow Eagles to brush "the dirt" off his clothes.

We then returned to the corollary of our assumption about the creation of conflict. Just as competition generates friction, working in a common endeavor should promote harmony. It seemed to us, considering group relations in the everyday world, that where harmony between groups is established, the most decisive factor is the existence of "superordinate" goals which have a compelling appeal for both but which neither could achieve without the other. To test this hypothesis experimentally, we created a series of urgent, and natural, situations which challenged our boys.

One was a breakdown in the water supply. Water came to our camp in pipes from a tank about a mile away. We arranged to interrupt it and then called the boys together to inform them of the crisis. Both groups promptly volunteered to search the water line for the trouble. They worked together harmoniously, and before the end of the afternoon they had located and corrected the difficulty.

A similar opportunity offered itself when the boys requested a movie. We told them that the camp could

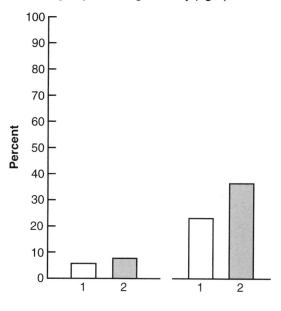

FIGURE 2 / During conflict between the two groups in the Robber's Cave experiment there were few friendships between cabins (*left*). After cooperation toward common goals had restored good feelings, the number of friendships between groups rose significantly (*right*).

not afford to rent one. The two groups then got together, figured out how much each group would have to contribute, chose the film by a vote and enjoyed the showing together.

One day the two groups went on an outing at a lake some distance away. A large truck was to go to town for food. But when everyone was hungry and ready to eat, it developed that the truck would not start (we had taken care of that). The boys got a rope—the same rope they had used in their acrimonious tug-of-war—and all pulled together to start the truck.

These joint efforts did not immediately dispel hostility. At first the groups returned to the old bickering and name-calling as soon as the job in hand was finished. But gradually the series of cooperative acts reduced friction and conflict. The members of the two groups began to feel more friendly to each other. For example, a Rattler whom the Eagles disliked for

FIGURE 3 / Sociograms represent patterns of friendship choice within the fully developed groups. One-way friendships are indicated by broken arrows; reciprocated friendships, by solid lines. Leaders were among those highest in the popularity scale. Bulldogs (*left*) had a close-knit organization with good group spirit. Low-ranking members participated less in the life of the group but were not rejected. Red Devils (*right*) lost the tournament of games between the groups. They had less group unity and were sharply stratified.

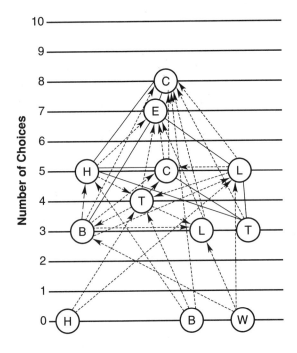
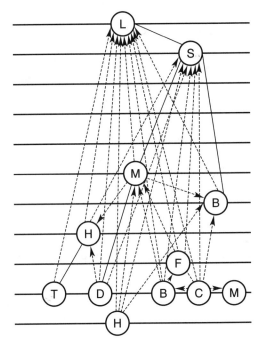

his sharp tongue and skill in defeating them became a "good egg." The boys stopped shoving in the meal line. They no longer called each other names, and sat together at the table. New friendships developed between individuals in the two groups.

In the end the groups were actively seeking opportunities to mingle, to entertain and "treat" each other. They decided to hold a joint campfire. They took turns presenting skits and songs. Members of both groups requested that they go home together on the same bus, rather than on the separate buses in which they had come. On the way the bus stopped for refreshments. One group still had five dollars which they had won as a prize in a contest. They decided to spend this sum on refreshments. On their own initiative they invited their former rivals to be their guests for malted milks.

Our interviews with the boys confirmed this change. From choosing their "best friends" almost

exclusively in their own group, many of them shifted to listing boys in the other group as best friends (see Fig. 2). They were glad to have a second chance to rate boys in the other group, some of them remarking that they had changed their minds since the first rating made after the tournament. Indeed they had. The new ratings were largely favorable (see Fig. 4).

Efforts to reduce friction and prejudice between groups in our society have usually followed rather different methods. Much attention has been given to bringing members of hostile groups together socially, to communicating accurate and favorable information about one group to the other, and to bringing leaders of groups together to enlist their influence. But as everyone knows, such measures sometimes reduce inter-group tensions and sometimes do not. Social contacts, as our experiments demonstrated, may only serve as occasions for intensifying conflict. Favorable information about a disliked group may be ignored or reinterpreted to fit stereotyped notions about the group. Leaders cannot act without regard for the prevailing temper in their own groups.

What our limited experiments have shown is that the possibilities for achieving harmony are greatly enhanced when groups are brought together to work toward common ends. Then favorable information about a disliked group is seen in a new light, and leaders are in a position to take bolder steps toward cooperation. In short, hostility gives way when groups pull together to achieve overriding goals which are real and compelling to all concerned.

REFERENCE

Sherif, M. & Sherif, C. W. (1953). *Groups in harmony and tension*. New York: Harper & Brothers.

FIGURE 4 / **Negative ratings of each group by the other were common during the period of conflict (*left*) but decreased when harmony was restored (*right*). The graphs show percent who thought that *all* (rather than *some* or *none*) of the other group were cheaters, sneaks, etc.**

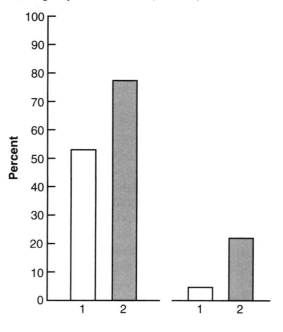

CRITICAL THINKING QUESTIONS

1. Design a laboratory experiment that would examine the development of prejudice in a more controlled fashion than was possible in the Sherif study. What are the pros and cons of the methodology used in this study as compared to a standard laboratory experiment that could be used to examine the same topic?

2. From your reading of the article, how fair (unbiased) were the observations made by the experimenters? Do you think it is possible that the experimenters may have unintentionally and subtly influenced the processes that they were observing, or were precautions taken to avoid this potential pitfall? Explain your answers.

3. What are the implications of this study for reducing prejudice in real life? Would the method used in the study work in the real world? Why or why not? Would the strength of the prejudice, as well as how long it has been held, influence how successful such prejudice-reduction techniques would be? Explain your answers.

ADDITIONAL RELATED READINGS

Carter, C., & Rice, C. L. (1997). Acquisition and manifestation of prejudice in children. *Journal of Multicultural Counseling and Development, 25,* 185–194.

Pettigrew, T. F. (1997). Generalized intergroup contact effects on prejudice. *Personality and Social Psychology Bulletin, 23,* 173–185.

ARTICLE 18 _____

Let us assume that we all want to avoid prejudiced thinking and behavior as much as possible, trying instead to view people as individuals, not just as members of certain groups. How can we do this?

Perhaps one way would be to focus consciously on the behavior or characteristics of each *person,* trying to ignore what we already know about the group to which he or she belongs. The only problem with this approach is that membership in a group may influence our judgment about that person in very subtle ways. For example, while we may feel that we are being objective, looking only at the facts, the very facts we see may be influenced by the person's group identity. Thus, a given behavior may be viewed very differently, depending on who is displaying it.

When we think of prejudice resulting in a biased evaluation, we usually think of a *negative* evaluation being made. Can prejudice also result in a more *positive* judgment being made about a person based solely on his or her membership in a particular group? The following article by Kent D. Harber examines the evidence for a positive bias in evaluating minorities. It turns out that this positive bias occurs only under certain conditions. When it does occur, however, the implications for a negative impact on minorities are tremendous.

Feedback to Minorities
Evidence of a Positive Bias
■ Kent D. Harber

This research tested the prediction that Whites supply more lenient feedback to Blacks than to fellow Whites. In Study 1, White undergraduates were led to believe that they were giving feedback on essays written by either a Black or a White fellow student. As predicted, feedback was less critical when the supposed feedback recipient was Black rather than White. It was also predicted that the feedback bias would be selective for subjective evaluative domains (i.e., essay content) in contrast to objective evaluative domains (i.e., essay mechanics). An interaction between recipient race and evaluative domain confirmed this prediction. The domain-specific quality of the feedback bias suggests that the bias may arise from social motives rather than from more automatic processes. Study 2 replicated these results.

The literature on intergroup evaluation has been exhaustive in mapping out the nature and causes of biased assessments of minority groups by Whites (for reviews, see Devine, 1989; Gaertner & Dovidio, 1986; Pulakos, White, Oppler, & Borman, 1989). However, in nearly all studies of interracial evaluation, White reviewers have supplied their judgments of minority persons to research staff or to some other third party. Interracial feedback, in which Whites evaluate the performance of a minority person and then communicate their assessments back to this person, has received scant empirical review.[1]

An important way in which interracial feedback may differ from other evaluation modes concerns the direction of evaluative biases. Research on nonfeedback evaluations often shows a propensity among Whites to judge minority targets negatively (e.g., Henderson-King & Nisbett, 1997; Kraiger & Ford, 1985; Lambert, Cronen, Chasteen, & Lickel, 1996). However, evaluations communicated in a feedback

Reprinted from *Journal of Personality and Social Psychology,* 1998, *74*(3), 622–628. Copyright © 1998 by the American Psychological Association. Reprinted with permission.

encounter may be biased in the opposite direction, such that Whites are selectively lenient when criticizing minorities. This is because of social challenges that, in kind or in degree, distinguish feedback delivery from other evaluation modes.

The literature on direct intergroup communications reveals a host of concerns that may lead Whites to temporize interracial feedback. These include Whites' wishes to display egalitarian values to others (Carver, Glass, & Katz, 1978) or to themselves (Devine, Montieth, Zuwerink, & Elliot, 1991; Dutton & Lake, 1973; Gaertner & Dovidio, 1986). Interracial feedback may also be informed by a *norm to be kind* (Hastorf, Northcraft, & Piucciotto, 1979) or by sympathy motives (Jones et al., 1984), which dissuade the nonstigmatized from directly criticizing members of disadvantaged groups. Finally, feedback encounters with minorities may arouse in Whites feelings of generalized awkwardness (Stephan & Stephan, 1985) or discomforting ambivalence (Katz, 1981). In such situations, Whites may mask underlying unease with overtly positive communications (Jones et al., 1984; Weitz, 1972).

There are also automatic processes that might interfere with feedback delivery. For example, Whites' negative stereotypes of minority persons' capabilities may cause Whites to shift their evaluative standards down (Biernat & Manis, 1994; Biernat, Manis, & Nelson, 1991) when supplying interracial feedback. Similarly, high standards selectively applied to fellow Whites may lead to expectancy effects (Bettencourt, Dill, Greathouse, Charlton, & Mulholland, 1997; Jussim, Coleman, & Lerch, 1987), such that Whites judge members of their own group more harshly than members of other groups for work considered substandard. These more cognitive mechanisms have been shown to mask latent, and negative, discrimination toward stereotyped groups.

Collectively, these various research approaches suggest that Whites may place a positive bias on the feedback they deliver to Blacks. The present research was intended to demonstrate that such a bias exists. In two experiments, White participants were asked to review a poorly written essay supposedly composed by either a Black or a White fellow student. Participants were led to believe that their comments would be returned directly to the writer. Feedback directed toward a "Black" writer was predicted to be more positive than feedback directed toward a "White" writer.

In addition to demonstrating the presence of a positive feedback bias, this research also was intended to identify limiting conditions that determine when the bias will occur. It did so by examining differences in feedback directed toward subjective and objective areas of evaluation. In regard to writing, *subjective evaluation* applies largely to the content of composition (e.g., strength of argument and originality of ideas), whereas *objective evaluation* addresses the mechanics of composition (e.g., grammar, spelling, and usage).

These two evaluative domains differ in the interpersonal challenges that they present to the feedback supplier. Content, according to experts in the field of writing instruction, is more interpersonally difficult to criticize than is mechanics (Shaughnessy, 1976). This is because there are few established guidelines for evaluating content, whereas mechanics have standardized referents such as dictionaries and stylebooks. Such referents supply external justification for criticism and thereby shield critics from the appearance of partiality. In addition, the content of writing often reflects on a writer's thinking and beliefs, which are more central personal attributes (cf. Weiner, Russell, & Lerman, 1979) than are grammatical skills. The faulting of content may therefore present ad hominem connotations that do not attend criticisms of mechanics. In fact, college students rate content as more difficult to critique than mechanics, citing the ad hominem implications and lack of external justification associated with this domain (Harber, 1995).

Because content lacks established standards of evaluation while also presenting the risk of implying ad hominem attacks it may be less "socially judgable" (cf. Yzerbyt, Schadron, Leyens, & Rocher, 1994) than mechanics. That is, it may lack the standards and norms that insulate judges from untoward appearances. The research on Whites' interracial concerns, cited above, suggests that Whites are likely to exercise particular caution when supplying interracial feedback in a less socially judgable domain. For these reasons, the feedback bias is expected to be revealed by an interaction, such that the predicted lenience in feedback to Black essay writers will appear most strongly in the evaluation of essay content.

STUDY 1

The primary purpose of this study was to demonstrate that feedback from Whites to Blacks is positively biased. A poorly composed writing sample was therefore predicted to be more favorably evaluated when its author was identified as Black rather than White. In addition, this study was designed to detect an interaction between writer race (Black vs. White) and evaluative domain (content vs. mechanics), revealing selective lenience in content-related feedback to a Black writer. This is because the ad hominem implications that content criticisms may convey, and relative lack of uniform justifications that they supply (Shaughnessy, 1976), may arouse Whites' intergroup concerns.

Method

Participants   Ninety-two White undergraduate psychology students (44 men and 48 women) participated in this study. Participants were tested individually in 1-hr sessions and received course-completion credit as compensation for their time.

Stimulus Materials   Substandard essay.   Participants' principal task involved reviewing one of two editorial-style essays that were, by design, filled with grammatical errors and content flaws. Two separate essay topics were developed to control for any artifacts arising from essay theme. One essay, entitled "TV Violence," discussed television's contribution to criminality, and the second essay, entitled "Interest in the Environment," commented on public apathy toward environmental issues. The essays were of comparable quality, length, format, and, to the extent possible, structure and tone.

Writer demographics sheet.   This form was used to unobtrusively introduce the fictive writer's race. The writer demographics sheet consisted of a number of self-description questions and the supposed writer's handwritten responses to these questions. These responses described the writer as a female 1st-year student interested in political science, currently living in a large dormitory but planning to live in a sorority the following year. There were two versions of this form, which were identical in all respects except how a

question concerning campus affiliations was answered. In the Black writer condition, this question was answered with "Black Students Union," and in the White writer condition, "None" was the reply. The demographics at this university are such that a female sorority pledge living in the indicated dormitory is almost certain to be White, unless otherwise indicated.

Procedure   Cover story.   Participants were greeted by the experimenter in a waiting area serving a suite of laboratory rooms. After completing standard experimental-consent forms, participants were taken to one of these rooms, where they were given the study's cover story. The gist of this story was that the research was designed to explore peer tutoring. Participants were told that their contribution to this research would involve reading and critiquing an essay written by a fellow student who was enrolled in a writing skills workshop. Participants were instructed to pen their editorial comments onto the essay. They were told that the copyedited essay would then be returned to the essay writer. Finally, participants were told that the essay writer was fully apprised of these procedures and was expecting to receive the participants' commentary on the essay. After supplying this cover story, the experimenter told the participants that although the writer's name would not be revealed, confidentiality concerns were still paramount. For this reason the participants were asked to review and sign a peer review confidentiality form. In actuality, this form served only to buttress the cover story.

Editing task.   Participants were next taken to an adjoining experiment room where they could review their assigned essay in privacy. Once seated, participants were informed that their writer's assignment was to compose a two-page editorial-style essay on a topic of the writer's choice. Participants were then handed a copy of either the TV violence essay or the environmental interest essay, according to a randomization schedule. The participants were again reminded to read through the entire essay and to comment on spelling, grammar, structure, and content, as well as anything else that appeared to deserve comment.

Writer race manipulation.   Before allowing the participants to begin their essay critiques, the experimenter introduced the writer demographics sheet as follows:

> *You know, in most peer tutoring situations the participants know something about each other. Because that's not possible here, we have had writers fill out this form that asks general questions about them. You should read this form over first, in order to get an idea about your writer.*

At this point participants were given either the Black writer or the White writer version of the writer demographics sheet, according to a randomization schedule. The experimenter left the room at this point, with final instructions that the participants should take as much time as needed to conduct the essay review, and to notify the experimenter when the critiquing was done.

Dependent measures. Participants' copyediting and margin comments were the first outcome measure of this study. After supplying their essay critiques, the participants were next asked to fill out a brief writer's evaluation form. The form consisted of three scales that addressed essay content, mechanics, and overall quality. Each scale contained the following seven options regarding how much added work these essay features required: *none at all, very little, little, moderate, fair amount, much, very much.* The participants were told that this form would go directly to the essay writer and that no one else would see it. To further the impression that the form was a confidential channel between the participants and the writer, the experimenter supplied participants with an envelope with which to seal the writer's evaluation form after completing its three scales.

Debriefing. After all dependent measures were completed, participants were questioned to ascertain the effectiveness of manipulations and to probe for suspicion. Participants were then debriefed, verbally and in writing, regarding the purpose and design of the experiment.

Data Scoring Participants' copyediting comments were coded for positive and negative content comments and for positive and negative mechanics comments. Although coders were aware of the hypothesis guiding the experiment, they were blind to participant condition. Interrater coding reliability was satisfactory for each of these dimensions (content positive $\alpha = .98$, content negative $\alpha = .69$, and mechanics negative $\alpha = .97$). Neither coder found any instances of positive mechanics comments. Participants' negative content comments were subtracted from their positive content comments, and their negative mechanics comments were subtracted from their positive mechanics comments (i.e., from zero). This yielded composite content and mechanics scores, necessary for analyzing the predicted interaction between writer race and evaluative domain (i.e., content vs. mechanics). Finally, because mechanics received many more comments than did content, raw comment totals were transformed into standard (z) units. Inferential analyses were conducted on these standard scores.

Results and Discussion

This study was intended to reveal an interaction between writer race and evaluative domain (i.e., content vs. mechanics).

This interaction was predicted to occur both in the writer's evaluation form ratings that participants believed were being transmitted directly from them to the essay writer and in participants' copyediting comments. The interaction was assessed using a mixed-design repeated measures analysis of variance (ANOVA), with evaluative domain (content vs. mechanics) as the within-subjects factor and writer race as the between-subjects factor.

Preliminary Analyses There were no significant sex differences in any of the outcome measures, and men's and women's data were therefore collapsed across experimental conditions. The TV violence essay and the environmentalism essay received comparable reviews, and there were no Writer Race × Essay Topic interactions. Data were therefore consolidated across this variable.

Manipulation Checks *Race of writer manipulation.* During debriefing, all participants were asked to recall the writer's race in order to confirm that participants had registered this central design feature. Two participants failed to make the correct identification (1 in the Black-writer condition and 1 in the White-writer condition). Their data were therefore deleted from the study.

Overall believability. Participants rated their level of suspicion as moderate (2.5 on a 5-point scale where 1 = *not at all,* 5 = *a lot*).[2] Suspicion did not significantly differ by experimental condition, $F(1, 88) = 1.27, p = .26$, or by participant sex, $F(1, 88) = 1.51, p = .23$.

Main Analyses   Writer's evaluation form. The writer's evaluation form consisted of three rating scales on which the participant indicated how much additional work the writer should dedicate to essay mechanics, content, and overall quality. Data from this measure verified the predicted Writer Race × Evaluative Domain interaction, $F(1, 88) = 14.62, p = .004$ (see Figure 1). Simple effects tests showed that essay content was rated more favorably when the supposed author was Black rather than White, $F(1, 88) = 9.59, p = .003$. In contrast, ratings of essay mechanics

did not significantly differ as a function of writer race, $F(1, 88) = 0.53, p = .46$. Ratings in regard to the overall quality of the essay did not differ as a function of writer race, $F(1, 88) = 1.00, p = .31$.

Essay comments. Review of participants' copy-editing comments also demonstrates the predicted interaction between writer race and evaluative domain (content vs. mechanics), $F(1, 88) = 5.70, p < .03$. This interaction is displayed in Figure 2. Simple effects tests showed that participants in the Black writer condition rated essay content more favorably ($M = .85$) than did participants in the White writer condition ($M = .14$), $t(89) = 3.67, p < .001$. In contrast to feedback on content, evaluation of essay mechanics showed that comments regarding Black writer mechanics ($M = .26$) did not significantly differ from those regarding White writer mechanics ($M = .22$), $t(89) = .15, p = .87$.

The separate contributions of positive and negative content comments were explored to better understand the nature of the domain-specific nature of the bias. This analysis revealed an interaction between

FIGURE 1 / The favorableness of grade-like ratings transmitted to the supposed essay writer, as a function of the supposed writer's race and evaluative domain (content vs. mechanics). Note that ratings have been reverse coded for purposes of interpretability. Also note the actual scale ranged from 1 (*lowest rating*) to 7 (*highest rating*) points.

FIGURE 2 / The favorableness of copyediting comments as a function of the supposed writer's race and evaluative domain (content vs. mechanics). Note that favorableness is a composite score composed of positive comments minus negative comments.

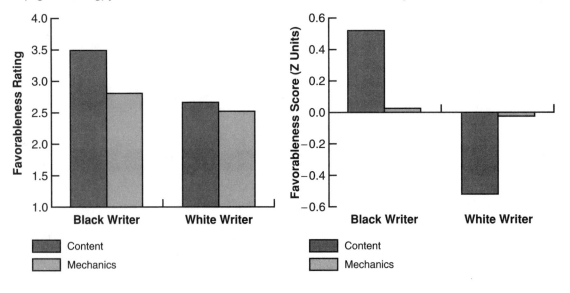

writer race and the valence of criticism, $F(1, 88) = 8.40$, $p = .006$. One-way ANOVAs showed that participants in the Black writer condition supplied more positive content comments ($M = 2.09$ vs. $M = 1.04$), $F(1, 87) = 4.74$, $p < .04$, and fewer negative content comments ($M = 1.04$ vs. $M = 2.26$), $F(1, 87) = 5.65$, $p < .03$, than did participants in the White writer condition.

Summary comments. Nearly half of the experimental participants (46%) concluded their essay critiques with short summary notes to the fictive writer. These added comments were not an anticipated outcome. Investigation of them showed that they were more commonly supplied by participants in the White writer condition (59%) than by those in the Black writer condition (36%), $\chi^2 (1) = 4.15$, $p = .04$. The evaluative tone of these comments was judged by a rater blind to experimental condition. Comments addressed to the Black writer were more supportive than were those directed to the White writer, $F(1, 53) = 6.46$, $p = .02$. For example, participants in the Black writer condition were more likely to tell the writer how much they enjoyed reading the editorial or how much potential they saw in the essay. On the other hand, participants in the White writer condition could on occasion be quite harsh, as for example the participant who wrote, "When I read college work this bad I just want to lay my head down on the table and cry." Such baldly negative comments were never made by participants in the Black writer condition.

Cumulatively, these results confirm that Whites supply more positive feedback to Blacks than to fellow Whites, and that this feedback bias is selective for essay content.

STUDY 2

The results of Study 1, although consistent with predictions, contrast with a number of meta-analytic reviews showing Whites to rate Blacks less favorably than fellow Whites (Ford, Kraiger, & Schechtman, 1986; Kraiger & Ford, 1985; Landy & Farr, 1980; Sackett & DuBois, 1991). However, these meta-analyses included few feedback studies, and no studies in which feedback biases were empirically examined. Instead, these reviews (which collectively include over 100 samples) focused primarily on biases that arose in

third-party contexts, which are less likely to pose the interpersonal considerations that may lead to a positive feedback bias. Nonetheless, the distinctiveness of the results obtained in Study 1 recommended their replication. Study 2 served as an attempt to reconfirm the positive feedback bias.[3]

Method

Participants One hundred three female undergraduates participated in this study. Only women were recruited because females' greater interpersonal sensitivities (e.g., Davis & Oathout, 1987) promised greater reactivity to the experimental designs. Participation was not restricted to psychology undergraduates, thereby broadening the inferential scope of this study. Participants were tested individually and received $8 for 1 hr of experimental participation. Data coding and analyses followed procedures used in Study 1.

Procedure The procedure of this study was largely identical to that of Study 1. Participants received the same cover story, reviewed the same materials, and completed the same dependent measures tasks as was done in Study 1.

Results and Discussion

Preliminary Analyses Data were excluded from 1 participant in the Black writer condition and 3 participants in the White writer condition who either failed to make the correct race identification, or who refused to report what race they believed the writer to be. Overall suspicion reported during debriefing was low. The mean overall suspicion rating was 1.53 on a 5-point scale (1 = *no suspicion,* 5 = *extreme suspicion*). Suspicion did not vary by the fictive writer's race, $F(1, 97) = .62$, $p = ns$.

Replication of the Feedback Bias This experiment largely replicated the effects detected in Study 1. The writer evaluation form reconfirmed the interaction between writer race and evaluative domain, $F(1, 97) = 5.93$, $p = .02$. Participants in the Black writer condition more favorably rated essay content than did participants in the White writer condition, $F(1, 97) =$

5.37, p = .02. In contrast, the between-groups differences in regard to mechanics ratings were not significant, $F(1, 97)$ = 1.82, p = .19. Participants' copyediting comments show that participants in the Black writer condition more leniently reviewed content than did their counterparts in the White writer condition, $F(1, 97)$ = 4.45, p = .04. There was no between-groups difference in mechanics ratings, $F(1, 97)$ = .41, p = .52. The interaction between race and evaluative domain, although in the predicted direction, was not significant, $F(1, 97)$ = 1.54, p = .22. However, a meta-analysis (Fisher Combined Test in Wolf, 1986) that combined the Writer Race × Evaluative Domain interactions computed in Studies 1 and 2 showed this effect to be reliable, $\chi^2(4)$ = 10.04, p < .05.

Analysis of the positive and negative content comments replicated the interaction found in Study 1, $F(1, 97)$ = 4.35, p < .04. Simple effects tests showed, as nonsignificant trends, that participants in the Black writer condition supplied both more positive content comments, $F(1, 97)$ = 2.23, p < .14, and fewer negative essay comments, $F(1, 97)$ = 2.34, p < .14, than did participants in the White writer condition. When these results are combined with those from Study 1 (Fisher Combined Test), the effects are clearly reliable for both positive content comments, $\chi^2(4)$ = 10.38, p < .05, and negative content comments, $\chi^2(4)$ = 10.96, p < .05.

Overall, results from Study 2 suggest that the feedback bias is a robust phenomenon and that it is most likely to be expressed in feedback that addresses subjective areas of evaluation (e.g., essay content) where intergroup concerns are more likely to be elevated.

GENERAL DISCUSSION

This research tested the prediction that Whites supply more lenient feedback to Blacks than to fellow Whites. Results provide consistent evidence that this positive feedback bias exists. In two separate experiments, White undergraduates gave more favorable feedback on poorly written essays when the author was described as Black rather than White.

These studies were also intended to identify the conditions in which the bias is expressed. As expected, the feedback bias affected the evaluation of a subjective evaluative domain (i.e., essay content) but had no influence on an objective evaluative domain (i.e., essay mechanics). Examination of content comments shows that Whites selectively supply Blacks more praise, and less criticism, in this domain. The interaction between writer race and evaluative domain was evident in participants' copyediting comments and in their grade-like ratings to the writer.

The domain specificity of the bias was predicted to occur for two complementary reasons (cf. Shaughnessy, 1976). Content criticisms, which address writers' quality of reasoning and coherence of beliefs, can suggest personalized attacks. Mechanics criticisms, which deal with the more neutral topics of spelling and grammar, are less likely to raise such ad hominem implications. Second, there are few objective rules or standard referents that justify content criticisms, whereas such guidelines do exist for evaluating mechanics (e.g., dictionaries and stylebooks). These liabilities of criticizing content may arouse Whites' intergroup concerns (e.g., of appearing racist, of violating internalized values), leading Whites to temper feedback to Blacks.

Alternative Explanations for the Feedback Bias

Social–cognitive approaches have also identified circumstances in which Whites will display evaluative lenience toward Blacks. Out-group polarization theory (Linville, 1982; Linville & Jones, 1980), for example, has shown that people accentuate their evaluations of out-group members, exaggerating both the outsider's successes and failures. White participants in the feedback studies did exaggerate their ratings of Blacks' written work, but not in the direction out-group polarization would predict. Substandard essays supposedly authored by a Black were consistently reviewed more favorably than were essays supposedly written by a White. According to polarization theory, the essays' poor quality should have led to accentuated criticism, rather than elevated praise, of Black writers' performances.

Shifting standards research (Biernat & Manis, 1994) supplies another cognitively based explanation for the feedback bias. According to this theory, evaluations of stereotyped groups are calibrated to group-based stereotypes. Thus, Whites' negative stereotypes about Blacks' verbal skills should cause Whites to employ less exacting standards when reviewing Blacks' verbal performances.[4] Biernat and Manis (1994) and Biernat and Kobrynowicz (1997) reported data consistent with this prediction.

A key qualification of the shifting standards approach is that its expression is limited to subjective metrics, which permit within-group comparisons (e.g., a target Black in relation to all other Blacks), and does not extend to objective scales, which force raters to evaluate in-group and out-group members using a common frame of reference. The present research also distinguished between subjective and objective evaluations. However, there is a critical difference between the feedback studies and the shifting standards research in how *subjective* and *objective* criteria are defined. In the feedback studies, the terms *subjective* and *objective* refer to the performance being evaluated (e.g., reasoning vs. grammar), whereas in the shifting standards research these terms refer to metrics used to judge performance (e.g., qualitative vs. quantitative ratings).

The orthogonal relationship between these different uses of the terms *subjective* and *objective* is evident in the present research. Feedback on essay content, which is a subjective performance domain, revealed the positive bias on both a subjective metric (i.e., the writer evaluation form) and on an objective one (i.e., the number of content-related copyediting comments). In contrast, feedback on mechanics, which is an objective performance domain, showed no race effects on either the subjective or the objective measures.

Expectancy-violation theory (Bettencourt et al., 1997; Jussim et al., 1987) would predict that Whites would more harshly criticize fellow Whites than Blacks, especially when evaluating subpar work such as the essays used in this study. However, expectancy-violation theory and its demonstrations are limited to affective and global judgments (e.g., how one feels about the person being evaluated); it fails to account for judgments relating to specific skills or qualifications (Bettencourt et al., 1997). In contrast, the feedback studies focused exclusively on judgments of actual performance. In addition, the domain selectivity of the feedback bias is not readily explained by expectancy violation, which, again, is limited to global

evaluations. Finally, expectancy effects, as applicable to the evaluations of substandard work, are generally revealed in a propensity to overcriticize the in-group (Bettencourt et al., 1997). However, the feedback bias was demonstrated by more positive content comments to the out-group, as well as more negative content comments to the in-group.

Why do results in the feedback studies contrast with these other approaches?[5] A likely explanation is that the feedback studies introduced a level of social consequence that these more cognitive paradigms did not present. Feedback study participants believed that they were communicating their essay criticisms directly to the essay authors rather than to an emotionally disinterested experimenter. This may have made salient one or more of the manifold intergroup concerns which cause Whites to approach Blacks with extra caution and conciliation. Participants in out-group polarization, shifting standards, and expectancy-violation studies were not faced with the social constraints that direct feedback entails. As a result, these participants may have been influenced more by automatic processes than by intergroup considerations.

Limitations of the Research

There are qualifications to the present research that should be noted. The causal role of intergroup concerns, although implicated by the domain specificity of the bias, remains to be more firmly established and more narrowly specified. In addition, it is unclear whether the feedback bias extends to settings other than the university environment in which it was observed, to encounters where the feedback supplier and feedback recipient are of unequal social status (e.g., teacher–pupil) rather than being college peers, or to work of high as well as low merit (e.g., Biernat & Kobrynowicz, 1997). These unresolved issues suggest further areas of research.

Educational Costs of Biased Feedback

The positive feedback bias may present serious costs for minorities. Inflated praise and insufficient criticism may dissuade minority students from striving toward greater achievement levels and may misrepresent the level of effort and mastery that academic and professional advancement entail (see Massey, Scott, & Dornbusch, 1975, for elaboration). Biased feedback may also deprive minority students of the mental challenge that educators (e.g., Sommers, 1982) have cited as critical for intellectual growth. Steele (1992, 1995) noted that Black college students, in particular, are subject to low expectations and insufficient challenge and that they suffer both academically and psychologically as a result.

Distrust of positive feedback, even that which is deserved, presents a corollary cost of a positive feedback bias. Crocker, Voelkl, Testa, and Major (1991) found that Blacks may be wary of Whites' praise, so much so that the receipt of it can depress their self-esteem. Significantly, the depressing effects that White praise had on Crocker et al.'s Black participants occurred only when these participants received feedback from a White who, supposedly, knew of their racial identity. Blacks who received positive feedback from a White in a race-blind condition showed elevated self-esteem.[6] Crocker et al. believe that Black participants in the race-aware condition regarded praise as a sign of the White feedback supplier's racial concerns, rather than as reliable testimony to the quality of their own efforts.

This catalogue of potential liabilities suggests that a positive feedback bias may lead to negative consequences for minorities. Although the present demonstration was conducted in an educational context, the bias may also arise in work settings, social gatherings, or any other circumstance where intergroup evaluations occur. For these reasons, it is important to learn more about the bias and to determine how it can be addressed.

REFERENCES

Bettencourt, B. A., Dill, K. E., Greathouse, S. A., Charlton, K., & Mulholland, A. (1997). Evaluations of ingroup and outgroup members: The role of category-based expectancy violation. *Journal of Experimental Social Psychology, 33,* 244–275.

Biernat, M., & Kobrynowicz, D. (1997). Gender- and race-based standards of competence: Lower minimum standards by higher ability standards for devalued groups. *Journal of Personality and Social Psychology, 72,* 544–557.

Biernat, M., & Manis, M. (1994). Shifting standards and stereotype-based judgments. *Journal of Personality and Social Psychology, 66,* 5–20.

Biernat, M., Manis, M., & Nelson, T. (1991). Stereotypes and standards of judgment. *Journal of Personality and Social Psychology, 60,* 485–499.

Carver, C. S., Glass, D. G., & Katz, I. (1978). Favorable evaluations of Blacks and the handicapped: Positive prejudice, unconscious denial, or social desirability? *Journal of Applied Social Psychology, 8,* 97–106.

Crocker, J., Voelkl, K., Testa, M., & Major, B. (1991). Social stigma: The affective consequences of attributional ambiguity *Journal of Personality and Social Psychology, 60,* 218–228.

Davis, M., & Oathout, H. (1987). Maintenance of satisfaction in romantic relationships: Empathy and relational competence. *Journal of Personality and Social Psychology, 53,* 397–410.

Devine, P. G. (1989). Stereotypes and prejudice: Their automatic and controlled components. *Journal of Personality and Social Psychology, 56,* 5–18.

Devine, P. G., Montieth, M. J., Zuwerink, J. R., & Elliot, A. J. (1991). Prejudice with and without compunction. *Journal of Personality and Social Psychology, 60,* 817–830.

Dutton, D. G., & Lake, R. A. (1973). Threat of own prejudice and reverse discrimination in interracial situations. *Journal of Personality and Social Psychology, 28,* 94–100.

Feldman, R. S., & Donahoe, L. F. (1978). Non-verbal communication of affect in interracial dyads. *Journal of Educational Psychology, 70,* 979–987.

Feldman, R. S., & Orchowsky, S. (1979). Race and performance of students as determinants of teacher nonverbal behavior. *Contemporary Educational Psychology, 4,* 324–333.

Ford, J. K., Kraiger, K., & Schechtman, S. L. (1986). Study of race effects in objective indices and subjective evaluations of performance: A meta-analysis of performance criteria. *Psychological Bulletin, 99,* 330–337.

Gaertner, S., & Dovidio, J. (1986). The aversive form of racism. In J. F. Dovidio & S. L. Gaertner (Eds.), *Prejudice, discrimination, and racism* (pp. 61–90). San Diego, CA: Academic Press.

Harber, K. D. (1995). *Unbiased ratings of race-biased essay critiques: Further evidence of an interrace positive feedback bias.* Unpublished raw data. Stanford University, Stanford, CA.

Hastorf, A. H., Northcraft, G., & Piucciotto, S. (1979). Helping the handicapped: How realistic is the performance feedback received by the physically handicapped?

Personality and Social Psychology Bulletin, 5, 373–376.

Henderson-King, E. J., & Nisbett, R. E. (1997). Anti-Black prejudice as a function of exposure to the negative behavior of a single Black person. *Journal of Personality and Social Psychology, 71,* 654–664.

Jones, E., Farina, A., Hastorf, A., Markus, H., Miller, D., & Scott, R. (1984). *Social stigma: The psychology of marked relationships.* New York: Freeman.

Jussim, L., Coleman, L. M., & Lerch, L. (1987). The nature of stereotypes: A comparison and integration of three theories. *Journal of Personality and Social Psychology, 52,* 536–546.

Katz, I. (1981). *Stigma: A social psychological analysis.* Hillsdale, NJ: Erlbaum.

Kraiger, K., & Ford, J. K. (1985). A meta-analysis of ratee race effects in performance ratings. *Journal of Applied Psychology, 70,* 56–65.

Lambert, A. J., Cronen, S., Chasteen, A. L., & Lickel, B. (1996). Private vs. public expressions of prejudice. *Journal of Experimental Social Psychology, 32,* 437–459.

Landy, F. J., & Farr, J. L. (1980). Performance rating. *Psychological Bulletin, 87,* 72–102.

Linville, P. W. (1982). The complexity–extremity effect and age-based stereotyping. *Journal of Personality and Social Psychology, 42,* 193–211.

Linville, P. W., & Jones, E. E. (1980). Polarized appraisals of out-group members. *Journal of Personality and Social Psychology, 38,* 689–703.

Massey, G., Scott, V., & Dornbusch, S. (1975, November). Racism without racists: Institutional racism in urban schools. *The Black Scholar,* pp. 10–19.

Pulakos, E. D., White, L. A., Oppler, S. H., & Borman, W. C. (1989). Examination of race and sex effects on performance ratings. *Journal of Applied Psychology, 74,* 770–780.

Rubovitz, P. C., & Maehr, M. L. (1973). Pygmalion Black and White. *Journal of Personality and Social Psychology, 25,* 210–218.

Sackett, P. R., & DuBois, C. L. Z. (1991). Rater–ratee effects on performance evaluation. Challenging meta-analytic conclusions. *Journal of Applied Psychology, 76,* 873–877.

Shaughnessy, M. (1976). Basic writing. In G. Tate (Ed.), *Teaching composition: Ten bibliographical essays* (pp. 102–134). Fort Worth, TX: Texas Christian University Press.

Sommers, N. (1982). Responding to student writing. *College Composition and Communication, 33,* 148–156.

Steele, C. (1988). The psychology of self-affirmation: Sustaining the integrity of the self. In L. Berkowitz (Ed.), *Advances in experimental social psychology* (Vol. 21, pp. 261–302). San Diego, CA: Academic Press.

Steele, C. (1992, April). Race and the schooling of Black Americans. *The Atlantic Monthly,* 68–78.

Steele, C. (1995, August 31). Black students live down to expectations. *New York Times,* p. A15.

Stephan, W. G., & Stephan, C. W. (1985). Inter-group anxiety. *Journal of Social Issues, 41,* 157–175.

Taylor, M. C. (1979). Race, sex, and the expression of self-fulfilling prophecies in a laboratory teaching situation. *Journal of Personality and Social Psychology, 37,* 897–912.

Weiner, B., Russell, D., & Lerman, D. (1979). The cognition–emotion process in achievement-related contexts. *Journal of Personality and Social Psychology, 37,* 1211–1220.

Weitz, S. (1972). Attitude, voice, and behavior. A repressed affect model of interracial interaction. *Journal of Personality and Social Psychology, 24,* 14–21.

Wolf, F. M. (1986). *Meta-analysis: Quantitative methods for research synthesis* (Sage Quantitative Applications in the Social Sciences Series No. 07-059). Beverly Hills, CA: Sage.

Word, C., Zanna, M., & Cooper, J. (1974). The nonverbal mediation of self-fulfilling prophesies in interracial interaction. *Journal of Experimental Social Psychology, 10,* 109–120.

Yzerbyt, V., Schadron, G., Leyens, J.-P., & Rocher, S. (1994). Social judgability: The impact of meta-informational cues on the use of stereotypes. *Journal of Personality and Social Psychology, 66,* 48–55.

This research is based on my doctoral thesis, submitted to the Department of Psychology at Stanford University. The research was conducted at the Institute for Social Research, University of Michigan, where I was a visiting doctoral student. This research was supported by a Russell Sage Foundation grant for the schooling of women and Black Americans and by National Institutes of Health Training Grant 5 T32 H107456-15. I thank Claude Steele, Richard Nisbett, and Edwin Fisher, Jr., for their sponsorship of this research. I also appreciate the exceedingly helpful comments on a draft of this article from Dov Cohen and Alan Lambert, as well as the advice I received from Donna Henderson-King, Eaaron Henderson-King, Carla Herrera, Donald Hills, Markus Kemmelmeier, Barbel Knauper, and Piotr Winkielman. Finally, I am grateful to the host of undergraduate research assistants without whose help this research could not have been done.

ENDNOTES

1. The few experimental studies that have explored this topic have generally identified biases (positive and negative) in expressions of liking and responsiveness (Feldman & Donahoe, 1978; Feldman & Orchowsky, 1979; Taylor, 1979; Word, Zanna, & Cooper, 1974). Only Rubovitz and Maehr (1973) reported a bias

in performance feedback, and this had a negative valence. However, they did not control for actual performance, thus limiting the interpretability of their results.

2. Participant pool policy at this institution requires that only those students who agree to participate in deception research be eligible for deception studies.

3. This study also sought to show that self-affirmation (Steele, 1988) would influence the feedback bias. The self-affirmation manipulation, however, had no significant effect.

4. Significantly, these evaluative shifts have been associated only with a deceptive impartiality that masks underlying negative biases, but not with heightened lenience toward Blacks.

5. Other cognitive theories also address positive biases (for reviews, see Biernat & Kobrynowicz, 1997; Jussim, Coleman, & Lerch, 1987). However, those addressed here subsume many of these other theories and appear most closely related to the present research.

6. White participants, across experimental conditions, displayed enhanced self-esteem when praised.

CRITICAL THINKING QUESTIONS

1. Consider how the research questions addressed in this study could be investigated without using paper-and-pencil stimulus materials. Design such a study.

2. The study did not measure the subjects' prejudice levels towards blacks. Do you think the behaviors exhibited by the subjects would differ for high- versus low-prejudice individuals? Why or why not?

3. The author of the article indicates several limitations of the research, including whether the same results would be obtained if the feedback supplier and feedback recipient were of unequal status (such as a teacher and a pupil), rather than peers. What would you hypothesize regarding this issue? Design a study to test your hypothesis.

4. The author of the article mentions a number of potential costs associated with biased feedback. Expand on this notion by addressing other negative impacts of biased feedback.

5. Do you think that positively biased feedback occurs in other settings, as well, including work and casual social interactions? How might these biases be manifested in those settings? How could you test these possibilities?

6. Suppose African-American subjects were used in the experiment? Would the results be the same or different? Why?

Chapter Seven

INTERPERSONAL ATTRACTION

T HE TOPIC OF *interpersonal attraction* is one to which most people can directly relate: Whom do we come to like and why? The research on factors affecting attraction has gone in several directions. One major thrust has been to identify the conditions that are important in determining if two people will like one another. Many factors have been identified, but two very important ones are physical attractiveness and attitude similarity.

"The Biology of Beauty," Article 19, summarizes the large impact that physical attractiveness has on our judgments of other people and how these preferences may be biologically rooted in our evolutionary past. Most of us may feel reluctant to admit that such factors play an important role. After all, we should not judge people by superficial characteristics, such as how they look. Nonetheless, a large body of research suggests that we do exactly that.

Our judgments of physical attractiveness is not just limited to selecting potential partners, however. It may also influence what other characteristics we ascribe to attractive people based solely on their looks. Article 20, "What Is Beautiful Is Good," is a classic demonstration of how positive stereotypes are associated with physical attractiveness. Given the pervasiveness of this effect of physical attractiveness, the practical implications for how we deal with and judge others in our daily lives are indeed important.

Finally, Article 21 demonstrates that attraction is based on more than looks. "An Overview (and Underview) of Research and Theory within the Attraction Paradigm" presents a firsthand account of how the initial concept that having similar attitudes leads to feeling attraction evolved into the current model known as the *attraction paradigm*. Besides demonstrating how the model can be used to explain complex human relationships, this article also is an excellent example of how science and its theoretical models actually develop over time.

ARTICLE 19 _____

Physical attractiveness is perhaps the most widely researched topic in the area of interpersonal attraction. Part of this interest may be due to the importance of physical appearance in interpersonal interactions. When we meet a new person, physical appearance is the first thing we notice. Although perceptions of attractiveness are, to some extent, a matter of individual taste, some cultural stereotypes also define what constitutes attractiveness. Thus, another reason that attractiveness is so heavily investigated may be that it is relatively easy to get subjects to agree on what it means. Beauty is not just in the eye of the beholder, in other words.

Although attractiveness is something that can be readily observed about a person, most people would agree that it should not be used to make judgments about him or her. Indeed, most people would strongly protest the suggestion that how they see a person's values, skills, personality, or attributes may be influenced by what that person looks like. Yet a large body of literature developed over the years suggests that this indeed is the case. For example, research suggests that attractive people are rated more highly on a number of valued attributes; this is perhaps best summarized as the "what is beautiful is good" stereotype. Other studies have demonstrated that attractiveness may influence outcomes in serious situations. For example, attractive defendants are generally less likely to be convicted, and when they are convicted, they are more likely to receive lighter sentences than their less attractive counterparts.

The following article by Geoffrey Cowley discusses not only *what* we find attractive but also *why*. Rooted in evolutionary psychology, the article suggests that preferences regarding human beauty may be rooted in our biological past. Viewed in this light, our preferences for what we find beautiful may not be arbitrary or even culture specific but may have universal underpinnings.

The Biology of Beauty

■ Geoffrey Cowley

When it comes to choosing a mate, a female penguin knows better than to fall for the first creep who pulls up and honks. She holds out for the fittest suitor available—which in Antarctica means one chubby enough to spend several weeks sitting on newly hatched eggs without starving to death. The Asian jungle bird *Gallus gallus* is just as choosy. Males in that species sport gaily colored head combs and feathers, which lose their luster if the bird is invaded by parasites. By favoring males with bright ornaments, a hen improves her odds of securing a mate (and bearing offspring) with strong resistance to disease. For female scorpion flies, beauty is less about size or color than about symmetry. Females favor suitors who have well-matched wings—and with good reason. Studies show they're the most adept at killing prey and at defending their catch from competitors. There's no reason to think that any of these creatures understands its motivations, but there's a clear pattern to their preferences. "Throughout the animal world," says University of New Mexico ecologist Randy Thornhill, "attractiveness certifies biological quality."

Is our corner of the animal world different? That looks count in human affairs is beyond dispute. Studies have shown that people considered attractive fare better with parents and teachers, make more friends and more money, and have better sex with more (and more beautiful) partners. Every year, 400,000 Americans, including 48,000 men, flock to cosmetic surgeons. In other lands, people bedeck themselves with scars, lip plugs or bright feathers. "Every culture is a 'beauty culture,'" says Nancy Etcoff, a neuroscientist who is studying human attraction at the MIT Media Lab and writing a book on the subject. "I defy anyone to point to a society, any time in history or any place in the world, that wasn't preoccupied with beauty." The high-minded may dismiss our preening and ogling as distractions from things that matter, but the stakes can be enormous. "Judging beauty involves looking at another person," says University of Texas psychologist Devendra Singh, "and figuring out whether you want your children to carry that person's genes."

It's widely assumed that ideals of beauty vary from era to era and from culture to culture. But a harvest of new research is confounding that idea. Studies have established that people everywhere—regardless of race, class or age—share a sense of what's attractive. And though no one knows just how our minds translate the sight of a face or a body into rapture, new studies suggest that we judge each other by rules we're not even aware of. We may consciously admire Kate Moss's legs or Arnold's biceps, but we're also viscerally attuned to small variations in the size and symmetry of facial bones and the placement of weight on the body.

This isn't to say that our preferences are purely innate—or that beauty is all that matters in life. Most of us manage to find jobs, attract mates and bear offspring despite our physical imperfections. Nor should anyone assume that the new beauty research justifies the biases it illuminates. Our beautylust is often better suited to the Stone Age than to the Information Age; the qualities we find alluring may be powerful emblems of health, fertility and resistance to disease, but they say nothing about people's moral worth. The human weakness for what Thornhill calls "biological quality" causes no end of pain and injustice. Unfortunately, that doesn't make it any less real.

No one suggests that points of attraction never vary. Rolls of fat can signal high status in a poor society or low status in a rich one, and lip plugs go over better in the Kalahari than they do in Kansas. But local fashions seem to rest on a bedrock of shared preferences. You don't have to be Italian to find Michelangelo's David better looking than, say, Alfonse D'Amato. When British researchers asked women from England, China and India to rate pictures of Greek men, the women responded as if working from the same crib sheet. And when researchers at the University of Louisville showed a diverse collection of faces to whites, Asians and Latinos from 13 countries, the subjects' ethnic background scarcely affected their preferences.

To a skeptic, those findings suggest only that Western movies and magazines have overrun the world. But scientists have found at least one group that hasn't been exposed to this bias. In a series of groundbreaking experiments, psychologist Judith Langlois of the University of Texas, Austin, has shown that even infants share a sense of what's attractive. In the late '80s, Langlois started placing 3- and 6-month-old babies in front of a screen and showing them pairs of facial photographs. Each pair included one considered attractive by adult judges and one considered unattractive. In the first study, she found that the infants gazed significantly longer at "attractive" white female faces than at "unattractive" ones. Since then, she has repeated the drill using white male faces, black female faces, even the faces of other babies, and the same pattern always emerges. "These kids don't read Vogue or watch TV," Langlois says. "They haven't been touched by the media. Yet they make the same judgments as adults."

What, then, is beauty made of? What are the innate rules we follow in sizing each other up? We're obviously wired to find robust health a prettier sight than infirmity. "All animals are attracted to other animals that are healthy, that are clean by their standards and that show signs of competence," says Rutgers University anthropologist Helen Fisher. As far as anyone knows, there isn't a village on earth where skin lesions, head lice and rotting teeth count as beauty aids. But the rules get subtler than that. Like scorpion flies, we love symmetry. And though we generally favor average features over unusual ones, the people we find extremely beautiful share certain exceptional qualities.

When Randy Thornhill started measuring the wings of Japanese scorpion flies six years ago, he wasn't much concerned with the orgasms and infidelities of college students. But sometimes one thing leads to another. Biologists have long used bilateral symmetry—the extent to which a creature's right and left sides match—to gauge what's known as developmental stability. Given ideal growing conditions, paired features such as wings, ears, eyes and feet would come out matching perfectly. But pollution, disease and other hazards can disrupt development. As a result, the least resilient individuals tend to be the most lopsided. In chronicling the scorpion flies' daily struggles, Thornhill found that the bugs with the most symmetrical wings fared best in the competition for food and mates. To his amazement, females preferred symmetrical males even when they were hidden from view; evidently, their smells are more attractive. And when researchers started noting similar trends in other species, Thornhill turned his attention to our own.

Working with psychologist Steven Gangestad, he set about measuring the body symmetry of hundreds of college-age men and women. By adding up right-left disparities in seven measurements—the breadth of the feet, ankles, hands, wrists and elbows, as well as the breadth and length of the ears—the researchers scored each subject's overall body asymmetry. Then they had the person fill out a confidential questionnaire covering everything from temperament to sexual behavior, and set about looking for connections. They weren't disappointed. In a 1994 study, they found that the most symmetrical males had started having sex three to four years earlier than their most lopsided brethren. For both men and women, greater symmetry predicted a larger number of past sex partners.

That was just the beginning. From what they knew about other species, Thornhill and Gangestad predicted that women would be more sexually responsive to symmetrical men, and that men would exploit that advantage. To date, their findings support both suspicions. Last year they surveyed 86 couples and found that women with highly symmetrical partners were more than twice as likely to climax during intercourse (an event that may foster conception by ushering sperm into the uterus) than those with low-symmetry partners. And in separate surveys, Gangestad and

Thornhill have found that, compared with regular Joes, extremely symmetrical men are less attentive to their partners and more likely to cheat on them. Women showed no such tendency.

It's hard to imagine that we even notice the differences between people's elbows, let alone stake our love lives on them. No one carries calipers into a singles bar. So why do these measurements predict so much? Because, says Thornhill, people with symmetrical elbows tend to have "a whole suite of attractive features." His findings suggest that besides having attractive (and symmetrical) faces, men with symmetrical bodies are typically larger, more muscular and more athletic than their peers, and more dominant in personality. In a forthcoming study, researchers at the University of Michigan find evidence that facial symmetry is also associated with health. In analyzing diaries kept by 100 students over a two-month period, they found that the least symmetrical had the most physical complaints, from insomnia to nasal congestion, and reported more anger, jealousy and withdrawal. In light of all Thornhill and Gangestad's findings, you can hardly blame them.

If we did go courting with calipers, symmetry isn't all we would measure. As we study each other in the street, the office or the gym, our beauty radars pick up a range of signals. Oddly enough, one of the qualities shared by attractive people is their averageness. Researchers discovered more than a century ago that if they superimposed photographs of several faces, the resulting composite was usually better looking than any of the images that went into it. Scientists can now average faces digitally, and it's still one of the surest ways to make them more attractive. From an evolutionary perspective, a preference for extreme normality makes sense. As Langlois has written, "Individuals with average population characteristics should be less likely to carry harmful genetic mutations."

So far, so good. But here's the catch: while we may find average faces attractive, the faces we find most beautiful are not average. As New Mexico State University psychologist Victor Johnston has shown, they're extreme. To track people's preferences, Johnston uses a computer program called FacePrints. Turn it on, and it generates 30 facial images, all male or all female, which you rate on a 1–9 beauty scale.

The program then "breeds" the top-rated face with one of the others to create two digital offspring, which replace the lowest-rated faces in the pool. By rating round after round of new faces, you create an ever more beautiful population. The game ends when you award some visage a perfect 10. (If you have access to the World Wide Web, you can take part in a collective face-breeding experiment by visiting http://www-psych.nmsu.edu/~vic/faceprints/.)

For Johnston, the real fun starts after the judging is finished. By collecting people's ideal faces and comparing them to average faces, he can measure the distance between fantasy and reality. As a rule, he finds that an ideal female has a higher forehead than an average one, as well as fuller lips, a shorter jaw and a smaller chin and nose. Indeed, the ideal 25-year-old woman, as configured by participants in a 1993 study, had a 14-year-old's abundant lips and an 11-year-old's delicate jaw. Because her lower face was so small, she also had relatively prominent eyes and cheekbones.

The participants in that study were all college kids from New Mexico, but researchers have since shown that British and Japanese students express the same bias. And if there are lingering doubts about the depth of that bias, Johnston's latest findings should dispel them. In a forthcoming study, he reports that male volunteers not only consciously prefer women with small lower faces but show marked rises in brain activity when looking at pictures of them. And though Johnston has yet to publish specs on the ideal male, his unpublished findings suggest that a big jaw, a strong chin and an imposing brow are as prized in a man's face as their opposites are in a woman's.

Few of us ever develop the heart-melting proportions of a FacePrints fantasy. And if it's any consolation, beauty is not an all-or-nothing proposition. Madonna became a sex symbol despite her strong nose, and Melanie Griffith's strong jaw hasn't kept her out of the movies. Still, special things have a way of happening to people who approximate the ideal. We pay them huge fees to stand on windblown bluffs and stare into the distance. And past studies have found that square-jawed males not only start having sex earlier than their peers but attain higher rank in the military.

FIGURE 1 / Facial Fantasies. As a rule, average faces are more attractive than unusual ones. But when people are asked to develop ideal faces on a computer, they tend to exaggerate certain qualities.

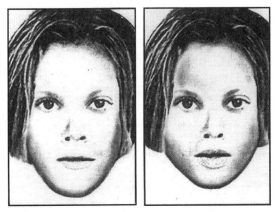

Average Proportions
This computer-generated face has the dimensions typical of Caucasian 20-year-olds.

Ideal Proportions
Most visions of the perfect female face have small jaws and abnormally lush lips.

Source: Victor Johnston, New Mexico State University. Used with permission.

None of this surprises evolutionary psychologists. They note that the facial features we obsess over are precisely the ones that diverge in males and females during puberty, as floods of sex hormones wash us into adulthood. And they reason that hormonal abundance would have been a good clue to mate value in the hunter-gatherer world where our preferences evolved. The tiny jaw that men favor in women is essentially a monument to estrogen—and, obliquely, to fertility. No one claims that jaws reveal a woman's odds of getting pregnant. But like breasts, they imply that she could.

Likewise, the heavy lower face that women favor in men is a visible record of the surge in androgens (testosterone and other male sex hormones) that turns small boys into 200-pound spear-throwers. An oversized jaw is biologically expensive, for the androgens required to produce it tend to compromise the immune system. But from a female's perspective, that should make jaw size all the more revealing. Evolutionists think of androgen-based features as "honest advertisements" of disease resistance. If a male can afford them without falling sick, the thinking goes, he must have a superior immune system in the first place.

No one has tracked the immune responses of men with different jawlines to see if these predictions bear out (Thornhill has proposed a study that would involve comparing volunteers' responses to a vaccine). Nor is it clear whether penis size figures into these equations. Despite what everyone thinks he knows on the subject, scientists haven't determined that women have consistent preferences one way or the other.

Our faces are our signatures, but when it comes to raw sex appeal, a nice chin is no match for a perfectly sculpted torso—especially from a man's perspective. Studies from around the world have found that while both sexes value appearance, men place more stock in it than women. And if there are social reasons for that imbalance, there are also biological ones. Just about any male over 14 can produce sperm, but a woman's ability to bear children depends on her age and hormone levels. Female fertility declines by two thirds between the ages of 20 and 44, and it's spent by 54. So while both sexes may eyeball potential partners, says Donald Symons, an anthropologist at the University of California in Santa Barbara, "a larger proportion of a woman's mate value can be detected from visual cues." Mounting evidence suggests there is no better cue than the relative contours of her waist and hips.

Before puberty and after menopause, females have essentially the same waistlines as males. But during puberty, while boys are amassing the bone and muscle of paleolithic hunters, a typical girl gains nearly 35 pounds of so-called reproductive fat around the hips and thighs. Those pounds contain roughly the 80,000 calories needed to sustain a pregnancy, and the curves they create provide a gauge of reproductive potential. "You have to get very close to see the details of a woman's face," says Devendra Singh, the University of Texas psychologist. "But you can see the shape of her body from 500 feet, and it says more about mate value."

Almost anything that interferes with fertility—obesity, malnutrition, pregnancy, meno-pause—changes a woman's shape. Healthy, fertile women typically have waist-hip ratios of .6 to .8, meaning their waists are 60 to 80 percent the size of their hips,

FIGURE 2 / Body Language. When men are asked to rank figures with various weights and waist-hip ratios (0.7 to 1.0), they favor a pronounced hourglass shape. The highest-ranked figures are N7, N8 and U7 (in that order). The lowest ranked is O10.

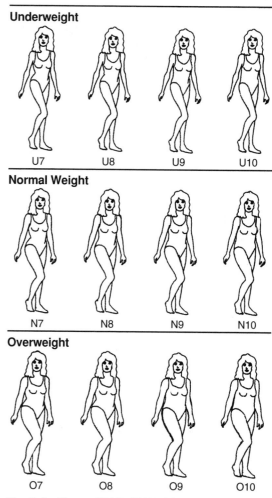

Underweight

U7   U8   U9   U10

Normal Weight

N7   N8   N9   N10

Overweight

O7   O8   O9   O10

The Order Chosen: (1) N7, (2) N8, (3) U7, (4) U8, (5) N9, (6) N10, (7) O7, (8) U9, (9) O8, (10) U10, (11) O9, (12) O10.

Source: Devendra Singh, University of Texas at Austin. Used with permission.

whatever their actual weight. To take one familiar example, a 36-25-36 figure would have a WHR of .7. Many women outside this range are healthy and capable of having children, of course. But as researchers in the Netherlands discovered in a 1993 study, even a slight increase in waist size relative to hip size can signal reproductive problems. Among 500 women who were attempting in vitro fertilization, the odds of conceiving during any given cycle declined by 30 percent with every 10 percent increase in WHR. In other words, a woman with a WHR of .9 was nearly a third less likely to get pregnant than one with a WHR of .8, regardless of her age or weight. From an evolutionary perspective, it's hard to imagine men not responding to such a revealing signal. And as Singh has shown repeatedly, they do.

Defining a universal standard of body beauty once seemed a fool's dream; common sense said that if spindly Twiggy and Rubens's girthy Three Graces could all excite admiration, then nearly anyone could. But if our ideals of size change from one time and place to the next, our taste in shapes is amazingly stable. A low waist-hip ratio is one of the few features that a long, lean Barbie doll shares with a plump, primitive fertility icon. And Singh's findings suggest the fashion won't change any time soon. In one study, he compiled the measurements of Playboy centerfolds and Miss America winners from 1923 to 1990. Their bodies got measurably leaner over the decades, yet their waist-hip ratios stayed within the narrow range of .68 to .72. (Even Twiggy was no tube; at the peak of her fame in the 1960s, the British model had a WHR of .73.)

The same pattern holds when Singh generates line drawings of different female figures and asks male volunteers to rank them for attractiveness, sexiness, health and fertility. He has surveyed men of various backgrounds, nationalities and ages. And whether the judges are 8-year-olds or 85-year-olds, their runaway favorite is a figure of average weight with a .7 WHR. Small wonder that when women were liberated from corsets and bustles, they took up girdles, wide belts and other waist-reducing contraptions. Last year alone, American women's outlays for shape-enhancing garments topped a half-billion dollars.

To some critics, the search for a biology of beauty looks like a thinly veiled political program. "It's the fantasy life of American men being translated into genetics," says poet and social critic Katha Pollitt. "You can look at any feature of modern life and make up a story about why it's genetic." In truth, says

Northwestern University anthropologist Micaela di Leonardo, attraction is a complicated social phenomenon, not just a hard-wired response. If attraction were governed by the dictates of baby-making, she says, the men of ancient Greece wouldn't have found young boys so alluring, and gay couples wouldn't crowd modern sidewalks. "People make decisions about sexual and marital partners inside complex networks of friends and relatives," she says. "Human beings cannot be reduced to DNA packets."

Homosexuality is hard to explain as a biological adaptation. So is stamp collecting. But no one claims that human beings are mindless automatons, blindly striving to replicate our genes. We pursue countless passions that have no direct bearing on survival. If we're sometimes attracted to people who can't help us reproduce, that doesn't mean human preferences lack any coherent design. A radio used as a doorstop is still a radio. The beauty mavens' mission—and that of evolutionary psychology in general—is not to explain everything people do but to unmask our biases and make sense of them. "Our minds have evolved to generate pleasurable experiences in response to some things while ignoring other things," says Johnston. "That's why sugar tastes sweet, and that's why we find some people more attractive than others."

The new beauty research does have troubling implications. First, it suggests that we're designed to care about looks, even though looks aren't earned and reveal nothing about character. As writer Ken Siman observes in his new book, "The Beauty Trip," "the kind [of beauty] that inspires awe, lust, and increased jeans sales cannot be evenly distributed. In a society where everything is supposed to be within reach, this is painful to face." From acne to birth defects, we wear our imperfections as thorns, for we know the world sees them and takes note.

A second implication is that sexual stereotypes are not strictly artificial. At some level, it seems, women are designed to favor dominant males over meek ones, and men are designed to value women for youthful qualities that time quickly steals. Given the slow pace of evolutionary change, our innate preferences aren't likely to fade in the foreseeable future. And if they exist for what were once good biological reasons, that doesn't make them any less nettlesome. "Men often forgo their health, their safety, their spare time and their family life in order to get rank," says Helen Fisher, the Rutgers anthropologist, "because unconsciously, they know that rank wins women." And all too often, those who can trade cynically on their rank do.

But do we have to indulge every appetite that natural selection has preserved in us? Of course not. "I don't know any scientist who seriously thinks you can look to nature for moral guidance," says Thornhill. Even the fashion magazines would provide a better compass.

With Karen Springen

CRITICAL THINKING QUESTIONS

1. Critically examine the explanations given by evolutionary psychology to explain people's beauty preferences. Are the arguments valid? As one critic notes in the article, "You can look at any feature of modern life and make up a story about why it's genetic." Defend your position.

2. The introduction to this article noted that people's beauty preferences may extend beyond simple mate selection and also be associated with hiring preferences, the likelihood of being convicted of a crime, and so on. What, if any, are the inherent risks involved whenever biological explanations are used to explain human behavior?

3. Why do you think the vast majority of the studies reported in the article concern *female* beauty? Why isn't the same amount of research being done on *male* attractiveness?

4. Based on your own experiences, is there a prejudice favoring attractive people? Provide evidence to support your point. Do you feel the effects of attractiveness are really as pervasive as suggested by the article? Why or why not? If being attractive has this great an impact, could this form of prejudice be reduced or eliminated or is it inevitable? Explain your answer.

ARTICLE 20 _____

It may seem obvious that looks matter when it comes to dating and mate selection. While many people would argue that physical attractiveness is not the only thing that they look for in a potential partner, few would argue that they are oblivious to appearance. Furthermore, according to Article 19—which considered how people's beauty preferences might have biological roots—there is fairly strong agreement as to what features people find attractive.

So, what is life like for people who happen to have the features that others find attractive? Are their lives significantly different from those of individuals who do not possess such good looks? Furthermore, do looks have any impact on people's lives outside the areas of dating and mating popularity? For example, compared to a less attractive counterpart, will an attractive person more likely be successful in the work world? Be a better parent? Be a happier person overall? The following classic article by Karen Dion, Ellen Berscheid, and Elaine Walster was one of the first studies to investigate the "what is beautiful is good" effect. As indicated in the article, attractiveness may convey a great many benefits to those people who possess it.

What Is Beautiful Is Good[1]

■ Karen Dion, Ellen Berscheid, and Elaine Walster

A person's physical appearance, along with his sexual identity, is the personal characteristic that is most obvious and accessible to others in social interaction. The present experiment was designed to determine whether physically attractive stimulus persons, both male and female, are (a) assumed to possess more socially desirable personality traits than physically unattractive stimulus persons and (b) expected to lead better lives (e.g., be more competent husbands and wives, be more successful occupationally, etc.) than unattractive stimulus persons. Sex of Subject × Sex of Stimulus Person interactions along these dimensions also were investigated. The present results indicate a "what is beautiful is good" stereotype along the physical attractiveness dimension with no Sex of Judge × Sex of Stimulus interaction. The implications of such a stereotype on self-concept development and the course of social interaction are discussed.

A person's physical appearance, along with his sexual identity, is the personal characteristic most obvious and accessible to others in social interaction. It is perhaps for this reason that folk psychology has always contained a multitude of theorems which ostensibly permit the forecast of a person's character and personality simply from knowledge of his outward appearance. The line of deduction advanced by most physiognomic theories is simply that "What is beautiful is good . . . [Sappho, Fragments, No. 101]," and that "Physical beauty is the sign of an interior beauty, a spiritual and moral beauty . . . [Schiller, 1882]."

Several processes may operate to make the soothsayers' prophecies more logical and accurate than would appear at first glance. First, it is possible that a correlation between inward character and appearance exists because certain personality traits influence one's appearance. For example, a calm, relaxed person may develop fewer lines and wrinkles than a tense, irritable person. Second, cultural stereotypes about the kinds of personalities appropriate for beautiful or ugly people may mold the personalities of these individuals. If casual acquaintances invariably assume that attractive individuals are more sincere, noble, and honest than unattractive persons, then attractive individuals should be habitually regarded with more respect than unattractive persons. Many have noted that one's self-concept develops from observing what oth-

Reprinted from *Journal of Personality and Social Psychology,* 1972, *24,* 285–290. Copyright © 1972 by the American Psychological Association. Reprinted with permission.

ers think about oneself. Thus, if the physically attractive person is consistently treated as a virtuous person, he may become one.

The above considerations pose several questions: (*a*) Do individuals in fact have stereotyped notions of the personality traits possessed by individuals of varying attractiveness? (*b*) To what extent are these stereotypes accurate? (*c*) What is the cause of the correlation between beauty and personality if, in fact, such a correlation exists?

Some observers, of course, deny that such stereotyping exists, and thus render Questions *b* and *c* irrelevant. Chief among these are rehabilitation workers (cf. Wright, 1960) whose clients possess facial and other physical disabilities. These researchers, however, may have a vested interest in believing that physical beauty is a relatively unimportant determinant of the opportunities an individual has available to him.

Perhaps more interestingly, it has been asserted that other researchers also have had a vested interest in retaining the belief that beauty is a peripheral characteristic. Aronson (1969), for example, has suggested that the fear that investigation might prove this assumption wrong has generally caused this to be a taboo area for social psychologists:

> As an aside, I might mention that physical attractiveness is rarely investigated as an antecedent of liking—even though a casual observation (even by us experimental social psychologists) would indicate that we seem to react differently to beautiful women than to homely women. It is difficult to be certain why the effects of physical beauty have not been studied more systematically. It may be that, at some levels, we would hate to find evidence indicating that beautiful women are better liked than homely women—somehow this seems undemocratic. In a democracy we like to feel that with hard work and a good deal of motivation, a person can accomplish almost anything. But, alas (most of us believe), hard work cannot make an ugly woman beautiful. Because of this suspicion perhaps most social psychologists implicitly prefer to believe that beauty is indeed only skin deep—and avoid the investigation of its social impact for fear they might learn otherwise [p. 160].

The present study was an attempt to determine if a physical attractiveness stereotype exists and, if so, to investigate the content of the stereotype along several dimensions. Specifically, it was designed to investigate (*a*) whether physically attractive stimulus persons, both male and female, are assumed to possess more *socially desirable personality traits* than unattractive persons and (*b*) whether they are expected to *lead better lives* than unattractive individuals. With respect to the latter, we wished to determine if physically attractive persons are generally expected to be better husbands and wives, better parents, and more successful socially and occupationally than less attractive persons.

Because it seemed possible that jealousy might attenuate these effects (if one is jealous of another, he may be reluctant to accord the other the status that he feels the other deserves), and since subjects might be expected to be more jealous of attractive stimulus persons of the same sex than of the opposite sex, we examined the Sex of Subject × Sex of Stimulus Person interactions along the dimensions described above.

METHOD

Subjects

Sixty students, 30 males and 30 females, who were enrolled in an introductory course in psychology at the University of Minnesota participated in this experiment. Each had agreed to participate in return for experimental points to be added to their final exam grade.

Procedure

When the subjects arrived at the designated rooms, they were introduced to the experiment as a study of accuracy in person perception. The experimenter stated that while psychological studies have shown that people do form detailed impressions of others on the basis of a very few cues, the variables determining the extent to which these early impressions are generally accurate have not yet been completely identified. The subjects were told that the purpose of the present study was to compare person perception accuracy of untrained college students with two other groups who had been trained in various interpersonal perception techniques, specifically graduate students in clinical psychology and clinical psychologists. The experimenter noted his belief that person perception accuracy is a general ability varying among people. Therefore, according to the experimenter, college students who are high on this ability may be as accurate as some professional clinicians when making first-impression judgments based on noninterview material.

The subjects were told that standard sets of photographs would be used as the basis for personality inferences. The individuals depicted in the photographs were said to be part of a group of college students currently enrolled at other universities who were participating in a longitudinal study of personality development scheduled to continue into adulthood. It would be possible, therefore, to assess the accuracy of each subject's judgments against information currently available on the stimulus persons and also against forthcoming information.

Stimulus materials. Following the introduction, each subject was given three envelopes. Each envelope contained one photo of a stimulus person of approximately the subject's own age. One of the three envelopes that the subject received contained a photograph of a physically attractive stimulus person; another contained a photograph of a person of average attractiveness; and the final envelope contained a photograph of a relatively unattractive stimulus person.[2] Half of our subjects received three pictures of girls; the remainder received pictures of boys.

To increase the generalizability of our findings and to insure that the general dimension of attractiveness was the characteristic responded to (rather than unique characteristics such as hair color, etc.), 12 different sets of three pictures each were prepared. Each subject received and rated only 1 set. Which 1 of the 12 sets of pictures the subject received, the order in which each of the three envelopes in the set were presented, and the ratings made of the person depicted, were all randomly determined.

Dependent variables. The subjects were requested to record their judgments of the three stimulus persons in several booklets.[3] The first page of each booklet cautioned the subjects that this study was an investigation of accuracy of person perception and that we were not interested in the subjects' tact, po-

liteness, or other factors usually important in social situations. It was stressed that it was important for the subject to rate the stimulus persons frankly.

The booklets tapped impressions of the stimulus person along several dimensions. First, the subjects were asked to open the first envelope and then to rate the person depicted on 27 different *personality traits* (which were arranged in random order).[4] The subjects' ratings were made on 6-point scales, the ends of which were labeled by polar opposites (i.e., exciting–dull). When these ratings had been computed, the subject was asked to open the second envelope, make ratings, and then open the third envelope.

In a subsequent booklet, the subjects were asked to assess the stimulus persons on five additional personality traits.[5] These ratings were made on a slightly different scale. The subjects were asked to indicate which stimulus person possessed the "most" and "least" of a given trait. The stimulus person thought to best represent a positive trait was assigned a score of 3; the stimulus person thought to possess an intermediate amount of the trait was assigned a score of 2; and the stimulus person thought to least represent the trait was assigned a score of 1.

In a previous experiment (see Endnote 3), a subset of items was selected to comprise an index of the *social desirability* of the personality traits assigned to the stimulus person. The subjects' ratings of each stimulus person on the appropriate items were simply summed to determine the extent to which the subject perceived each stimulus person as socially desirable.

In order to assess whether or not attractive persons are expected to lead happier and more successful lives than unattractive persons, the subjects were asked to estimate which of the stimulus persons would be most likely, and which least likely, to have a number of different life experiences. The subjects were reminded again that their estimates would eventually be checked for accuracy as the lives of the various stimulus persons evolved. The subjects' estimates of the stimulus person's probable life experiences formed indexes of the stimulus person's future happiness in four areas: (*a*) marital happiness (Which stimulus person is most likely to ever be divorced?); (*b*) parental happiness (Which stimulus person is most likely to be a good parent?); (*c*) social and professional happiness (Which stimulus person is most likely to experience deep personal fulfillment?); and (*d*) total happiness (sum of Indexes *a, b,* and *c*).

A fifth index, an occupational success index, was also obtained for each stimulus person. The subjects were asked to indicate which of the three stimulus persons would be most likely to engage in 30 different occupations. (The order in which the occupations were presented and the estimates made was randomized.) The 30 occupations had been chosen such that three status levels of 10 different general occupations were represented, three examples of which follow: Army sergeant (low status); Army captain (average status); Army colonel (high status). Each time a high-status occupation was foreseen for a stimulus person, the stimulus person was assigned a score of 3; when a moderate status occupation was foreseen, the stimulus person was assigned a score of 2; when a low-status occupation was foreseen, a score of 1 was assigned. The average status of occupations that a subject ascribed to a stimulus person constituted the score for that stimulus person in the occupational status index.

RESULTS AND DISCUSSION

Manipulation Check

It is clear that our manipulation of the relative attractiveness of the stimulus persons depicted was effective. The six unattractive stimulus persons were seen as less attractive than the average stimulus persons, who, in turn, were seen as less attractive than the six attractive stimulus persons. The stimulus persons' mean rankings on the attractiveness dimension were 1.12, 2.02, and 2.87, respectively. These differences were statistically significant ($F = 939.32$).[6]

Test of Hypotheses

It will be recalled that it was predicted that the subjects would attribute more socially desirable personality traits to attractive individuals than to average or unattractive individuals. It also was anticipated that jealousy might attenuate these effects. Since the subjects might be expected to be more jealous of stimulus persons of the same sex than of the opposite sex, we blocked both on sex of subject and sex of stimulus person. If jealousy attenuated the predicted main effect, a significant Sex of Subject × Sex of Stimulus Person interaction should be secured in addition to the main effect.

All tests for detection of linear trend and interaction were conducted via a multivariate analysis of variance. (This procedure is outlined in Hays, 1963.)

The means relevant to the hypothesis that attractive individuals will be perceived to possess more socially desirable personalities than others are reported in Table 1. Analyses reveal that attractive individuals were indeed judged to be more socially desirable than are unattractive ($F = 29.61$) persons. The Sex of Subject × Sex of Stimulus Person interac-

TABLE 1 / Traits Attributed to Various Stimulus Others

Trait Ascription[a]	Unattractive Stimulus Person	Average Stimulus Person	Attractive Stimulus Person
Social desirability of the stimulus person's personality	56.31	62.42	65.39
Occupational status of the stimulus person	1.70	2.02	2.25
Marital competence of the stimulus person	.37	.71	1.70
Parental competence of the stimulus person	3.91	4.55	3.54
Social and professional happiness of the stimulus person	5.28	6.34	6.37
Total happiness of the stimulus person	8.83	11.60	11.60
Likelihood of marriage	1.52	1.82	2.17

[a]The higher the number, the more socially desirable, the more prestigious an occupation, etc., the stimulus person is expected to possess.

tion was insignificant (interaction $F = .00$). Whether the rater was of the same or the opposite sex as the stimulus person, attractive stimulus persons were judged as more socially desirable.[7]

Furthermore, it was also hypothesized that the subjects would assume that attractive stimulus persons are likely to secure more prestigious jobs than those of lesser attractiveness, as well as experiencing happier marriages, being better parents, and enjoying more fulfilling social and occupational lives.

The means relevant to these predictions concerning the estimated future life experiences of individuals of varying degrees of physical attractiveness are also depicted in Table 1. As shown in the table, there was strong support for all of the preceding hypotheses save one. Attractive men and women were expected to attain more prestigious occupations than were those of lesser attractiveness ($F = 42.30$), and this expectation was expressed equally by raters of the same or the opposite sex as the stimulus person (interaction $F = .25$).

The subjects also assumed that attractive individuals would be more competent spouses and have happier marriages than those of lesser attractiveness ($F = 62.54$). (It might be noted that there is some evidence that this may be a correct perception. Kirkpatrick and Cotton (1951), reported that "well-adjusted" wives were more physically attractive than "badly adjusted" wives. "Adjustment," however, was assessed by friends' perceptions, which may have been affected by the stereotype evident here.)

According to the means reported in Table 1, it is clear that attractive individuals were not expected to be better parents ($F = 1.47$). In fact, attractive persons were rated somewhat lower than any other group of stimulus persons as potential parents, although no statistically significant differences were apparent.

As predicted, attractive stimulus persons were assumed to have better prospects for happy social and professional lives ($F = 21.97$). All in all, the attractive stimulus persons were expected to have more total happiness in their lives than those of lesser attractiveness ($F = 24.20$).

The preceding results did not appear to be attenuated by a jealousy effect (Sex of Subject × Stimulus Person interaction Fs = .01, .07, .21, and .05, respectively).

The subjects were also asked to estimate the likelihood that the various stimulus persons would marry early or marry at all. Responses were combined into a single index. It is evident that the subjects assumed that the attractive stimulus persons were more likely to find an acceptable partner than those of lesser attractiveness ($F = 35.84$). Attractive individuals were expected to marry earlier and to be less likely to remain single. Once again, these conclusions were reached by all subjects, regardless of whether they were of the same or opposite sex of the stimulus person (interaction $F = .01$).

The results suggest that a physical attractiveness stereotype exists and that its content is perfectly compatible with the "What is beautiful is good" thesis. Not only are physically attractive persons assumed to possess more socially desirable personalities than those of lesser attractiveness, but it is presumed that their lives will be happier and more successful.

The results also suggest that the physical attractiveness variable may have a number of implications for a variety of aspects of social interaction and influence. For example, it is clear that physically attractive individuals may have even more advantages in the dating market than has previously been assumed. In addition to an aesthetic advantage in marrying a beautiful spouse (cf. Josselin de Jong, 1952), potential marriage partners may also assume that the beautiful attract all of the world's material benefits and happiness. Thus, the lure of an attractive marriage partner should be strong indeed.

We do not know, of course, how well this stereotype stands up against contradictory information. Nor do we know the extent to which it determines the pattern of social interaction that develops with a person of a particular attractiveness level. Nevertheless, it would be odd if people did not behave toward others in accordance with this stereotype. Such behavior has been previously noted anecdotally. Monahan (1941) has observed that

> *Even social workers accustomed to dealing with all types often find it difficult to think of a normal, pretty girl as being guilty of a crime. Most people, for some inexplicable reason, think of crime in terms of abnormality in appearance, and I must say that beautiful women are not often convicted [p. 103].*

A host of other familiar social psychological dependent variables also should be affected in predictable ways.

In the above connection, it might be noted that if standards of physical attractiveness vary widely, knowledge of the content of the physical attractiveness stereotype would be of limited usefulness in predicting its effect on social interaction and the development of the self-concept. The present study was not designed to investigate the degree of variance in perceived beauty. (The physical attractiveness ratings of the stimulus materials were made by college students of a similar background to those who participated in this study.) Preliminary evidence (Cross & Cross, 1971) suggests that such differences in perceived beauty may not be as severe as some observers have suggested.

REFERENCES

Aronson, E. Some antecedents of interpersonal attraction. In W. J. Arnold & D. Levine (Eds.), *Nebraska Symposium on Motivation*, 1969, *17*, 143–177.

Cross, J. F., & Cross, J. Age, sex, race, and the perception of facial beauty. *Developmental Psychology*, 1971, *5*, 433–439.

Hays, W. L. *Statistics for psychologists.* New York: Holt, Rinehart & Winston, 1963.

Josselin de Jong, J. P. B. *Lévi-Strauss' theory on kinship and marriage.* Leiden, Holland: Brill, 1952.

Kirkpatrick, C., & Cotton, J. Physical attractiveness, age, and marital adjustment. *American Sociological Review*, 1951, *16*, 81–86.

Monahan, F. *Women in crime.* New York: Ives Washburn, 1941.

Schiller, J. C. F. *Essays, esthetical and philosophical, including the dissertation on the "Connexions between the animal and the spiritual in man."* London: Bell, 1882.

Wright, B. A. *Physical disability—A psychological approach.* New York: Harper & Row, 1960.

ENDNOTES

1. This research was financed in part by National Institute of Mental Health Grants MH 16729 to Berscheid and MH 16661 to Walster.

2. The physical attractiveness rating of each of the pictures was determined in a preliminary study. One hundred Minnesota undergraduates rated 50 yearbook pictures of persons of the opposite sex with respect to physical attractiveness. The criteria for choosing the 12 pictures to be used experimentally were (*a*) high-interrater agreement as to the physical attractiveness of the stimulus (the average interrater correlation for all of the pictures was .70); and (*b*) pictures chosen to represent the very attractive category and very unattractive category were not at the extreme ends of attractiveness.

3. A detailed report of the items included in these booklets is available. Order Document No. 01972 from the National Auxiliary Publication Service of the American Society for Information Science, c/o CCM Information Services, Inc., 909 3rd Avenue, New York, New York 10022. Remit in advance $5.00 for photocopies or $2.00 for microfiche and make checks payable to: Research and Microfilm Publications, Inc.

4. The subjects were asked how altruistic, conventional, self-assertive, exciting, stable, emotional, dependent, safe, interesting, genuine, sensitive, outgoing, sexually permissive, sincere, warm, sociable, competitive, obvious, kind, modest, strong, serious, sexually warm, simple, poised, bold, and sophisticated each stimulus person was.

5. The subjects rated stimulus persons on the following traits: friendliness, enthusiasm, physical attractiveness, social poise, and trustworthiness.

6. Throughout this report, $df = 1/55$.

7. Before running the preliminary experiment to determine the identity of traits usually associated with a socially desirable person (see Endnote 3), we had assumed that an exciting date, a nurturant person, and a person of good character would be perceived as quite different personality types. Conceptually, for example, we expected that an exciting date would be seen to require a person who was unpredictable, challenging, etc., while a nurturant person would be seen to be predictable and unthreatening. It became clear, however, that these distinctions were not ones which made sense to the subjects. There was almost total overlap between the traits chosen as representative of an exciting date, of a nurturant person, and a person of good or ethical character. All were strongly correlated with social desirability. Thus, attractive stimulus persons are assumed to be more exciting dates ($F = 39.97$), more nurturant individuals ($F = 13.96$), and to have better character ($F = 19.57$) than persons of lesser attractiveness.

CRITICAL THINKING QUESTIONS

1. The study used college students, presumably most of them ages 18 to 22. Do you think that the age of the subjects might influence the results? Why or why not? Design a study to test this possibility.

2. The study used photographs as stimulus materials. Do you think that the "what is beautiful is good" effect also would occur in face-to-face encounters? Or might the

judgments made in person somehow be different than those made by looking at photographs? How could you test this possibility?

3. The study indicated that physically attractive people are perceived as having more socially desirable traits and are expected to be more successful in life than their less attractive counterparts. Do you think that attractive people *actually* are more desirable and more successful in life? Why or why not? How could this question be tested?

4. Relate the results of this study to the information presented in Article 19. How would an evolutionary psychologist explain the results of the present study?

ADDITIONAL RELATED READINGS

McCall, M. (1997). Physical attractiveness and access to alcohol: What is beautiful does not get carded. *Journal of Applied Social Psychology, 27,* 453–462.

Wheller, L., & Kim, Y. (1997). What is beautiful is culturally good: The physical attractiveness stereotype has different content in collectivistic cultures. *Personality and Social Psychology Bulletin, 23,* 795–800.

ARTICLE 21 _____

As indicated in both Articles 19 and 20, physical attractiveness plays an important role in interpersonal attraction. But what other factors are important? Early research on the topic suggested that *propinquity,* or physical proximity to others, is an important initial determinate of attraction. For example, studies of friendship patterns in housing developments found that the most important determinant of who would become friends was how close people lived to one another.

But is propinquity enough? Obviously, not. It may provide the initial contact with another person, which, in turn, could be the basis for some relationship to develop, but something else is needed. One additional variable that is important in determining interpersonal attraction is *similarity.* Common sense suggests that we will invariably like people who are similar to ourselves. Again, early research, as well as everyday observation, seems to indicate that spouses and friends often hold similar attitudes.

Probably one of the most widely validated hypotheses in this area of research is that similarity leads to attraction. This is a very broad and highly replicated finding. It does not mean that it is *always* the case; there are exceptions when similarity does not lead to attraction. Nonetheless, this "similarity leads to liking" effect is a well-documented behavior and extends to many different areas beyond the simple similarity of attitudes.

Donn Byrne has been a major contributor over the years to the area of attraction research. In the article that follows, he discusses how the *attraction paradigm* developed as well as the current status of the concept. Byrne's article also is an excellent example of how knowledge really is advanced in psychology, not how it ideally is supposed to advance. Furthermore, the article describes how the original laboratory-based "similarity leads to liking" effect has been expanded to incorporate how these effects may operate in real-world adult attachment patterns.

An Overview (and Underview) of Research and Theory within the Attraction Paradigm

■ Donn Byrne

ABSTRACT

The initiation and subsequent development of what I once immodestly labeled 'the attraction paradigm' are described. Though an after-the-fact reconstruction of a given program of research and theory may appear to result from planful, rational, insightful, and even prescient actions, the actual process is more often a combination of multiple personal motives, semi-random input from a wide variety of sources, sheer luck, and semi-delusional tenacity. In any event, some highlights and landmarks of over 35 years of attraction research are summarized. The story includes the initial decision to investigate the effect of attitude similarity–dissimilarity

Reprinted from *Journal of Social and Personal Relationships,* 1997, *14*(3), 417–431. Copyright © 1997 Sage Publications, Ltd. Reprinted by permission.

on attraction, the gradual development of the linear function that specifies the relationship between seemingly diverse stimulus events and evaluative responses such as attraction, and the construction of a theoretical model that began with a focus on conditioning but was eventually expanded as 'the behaviour sequence,' incorporating cognitive constructs in order to deal with such interpersonal complexities as love. As a postscript, I describe our current efforts to place the components of adult attachment patterns within this model in an effort to predict more precisely various aspects of interpersonal relationships.

Over the years, I have frequently sought to describe how a body of research can grow and develop without necessarily encroaching on or being encroached on by the independent efforts of others to investigate the same or similar phenomena. We have offered such analogies as playing in one's own sandbox (Byrne, 1978) and laying out one's own yellow brick road through an opaque forest teeming with lions and tigers and bears (Clore & Byrne, 1974). More recently, while teaching a graduate attraction seminar, I happened upon a magazine ad for Erector Sets depicting a small boy engaged in a construction project, gazing TAT-like into space. It was a mildly epiphanic moment—the small boy was myself, and the construction process seemed to be an appropriate analogy for building a coherent conceptual model with consistent, interconnecting operations (Byrne, 1997). You may be as uninspired by the blinding clarity of this insight as were my students, but at least keep it in mind as we examine the attraction paradigm, past and present.

PLANNING DECADES OF RESEARCH IN ADVANCE?

Even in those blissful days when research funds flowed from what we hoped would be Washington's dedication to a never-ending fountain of truth, there was one aspect of the grant application process that seemed absolutely meaningless to me. The expectation that an investigator should be able to lay out a two-year or three-year research plan simply made no sense: I can describe what *has been done,* but not what *will be done.* My applications squeaked by only because I pretended to describe 'future research' that had already been conducted but not yet published along with a few unexciting and largely fictional proposals that seldom led anywhere. (If this confession means that I must return the money, I'm only kidding.) In the early stages of most subfields of social psychology and for an individual who is unsure about what he will do later this afternoon, there is little to be gained by designing a multi-year plan.

In the early stages of a paradigm, the ideas for any given investigation originate in a wide variety of unexpected sources—personal experiences and concerns (Byrne, 1997), a student's insight in a seminar (Byrne et al., 1969), my mother's criticism of presidential candidate George McGovern as being too 'wishy-washy' (Allgeier et al., 1979), or a student's vague interests that can be shaped, Skinner-like, into theoretical relevance (Byrne & Rhamey, 1965). In time (as a paradigm matures) research *can* be planful and purposeful; examples include hypotheses derived from theory (Smeaton et al., 1989) and the necessity to explain data that seem to be inconsistent with one's existing model (Byrne & Lamberth, 1971).

So, how did the attraction paradigm come to be? For any such endeavor to succeed, two interrelated factors are required:

An investigator must be committed to *operational* and *theoretical consistency* (Byrne, 1971). In many scientific fields, that statement would seem banal, obvious, and perhaps insulting; in much of social psychology, that same statement is an almost heretical admission of noncreativity.

The first factor, *operational consistency,* involves a simple, though often ignored rule. When progressing from one study to the next, an investigator should keep constant all operations except the single new element being studied. Francis Bacon alluded to such matters—at the beginning of the 17th century—as a necessity in order to avoid confounding the effects of two or more variables. Oddly enough, our graduate students seem to be taught about confounds within experiments much better than about confounds between experiments.

The second factor, *conceptual consistency,* refers to the need to incorporate any and all relevant findings into one's theoretical framework. Thus, findings should be interrelated not only empirically, but also conceptually. The reason that a given investigator selects a given theoretical approach is not clear, but it seems likely that we each rely in part on untestable meta-theoretical assumptions and in part on more explicit formulations such as learning theory, genetic determination, or cognitive consistency. Whatever the origins of a conceptual formulation and however much it is elaborated and altered over time, logical consistency is crucial. Otherwise, science would resemble a child's game in which the rules change from moment to moment to suit the individual player. Sometimes, of course, a finding does not fit the model, and the options include a reevaluation of the procedures and operations and, if necessary, a modification and expansion of the theoretical structure in order to take account of the anomaly. A more radical option, and a truly desperate last resort, is to conclude that there is a basic flaw in one's conceptual model. To date, I have resisted the latter option.

A general point to remember is that the first factor is of little value without a coherent theoretical framework while the second factor is of little value without a coherent empirical framework. Together, they provide the crucial components of scientific activity.

Now we consider what all this has to do with attraction research.

article while studying for my qualifying exams in Clinical Psychology even though its content had absolutely nothing to do with my chosen field. No matter—it made eminent sense and seemed both accurate and important. I ruminated about it many times over the next couple of years. Later, with a doctoral degree and a growing disinterest in clinical, I woke up early one hot Austin morning to the mockingbirds' trill, following one of the many legendary parties enjoyed by the Texas department. In addition to a headache, I had a realization (Byrne, 1979). Essentially, I decided I must follow Newcomb's lead with an investigation of the effect of attitude similarity on attraction. The specific topic was suggested by many observations of my father's evaluations of other people that were based on whether their views did or did not coincide with his own. That is, I had concluded long before that attitudes were among the determinants of attraction. Newcomb's paper easily convinced me that attitude similarity must involve reinforcement. These two beliefs led me to design an experiment to test the more accessible of the two. I might add that I heard the voice of James Earl Jones saying, 'Build a paradigm, and they will come.' The truth is, I had not yet learned about paradigms, very few decided to come to this particular corn field, and all I heard was the mockingbirds.

FROM A GENERAL INTEREST IN ATTRACTION TO EXPERIMENTATION ON A SPECIFIC PROBLEM

As discussed elsewhere (Byrne, 1997), the source of my abiding interest in attraction most likely began in childhood as the result of living in a peripatetic family whose frequent relocations took me to school after school where making (or not making) new friends presented an annual crisis. Though my first empirical research involved propinquity and acquaintanceship (Byrne & Buehler, 1955), my 'real' attraction research had its implicit beginning when I read Ted Newcomb's (1956) APA presidential address in which he touched on such matters as attraction and reinforcement. Specifically, he suggested that attraction between persons is a function of the extent to which reciprocal rewards are present in the interaction. For me, that was truly an 'aha!' experience. I read his

Selecting the Operations and Procedures Needed to Investigate the Effect of Attitude Similarity–Dissimilarity on Attraction

I eventually discovered that other psychologists had previously studied the similarity–attraction effect in an experimental setting: Schachter (1951) manipulated agreement in order to determine the relative amount of communication directed at group members with deviant vs non-deviant opinions, and Smith (1957, 1958) manipulated value similarity to determine its effect on acceptance and perceived similarity in the context of Heider's (1958) interpersonal theory. My blissful ignorance of this work afforded me the opportunity to create my own operations and procedures (Byrne, 1961). Only in retrospect is it now possible to identify this simple experiment as Landmark 1. I inadvertently initiated a new paradigm rather than working within an existing one.

A great deal of thought went into planning the research details because attraction appeared to be a central aspect of human behavior. I did not know at the time that this methodology would guide the experimental details of hundreds of future investigations (Griffitt & Byrne, 1970). The primary constraint was financial; as a new PhD, I had no grant money and no doctoral students. The department could afford to pay for paper and duplication but little else, so the independent and dependent variables had to remain within the technological boundaries set by the ditto machine.

The independent variable was attitude similarity, and the identification of appropriate attitude topics was provided by undergraduates in my classes who listed topics which they at one time or other discussed with friends and acquaintances; these issues were transformed into 26 7-point attitude items (agree–disagree, for–against, favor option A vs option B, etc.). The importance of these 26 issues was rated by other students, and the issues were perceived by them to range from relatively important (integration, God, and premarital sex) to relatively unimportant (western movies, music, and political affiliation).

The experimental procedure involved administering the attitude scale to students in class and later presenting the same students with what was purported to be a scale filled out by a same-sex fellow student in another class at the university (with the name and other identifying data about this stranger seemingly scissored out of the scale, imitating the military censors who cut passages out of my brother's letters from the Aleutian Islands during World War II). The ostensible purpose of the study was to determine just how much students could learn about one another from the limited information provided by an attitude scale. Besides being affordable, this method of presenting a bogus fellow student's attitudinal responses controlled many other variables that could have (and we now know *do* have) an influence on attraction such as physical attractiveness, age, height, ethnicity, educational background, nonverbal behaviour, etc. The scales of the 'other students' were prepared on my kitchen table with several different pens and pencils of various colors, making check marks and *x*s, writing large and small, left-handed and right-handed. In a between-subjects design, four experimental groups were created: some students were given a stranger who agreed with them on all 26 topics, others a stranger who disagreed on all 26 topics, still others a stranger agreeing on the 13 most important and disagreeing on the 13 least important topics, or agreeing on the 13 least important and disagreeing on the 13 most important topics. The limiting parameters (100% and 0%) and the inclusion of an intermediate degree of agreement (50%) were lucky happenstances, but of considerable value.

The dependent variable—attraction—consisted of two 7-point evaluative items borrowed from sociometric research (Lindzey & Byrne, 1968): how much one *likes* the other person and the degree to which one would *enjoy working with* that person. These items were preceded on the Interpersonal Judgment Scale by four additional items designed to support the cover story, by asking for perceptions of the stranger's intelligence, knowledge of current events, morality, and adjustment.

The highly significant results were based on several fortuitous aspects of the experiment: attitudinal stimuli actually do exert a powerful effect on interpersonal evaluations, the experimenter's false assertion that another student had filled out the bogus scale turned out to be believable, and the response measure was perceived as straightforward and unambiguous. Though the original data were not presented in the following way, Table 1 provides clues as to why this research might catch one's attention.

TABLE 1 / Mean Evaluative Responses as a Function of Percentage of Similar Attitudes Expressed by a Stranger

| | Attitudinal Condition | | |
| | Similarity | | |
Evaluation	0%	50%	100%
Attraction	4.41	7.20	13.00
Intelligence	3.06	3.93	5.63
Knowledge	2.65	3.56	4.65
Morality	3.47	4.33	5.76
Adjustment	2.71	3.50	6.00

Note: Based on data reported in Byrne (1961). The attraction scale ranges from 2 (least positive) to 14 (most positive), while the four other scales range from 1 (least positive) to 7.

Observe that the evaluations of strangers appear to be affected by degree of similarity, and statistical analysis confirms this impression. The effect of topic importance was, to my surprise, much weaker than had been assumed, suggesting the unexpected possibility that attitudinal content does not matter greatly in this context. Thus, the two intermediate (50% similarity) groups could reasonably be collapsed into one. The progression of attraction means across the three conditions suggests that no similarity, intermediate similarity, and total similarity represent three points along a stimulus continuum. That observation may seem obvious now, but at the time, it was closer to 'hmm . . . I wonder.'

Stumbling across the Linear Function

With the powerful rewards provided by statistical significance plus a publication in an APA journal, the probability of continuing to pan for scientific gold in this particular creek bed greatly increased. As should be expected, however, alternative explanations can be proffered even for the apparently clear-cut findings of a simple experiment. Almost immediately, a valid criticism was raised. Many of the attitudinal positions (pro-God, anti-integration, pro-westerns, pro-rock music, etc.) were perceived to be the overwhelming consensus of Texas undergraduates. A quick check of these subjects' attitudinal responses verified this hypothesis of attitude homogeneity. So, rather than manipulating attitude similarity–dissimilarity as I intended, perhaps I had unintentionally varied normality–deviancy.

The test of this possibility became Landmark 2 (Byrne, 1962). The seven attitude items eliciting the most diverse responses were selected from the original 26. At that time and place, student opinion was evenly divided about such topics as racial integration in public schools, smoking, and the goal of making money. Presumably, if normality–deviancy were the crucial independent variable rather than similarity–dissimilarity, agreement–disagreement on these seven controversial topics would *not* affect attraction. If, in contrast, similarity–dissimilarity continued to affect attraction under these conditions, it might be useful to explore the effect of several degrees of intermediate similarity beyond 50%. So, the procedures of the first study were repeated using the 7-item attitude scale,

and this time the between-subjects design involved eight groups in which strangers expressed either seven similar and no dissimilar attitudes, six similar and one dissimilar attitude, etc., continuing to no similar and seven dissimilar attitudes. The findings were unambiguous in that the similarity–dissimilarity manipulation had the hypothesized effect on attraction, ruling out the alternative normal–deviant interpretation Also, the eight attraction means were neatly ordered in terms of the stranger's similarity (with only one minor and nonsignificant inversion).

You may have noticed that this second experiment, to my embarrassment, incorporated the common methodological weakness described earlier. Because I did not know then what I know now, in moving from the initial 26-attitude experiment to the 7-attitude experiment, not only were the topics chosen on the basis of yielding diverse opinions (the new variable being investigated) but the total number of attitude topics was changed from 26 to 7 (a second, confounding new variable). Had there been a failure to replicate the original findings, the explanation could have been either the absence of normal deviant topics or the reduced scale length, and additional research would have been needed to provide clarification. Thanks to blind luck, the similarity effect *was* replicated, and we also had tentative evidence that the number of attitudes (at least between 7 and 26) was irrelevant.

For the next few years, we spent a lot of time fooling around with attitude similarity in the context of such variables as racial prejudice (Byrne & Wong, 1962), real and assumed similarity of spouses (Byrne & Blaylock, 1963), and dispositional mediators of the similarity–attraction relationship (Byrne, 1965), along with research unrelated to attraction. Such activity kept us off the streets, provided tenure for me and degrees for students, and convincingly demonstrated that consistent operations are a prerequisite for consistent findings. Something, however, was lacking. Our research seemed to be moving 'horizontally' rather than 'vertically.'

A breakthrough occurred when we decided to identify the stimulus in the attitude studies more precisely by pursuing a seemingly arcane question. Specifically, we wanted to determine whether the attitude–attraction effect was determined by the relative number of similar vs dissimilar attitudes expressed by a stranger, the total number of similar attitudes communicated by that individual, or some combination of the two. This was obviously not theory-driven research in that each of the three possible outcomes was compatible with reinforcement–affect theory. In any event, Landmark 3 in this paradigm (Byrne & Nelson, 1965) was an experiment involving four levels of relative similarity (the proportion of similar attitudes was either .33, .50, .67, or 1.00) and three levels varying the number of similar attitudes (4, 8, or 16). In order to create each of the resulting 12 conditions, it was necessary to use attitude scales varying in length from 4 to 48 items. We found that proportion had a highly significant effect on attraction, but neither the number of similar attitudes nor the interaction between proportion and number was significant.

An immediate implication of this finding was that all of our data (representing almost 800 research participants) from previous experiments could be combined (despite the utilization of attitude scales of varying content and varying length) permitting us to plot the functional relationship between proportion of similar attitudes and attraction. My colleagues in learning were plotting functions, so I wanted attraction research to resemble what the big boys and girls do. The result was the now notorious linear function: $Y = 5.44X + 6.62$, in which Y is attraction, X is proportion of similar attitudes, 5.44 is the empirically derived slope, and 6.62 is the empirically derived Y-intercept. That was so aesthetically pleasing that I would have been glad to erect a plaque with the linear function chiseled on it just outside of Mezes Hall, near the statue of Governor Hogg (father of Miss Ima—true trivia), but I settled for an inscribed tie clasp kindly given to me by my students.

Why was this stuff important? It took me a while to articulate a satisfactory answer. Back when I was only an eighth grader at Washington Junior High in Bakersfield, Kenneth Spence (1944) published a most impressive and still extremely relevant paper about theory construction in psychology. I was unaware of it until more than two decades had passed, but let me quote two brief passages that strongly influenced how I came to interpret attraction research:

In some areas of knowledge, for example present day physics, theories serve primarily to bring into functional connection with one another empirical laws which prior to their formulation had been isolated

realms of knowledge. The physicist is able to isolate, experimentally, elementary situations, i.e., situations in which there are a limited number of variables, and thus finds it possible to infer or discover descriptive, low-order laws. Theory comes into play for the physicist when he attempts to formulate more abstract principles which will bring these low-order laws into relationship with one another. . . . (pp. 47–8)

Without the generalizations which theories aim to provide we would never be in a position to predict behavior, for knowledge of particular events does not provide us with a basis for prediction when the situation differs in the least degree. The higher the level of abstraction that can be obtained the greater will be both the understanding and the actual control achieved. (p. 62)

Eureka! Science begins with simple, isolated, controllable situations in which it is possible to establish lawful relationships; then, the progression is from simple to complex, specific to general. I finally understood what I was doing.

'Low-order laws' may be common in science, including other fields of psychology, but they have not been all that common in social psychology. Perhaps the non-normative nature of our research strategy had something to do with the apparent irritation expressed over the years by various colleague in response to experiments in 'elementary situations,' the easily replicable similarity effect, and the lawful mathematical function (Aronson & Worchel, 1966; Rosenbaum, 1986; Sunnafrank, 1992). Graduate students often ask me why this work continues to evoke attack, but I honestly do not know why annoyance persists. Indifference maybe, but not annoyance. Leaving aside emotions, the original proportion–attraction formula was about as low-order as you can get, but that of course was only the beginning.

The utility of a law is ultimately defined by its generality. Thus, if this linear function were found to apply only to paper-and-pencil attitude presentations in the context of a spurious cover story given to Texas undergraduates who indicated attraction by making check marks on two 7-point scales, its value in the great scheme of things would be slim to none. To determine whether we were dealing with something more wide-reaching than that, it was essential to conduct a great many experiments that provided overwhelming evidence as to the generality of the relationship—to diverse attitudes (Byrne & Nelson, 1964) as well as other kinds of similarity (Byrne et al., 1966a, 1967) presented in various stimulus modes and contexts (Byrne & Clore, 1966) to quite different populations (Byrne & Griffitt, 1966; Byrne et al., 1969, 1971) in which attraction was measured in a variety of ways (Byrne et al., 1971). We also extended the findings to relatively complex 'real-life' settings such as computer dates (Byrne et al., 1970) and short-term residents of fall-out shelters (Griffitt & Veitch, 1974). Had we not conducted such research, the issue of generality would have been raised (and validly so) as a major limitation of this research. Had generality been lacking, I'm willing to bet that multiple cries of 'I told you so!' would have rung out across the fruited plains. Nevertheless, when generality became so obvious that we could describe the relationship as 'ubiquitous,' some colleagues concluded that we were unimaginatively studying the same thing over and over. As one anonymous reviewer put it, 'Surely, before we read more of Byrne's work he should tell us what to do with it' (Byrne, 1971: 278)—a tempting invitation indeed. Tongue-in-cheek, I confided to one such critic that my next major project involved determining the effect on attraction of Tuesday vs Wednesday. Perhaps he is still waiting for that imaginary article to appear, so that he can be appalled.

In defense of the critics, let me state candidly that there is a good reason for the lack of excitement generated by the search for the low-level generality of a low-order law. To find that changes in content, stimulus mode, populations, and response measures do *not* change the predictable relationship between similarity and attraction is actually not very exciting. OK, it's dull. What's good enough for Vice President Gore is good enough for psychological research. If the goal of behavioral science is prediction rather than excitement, however, these investigations were necessary. Analogously, when trying to build a multi-storied elevator with an Erector Set, work on the base also fails to raise one's pulse rate, but if you skip that step, the exciting generator is likely to wobble and fall.

There is, however, a bit more to the attraction paradigm than the seeming ubiquity of the effect of similarity on attraction. Empirical consistency and generality are nice, and they renew one's faith in the predictability of human behavior, but theoretical consistency and generality constitute the big enchilada. With an encompassing theoretical framework, it should be possible to account for a great many quite different phenomena. If so, we must redefine attitude similarity as simply one representative of a much broader class of stimulus events and attraction as simply one representative of a much broader class of response events. Watch out! This is where conceptualizations based on simple, limited experiments can metamorphose into far-reaching explanations of almost everything.

Donn Tries to Explain It All: From Classical Conditioning to the Behavior Sequence

According to Newcomb, interpersonal rewards constitute an essential element in determining attraction. In our work, therefore, similar attitudes were assumed to act as rewards and dissimilar attitudes as punishments because they satisfied or failed to satisfy the effectance motive (Byrne & Clore, 1967; Byrne et al., 1966b). We tossed in the assumption that positive affect is elicited by rewards and negative affect by punishments. It was further assumed that positive affect resulted in a positive evaluative response and negative affect in a negative evaluative response. At its simplest level, the previous statement means that people like feeling good and dislike feeling bad.

To apply such constructs to attraction, it was necessary to incorporate associational learning. In brief, our early attraction experiments were conceptualized as employing attitude statements (unconditioned stimuli) to elicit implicit affective responses (unconditioned responses) that were associated temporally and spatially with a stranger (classical conditioning) who became the conditioned stimulus for implicit affective responses (conditioned responses) which determined implicit evaluative responses that, in turn, were reflected in overt evaluative responses such as attraction.

An additional aspect of this process was the fact that subjects were presented with a mixed array of similar and dissimilar attitudes eliciting both positive and negative affective responses. These units of affect were assumed to be combined in some kind of internal calculus that resulted in a single evaluative response. It was proposed that the formula for the linear function simply reflects how people may be wired to combine varying numbers of positive and negative events to reach an evaluation—don't blame me.

Among the many implications of this model is the prediction that quite different types of stimulus events (attitudes, personal evaluations, physical appearance, race, etc. along with pre-existing mood, room temperature, background music, etc.) would be expected to elicit affective responses that vary not only in valence but also in magnitude. Just as in the simple situation in which magnitude is more or less constant, the affective responses must be combined, yielding an evaluative response expressed as attraction. In Landmark 4, Byrne & Rhamey (1965) investigated the relative effects on attraction of attitude similarity and personal evaluations, yielding a more general conceptualization of stimulus events and a revised and more general combinatorial formula:

$$Y = m\left[\frac{\Sigma\,(P \times M)}{\Sigma\,(P \times M) + S\,(N \times M)}\right] + k$$

in which Y represents any evaluative response, P and N represent units of positive and negative affect (each of which is multiplied by its magnitude, M, and then summed); m and k are the empirically derived constants indicating the slope and Y-intercept of the linear function. In a leap along the dimension from low to high abstraction, we were now describing evaluation as a linear function of proportion of weighted positive affect. Attitude similarity and attraction thus represented only a specific example of this more general conceptualization.

As a depiction of behavior, the model specifies that any stimulus that elicits an affective response or that is associated with an affective response is evaluated on the basis of the relative number and the relative strength of positive and negative units of affect. Any evaluation-relevant behavior such as attraction, physical proximity, dating, marriage, purchasing, judging, voting, etc. is determined by the effects of two mediators: implicit affective responses and implicit evaluative responses.

Further, affect, evaluation, and reinforcement are conceptualized as three interactive constructs. A great many non-obvious predictions follow from this triangular hypothesis. For example: (I) Any variable that is found to have an effect on evaluative responses should elicit affect (e.g. Clore & Gormly, 1974) and serve a reinforcement function in a learning paradigm (e.g. Golightly & Byrne, 1964); (II) Any variable that is found to elicit affective responses should have an effect on evaluative responses (e.g. Fisher & Byrne, 1975; Griffitt, 1970) and serve a reinforcement function in a learning paradigm (e.g. Griffitt & Kaiser, 1978); and (III) Any variable that serves a reinforcement function in a learning paradigm should have an effect on evaluative responses and elicit affective responses (e.g. McDonald, 1962).

Despite my infatuation with this model, it was not sufficiently inclusive to deal with complex aspects of human interactions. As was noted from time to time, people think as well as feel. As a result, cognitive variables can modify and even override emotional considerations. Perhaps the simplest illustration is going to the dentist; despite negative affect, we periodically make appointments (however reluctantly), enter the dental office, sit in the designated chair, undergo varying degrees of discomfort and pain, and then pay money to the individual who did this to us. Rather than basing our actions on affect, such behavior is determined by what we know and believe about dental hygiene, our expectations about the long-term negative consequences of avoiding this very unpleasant task, and our ability to imagine what it is like to undergo root canal surgery or wear dentures. Further, some activities (e.g. love, sex, aggression) seem to be partially influenced by the extent to which the individual is physiologically aroused, as indicated by a rapid heart beat, the production of adrenalin, vasoconstriction or vasodilatation, and the presence of moisture on the epidermis. The probability of approach vs avoidance–evaluative behavior, then, is based on positive and negative factors of varying magnitude associated with six mediators: affect, evaluation, cognition, expectancy, fantasy, and arousal. Some of these constructs may be redundant, additional ones may have to be added in the future, and the way in which the elements interact must be determined with greater precision than has so far been done. In other words, this model, labeled the *behavior sequence*, represents a work in progress (Byrne, 1982; Byrne & Kelley, 1981; Byrne & Schulte, 1990).

For the record, the need for this kind of expansion of the affect–evaluation model was first made clear to me when I heard Elaine Hatfield outline a theory of passionate love at a symposium in New London, Connecticut (Hatfield, 1971). A second impetus was provided by research attempting to predict contraceptive behavior (Byrne & Fisher, 1983), coercive sexuality (Hogben et al., 1996) and interpersonal relationships (Smith et al., 1993).

Empirical landmarks are easier to label than theoretical ones. Because conceptual formulations develop and expand, they must change over time as can be traced through Byrne & Clore (1970), Byrne (1971), Clore & Byrne (1974) and Byrne (1992).

Work in Progress: Adult Attachment Patterns as Mediators in the Behavior Sequence

Our empirical efforts have previously been concentrated on the affect–evaluation portion of the behavior sequence. Currently, our group has begun exploring the role of infant attachment patterns as first described by Bowlby (1969), further developed by Ainsworth et al. (1978), and extended to adult interpersonal behavior by, among others, Shaver & Hazan (1994). With attachment concepts, the remaining portions of the behavior sequence become essential.

At the moment, we are pursuing the formulations of Bartholomew and her associates (Bartholomew, 1990; Bartholomew & Horowitz, 1991; Griffin & Bartholomew, 1994a, 1994b). Briefly, two underlying positive–negative dimensions (based on early experiences with one's primary caregiver) are proposed: perceptions of self and perceptions of other people. That is, people differ in assessing their self-worth and also in assessing the trustworthiness of others.

These two dimensions were hypothesized to be orthogonal, and recent work at Albany by Stephanie McGowan and Lisa Daniels confirms their independence. When considered simultaneously, the dimensions yield four quadrants into which individuals can be categorized with respect to perceptions of self and others. (1) Those on the positive end of each dimension, a *secure* attachment pattern, have a positive self-image and expect other people to be trustworthy and supportive. Such individuals have good interpersonal skills, deal well with others, and easily establish and maintain positive relationships; (2) Those on the negative end of each dimension, a *fearful* attachment pattern, perceive themselves in negative terms and expect the worst of others. Their interpersonal skills are inadequate, other people pose a threat, and relationships are avoided; (3) Those who perceive themselves negatively but are positive about others have a *preoccupied* (or *clingy*) attachment pattern; they get involved in relationships but feel they are unworthy so are anxious and ambivalent about interacting with a partner; and (4) Those who have a positive opinion of themselves but distrust other people, a *dismissing* attachment pattern, are hesitant to become involved in relationships, but when they do they feel that they deserve better because they are suspicious about the motives and intentions of the partner.

As illustrated in Figure 1, p. 211, the characteristics associated with adult attachment patterns can be conceptualized as responses to generalized or specific others with respect to basic differences in affect, evaluations, beliefs, expectancies, and fantasies, plus differences in the kind of arousal generated by interpersonal situations.

Those involved in attachment research are well aware of the lack of conceptual and empirical consistency in that there is disagreement about whether there are three basic attachment patterns or four along with disagreement about the choice of instruments with which to measure such patterns. Our first step, therefore, is simply to assume there are four patterns and then to do our best to create, borrow, and adapt measuring techniques that we can use thereafter in a consistent fashion. We will be able to test a variety of hypotheses dealing with individual differences in attachment as predictors of interpersonal behavior.

With respect to planning ahead, I can more or less tentatively articulate what we will be doing next. As to the specifics of what will happen after that, however, I don't have a clue. Well, maybe a bit of a clue. Stay tuned.

REFERENCES

Ainsworth, M. D. S., Blehar, M. C., Waters, E. & Wall, S. (1978) *Patterns of Attachment.* Hillsdale, NJ: Erlbaum.

Allgeier, A. R., Byrne, D., Brooks, B. & Revnes, D. (1979) 'The Waffle Phenomenon: Negative Evaluation of

FIGURE 1 / An example of the way in which concepts generated by research on attachment patterns can be incorporated within the Behavior Sequence. Beyond providing a descriptive heuristic, this analysis also suggests some of the specific variables hypothesized to be most relevant to initiating or failing to initiate a relationship when one individual encounters another.

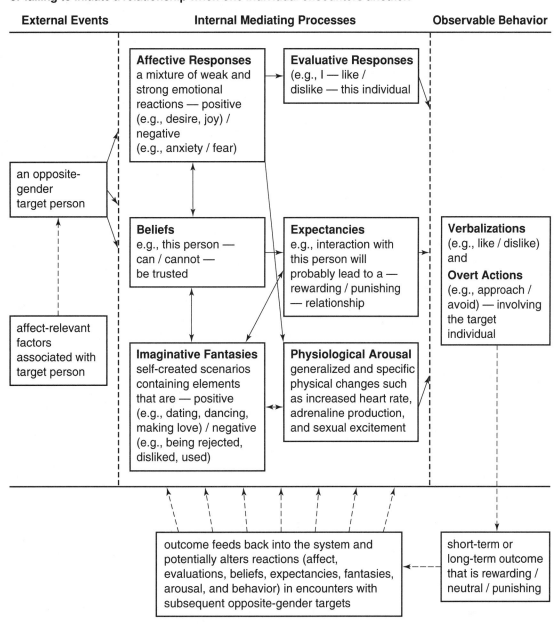

Those Who Shift Attitudinally,' *Journal of Applied Social Psychology* 9: 170–82.

Aronson, E. & Worchel, P. (1966) 'Similarity versus Liking as Determinants of Interpersonal Attractiveness,' *Psychonomic Science* 5: 157–8.

Bartholomew, K. (1990) 'Avoidance of Intimacy: An Attachment Perspective,' *Journal of Social and Personal Relationships* 7: 147–78.

Bartholomew, K. & Horowitz, L. M. (1991) 'Attachment Styles among Young Adults: A Test of a Four Category Model,' *Journal of Personality and Social Psychology* 61: 226–44.

Bowlby, J. (1969) *Attachment and Loss. Vol. 1. Attachment.* New York: Basic Books.

Byrne, D. (1961) 'Interpersonal Attraction and Attitude Similarity,' *Journal of Abnormal and Social Psychology* 62: 713–15.

Byrne, D. (1962) 'Response to Attitude Similarity as a Function of Affiliation Need,' *Journal of Personality* 30: 164–77.

Byrne, D. (1965) 'Authoritarianism and Response to Attitude Similarity–Dissimilarity,' *Journal of Social Psychology* 66: 251–6.

Byrne, D. (1971) *The Attraction Paradigm.* New York: Academic Press.

Byrne, D. (1978) 'Separation, Integration, or Parallel Play?' *Personality and Social Psychology Bulletin* 4: 498–9.

Byrne, D. (1979) 'This Week's Citation Classic,' *Current Contents* (12 February): 16.

Byrne, D. (1982) 'Predicting Human Sexual Behavior,' *The G. Stanley Hall Lecture Series* 2: 207–54.

Byrne, D. (1992) 'The Transition from Controlled Laboratory Experimentation to Less Controlled Settings: Surprise! Additional Variables Are Operative,' *Communication Monographs* 59: 190–8.

Byrne, D. (1997) 'Why Would Anyone Conduct Research on Sexual Behavior?' in G. G. Brannigan, E. R. Allgeier & A. R. Allgeier (eds) *The Sex Scientists.* New York: McGraw-Hill.

Byrne, D., Baskett, G. D. & Hodges, L. (1971) 'Behavioral Indicators of Interpersonal Attraction,' *Journal of Applied Social Psychology* 1: 137–49.

Byrne, D. & Blaylock, B. (1963) 'Similarity and Assumed Similarity of Attitudes among Husbands and Wives,' *Journal of Abnormal and Social Psychology* 67: 636–40.

Byrne, D. & Buehler, J. A. (1955) 'A Note on the Influence of Propinquity upon Acquaintanceships,' *Journal of Abnormal and Social Psychology* 51: 147–8.

Byrne, D. & Clore, G. L. (1966) 'Predicting Interpersonal Attraction toward Strangers Presented in Three Different Stimulus Modes,' *Psychonomic Science* 4: 239–40.

Byrne, D. & Clore, G. L. (1967) 'Effectance Arousal and Attraction,' *Journal of Personality and Social Psychology* 6(4) (Whole No. 638).

Byrne, D. & Clore, G. L. (1970) 'A Reinforcement Model of Evaluative Responses,' *Personality: An International Journal* 1: 103–28.

Byrne, D., Clore, G. L. & Worchel, P. (1966a) 'The Effect of Economic Similarity-Dissimilarity on Interpersonal Attraction,' *Journal of Personality and Social Psychology* 4: 220–4.

Byrne, D., Erwin, C. R. & Lamberth, J. (1970) 'Continuity between the Experimental Study of Attraction and Real-Life Computer Dating,' *Journal of Personality and Social Psychology* 16: 157–65.

Byrne, D. & Fisher, W. A. (eds) (1983) *Adolescents, Sex, and Contraception.* Hillsdale, NJ: Erlbaum.

Byrne, D., Gouaux, C., Griffitt, W., Lamberth, J., Murakawa, N., Prasad, M. B., Prasad, A. & Ramirez, M., III (1971) 'The Ubiquitous Relationship: Attitude Similarity and Attraction. A Cross-Cultural Study,' *Human Relations* 24: 201–7.

Byrne, D. & Griffitt, W. (1966) 'A Developmental Investigation of the Law of Attraction,' *Journal of Personality and Social Psychology* 4: 699–702.

Byrne, D., Griffitt, W., Hudgins, W. & Reeves, K. (1969) 'Attitude Similarity–Dissimilarity and Attraction: Generality beyond the College Sophomore,' *Journal of Social Psychology* 79: 155–61.

Byrne, D., Griffitt, W. & Stefaniak, D. (1967) 'Attraction and Similarity of Personality Characteristics,' *Journal of Personality and Social Psychology* 5: 82–90.

Byrne, D. & Kelley, K. (1981) *An Introduction to Personality.* 3rd edn. Englewood Cliffs, NJ: Prentice-Hall.

Byrne, D. & Lamberth, J. (1971) 'Cognitive and Reinforcement Theories as Complementary Approaches to the Study of Attraction,' in B. I. Murstein (ed.) *Theories of Attraction and Love,* pp. 59–84. New York: Springer.

Byrne, D., Lamberth, J., Palmer, J. & London, O. (1969) 'Sequential Effects as a Function of Explicit and Implicit Interpolated Attraction Responses,' *Journal of Personality and Social Psychology* 13: 70–8.

Byrne, D. & Nelson, D. (1964) 'Attraction as a Function of Attitude Similarity-Dissimilarity: The Effect of Topic Importance,' *Psychonomic Science* 1: 93–4.

Byrne, D. & Nelson, D. (1965) 'Attraction as a Linear Function of Proportion of Positive Reinforcements,' *Journal of Personality and Social Psychology* 1: 659–63.

Byrne, D., Nelson, D. & Reeves. K. (1966b) 'Effects of Consensual Validation and Invalidation on Attraction as a Function of Verifiability,' *Journal of Experimental Social Psychology* 2: 98–107.

Byrne, D. & Rhamey, R. (1965) 'Magnitude of Positive and Negative Reinforcements as Determinant of Attraction,' *Journal of Personality and Social Psychology* 2: 884–9.

Byrne, D. & Schulte, L. (1990) 'Personality Dispositions as Mediators of Sexual Responses,' *Annual Review of Sex Research* 1: 93–117.

Byrne, D. & Wong, T. J. (1962) 'Racial Prejudice, Interpersonal Attraction, and Assumed Dissimilarity of Attitudes,' *Journal of Abnormal and Social Psychology* 65: 246–53.

Clore, G. L. & Byrne, D. (1974) 'A Reinforcement–Affect Model of Attraction,' in T. L. Huston (ed.) *Foundations of Interpersonal Attraction,* pp. 143–70. New York: Academic Press.

Clore, G. L. & Gormly, J. B. (1974) 'Knowing, Feeling, and Liking: A Psychophysiological Study of Attraction,' *Journal of Research in Personality* 8: 218–30.

Fisher, J. D. & Byrne, D. (1975) 'Too Close for Comfort: Sex Differences in Response to Invasions of Personal Space,' *Journal of Personality and Social Psychology* 32: 15–21.

Golightly, C. & Byrne, D. (1964) 'Attitude Statements as Positive and Negative Reinforcements,' *Science* 146: 798–9.

Griffin, D. W. & Bartholomew, K. (1994a) 'The Metaphysics of Measurement: The Case of Adult Attachment,' in K. Bartholomew & D. Perlman (eds) *Advances in Personal Relationships Vol. 5. Attachment Processes in Adulthood,* pp. 17–52. London: Jessica Kingsley.

Griffin, D. W. & Bartholomew, K. (1994b) 'Models of the Self and Other: Fundamental Dimensions Underlying Measures of Adult Attachment,' *Journal of Personality and Social Psychology* 67: 430–45.

Griffitt, W. (1970) 'Environmental Effects on Interpersonal Affective Behavior: Ambien Effective Temperature and Attraction,' *Journal of Personality and Social Psychology* 15: 240–4.

Griffitt, W. & Byrne, D. (1970) 'Procedures in the Paradigmatic Study of Attitude and Attraction,' *Representative Research in Social Psychology* 1: 33–48.

Griffitt, W. & Kaiser, D. L. (1978) 'Affect, Sex Guilt, Gender, and the Rewarding–Punishing Effects of Erotic Stimuli,' *Journal of Personality and Social Psychology* 36: 850–8.

Griffitt, W. & Veitch, R. (1974) 'Preacquaintance Attitude Similarity and Attraction Revisited: Ten Days in a Fall-Out Shelter,' *Sociometry* 37: 163–73.

Hatfield (Walster), E. (1971) 'Passionate Love,' in B. I. Murstein (ed.) *Theories of Attraction and Love,* pp. 85–99. New York: Springer.

Heider, F. (1958) *The Psychology of Interpersonal Relations.* New York: Wiley.

Hogben, M., Byrne, D. & Hamburger, M. E. (1996) 'Coercive Heterosexual Sexuality in Dating Relationships of College Students: Implications of Differential Male–Female Experiences,' *Journal of Psychology and Human Sexuality* 8: 69–78.

Lindzey, G. & Byrne, D. (1968) 'Measurement of Social Choice and Interpersonal Attractiveness,' in G. Lindsey & E. Aronson (eds) *Handbook of Social Psychology,* Vol. 2, pp. 452–525. Reading, MA: Addison-Wesley.

McDonald, R. D. (1962) 'The Effect of Reward–Punishment and Affiliation Need on Interpersonal Attraction,' unpublished PhD thesis, University of Texas.

Newcomb, T. M. (1956) 'The Prediction of Interpersonal Attraction,' *American Psychologist* 11: 575–86.

Rosenbaum, M. E. (1986) 'On the Nondevelopment of Relationships,' *Journal of Personality and Social Psychology* 51: 1156–66.

Schachter, S. (1951) 'Deviation, Rejection, and Communication,' *Journal of Abnormal and Social Psychology* 46: 190–207.

Shaver, P. R. & Hazan, C. (1994) 'Attachment,' in A. L. Weber & J. H. Harvey (eds) *Perspectives on Close Relationships,* pp. 110–30. Boston: Allyn and Bacon.

Smeaton, G., Byrne, D. & Murnen, S. K. (1989) 'The Revulsion Hypothesis Revisited: Similarity Irrelevance or Dissimilarity Bias?' *Journal of Personality and Social Psychology* 56: 54–9.

Smith, A. J. (1957) 'Similarity of Values and Its Relation to Acceptance and the Projection of Similarity,' *Journal of Psychology* 43: 251–60.

Smith, A. J. (1958) 'Perceived Similarity and the Projection of Similarity: The Influence of Valence,' *Journal of Abnormal and Social Psychology* 57: 376–9.

Smith, E. R., Byrne, D., Becker, M. A. & Przybyla, D. P. J. (1993) 'Sexual Attitudes of Male and Females as Predictors of Interpersonal Attraction and Marital Compatibility,' *Journal of Applied Social Psychology* 23: 1011–34.

Spence, K. W. (1944) 'The Nature of Theory Construction in Contemporary Psychology,' *Psychological Review* 51: 47–68.

Sunnafrank, M. (1992) 'On Debunking the Attitude Similarity Myth,' *Communication Monographs* 59: 164–79.

The research described in this article represents many collaborative efforts, most especially with my doctoral students over the years beginning with my first PhD, Roy McDonald, and continuing to my most recent, Matthew Hogben, plus those who came after Roy and before Matthew, those now in graduate school, and those still to come. If it were customary, this paper would be dedicated to all of these individuals.

CRITICAL THINKING QUESTIONS

1. Apply the attraction sequence found in Figure 1 (p. 211) of the article to an actual romantic relationship that you have been in. Identify the different components of the attraction process, as described in the model. Explain how the model either does or does not help explain why that attraction developed or failed to develop.

2. Do you think the attraction sequence model applies equally well to friendship formation and to romantic attraction? What do you see as the possible similarities and differences between these two types of attraction? Explain your answers.

3. The attraction sequence may help explain how initial attractions develop. How might this model be applied to long-term relationships? What additional factors might come into play?

4. Elaborate on the "Internal Mediating Processes" outlined in Figure 1. What specific factors may be involved in these processes (in addition to the ones already listed in the figure)?

5. In your view, how typical is the description of how the theoretical construct of *attraction* evolved? Have you ever encountered another example of how some idea was developed in science that sounds similar to the process described in the article? Explain your answers.

Chapter Eight

CLOSE RELATIONSHIPS
Friendship, Love, and Sexuality

OF ALL THE interactions that occur between human beings, perhaps none is more capable of producing such intense feelings as love. If we look at how often love is portrayed in the popular media, we get the definite impression that it is a major concern, almost a preoccupation, of most people. However, if we look at the literature in social psychology, we might get a very different impression. Until recently, the topic of love was largely ignored in the research literature.

Some of the reluctance to study this common human experience may be due to the difficulty of the subject matter. What is love? How do you measure it? However, there also may have been some bias in not considering love to be an appropriate research topic. Article 22, "The Lessons of Love," examines the evolution of research on love and summarizes what researchers now know (and do not know) about this seemingly mysterious experience.

After meeting someone who catches your attention, and then deciding that you would like to get to know him or her better, comes a big step: asking the person out. So you take the chance and ask for a date. Which response to your request would increase your liking of the recipient of your request the most: The person enthusiastically accepts your offer, or the person first plays "hard to get" and then later accepts your invitation? Much folk wisdom would suggest the value of not appearing too eager. But does that hard-to-get strategy actually work? Article 23, "Playing Hard to Get," is an amusing classic article that addresses this dating dilemma.

Most of us would agree that it is very difficult to sustain a healthy relationship without trust. But what produces trust in a relationship? Is it based on the behavior of the other person, so that, in a sense, he or she earns the right to be trusted? Or is trusting part of personality, such that some people are more willing to trust than others? Article 24, "Assessments of Trust in Intimate Relationships and the Self-Perception Process," examines the issue of trust and some of the factors that impact its development. The article includes some important implications about the effectiveness of certain trust-enhancing exercises, such as those used in marital counseling.

ARTICLE 22 _____

What is *love?* The topic certainly has been and continues to be a popular one in the realms of philosophy, theology, and the arts. In spite of the high value that people place on this experience, social scientists did not begin to investigate this topic until recently for a variety of reasons. First and foremost is the subject matter itself. What, exactly, is love? How can someone begin to define it, let alone measure it? But there were other reasons why the question was not addressed. For one thing, many people thought that the very importance of this feeling is why it should not be addressed. Perhaps love is too private and best left alone.

The first scientific studies of love began about a quarter century ago. Since then, a great deal of research has shed considerable light on the subject. Besides being embraced as a legitimate subject of study for its own sake, the investigation of love perhaps came of age because of certain changes in society. Specifically, as the divorce rate began to soar, it became more urgent to understand what role love plays in the beginning (and ending) of a relationship.

The following article by Beth Livermore provides an excellent overview of the origins of the study of love as well as some of the contemporary knowledge of why, when, and how people fall in love. As the article illustrates, love is not a single concept but rather takes on many different faces. The article also points out that contrary to many popular ideas, men and women have a lot more in common when it comes to love than many people might think.

The Lessons of Love

■ Beth Livermore

As winter thaws, so too do icicles on cold hearts. For with spring, the sap rises—and resistance to love wanes. And though the flame will burn more of us than it warms, we will return to the fire—over and over again.

Indeed, love holds central in everybody's everyday. We spend years, sometimes lifetimes pursuing it, preparing for it, longing for it. Some of us even die for love. Still, only poets and songwriters, philosophers and playwrights have traditionally been granted license to sift this hallowed preserve. Until recently. Over the last decade and a half, scientists have finally taken on this most elusive entity. They have begun to parse out the intangibles, the *je ne sais quoi* of love. The word so far is—little we were sure of is proving to be true.

OUT OF THE LAB, INTO THE FIRE

True early greats, like Sigmund Freud and Carl Rogers, acknowledged love as important to the human experience. But not till the 1970s did anyone attempt to define it—and only now is it considered a respectable topic of study.

One reason for this hesitation has been public resistance. "Some people are afraid that if they look too close they will lose the magic," says Arthur Aron, Ph.D., professor of psychology at the University of California, Santa Cruz. "Others believe we know all that we need to know." But mostly, to systematically study love has been thought impossible, and therefore a waste of time and money.

No one did more to propagate this false notion than former United States Senator William Proxmire of Wisconsin, who in 1974 launched a very public campaign against the study of love. As a member of the Senate Finance Committee, he took it upon himself to ferret out waste in government spending. One of the first place he looked was the National Science Foundation, a federal body that both funds research and promotes scientific progress.

Upon inspection, Proxmire found that Ellen Berscheid, Ph.D., a psychologist at the University of Minnesota who had already broken new ground scrutinizing the social power of physical attractiveness, had secured an $84,000 federal grant to study relationships. The proposal mentioned romantic love. Proxmire loudly denounced such work as frivolous—tax dollars ill spent.

The publicity that was given Proxmire's pronouncements not only cast a pall over all behavioral science research, it set off an international firestorm around Berscheid that lasted the next two years. Colleagues were fired. Her office was swamped with hate mail. She even received death threats. But in the long run, the strategy backfired, much to Proxmire's chagrin. It generated increased scientific interest in the study of love, propelling it forward, and identified Berscheid as the keeper of the flame. Scholars and individuals from Alaska to then-darkest Cold War Albania sent her requests for information, along with letters of support.

Berscheid jettisoned her plans for very early retirement, buttoned up the country house, and, as she says, "became a clearinghouse" for North American love research. "It became eminently clear that there were people who really did want to learn more about love. And I had tenure."

PUTTING THE SOCIAL INTO PSYCHOLOGY

This incident was perfectly timed. For during the early 1970s, the field of social psychology was undergoing a revolution of sorts—a revolution that made the study of love newly possible.

For decades behaviorism, the school of psychology founded by John B. Watson, dominated the field.

Watson argued that only overt actions capable of direct observation and measurement were worthy of study. However, by the early seventies, dissenters were openly calling this approach far too narrow. It excluded unobservable mental events such as ideas and emotions. Thus rose cognitive science, the study of the mind, or perception, thought, and memory. Now psychologists were encouraged to ask human subjects what they thought and how they felt about things. Self-report questionnaires emerged as a legitimate research tool. Psychologists were encouraged to escape laboratory confines—to study real people in the real world. Once out there, they discovered that there was plenty to mine.

Throughout the seventies, soaring divorce rates, loneliness, and isolation began to dominate the emotional landscape of America. By the end of that decade, love had become a pathology. No longer was the question "What is love?" thought to be trivial. "People in our culture dissolve unions when love disappears, which has a lasting effect on society," says Berscheid. Besides, "we already understood the mating habits of the stickleback fish." It was time to turn to a new species.

Today there are hundreds of research papers on love. Topics range from romantic ideals to attachment styles of the young and unmarried. "There were maybe a half dozen when I wrote my dissertation on romantic attraction in 1969," reports Aron. These days, a national association and an international society bring "close relationship" researchers close together annually. Together or apart they are busy producing and sharing new theories, new questionnaires to use as research instruments, and new findings. Their unabashed aim: to improve the human condition by helping us to understand, to repair, and to perfect our love relationships.

SO WHAT *IS* LOVE?

"If there is anything that we have learned about love it is its variegated nature," says Clyde Hendrick, Ph.D., of Texas Tech University in Lubbock. "No one volume or theory or research program can capture love and transform it into a controlled bit of knowledge."

Instead, scholars are tackling specific questions about love in the hopes of nailing down a few facets at a time. The expectation is that every finding will be a building block in the base of knowledge, elevating understanding.

Elaine Hatfield, Ph.D., now of the University of Hawaii, has carved out the territory of passionate love. Along with Berscheid, Hatfield was at the University of Minnesota in 1964 when Stanley Schacter, formerly a professor there and still a great presence, proposed a new theory of emotion. It said that any emotional state requires two conditions: both physiological arousal and relevant situational cues. Already studying close relationships, Hatfield and Berscheid were intrigued. Could the theory help to explain the turbulent, all-consuming experience of passionate love?

Hatfield has spent a good chunk of her professional life examining passionate love, "a state of intense longing for union with another." In 1986, along with sociologist Susan Sprecher, she devised the Passionate Love Scale (PLS), a questionnaire that measures thoughts and feelings she previously identified as distinctive of this "emotional" state.

Lovers rate the applicability of a variety of descriptive statements. To be passionately in love is to be preoccupied with thoughts of your partner much of the time. Also, you likely idealize your partner. So those of you who are passionately in love would, for example, give "I yearn to know all about—" a score somewhere between "moderately true" and "definitely true" on the PLS.

The quiz also asks subjects if they find themselves trying to determine the other's feelings, trying to please their lover, or making up excuses to be close to him or her—all hallmarks of passionate, erotic love. It canvasses for both positive and negative feelings. "Passionate lovers," explains Hatfield, "experience a roller coaster of feelings: euphoria, happiness, calm, tranquility, vulnerability, anxiety, panic, despair."

Passionate love, she maintains, is kindled by "a sprinkle of hope and a large dollop of loneliness, mourning, jealousy, and terror." It is, in other words, fueled by a juxtaposition of pain and pleasure. According to psychologist Dorothy Tennov, who interviewed some 500 lovers, most of them expect their romantic experiences to be bittersweet. For a full 10

percent of them, previous romantic relationships proved so painful that they hope never to love again.

Contrary to myths that hold women responsible for romance, Hatfield finds that both males and females love with equal passion. But men fall in love faster. They are, thus, more romantic. Women are more apt to mix pragmatic concerns with their passion.

And people of all ages, even four-year-old children, are capable of "falling passionately in love." So are people of any ethnic group and socioeconomic stratum capable of passionate love.

Hatfield's most recent study, of love in three very different cultures, shows that romantic love is not simply a product of the Western mind. It exists among diverse cultures worldwide.

Taken together, Hatfield's findings support the idea that passionate love is an evolutionary adaptation. In this scheme, passionate love works as a bonding mechanism, a necessary kind of interpersonal glue that has existed since the start of the human race. It assures that procreation will take place and that the human species will be perpetuated.

UP FROM THE SWAMP

Recent anthropological work also supports this notion. In 1991, William Jankowiak, Ph.D., of the University of Nevada in Las Vegas, and Edward Fischer, Ph.D., of Tulane University published the first study systematically comparing romantic love across 166 cultures.

They looked at folklore, indigenous advice about love, tales about lovers, love potion recipes—anything related. They found "clear evidence" that romantic love is known in 147, or 89 percent, of cultures. Further, Jankowiak suspects that the lack of proof in the remaining 19 cultures is due more to field workers' oversights than to the absence of romance.

Unless prompted, few anthropologists recognize romantic love in the populations that they study, explains Jankowiak. Mostly because romance takes different shapes in different cultures, they do not know what to look for. They tend to recognize romance only in the form it takes in American culture—a progressive phenomenon leading from flirtation to marriage. Elsewhere, it may be a more fleeting fancy.

Still, reports Jankowiak, "when I ask them specific questions about behavior, like 'Did couples run away from camp together?', almost all of them have a positive response."

For all that, there is a sizable claque of scholars who insist that romantic love is a cultural invention of the last 200 years or so. They point out that few cultures outside the West embrace romantic love with the vigor that we do. Fewer still build marriage, traditionally a social and economic institution, on the individualistic pillar of romance.

Romantic love, this thinking holds, consists of a learned set of behaviors; the phenomenon is culturally transmitted from one generation to the next by example, stories, imitation, and direct instruction. Therefore, it did not rise from the swamps with us, but rather evolved with culture.

THE ANXIOUS ARE ITS PREY

Regardless whether passionate, romantic love is universal or unique to us, there is considerable evidence that what renders people particularly vulnerable to it is anxiety. It whips up the wherewithal to love. And anxiety is not alone; in fact, there are a number of predictable precursors to love.

To test the idea that emotions such as fear, which produces anxiety, can amplify attraction, Santa Cruz's Arthur Aron recorded the responses of two sets of men to an attractive woman. But one group first had to cross a narrow 450-foot-long bridge that swayed in the wind over a 230-foot drop—a pure prescription for anxiety. The other group tromped confidently across a seemingly safe bridge. Both groups encountered Miss Lovely, a decoy, as they stepped back onto terra firma.

Aron's attractive confederate stopped each young man to explain that she was doing a class project and asked if he would complete a questionnaire. Once he finished, she handed him her telephone number, saying that she would be happy to explain her project in greater detail.

Who called? Nine of the 33 men on the suspension bridge telephoned, while only two of the men on the safe bridge called. It is not impossible that the callers simply wanted details on the project, but Aron suspects instead that a combustible mix of excitement and anxiety prompted the men to become interested in their attractive interviewee.

Along similar if less treacherous lines, Aron has most recently looked at eleven possible precursors to love. He compiled the list by conducting a comprehensive literature search for candidate items. If you have a lot in common with or live and work close to someone you find attractive, your chances of falling in love are good, the literature suggests.

Other general factors proposed at one time or another as good predictors include being liked by the other, a partner's positive social status, a partner's ability to fill your needs, your readiness for entering a relationship, your isolation from others, mystery, and exciting surroundings or circumstances. Then there are specific cues, like hair color, eye expression, and face shape.

To test the viability and relative importance of these eleven putative factors, Aron asked three different groups of people to give real-life accounts of falling in love. Predictably, desirable characteristics, such as good looks and personality, made the top of the list. But proximity, readiness to develop a relationship, and exciting surroundings and circumstances ranked close behind.

The big surprise: reciprocity. Love is at heart a two-way event. The perception of being liked ranked just as high as the presence of desirable characteristics in the partner. "The combination of the two appears to be very important," says Aron. In fact, love just may not be possible without it.

Sprecher and his colleagues got much the same results in a very recent cross-cultural survey. They and their colleagues interviewed 1,667 men and women in the U.S., Russia, and Japan. They asked the people to think about the last time they had fallen in love or been infatuated. Then they asked about the circumstance that surrounded the love experience.

Surprisingly, the rank ordering of the factors was quite similar in all three cultures. In all three, men and women consider reciprocal liking, personality, and physical appearance to be especially important. A partner's social status and the approval of family and friends are way down the list. The cross-cultural validation of predisposing influences suggests that reciprocal liking, desirable personality and physical features may be universal elements of love, among the *sine qua non* of love, part of its heart and soul.

FRIENDSHIP OVER PASSION

Another tack to the intangible of love is the "prototype" approach. This is the study of our conceptions of love, what we "think" love is.

In 1988, Beverly Fehr, Ph.D., of the University of Winnipeg in Canada conducted a series of six studies designed to determine what "love" and "commitment" have in common. Assorted theories suggested they could be anything from mutually inclusive to completely separate. Fehr asked subjects to list characteristics of love and to list features of commitment. Then she asked them to determine which qualities were central and which more peripheral to each.

People's concepts of the two were to some degree overlapping. Such elements as trust, caring, respect, honesty, devotion, sacrifice, and contentment were deemed attributes of both love and commitment. But such other factors as intimacy, happiness, and a desire to be with the other proved unique to love (while commitment alone demanded perseverance, mutual agreement, obligation, and even a feeling of being trapped).

The findings of Fehr's set of studies, as well as others', defy many expectations. Most subjects said they consider caring, trust, respect, and honesty central to love—while passion-related events like touching, sexual passion, and physical attraction are only peripheral. "They are not very central to our concept of love," Fehr shrugs.

Recently, Fehr explored gender differences in views of love—and found remarkably few. Both men and women put forth friendship as primary to love. Only in a second study, which asked subjects to match their personal ideal of love to various descriptions, did any differences show up. More so than women, men tended to rate erotic, romantic love closer to their personal conception of love.

Still, Fehr is fair. On the whole, she says, "the essence, the core meaning of love differs little." Both genders deem romance and passion far less important than support and warm fuzzies. As even Nadine Crenshaw, creator of steamy romance novels, has re-

marked, "love gets you to the bathroom when you're sick."

LOVE ME TENDER

Since the intangible essence of love cannot be measured directly, many researchers settle for its reflection in what people do. They examine the behavior of lovers.

Clifford Swensen, Ph.D., professor of psychology at Purdue University, pioneered this approach by developing a scale with which to measure lovers' behavior. He produced it from statements people made when asked what they did for, said to, or felt about people they loved . . . and how these people behaved towards them.

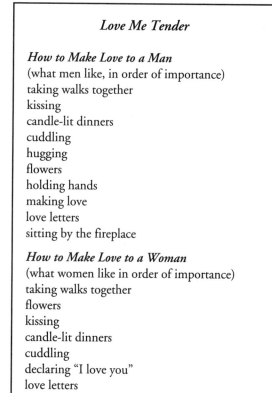

Love Me Tender

How to Make Love to a Man
(what men like, in order of importance)
taking walks together
kissing
candle-lit dinners
cuddling
hugging
flowers
holding hands
making love
love letters
sitting by the fireplace

How to Make Love to a Woman
(what women like in order of importance)
taking walks together
flowers
kissing
candle-lit dinners
cuddling
declaring "I love you"
love letters
slow dancing
hugging
giving surprise gifts

Being supportive and providing encouragement are important behaviors to all love relationships—whether with a friend or mate, Swensen and colleagues found. Subjects also gave high ratings to self-disclosure, or talking about personal matters, and a sense of agreement on important topics.

But two categories of behaviors stood out as unique to romantic relationships. Lovers said that they expressed feelings of love verbally; they talked about how they enjoyed being together, how they missed one another when apart, and other such murmurings. They also showed their affection through physical acts like hugging and kissing.

Elaborating on the verbal and physical demonstrations of love, psychologist Raymond Tucker, Ph.D., of Bowling Green State University in Ohio probed 149 women and 48 men to determine "What constitutes a romantic act?" He asked subjects, average age of 21, to name common examples. There was little disagreement between the genders.

Both men and women most often cited "taking walks" together. For women, "sending or receiving flowers" and "kissing" followed close on its heels, then "candle-lit dinners" and "cuddling." Outright declarations of "I love you" came in a distant sixth. (Advisory to men: The florists were right all along. Say it with flowers instead.)

For men, kissing and "candle-lit dinners" came in second and third. If women preferred demonstrations of love to outright declarations of it, men did even more so; "hearing and saying 'I love you'" didn't even show up among their top ten preferences. Nor did "slow dancing" or "giving or receiving surprise gifts," although all three were on the women's top-ten list. Men likewise listed three kinds of activity women didn't even mention: "holding hands," "making love"—and "sitting by the fireplace." For both sexes, love is more tender than most of us imagined.

All in all, says Tucker, lovers consistently engage in a specific array of actions. "I see these items show up over and over and over again." They may very well be the bedrock behaviors of romantic love.

SIX COLORS OF LOVE

That is not to say that once in love we all behave alike. We do not. Each of us has a set of attitudes toward love that colors what we do. While yours need not match your mate's, you best understand your partner's approach. It underlies how your partner is likely to treat you.

There are six basic orientations toward love, Canadian sociologist John Allen Lee first suggested in 1973. They emerged from a series of studies in which subjects matched story cards, which contain statements projecting attitudes, to their own personal relationships. In 1990 Texas Tech's Clyde Hendrick, along with wife/colleague Susan Hendrick, Ph.D., produced a Love Attitude Scale to measure all six styles. You may embody more than one of these styles. You are also likely to change style with time and circumstance.

You may, for example, have spent your freewheeling college years as an Eros lover, passionate and quick to get involved, setting store on physical attraction and sexual satisfaction. Yet today you may find yourself happy as a Storge lover, valuing friendship-based love, preferring a secure, trusting relationship with a partner of like values.

There are Ludus lovers, game-players who like to have several partners at one time. Their partners may be very different from one another, as Ludus does not act on romantic ideals. Mania-type lovers, by contrast, experience great emotional highs and lows. They are very possessive—and often jealous. They spend a lot of their time doubting their partner's sincerity.

Pragma lovers are, well, pragmatic. They get involved only with the "right" guy or gal—someone who fills their needs or meets other specifications. This group is happy to trade drama and excitement for a partner they can build a life with. In contrast, Agape, or altruistic, lovers form relationships because of what they may be able to give to their partner. Even sex is not an urgent concern of theirs. "Agape functions on a more spiritual level," Hendrick says.

The Hendricks have found some gender difference among love styles. In general, men are more ludic, or game-playing. Women tend to be more storgic, more pragmatic—and more manic. However, men and women seem to be equally passionate and altruistic in their relationships. On the whole, say the Hendricks, the sexes are more similar than different in style.

Personality traits, at least one personality trait, is strongly correlated to love style, the Hendricks have

The Colors of Love

How do I love thee? At least six are the ways.

There is no one type of love; there are many equally valid ways of loving. Researchers have consistently identified six attitudes or styles of love that, to one degree or another, encompass our conceptions of love and color our romantic relationships. They reflect both fixed personality traits and more malleable attitudes. Your relative standing on these dimensions may vary over time—being in love NOW will intensify your responses in some dimensions. Nevertheless studies show that for most people, one dimension of love predominates.

Answering the questions below will help you identify your own love style, one of several important factors contributing to the satisfaction you feel in relationships. You may wish to rate yourself on a separate sheet of paper. There are no right or wrong answers, nor is there any scoring system. The test is designed to help you examine your own feelings and to help you understand your own romantic experiences.

After you take the test, if you are currently in a relationship, you may want to ask your partner to take the test and then compare your responses. Better yet, try to predict your partner's love attitudes before giving the test to him or her.

Studies show that most partners are well-correlated in the areas of love passion and intensity (Eros), companionate or friendship love (Storge), dependency (Mania), and all-giving or selfless love (Agape). If you and your partner aren't a perfect match, don't worry. Knowing your styles can help you manage your relationship.

Directions: Listed below are several statements that reflect different attitudes about love. For each statement, fill in the response on an answer sheet that indicates how much you agree or disagree with that statement. The items refer to a specific love relationship. Whenever possible, answer the questions with your current partner in mind. If you are not currently dating anyone, answer the questions with your most recent partner in mind. If you have never been in love, answer in terms of what you think your responses would most likely be.

For Each Statement:
A = Strongly agree with the statement
B = Moderately agree with the statement
C = Neutral, neither agree nor disagree
D = Moderately disagree with the statement
E = Strongly disagree with the statement

Eros

Measures passionate love as well as intimacy and commitment. It is directly and strongly correlated with satisfaction in a relationship, a major ingredient in relationship success. Eros gives fully, intensely, and takes risks in love; it requires substantial ego strength. Probably reflects secure attachment style.

1. My partner and I were attracted to each other immediately after we first met.
2. My partner and I have the right physical "chemistry" between us.
3. Our lovemaking is very intense and satisfying.
4. I feel that my partner and I were meant for each other.
5. My partner and I became emotionally involved rather quickly.
6. My partner and I really understand each other.
7. My partner fits my ideal standards of physical beauty/handsomeness.

Ludus

Measures love as an interaction game to be played out with diverse partners. Relationships do not have great depth of feeling. Ludus is wary of emotional intensity from others and has a manipulative or cynical quality to it. Ludus is negatively related to satisfaction in relationships. May reflect avoidant attachment style.

8. I try to keep my partner a little uncertain about my commitment to him/her.
9. I believe that what my partner doesn't know about me won't hurt him/her.

10. I have sometimes had to keep my partner from finding out about other partners.
11. I could get over my affair with my partner pretty easily and quickly.
12. My partner would get upset if he/she knew of some of the things I've done with other people.
13. When my partner gets too dependent on me, I want to back off a little.
14. I enjoy playing the "game of love" with my partner and a number of other partners.

Storge

Reflects an inclination to merge love and friendship. Storgic love is solid, down to earth, presumably enduring. It is evolutionary, not revolutionary, and may take time to develop. It is related to satisfaction in long-term relationships.

15. It is hard for me to say exactly when our friendship turned to love.
16. To be genuine, our love first required caring for awhile.
17. I expect to always be friends with my partner.
18. Our love is the best kind because it grew out of a long friendship
19. Our friendship merged gradually into love over time.
20. Our love is really a deep friendship, not a mysterious, mystical emotion.
21. Our love relationship is the most satisfying because it developed from a good friendship.

Pragma

Reflects logical, "shopping list" love, rational calculation with a focus on desired attributes of a lover. Suited to computer-matched dating. Related to satisfaction in long-term relationships.

22. I considered what my partner was going to become in life before I committed myself to him/her.
23. I tried to plan my life carefully before choosing my partner.
24. In choosing my partner, I believed it was best to love someone with a similar background.
25. A main consideration in choosing my partner was how he/she would reflect on my family.
26. An important factor in choosing my partner was whether or not he/she would be a good parent.
27. One consideration in choosing my partner was how he/she would reflect on my career.
28. Before getting very involved with my partner, I tried to figure out how compatible his/her hereditary background would be with mine in case we ever had children.

Mania

Measures possessive, dependent love. Associated with high emotional expressiveness and disclosure, but low self-esteem; reflects uncertainty of self in the relationship. Negatively associated with relationship satisfaction. May reflect anxious/ambivalent attachment style.

29. When things aren't right with my partner and me, my stomach gets upset.
30. If my partner and I break up, I would get so depressed that I would even think of suicide.
31. Sometimes I get so excited about being in love with my partner that I can't sleep.
32. When my partner doesn't pay attention to me, I feel sick all over.
33. Since I've been in love with my partner, I've had trouble concentrating on anything else.
34. I cannot relax if I suspect that my partner is with someone else.
35. If my partner ignores me for a while, I sometimes do stupid things to try to get his/her attention back.

Agape

Reflects all-giving, selfless, nondemanding love. Associated with altruistic, committed, sexually idealistic love. Like Eros, tends to flare up with "being in love now."

36. I try to always help my partner through difficult times.
37. I would rather suffer myself than let my partner suffer.
38. I cannot be happy unless I place my partner's happiness before my own.
39. I am usually willing to sacrifice my own wishes to let my partner achieve his/hers.
40. Whatever I own is my partner's to use as he/she chooses.
41. When my partner gets angry with me, I still love him/her fully and unconditionally.
42. I would endure all things for the sake of my partner.

Adapted from Hendrick, Love Attitude Scale.

discovered. People with high self-esteem are more apt to endorse eros, but less likely to endorse mania than other groups. "This finding fits with the image of a secure, confident eros lover who moves intensely but with mutuality into a new relationship," they maintain.

When they turned their attention to ongoing relationships, the Hendricks' found that couples who stayed together over the course of their months-long study were more passionate and less game-playing than couples who broke up. "A substantial amount of passionate love" and "a low dose of game-playing" love are key to the development of satisfying relationships—at least among the college kids studied.

YOUR MOTHER MADE YOU DO IT

The love style you embrace, how you treat your partner, may reflect the very first human relationship you ever had—probably with Mom. There is growing evidence supporting "attachment theory," which holds that the rhythms of response by a child's primary caregiver affect the development of personality and influence later attachment processes, including adult love relationships.

First put forth by British psychiatrist John Bowlby in the 1960s and elaborated by American psychologist Mary Ainsworth, attachment theory is the culmination of years of painstaking observation of infants and their adult caregivers—and those separated from them—in both natural and experimental situations. Essentially it suggests that there are three major patterns of attachment; they develop within the first year of life and stick with us, all the while reflecting the responsiveness of the caregiver to our needs as helpless infants.

Those whose mothers, or caregivers, were unavailable or unresponsive may grow up to be detached and nonresponsive to others. Their behavior is Avoidant in relationships. A second group takes a more Anxious-Ambivalent approach to relationships, a response set in motion by having mothers they may not have been able to count on—sometimes responsive, other times not. The lucky among us are Secure in attachment, trusting and stable in relationships, prob-

ably the result of having had consistently responsive care.

While attachment theory is now driving a great deal of research on children's social, emotional, and cognitive development, University of Denver psychologists Cindy Hazan and Philip Shaver set out not long ago to investigate the possible effect of childhood relationships on adult attachments. First, they developed descriptive statements that reflect each of the three attachment styles. Then they asked people in their community, along with college kids, which statements best describe how they relate to others. They asked, for example, about trust and jealousy, about closeness and desire for reciprocation, about emotional extremes.

The distribution of the three attachment styles has proved to be about the same in grown-ups as in infants, the same among collegians as the fully fledged. More than half of adult respondents call themselves Secure; the rest are split between Avoidant and Ambivalent. Further, their adult attachment patterns predictably reflect the relationship they report with their parents. Secure people generally describe their parents as having been warm and supportive. What's more, these adults predictably differ in success at romantic love. Secure people reported happy, long-lasting relationships. Avoidants rarely found love.

Secure adults are more trusting of their romantic partners and more confident of a partner's love, report Australian psychologists Judith Feeney and Patricia Noller of the University of Queensland. The two surveyed nearly 400 college undergraduates with a questionnaire on family background and love relationships, along with items designed to reveal their personality and related traits.

In contrast to the Secure, Avoidants indicated an aversion to intimacy. The Anxious-Ambivalent participants were characterized by dependency and what Feeney and Noller describe as "a hunger" for commitment. Their approach resembles the Mania style of love. Each of the three groups reported differences in early childhood experience that could account for their adult approach to relationships. Avoidants, for example, were most likely to tell of separations from their mother.

It may be, Hazan and Shaver suggest, that the world's greatest love affairs are conducted by the Anxious-Ambivalents—people desperately searching for a kind of security they never had.

THE MAGIC NEVER DIES

Not quite two decades into the look at love, it appears as though love will not always mystify us. For already we are beginning to define what we think about it, how it makes us feel, and what we do when we are in love. We now know that it is the insecure, rather than the confident, who fall in love more readily. We know that outside stimuli that alter our emotional state can affect our susceptibility to romance; it is not just the person. We now know that to a certain extent your love style is set by the parenting you received. And, oh yes, men are more quickly romantic than women.

The best news may well be that when it comes to love, men and women are more similar than different. In the face of continuing gender wars, it is comforting to think that men and women share an important, and peaceful, spot of turf. It is also clear that no matter how hard we look at love, we will always be amazed and mesmerized by it.

CRITICAL THINKING QUESTIONS

1. In U.S. contemporary society, what role does love play in the decision to get married? What role *should* it play? Has love always been at the core of a decision to marry? Present your personal views on the relationship of love and marriage. What about a marriage where love is gone? Is that a valid reason to get divorced? Explain your answers.
2. Take a look at the six styles of love described in the article. By examining a popular media source, such as television or the movies, determine what type or types of love seem to be portrayed most often. Do you think these media portrayals of love have an impact on how people view love? Explain your answers.
3. One continuing controversy acknowledged in the article is whether passionate, romantic love is a fairly recent cultural invention or if it has been around for a very long time. Find and summarize evidence to support either one of these contentions.
4. The article notes that most of the studies reported in it were done with college students. Do you think that the nature of love is constant with age, or does it somehow change? Defend your position.
5. What are the differences between romantic love and infatuation? How could you test the differences (if any) between them? Would there be any real value in conducting such a study? Why?
6. How can you relate the information contained in this article on love to an understanding of why the divorce rate has increased over the last several decades?
7. Is *love* the ultimate of *like?* Or is it qualitatively a different experience? Explain.

ARTICLE 23 ⎯⎯⎯⎯⎯⎯⎯⎯⎯⎯⎯⎯⎯⎯⎯⎯⎯⎯⎯

Wanting to love and be loved is perhaps the most profound and universal human longing. As personal experience teaches us, and as the previous reading (Article 22) elaborated on, love is not only a highly desired and sought after state but it also may actually be necessary for our very well-being. Yet exactly what love means and how it is expressed and felt may be something that differs in each of us.

Let's back up a step. Before talking about a deep and profound love for another person, what about the initial stages that may precede it? In other words, what are the factors involved in the initial attraction to another potential romantic partner? People vary considerably in what they find attractive and desirable in another person, but there are common dimensions that seem to be fairly universal. Again, Article 22 elaborated on many of these, such as the importance of physical attractiveness and certain personality traits such as intelligence.

Suppose that you have just met someone who has caught your attention. You are interested enough that you want to ask the person out on a date. Whether you are the iniator or the recipient of the request, a date often creates a set of mixed feelings. On one hand, the potential pleasure that one can have in a successful relationship is highly desirable. On the other hand, most people do not like rejection, and any such beginning also carries with it the possibility of an end.

All right, so he finally asks her out. (Although females certainly initiate dates, research still shows that males typically take this first step in U.S. culture.) How does she respond to his request? Obviously, she can say no. If she says yes, however, there are many ways that it can be said. Which do you think would be most favorably received by the man—someone who enthusiastically and without hesitation says "Yes. I thought you'd never ask" or someone who plays hard to get, ultimately accepting the invitation but only after some hesitation or convincing?

Folk advice going back thousands of years states that playing hard to get might be the way to proceed. As this classic article by Elaine Hatfield, G. William Walster, Jane Piliavin, and Lynn Schmidt indicates, however, that might not be the best advice to follow.

"Playing Hard to Get"
Understanding an Elusive Phenomenon

■ Elaine Hatfield, G. William Walster, Jane Piliavin, and Lynn Schmidt

According to folklore, the woman who is hard to get is a more desirable catch than the woman who is too eager for an alliance. Five experiments were conducted to demonstrate that individuals value hard-to-get dates more than easy-to-get ones. All five experiments failed. In Experiment VI, we finally gained an understanding of this elusive phenomenon. We proposed that two components contribute to a woman's desirability: (a) how hard the woman is for the subject to get and (b) how hard she is for other men to get. We predicted that the selectively hard-to-get woman (i.e.; a woman who is easy for the subject to get but hard for all other men to get) would be

Reprinted from *Journal of Personality and Social Psychology,* 1973, *26,* 113–121. Copyright © 1973 by the American Psychological Association. Reprinted by permission.

preferred to either a uniformly hard-to-get woman, a uniformly easy-to-get woman, or a woman about which the subject has no information. This hypothesis received strong support. The reason for the popularity of the selective woman was evident. Men ascribe to her all of the assets of uniformly hard-to-get and the uniformly easy-to-get women and none of their liabilities.

According to folklore, the woman who is hard to get is a more desirable catch than is the woman who is overly eager for alliance. Socrates, Ovid, Terence, the *Kama Sutra,* and Dear Abby all agree that the person whose affection is easily won is unlikely to inspire passion in another. Ovid, for example, argued:

> *Fool, if you feel no need to guard your girl for her own sake, see that you guard her for mine, so I may want her the more. Easy things nobody wants, but what is forbidden is tempting. . . . Anyone who can love the wife of an indolent cuckold, I should suppose, would steal buckets of sand from the shore. (pp. 65–66)*

When we first began our investigation, we accepted cultural lore. We assumed that men would prefer a hard-to-get woman. Thus, we began our research by interviewing college men as to why they preferred hard-to-get women. Predictably, the men responded to experimenter demands. They explained that they preferred hard-to-get women because the elusive woman is almost inevitably a valuable woman. They pointed out that a woman can only afford to be "choosy" if she is popular—and a woman is popular for some reason. When a woman is hard to get, it is usually a tip-off that she is especially pretty, has a good personality, is sexy, etc. Men also were intrigued by the challenge that the elusive woman offered. One can spend a great deal of time fantasizing about what it would be like to date such a woman. Since the hard-to-get woman's desirability is well recognized, a man can gain prestige if he is seen with her.

An easy-to-get woman, on the other hand, spells trouble. She is probably desperate for a date. She is probably the kind of woman who will make too many demands on a person; she might want to get serious right away. Even worse, she might have a "disease."

In brief, nearly all interviewees agreed with our hypothesis that a hard-to-get woman is a valuable woman, and they could supply abundant justification

for their prejudice. A few isolated men refused to cooperate. These dissenters noted that an elusive woman is not always more desirable than an available woman. Sometimes the hard-to-get woman is not only hard to get—she is *impossible* to get, because she is misanthropic and cold. Sometimes a woman is easy to get because she is a friendly, outgoing woman who boosts one's ego and insures that dates are "no hassle." We ignored the testimony of these deviant types.

We then conducted five experiments designed to demonstrate that an individual values a hard-to-get date more highly than an easy-to-get date. All five experiments failed.

THEORETICAL RATIONALE

Let us first review the theoretical rationale underlying these experiments.

In Walster, Walster, and Berscheid (1971) we argued that if playing hard to get does increase one's desirability, several psychological theories could account for this phenomenon:

1. Dissonance theory predicts that if a person must expend great energy to attain a goal, one is unusually appreciative of the goal (see Aronson and Mills, 1959; Gerard and Mathewson, 1966; Zimbardo, 1965). The hard-to-get date requires a suitor to expend more effort in her pursuit than he would normally expend. One way for the suitor to justify such unusual effort is by aggrandizing her.

2. According to learning theory, an elusive person should have two distinct advantages: (*a*) Frustration may increase drive—by waiting until the suitor has achieved a high sexual drive state, heightening his drive level by introducing momentary frustration, and then finally rewarding him, the hard-to-get woman can maximize the impact of the sexual reward she provides (see Kimball, 1961, for evidence that frustration does energize behavior and does increase the impact of appropriate rewards). (*b*) Elusiveness and value may be associated—individuals may have discovered through frequent experience that there is more competition for socially desirable dates than for undesirable partners. Thus, being "hard to get" comes to be associated with "value." As a consequence, the conditional stimulus (CS) of being hard to get generates a fractional antedating goal response and a frac-

tional goal response, which leads to the conditioned response of liking.

3. In an extension of Schachterian theory, Walster (1971) argued that two components are necessary before an individual can experience passionate love; (*a*) He must be physiologically aroused; and (*b*) the setting must make it appropriate for him to conclude that his aroused feelings are due to love. On both counts, the person who plays hard to get might be expected to generate unusual passion. Frustration should increase the suitor's physiological arousal, and the association of "elusiveness" with "value" should increase the probability that the suitor will label his reaction to the other as "love."

From the preceding discussion, it is evident that several conceptually distinct variables may account for the hard-to-get phenomenon. In spite of the fact that we can suggest a plethora of reasons as to why the playing hard-to-get strategy might be an effective strategy, all five studies failed to provide any support for the contention that an elusive woman is a desirable woman. Two experiments failed to demonstrate that outside observers perceive a hard-to-get individual as especially "valuable." Three experiments failed to demonstrate that a suitor perceives a hard-to-get date as especially valuable.

Walster, Walster, and Berscheid (1971) conducted two experiments to test the hypothesis that teenagers would deduce that a hard-to-get boy or girl was more socially desirable than was a teenager whose affection could be easily obtained. In these experiments high school juniors and seniors were told that we were interested in finding out what kind of first impression various teenagers made on others. They were shown pictures and biographies of a couple. They were told how romantically interested the stimulus person (a boy or girl) was in his partner after they had met only four times. The stimulus person was said to have liked the partner "extremely much," to have provided no information to us, or to have liked the partner "not particularly much." The teenagers were then asked how socially desirable both teenagers seemed (i.e., how likable, how physically attractive, etc.). Walster, Walster, and Berscheid, of course, predicted that the more romantic interest the stimulus person expressed in a slight acquaintance, the less socially desirable that stimulus person would appear to an outside observer.

The results were diametrically opposed to those predicted. The more romantic interest the stimulus person expressed in an acquaintance, the *more* socially desirable teenagers judged him to be. Restraint does not appear to buy respect. Instead, it appears that "All the world *does* love a lover."

Lyons, Walster, and Walster (1971) conducted a field study and a laboratory experiment in an attempt to demonstrate that men prefer a date who plays hard to get. Both experiments were conducted in the context of a computer matching service. Experiment III was a field experiment. Women who signed up for the computer matching program were contacted and hired as experimenters. They were then given precise instructions as to how to respond when their computer match called them for a date. Half of the time they were told to pause and think for 3 seconds before accepting the date. (These women were labeled "hard to get.") Half of the time they were told to accept the date immediately. (These women are labeled "easy to get.") The data indicated that elusiveness had no impact on the man's liking for his computer date.

Experiment IV was a laboratory experiment. In this experiment, Lyons et al. hypothesized that the knowledge that a woman is elusive gives one indirect evidence that she is socially desirable. Such indirect evidence should have the biggest impact when a man has no way of acquiring *direct* evidence about a coed's value or when he has little confidence in his own ability to assess value. When direct evidence is available, and the man possesses supreme confidence in his ability to make correct judgments, information about a woman's elusiveness should have little impact on a man's reaction to her. Lyons et al. thus predicted that when men lacked direct evidence as to a woman's desirability, a man's self-esteem and the woman's elusiveness should interact in determining his respect and liking for her. Lyons et al. measured males' self-esteem via Rosenberg's (1965) measure of self-esteem, Rosenfeld's (1964) measure of fear of rejection, and Berger's (1952) measure of self-acceptance.

The dating counselor then told subjects that the computer had assigned them a date. They were asked to telephone her from the office phone, invite her out, and then report their first impression of her. Presumably the pair would then go out on a date and eventually give us further information about how successful our computer matching techniques had been. Actually, all men were assigned a confederate as a date. Half of the time the woman played hard to get. When the man asked her out she replied:

Mmm [slight pause] No, I've got a date then. It seems like I signed up for that Date Match thing a long time ago and I've met more people since then—I'm really pretty busy all this week.

She paused again. If the subject suggested another time, the confederate hesitated only slightly, then accepted. If he did not suggest another time, the confederate would take the initiative of suggesting: "How about some time next week—or just meeting for coffee in the Union some afternoon?" And again, she accepted the next invitation. Half of the time, in the easy-to-get condition, the confederate eagerly accepted the man's offer of a date.

Lyons et al. predicted that since men in this blind date setting lacked direct evidence as to a woman's desirability, low-self-esteem men should be more receptive to the hard-to-get woman than were high-self-esteem men. Although Lyons et al.'s manipulation checks indicate that their manipulations were successful and their self-esteem measure was reliable, their hypothesis was not confirmed. Elusiveness had no impact on liking, regardless of subject's self-esteem level.

Did we give up our hypothesis? Heavens no. After all, it had only been disconfirmed four times.

By Experiment V, we had decided that perhaps the hard-to-get hypothesis must be tested in a sexual setting. After all, the first theorist who advised a woman to play hard to get was Socrates; his pupil was Theodota, a prostitute. He advised:

They will appreciate your favors most highly if you wait till they ask for them. The sweetest meats, you see, if served before they are wanted seem sour, and to those who had enough they are positively nauseating; but even poor fare is very welcome when offered to a hungry man. [Theodota inquired] And how can I make them hungry for my fare? [Socrates' reply] Why, in the first place, you must not offer it to them when they have had enough—but prompt them by behaving as a model of Propriety, by a show of reluctance to

yield, and by holding back until they are as keen as can be; and then the same gifts are much more to the recipient than when they're offered before they are desired. (see Xenophon, p. 48)

Walster, Walster, and Lambert (1971) thus proposed that a prostitute who states that she is selective in her choice of customers will be held in higher regard than will be the prostitute who admits that she is completely unselective in her choice of partners.

In this experiment, a prostitute served as the experimenter. When the customer arrived, she mixed a drink for him; then she delivered the experimental manipulation. Half of the time, in the hard-to-get condition, she stated, "Just because I see you this time it doesn't mean that you can have my phone number or see me again. I'm going to start school soon, so I won't have much time, so I'll only be able to see the people that I like the best." Half of the time, in the easy-to-get condition, she did not communicate this information. From this point on, the prostitute and the customer interacted in conventional ways.

The client's liking for the prostitute was determined in two ways: First, the prostitute estimated how much the client had seemed to like her. (Questions asked were, for example, How much did he seem to like you? Did he make arrangements to return? How much did he pay you?) Second, the experimenter recorded how many times within the next 30 days the client arranged to have sexual relations with her.

Once again we failed to confirm the hard-to-get hypothesis. If anything, those clients who were told that the prostitute did not take just anyone were *less* likely to call back and liked the prostitute less than did other clients.

At this point, we ruefully decided that we had been on the wrong track. We decided that perhaps all those practitioners who advise women to play hard to get are wrong. Or perhaps it is only under very special circumstances that it will benefit one to play hard to get.

Thus, we began again. We reinterviewed students—this time with an open mind. This time we asked men to tell us about the advantages *and* disadvantages of hard-to-get and easy-to-get women. This time replies were more informative. According to reports, choosing between a hard-to-get woman and an easy-to-get woman was like choosing between Scylla and Charybdis—each woman was uniquely desirable and uniquely frightening.

Although the elusive woman was likely to be a popular prestige date, she presented certain problems. Since she was not particularly enthusiastic about you, she might stand you up or humiliate you in front of your friends. She was likely to be unfriendly, cold, and to possess inflexible standards.

The easy-to-get woman was certain to boost one's ego and to make a date a relaxing, enjoyable experience, but . . . Unfortunately, dating an easy woman was a risky business. Such a woman might be easy to get, but hard to get rid of. She might "get serious." Perhaps she would be so oversexed or overaffectionate in public that she would embarrass you. Your buddies might snicker when they saw you together. After all, they would know perfectly well why you were dating *her*.

The interlocking assets and difficulties envisioned when they attempted to decide which was better—a hard-to-get or an easy-to-get woman—gave us a clue as to why our previous experiments had not worked out. The assets and liabilities of the elusive and the easy dates had evidently generally balanced out. On the average, then, both types of women tended to be equally well liked. When a slight difference in liking did appear, it favored the easy-to-get woman.

It finally impinged on us that there are *two* components that are important determinants of how much a man likes a woman: (*a*) How hard or easy she is for him to get, and (*b*) how hard or easy she is for *other men* to get. So long as we were examining the desirability of women who were hard or easy for everyone to get, things balanced out. The minute we examined other possible configurations, it became evident that there is one type of woman who can transcend the limitations of the uniformly hard-to-get or the uniformly easy-to-get woman. If a woman has a reputation for being hard to get, but for some reason she is easy for the subject to get, she should be maximally appealing. Dating such a woman should insure one of great prestige; she is, after all, hard to get. Yet, since she is exceedingly available to the subject, the dating situation should be a relaxed, rewarding experience. Such a *selectively* hard-to-get woman possesses the

assets of both the easy-to-get and the hard-to-get women, while avoiding all of their liabilities.

Thus, in Experiment VI, we hypothesized that a selectively hard-to-get woman (i.e., a woman who is easy for the subject to get but very hard for any other man to get) will be especially liked by her date. Women who are hard for everyone—including the subject—to get, or who are easy for everyone to get—or control women, about whom the subject had no information—will be liked a lesser amount.

METHOD

Subjects were 71 male summer students at the University of Wisconsin. They were recruited for a dating research project. This project was ostensibly designed to determine whether computer matching techniques are in fact more effective than is random matching. All participants were invited to come into the dating center in order to choose a date from a set of five potential dates.

When the subject arrived at the computer match office, he was handed folders containing background information on five women. Some of these women had supposedly been "randomly" matched with him; others had been "computer matched" with him. (He was not told which women were which.)

In reality, all five folders contained information about fictitious women. The first item in the folder was a "background questionnaire" on which the woman had presumably described herself. This questionnaire was similar to one the subject had completed when signing up for the match program. We attempted to make the five women's descriptions different enough to be believable, yet similar enough to minimize variance. Therefore, the way the five women described themselves was systematically varied. They claimed to be 18 or 19 years old; freshmen or sophomores; from a Wisconsin city, ranging in size from over 500,000 to under 50,000; 5 feet 2 inches to 5 feet 4 inches tall; Protestant, Catholic, Jewish or had no preference; graduated in the upper 10 to 50 percent of their high school class; and Caucasians who did not object to being matched with a person of another race. The women claimed to vary on a political spectrum from "left of center" through "moderate" to "near right of center"; to place little or no importance on politics and religion; and to like recent popular movies. Each woman listed four or five activities she liked to do on a first date (i.e., go to a movie, talk in a quiet place, etc.).

In addition to the background questionnaire, three of the five folders contained five "date selection forms." The experimenter explained that some of the women had already been able to come in, examine the background information of their matches, and indicate their first impression of them. Two of the subject's matches had not yet come in. Three of the women had already come in and evaluated the subject along with her four other matches. These women would have five date selection forms in their folders. The subject was shown the forms, which consisted of a scale ranging from "definitely do *not* want to date" (–10) to "definitely want to date" (+10). A check appeared on each scale. Presumably the check indicated how much the woman had liked a given date. (At this point, the subject was told his identification number. Since all dates were identified by numbers on the forms, this identification number enabled him to ascertain how each date had evaluated both him and her four other matches.)

The date selection forms allowed us to manipulate the elusiveness of the woman. One woman appeared to be uniformly hard to get. She indicated that though she was willing to date any of the men assigned to her, she was not enthusiastic about any of them. She rated all five of her date choices from +1 to +2, including the subject (who was rated 1.75).

One woman appeared to be uniformly easy to get. She indicated that she was enthusiastic about dating all five of the men assigned to her. She rated her desire to date all five of her date choices +7 to +9. This included the subject, who was rated 8.

One woman appeared to be easy for the subject to get but hard for anyone else to get (i.e., the selectively hard-to-get woman). She indicated minimal enthusiasm for four of her date choices, rating them from +2 to +3, and extreme enthusiasm (+8) for the subject.

Two women had no date selection forms in their folders (i.e., no information women).

Naturally, each woman appeared in each of the five conditions.

The experimenter asked the man to consider the folders, complete a "first impression questionnaire"

for each woman, and then decide which *one* of the women he wished to date. (The subject's rating of the dates constitute our verbal measure of liking; his choice in a date constitutes our behavioral measure of liking.)

The experimenter explained that she was conducting a study of first impressions in conjunction with the dating research project. The study, she continued, was designed to learn more about how good people are at forming first impressions of others on the basis of rather limited information. She explained that filling out the forms would probably make it easier for the man to decide which one of the five women he wished to date.

The first impression questionnaire consisted of three sections:

Liking for Various Dates   Two questions assessed subjects' liking for each woman: "If you went out with this girl, how well do you think you would get along?"—with possible responses ranging from "get along extremely well" (5) to "not get along at all" (1)—and "What was your overall impression of the girl?"—with possible responses ranging from "extremely favorable" (7) to "extremely unfavorable" (1). Scores on these two questions were summed to form an index of expressed liking. This index enables us to compare subjects' liking for each of the women.

Assets and Liabilities Ascribed to Various Dates   We predicted that subjects would prefer the selective woman, because they would expect her to possess the good qualities of both the uniformly hard-to-get and the uniformly easy-to-get woman, while avoiding the bad qualities of both her rivals. Thus, the second section was designed to determine the extent to which subjects imputed good and bad qualities to the various dates.

This section was comprised of 10 pairs of polar opposites. Subjects were asked to rate how friendly–unfriendly, cold–warm, attractive–unattractive, easy-going–rigid, exciting–boring, shy–outgoing, fun-loving–dull, popular–unpopular, aggressive–passive, selective–nonselective each woman was. Ratings were made on a 7-point scale. The more desirable the trait ascribed to a woman, the higher the score she was given.

Liabilities Attributed to Easy-to-Get Women   The third scale was designed to assess the extent to which subjects attributed selected negative attributes to each woman. The third scale consisted of six statements:

> She would more than likely do something to embarrass me in public.
>
> She probably would demand too much attention and affection from me.
>
> She seems like the type who would be too dependent on me.
>
> She might turn out to be too sexually promiscuous.
>
> She probably would make me feel uneasy when I'm with her in a group.
>
> She seems like the type who doesn't distinguish between the boys she dates. I probably would be "just another date."

Subjects were asked whether they anticipated any of the above difficulties in their relationship with each woman. They indicated their misgivings on a scale ranging from "certainly true of her" (1) to "certainly not true of her" (7).

The experimenter suggested that the subject carefully examine both the background questionnaires and the date selection forms of all potential dates in order to decide whom he wanted to date. Then she left the subject. (The experimenter was, of course, unaware of what date was in what folder.)

The experimenter did not return until the subject had completed the first impression questionnaires. Then she asked him which woman he had decided to date.

After his choice had been made, the experimenter questioned him as to what factors influenced his choice. Frequently men who chose the selectively easy-to-get woman said that "She chose me, and that made me feel really good" or "She seemed more selective than the others." The uniformly easy-to-get woman was often rejected by subjects who complained "She must be awfully hard up for a date—she really would take anyone." The uniformly hard-to-get woman was once described as a "challenge" but more often rejected as being "snotty" or "too picky."

At the end of the session, the experimenter debriefed the subject and then gave him the names of five actual dates who had been matched with him.

RESULTS

We predicted that the selectively hard-to-get woman (easy for me but hard for everyone else to get) would be liked more than women who were uniformly hard to get, uniformly easy to get, or neutral (the no information women). We had no prediction as to whether or not her three rivals would differ in attractiveness. The results strongly support our hypothesis.

Dating Choices

When we examine the men's choices in dates, we see that the selective woman is far more popular than any of her rivals. (See Table 1.) We conducted a chi-square test to determine whether or not men's choices in dates were randomly distributed. They were not ($\chi^2 = 69.5$, $df = 4$, $p < .001$). Nearly all subjects preferred to date the selective woman. When we compare the frequency with which her four rivals (combined) are chosen, we see that the selective woman does get far more than her share of dates ($\chi^2 = 68.03$, $df = 1$, $p < .001$).

We also conducted an analysis to determine whether or not the women who are uniformly hard to

TABLE 1 / Men's Choices in a Date

Item	Selectively Hard to Get	Uniformly Hard to Get	Uniformly Easy to Get	No Information for No. 1	No Information for No. 2
Number of men choosing to date each woman	42	6	5	11	7

get, uniformly easy to get, or whose popularity is unknown, differed in popularity. We see that they did not ($\chi^2 = 2.86$, $df = 3$).

Liking for the Various Dates

Two questions tapped the men's romantic liking for the various dates: (*a*) "If you went out with this woman, how well do you think you'd get along?"; and (*b*) "What was your overall impression of the woman?" Scores on these two indexes were summed to form an index of liking. Possible scores ranged from 2 to 12.

A contrast was then set up to test our hypothesis that the selective woman will be preferred to her rivals. The contrast that tests this hypothesis is of the form $\Gamma_1 = 4\mu$ (selectively hard to get) $- 1$ (uniformly hard to get) $- 2\mu$ (neutral). We tested the hypothesis $\Gamma_1 = 0$ against the alternative hypothesis $\Gamma_1 \neq 0$. An explanation of this basically simple procedure may be found in Hays (1963). If our hypothesis is true, the preceding contrast should be large. If our hypothesis is false, the resulting contrast should not differ significantly from 0. The data again provide strong support for the hypothesis that the selective woman is better liked than her rivals ($F = 23.92$, $df = 1/70$, $p < .001$).

Additional Data Snooping

We also conducted a second set of contrasts to determine whether the rivals (i.e., the uniformly hard-to-get woman, the uniformly easy-to-get woman, and the control woman) were differentially liked. Using the procedure presented by Morrison (1967) in chapter 4, the data indicate that the rivals are differentially liked ($F = 4.43$, $df = 2/69$). As Table 2 indicates, the uniformly hard-to-get woman seems to be liked slightly less than the easy-to-get or control woman.

In any attempt to explore data, one must account for the fact that observing the data permits the researcher to capitalize on chance. Thus, one must use simultaneous testing methods so as not to spuriously inflate the probability of attaining statistical significance. In the present situation, we are interested in comparing the means of a number of dependent measures, namely the liking for the different women in the dating situation. To perform post hoc multiple comparisons in this situation, one can use a transformation of Hotelling's t^2 statistic, which is distributed as F. The procedure is directly analogous to Scheffé's multiple-comparison procedure for independent groups, except where one compares means of a number of dependent measures.

TABLE 2 / Men's Reactions to Various Dates

	Type of Date			
Item	Selectively Hard to Get	Uniformly Hard to Get	Uniformly Easy to Get	No Information
Men's liking for dates	9.41[a]	7.90	8.53	8.58
Evaluation of women's assets and liabilities				
Selective[b]	5.23	4.39	2.85	4.30
Popular[b]	4.83	4.58	4.65	4.83
Friendly[c]	5.58	5.07	5.52	5.37
Warm[c]	5.15	4.51	4.99	4.79
Easy Going[c]	4.83	4.42	4.82	4.61
Problems expected in dating	5.23[d]	4.86	4.77	4.99

[a]The higher the number, the more liking the man is expressing for the date.
[b]Traits we expected to be ascribed to the selectively hard-to-get and the uniformly hard-to-get dates.
[c]Traits we expected to be ascribed to the selectively hard-to-get and the uniformly easy-to-get dates.
[d]The higher the number the *fewer* the problems the subject anticipates in dating.

To make it abundantly clear that the main result is that the discriminating woman is better liked than each of the other rivals, we performed an additional post hoc analysis, pitting each of the rivals separately against the discriminating woman. In these analyses, we see that the selective woman is better liked than the woman who is uniformly easy to get ($F = 3.99$, $df = 3/68$), than the woman who is uniformly hard to get ($F = 9.47$, $df = 3/68$), and finally, than the control women ($F = 4.93$, $df = 3/68$).

Thus, it is clear that although there are slight differences in the way rivals are liked, these differences are small, relative to the overwhelming attractiveness of the selective woman.

Assets and Liabilities Attributed to Dates

We can now attempt to ascertain *why* the selective woman is more popular than her rivals. Earlier, we argued that the selectively hard-to-get woman should occupy a unique position; she should be assumed to possess all of the virtues of her rivals, but none of their flaws.

The virtues and flaws that the subject ascribed to each woman were tapped by the polar–opposite scale. Subjects evaluated each woman on 10 characteristics.

We expected that subjects would associate two assets with a uniformly hard-to-get woman: Such a woman should be perceived to be both "selective" and "popular." Unfortunately, such a woman should also be assumed to possess three liabilities—she should be perceived to be "unfriendly," "cold," and "rigid." Subjects should ascribe exactly the opposite virtues and liabilities to the easy-to-get woman: Such a woman should possess the assets of "friendliness," "warmth," and "flexibility," and the liabilities of "unpopularity" and "lack of selectivity." The selective woman was expected to possess only assets: She should be perceived to be as "selective" and "popular" as the uniformly elusive woman, and as "friendly," "warm," and "easy-going" as the uniformly easy woman. A contrast was set up to test this specific hypothesis. (Once again, see Hays for the procedure.) This contrast indicates that our hypothesis is confirmed ($F = 62.43$, $df = 1/70$). The selective woman is rated most like the uniformly hard-to-get woman on the first two positive characteristics and most like the uniformly easy-to-get woman on the last three characteristics.

For the reader's interest, the subjects' ratings of all five women's assets and liabilities are presented in Table 2.

Comparing the Selective and the Easy Women

Scale 3 was designed to assess whether or not subjects anticipated fewer problems when they envisioned dating the selective woman than when they envisioned dating the uniformly easy-to-get woman. On the basis of pretest interviews, we compiled a list of many of the concerns men had about easy women (e.g., "She would more than likely do something to embarrass me in public.").

We, of course, predicted that subjects would experience more problems when contemplating dating the uniformly easy woman than when contemplating dating a woman who was easy for *them* to get, but hard for anyone else to get (i.e., the selective woman).

Men were asked to say whether or not they envisioned each of the difficulties were they to date each of the women. Possible replies varied from 1 (certainly true of her) to 7 (certainly not true of her). The subjects' evaluations of each woman were summed to form an index of anticipated difficulties. Possible scores ranged from 6 to 42.

A contrast was set up to determine whether the selective woman engendered less concern than the uniformly easy-to-get woman. The data indicate that she does ($F = 17.50$, $df = 1/70$). If the reader is interested in comparing concern engendered by each woman, these data are available in Table 2.

The data provide clear support for our hypotheses: The selective woman is strongly preferred to any of her rivals. The reason for her popularity is evident. Men ascribe to her all of the assets of the uniformly hard-to-get and the uniformly easy-to-get women, and none of their liabilities.

Thus, after five futile attempts to understand the "hard-to-get" phenomenon, it appears that we have finally gained an understanding of this process. It appears that a woman can intensify her desirability if she acquires a reputation for being hard-to-get and then, by her behavior, makes it clear to a selected romantic partner that she is attracted to him.

In retrospect, especially in view of the strongly supportive data, the logic underlying our predictions sounds compelling. In fact, after examining our data, a colleague who had helped design the five ill-fated experiments noted that, "That is exactly what I would have predicted" (given his economic view of man). Unfortunately, we are all better at postdiction than prediction.

REFERENCES

Aronson, E., and Mills, J. The effect of severity of initiation on liking for a group. *Journal of Abnormal and Social Psychology,* 1959, **67,** 31–36.

Berger, E. M. The relation between expressed acceptance of self and expressed acceptance of others. *Journal of Abnormal and Social Psychology,* 1952, **47,** 778–782.

Gerard, H. B. and Mathewson, G. C. The effects of severity of initiation and liking for a group: A replication. *Journal of Experimental Social Psychology,* 1966, **2,** 278–287.

Hays, W. L. *Statistics for psychologists.* New York: Holt, Rinehart, 1963.

Kimball, G. A. *Hilgard and Marquis' conditioning and learning.* New York: Appleton-Century-Crofts, 1961.

Lyons, J., Walster, and Walster, G. W. Playing hard-to-get: An elusive phenomenon University of Wisconsin, Madison: Author, 1971. (Mimeo)

Morrison, D. F. *Multivariate statistical methods.* New York: McGraw-Hill, 1967.

Ovid. *The art of love.* Bloomington: University of Indiana Press, 1963.

Rosenberg, M. *Society and the adolescent self image.* Princeton, N.J.: Princeton University Press, 1965.

Rosenfeld, H. M. Social choice conceived as a level of aspiration. *Journal of Abnormal and Social Psychology,* 1964, **68,** 491–499.

Walster, E. Passionate love. In B. I. Murstein (Ed.), *Theories of attraction and love.* New York: Springer, 1971.

Walster, E., Walster, G. W., and Berscheid, E. The efficacy of playing hard-to-get. *Journal of Experimental Education,* 1971, **39,** 73–77.

Walster, G. W., and Lambert, P. Playing hard-to-get: A field study. University of Wisconsin, Madison: Author, 1971. (Mimeo)

Xenophon. *Memorabilia.* London: Heinemann, 1923.

Zimbardo, P. G. The effect of effort and improvisation on self persuasion produced by role-playing. *Journal of Experimental Social Psychology,* 1965, **1,** 103–120.

This research was supported in part by National Science Foundation Grants GS 2932 and GS 30822X and in part by National Institute for Mental Health Grant MH 16661.

CRITICAL THINKING QUESTIONS

1. Nonsignificant results are difficult to interpret in research. For example, if a woman playing hard to get is not viewed differently from one playing "easy," is there really no difference? Why or why not? Or is it possible that the experimental manipulation (how playing hard to get or easy were varied in the study) was not strong enough to produce an effect? Discuss this possibility by examining how playing hard to get was manipulated in the first five experiments reported in this article.

2. Are ethical issues involved in any of the studies? In particular, what are your views of Study 5, which involved the services of a prostitute?

3. This study ultimately determined that selectively hard-to-get women were most preferred by the men. Do you think the reverse is true—that women most prefer selectively hard-to-get men? Why or why not?

4. Do you think that the results of this study could be generalized to the sexual arena (i.e., when it comes to sex, a selectively hard-to-get woman would be preferred over either a hard-to-get or easy-to-get woman)? Explain.

ADDITIONAL RELATED READINGS

Keenan, J. P., Gallup, G. G., Goulet, N., & Kulkarni, M. (1997). Attributions of deception in human mating strategies. *Journal of Social Behavior and Personality, 12,* 45–52.

Ruvolo, A. P., & Brennan, C. J. (1997). What's love got to do with it? Close relationships and perceived growth. *Personality and Social Psychology Bulletin, 23,* 814–823.

ARTICLE 24 _____

Trust is a critical part of any relationship, whether one between friends or between lovers. Without trust, it would be difficult to maintain a satisfying, ongoing relationship. But what produces trust? Is it part of a person's core attributes, such that some people are inherently more trusting than others? Or does the willingness to trust depend on the situation as well as the actions of the other person in the relationship? The former explanation is known as a *dispositional* attribution, in which trusting is viewed as part of the person's stable personality, while the latter is known as a *situational* attribution, in which trusting is a function of the setting or context, rather than being a fixed factor.

So, which approach best explains our willingness to trust? It turns out to be a combination of the two. Trust, as a dispositional variable, exists along a continuum, with some people being exceptionally trusting and others being very nontrusting. Yet situational factors also play a role. Even a naturally trusting individual can lose his or her trust for a specific person, depending on the behavior of the latter.

Another factor also can influence the existence of trust: Our level of trust of our partners may be more a function of our own trusting behaviors, rather than the actions of our partners. According to *self-perception theory*, attitudes (like trust) can be influenced by how we see ourselves behaving. In other words, if I treat you in a trusting manner, then my attitude toward you becomes one of trust. In this case, the trusting behavior precedes the trusting attitude.

The following article by Ann Marie Zak, Joel A. Gold, Richard M. Ryckman, and Ellen Lenney examines the assessment of trust in intimate relationships based on a number of factors, including the impact of self-perception. Most studies on trust are correlational in nature and thus unable to determine the cause-and-effect sequence between trusting attitudes and trusting behaviors. This study is notable in that it uses experimental methodology to examine the trust process in relationships.

Assessments of Trust in Intimate Relationships and the Self-Perception Process

■ Ann Marie Zak, Joel A. Gold, Richard M. Ryckman, and Ellen Lenney

ABSTRACT. Assessments of trust in intimate relationships are often based on perceptions of a partner's behaviors; however, people's own actions, increased self-awareness, and individual differences (e.g., exchange or communal orientation) may also affect their trust in their partners. Communally or exchange-oriented members of heterosexual dating couples, students in a U.S. university, displayed either trusting or irrelevant behaviors under conditions of increased self-awareness. They then completed measures of interpersonal trust. The participants' trusting behaviors significantly determined their level of trust; heightened self-awareness and a communal orientation further enhanced the participants' trust in their partners.

Interpersonal trust is an essential aspect of healthy human relationships (Butler, 1986). Placing one's confidence in another person promotes many effec-

Reprinted from *The Journal of Social Psychology, 138,* 217–228, 1998. Reprinted with permission of the Helen Dwight Reid Educational Foundation. Published by Heldref Publications, 1319 Eighteenth St., N.W., Washington, D.C. 20036-1802. Copyright © 1998.

tive interactions, ranging from those between colleagues to those between lovers. Although investigators (Johnson-George & Swap, 1982; Larzelere & Huston, 1980) have examined trust between partners in heterosexual relationships, apparently only Holmes (1990, 1991) has introduced a fully developed model that outlines the processes by which such trust evolves.

Holmes and Rempel (1989) recognized individual differences in the nature of trust, but they emphasized that trust can be relationship-specific, that is, represented by confident expectations of positive outcomes from a particular intimate partner. People in trusting relationships expect their partners to care and respond to their needs, both present and future. Holmes and Rempel also posited that trust grows in accordance with social exchange principles: One partner trusts the other only a little at the beginning of the relationship, the other responds by trusting a bit more as time passes, and this exchange of increasing trust continues. As it develops, trust often proceeds through three distinct categories of expectations, according to Holmes and Rempel.

The first category, predictability, begins as each partner observes the other's behaviors. If one partner repeatedly fulfills his or her promises and usually acts positively, the other will view those behaviors as predictable. On the other hand, when individuals find that they never know what their partners will do next, they will not decide that their partners behave consistently.

After one partner witnesses enough consistently positive behaviors by the other, trust can move to the second category, dependability, which refers to a partner's general traits rather than to the predictability of specific actions. After people see their partners behaving predictably, they begin to consider the partners reliable or dependable.

The final abstract category of expectations, faith, evolves as partners grow confident that their relationships will last. Once individuals have decided that their partners are predictable and dependable, they can begin to feel secure about the future of the relationship. Decisions about faith represent a shift from expectations about a partner's current traits to expectations about his or her general motives concerning the value, present and future, of the relationship.

Overall, Holmes and Rempel (1989) argued that trust is based on perceptions of a partner's behaviors. If people believe that their partners are predictable and dependable and show faith in the future of their relationships, they learn to trust their partners. It is also possible, however, that individuals' own behaviors, independent of the behaviors of the partners, at times play a primary role in determining the extent to which they trust their partners. According to self-perception theory (Bem, 1972), individuals often infer their beliefs by examining their own behavior. Thus, trust may develop through a self-perception process in which people decide, after engaging in a trusting action, that they trust their partners. Like self-disclosure, consent for a partner to engage in an activity that others find threatening may be viewed as proof of trust in one's mate.

The tendency to develop trust through a self-perception process may also be enhanced by situational variables. Specifically, a state of increased, objective self-awareness should affect the self-perception process in two different ways: First, Hull and Levy (1979) found that heightened self-awareness produced by mirrors increases attitude–behavior consistency. Second, individuals in a state of objective self-awareness view themselves as an observer would view them. From the perspective of the actor–observer bias, this state should lead to dispositional rather than situational attributions; Scheir and Carver's (1977) research has supported this assumption.

Along with the situational variable of self-awareness, individual differences in exchange or communal orientation in perceptions of interpersonal relationships may also affect the operation of self-perception processes in the development of trust. Vanyperen and Buunk (1991) as well as Clark, Ouellette, Powell, and Milberg (1987) have suggested that individuals who focus on their partners' needs rather than on fair exchange in their relationships are more satisfied with their own actions than individuals who continually check their inputs and outputs against those of their partners. For persons who are communally oriented, trust is not a function of ensuring that their partners respond in kind to their own trusting actions; although communally oriented individuals may examine their partners' behaviors, they do so only to determine whether those behaviors reveal information about their partners' needs, not to assess them as a basis for trust. Persons who score high on communal orientation are focused exclusively on their partners' needs without concern over whether the partners are "keeping up" with them in matters of trust. Thus, communally oriented people should be more likely than exchange-oriented people to develop trust through their own actions.

Although self-perception theory states that one's own behaviors lead to internalized attitude change, it has also been argued that one's own actions may lead to a change in publicly reported beliefs only. According to Tedeschi, Schlenker, and Bonoma's (1977) impression management theory, people are motivated to appear consistent in front of others; therefore, after a particular behavior, they later report changes in attitudes that match the performed behavior, although their private attitudes have not necessarily changed. In terms of the present issue, if people exhibit trusting behaviors in front of others, they may publicly report more trust in their partners to appear consistent. Although the empirical evidence supporting impression management theory is inconclusive (Brehm & Kassin, 1991), it is a plausible rival hypothesis to a self-perception explanation.

We based the present study on the following hypotheses:

> *Hypothesis 1:* The participants who perform trusting behaviors or learn that their partners have done so will experience greater trust than those in the irrelevant, or nonthreatening, behavior condition.

> *Hypothesis 2:* The participants who act in a trusting manner themselves will trust their partners more than will those who learn that their partners act in a trusting manner.

> *Hypothesis 3:* No differences will occur between the participants who anonymously report their levels of trust and those in other trust conditions. (The purpose of Hypothesis 3 was to rule out an impression management explanation for increased trust.)

> *Hypothesis 4:* Increased self-awareness and communal orientation of the participants will predict greater trust in partners than will lack of self-awareness and an exchange orientation.

METHOD

U.S. students who were members of heterosexual dating relationships participated in this experiment. The design was a 2 (male/female) × 2 (relationship orientation: high/low exchange) × 2 (actor/recipient) × 4 (type of behavior: trusting with mirror, trusting with no mirror, trusting + anonymity with no mirror, irrelevant with no mirror) factorial experiment. All the participants first completed a measure of relationship orientation, which assesses individual differences along an exchange–communal dimension. Then we randomly assigned them to conditions where they (a) exhibited either trusting or irrelevant behaviors with or without a mirror; or (b) learned, with or without a mirror, that their partners had exhibited either trusting or irrelevant behaviors. We assigned both the male and the female members of each couple to the same condition. The participants then completed measures of trust.

Participants

The volunteer participants were members of 64 heterosexual couples recruited from psychology, human development, and human sexuality classes at the University of Maine. The announcements stressed that the study concerned relationships and that the participants must bring their partners, although their partners did not have to be students to participate. Among the entire sample of 128 participants, ages ranged from 18 to 47 years (*M* = 21 years, *SD* = 5.7). The participants had been dating from 1 to 96 months (*M* = 21 months, *SD* = 5.1). Of the total sample, 96% were Caucasian.

Measures

In an initial group session, the participants completed a battery of personality inventories; they then signed up for a time to return for a second session. Embedded among the tests was the Relationship Orientation Scale (Zak & Gold, 1991), which was developed to assess on a single continuum aspects of both exchange and communal orientation. We modified 7 items from Murstein, Wadlin, and Bond's Exchange Orientation Scale (1987) to reflect preferences for exchange (or nonexchange) in a particular relationship, and we reworded 4 items from the Communal Orientation Scale (Clark et al., 1987) to reflect preferences for helping without expecting anything in return. We combined these 11 items to form the acceptably reliable Relationship Orientation Scale, coefficient alpha = .76 (Zak & Gold).

The participants responded to the Relationship Orientation Scale on a 19-point scale ranging from *strongly disagree* (1) to *strongly agree* (19); higher scores reflected greater tendencies toward an exchange orientation. Examples of items from that scale include "I usually remember if I owe my partner a favor or if he/she owes me a favor" (an exchange-oriented item) and "I would go out of my way to aid my partner should the need arise, without expecting repayment" (a communally oriented item; item scoring reversed).

Procedure

Individual couples reported for the second session and were met by a male and a female experimenter. The male and female participants were then taken to separate laboratory rooms by experimenters of the same gender. The experimenters then proceeded with the behavioral manipulation.

Actors in the Trusting Behavior Conditions   The experimenters gave the participants the following information:

> Originally, we were interested in whether dancing to slow, soft rock music influences relationship variables. So, at this point, we were going to ask you and your partner to move to a special laboratory across the hall and dance to music like that recorded by Debbie Gibson and Madonna. Then we were going to ask you to fill out a survey that measured relationship variables. However, now we have enough data on couples dancing and instead need data on one member of a couple dancing with an opposite-sex stranger and how that influences relationship variables. Your partner has been randomly assigned to dance with a member of the opposite sex. The other experimenter and I will not be in the room; instead your partner and the other male (female) will be alone, and after about 20 minutes, your partner will fill out a survey that measures beliefs about relationships. During the dancing

session, we have several surveys that you could complete. Since we have changed the nature of the study, I have to ask you if you would mind if your partner dances in the situation I have described.

The experimenters waited for the participants' responses; none of the participants refused to allow their partners to dance with the stranger. After telling the participants that they were going to alert their partners to their decisions, the experimenters left the room for a brief period.

Recipients in the Trusting Behavior Conditions   The participants were given the same information as those in the actor conditions, but the roles were reversed: In this condition, each partner would supposedly be asked if he or she allowed the present participant (recipient) to dance with the stranger. The experimenters then left the room for a brief period. Although the experimenters did not contact the partners, they returned to tell the participants that their partners did not mind if the participants danced.

After the manipulation, the experimenters asked both partners, who remained in separate rooms, to complete the dependent measures, the Trust Scale (Rempel, Holmes, & Zanna, 1985) and the Dyadic Trust Scale (Larzelere & Huston, 1980).

Trusting Behavior + Anonymity Condition   The procedure for these participants was identical to the procedure for actors and recipients, except for the addition of the following instructions before completion of the dependent measures:

> Before you [your partner] dance[s] and we later measure perceptions of relationships, we would like you to complete these surveys. Keep in mind that your responses are completely confidential—in no way will I or the other experimenter know how you personally scored. The data are coded by number only to ensure anonymity; your name will never be linked to the data.

Actors and Recipients in the Irrelevant Behavior Condition   The protocols for these groups were the same as those for the actors and recipients in the trusting behavior groups except that we told the participants that we now needed data on one member of a couple listening to music rather than dancing with a member of the opposite sex.

Self-Awareness Manipulation Self-awareness was induced for actors and recipients in an additional trusting behavior condition that included a mirror. In a room filled with boxes and folders, the participants were seated in front of a large mirror and told that another researcher must have left his supplies in that particular laboratory.

The mirror-absent condition was identical to the mirror-present condition with the exception that the mirror had been turned so that only its back was showing. These participants were also told that another researcher must have left his supplies in that particular laboratory.

Dependent Measures All the participants first completed Rempel, Holmes, and Zanna's (1985) 17-item Trust Scale. To allow for more response variability, we changed the 7-point response format to a 19-point format ranging from *strongly disagree* (1), through *neutral* (10), to *strongly agree* (19). The Trust Scale consists of items such as "My partner behaves in a very consistent manner," "I can rely on my partner to keep the promises he/she makes to me," and "Though times may change and the future is uncertain, I know my partner is ready and willing to offer me strength and support"; those items measure predictability, dependability, and faith, respectively. The participants then completed Larzelere and Huston's (1980) Dyadic Trust Scale, an eight-item scale ranging from *strongly disagree* (1) to *strongly agree* (7). Sample items from the Dyadic Trust Scale are "My partner treats me fairly and justly" and "I feel that my partner can be counted on to help me."

Debriefing

After the participants completed the dependent measures, the experimenters questioned them about their reactions to the manipulations. All the participants reported that they believed that the dancing or listening-to-music session would occur; no participant discerned the true purpose of the manipulations. In an extensive debriefing, we told the participants that they would not really be asked to dance or listen to music;

we told them that we were interested in whether trusting behaviors influence trust. We explained that allowing a partner to dance with a member of the opposite sex is a trusting behavior. Because both members of each couple were assigned to the same condition, we stressed that in the actor groups, we did not notify the participants' partners of their decisions; similarly, in the recipient groups, we did not ask the participants' partners if they would allow them to dance or listen to music. The experimenter apologized for the deceptions, answered questions, and thanked all the participants. No participant reported negative feelings about the experiment.

RESULTS

Scoring and Data Reduction

The Relationship Orientation Scale It was impossible to recruit all of the participants early in the study; consequently, all relationship-orientation scores were not available before we assigned the participants to the experimental conditions. Therefore, after all 64 couples had participated in the experiment, we computed their relationship-orientation scores and performed a median split. Coefficient alpha for the 11-item Relationship Orientation Scale was .72.

Trust Measures Coefficient alpha was .79 for the 17-item Trust Scale and .76 for the 8-item Dyadic Trust Scale. Because the scales were correlated substantially, $r(128) = .67$, $p < .001$, we standardized each item on both scales to put them into common units; we combined and averaged all items for convergent validity to form an overall measure of trust. This 25-item trust measure was highly reliable, with a coefficient alpha of .88.

Analyses

We performed a 4 (type of behavior: trusting with mirror, trusting with no mirror, trusting + anonymity with no mirror, irrelevant with no mirror) × 2 (actor/recipient) × 2 (relationship orientation: high/low exchange) × 2 (male/female) analysis of variance (ANOVA) on the mean trust scores. No sex differences emerged; hence, we collapsed the data across

TABLE 1 / Means and Standard Deviations of Trust Scores, across Behaviors

Orientation	Behavior			
	Trusting + Mirror	Trusting + No Mirror	Trusting + No Mirror + Anonymity	Irrelevant
	Actors			
Communal				
M	.673	.420	.280	.036
SD	.071	.219	.221	.345
Exchange				
M	.419	.078	.068	−.804
SD	.250	.352	.189	.806
	Recipients			
Communal				
M	.306	.019	.081	−.399
SD	.228	.252	.232	.443
Exchange				
M	.058	−.231	−.140	−.764
SD	.352	.439	.223	.374

Note: Higher means indicate greater trust in a partner. Means are expressed as standard scores.

sex. The means and standard deviations for all conditions are reported in Table 1.

Hypothesis 1 was supported; there was a significant main effect for type of behavior, $F(3, 96) = 28.69$, $p < .001$. An a priori contrast revealed that the participants in the combined trusting-behavior groups scored significantly higher on trust ($M = .155$) than did the participants in the irrelevant-behavior group ($M = −.465$), $F(1, 124) = 7.9$, $p < .01$. Post hoc tests via Scheffé (.05) revealed that trust scores were significantly higher in each of the trusting-behavior conditions ($Ms = .364, .286,$ and $.289$ for mirror, no mirror, and no mirror/anonymous, respectively) than in the irrelevant-behavior condition ($M = −.465$).

Hypothesis 2 was also supported; the actor–recipient main effect was significant, $F(1, 96) = 15.18$, $p < .001$; the actors experienced greater trust ($M = .133$) in their partners than the recipients did ($M = −.133$).

There was also evidence supporting Hypothesis 3; a nonsignificant a priori contrast between the trusting-behavior group with no mirror ($M = .043$) and the trusting-behavior + anonymity group with no mirror ($M = .032$) reduced the plausibility of an impression management interpretation for increased trust.

Providing support for Hypothesis 4, post hoc Scheffé tests (.05) revealed that the scores in the trusting-behavior condition with mirror ($M = .390$) were significantly higher than those in either the trusting-behavior condition with no mirror ($M = .043$) or the trusting-behavior + anonymity condition with no mirror ($M = .032$). Last, the main effect for relationship orientation achieved significance, $F(1, 96) = 29.73$, $p < .001$; the communally oriented participants reported more trust in their partners ($M = .176$) than did the exchange oriented participants ($M = −.181$).

DISCUSSION

Previous U.S. researchers have used only correlational designs to study trust. By inducing trusting behaviors in the present research, we showed the immediate impact of such behaviors on trust among U.S. couples. Consistent with the first hypothesis, our results demonstrated that trusting behaviors, whether exhibited by oneself or by one's partner, lead to significantly greater trust in a partner than do irrelevant actions.

Our second hypothesis was also supported: A person's own trusting actions induce trust in the actor; furthermore, their effect is significantly greater than the effect produced by knowledge of one's partner's trusting behaviors. This finding is consistent with a self-perception explanation (Bem, 1972): People may sometimes infer trust more from their own actions than from those of their partners. Our intention in this research, however, was not to demonstrate the superiority of the self-perception perspective to Holmes's social-exchange model or to offer it as a more powerful theoretical alternative. Instead, the data supporting the self-perception perspective suggest that it may be useful to modify Holmes' model to include a self-perception component. For example, partners in the state of intense passion called *limerence* (Tennov, 1979) or romantic love (Hatfield & Walster, 1981) are typically blind to imperfections in their loved ones (Gold et al., 1984; McClanahan et al., 1990). Consequently, fueled by their passion, people may discount, or even ignore, their partners' lack of trusting behaviors and use their own trusting behaviors as the critical criteria in judging interpersonal trust. Later, as their passion wanes (Sternberg, 1986), they may adopt a view of their partners based more on the mutual exchange or "tit-for-tat" strategy proposed by Holmes. In fact, Holmes and Rempel (1989) themselves claim that early in relationships, partners may experience "blind trust" in one another without much behavioral evidence. Self-perception may account for such blind trust. If one forms beliefs only on the basis of one's own behaviors and ignores relevant partner data, such behavior could be a function of blind trust.

In regard to the third hypothesis, that impression management may be a plausible rival to self-perception as an explanation of the actor results, the lack of differences between the participants who displayed trusting behavior after reminders that their responses were completely anonymous and the participants who were not so reminded provides strong evidence for the self-perception position. Thus, it seems likely that private, internalized trusting beliefs were changed in the present study.

Concerning the fourth hypothesis, both the mirror manipulation, designed to increase objective self-awareness, and the variable of relationship orientation yielded unexpected results: When trusting behaviors occurred in front of a mirror, they resulted in even greater trusting-behavior effects, but these effects occurred under both the actor and the recipient conditions. Because the purpose of the mirror was to produce increased objective self-awareness and, consequently, to increase the self-perception effect upon trust, the enhanced trust thereby created in the receiver conditions was not anticipated.

Theoretically, the mirror should have focused the actors' attention on their own behaviors, making them more like observers and leading to dispositional attributions and consequently greater trust scores. Because they were viewing themselves as the recipients of trusting actions, the process for the receivers should have led to a stronger belief in their own trustworthiness rather than to an increase in trust toward their partners. Perhaps increased feelings of being trusted by their partners then led individuals to increase their own trust in their partner for three reasons: First, the recipients of trusting behaviors may have felt pressure to reciprocate the confidence of their partners. Second, they may have believed that they had power over their partners that caused their partners to act in trusting ways. Third, they may have been convinced that because their partners' trust was evidence of an overall positive orientation toward the recipients, they should in turn trust their partners. According to these explanations, increased self-awareness would increase trust directly for the actors and more indirectly for the recipients.

We expected communally oriented participants to be more likely than exchange-oriented participants to develop trust through their own actions; however, since relationship orientation did not interact with the experimental variables, that expectation was not confirmed. On the other hand, relationship orientation was related to the participants' trust in their partners: The communally oriented participants reported greater trust than did the exchange-oriented participants. Possibly, their lack of emphasis on behavioral reciprocation enabled the former to trust their partners more because they developed trust. Also, the communal participants may have had blind faith in their partners, which led to increased trust in their mates. Communal orientation and trust may also have been related because both are properties of healthy, well-functioning relationships.

Although this research is limited because the sample was composed primarily of U.S. undergraduates, our findings may have implications for one specific area: the contractual approach to marital therapy. According to this approach, distressed couples are encouraged to develop behavioral contracts designed to promote fair exchange in relationships by focusing on the relation of a partner's actions to one's own. Although Epstein and Baucom (1989) and Hahlweg and Markman (1988) found merit in this method, Weiss (1974) pointed out long ago that this form of contracting may not be effective in promoting trust and satisfaction in severely distressed couples. The contingent relationship between each partner's behavior change agreements creates a "who goes first" problem; neither partner is likely to change under such conditions if intense mistrust exists between them. Thus, Weiss recommended "good faith" contracting as an alternative therapeutic procedure. With this procedure, both partners initiate positive changes in their behaviors, including those involving trust, independently of what the other party does. Jacobson and Holtzworth-Munroe (1986) noted that these self-initiated behavior changes are likely to be viewed by the actor as voluntary and eventually reflective of a positive, trusting attitude. Research by Jacobson (1978, 1984) showed that the "good faith" procedure does indeed promote general satisfaction and trust in the relationship. Although the process underlying the increases in trust is left unspecified, it seems reasonable, in light of the present study, that a self-perception component may be at least partially responsible for the development of greater overall trust.

REFERENCES

Bem, D. J. (1972). Self-perception theory. In L. Berkowitz (Ed.), *Advances in experimental social psychology* (Vol. 6). San Diego: Academic Press.

Brehm, S. S., & Kassin, S. M. (1991). *Social psychology* (pp. 480–483). Boston, MA: Houghton-Mifflin.

Butler, J. K. (1986). Reciprocity of dyadic trust in close male-female relationships. *The Journal of Social Psychology, 126,* 579–591.

Clark, M. S., Ouellette, R., Powell, M. C., & Milberg, S.

(1987). Recipient's mood, relationship type, and helping. *Journal of Personality and Social Psychology, 53,* 94–103.

Epstein, N., & Baucom, D. H. (1989). Cognitive-behavioral marital therapy. In A. Freeman, K. M. Simon, L. E. Beutler, & H. Arkowitz (Eds.), *Comprehensive handbook of cognitive therapy* (pp. 491–513). New York: Plenum Press.

Gold, J. A. (1984). Romantic mood induction and attraction to a dissimilar other: Is love blind? *Personality and Social Psychology Bulletin, 10,* 358–368.

Hahlweg, K., & Markman, H. J. (1988). Effectiveness of behavioral marital therapy: Empirical status of behavioral techniques in preventing and alleviating marital distress. *Journal of Consulting and Clinical Psychology, 56,* 440–447.

Hatfield, E., & Walster, G. W. (1981). *A new look at love.* Reading, MA: Addison-Wesley.

Holmes, J. G. (1990, April). *Memory for relationship events: Reconstructions that perpetuate attitudes toward a partner.* Paper presented at The International Conference on Personal Relationships, Oxford, England.

Holmes, J. G. (1991). Trust and the appraisal process in close relationships. In W. H. Jones & D. Perlman (Eds.), *Advances in personality relationships* (Vol. 2, pp. 57–106). London: Jessica Kingsley.

Holmes, J. G., & Rempel, J. K. (1989). Trust in close relationships. In C. Hendrick (Ed.), *Review of personality and social psychology: Close relationships* (Vol. 10). Newbury Park, CA: Sage.

Hull, J., & Levy, A. (1979). The organizational functions of the self. *Journal of Personality and Social Psychology, 37,* 756–768.

Jacobson, N. S. (1978). Specific and nonspecific factors in the effectiveness of a behavioral approach to the treatment of marital discord. *Journal of Consulting and Clinical Psychology, 46,* 442–452.

Jacobson, N. S. (1984). A component analysis of behavioral marital therapy: The relative effectiveness of behavior exchange and communication/problem-solving training. *Journal of Consulting and Clinical Psychology, 52,* 295–305.

Jacobson, N. S., & Holtzworth-Munroe, A. (1986). Marital therapy: A social learning-cognitive perspective. In N. S. Jacobson & A. S. Gurman (Eds.), *Clinical handbook of marital therapy.* New York: Guilford.

Johnson-George, C., & Swap, W. C. (1982). Measurement of specific interpersonal trust: Construction and validation of a scale to assess trust in a specific other. *Journal of Personality and Social Psychology, 43,* 1306–1317.

Larzelere, R. E., & Huston, T. L. (1980). The Dyadic Trust

Scale: Toward understanding interpersonal trust in close relationships. *Journal of Marriage and the Family, 42,* 595–604.

McClanahan, K. K. (1990). Infatuation and attraction to a dissimilar other: Why is love blind? *The Journal of Social Psychology, 130,* 433–445.

Murstein, B. I., Wadlin, R., & Bond, C. I. (1987). The revised Exchange Orientation Scale. *Small Group Behavior, 18,* 212–223.

Rempel, J. K., Holmes, J. G., & Zanna, M. P. (1985). Trust in close relationships. *Journal of Personality and Social Psychology, 49,* 95–112.

Scheir, M. F., & Carver, C. S. (1977). Self-focused attention and the experience of emotion: Attraction, repulsion, elation, and depression. *Journal of Personality and Social Psychology, 35,* 625–636.

Sternberg, R. J. (1986). A triangular theory of love. *Psychological Review, 93,* 119–135.

Tedeschi, J. T., Schlenker, B. R., & Bonoma, T. V. (1971). Cognitive dissonance: Private rationalization or public spectacle? *American Psychologist, 26,* 685–695.

Tennov, D. (1979). *Love and limerence: The experience of being in love.* New York: Stein & Day.

Vanyperen, N. W., & Buunk, B. P. (1991). Equity theory and exchange and communal orientation from a cross-national perspective. *The Journal of Social Psychology, 131,* 5–20.

Weiss, R. L. (1974). Contractual models for negotiation training in marital dyads. *Journal of Marriage and the Family, 36,* 321–331.

Zak, A. M., & Gold, J. A. (1991). *Relation styles revised.* Unpublished manuscript, University of Maine.

The authors express much gratitude to Robert Milardo for his insightful comments during all phases, to Cathy Loomis for her help on a previous draft of this article, and to Mark Pellowski for his help in testing the participants.

CRITICAL THINKING QUESTIONS

1. The article states that "early in relationships, partners may experience 'blind trust' in one another without much behavioral evidence. Self-perception may account for such blind trust." Examine a significant relationship that you have been in by considering your understanding of trust and the self-perception process. Do your own experiences support or refute the information presented in the article? Explain your answers.

2. Trust is an integral part of any intimate relationship. Based on the information in the article, what can people do to enhance the level of trust in a relationship? Is their a potential downside to these trust-enhancing actions? If so, what might it be?

3. The study used a mirror to induce self-awareness. How else might self-awareness be heightened?

4. Design a nonlaboratory study for examining the role of self-perception on the development of trust in a relationship.

5. The article examined trust in intimate relationships. Does the issue of trust work the same way in all relationships? Or is the nature of trust and how it is attained somehow different in other types of relationships, such as between friends or between work partners? Explain your answers.

Chapter Nine

SOCIAL INFLUENCE

SOCIAL INFLUENCE IS the process of inducing change in other people. Sometimes social change results from direct orders to do something, such as when a military officer gives an order to a subordinate. When this happens, we call it *obedience*. Basic to situations involving obedience is some sort of power, either real or imagined, that the person giving the orders has over the person obeying him or her.

Not all social influence is due to direct orders from people in positions of authority. Instead, we may simply ask that a person do something for us. *Compliance* is when a person does something just because he or she was asked to, not because the requestor had any type of power over him or her.

Finally, social influence also operates in a very subtle way when people follow *norms,* or generally expected ways of behaving in certain situations. For example, when you are in an elevator, what do you do? Most likely, you face forward and stare at the numbers. *Conformity* occurs in many situations where norms exist for proper behavior. In a sense, conformity is the lifeblood of a society, for without conformity to rules, society could not exist.

The articles selected for this chapter primarily deal with obedience and compliance, although issues of conformity also can be found. Article 25, "The Education of a Torturer," gives a chilling account of what types of social influence go into the transformation of a normal human being into someone capable of inflicting the most hideous punishment and pain on someone else. As the article notes, the transformation is not due just to obedience to authority but also to compliance to requests and conformity to the norms of the torturer subculture.

Article 26, a classic work on obedience to authority, is perhaps one of the most widely known studies in the field of social psychology. "Behavioral Study of Obedience" seeks to demonstrate experimentally that the average person could be induced to harm another person simply by being ordered to do so by someone in a position of authority. The large number of people who fully obeyed orders is surprising.

Finally, Article 27, "The Use of Metacommunication in Compliance: Door-in-the-Face and Single-Request Strategies," examines a well-known social influence technique—the door-in-the-face—with a new dynamic introduced: whether the person being asked a favor is asked to comment on the appropriateness of the request.

ARTICLE 25 _____

When people read about a horrendous act that has been committed, they naturally think that the person who committed it is somehow deranged or inhuman. Sometimes that is indeed the case, as when a psychotic commits an act under orders he or she has supposedly received during hallucinations. Personal pathology and mental illness are certainly involved in many of the hideous acts that people commit. But are personality or psychological factors always the cause of such behavior? Is it possible that an otherwise normal individual may commit an abnormal, sick act not because there is something wrong with him or her but because of the situation he or she might be in?

History is full of examples of normal people who have committed abnormal acts. For example, warfare has often induced otherwise normal, nonviolent people not only to kill but also to commit atrocities. Yet the suggestion that somehow anyone placed in the same situation may act the same way is repugnant. It might be a lot more personally comforting to believe that people who do bad things are somehow different from us. We, after all, are good and certainly incapable of being mass murderers. Only other people who are either sick or are somehow overly conforming could do such things. In other words, we tend to attribute others' acts to their disposition—that is, some personality or other enduring trait causes them to act that way.

In this article, Janice T. Gibson and Mika Haritos-Fatouros present both field and experimental research to suggest that perhaps it is not so much individual characteristics (disposition) that result in people performing terrible acts but rather the situation that produces the behavior. The authors review the step-by-step process of taking a normal person who does not enjoy hurting other people and transforming him into a torturer. Similar steps of inducing obedience found in other studies also are presented. If you strongly believe that a torturer is somehow different from other people, this article may make you think again.

The Education of a Torturer

■ Janice T. Gibson and Mika Haritos-Fatouros

Torture—for whatever purpose and in whatever name—requires a torturer, an individual responsible for planning and causing pain to others. "A man's hands are shackled behind him, his eyes blindfolded," wrote Argentine journalist Jacobo Timerman about his torture by Argentine army extremists. "No one says a word. Blows are showered . . . [He is] stripped, doused with water, tied . . . And the application of electric shocks begins. It's impossible to shout—you howl." The governments of at least 90 countries use similar methods to torture people all over the world, Amnesty International reports.

What kind of person can behave so monstrously to another human being? A sadist or a sexual deviant? Someone with an authoritarian upbringing or who was abused by parents? A disturbed personality affected somehow by hereditary characteristics?

On the contrary, the Nazis who tortured and killed millions during World War II "weren't sadists or killers by nature," Hannah Arendt reported in her book *Eichmann in Jerusalem.* Many studies of Nazi behavior concluded that monstrous acts, despite their horrors, were often simply a matter of faithful bureaucrats slavishly following orders.

Reprinted from *Psychology Today,* 1986 (November), *20,* 50–58. Reprinted with permission from *Psychology Today* magazine. Copyright © 1986 (Sussex Publishers, Inc.).

In a 1976 study, University of Florida psychologist Molly Harrower asked 15 Rorschach experts to examine ink-blot test reports from Adolph Eichmann, Rudolf Hess, Hermann Goering and five other Nazi war criminals, made just before their trials at Nuremberg. She also sent the specialists Rorschach reports from eight Americans, some with well-adjusted personalities and some who were severely disturbed, without revealing the individuals' identities. The experts were unable to distinguish the Nazis from the Americans and judged an equal number of both to be well-adjusted. The horror that emerges is the likelihood that torturers are not freaks; they are ordinary people.

Obedience to what we call the "authority of violence" often plays an important role in pushing ordinary people to commit cruel, violent and even fatal acts. During wartime, for example, soldiers will follow orders to kill unarmed civilians. Here, we will look at the way obedience and other factors combine to produce willing torturers.

Twenty-five years ago, the late psychologist Stanley Milgram demonstrated convincingly that people unlikely to be cruel in everyday life will administer pain if they are told to by someone in authority. In a famous experiment, Milgram had men wearing laboratory coats direct average American adults to inflict a series of electric shocks on other people. No real shocks were given and the "victims" were acting, but the people didn't know this. They were told that the purpose of the study was to measure the effects of punishment on learning. Obediently, 65 percent of them used what they thought were dangerously high levels of shocks when the experimenter told them to. While they were less likely to administer these supposed shocks as they were moved closer to their victims, almost one-third of them continued to shock when they were close enough to touch.

This readiness to torture is not limited to Americans. Following Milgram's lead, other researchers found that people of all ages from a wide range of countries were willing to shock others even when they had nothing to gain by complying with the command or nothing to lose by refusing it. So long as someone else, an authority figure, was responsible for the final outcome of the experiment, almost no one absolutely refused to administer shocks. Each study

also found, as Milgram had, that some people would give shocks even when the decision was left up to them.

Milgram proposed that the reasons people obey or disobey authority fall into three categories. The first is personal history family or school backgrounds that encourage obedience or defiance. The second, which he called "binding," is made up of ongoing experiences that make people feel comfortable when they obey authority. Strain, the third category, consists of bad feelings from unpleasant experiences connected with obedience. Milgram argued that when the binding factors are more powerful than the strain of cooperating, people will do as they are told. When the strain is greater, they are more likely to disobey.

This may explain short-term obedience in the laboratory, but it doesn't explain prolonged patterns of torture during wartime or under some political regimes. Repeatedly, torturers in Argentina and elsewhere performed acts that most of us consider repugnant, and in time this should have placed enough strain on them to prevent their obedience. It didn't. Nor does Milgram's theory explain undirected cruel or violent acts, which occur even when no authority orders them. For this, we have developed a more comprehensive learning model; for torture, we discovered, can be taught (see "Teaching to Torment," this article).

We studied the procedures used to train Greek military police as torturers during that country's military regime from 1967 through 1974. We examined the official testimonies of 21 former soldiers in the ESA (Army Police Corps) given at their 1975 criminal trials in Athens; in addition, Haritos-Fatouros conducted in-depth interviews with 16 of them after their trials. In many cases, these men had been convicted and had completed prison sentences. They were all leading normal lives when interviewed. One was a university graduate, five were graduates of higher technical institutes, nine had completed at least their second year of high school and only one had no more than a primary school education.

All of these men had been drafted, first into regular military service and then into specialized units that required servicemen to torture prisoners. We found no record of delinquent or disturbed behavior before their military service. However, we did find several features of the soldiers' training that helped to turn them into willing and able torturers.

The initial screening for torturers was primarily based on physical strength and "appropriate" political beliefs, which simply meant that the recruits and their families were anticommunists. This ensured that the men had hostile attitudes toward potential victims from the very beginning.

Once they were actually serving as military police, the men were also screened for other attributes. According to former torturer Michaelis Petrou, "The most important criterion was that you had to keep your mouth shut. Second, you had to show aggression. Third, you had to be intelligent and strong. Fourth, you had to be 'their man,' which meant that you would report on the others serving with you, that [the officers] could trust you and that you would follow their orders blindly."

Binding the recruits to the authority of ESA began in basic training, with physically brutal initiation rites. Recruits themselves were cursed, punched, kicked and flogged. They were forced to run until they collapsed and prevented from relieving themselves for long stretches of time. They were required to swear allegiance to a symbol of authority used by the regime (a poster of a soldier superimposed on a large phoenix rising from its own ashes), and they had to promise on their knees to obey their commander-in-chief and the military revolution.

While being harassed and beaten by their officers, servicemen were repeatedly told how fortunate they were to have joined the ESA, the strongest and most important support of the regime. They were told that an ESA serviceman's action is never questioned: "You can even flog a major." In-group language helped the men to develop elitist attitudes. Servicemen used

---

Teaching to Torment

There are several ways to teach people to do the unthinkable, and we have developed a model to explain how they are used. We have also found that college fraternities, although they are far removed from the grim world of torture and violent combat, use similar methods for initiating new members, to ensure their faithfulness to the fraternity's rules and values. However, this unthinking loyalty can sometimes lead to dangerous actions: Over the past 10 years, there have been countless injuries during fraternity initiations and 39 deaths. These training techniques are designed to instill unquestioning obedience in people, but they can easily be a guide for an intensive course in torture.

1. Screening to find the best prospects: normal, well-adjusted people with the physical, intellectual and, in some cases, political attributes necessary for the task.
2. Techniques to increase binding among these prospects:

- Initiation rites to isolate people from society and introduce them to a new social order, with different rules and values.
- Elitist attitudes and "in-group" language, which highlight the differences between the group and the rest of society.

3. Techniques to reduce the strain of obedience:

- Blaming and dehumanizing the victims, so it is less disturbing to harm them.
- Harassment, the constant physical and psychological intimidation that prevents logical thinking and promotes the instinctive responses needed for acts of inhuman cruelty.
- Rewards for obedience and punishments for not cooperating.
- Social modeling by watching other group members commit violent acts and then receive rewards.
- Systematic desensitization to repugnant acts by gradual exposure to them, so they appear routine and normal despite conflicts with previous moral standards.

nicknames for one another and, later, they used them for victims and for the different methods of torture. "Tea party" meant the beating of a prisoner by a group of military police using their fists, and "tea party with toast" meant more severe group beatings using clubs. Gradually, the recruits came to speak of all people who were not in their group, parents and families included, as belonging to the "outside world."

The strain of obedience on the recruits was reduced in several ways. During basic training, they were given daily "national ethical education" lectures that included indoctrination against communism and enemies of the state. During more advanced training, the recruits were constantly reminded that the prisoners were "worms," and that they had to "crush" them. One man reported that when he was torturing prisoners later, he caught himself repeating phrases like "bloody communists!" that he had heard in the lectures.

The military police used a carrot-and-stick method to further diminish the recruits' uneasiness about torture. There were many rewards, such as relaxed military rules after training was completed, and torturers often weren't punished for leaving camp without permission. They were allowed to wear civilian clothes, to keep their hair long and to drive military police cars for their personal use. Torturers were frequently given a leave of absence after they forced a confession from a prisoner. They had many economic benefits as well, including free bus rides and restaurant meals and job placement when military service was over. These were the carrots.

The sticks consisted of the constant harassment, threats and punishment for disobedience. The men were threatened and intimidated, first by their trainers, then later by senior servicemen. "An officer used to tell us that if a warder helps a prisoner, he will take the prisoner's place and the whole platoon will flog him," one man recalled. Soldiers spied on one another, and even the most successful torturers said that they were constantly afraid.

"You will learn to love pain," one officer promised a recruit. Sensitivity to torture was blunted in several steps. First, the men had to endure it themselves, as if torture were a normal act. The beatings and other torments inflicted on them continued and became worse. Next, the servicemen chosen for the Persecu-

tion Section, the unit that tortured political prisoners, were brought into contact with the prisoners by carrying food to their cells. The new men watched veteran soldiers torture prisoners, while they stood guard. Occasionally, the veterans would order them to give the prisoners "some blows."

At the next step, the men were required to participate in group beatings. Later, they were told to use a variety of torture methods on the prisoners. The final step, the appointment to prison warder or chief torturer, was announced suddenly by the commander-in-chief, leaving the men no time to reflect on their new duties.

The Greek example illustrates how the ability to torture can be taught. Training that increases binding and reduces strain can cause decent people to commit acts, often over long periods of time, that otherwise would be unthinkable for them. Similar techniques can be found in military training all over the world, when the intent is to teach soldiers to kill or perform some other repellent act. We conducted extensive interviews with soldiers and ex-soldiers in the U.S. Marines and the Green Berets, and we found that all the steps in our training model were part and parcel of elite American military training. Soldiers are screened for intellectual and physical ability, achievement and mental health. Binding begins in basic training, with initiation rites that isolate trainees from society, introduce them to new rules and values and leave them little time for clear thinking after exhausting physical exercise and scant sleep. Harassment plays an important role, and soldiers are severely punished for disobedience, with demerits, verbal abuse, hours of calisthenics and loss of eating, sleeping and other privileges.

Military training gradually desensitizes soldiers to violence and reduces the strain normally created by repugnant acts. Their revulsion is diminished by screaming chants and songs about violence and killing during marches and runs. The enemy is given derogatory names and portrayed as less than human; this makes it easier to kill them. Completing the toughest possible training and being rewarded by "making it" in an elite corps bring the soldiers confidence and pride, and those who accomplish this feel they can do anything. "Although I tried to avoid killing, I learned to have confidence in myself and was never afraid," said a former Green Beret who served in Vietnam. "It was part of the job. . . . Anyone who goes through that kind of training could do it."

The effectiveness of these techniques, as several researchers have shown, is not limited to the army. History teacher Ronald Jones started what he called the Third Wave movement as a classroom experiment to show his high school students how people might have become Nazis in World War II. Jones began the Third Wave demonstration by requiring students to stand at attention in a unique new posture and follow strict new rules. He required students to stand beside their desks when asking or answering questions and to begin each statement by saying, "Mr. Jones." The students obeyed. He then required them to shout slogans, "Strength through discipline!" and "Strength through community!" Jones created a salute for class members that he called the Third Wave: the right hand raised to the shoulder with fingers curled. The salute had no meaning, but it served as a symbol of group belonging and a way of isolating members from outsiders.

The organization expanded quickly from 20 original members to 100. The teacher issued membership cards and assigned students to report members who didn't comply with the new rules. Dutifully, 20 students pointed accusing fingers at their classmates.

Then Jones announced that the Third Wave was a "nationwide movement to find students willing to fight for political change," and he organized a rally, which drew a crowd of 200 students. At the rally, after getting students to salute and shout slogans on command, Jones explained the true reasons behind the Third Wave demonstration. Like the Nazis before them, Jones pointed out, "You bargained your freedom for the comfort of discipline."

The students, at an age when group belonging was very important to them, made good candidates for training. Jones didn't teach his students to commit atrocities, and the Third Wave lasted for only five days; in that time, however, Jones created an obedient group that resembled in many ways the Nazi youth groups of World War II (see "The Third Wave: Nazism in a High School," *Psychology Today*, July 1976).

Psychologists Craig Haney, W. Curtis Banks and Philip Zimbardo went even further in a remarkable simulation of prison life done at Stanford University.

With no special training and in only six days' time, they changed typical university students into controlling, abusive guards and servile prisoners.

The students who agreed to participate were chosen randomly to be guards or prisoners. The mock guards were given uniforms and nightsticks and told to act as guards. Prisoners were treated as dangerous criminals: Local police rounded them up, fingerprinted and booked them and brought them to a simulated cell block in the basement of the university psychology department. Uniformed guards made them remove their clothing, deloused them, gave them prison uniforms and put them in cells.

The two groups of students, originally found to be very similar in most respects, showed striking changes within one week. Prisoners became passive, dependent and helpless. In contrast, guards expressed feelings of power, status and group belonging. They were aggressive and abusive within the prison, insulting and bullying the prisoners. Some guards reported later that they had enjoyed their power, while others said they had not thought they were capable of behaving as they had. They were surprised and dismayed at what they had done: "It was degrading. . . . To me, those things are sick. But they [the prisoners] did everything I said. They abused each other because I requested them to. No one questioned my authority at all."

The guards' behavior was similar in two important ways to that of the Greek torturers. First, they dehumanized their victims. Second, like the torturers, the guards were abusive only when they were within the prison walls. They could act reasonably outside the prisons because the two prison influences of binding and reduced strain were absent.

All these changes at Stanford occurred with no special training, but the techniques we have outlined were still present. Even without training, the student guards "knew" from television and movies that they were supposed to punish prisoners; they "knew" they were supposed to feel superior; and they "knew" they were supposed to blame their victims. Their own behavior and that of their peers gradually numbed their sensitivity to what they were doing, and they were rewarded by the power they had over their prisoners.

There is no evidence that such short-term experiments produce lasting effects. None were reported from either the Third Wave demonstration or the Stanford University simulation. The Stanford study, however, was cut short when depression, crying and psychosomatic illnesses began to appear among the students. And studies of Vietnam veterans have revealed that committing abhorrent acts, even under the extreme conditions of war, can lead to long-term problems. In one study of 130 Vietnam veterans who came to a therapist for help, almost 30 percent of them were concerned about violent acts they had committed while in the service. The veterans reported feelings of anxiety, guilt, depression and an inability to carry on intimate relationships. In a similar fashion, after the fall of the Greek dictatorship in 1974, former torturers began to report nightmares, irritability and episodes of depression.

"Torturing became a job," said former Greek torturer Petrou. "If the officers ordered you to beat, you beat. If they ordered you to stop, you stopped. You never thought you could do otherwise." His comments bear a disturbing resemblance to the feelings expressed by a Stanford guard: "When I was doing it, I didn't feel regret. . . . I didn't feel guilt. Only afterwards, when I began to reflect . . . did it begin to dawn on me that this was a part of me I hadn't known before."

We do not believe that torture came naturally to any of these young men. Haritos-Fatouros found no evidence of sadistic, abusive or authoritarian behaviors in the Greek soldiers' histories prior to their training. This, together with our study of Marine training and the Stanford and Third Wave studies, leads to the conclusion that torturers have normal personalities. Any of us, in a similar situation, might be capable of the same cruelty. One probably cannot train a deranged sadist to be an effective torturer or killer. He must be in complete control of himself while on the job.

CRITICAL THINKING QUESTIONS

1. What are the real implications of the studies summarized in the article? Could anyone, including you, be induced to do the same things if you were put into the same situations? Does it really mean that personality and perhaps free will have nothing to do with whether you choose to obey the orders? Or is free choice not really possible in such situations? Support your answers.

2. If inhuman behaviors can be induced by the techniques used to get torturers to do their deeds, does that mean that people should not be held responsible for the things they do? Would a defense of "I was conditioned to do it" absolve an individual of personal responsibility for his or her actions? Explain your responses.

3. The article seemed to suggest that it is fairly easy to get people to do some terrible things under the right set of conditions. How could you prevent such effects? For example, would forewarning people about possible recrimination lessen the likelihood that they would be influenced by the process?

ARTICLE 26 _____

Stanley Milgram's article "Behavioral Study of Obedience" was one of his first describing a series of studies investigating the conditions that produce obedience to authority. This study, as well as Milgram's subsequent research, is truly classic. In fact, if you asked someone who has had only minimal exposure to the field of social psychology about landmark research, this study would perhaps come to mind.

Part of the widespread interest in Milgram's work is due to the implications it has. Basically, Milgram took a group of male volunteers from various backgrounds and ages and induced them to perform acts that appeared to harm another person. Nearly two-thirds of the subjects were fully obedient, continuing to give shocks even though it was apparent that they were harming the victim. Does that mean that just about anyone could be made to do the same? More importantly, while reading the article, keep in mind the actual situation confronting the subjects: What would have happened to them if they had refused to obey? Would the effect demonstrated by Milgram be greater for real-life situations, where there might be punishments for failing to obey?

Besides the implications of the research, Milgram's work on obedience also has attracted considerable interest over the years because of the ethical issues raised. When reading the article, try to put yourself in the shoes of the subjects: How would you feel if you volunteered for a study on learning and instead walked out of the experiment an hour later with the realization that you were willing to harm someone just because an authority figure told you to do so? Think about the ethical issues involved in the study, including the issue of debriefing subjects following an experiment.

Behavioral Study of Obedience

■ Stanley Milgram

This chapter describes a procedure for the study of destructive obedience in the laboratory. It consists of ordering a naive S to administer increasingly more severe punishment to a victim in the context of a learning experiment. Punishment is administered by means of a shock generator with thirty graded switches ranging from Slight Shock to Danger: Severe Shock. The victim is a confederate of the E. The primary dependent variable is the maximum shock the S is willing to administer before he refuses to continue further. Twenty-six Ss obeyed the experimental commands fully, and administered the highest shock on the generator. Fourteen Ss broke off the experiment at some point after the victim protested and refused to provide further answers. The procedure created extreme levels of nervous tension in some Ss. Profuse sweating, trembling and stuttering were typical expressions of this emotional disturbance. One unexpected sign of tension—yet to be explained—was the regular occurrence of nervous laughter, which in some Ss developed into uncontrollable seizures. The variety of interesting behavioral dynamics observed in the experiment, the reality of the situation for the S, and the possibility of parametric variation within the framework of the procedure, point to the fruitfulness of further study.

Obedience is as basic an element in the structure of social life as one can point to. Some system of authority is a requirement of all communal living, and it is only the man dwelling in isolation who is not forced to respond, through defiance or submission, to the commands of others. Obedience, as a determinant of behavior, is of particular relevance to our time. It has been reliably established that from 1933–1945 millions of innocent persons were systematically slaughtered on command. Gas chambers were built, death camps were guarded, daily quotas of corpses were produced with the same efficiency as the manufacture of appliances. These inhumane policies may have originated in the mind of a single person, but they could only be carried out on a massive scale if a very large number of persons obeyed orders.

Obedience is the psychological mechanism that links individual action to political purpose. It is the dispositional cement that binds men to systems of authority. Facts of recent history and observation in daily life suggest that for many persons obedience may be a deeply ingrained behavior tendency, indeed, a prepotent impulse overriding training in ethics, sympathy, and moral conduct. C. P. Snow (1961) points to its importance when he writes:

> When you think of the long and gloomy history of man, you will find more hideous crimes have been committed in the name of obedience than have ever been committed in the name of rebellion. If you doubt that, read William Shirer's "Rise and Fall of the Third Reich." The German Officer Corps were brought up in the most rigorous code of obedience . . . in the name of obedience they were party to, and assisted in, the most wicked large scale actions in the history of the world. (p. 24)

While the particular form of obedience dealt with in the present study has its antecedents in these episodes, it must not be thought all obedience entails acts of aggression against others. Obedience serves numerous productive functions. Indeed, the very life of society is predicated on its existence. Obedience may be ennobling and educative and refer to acts of charity and kindness, as well as to destruction.

GENERAL PROCEDURE

A procedure was devised which seems useful as a tool for studying obedience (Milgram, 1961). It consists of ordering a naive subject to administer electric shock to a victim. A simulated shock generator is used, with 30 clearly marked voltage levels that range from 15 to 450 volts. The instrument bears verbal designations that range from Slight Shock to Danger: Severe Shock. The responses of the victim, who is a trained confederate of the experimenter, are standardized. The orders to administer shocks are given to the naive subject in the context of a "learning experiment" ostensibly set up to study the effects of punishment on memory. As the experiment proceeds the naive subject is commanded to administer increasingly more intense shocks to the victim, even to the point of reaching the level marked Danger: Severe Shock. Internal resistances become stronger, and at a certain point the subject refuses to go on with the experiment. Behavior prior to this rupture is considered "obedience," in that the subject complies with the commands of the experimenter. The point of rupture is the act of disobedience. A quantitative value is assigned to the subject's performance based on the maximum intensity shock he is willing to administer before he refuses to participate further. Thus for any particular subject and for any particular experimental condition the degree of obedience may be specified with a numerical value. The crux of the study is to systematically vary the factors believed to alter the degree of obedience to the experimental commands.

The technique allows important variables to be manipulated at several points in the experiment. One may vary aspects of the source of command, content and form of command, instrumentalities for its execution, target object, general social setting, etc. The problem, therefore, is not one of designing increasingly more numerous experimental conditions, but of selecting those that best illuminate the process of obedience from the sociopsychological standpoint.

RELATED STUDIES

The inquiry bears an important relation to philosophic analyses of obedience and authority (Arendt, 1958; Friedrich, 1958; Weber, 1947), an early experimental study of obedience by Frank (1944), studies in "authoritarianism" (Adorno, Frenkel-Brunswik, Levinson, and Sanford, 1950; Rokeach, 1961), and a recent series of analytic and empirical studies in social power (Cartwright, 1959). It owes much to the long concern with *suggestion* in social psychology, both in its normal forms (e.g., Binet, 1900) and in its clinical manifestations (Charcot, 1881). But it derives, in the first instance, from direct observation of a social fact; the individual who is commanded by a legitimate authority ordinarily obeys. Obedience comes easily and often. It is a ubiquitous and indispensable feature of social life.

METHOD

Subjects

The subjects were 40 males between the ages of 20 and 50, drawn from New Haven and the surrounding communities. Subjects were obtained by a newspaper advertisement and direct mail solicitation. Those who responded to the appeal believed they were to participate in a study of memory and learning at Yale University. A wide range of occupations is represented in the sample. Typical subjects were postal clerks, high school teachers, salesmen, engineers, and laborers. Subjects ranged in educational level from one who had not finished elementary school, to those who had doctorate and other professional degrees. They were paid $4.50 for their participation in the experiment. However, subjects were told that payment was simply for coming to the laboratory, and that the money was theirs no matter what happened after they arrived. Table 1 shows the proportion of age and occupational types assigned to the experimental condition.

Personnel and Locale

The experiment was conducted on the grounds of Yale University in the elegant interaction laboratory. (This detail is relevant to the perceived legitimacy of the experiment. In further variations, the experiment was dissociated from the university, with consequences for performance.) The role of experimenter was played by a 31-year-old high school teacher of biology. His manner was impassive, and his appearance somewhat stern throughout the experiment. He was dressed in a gray technician's coat. The victim was played by a 47-year-old accountant, trained for the role; he was of Irish-American stock, whom most observers found mild-mannered and likable.

Procedure

One naive subject and one victim (an accomplice) performed in each experiment. A pretext had to be devised that would justify the administration of electric shock by the naive subject. This was effectively accomplished by the cover story. After a general introduction on the presumed relation between punishment and learning, subjects were told:

> But actually, we know very little *about the effect of punishment on learning, because almost no truly scientific studies have been made of it in human beings.*
>
> *For instance, we don't know how* much *punishment is best for learning—and we don't know how much difference it makes as to who is giving the punishment, whether an adult learns best from a younger or an older person than himself—or many things of that sort.*
>
> *So in this study we are bringing together a number of adults of different occupations and ages. And we're asking some of them to be teachers and some of them to be learners.*
>
> *We want to find out just what effect different people have on each other as teachers and learners,*

TABLE 1 / Distribution of Age and Occupational Types in the Experiment

Occupations	20–29 Years n	30–39 Years n	40–50 Years n	Percentage of Total (Occupations)
Workers, skilled and unskilled	4	5	6	37.5
Sales, business, and white-collar	3	6	7	40.0
Professional	1	5	3	22.5
Percentage of total (age	20	40	40	

Note: Total n = 40.

and also what effect punishment *will have on learning in this situation.*

Therefore, I'm going to ask one of you to be the teacher here tonight and the other one to be the learner.

Does either of you have a preference?

Subjects then drew slips of paper from a hat to determine who would be the teacher and who would be the learner in the experiment. The drawing was rigged so that the naive subject was always the teacher and the accomplice always the learner. (Both slips contained the word "Teacher.") Immediately after the drawing the teacher and learner were taken to an adjacent room and the learner was strapped into an "electric chair" apparatus.

The experimenter explained that the straps were to prevent excessive movement while the learner was being shocked. The effect was to make it impossible for him to escape from the situation. An electrode was attached to the learner's wrist, and electrode paste was applied "to avoid blisters and burns." Subjects were told that the electrode was attached to the shock generator in the adjoining room.

In order to improve credibility the experimenter declared, in response to a question by the learner: "Although the shocks can be extremely painful, they cause no permanent tissue damage."

Learning Task   The lesson administered by the subject was a paired-associate learning task. The subject read a series of word pairs to the learner, and then read the first word of the pair along with four terms. The learner was to indicate which of the four terms had originally been paired with the first word. He communicated his answer by pressing one of four switches in front of him, which in turn lit up one of four numbered quadrants in an answer-box located atop the shock generator.

Shock Generator   The instrument panel consists of 30 lever switches set in a horizontal line. Each switch is clearly labeled with a voltage designation that ranges from 15 to 450 volts. There is a 15-volt increment from one switch to the next going from left to right. In addition, the following verbal designations are clearly indicated for groups of four

switches going from left to right: Slight Shock, Moderate Shock, Strong Shock, Very Strong Shock, Intense Shock, Extreme Intensity Shock, Danger: Severe Shock. (Two switches after this last designation are simply marked XXX.)

Upon depressing a switch: a pilot light corresponding to each switch is illuminated in bright red; an electric buzzing is heard; an electric blue light, labeled "voltage energizer," flashes; the dial on the voltage meter swings to the right; various relay clicks are sounded.

The upper left-hand corner of the generator is labeled Shock Generator, Type ZLB, Dyson Instrument Company, Waltham, Mass. Output 15 Volts–450 Volts.

Details of the instrument were carefully handled to insure an appearance of authenticity. The panel was engraved by precision industrial engravers, and all components were of high quality. No subject in the experiment suspected that the instrument was merely a simulated shock generator.[1]

Sample Shock   Each naive subject is given a sample shock on the shock generator, prior to beginning his run as teacher. This shock is always 45 volts, and is applied by pressing the third switch of the generator. The shock is applied to the wrist of the naive subject, and has its source in a 45-volt battery wired into the generator. This further convinces the subject of the authenticity of the generator.

Shock Instructions   The subject is told to administer a shock to the learner each time he gives a wrong response. Moreover—and this is the key command—the subject is instructed to "move one lever higher on the shock generator each time the learner flashes a wrong answer." He is also instructed to announce the voltage level before administering a shock. This serves to continually remind subjects of the increasing intensity of shocks administered to the learner.

Preliminary and Regular Run   Pretests revealed that the procedure of reading words and administering shocks requires some practice before it can be handled smoothly. Therefore, immediately preceding the regular run, the teacher is given a preliminary series of 10 words to read to the learner. There are 3 neutral words in the practice series (i.e., words that the learner answers correctly), so that shocks are administered for 7 of the words, with the maximum shock at 105 volts (moderate shock). Almost all subjects master the procedure by the time the preliminary run is over.

Subjects are then presented with a second list, and are told that the procedure is the same as for the first list; the experimenter adds, however:

When you get to the bottom of the list, repeat it over again, and continue giving shocks, until the learner has learned all the pairs correctly.

The experimenter instructs the subject to

start from 15 volts and increase the shock level one step each time the learner gives a wrong answer.

Feedback from the Victim   In all conditions the learner gives a predetermined set of responses to the word pair test, based on a schedule of approximately three wrong answers to one correct answer. In the present experimental condition no vocal response or other sign of protest is heard from the learner until Shock Level 300 is reached. When the 300-volt shock is administered, the learner pounds on the wall of the room in which he is bound to the electric chair. The pounding can be heard by the subject. From this point on, the learner's answers no longer appear on the four-way panel.

At this juncture, subjects ordinarily turn to the experimenter for guidance. The experimenter instructs the subject to treat the absence of a response as a wrong answer, and to shock the subject according to the usual schedule. He advises the subjects to allow 5–10 seconds before considering no response as a wrong answer, and to increase the shock level one step each time the learner fails to respond correctly. The learner's pounding is repeated after the 315-volt shock is administered; afterwards he is not heard from, nor do his answers reappear on the four-way signal box.

Experimenter Feedback   At various points in the experiment the subject may turn to the experimenter for advice on whether he should continue to administer shocks. Or he may indicate that he does not wish to go on. It was important to standardize the experimenter's responses to these inquiries and reactions.

If the subject indicated his unwillingness to go on, the experimenter responded with a sequence of "prods," using as many as necessary to bring the subject into line.

Prod 1: Please continue or *Please go on.*
Prod 2: The experiment requires that you continue.
Prod 3: It is absolutely essential that you continue.
Prod 4: You have no other choice, you must *go on.*

The prods were always made in sequence: Only if Prod 1 had been unsuccessful, could Prod 2 be used. If the subject refused to obey the experimenter after Prod 4, the experiment was terminated. The experimenter's tone of voice was at all times firm, but not impolite. The sequence was begun anew on each occasion that the subject balked or showed reluctance to follow orders.

Special Prods   If the subject asked if the learner was liable to suffer permanent physical injury, the experimenter said:

Although the shocks may be painful, there is no permanent tissue damage, so please go on. [Followed by Prods 2, 3, and 4 if necessary.]

If the subject said that the learner did not want to go on, the experimenter replied:

Whether the learner likes it or not, you must go on until he has learned all the word pairs correctly. So please go on. [Followed by Prods 2, 3, and 4 if necessary.]

Dependent Measures

The primary dependent measure for any subject is the maximum shock he administers before he refuses to go any further. In principle this may vary from 0 (for a subject who refuses to administer even the first shock) to 30 (for a subject who administers the highest shock on the generator). A subject who breaks off the experiment at any point prior to administering the thirtieth shock level is termed a *defiant* subject. One who complies with experimental commands fully, and proceeds to administer all shock levels commanded, is termed an *obedient* subject.

Further Records   With few exceptions, experimental sessions were recorded on magnetic tape. Occasional photographs were taken through one-way mirrors. Notes were kept on any unusual behavior occurring during the course of the experiments. On occasion, additional observers were directed to write objective descriptions of the subjects' behavior. The latency and duration of shocks were measured by accurate timing devices.

Interview and Dehoax Following the experiment, subjects were interviewed; open-ended questions, projective measures, and attitude scales were employed. After the interview, procedures were undertaken to assure that the subject would leave the laboratory in a state of well being. A friendly reconciliation was arranged between the subject and the victim, and an effort was made to reduce any tensions that arose as a result of the experiment.

RESULTS

Preliminary Notions

Before giving an account of the experimental results, it is instructive to consider how persons predict others will perform when commanded to administer powerful shocks to another person. Fourteen Yale seniors, all psychology majors, were provided with a detailed description of the experimental situation. They were asked to reflect carefully on it, and to predict the behavior of 100 hypothetical subjects. More specifically, they were instructed to plot the distribution of obedience of "100 Americans of diverse occupations, and ranging in age from 20 to 50 years," who were placed in the experimental situation.

There was considerable agreement among the respondents on the expected behavior of hypothetical subjects. All respondents predicted that only an insignificant minority would go through to the end of the shock series. (The estimates ranged from 0 to 3 percent; i.e., the most "pessimistic" member of the class predicted that of 100 persons, 3 would continue through to the most potent shock available on the shock generator—450 volts.) The class mean was 1.2 percent. The question was also posed informally to colleagues of the author, and the most general feeling was that few if any subjects would go beyond the designation Very Strong Shock.

Result of Experiment 1

Subjects Accept Situation With few exceptions subjects were convinced of the reality of the experimental situation, that they were administering shocks to another person, and the most potent shocks were extremely painful. In the post-experimental interview subjects were asked: "How painful to the learner were the last few shocks that you administered to him?" Subjects were instructed to indicate their answers on a printed 14-point scale ranging from "Not at all painful" to "Extremely painful." The modal response was 14 (Extremely painful) with the mean at 13.42.

Signs of Extreme Tension Many subjects showed signs of nervousness in the experimental situation, and especially upon administering the more powerful shocks. In a large number of cases the degree of tension reached extremes that are rarely seen in sociopsychological laboratory studies. Subjects were observed to sweat, tremble, stutter, bite their lips, groan, and dig their fingernails into their flesh. These were characteristic rather than exceptional responses to the experiment.

One sign of tension was the regular occurrence of nervous laughing fits. Fourteen of the 40 subjects showed definite signs of nervous laughter and smiling. The laughter seemed entirely out of place, even bizarre. Full-blown, uncontrollable seizures were observed for 3 subjects. On one occasion we observed a seizure so violently convulsive that it was necessary to call a halt to the experiment. The subject, a 46-year-old encyclopedia salesman, was seriously embarrassed by his untoward and uncontrollable behavior. In the post-experimental interviews subjects took pains to point out that they were not sadistic types, and that the laughter did not mean they enjoyed shocking the victim.

Distribution of Scores It had been conjectured that persons would not, in general, agree to administer shocks beyond the level designated as Very Strong Shock. The distribution of maximum shocks for this experiment is shown in Table 2. The obtained distribution of scores deviates radically from the prediction.

Upon command of the experimenter, each of the 40 subjects went beyond the expected breakoff point.

TABLE 2 / Distribution of Breakoff Points

Verbal Designation and Voltage Indication	Number of Subjects for Whom This Was Maximum Shock
Slight Shock	
15	
30	0
45	0
60	0
Moderate Shock	
75	0
90	0
105	0
120	0
Strong Shock	
135	0
150	0
165	0
180	0
Very Strong Shock	
195	0
210	0
225	0
240	0
Intense Shock	
255	0
270	0
285	0
300	5
Extreme Intensity Shock	
315	4
330	2
345	1
360	1
Danger: Severe Shock	
375	1
390	0
405	0
420	0
XXX	
435	0
450	26

No subject stopped prior to administering Shock Level 20. (At this level—300 volts—the victim kicks on the wall and no longer provides answers to the teacher's multiple-choice questions.)

Of the 40 subjects, 5 refused to obey the experimental commands beyond the 300-volt level. Four more subjects administered one further shock, and then refused to go on. Two broke off at the 330-volt level, and 1 each at 345, 360, and 375 volts. Thus a total of 14 subjects defied the experimenter. It is instructive to reprint their remarks at the point of defiance, as transcribed from the tape recordings:

> *[0124] I think he's trying to communicate, he's knocking . . . Well it's not fair to shock the guy . . . these are terrific volts. I don't think this is very humane . . . Oh, I can't go on with this; no, this isn't right. It's a hell of an experiment. The guy is suffering in there. No, I don't want to go on. This is crazy. [Subject refused to administer more shocks.]*
>
> *[0123] He's hanging in there. I'm gonna chicken out. I'd like to continue, but I can't do that to a man . . . I'm sorry I can't do that to a man. I'll hurt his heart. You take your check . . . No really, I couldn't do it.*

These subjects were frequently in a highly agitated and even angered state. Sometimes, verbal protest was at a minimum, and the subject simply got up from his chair in front of the shock generator, and indicated that he wished to leave the laboratory.

Of the 40 subjects, 26 obeyed the orders of the experimenter to the end, proceeding to punish the victim until they reached the most potent shock available on the shock generator. At that point, the experimenter called a halt to the session. (The maximum shock is labeled 450 volts, and is two steps beyond the designation: Danger: Severe Shock.) Although obedient subjects continued to administer shocks, they often did so under extreme stress. Some expressed reluctance to administer shocks beyond the 300-volt level, and displayed fears similar to those who defied the experimenter; yet they obeyed.

After the maximum shocks had been delivered, and the experimenter called a halt to the proceedings, many obedient subjects heaved sighs of relief, mopped their brows, rubbed their fingers over their eyes, or nervously fumbled cigarettes. Some shook their heads, apparently in regret. Some subjects had remained calm throughout the experiment, and displayed only minimal signs of tension from beginning to end.

DISCUSSION

The experiment yielded two findings that were surprising. The first finding concerns the sheer strength of obedient tendencies manifested in this situation. Subjects have learned from childhood that it is a fundamental breach of moral conduct to hurt another person against his will. Yet, 26 subjects abandon this tenet in following the instructions of an authority who has no special powers to enforce his commands. To disobey would bring no material loss to the subject; no punishment would ensue. It is clear from the remarks and outward behavior of many participants that in punishing the victim they are often acting against their own values. Subjects often expressed deep disapproval of shocking a man in the face of his objections, and others denounced it as stupid and senseless. Yet the majority complied with the experimental commands. This outcome was surprising from two perspectives: first, from the standpoint of predictions made in the questionnaire described earlier. (Here, however, it is possible that the remoteness of the respondents from the actual situation, and the difficulty of conveying to them the concrete details of the experiment, could account for the serious underestimation of obedience.)

But the results were also unexpected to persons who observed the experiment in progress, through one-way mirrors. Observers often uttered expressions of disbelief upon seeing a subject administer more powerful shocks to the victim. These persons had a full acquaintance with the details of the situation, and yet systematically underestimated the amount of obedience that subjects would display.

The second unanticipated effect was the extraordinary tension generated by the procedures. One might suppose that a subject would simply break off or continue as his conscience dictated. Yet, this is very far from what happened. There were striking reactions of tension and emotional strain. One observer related:

I observed a mature and initially poised businessman enter the laboratory smiling and confident. Within 20 minutes he was reduced to a twitching, stuttering wreck, who was rapidly approaching a point of nervous collapse. He constantly pulled on his earlobe, and twisted his hands. At one point he pushed his fist into his forehead and muttered: "Oh God, let's stop it." And yet he continued to respond to every word of the experimenter and obeyed to the end.

Any understanding of the phenomenon of obedience must rest on an analysis of the particular conditions in which it occurs. The following features of the experiment go some distance in explaining the high amount of obedience observed in the situation.

1. The experiment is sponsored by and takes place on the grounds of an institution of unimpeachable reputation, Yale University. It may be reasonably presumed that the personnel are competent and reputable. The importance of this background authority is now being studied by conducting a series of experiments outside of New Haven, and without any visible ties to the university.

2. The experiment is, on the face of it, designed to attain a worthy purpose—advancement of knowledge about learning and memory. Obedience occurs not as an end in itself, but as an instrumental element in a situation that the subject construes as significant, and meaningful. He may not be able to see its full significance, but he may properly assume that the experimenter does.

3. The subject perceives that the victim has voluntarily submitted to the authority system of the experimenter. He is not (at first) an unwilling captive impressed for involuntary service. He has taken the trouble to come to the laboratory presumably to aid the experimental research. That he later becomes an involuntary subject does not alter the fact that, initially, he consented to participate without qualification. Thus he has in some degree incurred an obligation toward the experimenter.

4. The subject, too, has entered the experiment voluntarily, and perceives himself under obligation to aid the experimenter. He has made a commitment, and to disrupt the experiment is a repudiation of this initial promise of aid.

5. Certain features of the procedure strengthen the subject's sense of obligation to the experimenter.

For one, he has been paid for coming to the laboratory. In part this is canceled out by the experimenter's statement that:

Of course, as in all experiments, the money is yours simply for coming to the laboratory. From this point on, no matter what happens, the money is yours.[2]

6. From the subject's standpoint, the fact that he is the teacher and the other man the learner is purely a chance consequence (it is determined by drawing lots) and he, the subject, ran the same risk as the other man in being assigned the role of learner. Since the assignment of positions in the experiment was achieved by fair means, the learner is deprived of any basis of complaint on this count. (A similar situation obtains in Army units, in which—in the absence of volunteers—a particularly dangerous mission may be assigned by drawing lots, and the unlucky soldier is expected to bear his misfortune with sportsmanship.)

7. There is, at best, ambiguity with regard to the prerogatives of a psychologist and the corresponding rights of his subject. There is a vagueness of expectation concerning what a psychologist may require of his subject, and when he is overstepping acceptable limits. Moreover, the experiment occurs in a closed setting, and thus provides no opportunity for the subject to remove these ambiguities by discussion with others. There are few standards that seem directly applicable to the situation, which is a novel one for most subjects.

8. The subjects are assured that the shocks administered to the subject are "painful but not dangerous." Thus they assume that the discomfort caused the victim is momentary, while the scientific gains resulting from the experiment are enduring.

9. Through Shock Level 20 the victim continues to provide answers on the signal box. The subject may construe this as a sign that the victim is still willing to "play the game." It is only after Shock Level 20 that the victim repudiates the rules completely, refusing to answer further.

These features help to explain the high amount of obedience obtained in this experiment. Many of the arguments raised need not remain matters of speculation, but can be reduced to testable propositions to be confirmed or disproved by further experiments.[3]

The following features of the experiment concern the nature of the conflict which the subject faces.

10. The subject is placed in a position in which he must respond to the competing demands of two persons: the experimenter and the victim. The conflict must be resolved by meeting the demands of one or the other; satisfaction of the victim and the experimenter are mutually exclusive. Moreover, the resolution must take the form of a highly visible action, that of continuing to shock the victim or breaking off the experiment. Thus the subject is forced into a public conflict that does not permit any completely satisfactory solution.

11. While the demands of the experimenter carry the weight of scientific authority, the demands of the victim spring from his personal experience of pain and suffering. The two claims need not be regarded as equally pressing and legitimate. The experimenter seeks an abstract scientific datum; the victim cries out for relief from physical suffering caused by the subject's actions.

12. The experiment gives the subject little time for reflection. The conflict comes on rapidly. It is only minutes after the subject has been seated before the shock generator that the victim begins his protests. Moreover, the subject perceives that he has gone through but two-thirds of the shock levels at the time the subject's first protests are heard. Thus he understands that the conflict will have a persistent aspect to it, and may well become more intense as increasingly more powerful shocks are required. The rapidity with which the conflict descends on the subject, and his realization that it is predictably recurrent may well be sources of tension to him.

13. At a more general level, the conflict stems from the opposition of two deeply ingrained behavior dispositions: first, the disposition not to harm other people, and second, the tendency to obey those whom we perceive to be legitimate authorities.

REFERENCES

Adorno, T., Frenkel-Brunswik, Else, Levinson, D. J., and Sanford, R. N. *The authoritarian personality.* New York: Harper, 1950.

Arendt, H. What was authority? In C. J Friedrich (ed.), *Authority*. Cambridge: Harvard Univer. Press, 1958. Pp. 81–112.

Binet, A. *La suggestibilité*. Paris: Schleicher, 1900.

Buss, A. H. *The psychology of aggression*. New York: Wiley, 1961.

Cartwright, S. (ed.) *Studies in social power*. Ann Arbor: University of Michigan Institute for Social Research, 1959.

Charcot, J. M. *Oeuvres complètes*. Paris: Bureaux du Progrès Médical, 1881.

Frank, J. D. Experimental studies of personal pressure and resistance. *J. Gen. Psychol.* 1944, *30*, 23–64.

Freidrich, C. J. (ed.) *Authority*. Cambridge: Harvard Univer. Press, 1958.

Milgram, S. Dynamics of obedience. Washington: National Science Foundation, 25 January 1961. (Mimeo).

Milgram, S. Some conditions of obedience and disobedience to authority. *Hum. Relat.,* 1965, *18*, 57–76.

Rokeach, M. Authority, authoritarianism, and conformity. In I. A. Berg and B. M. Bass (eds.), *Conformity and deviation*. New York: Harper, 1961. Pp. 230–257.

Snow, C. P. Either-or. *Progressive,* 1961 (Feb.) 24.

Weber, M. *The theory of social and economic organization*. Oxford: Oxford Univer. Press, 1947.

ENDNOTES

1. A related technique, making use of a shock generator, was reported by Buss (1961) for the study of aggression in the laboratory. Despite the considerable similarity of technical detail in the experimental procedures, each investigator proceeded in ignorance of the other's work. Milgram provided plans and photographs of his shock generator, experimental procedure, and first results in a report to the National Science Foundation in January 1961. This report received only limited circulation. Buss reported his procedure six months later, but to a wider audience. Subsequently, technical information and reports were exchanged. The present article was first received in the editor's office on December 27, 1961; it was resubmitted with deletions on July 27, 1962.

2. Forty-three subjects, undergraduates at Yale University, were run in the experiment without payment. The results are very similar to those obtained with paid subjects.

3. A series of recently completed experiments employing the obedience paradigm is reported in Milgram (1965).

This research was supported by a grant (NSF G-17916) from the National Science Foundation. Exploratory studies conducted in 1960 were supported by a grant from the Higgins Fund at Yale University. The research assistance of Alan E. Elms and Jon Wayland is gratefully acknowledged.

CRITICAL THINKING QUESTIONS

1. What are the ethical implications of this study? In particular, are you satisfied that no lasting harm was done to the participants? Would the debriefing at the end of the experiment be sufficient to eliminate any long-term problems from participation in the study? What about short-term effects? Many of the subjects obviously suffered during the experiment. Was the infliction of this distress on the subjects justified? Support your answers. (*Note:* For a good discussion of the ethics of the study, see the Baumrind and Milgram articles cited on the next page.)

2. What are the implications of this study for people accused of committing atrocities? Suppose that the results of this study had been known when the Nazi war criminals were put on trial in Nuremburg. Could the information have been used in their defense? Do the results remove some of the personal responsibility that people have for their actions? Explain your answers.

3. Subjects were paid a nominal amount for participation in the study. They were told that the money was theirs to keep simply because they showed up, regardless of what happened after they arrived. Do you think that this payment was partly responsible for the findings? Why or why not? Do you think that paying someone, no matter how small the amount, somehow changes the dynamics of the situation? Explain.

ADDITIONAL RELATED READINGS

Baumrind, D. (1964). Some thoughts on ethics of research after reading Milgram's "Behavioral study of obedience." *American Psychologist, 19,* 421–423.

Blass, T. (1991). Understanding behavior in the Milgram obedience experiment: The role of personality, situations, and their interactions. *Journal of Personality and Social Psychology, 60,* 398–413.

Milgram, S. (1964). Issues in the study of obedience: A reply to Baumrind. *American Psychologist, 19,* 848–852.

ARTICLE 27 _____

As indicated in the introduction to this chapter, one of the areas of social influence that has been investigated is *compliance*. Unlike attempts at social influence, which may involve either orders to do something (such as in Milgram's study, Article 26) or subtle attempts at manipulation (such as reported in Article 25), compliance involves an explicit request for a person to do something.

Suppose you would like someone to do something for you. How can you make a request of that person in a way that will increase the probability of his or her saying yes? One technique, long known to salespeople, is first to get a person to agree to a small request and then make progressively larger requests. This approach, known as the *foot-in-the-door technique,* relies on making such a small initial request that the person cannot refuse. But once he or she has made the commitment to comply with the small request, it appears that it is much more difficult for the person to refuse larger subsequent requests.

Why does this strategy work? There are several possible explanations, but the dominant one is that it concerns the process of self-perception. According to *self-perception theory,* we infer our attitudes from observing our behavior. Thus, if I comply with the initial (but small) request, I may see myself as someone who cooperates or helps with requests. Consequently, when confronted with a larger request, I may be more likely to comply because of my attitude that I am a helping, cooperative person.

As effective as the foot-in-the-door strategy is, it turns out that a totally opposite strategy also is effective in bringing about compliance to a request. The *door-in-the-face technique* starts out with a large request, one that is likely to be refused. Then, a second, more reasonable request is made. Again, salespeople (as well as social psychologists) know this is an effective social influence technique.

Why does this strategy work? Part of the reason may be a sort of *contrast effect;* that is, compared to the initial request, the second request seems a lot smaller and more reasonable. However, the process may also involve what is known as *reciprocal concession,* which refers to a norm in bargaining that if one person makes a concession, then the other should reciprocate with a concession of his or her own. The requestor who lowered his or her initial request may be seen as having made a concession and thereby activate this process.

The following article by Michael E. Patch, Vicki R. Hoang, and Anthony J. Stahelski is a contemporary example of research on the door-in-the-face technique, which was first experimentally tested more than three decades ago. This article adds to the compliance equation the issue of *metacommunication,* which refers to the act of communicating about the communication or the relationship implied in the communication. In other words, if I asked you a question and then asked you how appropriate that question was, your response would be a metacommunication in that you would be discussing what you felt was and was not appropriate in terms of our social relationship. As the article indicates, using metacommunication language may be an effective way of increasing compliance to a request independent of a door-in-the-face process operating.

The Use of Metacommunication in Compliance
Door-in-the-Face and Single-Request Strategies

■ Michael E. Patch, Vicki R. Hoang, and Anthony J. Stahelski

ABSTRACT. Investigation of compliance techniques has generally overlooked a dynamic involving a target's dilemma over directly commenting about the imposition of the requester's behavior. Such behavior is generally classified as being metacommunicative in nature. In two studies, the authors tested the hypothesis that compliance can be enhanced when the target is asked to metacommunicate about the appropriateness of an imposition in order to refuse it. American participants were exposed to door-in-the-face (DITF) and single-request strategies that used either metacommunicative or standard language. Although metacommunicative DITF strategies yielded significant compliance effects, the obtained levels were not significantly greater than those of standard DITF strategies. However, when communication style (metacommunicative language) was considered independent of strategy, significant overall effects were found. Therefore, the use of metacommunicative binds in the language of single requests may facilitate compliance.

The study of compliance seems to underscore human vulnerability to blatant, if not inappropriate, imposition by complete strangers. However, although techniques for achieving compliance have focused on a variety of theoretical facilitating factors, researchers have not generally addressed a target person's reluctance to confront the fact of the imposition itself. A case in point, and a primary focus of this research, is the door-in-the-face (DITF) technique. This reluctance was first described by Cialdini et al. (1975), who suggested that a moderate request will yield greater compliance when followed by refusal to a larger request because a target person feels obliged to make a reciprocal concession. Subsequent explanations of the DITF technique have concerned both the target's self-presentation needs (Pendleton & Batson, 1979) and

perceived contrast between the two requests (Miller, Seligman, Clark, & Bush, 1976), but none of these views fully addresses the basic dilemma that a target must face. More specifically, when an understood social distance has been violated by a stranger, the target must often decide whether or not to comment openly about such an imposition.

The imposition by a requester can force a target to consider a response that is metacommunicative (MC). As generally defined (Ruesch & Bateson, 1951; Scheflen, 1973; Watzlawick, Bavelas, & Jackson, 1967), such a response involves commenting on the appropriateness of ongoing behavior and thus establishes what is or is not acceptable in any given context. This kind of response is useful for the regulation of any potential target's social boundaries (Patch, 1995); however, its execution is both confrontational and uncomfortable, often to the point of being considered taboo behavior (Baxter & Wilmot, 1985; Parks, 1982). The target may be spared this burden if the imposition is framed with an acknowledgment of social distance that allows ample room and comfort for refusal (see Brown & Levinson, 1978, on negative politeness), but this appears not to be the case when a DITF strategy is used. Here, consistent with the analysis of Cialdini et al. (1975), the requester's second request may often convey a claim of being reasonable and appropriate in its immediate context. If a metacommunicative response is necessary to refute that claim, any reluctance by the target to do so may make refusal more difficult.

Herein lies the central proposition of the present study. A requester's strategy can be specifically designed to capitalize on the target's reluctance to metacommunicate. It is possible to capitalize on the target's reluctance when the question of request ap-

Reprinted from *The Journal of Social Psychology, 137,* 88–94, 1997. Reprinted with permission of the Helen Dwight Reid Educational Foundation. Published by Heldref Publications, 1219 Eighteenth Street, N.W., Washington, D.C. 20036-1802. Copyright © 1997.

propriateness is made explicit to the target, inducing that person to choose between characterizing a request as inappropriate or complying with it. As a consequence, compliance can theoretically be facilitated whenever such a *metacommunicative bind* is established. Asked to challenge the appropriateness of a request in order to refuse it, a person may become more likely to comply with the request in order to resolve the dilemma.

In the two studies reported here, we attempted to determine (a) if DITF compliance can be enhanced when the metacommunicative bind is made more salient to the target and (b) if the metacommunicative bind might operate in single-request strategies without the aid of sequential request dynamics. To maximize their salience in both DITF and single-request strategies, we designed the techniques used here to constrain and focus the target's response options on the appropriateness of the request behavior in a relationship context rather than on the intrinsic cost or difficulty of the request itself. Thus, the key manipulation was whether the requester invoked this metacommunicative issue as the baseline request was made. The basic hypothesis was that compliance would be increased when a target was asked to metacommunicate in order to refuse.

METHOD

Operational Definitions and Pretesting

The first task was the development of the metacommunicative influence strategies. The starting point was, therefore, the use of specific language—key words and phrases—that are considered, by definition, to be metacommunicative in nature. Based on criteria suggested by Scheflen (1973), we deemed two aspects fundamental to the task: (a) reference to the immediate behavior at hand (the request for compliance) and (b) reference to the specific relationship (strangers) that was involved. Both are used when a requester either acknowledges that his or her request may not be appropriate or asks the target to comment on that appropriateness. The latter aspect was used in the present research. For example, targets were asked to "please tell me if I'm pressuring you" or to say if the request seemed "inappropriate between strangers."

As a check on this type of manipulation, we obtained participant feedback to both written simulations and videotaped versions of the various strategies from pilot studies. It was necessary to determine that the effectiveness of any metacommunicative strategy was not simply a matter of effective politeness, which might make the requester seem more likable. To this end, we obtained target likability ratings in the preliminary work to establish that requesters using metacommunicative language did not have any significant advantage in this regard. Consequently, we began the main research with some confidence that affective reactions to the requesters themselves would not explain differences between the various strategy conditions.

Participants

The samples included U.S. men and women taken from student and nonstudent populations. However, based on preliminary findings, we did not systematically explore gender and population differences. The participants were approached randomly in two different field settings (at a shopping mall for the first study and on the campus of a large university for the second study); there were 90 participants in the first study and 176 in the second study.

Procedure

The basic procedures, derived from the pilot phase of the research, were essentially the same for both studies. Each target participant was approached by a single requester when he or she was alone and, in the judgment of the requester, not ostensibly moving to some other destination (e.g., a class) at that moment. At that point, using either metacommunicative or standard versions of the requests described below, the requester made the influence attempt.

We designed the metacommunicative versions of the requests to confound the two basic issues facing the target, namely, whether to comment on the appropriateness of the requester's behavior and whether to comply with the request. The target was told, "Tell me if this is inappropriate" or "Tell me if I'm pressuring you" before he or she could respond to the baseline request. In effect then, the option of refusal became linked to comment on the requester's behavior.

We assessed compliance by noting whether the target made an affirmative or negative response to the request; for metacommunicative versions, a negative response would have been scored for any participant who indicated that the requester's behavior was inappropriate. Once the requester had obtained commitments, participants were in most cases simply told that they might be contacted at a future time, but no behavioral follow-ups were actually pursued.

Design

In the first study, we used various requests and metacommunicative language in a one-factor design to compare the explicit metacommunicative MC/DITF, DITF, and control-request strategies. In the second study, we manipulated strategy and communication style (metacommunicative or standard language) independently in a two-factor design. The four resulting strategy conditions were thus MC/DITF, DITF, MC/control, and control request.

Scripts of what was said to target participants in the various conditions (metacommunicative language shown in italics) of the two studies were as follows.

Study 1

1. MC/DITF: "We are trying to encourage community awareness in promoting environmental health and are looking for people to hand out 100 flyers to family, friends, and coworkers. Issues covered in the handout include such issues as recycling and elimination of toxic household products. Would you be willing to give us your address so that we might send you these handouts to distribute? (REFUSAL) Would you be willing to distribute 10 flyers then? *I realize that this is a strange request seeing that you do not know who I am, but I really would appreciate your help. I hope that I am not pressuring you with this request. If I am, please tell me.*"

2. DITF: The same as Condition 1, but the italicized metacommunicative (MC) line was excluded.

3. Control moderate request: Only the smaller request of Condition 1 was made (distribute 10 flyers).

Study 2

1. MC/DITF: "I'm part of a student group concerned with student interests such as campus social events and parking. We need to conduct some in-depth interviews with a few students to help us define where the most serious problems are. Would you be able to give us a couple of hours of your time some afternoon this week? (REFUSAL) *This is kind of awkward. There is something else I'd like to ask of you, but tell me if even this seems inappropriate between strangers.* Is it possible you could at least give us about 20 minutes of your time to fill out a questionnaire regarding activities and problems here on campus?"

2. DITF: The same as Condition 1, but the MC line was excluded.

3. MC/control: The same as Condition 1, but the larger request (couple hours of your time) was excluded. We used only the smaller request (20 minutes of your time), preceded by the MC line.

4. Control moderate request: We used only the smaller request of Condition 1.

RESULTS

Table 1 contains compliance frequencies obtained in the first study. A chi-square test of independence performed on these data yielded a significant Strategy × Compliance effect, $\chi^2(1, N = 90) = 13.89, p < .001$. However, although it is evident that differences in compliance between the MC/DITF and DITF strategies were in the expected direction, planned orthogonal contrasts did not confirm our basic hypothesis; communication style did not have a significant effect on DITF compliance frequencies.

The results of the second study, which varied metacommunication across DITF and single-request conditions, indicate a significant effect of communication style. For these compliance frequencies, we used a three-factor chi-square analysis (Strategy × Communication Style × Compliance; see Table 2). Consistent with the original hypothesis, we obtained significant chi-squares for both Strategy × Compliance, $\chi^2(1, N = 176) = 10.32, p < .01$, and Communication Style × Compliance, $\chi^2(1, N = 176) = 3.96, p < .05$. As in the first study, the MC/DITF and DITF conditions could not be statistically differentiated, as

TABLE 1 / Compliance Frequencies for Study 1

	Strategy		
Frequency	MC/DITF	DITF	Control
Comply	23	19	9
Not comply	7	11	21

Note: MC = metacommunicative. DITF = door-in-the-face.

TABLE 2 / Compliance Frequencies for Study 2

	Strategy	
Communication Style	DITF	Control
Metacommunicative		
Comply	25	18
Not comply	19	26
Standard		
Comply	22	8
Not comply	22	36

Note: DITF = door-in-the-face.

hypothesized. Nonetheless, the nonsignificance of the expected Strategy × Communication Style × Compliance interaction suggests that the effect of communication style was not restricted to the DITF strategy conditions. Noteworthy in this pattern is the observation from Table 2 that compliance with the metacommunicative single-request strategy appreciably exceeded that of the standard single-request control.

DISCUSSION

Our hypothesis was that strategies that requested a metacommunicative response in order for a participant to refuse a request would yield greater compliance than those that did not. In the first study, although frequency of compliance to the MC/DITF exceeded that to the DITF, the difference was not significant. However, in the second study, in which we manipulated strategy and communication style independently, the effect of the metacommunicative bind was clearly in evidence. In Study 2, compliance was significantly greater across DITF and control conditions where a metacommunicative response was requested. This evidence, however, would seem to say more about the effectiveness of metacommunicative request strategies in general than about the MC/DITF strategy in particular. It appears that a target who is asked to comment explicitly on the appropriateness of any single request may often find it less distressing to comply than to engage in a metacommunicative confrontation with the requester.

The precise effect of the metacommunicative language manipulation is not entirely clear at this point. Initially, there was concern that such language, by facilitating ritualistic social distance (Brown & Levinson, 1978), might simply serve to make the requester seem more polite and likable. Although this possibility cannot be discounted entirely, preliminary checks yielded no differences in evaluations of likability for requesters who used metacommunicative language and those who did not. This finding is consistent with our assumption that the key ingredient in the metacommunicative strategy is indeed the target's involvement rather than the requester's self-presentation. Thus, compliance seemed to be enhanced, not because the requester commented on the appropriateness of his or her own behavior (using what Brown and Levinson call negative politeness), but because the target was asked to make that comment. Future researchers should explore the target's specific affective reaction to a request for metacommunicative comment, as well as his or her perception of the link between that comment and refusal.

Finally, although the evidence obtained here suggests an important mechanism for obtaining compliance in a limited context, the general applicability of this effect has yet to be determined. Metacommunicative behavior has been conceptualized as confrontational and face threatening, but such dynamics vary widely across different relational contexts and particularly across different societies. Thus, it is important for subsequent researchers to chart carefully when and where metacommunicative binds can be effectively established.

REFERENCES

Baxter, L. A., & Wilmot, W. W. (1985). Taboo topics in close relationships. *Journal of Social and Personal Relationships, 2,* 253–269.

Brown, P., & Levinson, S. (1978). Universals in language usage: Politeness phenomena. In E. Goody (Ed.), *Questions and politeness: Strategies in social interaction* (pp. 56–289). New York: Cambridge University Press.

Cialdini, R. B., Vincent, J. E., Lewis, S. K., Catalan, J., Wheeler, D., & Darby, B. L. (1975). Reciprocal concessions procedure for inducing compliance: The door-in-the-face technique. *Journal of Personality and Social Psychology, 31,* 206–215.

Miller, R. L., Seligman, C., Clark, N. T., & Bush, M. (1976). Perceptual contrast versus reciprocal concessions as mediators of induced compliance. *Canadian Journal of Behavioral Science, 8,* 401–409.

Parks, M. R. (1982). Ideology in interpersonal communication: Off the couch and into the world. *Communication yearbook* (Vol. 5, pp. 79–107). New Brunswick, NJ: Transaction Books.

Patch, M. E. (1995). The effect of asymmetrical use of metacommunicative behavior on judgments of power. *The Journal of Social Psychology, 135,* 747–753.

Pendleton, M. G., & Batson, C. D. (1979). Self-presentation and the door-in-the-face technique for inducing compliance. *Personality and Social Psychology Bulletin, 5,* 77–81.

Ruesch, J., & Bateson, G. (1951). *Communication: The social matrix of psychiatry.* New York: Norton.

Scheflen, A. E. (1973). *How behavior means.* New York: Jordan & Breach.

Watzlawick, K., Bavelas, J. B., & Jackson, D. D. (1967). *Pragmatics of human communication: A study of interactional patterns, pathologies and paradoxes.* New York & London: Norton.

CRITICAL THINKING QUESTIONS

1. This article suggested that social influence may be increased by employing a *metacommunicative bind.* Describe other possible situations of social influence in which people's responses might be influenced by creating such a bind.

2. As indicated in the article, the generalizability of the effect described has yet to be determined. What do you see as the next step in the process of investigation? What should be examined, and how would you go about conducting such a study? Explain your answers.

3. Design a study to test whether the effect was due to the requestor's seeming more polite and likeable when he or she used metacommunicative binds or to the bind itself.

4. Social psychology texts describe several other well-known social influence techniques, such as the *foot-in-the-door,* the *that's-not-all,* and the *low-balling* techniques. Relate the concepts of this article to any or all of these other techniques.

Chapter Ten

PROSOCIAL BEHAVIOR

Help. IT IS something that we all need at some time in our lives, and hopefully, it is something that we all give to others. Dramatic examples of helping or failing to help are not hard to find in the mass media. Consider the various published accounts of people needing help yet receiving none versus those of people who risk their own lives to help strangers.

Why do people help or not help? Is helpfulness a personality trait, so that some people are simply helpful individuals who give assistance in a variety of settings? Or does it have more to do with the specific situation, so that a person who helps in one situation is not necessarily more likely to help in another? Or perhaps these two factors somehow interact with one another, so that people with a certain type of personality in a certain type of situation are more likely to help than others.

The research in this area of social psychology has gone in several directions. Article 28, "Cities with Heart," looks at differential rates of helpfulness in cities of different sizes. The article suggests that a number of factors, including stress and sense of community, may affect people's willingness to help. Where people currently are living, rather than where they grew up, seems to be a key factor in determining their willingness to help others.

Article 29, "From Jerusalem to Jericho," is a classic example of a study that examines both situational and personality factors as influences on helping behavior. It turns out that both factors may be operating, with situational factors determining whether people will offer help in the first place and dispositional factors determining the character of the helping response.

Finally, Article 30, "The Sweet Smell of . . . Helping," takes the study of helping behavior out of the laboratory and into your neighborhood shopping mall to consider whether the presence of pleasant aromas increases levels of helpfulness. This article is yet another example of how situational factors—in this case, an environmental fragrance—can influence prosocial behavior.

ARTICLE 28 _____

Why do people help or not help others in need? Psychologists studying prosocial behavior have examined a number of sources that can influence helping behavior. One of these factors is the potential costs and benefits of helping: How much time will it take? Is any potential danger involved? Will I feel guilty if I don't help? Will other people think better of me if I do help? Together, questions like these influence the likelihood of one person offering another assistance.

A second set of factors concerns the mood of the potential helper. Simply put, people who are in a good mood are more likely to offer help, whereas people who are stressed out are less likely to help.

The third set of factors concerns people's ability to empathize with others. Namely, the greater the perceived similarity between two individuals, the greater the likelihood that one will help the other. Moreover, this ability to empathize interacts with other factors, such as the mood of the individual or the perception of potential harm in offering assistance.

The following article by Robert V. Levine examines whether people's willingness to help strangers is related to the size of the city in which they live. Anecdotal reports of the callousness of residents of big cities abound; almost everyone has heard a report of a big-city dweller literally stepping over someone on the street without offering any assistance. But is that usually the case? Levine's study tested the helping responses of people in 36 cities using a number of measures. As it turns out, large cities did indeed have lower rates of helping than small cities. Some of the possible reasons for this finding—such as people's sense of community, pace of life, and stress—are considered in the article.

Cities with Heart

■ Robert V. Levine

Thomas Wolfe once wrote that city people "have no manners, no courtesy, no consideration for the rights of others, and no humanity." Here in post–Rodney King America, most of us would agree that urban residents see more than their share of human nature's nastier side. Ample evidence demonstrates that the rates of crime and violence rise with population density.

But what of the benevolent side of city people? While growing up in New York City, I was taught that big cities simply have more of everything, both good and bad. Of course, there were more criminals. But I was assured that beneath the seemingly harsh exteriors, you would find as many compassionate hearts as in any small town.

Over the past two years, my research group—students Todd Martinez, Gary Brase, Kerry Sorenson, and other volunteers—spent much of their summer vacations traveling nationwide conducting these experiments. We compared the frequency of helpful acts in various places to answer two basic questions. First, how does overall helping compare from one city and region to another? Second, which characteristics of communities best predict how helpful residents are toward strangers?

WHERE DO PEOPLE HELP?

The team conducted six different experiments in 36 cities of various sizes in all four regions of the country:

Reprinted from *American Demographics* magazine (October 1993, pp. 46–50, 54) with permission. © 1993 American Demographics, Inc., Ithaca, NY.

Dropped a Pen   Walking at a moderate pace, the researcher approached a solitary pedestrian passing in the opposite direction. When 15 to 20 feet away, the researcher reached into his pocket, "accidentally" dropped his pen behind him, and continued walking. Helping was scored on a five-point scale, ranging from no help offered to picking up the pen and running back to hand it to the researcher.

Helping a Blind Person across the Street   Researchers dressed in dark glasses and carrying white canes acted the role of blind persons needing help crossing the street. Just before the light turned green, they stepped up to the corner, held out their cane, and waited for help. A trial was terminated after 60 seconds or when the light turned red, whichever came first. Helping was measured on a two-point scale: helped or did not help.

A Hurt Leg   Walking with a heavy limp and wearing a large, clearly visible leg brace, researchers "accidentally" dropped and then unsuccessfully struggled to reach down for a pile of magazines as they came within 20 feet of a passing pedestrian. Helping was scored on a three-point scale ranging from no help to picking up the magazines and asking to be of further assistance.

Change for a Quarter   With a quarter in full view, researchers approached pedestrians passing in the opposite direction and asked politely if they could make change. Responses were scored on a four-point scale ranging from totally ignoring the request to stopping to check for change.

Lost Letter   A neat handwritten note reading, "I found this next to your car," was placed on a stamped envelope addressed to the researcher's home. The envelope was then left on the windshield of a randomly selected car parked at a meter in a main shopping area. The response rate was measured by the share of letters that later arrived because people were helpful enough to mail them.

United Way Contributions   As a general measure of charitable contributions, we looked at 1990 per capita contributions to United Way campaigns in each city.

The researchers conducted the experiments in downtown areas on clear summer days during primary business hours, targeting a relatively equal number of able-bodied men and women pedestrians. They conducted 379 trials of the blind-person episode; approached approximately 700 people in each of the dropped-pen, hurt-leg, and asking-for-change episodes; and left a total of 1,032 "lost" letters.

NEW YORK, NEW YORK

New York State is home to both the most and least helpful of the 36 cities. Rochester ranks first, closely followed by a group of small and medium-sized cities in the South and Midwest. New York City ranks last.

Generally speaking, the study did not find much difference from city to city. At the extremes, however, the differences are dramatic. In the dropped-pen situation, a stranger would have lost more than three times as many pens in Chicago as in Springfield, Massachusetts. Nearly 80 percent of passersby checked their pockets for change in first-place Louisville, compared with 11 percent in last-place Paterson, New Jersey. Fresno came in dead last on two measures, returning only half (53 percent) as many letters as did San Diego (100 percent). Also, Fresno's per capita contribution to United Way is less than one-tenth that of front-runner Rochester.

Why are people so much less helpful in some places than in others? Studies have shown that urban dwellers are more likely than rural people to do each other harm. Our results indicate that they are also less likely to do them good. This unwillingness to help increases with the degree of "cityness." In other words, density drives strangers apart.

"Cities give not the human senses room enough," wrote Ralph Waldo Emerson. Urban theorists have long argued that crowding brings out our worst nature, and these data support that notion. Places with lower population densities are far more likely to offer help, particularly in situations that call for face-to-face, spontaneous responses such as a dropped pen, a hurt leg, or the need for change. Research shows that squeezing many people into a small space leads to feelings of alienation, anonymity, and social isolation. At the same time, feelings of guilt, shame, and social commitment tend to decline. Ultimately, people feel

Helping Behavior

Disregard for strangers seems to increase with population density and environmental stress.

(36 cities ranked by overall score for helping behavior, and population density rank, environmental stress rank, and pace of life rank)

	Overall Helping Rank	Lowest Population Density	Least Environmental Stress	Fastest Pace of Life
1	Rochester, NY	Bakersfield, CA	East Lansing, MI	Boston, MA
2	East Lansing, MI	Fresno, CA	Indianapolis, IN	Buffalo, NY
3	Nashville, TN	Santa Barbara, CA	Worcester, MA	New York, NY
4	Memphis, TN	Shreveport, LA	Atlanta, GA	Salt Lake City, UT
5	Houston, TX	Chattanooga, TN	Buffalo, NY	Columbus, OH
6	Chattanooga, TN	Knoxville, TN	Memphis, TN	Worcester, MA
7	Knoxville, TN	Nashville, TN	San Francisco, CA	Providence, RI
8	Canton, OH	East Lansing, MI	Shreveport, LA	Springfield, MA
9	Kansas City, MO	Sacramento, CA	Springfield, MA	Rochester, NY
10	Indianapolis, IN	Kansas City, MO	Boston, MA	Kansas City, MO
11	St. Louis, MO	Rochester, NY	Kansas City, MO	St. Louis, MO
12	Louisville, KY	Columbus, OH	Nashville, TN	Houston, TX
13	Columbus, OH	Canton, OH	Providence, RI	Paterson, NJ
14	Detroit, MI	Indianapolis, IN	Rochester, NY	Bakersfield, CA
15	Santa Barbara, CA	Louisville, KY	Chicago, IL	Atlanta, GA
16	Dallas, TX	Memphis, TN	Louisville, KY	Detroit, MI
17	Worcester, MA	St. Louis, MO	Paterson, NJ	Youngstown, OH
18	Springfield, MA	Worcester, MA	Chattanooga, TN	Indianapolis, IN
19	San Diego, CA	Youngstown, OH	Columbus, OH	Chicago, IL
20	San Jose, CA	Springfield, MA	Dallas, TX	Philadelphia, PA
21	Atlanta, GA	Atlanta, GA	Knoxville, TN	Louisville, TN
22	Bakersfield, CA	Dallas, TX	Salt Lake City, UT	Canton, OH
23	Buffalo, NY	San Diego, CA	Detroit, MI	Knoxville, TN
24	Salt Lake City, UT	Houston, TX	Houston, TX	San Francisco, CA
25	Boston, MA	Salt Lake City, UT	Los Angeles, CA	Chattanooga, TN
26	Shreveport, LA	Buffalo, NY	Philadelphia, PA	Dallas, TX
27	Providence, RI	Providence, RI	San Jose, CA	Nashville, TN
28	Philadelphia, PA	Detroit, MI	Bakersfield, CA	San Diego, CA
29	Youngstown, OH	San Jose, CA	Fresno, CA	East Lansing, MI
30	Chicago, IL	Philadelphia, PA	New York, NY	Fresno, CA
31	San Francisco, CA	Boston, MA	Sacramento, CA	Memphis, TN
32	Sacramento, CA	San Francisco, CA	San Diego, CA	San Jose, CA
33	Fresno, CA	Los Angeles, CA	St. Louis, MO	Shreveport, LA
34	Los Angeles, CA	Paterson, NJ	Santa Barbara, CA*	Sacramento, CA
35	Paterson, NJ	Chicago, IL	Canton, OH*	Los Angeles, CA
36	New York, NY	New York, NY	Youngstown, OH*	Santa Barbara, CA*

Note: See Behind the Numbers for explanation of overall helping score. Boxes denote ties.

*Data not available

Source: Environmental stress rank is based on Zero Population Growth. Environmental Stress Index, 1991; and author's research.

Towns with Pity

Rochester places first in only one measure of helping behavior, but it ranks first overall.

(36 cities ranked by overall score for helping behavior, and ranks for individual tests of helping behavior, 1992)

	Overall Helping Rank	Dropped Pen	Hurt Leg	Make Change	Blind Person	Lost Letter	United Way
1	Rochester, NY	Springfield, MA	Chattanooga, TN	Louisville, MO	Kansas City, MO	San Diego, CA	Rochester, NY
2	East Lansing, MI	Santa Barbara, CA	Fresno, CA	Houston, TX	Knoxville, TN	Detroit, MI	Chattanooga, TN
3	Nashville, TN	East Lansing, MI	Nashville, TN	Knoxville, TN	Rochester, NY	East Lansing, MI	Columbus, OH
4	Memphis, TN	Louisville, KY	Sacramento, CA	Canton, OH	Bakersfield, CA	Indianapolis, IN	Indianapolis, IN
5	Houston, TX	San Francisco, CA	Shreveport, LA	Detroit, MI	Dallas, TX	Worcester, MA	St. Louis, MO
6	Chattanooga, TN	Memphis, TN	Memphis, TN	East Lansing, MI	Nashville, TN	Knoxville, TN	Kansas City, MO
7	Knoxville, TN	Dallas, TX	San Diego, CA	Boston, MA	Chicago, IL	Canton, OH	Philadelphia, PA
8	Canton, OH	Houston, TX	Providence, RI	Nashville, TN	Columbus, OH	Columbus, OH	Dallas, TX
9	Kansas City, MO	Salt Lake City, UT	San Jose, CA	Worcester, MA	East Lansing, MI	San Francisco, CA	Nashville, TN
10	Indianapolis, IN	Bakersfield, CA	Canton, OH	Santa Barbara, CA	Indianapolis, IN	San Jose, CA	Boston, MA
11	St. Louis, MO	Detroit, MI	Kansas City, MO	Buffalo, NY	St. Louis, MO	Chattanooga, TN	Springfield, MA
12	Louisville, KY	Canton, OH	Atlanta, GA	Kansas City, MO	Memphis, TN	Rochester, NY	Canton, OH
13	Columbus, OH	Knoxville, TN	Houston, TX	Rochester, NY	Buffalo, NY	Salt Lake City, UT	Atlanta, GA
14	Detroit, MI	Nashville, TN	Paterson, NJ	San Jose, CA	Houston, TX	St. Louis, MO	Worcester, MA
15	Santa Barbara, CA	St. Louis, MO	St. Louis, MO	Indianapolis, IN	Atlanta, GA	Los Angeles, CA	Louisville, MO
16	Dallas, TX	Indianapolis, IN	Bakersfield, CA	Chattanooga, TN	New York, NY	Louisville, KY	Memphis, TN
17	Worcester, MA	San Diego, CA	Youngstown, OH	Memphis, TN	Santa Barbara, CA	Memphis, TN	Buffalo, NY
18	Springfield, MA	Worcester, MA	Rochester, NY	Bakersfield, CA	Louisville, KY	Santa Barbara, CA	Detroit, MI
19	San Diego, CA	Atlanta, GA	Santa Barbara, CA	Salt Lake City, UT	Canton, OH	Youngstown, OH	Houston, TX
20	San Jose, CA	Rochester, NY	Detroit, MI	Columbus, OH	Philadelphia, PA	Houston, TX	Knoxville, TN
21	Atlanta, GA	Fresno, CA	East Lansing, MI	Springfield, IL	Shreveport, LA	Sacramento, CA	San Jose, CA
22	Bakersfield, CA	Paterson, NJ	Salt Lake City, UT	St. Louis, MO	Providence, RI	Buffalo, NY	East Lansing, MI
23	Buffalo, NY	Kansas City, MO	Dallas, TX	Fresno, CA	Detroit, MI	Dallas, TX	Chicago, IL
24	Salt Lake City, UT	Los Angeles, CA	Springfield, IL	Shreveport, LA	Los Angeles, CA	Kansas City, MO	San Francisco, CA
25	Boston, MA	Sacramento, CA	Boston, MA	Youngstown, OH	San Jose, CA	Nashville, TN	Providence, RI
26	Shreveport, LA	Shreveport, LA	Worcester, MA	Dallas, TX	Worcester, MA	New York, NY	Santa Barbara, CA
27	Providence, RI	Chattanooga, TN	Chicago, IL	Los Angeles, CA	Chattanooga, TN	Springfield, IL	Youngstown, OH
28	Philadelphia, PA	Columbus, OH	Indianapolis, IN	Philadelphia, PA	San Francisco, CA	Philadelphia, PA	San Diego, CA
29	Youngstown, OH	Boston, MA	Columbus, OH	Atlanta, GA	Youngstown, OH	Chicago, IL	New York, NY
30	Chicago, IL	Philadelphia, PA	Knoxville, TN	San Diego, CA	Boston, MA	Providence, RI	Los Angeles, CA
31	San Francisco, CA	Providence, RI	Buffalo, NY	Chicago, IL	Fresno, CA	Atlanta, GA	Sacramento, CA
32	Sacramento, CA	San Jose, CA	Louisville, KY	Providence, RI	Paterson, NJ	Boston, MA	Salt Lake City, UT
33	Fresno, CA	Youngstown, OH	Philadelphia, PA	San Francisco, CA	Sacramento, CA	Paterson, NJ	Shreveport, LA
34	Los Angeles, CA	Buffalo, NY	San Francisco, CA	Sacramento, CA	San Diego, CA	Shreveport, LA	Paterson, NJ
35	Paterson, NJ	New York, NY	New York, NY	New York, NY	Springfield, MA	Bakersfield, CA	Bakersfield, CA
36	New York, NY	Chicago, IL	Los Angeles, CA	Paterson, NJ	Salt Lake City, UT	Fresno, CA	Fresno, CA

Note: See text for explanation of individual helping tests. Boxes denote ties. See Behind the Numbers for explanation of overall helping score.
Source: 1990 per capita contributions to the United Way campaigns in each city; and author's research.

less responsible for their behavior toward others—especially strangers.

Population density has direct psychological effects on people. It also leads to stressful conditions that can take a toll on helping behavior. For example, people are less helpful in cities that have higher costs of living. These high costs are, in turn, related to population density, because the laws of supply and demand drive up the prices of land and other resources when they are limited.

High concentrations of people also produce stress on the environment. We compared our findings with Zero Population Growth's Environmental Stress Index, which rates the environmental quality of cities. As predicted, people were less helpful in environmentally stressed-out cities.

Stressful situations and their consequent behaviors ultimately sustain one another. Violent crime results from stressful conditions but is itself a source of urban stress. Ultimately, inaction becomes the norm. Big cities see more of the worst and less of the best of human nature.

One characteristic that does not affect helping behavior is the general pace of life. In a previous study of the same cities, we looked at four indicators of the pace of life: walking speed, work speed, speaking speed, and clock and watch accuracy. Since helping people essentially demands a sacrifice of time, people who live in cities where time is at a premium would presumably be less helpful.

Yet there is no consistent relationship between a city's pace of life and its helpfulness. Some cities fit the expected pattern. New York, for example, has the third-fastest pace of life and is the least helpful place. But Rochester has the ninth-fastest pace, and its people are most helpful. Laid-back Los Angeles, the slowest city, is also one of the least helpful, ranking 34th.

Todd Martinez, who gathered data in both New York City and (pre–Rodney King situation) Los Angeles, was acutely aware of the differences between the two cities. "I hated doing L.A. People looked at me but just didn't seem to want to bother," he says. "For a few trials, I was acting the hurt-leg episode on a narrow sidewalk with just enough space for a person to squeeze by. After I dropped my magazines, one man walked up very close to me, checked out the situation, and then sidestepped around me without a word.

"Los Angeles was the only city that I worked where I found myself getting frustrated and angry when people didn't help. In New York, for some reason, I never took it personally. People looked like they were too busy to help. It was as if they saw me, but didn't really notice me or anything else around them."

To real-life strangers in need, of course, thoughts are less important than actions. The bottom line is that a stranger's prospects are just as bleak in New York as in Los Angeles. People either find the time to help or they don't.

ROCHESTER'S SECOND WIN

More than 50 years ago, sociologist Robert Angell combined a series of statistics from the 1940 census to assess the 'moral integration' of 43 U.S. cities. Angell measured the degree to which citizens were willing to sacrifice their own private interests for the public good ("Welfare Effort Index") and the frequency with which people violated one another's person and property ("Crime Index"). Angell's methods are not comparable with the current study, but to our astonishment, Rochester also ranked number one on Angell's moral integration index in 1940.

Harry Reis, a psychology professor at the University of Rochester who grew up in New York City, is "not the least bit surprised" by the performance of his adopted home. "I like to describe Rochester as a nice place to live—in both the best and the mildest sense of the word," he says. "It's very traditional and not always very innovative. But it's a town where the social fabric hasn't deteriorated as much as in other places. Unlike New York City, people here don't laugh when you speak of ideals like 'family values.' They take their norms of social responsibility seriously."

Even when people do help in New York City, their altruism sometimes takes a hard edge. On the lost-letter measure, many of the envelopes we received from people had been opened. In almost all cases, the finder had resealed the envelope or mailed the letter in a new one. Sometimes they even attached notes, usually apologizing for opening the letter. Only from New York City, however, did we receive an envelope with its entire side ripped and left open. On the back of the letter, the "helper" had scribbled, in Spanish, a very nasty accusation about the researcher's mother. Below that, he or she added in straightforward English: "F— you." It is fascinating to imagine this angry New Yorker, perhaps cursing while walking to the mailbox, yet feeling compelled by the norm of social responsibility to assist a stranger. Ironically, this rudely returned letter added to New York's helpfulness score.

While growing up in New York City, I was taught by loving, caring people to ignore the cries of strangers. I learned to walk around people stretched unconscious on sidewalks, because I was told that they just need to "sleep it off." I learned to ignore screams from fighting couples: "they don't want your help." And I was warned to disregard the ramblings of mentally disturbed street people because "you never know how they'll react." The ultimate message: "Don't get involved."

Do our data prove that urbanites are less caring people? Perhaps not. For one thing, no comparable data from small towns exist to show that people there are more helpful than are urbanites. Furthermore, city dwellers we talked with claimed over and over that they care deeply about the needs of strangers, but that the realities of city living prohibit them from reaching out. Many are simply afraid to make contact with strangers. Some are concerned that others might not want unsolicited help. They claim that the stranger might be afraid of outside contact or, in some cases, that it would be patronizing or insulting to offer them help. People speak with nostalgia about the past, when they thought nothing of picking up hitchhikers or arranging a square meal for a hungry stranger. Many express frustration—even anger—that life today deprives them of the satisfaction of feeling like good Samaritans.

To some degree, these may be the rationalizations of unwilling helpers trying to preserve a benevolent self-image. But the evidence, in fact, indicates that helping is affected less by people's inherent nature than by the environment. Studies reveal that seemingly minor changes in a situation can drastically affect helping behavior. In particular, the size of the place where one was raised has less to do with how helpful one is than does the size of one's current home. In other words, small-town natives and urbanites are both less likely to offer help in urban areas.

The future of urban helping may not be as bleak as it seems. Just as the environment can inhibit helping behavior, researchers are currently exploring ways to modify the environment to encourage it. Experiments have found that increasing the level of personal responsibility people feel in a situation increases the likelihood they will help. It also helps to make people feel guilty when they don't help others.

A little more than a century ago, John Habberton wrote: "Nowhere in the world are there more charitable hearts with plenty of money behind them than in large cities, yet nowhere else is there more suffering." The current status of helping activity in our cities is dismal. But helping, like language and other human skills, is a learned behavior.

Research indicates that children who are exposed to altruistic models on television tend to follow suit. Just think how much good it could do them to see positive role models in real life.

Behind the Numbers   Three large, medium, and smaller cities were sampled in each of the four census-defined regions of the U.S. (Northeast, North Central, South, and West). Travel distance within each region was a factor in selection of cities. The data for the five experiments were collected in two or more locations, in downtown areas during main business hours, on clear days during the summer months of 1990 and 1991. For the three measures that required approaching pedestrians, only individuals walking alone were selected. Children apparently under 17 years old, handicapped, very old people, and people with heavy packages were excluded. For the purposes of analysis, each of the 36 cities was treated as a single subject. For each city, the six measures of helping were converted to standardized scores, to which the value "10" was added to eliminate negative values. These adjusted standardized scores were then averaged to produce the overall helping score.

CRITICAL THINKING QUESTIONS

1. Levine's study examined people's willingness to help strangers in nonemergency situations. Do you think there would be similar city-size differences in helping behavior if emergency situations were used? Why or why not? How could this possibility be tested?

2. The cities used in the study varied considerably in size, but they all were cities. What differences, if any, would you expect in helping behavior between more rural areas and the smaller cities listed in the article? Why? Could the same methodologies used in the study also work in a rural setting? Explain your answers.

3. Levine suggested a number of possible reasons for his findings about the relationship between helpfulness and city size. What other possible reasons may account for the findings?

4. The article indicated that the most important factor in determining people's helpfulness is where they currently live, not where they grew up. This finding is, of course, correlational in nature. Design a study to test whether a person's willingness to help changes once he or she moves to a different environment, such as from a small city to a large one or vice versa.

ARTICLE 29 _____

Many variables can potentially influence whether an individual will help someone in need. One such factor, the size of the city in which the person is living, was discussed in the previous article. But what other factors may influence prosocial behavior?

Broadly speaking, two types of determinants can be considered. The first concerns *situational* factors: What circumstances surrounding the specific situation may affect helping behavior? The second variable concerns *dispositions:* To what extent are decisions to help due to relatively permanent personality factors? In other words, are some people more likely to help than others because of their unique personality makeup? Or does the situation, rather than personality, influence helping?

In "From Jerusalem to Jericho," John M. Darley and C. Daniel Batson examine both situational and dispositional variables in an experiment modeled after a biblical parable. Specifically, the study looks at helping as influenced by situational variables—whether the subjects were in a hurry and what they were thinking at the time—and dispositional variables—the religious orientations of the subjects. This classic article is interesting not only because of the methodology used but also because of the important implications of the results.

"From Jerusalem to Jericho"
A Study of Situational and Dispositional Variables in Helping Behavior

■ John M. Darley and C. Daniel Batson

The influence of several situational and personality variables on helping behavior was examined in an emergency situation suggested by the parable of the Good Samaritan. People going between two buildings encountered a shabbily dressed person slumped by the side of the road. Subjects in a hurry to reach their destination were more likely to pass by without stopping. Some subjects were going to give a short talk on the parable of the Good Samaritan, others on a nonhelping relevant topic; this made no significant difference in the likelihood of their giving the victim help. Religious personality variables did not predict whether an individual would help the victim or not. However, if a subject did stop to offer help, the character of the helping response was related to his type of religiosity.

Helping other people in distress is, among other things, an ethical act. That is, it is in act governed by ethical norms and precepts taught to children at home, in school, and in church. From Freudian and other personality theories, one would expect individual differences in internalization of these standards that would lead to differences between individuals in the likelihood with which they would help others. But recent research on bystander intervention in emergency situations (Bickman, 1969; Darley & Latané, 1968; Korte, 1969; but see also Schwartz & Clausen, 1970) has had bad luck in finding personality determinants of helping behavior. Although personality variables that one might expect to correlate with helping behavior have been measured (Machiavellianism, authoritarianism, social desirability, alienation, and social responsibility), these were not predictive of helping. Nor was this due to a generalized lack of predictability in the helping situation examined, since variations in the experimental situation, such as the

Reprinted from *Journal of Personality and Social Psychology*, 1973, *27*, 100–108. Copyright © 1973 by the American Psychological Association. Reprinted by permission.

availability of other people who might also help, produced marked changes in rates of helping behavior. These findings are reminiscent of Hartshorne and May's (1928) discovery that resistance to temptation, another ethically relevant act, did not seem to be a fixed characteristic of an individual. That is, a person who was likely to be honest in one situation was not particularly likely to be honest in the next (but see also Burton, 1963).

The rather disappointing correlation between the social psychologist's traditional set of personality variables and helping behavior in emergency situations suggests the need for a fresh perspective on possible predictors of helping and possible situations in which to test them. Therefore, for inspiration, we turned to the Bible, to what is perhaps the classical helping story in the Judeo-Christian tradition, the parable of the Good Samaritan. The parable proved of value in suggesting both personality and situational variables relevant to helping.

"And who is my neighbor?" Jesus replied, "A man was going down from Jerusalem to Jericho, and he fell among robbers, who stopped him and beat him, and departed, leaving him half dead. Now by chance a priest was going down the road; and when he saw him he passed by on the other side. So likewise a Levite, when he came to the place and saw him, passed by on the other side. But a Samaritan, as he journeyed, came to where he was; and when he saw him, he had compassion, and went to him and bound his wounds, pouring on oil and wine; then he set him on his own beast and brought him to an inn, and took care of him. And the next day he took out two dennarii and gave them to the innkeeper, saying, "Take care of him; and whatever more you spend, I will repay you when I come back." Which of these three, do you think, proved neighbor to him who fell among the robbers? He said, "The one who showed mercy on him." And Jesus said to him, "Go and do likewise." (Luke 10: 29–37 RSV)

To psychologists who reflect on the parable, it seems to suggest situational and personality differences between the nonhelpful priest and Levite and the helpful Samaritan. What might each have been thinking and doing when he came upon the robbery victim on that desolate road? What sort of persons were they?

One can speculate on differences in thought. Both the priest and the Levite were religious functionaries who could be expected to have their minds occupied with religious matters. The priest's role in religious activities is obvious. The Levite's role, although less obvious, is equally important: The Levites were necessary participants in temple ceremonies. Much less can be said with any confidence about what the Samaritan might have been thinking, but, in contrast to the others, it was most likely not of a religious nature, for Samaritans were religious outcasts.

Not only was the Samaritan most likely thinking about more mundane matters than the priest and Levite, but, because he was socially less important, it seems likely that he was operating on a quite different time schedule. One can imagine the priest and Levite, prominent public figures, hurrying along with little black books full of meetings and appointments, glancing furtively at their sundials. In contrast, the Samaritan would likely have far fewer and less important people counting on him to be at a particular place at a particular time, and therefore might be expected to be in less of a hurry than the prominent priest or Levite.

In addition to these situational variables, one finds personality factors suggested as well. Central among these, and apparently basic to the point that Jesus was trying to make, is a distinction between types of religiosity. Both the priest and Levite are extremely "religious." But it seems to be precisely their type of religiosity that the parable challenges. At issue is the motivation for one's religion and ethical behavior. Jesus seems to feel that the religious leaders of his time, though certainly respected and upstanding citizens, may be "virtuous" for what it will get them, both in terms of the admiration of their fellowmen and in the eyes of God. New Testament scholar R. W. Funk (1966) noted that the Samaritan is at the other end of the spectrum:

The Samaritan does not love with side glances at God. The need of neighbor alone is made self-evident, and the Samaritan responds without other motivation. (pp. 218–219)

That is, the Samaritan is interpreted as responding spontaneously to the situation, not as being preoccupied with the abstract ethical or organizational do's and don'ts of religion as the priest and Levite would seem to be. This is not to say that the Samaritan is portrayed as irreligious. A major intent of the parable would seem to be to present the Samaritan as a religious and ethical example, but at the same time to contrast his type of religiosity with the more common conception of religiosity that the priest and Levite represent.

To summarize the variables suggested as affecting helping behavior by the parable, the situational variables include the content of one's thinking and the amount of hurry in one's journey. The major dispositional variable seems to be differing types of religiosity. Certainly these variables do not exhaust the list that could be elicited from the parable, but they do suggest several research hypotheses.

Hypothesis 1   The parable implies that people who encounter a situation possibly calling for a helping response while thinking religious and ethical thoughts will be no more likely to offer aid than persons thinking about something else. Such a hypothesis seems to run counter to a theory that focuses on norms as determining helping behavior because a normative account would predict that the increased salience of helping norms produced by thinking about religious and ethical examples would increase helping behavior.

Hypothesis 2   Persons encountering a possible helping situation when they are in a hurry will be less likely to offer aid than persons not in a hurry.

Hypothesis 3   Concerning types of religiosity, persons who are religious in a Samaritan-like fashion will help more frequently than those religious in a priest or Levite fashion.

Obviously, this last hypothesis is hardly operationalized as stated. Prior research by one of the investigators on types of religiosity (Batson, 1971), however, led us to differentiate three distinct ways of being religious: (a) for what it will gain one (cf. Freud, 1927, and perhaps the priest and Levite), (b) for its own intrinsic value (cf. Allport & Ross, 1967), and (c) as a response to and quest for meaning in one's everyday life (cf. Batson, 1971). Both of the latter conceptions would be proposed by their exponents as related to the

more Samaritanlike "true" religiosity. Therefore, depending on the theorist one follows, the third hypothesis may be stated like this: People (a) who are religious for intrinsic reasons (Allport & Ross, 1967) or (b) whose religion emerges out of questioning the meaning of their everyday lives (Batson, 1971) will be more likely to stop to offer help to the victim.

The parable of the Good Samaritan also suggested how we would measure people's helping behavior— their response to a stranger slumped by the side of one's path. The victim should appear somewhat ambiguous—dressed, possibly in need of help, but also possibly drunk or even potentially dangerous.

Further, the parable suggests a means by which the incident could be perceived as a real one rather than part of a psychological experiment in which one's behavior was under surveillance and might be shaped by demand characteristics (Orne, 1962), evaluation apprehension (Rosenberg, 1965), or other potentially artifactual determinants of helping behavior. The victim should be encountered not in the experimental context but on the road between various tasks.

METHOD

In order to examine the influence of these variables on helping behavior, seminary students were asked to participate in a study on religious education and vocations. In the first testing session, personality questionnaires concerning types of religiosity were administered. In a second individual session, the subject began experimental procedures in one building and was asked to report to another building for later procedures. While in transit, the subject passed a slumped "victim" planted in an alleyway. The dependent variable was whether and how the subject helped the victim. The independent variables were the degree to which the subject was told to hurry in reaching the other building and the talk he was to give when he arrived there. Some subjects were to give a talk on the jobs in which seminary students would be most effective, others, on the parable of the Good Samaritan.

Subjects

The subjects for the questionnaire administration were 67 students at Princeton Theological Seminary.

Forty-seven of them, those who could be reached by telephone, were scheduled for the experiment. Of the 47, 7 subjects' data were not included in the analyses—3 because of contamination of the experimental procedures during their testing and 4 due to suspicion of the experimental situation. Each subject was paid $1 for the questionnaire session and $1.50 for the experimental session.

Personality Measures

Detailed discussion of the personality scales used may be found elsewhere (Batson, 1971), so the present discussion will be brief. The general personality construct under examination was religiosity. Various conceptions of religiosity have been offered in recent years based on different psychometric scales. The conception seeming to generate the most interest is the Allport and Ross (1967) distinction between "intrinsic" versus "extrinsic" religiosity (cf. also Allen & Spilka, 1967, on "committed" versus "consensual" religion). This bipolar conception of religiosity has been questioned by Brown (1964) and Batson (1971), who suggested three-dimensional analyses instead. Therefore, in the present research, types of religiosity were measured with three instruments which together provided six separate scales; (a) a *doctrinal orthodoxy* (D-O) scale patterned after that used by Glock and Stark (1966), scaling agreement with classic doctrines of Protestant theology; (b) the Allport-Ross *extrinsic* (AR-E) scale, measuring the use of religion as a means to an end rather than as an end in itself; (c) the Allport-Ross *intrinsic* (AR-I) scale, measuring the use of religion as an end in itself; (d) the *extrinsic external* scale of Batson's Religious Life Inventory (RELI-EE), designed to measure the influence of significant others and situations in generating one's religiosity; (e) the *extrinsic internal* scale of the Religious Life Inventory (RELI-EI), designed to measure the degree of "driveness" in one's religiosity; and (f) the *intrinsic* scale of the Religious Life Inventory (RELI-I), designed to measure the degree to which one's religiosity involves a questioning of the meaning of life arising out of one's interactions with his social environment. The order of presentation of the scales in the questionnaire was RELI, AR, D-O.

Consistent with prior research (Batson, 1971), a principal-component analysis of the total scale scores

and individual items for the 67 seminarians produced a theoretically meaningful, orthogonally rotated three-component structure with the following loadings:

Religion as means received a single very high loading from AR-E (.903) and therefore was defined by Allport and Ross's (1967) conception of this scale as measuring religiosity as a means to other ends. This component also received moderate negative loadings from D-O (−.400) and AR-I (−.372) and a moderate positive loading from RELI-EE (.301).

Religion as an end received high loadings from RELI-EI (.874), RELI-EE (.725), AR-I (.768), and D-O (.704). Given this configuration, and again following Allport and Ross's conceptualization, this component seemed to involve religiosity as an end in itself with some intrinsic value.

Religion as quest received a single very high loading from RELI-I (.945) and a moderate loading from RELI-EE (.75). Following Batson, this component was conceived to involve religiosity emerging out of an individual's search for meaning in his personal and social world.

The three religious personality scales examined in the experimental research were constructed through the use of complete-estimation factor score coefficients from these three components.

Scheduling of Experimental Study

Since the incident requiring a helping response was staged outdoors, the entire experimental study was run in 3 days, December 14–16, 1970, between 10 A.M. and 4 P.M. A tight schedule was used in an attempt to maintain reasonably consistent weather and light conditions. Temperature fluctuation according to the *New York Times* for the 3 days during these hours was not more than 5 degrees Fahrenheit. No rain or snow fell, although the third day was cloudy, whereas the first two were sunny. Within days the subjects were randomly assigned to experimental conditions.[1]

Procedure

When a subject appeared for the experiment, an assistant (who was blind with respect to the personality scores) asked him to read a brief statement which explained that he was participating in a study of the vocational careers of seminary students. After developing the rationale for the study, the statement read:

What we have called you in for today is to provide us with some additional material which will give us a clearer picture of how you think than does the questionnaire material we have gathered thus far. Questionnaires are helpful, but tend to be somewhat oversimplified. Therefore, we would like to record a 3–5 minute talk you give based on the following passage. . . .

Variable 1: Message In the task-relevant condition the passage read,

With increasing frequency the question is being asked: What jobs or professions do seminary students subsequently enjoy most, and in what jobs are they most effective? The answer to this question used to be so obvious that the question was not even asked. Seminary students were being trained for the ministry, and since both society at large and the seminary student himself had a relatively clear understanding of what made a "good" minister, there was no need even to raise the question of for what other jobs seminary experience seems to be an asset. Today, however, neither society nor many seminaries have a very clearly defined conception of what a "good" minister is or of what sorts of jobs and professions are the best context in which to minister. Many seminary students, apparently genuinely concerned with "ministering," seem to feel that it is impossible to minister in the professional clergy. Other students, no less concerned, find the clergy the most viable profession for ministry. But are there other jobs and/or professions for which seminary experience is an asset? And, indeed, how much of an asset is it for the professional ministry? Or, even more broadly, can one minister through an "establishment" job at all?

In the helping-relevant condition, the subject was given the parable of the Good Samaritan exactly as printed earlier in this article. Next, regardless of condition, all subjects were told,

You can say whatever you wish based on the passage. Because we are interested in how you think on your feet, you will not be allowed to use notes in giving the

talk. Do you understand what you are to do? If not, the assistant will be glad to answer questions.

After a few minutes the assistant returned, asked if there were any questions, and then said:

Since they're rather tight on space in this building, we're using a free office in the building next door for recording the talks. Let me show you how to get there [draws and explains map on 3 × 5 card]. This is where Professor Steiner's laboratory is. If you go in this door [points at map], there's a secretary right here, and she'll direct you to the office we're using for recording. Another of Professor Steiner's assistants will set you up for recording your talk. Is the map clear?

Variable 2: Hurry In the high-hurry condition the assistant then looked at his watch and said, "Oh, you're late. They were expecting you a few minutes ago. We'd better get moving. The assistant should be waiting for you so you'd better hurry. It shouldn't take but just a minute." In the intermediate-hurry condition he said, "The assistant is ready for you, so please go right over." In the low-hurry condition, he said, "It'll be a few minutes before they're ready for you, but you might as well head on over. If you have to wait over there, it shouldn't be long."

The Incident When the subject passed through the alley, the victim was sitting slumped in a doorway, head down, eyes closed, not moving. As the subject went by, the victim coughed twice and groaned, keeping his head down. If the subject stopped and asked if something was wrong or offered to help, the victim, startled and somewhat groggy, said, "Oh, thank you [cough]. . . . No, it's all right. [Pause] I've got this respiratory condition [cough]. . . . The doctor's given me these pills to take, and I just took one. . . . If I just sit and rest for a few minutes I'll be O.K. . . . Thanks very much for stopping though [smiles weakly]." If the subject persisted, insisting on taking the victim inside the building, the victim allowed him to do so and thanked him.

Helping Ratings The victim rated each subject on a scale of helping behavior as follows:

0 = failed to notice the victim as possibly in need at all; 1 = perceived the victim as possibly in need but did not offer aid; 2 = did not stop but helped indi-

rectly (e.g., by telling Steiner's assistant about the victim); 3 = stopped and asked if victim needed help; 4 = after stopping, insisted on taking the victim inside and then left him.

The victim was blind to the personality scale scores and experimental conditions of all subjects. At the suggestion of the victim, another category was added to the rating scales, based on his observations of the pilot subjects' behavior:

5 = after stopping, refused to leave the victim (after 3–5 minutes) and/or insisted on taking him somewhere outside experimental context (e.g., for coffee or to the infirmary).

(In some cases it was necessary to distinguish Category 0 from Category 1 by the postexperimental questionnaire and Category 2 from Category 1 on the report of the experimental assistant.)

This 6-point scale of helping behavior and a description of the victim were given to a panel of 10 judges (unacquainted with the research) who were asked to rank order the (unnumbered) categories in terms of "the amount of helping behavior displayed toward the person in the doorway." Of the 10, 1 judge reversed the order of Categories 0 and 1. Otherwise there was complete agreement with the ranking implied in the presentation of the scale above.

The Speech   After passing through the alley and entering the door marked on the map, the subject entered a secretary's office. She introduced him to the assistant who gave the subject time to prepare and privately record his talk.

Helping Behavior Questionnaire   After recording the talk, the subject was sent to another experimenter, who administered "an exploratory questionnaire on personal and social ethics." The questionnaire contained several initial questions about the interrelationship between social and personal ethics, and then asked three key questions: (a) "When was the last time you saw a person who seemed to be in need of help?" (b) "When was the last time you stopped to help someone in need?" (c) "Have you had experience helping persons in need? If so, outline briefly." These data were collected as a check on the victim's ratings

of whether subjects who did not stop perceived the situation in the alley as one possibly involving need or not.

When he returned, the experimenter reviewed the subject's questionnaire, and, if no mention was made of the situation in the alley, probed for reactions to it and then phased into an elaborate debriefing and discussion session.

Debriefing

In the debriefing, the subject was told the exact nature of the study, including the deception involved, and the reasons for the deception were explained. The subject's reactions to the victim and to the study in general were discussed. The role of situational determinants of helping behavior was explained in relation to this particular incident and to other experiences of the subject. All subjects seemed readily to understand the necessity for the deception, and none indicated any resentment of it. After debriefing, the subject was thanked for his time and paid, then he left.

RESULTS AND DISCUSSION

Overall Helping Behavior

The average amount of help that a subject offered the victim, by condition, is shown in Table 1. The unequal-N analysis of variance indicates that while the hurry variable was significantly ($F = 3.56$, $df = 2.34$, $p < .05$) related to helping behavior, the message variable was not. Subjects in a hurry were likely to offer less help than were subjects not in a hurry. Whether the subject was going to give a speech on the parable of the Good Samaritan or not did not significantly affect his helping behavior on this analysis.

Other studies have focused on the question of whether a person initiates helping action or not, rather than on scaled kinds of helping. The data from the present study can also be analyzed on the following terms: Of the 40 subjects, 16 (40%) offered some form of direct or indirect aid to the victim (Coding Categories 2–5), 24 (60%) did not (Coding Categories 0 and 1). The percentages of subjects who offered aid by situational variable were, for low hurry, 63%

offered help, intermediate hurry 45%, and high hurry 10%, for helping-relevant message 53%, task-relevant message 29%. With regard to this more general question of whether help was offered or not, an unequal-N analysis of variance (arc sine transformation of percentages of helpers, with low- and intermediate-hurry conditions pooled) indicated that again only the hurry main effect was significantly ($F = 5.22$, $p < .05$) related to helping behavior; the subjects in a hurry were more likely to pass by the victim than were those in less of a hurry.

Reviewing the predictions in the light of these results, the second hypothesis, that the degree of hurry a person is in determines his helping behavior, was supported. The prediction involved in the first hypothesis concerning the message content was based on the parable. The parable itself seemed to suggest that thinking pious thoughts would not increase helping. Another and conflicting prediction might be produced by a norm salience theory. Thinking about the parable should make norms for helping salient and therefore produce more helping. The data, as hypothesized, are more congruent with the prediction drawn from the parable. A person going to speak on the parable of the Good Samaritan is not significantly more likely to stop to help a person by the side of the road than is a person going to talk about possible occupations for seminary graduates.

Since both situational hypotheses are confirmed, it is tempting to stop the analysis of these variables at this point. However, multiple regression analysis procedures were also used to analyze the relationship of all of the independent variables of the study and the helping behavior. In addition to often being more statistically powerful due to the use of more data information, multiple regression analysis has an advantage over analysis of variance in that it allows for a comparison of the relative effect of the various independent variables in accounting for variance in the dependent variable. Also, multiple regression analysis can compare the effects of continuous as well as nominal independent variables on both continuous and nominal dependent variables (through the use of point biserial correlations, r_{pb}) and shows considerable robustness to violation of normality assumptions (Cohen, 1965, 1968). Table 2 reports the results of the multiple regression analysis using both help versus no help and the graded helping scale as dependent measures. In this table the overall equation Fs show the F value of the entire regression equation as a particular row variable enters the equation. Individual variable Fs were computed with all five independent variables in the equation. Although the two situational variables, hurry and message condition, correlated more highly with the dependent measure than any of the religious dispositional variables, only hurry was a significant predictor of whether one will help or not (column 1) or of the overall amount of help given (column 2). These results corroborate the findings of the analysis of variance.[2]

Notice also that neither form of the third hypothesis, that types of religiosity will predict helping, received support from these data. No correlation between the various measures of religiosity and any form of the dependent measure ever came near statistical significance, even though the multiple regression analysis procedure is a powerful and not particularly conservative statistical test.

TABLE 1 / Means and Analysis of Variance of Graded Helping Responses

		M		
		Hurry		Sum-
Message	Low	Medium	High	mary
Helping relevant	3.800	2.000	1.000	2.263
Task relevant	1.667	1.667	.500	1.333
Summary	3.000	1.818	.700	

Analysis of Variance				
Source	SS	df	MS	F
Message (A)	7.766	1	7.766	2.65
Hurry (B)	20.884	2	10.442	3.50*
A x B	5.237	2	2.619	.89
Error	99.633	34	2.930	

Note: N = 40.
*$p < .05$.

Personality Difference among Subjects Who Helped

To further investigate the possible influence of personality variables, analyses were carried out using only the data from subjects who offered some kind of help to the victim. Surprisingly (since the number of these subjects was small, only 16) when this was done, one religiosity variable seemed to be significantly related to the kind of helping behavior offered. (The situational variables had no significant effect.) Subjects high on the religion as quest dimension appear likely, when they stop for the victim, to offer help of a more tentative or incomplete nature than are subjects scoring low on this dimension ($r = -.53, p < .05$).

This result seemed unsettling for the thinking behind either form of Hypothesis 3. Not only do the data suggest that the Allport-Ross-based conception of religion as *end* does not predict the degree of helping, but the religion as quest component is a significant predictor of offering less help. This latter result seems counterintuitive and out of keeping with previous research (Batson, 1971), which found that this type of religiosity correlated positively with other socially valued characteristics. Further data analysis, however, seemed to suggest a different interpretation of this result.

It will be remembered that one helping coding category was added at the suggestion of the victim after his observation of pilot subjects. The correlation of religious personality variables with helping behavior dichotomized between the added category (1) and all of the others (0) was examined. The correlation between religion as quest and this dichotomous helping scale was essentially unchanged ($rpb = -.54, p < .05$). Thus, the previously found correlation between the helping scale and religion as quest seems to reflect the tendency of those who score low on the quest dimension to offer help in the added helping category.

What does help in this added category represent? Within the context of the experiment, it represented an embarrassment. The victim's response to persistent offers of help was to assure the helper he was all right, had taken his medicine, just needed to rest for a minute or so, and, if ultimately necessary, to request the helper to leave. But the *super* helpers in this added category often would not leave until the final appeal was repeated several times by the victim (who was growing increasingly panicky at the possibility of the arrival of the next subject). Since it usually involved the subject's attempting to carry through a preset plan (e.g., taking the subject for a cup of coffee or revealing to him the strength to be found in Christ), and did not allow information from the victim to change that plan, we originally labeled this kind of helping as rigid—an interpretation supported by its increased likelihood among highly doctrinal orthodox subjects

TABLE 2 / Stepwise Multiple Regression Analysis

	Help vs. No Help					Graded Helping			
	Individual Variable		Overall Equation			Individual Variable		Variable Equation	
Step	r [a]	F	R	F	Step	r	F	R	F
1. Hurry[b]	−.37	4.537*	.37	5.884*	1. Hurry	−.42	6.665*	.42	8.196**
2. Message[c]	.25	1.495	.41	3.834*	2. Message	.25	1.719	.46	5.083*
3. Religion as quest	−.03	.081	.42	2.521	3. Religion as quest	−.16	1.297	.50	3.897*
4. Religion as means	−.03	.003	.42	1.838*	4. Religion as means	−.08	.018	.50	2.848*
5. Religion as end	.06	.000	.42	1.430	5. Religion as end	−.07	.001	.50	2.213

Note: $N = 40$. Helping is the dependent variable. $df = 1/34$.
[a]Individual variable correlation coefficient is a point biserial where appropriate.
[b]Variables are listed in order of entry into stepwise regression equations.
[c]Helping-relevant message is positive.
*$p < .05$.
**$p < .01$.

($r = .63, p < .01$). It also seemed to have an inappropriate character. If this more extreme form of helping behavior is indeed effectively less helpful, then the second form of Hypothesis 3 does seem to gain support.

But perhaps it is the experimenters rather than the super helpers who are doing the inappropriate thing; perhaps the best characterization of this kind of helping is as different rather than as inappropriate. This kind of helper seems quickly to place a particular interpretation on the situation, and the helping response seems to follow naturally from this interpretation. All that can safely be said is that one style of helping that emerged in this experiment was directed toward the presumed underlying needs of the victim and was little modified by the victim's comments about his own needs. In contrast, another style was more tentative and seemed more responsive to the victim's statements of his need.

The former kind of helping was likely to be displayed by subjects who expressed strong doctrinal orthodoxy. Conversely, this fixed kind of helping was unlikely among subjects high on the religion as quest dimension. These latter subjects, who conceived their religion as involving an ongoing search for meaning in their personal and social world, seemed more responsive to the victim's immediate needs and more open to the victim's definitions of his own needs.

CONCLUSION AND IMPLICATIONS

A person not in a hurry may stop and offer help to a person in distress. A person in a hurry is likely to keep going. Ironically, he is likely to keep going even if he is hurrying to speak on the parable of the Good Samaritan, thus inadvertently confirming the point of the parable. (Indeed, on several occasions, a seminary student going to give his talk on the parable of the Good Samaritan literally stepped over the victim as he hurried on his way!)

Although the degree to which a person was in a hurry had a clearly significant effect on his likelihood of offering the victim help, whether he was going to give a sermon on the parable or on possible vocational roles of ministers did not. This lack of effect of sermon topic raises certain difficulties for an explanation of helping behavior involving helping norms and their

salience. It is hard to think of a context in which norms concerning helping those in distress are more salient than for a person thinking about the Good Samaritan, and yet it did not significantly increase helping behavior. The results were in the direction suggested by the norm salience hypothesis, but they were not significant. The most accurate conclusion seems to be that salience of helping norms is a less strong determinant of helping behavior in the present situation than many, including the present authors, would expect.

Thinking about the Good Samaritan did not increase helping behavior, but being in a hurry decreased it. It is difficult not to conclude from this that the frequently cited explanation that ethics becomes a luxury as the speed of our daily lives increases is at least an accurate description. The picture that this explanation conveys is of a person seeing another, consciously noting his distress, and consciously choosing to leave him in distress. But perhaps this is not entirely accurate, for, when a person is in a hurry, something seems to happen that is akin to Tolman's (1948) concept of the "narrowing of the cognitive map." Our seminarians in a hurry noticed the victim in that in the postexperiment interview almost all mentioned him as, on reflection, possibly in need of help. But it seems that they often had not worked this out when they were near the victim. Either the interpretation of their visual picture as a person in distress or the empathic reactions usually associated with that interpretation had been deferred because they were hurrying. According to the reflections of some of the subjects, it would be inaccurate to say that they realized the victim's possible distress, then chose to ignore it; instead, because of the time pressures, they did not perceive the scene in the alley as an occasion for an ethical decision.

For other subjects it seems more accurate to conclude that they decided not to stop. They appeared aroused and anxious after the encounter in the alley. For these subjects, what were the elements of the choice that they were making? Why were the seminarians hurrying? Because the experimenter, *whom the subject was helping* was depending on him to get to a particular place quickly. In other words, he was in conflict between stopping to help the victim and continuing on his way to help the experimenter. And this is often true of people in a hurry; they hurry because somebody depends on their being somewhere. Conflict, rather than callousness, can explain their failure to stop.

Finally, as in other studies, personality variables were not useful in predicting whether a person helped or not. But in this study, unlike many previous ones, considerable variations were possible in the kinds of help given, and these variations did relate to personality measures—specifically to religiosity of the quest sort. The clear light of hindsight suggests that the dimension of kinds of helping would have been the appropriate place to look for personality differences all along; *whether* a person helps or not is an instant decision likely to be situationally controlled. How a person helps involves a more complex and considered number of decisions, including the time and scope to permit personality characteristics to shape them.

REFERENCES

Allen, R. O., & Spilka, B. Committed and consensual religion. A specification of religion-prejudice relationships. *Journal for the Scientific Study of Religion,* 1967, *6,* 191–206.

Allport, G. W., & Ross, J. M. Personal religious orientation and prejudice. *Journal of Personality and Social Psychology,* 1967, *5,* 432–443.

Batson, C. D. Creativity and religious development: Toward a structural-functional psychology of religion Unpublished doctoral dissertation, Princeton Theological Seminary, 1971.

Bickman, L. B. The effect of the presence of others on bystander intervention in an emergency. Unpublished doctoral dissertation, City College of the City University of New York, 1969.

Brown, L. B. Classifications of religious orientation. *Journal for the Scientific Study of Religion,* 1964, *4,* 91–99.

Burton, R. V. The generality of honesty reconsidered. *Psychological Review,* 1963, *70,* 481–499.

Cohen, J. Multiple regression as a general data-analytic system. *Psychological Bulletin,* 1968, *70,* 426–443.

Cohen, J. Some statistical issues in psychological research. In B. B. Wolman (Ed.), *Handbook of clinical psychology.*

New York: McGraw-Hill, 1965.

Darley, J. M., & Latané, B. Bystander intervention in emergencies: Diffusion of responsibility. *Journal of Personality and Social Psychology,* 1968, *8,* 377–383.

Freud, S. *The future of an illusion.* New York: Liveright, 1953.

Funk, R. W. *Language, hermeneutic, and word of God.* New York: Harper & Row, 1966.

Glock, C. Y., & Stark, R. *Christian beliefs and anti-Semitism.* New York: Harper & Row, 1966.

Hartshorne, H., & May, M. A. *Studies in the nature of character.* Vol. 1. *Studies in deceit.* New York: Macmillan, 1928.

Korte, C. Group effects on help-giving in an emergency. *Proceedings of the 77th Annual Convention of the American Psychological Association,* 1969, *4,* 383–384. (Summary)

Orne, M. T. On the social psychology of the psychological experiment: With particular reference to demand characteristics and their implications. *American Psychologist,* 1962, *17,* 776–783.

Rosenberg, M. J. When dissonance fails: On eliminating evaluation apprehension from attitude measurement. *Journal of Personality and Social Psychology,* 1965, *1,* 28–42.

Schwartz, S. H., & Clausen, G. T. Responsibility, norms, and helping in an emergency. *Journal of Personality and Social Psychology,* 1970, *16,* 299–310.

Tolman, E. C. Cognitive maps in rats and men. *Psychological Review,* 1948, *55,* 189–208.

ENDNOTES

1. An error was made in randomizing that increased the number of subjects in the intermediate-hurry conditions. This worked against the prediction that was most highly confirmed (the hurry prediction) and made no difference to the message variable tests.
2. To check the legitimacy of the use of both analysis of variance and multiple regression analysis, parametric analyses, on this ordinal data, Kendall rank correlation coefficients were calculated between the helping scale and the five independent variables. As expected t approximated the correlation quite closely in each case and was significant for hurry only (hurry $\tau -.38, p < .001$).

For assistance in conducting this research thanks are due Robert Wells, Beverly Fisher, Mike Shafto, Peter Sheras, Richard Detweiler, and Karen Glasser. The research was funded by National Science Foundation Grant GS-2293.

CRITICAL THINKING QUESTIONS

1. Being prompted to think of the parable of the Good Samaritan did not increase the subjects' helping behavior in this study, but being in a hurry actually decreased it. Suppose that you are in the business of soliciting money for a worthy purpose. What strategies could you use to maximize the money you receive, based on the implications of this study? Explain.

2. *Rush hour,* as the name implies, describes a time of day when people are in a hurry to get to or from work. Do you think that people would be less likely to help someone in need during rush hour than at other times of the day? What about on weekends? Design a study to test this possibility, being sure to address any ethical issues that may be involved.

3. Reading about the Good Samaritan had no impact on subsequent helping behavior. Do you think that reading an article such as this one would change people's helping behavior? Why or why not? Specifically, now that you know that being in a hurry will decrease the likelihood of your giving help, do you think that this awareness will make you more likely to give help in the future, even if you are in a hurry? Why or why not? If simply telling someone about the Good Samaritan was not enough to improve people's helping behavior, what might be more effective?

ADDITIONAL RELATED READINGS

Batson, C. D. (1996). "I've been there, too": Effect of empathy of prior experience with a need. *Personality and Social Psychology Bulletin, 22,* 474–482.

Batson, C. D., Cochran, P., Biederman, M., Blosser, J., Ryan, M., & Vogt, B. (1978). Failure to help when in a hurry: Callousness or conflict? *Personality and Social Psychology Bulletin, 4,* 97–101.

Batson, C. D., Sager, K., Garst, E., & Kang, M. (1997). Is empathy-induced helping due to self-other merging? *Journal of Personality and Social Psychology, 73,* 495–509.

ARTICLE 30 _____

Have you ever worn a perfume or cologne in the belief that it would enhance your attractiveness? The fragrance industry spends millions of dollars in advertising each year to convince us that having a pleasant scent can enhance our appeal. But might fragrance also have other effects on people? For example, can smelling a pleasant fragrance make us more likely to help others in need?

The suggestion that the presence of a fragrance can impact people's helping behavior is not that farfetched. For a number of years, psychologists have documented a variety of environmental factors that affect prosocial behavior. For example, research has indicated that environmental factors such as high temperatures and overcrowding have negative impacts on people's willingness to help. Perhaps how a place smells, which can be considered an environmental factor, can likewise influence helping behavior.

The following article by Robert A. Baron examines the impact of environmental fragrance on prosocial behavior. Specifically, the article tests how pleasant fragrances found at a shopping mall (such as those encountered around food stores) influence people's responses to requests for help. Moreover, the article also seeks to elaborate on the underlying mechanism of the pleasant odor/prosocial behavior connection, examining the possibility that pleasant odors may enhance positive affect, which, in turn, influences prosocial acts. Finally, the article is significant in that it tests the influence of pleasant fragrances on prosocial behavior in a real-world setting, unlike most studies on smell, which are conducted in a laboratory.

The Sweet Smell of . . . Helping
Effects of Pleasant Ambient Fragrance on Prosocial Behavior in Shopping Malls

■ Robert A. Baron

In a preliminary study, passersby in a large shopping mall were significantly more likely to help a same-sex accomplice (by retrieving a dropped pen or providing change for a dollar) when these helping opportunities took place in the presence of pleasant ambient odors (e.g., baking cookies, roasting coffee) than in the absence of such odors. Participants also reported significantly higher levels of positive affect in the presence of pleasant odors. In a second study, the order in which passersby were exposed to a helping opportunity and rated their current mood was systematically varied. Results similar to those of the first study were obtained; order of task had no effect on either mood or helping, but helping was significantly greater in the presence of pleasant fragrances than in their absence.

In addition, there was some evidence that fragrance-induced increments in helping were mediated by increments in positive affect.

Human beings have been using pleasant fragrances since the dawn of civilization. For example, when archaeologists excavate the tombs of Egyptian pharaohs—persons who lived thousands of years ago—they often find jars containing traces of fragrant oils (used for anointing one's body) and various forms of incense—substances that, when burned, release pleasant odors. These two major uses of fragrance have continued until the present. Current magazines are filled with ads for perfumes and colognes, and sales of

Reprinted from R. A. Baron, *Personality and Social Psychology Bulletin, 23,* pp. 498–503, copyright © 1997 by Sage Publications, Inc. Reprinted by permission of Sage Publications, Inc.

devices for releasing pleasant smells into the air have been rising steadily in recent years (Foderaro, 1988). Indeed, the present author has contributed in a small way to this activity. He has patented a device for enhancing indoor environments through air filtration, noise control, and the release of pleasant fragrances (Edwards, 1995).

Do pleasant fragrances actually yield the beneficial effects that many persons assume? This question has recently received increased attention from social psychologists (e.g., DeBono, 1992; Knasko, 1993; Ludvigson & Rottman, 1989; Warm, Dember, & Parasuraman, 1991). In one sense, this growing interest in the potential effects of pleasant odors represents a logical extension of a line of investigation that has continued for more than 20 years in social psychology: efforts to study the effects of environmental variables such as temperature (Anderson, Deuser, & DeNeve, 1995; Baron, 1983a), lighting (Baron, Rea, & Daniels, 1992; Gifford, 1988), noise (Becker et al., 1992), and air quality (Baron, 1987) on social behavior. Within this context, ambient fragrances merely constitute an additional aspect of the physical environment that may, potentially, influence behavior.

However, research on this topic also represents a scientific response to strong claims by aromatherapists and others to the effect that pleasant fragrances exert powerful (one might even say magical) effects on behavior (Tisserand, 1977). Social psychologists interested in effects of the physical environment find such claims disturbing because they rest largely on informal observation rather than systematic data. The present study and several previous experiments on the potential effects of pleasant odors (e.g., Baron & Bronfen, 1994; Baron & Thomley, 1994; Knasko, 1995; Warm et al., 1991) were undertaken to help replace such speculation with scientific knowledge.

Initial research by social psychologists on the effects of pleasant fragrances focused on their use as aids to personal grooming. Such research considered the question of whether individuals could enhance their attractiveness to others through the use of scented products such as perfumes and colognes (Baron, 1981, 1983b, 1986). More recently, researchers have turned their attention to the second use of fragrance noted above: its release into the air as a means of enhancing indoor environments. In this context,

pleasant odors are not associated with a specific person; rather, they are used simply to render indoor environments more pleasant. As noted earlier, research on this topic can be viewed as an extension of previous research on the effects of the physical environment on social behavior (cf. Baron, 1994; Bell, Fisher, Baum, & Green, 1996; Gifford, in press). The results of several recent studies on this topic (e.g., Warm et al., 1991; Dunn, Sleep, & Collett, 1995) indicate that ambient pleasant odors do indeed influence behavior. For example, in two related investigations (Baron & Bronfen, 1994; Baron & Thomley, 1994), participants worked on fairly complex cognitive tasks (forming words from scrambled letters; decoding messages) either in the presence or in the absence of several different odors previously rated as very pleasant by judges. Performance on these tasks was significantly better in the presence of these odors than in their absence. Further, when asked to help either the experimenter (by volunteering to participate in another study without compensation) or another participant, persons who worked in the presence of the pleasant odors showed significantly greater helping both immediately and at a later time (i.e., a higher proportion of persons exposed to pleasant fragrances completed a questionnaire at home on their own time and returned it to the experimenter).

Previous research also suggests one potential mechanism through which ambient fragrances might influence social behavior: by producing mild increments in positive affect. Several findings offer support for this possibility. First, in some recent studies (e.g., Baron & Thomley, 1994), participants exposed to pleasant odors reported higher levels of positive affect than those not exposed to such odors. Similarly, hospital patients exposed to pleasant odors report significantly greater improvements in mood than patients not exposed to such aromas (Dunn et al., 1995). Finally, exposure to pleasant fragrance has been found, in two studies, to increase helping to the same extent as receipt of a small, unexpected gift (Baron & Bronfen, 1994; Baron & Thomley, 1994). Because previous research indicates that receipt of a small gift produces increments in positive affect (cf. Isen, 1987; Spacapan & Oskamp, 1992), these findings suggest, through the method of *converging operations*, that the effects of pleasant odors on social behavior may also stem, at least in part, from fragrance-generated increments in positive affect (Garner, Hake, & Eriksen, 1956).

The present study was designed to both replicate and extend previous findings concerning the effects of pleasant odors on social behavior and to further investigate the possibility that such effects are mediated, to some degree, by fragrance-induced increments in positive affect. Specifically, it sought to determine whether effects similar to those reported in previous laboratory studies would also be obtained in a field setting and with helping tasks different in nature from those employed in previous investigations. To examine these questions, it was necessary to identify field locations where pleasant odors are present and where individuals can engage in spontaneous acts of helping. Shopping malls appeared to meet these requirements. In large malls, numerous businesses release pleasant odors into the air (e.g., bakeries, coffee-roasters, candle and scent retailers). Moreover, the high volume of shoppers provides ample opportunity to measure several forms of spontaneous helping behavior (cf. Levine, Martinez, Brase, & Sorenson, 1994).

On the basis of the studies described above, it was predicted that passersby would experience mild elevations in mood in the presence of pleasant odors and would, therefore, be more likely to engage in acts of spontaneous helping in the presence than in the absence of this environmental variable. To investigate this hypothesis and to establish appropriate methodology, a preliminary study was conducted. In this investigation, 232 passersby at a large shopping mall were exposed to one of two different opportunities to help a stranger: retrieving a pen dropped by an accomplice or providing the accomplice with change for $1. Immediately after exposure to one of these two helping opportunities, participants were approached by a second assistant and asked to rate their current mood on a simple 5-point scale (1 = *very bad,* 5 = *very good*). Results indicated that helping by passersby was significantly increased for both tasks by the presence of pleasant ambient fragrances ($p < .05$ in both instances). Moreover, persons exposed to pleasant fragrances reported being in a significantly more positive mood than persons not exposed to pleasant odors. Interpretation of these findings was rendered somewhat problematic, however, by the fact that in this preliminary study, all participants were first presented with an opportunity to help a stranger and then, after this, were asked to rate their current moods. Previous research indicates that helping others can produce increments in positive affect (e.g., Williamson & Clark, 1989). Thus it is possible that the higher levels of positive affect reported by participants in the pleasant-fragrance condition stemmed from their higher incidence of helping rather than from the presence of pleasant odors. To test this possibility, as well as to replicate the findings of the initial study, a second study—the one reported in detail here—was conducted.

METHOD

Participants and Design

Participants were 116 passersby in a large shopping mall. The study employed a $2 \times 2 \times 2$ factorial design based on the presence or absence of pleasant odors, gender of passersby, and order (mood measure first, helping opportunity second; helping opportunity first, mood measure second).

Overview   Passersby in a large shopping mall were approached by two accomplices of the same gender as themselves. One of these accomplices asked for change for $1. The second accomplice indicated that he or she was conducting a study of the air quality in the mall and then asked participants whether they smelled anything in the air and, if they did, to rate this odor on a 5-point scale ranging from 1 (*unpleasant*) to 5 (*very pleasant*). The second accomplice also asked participants to rate their current mood, again on a 5-point scale (1 = *very bad;* 5 = *very good*). The order in which these two interactions took place was systematically varied so that half of the participants were first asked for help and then asked to rate the air in the mall and their own mood, whereas for the remaining half, the order of these events was reversed.

Permission to collect data was obtained from the mall director. Permission was granted with one restriction: that accomplices approach only persons of the same gender as themselves. (The mall director was concerned that cross-gender requests for help might be perceived as "pick-up" attempts and would thus be annoying to shoppers.) Specific locations where the study would be conducted were identified so that security guards and store managers could be alerted to the presence of the researchers.

Fragrance   Prior to the start of the investigation, the author and several other persons (graduate students and a psychologist) visited the mall to identify areas containing and not containing pleasant odors. Locations with pleasant fragrance were near such businesses as Cinnabon (a bakery), Mrs. Field's Cookies (a bakery), and The Coffee Beanery (a coffee-roasting cafe). In contrast, locations without pleasant fragrance were generally located near clothing stores and similar establishments (e.g., Banana Republic, Nine West, and Chess King). Every effort was made to match locations containing fragrance with locations not containing fragrance in terms of volume of pedestrians, mix of nearby stores, lighting, and proximity to mall entrances. Original plans called for conducting the fragrance and no-fragrance conditions in the same locations at times of the day when the businesses in question were, or were not, emitting pleasant odors. However, this proved to be impossible because detectable odors were present near most of the odor-producing businesses at all hours of the day. For this reason, it proved necessary to conduct the fragrance and no-fragrance conditions in different, but closely matched, locations.

Request for Help and Measures of Helping   The accomplice approached an individual passerby and, showing a $1 bill, asked for change of this bill. Responses to the accomplice's request were scored as *helping* only if the passerby stopped and made change; all other responses (e.g., ignoring the accomplice, indicating verbally that the passerby did not have change) were scored as *no helping*. In all cases, the accomplices approached only passersby of their own gender who were walking toward them alone; passersby who were part of groups were not approached by the accomplices.

The study was conducted in the late morning (11:00 AM to 12:00 noon) and in mid-afternoon (2:00 PM to 4:00 PM) on weekdays. At these times, pedestrian traffic in the mall was moderate, and many passersby were alone rather than in groups.

Because of the questions asked of participants (e.g., "Do you smell anything?"), it was impossible to conceal from accomplices the fact that the study was concerned, in part, with the effects of odors. However, accomplices were unaware of the specific hypothesis under investigation and were carefully trained to behave in an identical manner across conditions and for all participants. Careful, unannounced observation of their behavior by the author confirmed that their behavior did not vary across conditions.

Additional Demographic Data   In addition to gender, observers recorded each participant's apparent age (20–30, 31–40, 41–50, 51–60, 61 and over), ethnic background (Caucasian, African American, Asian, Hispanic, American Indian, Asian Indian, other), and style of dress (very sloppy to formal).

RESULTS

Helping Behavior

To examine the effects of fragrance condition, task order, and gender on helping, a hierarchical loglinear analysis was conducted on the helping data. In this analysis, three variables—fragrance condition, order, and gender—as well as all two-way and three-way interactions between these variables were examined. This analysis employed a backward elimination procedure ($p = .05$). Results indicated that only removal of the main effect for fragrance condition produced a significant χ^2 for the goodness-of-fit test, $\chi^2(1) = 26.13$, $p < .001$. Neither removal of order, $\chi^2(1) = 0.18$, $p > .71$, nor gender, $\chi^2(1) = 0.34$, $p > .085$, produced significant effects, nor did removal of any of the two-way interactions or the three-way interaction produce significant effects. These findings indicate that a higher proportion of passersby helped the accomplice when pleasant fragrances were present than when they were absent and that this was true for both female and male passersby and occurred regardless of the order in which participants in the study were exposed to the helping request and asked to rate their current moods. The proportion of individuals who helped the accomplice in each condition is shown in Table 1.

TABLE 1 / Percentage of Passersby Who Helped the Accomplice as a Function of Presence of Pleasant Fragrance, Order, and Gender

	No Fragrance		Fragrance	
	Helping First	Mood First	Helping First	Mood First
Males	22.22	25.00	45.45	61.11
Females	16.67	12.50	60.87	59.09

Mood

An ANOVA in which fragrance, gender of participants, and order were the independent variables was performed on the data for self-reported mood. This analysis yielded one significant effect, that for fragrance condition, $F(1, 114) = 7.95$, $p < .01$. Participants exposed to pleasant fragrance reported higher levels of positive affect ($M = 4.11$) than those not exposed to pleasant fragrance ($M = 3.81$). No other effects in the analysis were significant.

Potential Mediating Role of Positive Affect

To examine the potential mediating role of positive affect (mood) with respect to the effects of pleasant fragrance on helping, procedures recommended by Baron and Kenny (1986) were adopted. These procedures involved a series of regression analyses. In the first, the proposed mediator (self-reported mood) was regressed on the independent variable (fragrance). In the second, the dependent variable (helping) was regressed on the independent variable (fragrance). Finally, in the third, the dependent variable (helping) was regressed on both the independent variable (fragrance) and the mediator (affect). According to Baron and Kenny, there would be evidence of mediation if the following findings emerged: (a) the independent variable affected the mediator in the first equation, (b) the independent variable affected the dependent variable in the second analysis, and (c) the mediator affected the dependent variable in the third equation, whereas the effect of the independent variable was reduced relative to the second analysis.

The results of these analyses indicated that fragrance condition was a significant predictor of mood ($\beta = -.253$, $t = -2.90$, $p < .005$) and was also a significant predictor of helping ($\beta = .119$, $t = 2.13$, $p < .05$). However, when the mediator (mood) was entered into the regression equation along with fragrance condition, fragrance condition was no longer a significant predictor of helping ($\beta = .158$ $t = 1.74$, $p > .08$). In other words, as required by the Baron and Kenny (1986) procedures, the effect of fragrance on the dependent variable was reduced relative to the second equation. Together, these findings offer some support for the suggestion that positive affect (i.e., current mood) mediates the effects of pleasant fragrance on helping. However, once again, this evidence should be interpreted with a degree of caution.

Participants' Awareness of Ambient Fragrance

Among participants in the fragrance condition, 64.4% reported smelling a fragrance. Among those in the no-fragrance condition, 35.6% reported smelling a fragrance, $\chi^2(1) = 4.93$, $p < .03$. Thus it appeared that participants were differentially aware of ambient fragrance in the two conditions.

Demographic Variables

A large majority of the shoppers were Caucasian, relatively young, and casually dressed. Analyses were performed to examine the potential effects of ethnic background, age, and style of dress on helping. None of these analyses yielded significant effects. Thus it appeared that within the limits imposed by the demographic characteristics of shoppers at this mall, the pleasant ambient fragrances exerted similar effects on passersby regardless of their ethnic background, age, or style of dress.

DISCUSSION

The present findings serve to replicate and extend those reported in previous research (e.g., Baron &

Bronfen, 1994; Baron & Thomley, 1994; Warm et al., 1991). As in earlier studies, pleasant odors in the air significantly influenced the behavior of participants. Specifically, passersby were more likely to help the accomplice when pleasant fragrances were present in the air than when they were absent. These findings were obtained in a field setting—a busy shopping mall—with tasks quite different from those employed in previous research. Moreover, they occurred regardless of the order in which participants were exposed to a helping opportunity and rated their current mood. Together, these findings suggest that the effects of pleasant ambient fragrances on behavior may be quite general in scope—that is, they may occur in a wide range of settings.

The present findings also provide additional support, albeit far from conclusive, for the suggestion that the effects of pleasant fragrances on social behavior stem, at least in part, from fragrance-induced increments in positive affect. Support for this suggestion is provided by the results of the regression analyses conducted in accordance with the Baron and Kenny (1986) model for testing mediating effects. These analyses indicated that fragrance condition was a significant predictor of current self-reported mood and a significant predictor of helping. However, this was no longer the case when mood was added to the regression equation. Although these results are consistent with the reasoning of the Baron and Kenny model, they should be interpreted with caution pending the collection of additional data. It should also be emphasized, once again, that there is no intention here of suggesting that affective states are the only potential mediator of pleasant fragrances. On the contrary, recent studies on the behavioral effects of fragrance suggest that other factors, too, may play a role (e.g., Knasko, 1993). Thus further research is clearly needed to obtain full understanding of the mechanisms through which pleasant fragrances influence behavior. What does seem clear from the present and previous findings, however, is that this environmental variable can indeed produce significant effects on some forms of social behavior.

At this point, it should be noted that the present findings are consistent with predictions derived from a model of the influence of affective states on social judgment proposed by Forgas (1995). According to

this affect infusion model, the extent to which affective states influence social judgments—and, therefore, many forms of social behavior—is partly a function of the processing demands of a given situation. According to this model, when individuals can make decisions on the basis of previously formed judgments or make them in accordance with strong motivational pressures to reach particular judgments, the potential for affect infusion is low: The impact of current affective states on such judgments will be minimal (Forgas, 1995, pp. 46–47). In contrast, when individuals engage in more substantive processing, the potential for affect infusion is greater. One set of conditions under which affect infusion is expected to occur is described by Forgas (1995, p. 47) as involving *heuristic processing*. In such situations individuals have neither prior evaluations nor strong motivational goals but do wish to make judgments as quickly and effortlessly as possible because they do not view the decisions as important or as requiring high levels of accuracy and because they have limited time at their disposal. In such situations, Forgas suggests, the potential for affect infusion is great.

It can be argued that this is precisely the kind of situation confronted by passersby in the present research: They were approached by an individual who made a simple and relatively uncontroversial request; the decision as to whether to help this person was not an important one; and passersby, who were all walking toward some destination, may have experienced at least moderate time pressures. According to the affect infusion model, this situation was one in which affect elicited by unrelated conditions or events (in this case by pleasant fragrances) could readily influence judgments about whether to help the accomplice. Indeed, in describing situations involving heuristic processing, Forgas (1995, p. 47) specifically calls attention to the potential impact of environmental variables that can influence affective states—for example, uncomfortably high temperatures.

In short, the affect infusion model provides one useful framework for interpreting the finding that pleasant fragrances influenced helping in the present research. In addition, this theoretical framework suggests future studies that could shed additional light on the potential role of positive affect as a mediator of such effects. According to the affect infusion model, pleasant fragrances (or other environmental variables) would be less likely to influence judgments and behavior in situations in which individuals can draw on previously formed judgments about helping. For example, in the present context, the impact of pleasant fragrances might be reduced if the person in need of help appeared to be either especially deserving of assistance (e.g., a child, a handicapped person) or especially undeserving of help (e.g., a person who appeared to be drunk or on drugs). Under these conditions, most persons would have previously formed judgments about helping—strongly favorable in the first instance, strongly unfavorable in the latter case. According to the affect infusion model, positive affect from other sources (e.g., pleasant fragrances) would be less likely to influence their tendency to help under these conditions.

In contrast, the potential for affect infusion would be considerably greater in situations in which passersby were required to engage in substantive processing—for instance, if they were asked to respond to survey questions dealing with important aspects of their personal lives or attitudes they view as important (Forgas, 1995). These and other predictions derived from the affect infusion model can be readily tested in further research. The results of such studies may well yield further evidence on the potential mediating role of positive affect with respect to the effects of pleasant fragrances on social behavior and social judgments.

REFERENCES

Anderson, C. A., Deuser, W. E., & DeNeve, K. M. (1995). Hot temperatures, hostile affect, hostile cognition, and arousal: Tests of a general model of affective aggression. *Personality and Social Psychology Bulletin, 21,* 434–448.

Baron, R. A. (1981). The role of olfaction in human social behavior: Effects of a pleasant scent on attraction and social perception. *Personality and Social Psychology Bulletin, 7,* 611–617.

Baron, R. A. (1983a). Aggression and heat: The "long hot summer" revisited. In A. Baum, S. Valins, & J. E. Singer (Eds.), *Advances in environmental research* (Vol. 1, pp. 173–196). Hillsdale, NJ: Lawrence Erlbaum.

Baron, R. A. (1983b). The "sweet smell of success"? The impact of pleasant artificial scents (perfume or cologne) on evaluations of job applications. *Journal of Applied Psychology, 68,* 709–713.

Baron, R. A. (1986). Self-presentation in job interviews: When there can be "too much of a good thing." *Journal of Applied Social Psychology, 16,* 16–28.

Baron, R. A. (1987). Effects of negative air ions on interpersonal attraction: Evidence for intensification effects. *Journal of Personality and Social Psychology, 52,* 547–553.

Baron, R. A. (1994). The physical environment of work settings: Effects on task performance, interpersonal relations, and job satisfaction. In B. M. Staw & L. L. Cummings (Eds.), *Research in organizational behavior* (Vol. 16, pp. 1–46). Greenwich, CT: JAI.

Baron, R. A., & Bronfen, M. I. (1994). A whiff of reality: Empirical evidence concerning the effects of pleasant fragrances on work-related behavior. *Journal of Applied Social Psychology, 24,* 1179–1203.

Baron, R. A., Rea, M. S., & Daniels, S. G. (1992). Effects of indoor lighting (illuminance and spectral distribution) on the performance of cognitive tasks and interpersonal behavior: The potential mediating role of positive affect. *Motivation and Emotion, 16,* 1–33.

Baron, R. A., & Thomley, J. (1994). A whiff of reality: Positive affect as a potential mediator of the effects of pleasant fragrances on task performance and helping. *Environment and Behavior, 26,* 766–784.

Baron, R. M., & Kenny, D. A. (1986). The mediator-moderator variable distinction in social psychological research: Conceptual, strategic, and statistical considerations. *Journal of Personality and Social Psychology, 51,* 1173–1192.

Becker, A. B., Warm, J. S., Dember, W. N., Sparnall, J., DeRonde, L., & Hancock, P. A. (1992). Effects of aircraft noise on vigilance performance and perceived workload. *Proceedings of the Human Factors Society, 35,* 1513–1517.

Bell, P. A., Fisher, J. D., Baum, A., & Green, T. E. (1996). *Environmental psychology* (4th ed.). New York: Holt, Rinehart, & Winston.

DeBono, K G. (1992). Pleasant scents and persuasion: An information processing approach. *Journal of Applied Social Psychology, 22,* 910–919.

Dunn, C., Sleep, J., & Collett, D. (1995). Sensing an improvement: An experimental study to evaluate the use of aromatherapy, massage, and periods of rest in an intensive care unit. *Journal of Advanced Nursing, 21,* 34–40.

Edwards, R. (1995). Pleasant aromas chase away those bitter moods. *APA Monitor, 26*(3), 20.

Foderaro, L. W. (1988, February 4). The fragrant house: An expanding market for every mood. *The New York Times,* pp. C1, C10.

Forgas, J. P. (1995). The affect infusion model (AIM): Review and an integrative theory of mood judgments. *Psychological Bulletin, 117,* 39–66.

Garner, W. R., Hake, H. W., & Eriksen, C. W. (1956). Operationism and the concept of perception. *Psychological Review, 63,* 149–159.

Gifford, R. (1988). Light, decor, arousal, comfort, and communication. *Journal of Environmental Psychology, 8,* 177–189.

Gifford, R. (in press). *Environmental psychology: Principles and practice* (2nd ed.). Boston: Allyn & Bacon.

Isen, A. M. (1987). Positive affect, cognitive processes, and social behavior. In L. Berkowitz (Ed.), *Advances in experimental social psychology* (Vol. 20, pp. 203–253). New York: Academic Press.

Knasko, S. C. (1993). Performance, mood, and health during exposure to intermittent odors. *Archives of Environmental Health, 48,* 305–308.

Knasko, S. C. (1995). *The behavior and perceptions of museum visitors: Effects of ambient-odor congruency and hedonics.* Unpublished manuscript, Monell Chemical Senses Center, Philadelphia, PA.

Levine, R. V., Martinez, T. S., Brase, G., & Sorenson, K. (1994). Helping in 36 U.S. cities. *Journal of Personality and Social Psychology, 67,* 69–82.

Ludvigson, H. W., & Rottman, T. R. (1989). Effects of ambient odors of lavender and cloves on cognition, memory, affect, and mood. *Chemical Senses, 14,* 525–536.

Spacapan, S., & Oskamp, S. (Eds.). (1992). *Helping and being helped.* Newbury Park, CA: Sage.

Tisserand, R. A. (1977). *The art of aromatherapy.* Rochester, VT: Healing Arts.

Warm, J. S., Dember, W. N., & Parasuraman, R. (1991). Effects of olfactory stimulation on performance and stress in a visual sustained attention task. *Journal of the Society of Cosmetic Chemists, 42,* 199–210.

Williamson, G. M., & Clark, M. S. (1989). Providing help and desired relationship type as determinants of changes in mood and self-evaluation. *Journal of Personality and Social Psychology, 56,* 722–734.

Author's Note: I wish to express my sincere appreciation to Preshant Desai, Karen Graham, Jackie Higgins, Jan Ketchum, David Lohrman, Janice Methé, Eric Mastriani, Darren Mansfield, Cynthia Munoz, Jessica Simonds, Nacole Simonds, and David Soler for their able assistance in collection of the data. I also wish to express my sincere appreciation to Mr. Charles Breidenbach, director of Crossgates Mall, for his kind permission to conduct this research. Finally, I wish to thank several anonymous reviewers, and especially the editor, Jack Dovidio, for exceptionally helpful comments and suggestions.

CRITICAL THINKING QUESTIONS

1. All of the pleasant fragrances employed in the study were food related. Do you think it is possible that the findings were somehow influenced by an association of fragrance with food? In other words, would pleasant smells generated by perfumes or scented candles produce the same effects? Design a study to test this possibility.

2. Design a further study to test the predictions derived from the *affect infusion model* discussed in the article.

3. Would the presence of pleasant smells influence prosocial behaviors of greater consequence than giving someone change—say, helping someone in an emergency situation? Why or why not? Explain.

4. In what other real-world settings might fragrance have an impact on prosocial behavior? How could these possibilities be tested?

5. In recent years, several manufacturers have marketed human *pheromes,* claiming that these substances have a powerful effect on attraction between people. Design a study to test whether pheromes (or indeed, any perfume) actually can impact people.

Chapter Eleven

AGGRESSION

Pɪᴄᴋ ᴜᴘ ᴀ ᴄᴏᴘʏ of today's newspaper. How much of it concerns acts of violence, whether from war, terrorism, homicide, or domestic violence? Aggression seems to be a fairly common part of modern life.

Now think about your own experiences. Chances are, you have not directly experienced a murder or assault. But what other types of aggressive behavior have you witnessed? Have you seen verbal aggression, where the intention was to hurt another person's feelings? Have you experienced cruelty in one form or another, where pain was experienced, even though no blood was shed?

Must aggression be part of life? Is it simply human nature and consequently something that cannot be changed? Or is it possible that the amount of aggression in the world could be reduced, if not actually eliminated?

Article 31, "Televised Violence and Kids," reports on long-term studies that indicate that watching violent television programs as children is a strong predictor of being aggressive as adults. However, the aggressive behavior of adults who watch the same types of violent programs may not be affected by the programs' content.

In contrast, Article 32, "Transmission of Aggression through Imitation of Aggressive Models," represents one of the earliest studies demonstrating that aggression is learned and in particular that the violence portrayed on television may contribute to aggressiveness in children. Since many behavioral patterns, such as aggression, may be learned in childhood, knowledge about what contributes to aggression can be used to help reduce those very behaviors.

Finally, Article 33 underscores the idea that aggression is not a single concept but refers to many different forms of behavior. "Cross-Cultural Evidence of Female Indirect Aggression" examines how boys and girls from four countries express aggression in different forms. This article also may have some implications for the question of whether aggression (or at least the form it takes) is simply part of human nature.

ARTICLE 31 _____

What causes aggression? Psychologists have asked that question for nearly a century now. In their search for an answer, several theoretical perspectives have emerged.

One such perspective holds that aggression is an innate tendency, something toward which people are biologically predisposed. This view, espoused by theorists such as Sigmund Freud, maintains that people periodically need to discharge a natural buildup of aggressive energy. Thus, human aggressiveness may be a normal and perhaps unavoidable fact of life.

A second view suggests that aggression is a drive to harm someone elicited by some external stimulus. In other words, certain external conditions, such as frustration, produce a tendency for people to want to harm or injure others.

Other theories of aggression maintain that aggressive behavior is purely the product of social learning. People are aggressive because they have *learned* how to be aggressive, perhaps by watching other people act in such a fashion.

Given these different theoretical perspectives on aggression, ask yourself these questions: If you were a parent and did not want your child to become an aggressive, hostile adult, what would you do? For example, if your child liked to watch television programs with a lot of violent content or to play video games that involved make-believe killing, would you discourage or limit such entertainment? Or would you allow it and perhaps even encourage it, since aggression is a natural human impulse that needs to be expressed in some fashion?

The following article from the *ISR Newsletter* discusses the work of Leonard Eron and L. Rowell Huesmann on the impact of viewing television programs on subsequent aggression. A unique feature of the research described in the article is that it is *longitudinal,* having tracked the subjects for more than a decade. As it turns out, children's television viewing of aggression did strongly correlate with their displaying aggressive behavior later in life. However, the amount of viewing of aggressive programs as adults seemed to have little influence on subsequent aggressive behavior.

Televised Violence and Kids
A Public Health Problem?
■ from *ISR Newsletter*

When Leonard Eron surveyed every 8-year-old child in Columbia County, New York, in 1960, he found something he wasn't looking for: an astonishing, and unmistakable, correlation between the amount of violence the youngsters saw on television and the aggressiveness of their behavior.

More than three decades and two follow-up studies later, after several related research projects and countless hearings and conferences, the work of Eron and his ISR colleague, L. Rowell Huesmann, has become an "overnight sensation." As leading researchers on the effects of media violence on the young, they have been making the rounds of TV talk and news programs and radio call-in shows, while fielding almost daily calls from reporters.

Their message is ultimately a simple one: Aggression is a learned behavior, it is learned at an early age, and media violence is one of its teachers. But because

Reprinted from *ISR Newsletter,* Vol. 18, No. 1, February 1994, pp. 5–7. © 1994 by the Regents of the University of Michigan Institute for Social Research. Reprinted by permission.

it is a learned behavior, there is hope that it can be unlearned, or never taught in the first place.

Both Eron and Huesmann are professors of psychology at the University of Michigan and research scientists at ISR's Research Center for Group Dynamics. Huesmann is also a professor of communication and acting chair of the Department of Communication. Their talents and interests have complemented each other since they met at Yale in the early 1970s. Eron's research interest is aggression, while Huesmann, who minored in mathematics as a U-M undergraduate in the early '60s, brings his prowess in data analysis and expertise in cognitive mechanisms and development to the team.

"I wanted to measure childrearing practices as they related to aggression" in the 1960 survey, says Eron. "The parents knew what the study was about and, in the interviews, we were asking sensitive questions about how parents punished their children, what their disagreements were, and so forth. So we wanted to buffer those with what we called 'Ladies' Home Journal' questions—Had they read Dr. Spock? How often did their child watch TV? What were his or her favorite shows?

"But the computer was unaware of our humor and analyzed those TV programs," he adds. "And, lo and behold, the more aggressive that kids were in school, the higher the violence content of the shows they watched."

But that still left the chicken-and-egg ambiguity. Did watching violent TV make kids more aggressive, or did more aggressive kids watch violent TV?

That's where time, and Huesmann, came in. In 1970, the U.S. Surgeon General formed a committee on television and social behavior, and asked Eron to re-survey as many of the Columbia County kids as he could find. Eron, in turn, sought the services of Huesmann, then an assistant professor at Yale.

"The analysis of long-term data on children's behavior required some sophisticated mathematical and statistical analysis," says Huesmann, "and that was the area in which I was trained."

The project also struck another responsive chord, he says: "The models that had been advanced to explain the long-term effects of television violence were lacking an explanation of how the effects of watching television violence could last way into adulthood."

So it was back to the Hudson Valley of upstate New York in 1971. They found about 500 of the now 19-year-olds from the original sample of 875 youngsters. The results were just as powerful, if not more so.

"The correlation between violence-viewing at age 8 and how aggressive the individual was at 19 was higher than the correlation between watching violence at age 8 and behaving aggressively at age 8," says Eron. "There was no correlation between violence-viewing at age 19 and aggressiveness at 19. It seems there was a cumulative effect going on here."

Its persistence was documented once more in 1981, when 400 of the subjects were surveyed again, along with 80 of their offspring. The 30-year-old men who had been the most aggressive when they were 8 had more arrests for drunk driving, more arrests for violent crime, were more abusive to their spouses . . . and had more aggressive children. And of the 600 subjects whose criminal justice records were reviewed, those who watched more violence on TV when they were 8 had been arrested more often for violent crimes, and self-reported more fights when consuming alcohol.

In other words, their viewing choices and behavior as 8-year-olds were better predictors of their behavior at age 30 than either what they watched on TV or how aggressively they behaved later in life.

"Children learn programs for how to behave that I call scripts," says Huesmann. "In a new social situation, how do you know how to behave? You search for scripts to follow. Where is a likely place for those scripts to come from? From what you've observed others doing in life, films, TV. So, as a child, you see a Dirty Harry movie, where the heroic policeman is shooting people right and left. Even years later, the right kind of scene can trigger that script and suggest a way to behave that follows it. Our studies have come up with a lot of evidence that suggests that's very possible. Moreover, we find that watching TV violence affects the viewer's beliefs and attitudes about how people are going to behave."

The longitudinal data were so compelling that the 1993 report of the American Psychological Association's Commission on Violence and Youth, which Eron chaired, stated unequivocally that there is "absolutely no doubt that higher levels of viewing violence on television are correlated with increased acceptance of aggressive attitudes and increased aggressive behavior."

"The evidence is overwhelming," says Eron. "The strength of the relationship is the same as cigarettes causing lung cancer. Is there any doubt about that?"

Only among those who profit from tobacco, just as TV and movie industry executives have generated most of the criticism of the ISR colleagues' work. While the media in general were fascinated by the damning data, especially after the APA report was released last August, the visual media in particular were equally eager to defend themselves and defuse the evidence.

This is not a message the industry wants to hear. Its position is that the off-on switch is the ultimate defense, and parents wield it. Eron says that's unrealistic.

"Parents can't do it all by themselves, especially in these days of single-parent families and two parents working," he says. "They can't be with their children all the time."

If the industry can't or won't regulate itself, should the government intervene? It's an obvious question to ask and a difficult one to answer, especially for believers in the First Amendment.

"The scientific evidence clearly shows that long-term exposure to TV violence makes kids behave more aggressively," says Huesmann, "but it doesn't show the same effect on adults. What you watch now won't have nearly the effect of what you saw when you were 8. What we're talking about is regulating what kids see, not adults, and there are reasonable precedents for this—alcohol and tobacco regulations, for example."

In their view, watching TV violence is every bit as dangerous to kids as smoking and drinking. They see it as a matter of public health, not free speech. And they are grimly amused by the industry's protestations of exculpability. "How can they say their programs have no effect on behavior when they're in the business of selling ads?" Eron asks.

Then there are those who wonder how it is that Detroit and Windsor, Ontario, which face each other across the Detroit River and receive the same TV signals, have such disparate crime rates. "If we said TV violence is the only cause, then they'd have an argument," says Eron. "But we don't say that."

They are, in fact, well aware that any number of psychological, physiological and macro-social factors are simmering in the stew of violence. "TV is really a minor part of our research," says Eron, "although it's gotten the most play. We're interested in how children learn aggression. Violence on TV is only one cause, but it's a cause we can do something about."

Two projects they are currently involved in show signs of making progress toward that end. Huesmann is directing the second phase of a study begun in 1977 that looks, he says, at "whether the effects of media violence generalize across different countries and cultures."

Researchers are collecting longitudinal data on subjects in Poland, Australia, Finland and Israel, as well as the United States. Meanwhile, Eron, Huesmann and three researchers at the University of Illinois (where Huesmann spent 20 years before returning to U-M in 1992) are conducting an ambitious study of inner-city schools "in which we are trying to change the whole school atmosphere," says Eron.

In the former study, almost 2,000 children were interviewed and tested in either first or third grade and for two consecutive years thereafter. "In all countries, the children who watched more violence were the more aggressive," says Huesmann. "This was a study showing that this was a real effect across countries and not a special, one-time study of Columbia County."

The only exceptions were found in Australia and Israel. In Australia, there was a correlation between watching violence and behaving aggressively, but it was not as persistent as in other countries. In Israel, the correlation was stronger for city-raised children than for those growing up in kibbutzes. Huesmann suspects that the communal nature of the kibbutz, with its attendant reinforcement of pro-social behaviors, neutralized the effect of televised violence. And Australia? "We have no good explanation," he says.

Perhaps the second phase, revisiting subjects who are now in their early 20s, will provide one. Interviewing is almost complete in the United States and Finland and began in Poland this winter as one of the collaborative projects between ISR and ISS [Institute for Social Studies], its Polish sibling. Work will begin in Israel near the end of 1994.

The project in Illinois attempts to measure the relative influence of multiple contexts, including schools, peers, families, and neighborhoods, and the cost-effectiveness of targeting each. "This is a public health model," says Eron, "from primary prevention to tertiary prevention."

Both teachers and students will be taught techniques for handling aggression and solving problems. Youngsters who are believed to be at high risk for becoming aggressive will also be seen in groups of six by research staffers. And half of those youngsters will receive family therapy as well, what Eron calls "an increased dosage" of treatment.

"We don't think just working with kids in the schools will help much," Eron says. "Studies show kids change attitudes, but there's no data to show they change behavior. In this program, we're trying to change the whole school atmosphere. We're also trying to see what the cost-effectiveness is. Is it enough to have a school program? Or do you always have to do family therapy, which is the most costly? Does it really add to the effectiveness of the treatment?"

The problem clearly isn't simple, but some of the data are nonetheless clear. "Over the years, Rowell and I have testified at many congressional hearings," says Eron, "and now it's having an effect. The public sentiment is there's too much of this stuff, and we've got the data to show it. I think we are having an impact, finally."

Eron himself estimates that TV is only responsible for perhaps 10% of the violent behavior in this country. "But," he says, "if we could reduce violence by 10%, that would be a great achievement."

CRITICAL THINKING QUESTIONS

1. People concerned with freedom of expression may object to the idea of the government regulating violent television content. What do you think of the contention stated in the article that aggression is a public health problem, so the government should do whatever it can to eliminate it, just as it does with other public health problems, such as smoking and drinking?

2. The so-called *v-chip* is a device that can be installed in a television and activated to block violent television programs from being received. Is this an effective solution to the problem of children being exposed to media violence? Why or why not?

3. Do you think that playing video games with violent characters and scenarios has the same impact on children as watching violent television programs? Why or why not? Design a study to test whether the two media have different effects on the aggressiveness of children.

4. Leonard Eron stated in the article that "TV is only responsible for perhaps 10% of the violent behavior in this country." Based on your observations and readings, what do you think accounts for the other 90%? Besides limiting or eliminating violent television programs, what, if anything, can be done to reduce the amount of violence in society? Explain your answers.

ARTICLE 32 _____

Think of the amount of time that a typical child spends in front of the television. Do you think that what that child sees on "the tube" influences his or her behavior to a great extent? Or is television more neutral—just entertainment with no lasting effects?

A major concern of parents and social psychologists alike is the impact of one particular aspect of television on children's subsequent behavior: aggression. If you have not done so in a long time, sit down and watch the Saturday morning cartoons or other programs shown after school or in the early evening, when children are most likely to be watching. How many of these programs involve some sort of violence? What are these shows teaching children, not only in terms of behaviors but also in terms of values?

The following article by Albert Bandura, Dorothea Ross, and Sheila A. Ross was one of the earliest studies to examine the impact of televised aggression on the behavior of children. In the more than 30 years since its publication, numerous other experiments have been conducted on the same topic. Article 31 provided some of the more recent evidence for the connection between children's viewing television violence and subsequently displaying aggressive behavior. Many additional studies also strongly suggest that viewing televised aggression has a direct impact on the aggressive behavior of its viewers. The research by Bandura and his colleagues helped initiate this important line of research.

Transmission of Aggression through Imitation of Aggressive Models[1]

■ Albert Bandura, Dorothea Ross, and Sheila A. Ross[2]

A previous study, designed to account for the phenomenon of identification in terms of incidental learning, demonstrated that children readily imitated behavior exhibited by an adult model in the presence of the model (Bandura & Huston, 1961). A series of experiments by Blake (1958) and others (Grosser, Polansky, & Lippitt, 1951; Rosenblith, 1959; Schachter & Hall, 1952) have likewise shown that mere observation of responses of a model has a facilitating effect on subjects' reactions in the immediate social influence setting.

While these studies provide convincing evidence for the influence and control exerted on others by the behavior of a model, a more crucial test of imitative learning involves the generalization of imitative response patterns to new settings in which the model is absent.

In the experiment reported in this paper, children were exposed to aggressive and nonaggressive adult models and were then tested for amount of imitative learning in a new situation in the absence of the model. According to the prediction, subjects exposed to aggressive models would reproduce aggressive acts resembling those of their models and would differ in this respect both from subjects who observed nonaggressive models and from who had no prior exposure to any models. This hypothesis assumed that subjects had learned imitative habits as a result of prior reinforcement, and these tendencies would generalize to some extent to adult experimenters (Miller & Dollard, 1941).

It was further predicted that observation of subdued nonaggressive models would have a generalized inhibiting effect on the subjects' subsequent behavior,

Reprinted from *Journal of Abnormal and Social Psychology*, 1961, *63*, 575–583.

and this effect would be reflected in a difference between the nonaggressive and the control groups, with subjects in the latter group displaying significantly more aggression.

Hypotheses were also advanced concerning the influence of the sex of model and sex of subjects on imitation. Fauls and Smith (1956) have shown that preschool children perceive their parents as having distinct preferences regarding sex appropriate modes of behavior for their children. Their findings, as well as informal observation, suggest that parents reward imitation of sex appropriate behavior and discourage or punish sex inappropriate imitative responses, e.g., a male child is unlikely to receive much reward for performing female appropriate activities, such as cooking, or for adopting other aspects of the maternal role, but these same behaviors are typically welcomed if performed by females. As a result of differing reinforcement histories, tendencies to imitate male and female models thus acquire differential habit strength. One would expect, on this basis, subjects to imitate the behavior of a same-sex model to a greater degree than a model of the opposite sex.

Since aggression, however, is a highly masculine-typed behavior, boys should be more predisposed than girls toward imitating aggression, the difference being most marked for subjects exposed to the male aggressive model.

METHOD

Subjects

The subjects were 36 boys and 36 girls enrolled in the Stanford University Nursery School. They ranged in age from 37 to 69 months, with a mean age of 52 months.

Two adults, a male and a female, served in the role of model, and one female experimenter conducted the study for all 72 children.

Experimental Design

Subjects were divided into eight experimental groups of six subjects each and a control group consisting of 24 subjects. Half the experimental subjects were exposed to aggressive models and half were exposed to models that were subdued and nonaggressive in their behavior. These groups were further subdivided into male and female subjects. Half the subjects in the aggressive and nonaggressive conditions observed same-sex models, while the remaining subjects in each group viewed models of the opposite sex. The control group had no prior exposure to the adult models and was tested only in the generalization situation.

It seemed reasonable to expect that the subjects' level of aggressiveness would be positively related to the readiness with which they imitated aggressive modes of behavior. Therefore, in order to increase the precision of treatment comparisons, subjects in the experimental and control groups were matched individually on the basis of ratings of their aggressive behavior in social interactions in the nursery school.

The subjects were rated on four five-point rating scales by the experimenter and a nursery school teacher, both of whom were well acquainted with the children. These scales measured the extent to which subjects displayed physical aggression, verbal aggression, aggression toward inanimate objects, and aggressive inhibition. The latter scale, which dealt with the subjects' tendency to inhibit aggressive reactions in the face of high instigation, provided a measure of aggression anxiety.

Fifty-one subjects were rated independently by both judges so as to permit an assessment of interrater agreement. The reliability of the composite aggression score, estimated by means of the Pearson product-moment correlation, was .89.

The composite score was obtained by summing the ratings on the four aggression scales; on the basis of these scores, subjects were arranged in triplets and assigned at random to one of two treatment conditions or to the control group.

Experimental Conditions

In the first step in the procedure subjects were brought individually by the experimenter to the experimental room and the model who was in the hallway outside the room was invited by the experimenter to come and join in the game. The experimenter then escorted the subject to one corner of the room, which was structured as the subject's play area. After seating the child at a small table, the experimenter demonstrated how the subject could design pictures with potato prints and picture stickers provided. The potato prints included a variety of geometrical forms; the stickers were attractive multicolor pictures of animals, flowers, and western figures to be pasted on a pastoral scene. These activities were selected since they had been established, by previous studies in the nursery school, as having high interest value for the children.

After having settled the subject in his corner, the experimenter escorted the model to the opposite corner of the room which contained a small table and chair, a tinker toy set, a mallet, and a 5-foot inflated Bobo doll. The experimenter explained that these were the materials provided for the model to play with and, after the model was seated, the experimenter left the experimental room.

With subjects in the *nonaggressive condition,* the model assembled the tinker toys in a quiet subdued manner totally ignoring the Bobo doll.

In contrast, with subjects in the *aggressive condition,* the model began by assembling the tinker toys but after approximately a minute had elapsed, the model turned to the Bobo doll and spent the remainder of the period aggressing toward it.

Imitative learning can be clearly demonstrated if a model performs sufficiently novel patterns of responses which are unlikely to occur independently of the observation of the behavior of a model and if a subject reproduces these behaviors in substantially identical form. For this reason, in addition to punching the Bobo doll, a response that is likely to be performed by children independently of a demonstration, the model exhibited distinctive aggressive acts which were to be scored as imitative responses. The model laid Bobo on its side, sat on it and punched it repeatedly in the nose. The model then raised the Bobo doll, picked up the mallet and struck the doll on the head. Following the mallet aggression, the model tossed the doll up in the air aggressively and kicked it about the room. This sequence of physically aggressive acts was repeated approximately three times, interspersed with verbally aggressive responses such as "Sock him in the nose . . . ," "Hit him down . . . ," "Throw him in the air . . . ," "Kick him . . . ," "Pow . . . ," and two nonaggressive comments, "He keeps coming back for more" and "He sure is a tough fella."

Thus in the exposure situation, subjects were provided with a diverting task which occupied their attention while at the same time insured observation of the model's behavior in the absence of any instructions to observe or to learn the responses in question. Since subjects could not perform the model's aggressive behavior, any learning that occurred was purely on an observational or covert basis.

At the end of 10 minutes, the experimenter entered the room, informed the subject that he would now go to another game room, and bid the model goodbye.

AGGRESSION AROUSAL

Subjects were tested for the amount of imitative learning in a different experimental room that was set off from the main nursery school building. The two experimental situations were thus clearly differentiated; in fact, many subjects were under the impression that they were no longer on the nursery school grounds.

Prior to the test for imitation, however, all subjects, experimental and control, were subjected to mild aggression arousal to insure that they were under some degree of instigation to aggression. The arousal experience was included for two main reasons. In the first place, observation of aggressive behavior exhibited by others tends to reduce the probability of aggression on the part of the observer (Rosenbaum & deCharms, 1960). Consequently, subjects in the aggressive condition, in relation both to the nonaggressive and control groups, would be under weaker instigation following exposure to the models. Second, if subjects in the nonaggressive condition expressed little aggression in the face of appropriate instigation, the presence of an inhibitory process would seem to be indicated.

Following the exposure experience, therefore, the experimenter brought the subject to an anteroom that contained these relatively attractive toys: a fire engine, a locomotive, a jet fighter plane, a cable car, a colorful spinning top, and a doll set complete with wardrobe, doll carriage, and baby crib. The experimenter explained that the toys were for the subject to play with but, as soon as the subject became sufficiently involved with the play material (usually in about 2 minutes), the experimenter remarked that these were her very best toys, that she did not let just anyone play with them, and that she had decided to reserve these toys for the other children. However, the subject could play with any of the toys that were in the next room. The experimenter and the subject then entered the adjoining experimental room.

It was necessary for the experimenter to remain in the room during the experimental session; otherwise a number of the children would either refuse to remain alone or would leave before the termination of the session. However, in order to minimize any influence her presence might have on the subject's behavior, the experimenter remained as inconspicuous as possible by busying herself with paper work at a desk in the far corner of the room and avoiding any interaction with the child.

Test for Delayed Imitation

The experimental room contained a variety of toys including some that could be used in imitative or nonimitative aggression, and others that tended to elicit predominantly nonaggressive forms of behavior. The aggressive toys included a 3-foot Bobo doll, a mallet and peg board, two dart guns, and a tether ball with a face painted on it which hung from the ceiling. The nonaggressive toys, on the other hand, included a tea set, crayons and coloring paper, a ball, two dolls, three bears, cars and trucks, and plastic farm animals.

In order to eliminate any variation in behavior due to mere placement of the toys in the room, the play material was arranged in a fixed order for each of the sessions.

The subject spent 20 minutes in this experimental room during which time his behavior was rated in terms of predetermined response categories by judges who observed the session through a one-way mirror in an adjoining observation room. The 20-minute session was divided into 5-second intervals by means of an electric interval timer, thus yielding a total number of 240 response units for each subject.

The male model scored the experimental sessions for all 72 children. Except for the cases in which he served as model, he did not have knowledge of the subjects' group assignments. In order to provide an estimate of interscorer agreement, the performances of half the subjects were also scored independently by

a second observer. Thus one or the other of the two observers usually had no knowledge of the conditions to which the subjects were assigned. Since, however, all but two of the subjects in the aggressive condition performed the models' novel aggressive responses while subjects in the other conditions only rarely exhibited such reactions, subjects who were exposed to the aggressive models could be readily identified through their distinctive behavior.

The responses scored involved highly specific concrete classes of behavior and yielded high interscorer reliabilities, the product-moment coefficients being in the .90s.

Response Measures

Three measures of imitation were obtained:

Imitation of physical aggression: This category included acts of striking the Bobo doll with the mallet, sitting on the doll and punching it in the nose, kicking the doll, and tossing it in the air.

Imitative verbal aggression: Subject repeats the phrases, "Sock him," "Hit him down," "Kick him," "Throw him in the air," or "Pow."

Imitative nonaggressive verbal responses: Subject repeats, "He keeps coming back for more," or "He sure is a tough fella."

During the pretest, a number of the subjects imitated the essential components of the model's behavior but did not perform the complete act, or they directed the imitative aggressive response to some object other than the Bobo doll. Two responses of this type were therefore scored and were interpreted as partially imitative behavior.

Mallet aggression: Subject strikes objects other than the Bobo doll aggressively with the mallet.

Sits on the Bobo doll: Subject lays the Bobo doll on its side and sits on it, but does not aggress toward it.

The following additional nonimitative aggressive responses were scored:

Punched Bobo doll: Subject strikes, slaps, or pushes the doll aggressively.

Nonimitative physical and verbal aggression: This category included physically aggressive acts directed toward objects other than the Bobo doll and any hostile remarks except for those in the verbal imitation category; e.g., "Shoot the Bobo," "Cut him," "Stupid ball," "Knock over people," "Horses fighting, biting."

Aggressive gun play: Subject shoots darts or aims the guns and fires imaginary shots at objects in the room.

Ratings were also made of the number of behavior units in which subjects played nonaggressively or sat quietly and did not play with any of the material at all.

RESULT

Complete Imitation of Models' Behavior

Subjects in the aggression condition reproduced a good deal of physical and verbal aggressive behavior resembling that of the models, and their mean scores differed markedly from those of subjects in the nonaggressive and control groups who exhibited virtually no imitative aggression (see Table 1).

Since there were only a few scores for subjects in the nonaggressive and control conditions (approximately 70% of the subjects had zero scores), and the assumption of homogeneity of variance could not be made, the Friedman two-way analysis of variance by ranks was employed to test the significance of the obtained differences.

The prediction that exposure of subjects to aggressive models increases the probability of aggressive behavior is clearly confirmed (see Table 2). The main effect of treatment conditions is highly significant both for physical and verbal imitative aggression. Comparison of pairs of scores by the sign test shows that the obtained over-all differences were due almost entirely to the aggression displayed by subjects who had been exposed to the aggressive models. Their scores were significantly higher than those of either the nonaggressive or control groups, which did not differ from each other (Table 2).

Imitation was not confined to the model's aggressive responses. Approximately one-third of the subjects in the aggressive condition also repeated the model's nonaggressive verbal responses while none of the subjects in either the nonaggressive or control groups made such remarks. This difference, tested by means of the Cochran Q test, was significant well beyond the .001 level (Table 2).

Partial Imitation of Models' Behavior

Differences in the predicted direction were also obtained on the two measures of partial imitation.

Analysis of variance of scores based on the subjects' use of the mallet aggressively toward objects other than the Bobo doll reveals that treatment conditions are a statistically significant course of variation (Table 2). In addition, individual sign tests show that both the aggressive and the control groups, relative to subjects in the nonaggressive condition, produced significantly more mallet aggression, the difference being particularly marked with regard to female subjects. Girls who observed nonaggressive models performed a mean number of 0.5 mallet aggression responses as compared to mean values of 18.0 and 13.1 for girls in the aggressive and control groups, respectively.

Although subjects who observed aggressive models performed more mallet aggression (M = 20.0) than their controls (M = 13. 3), the difference was not statistically significant.

With respect to the partially imitative response of sitting on the Bobo doll, the over-all group differences were significant beyond the .01 level (Table 2). Comparison of pairs of scores by the sign test procedure reveals that subjects in the aggressive group reproduced this aspect of the models' behavior to a greater extent than did the nonaggressive (p = .018) or the control (p = .059) subjects. The latter two groups, on the other hand, did not differ from each other.

Nonimitative Aggression

Analyses of variance of the remaining aggression measures (Table 2) show that treatment conditions did not influence the extent to which subjects engaged in aggressive gun play or punched the Bobo doll. The effect of conditions is highly significant ($\chi^2 r$ = 8.96, p < .02), however, in the case of the subjects' expression of nominative physical and verbal aggression. Further comparison of treatment pairs reveals that the main

TABLE 1 / Mean Aggression Scores for Experimental and Control Subjects

| | Experimental Groups | | | | |
| | Aggressive | | Nonaggressive | | |
Response Category	F Model	M Model	F Model	M Model	Control Groups
Imitative physical aggression					
Female subjects	5.5	7.2	2.5	0.0	1.2
Male subjects	12.4	25.8	0.2	1.5	2.0
Imitative verbal aggression					
Female subjects	13.7	2.0	0.3	0.0	0.7
Male subjects	4.3	12.7	1.1	0.0	1.7
Mallet aggression					
Female subjects	17.2	18.7	0.5	0.5	13.1
Male subjects	15.5	28.8	18.7	6.7	13.5
Punches Bobo doll					
Female subjects	6.3	16.5	5.8	4.3	11.7
Male subjects	18.9	11.9	15.6	14.8	15.7
Nonimitative aggression					
Female subjects	21.3	8.4	7.2	1.4	6.1
Male subjects	16.2	36.7	26.1	22.3	24.6
Aggressive gun play					
Female subjects	1.8	4.5	2.6	2.5	3.7
Male subjects	7.3	15.9	8.9	16.7	14.3

source of the over-all difference was the aggressive and nonaggressive groups which differed significantly from each other (Table 2), with subjects exposed to the aggressive models displaying the greater amount of aggression.

Influence of Sex of Model and Sex of Subjects on Imitation

The hypothesis that boys are more prone than girls to imitate aggression exhibited by a model was only partially confirmed. t tests computed for subjects in the aggressive condition reveal that boys reproduced more imitative physical aggression than girls ($t = 2.50$, $p < .01$). The groups do not differ, however, in their imitation of verbal aggression.

The use of nonparametric tests, necessitated by the extremely skewed distributions of scores for subjects in the nonaggressive and control conditions, preclude an over-all test of the influence of sex of model per se, and of the various interactions between the main effects. Inspection of the means presented in Table 1 for subjects in the aggression condition, however, clearly suggests the possibility of a Sex × Model interaction. This interaction effect is much more consistent and pronounced for the male model than for the female model. Male subjects, for example, exhibited more physical ($t = 2.07$, $p < .05$) and verbal imitative aggression ($t = 2.51$, $p < .05$), more nonimitative aggression ($t = 3.15$, $p < .025$), and engaged in significantly more aggressive gun play ($t = 2.12$, $p < .05$) following exposure to the aggressive male model than the female subjects. In contrast, girls exposed to the female model performed considerably more imitative verbal aggression and more nonimitative aggression than did the boys (Table 1). The variances, however, were equally large and with only a small N in each cell the mean differences did not reach statistical significance.

TABLE 2 / Significance of the Differences between Experimental and Control Groups in the Expression of Aggressive

Response Category	χ^2_r	Q	P	Aggressive vs. Nonaggressive p	Aggressive vs. Control p	Nonaggressive vs. Control p
				Comparison of Pairs of Treatment Conditions		
Imitative responses						
Physical aggression	27.17		< .001	< .001	< .001	.09
Verbal aggression	9.17		< .02	.004	.048	.09
Nonaggressive verbal responses		17.50	< .001	.004	.004	ns
Partial imitation						
Mallet aggression	11.06		< .01	.026	ns	.005
Sits on Bobo		13.44	< .01	.018	.059	ns
Nonimitative aggression						
Punches Bobo doll	2.87		ns			
Physical and verbal	8.96		< .02	.026	ns	ns
Aggressive gun play	2.75		ns			

Note: ns = nonsignificant.

Data for the nonaggressive and control subjects provide additional suggestive evidence that the behavior of the male model exerted a greater influence than the female model on the subjects' behavior in the generalization situation.

It will be recalled that, except for the greater amount of mallet aggression exhibited by the control subjects, no significant differences were obtained between the nonaggressive and control groups. The data indicate, however, that the absence of significant differences between these two groups was due primarily to the fact that subjects exposed to the nonaggressive female model did not differ from the controls on any of the measures of aggression. With respect to the male model, on the other hand, the differences between the groups are striking. Comparison of the sets of scores by means of the sign test reveals that, in relation to the control group, subjects exposed to the nonaggressive male model performed significantly less imitative physical aggression ($p = .06$), less imitative verbal aggression ($p = .002$), less mallet aggression ($p = .003$), less nonimitative physical and verbal aggression ($p = .03$) and they were less inclined to punch the Bobo doll ($p = .07$).

While the comparison of subgroups, when some of the over-all tests do not reach statistical significance, is likely to capitalize on chance differences, nevertheless the consistency of the findings adds support to the interpretation in terms of influence by the model.

Nonaggressive Behavior

With the exception of expected sex differences, Lindquist (1956) Type III analyses of variance of the nonaggressive response scores yielded few significant differences.

Female subjects spent more time than boys playing with dolls ($p < .001$), with the tea set ($p < .001$), and coloring ($p < .05$). The boys, on the other hand, devoted significantly more time than the girls to exploratory play with the guns ($p < .01$). No sex differences were found in respect to the subjects' use of the other stimulus objects, i.e., farm animals, cars, or tether ball.

Treatment conditions did produce significant differences on two measures of nonaggressive behavior that are worth mentioning. Subjects in the nonaggressive condition engaged in significantly more nonaggressive play with dolls than either subjects in the aggressive group ($t = 2.67$, $p < .02$), or in the control group ($t = 2.57$, $p < .02$).

Even more noteworthy is the finding that subjects who observed nonaggressive models spent more than twice as much time as subjects in aggressive condition ($t = 3.07$, $p < .01$) in simply sitting quietly without handling any of the play material.

DISCUSSION

Much current research on social learning is focused on the shaping of new behavior through rewarding and punishing consequences. Unless responses are emitted, however, they cannot be influenced. The results of this study provide strong evidence that observation of cues produced by the behavior of others is one effective means of eliciting certain forms of responses for which the original probability is very low or zero. Indeed, social imitation may hasten or short-cut the acquisition of new behaviors without the necessity of reinforcing successive approximations as suggested by Skinner (1953).

Thus subjects given an opportunity to observe aggressive models later reproduced a good deal of physical and verbal aggression (as well as nonaggressive responses) substantially identical with that of the model. In contrast, subjects who were exposed to nonaggressive models and those who had no previous exposure to any models only rarely performed such responses.

To the extent that observation of adult models displaying aggression communicates permissiveness for aggressive behavior, such exposure may serve to weaken inhibitory responses and thereby to increase the probability of aggressive reactions to subsequent frustrations. The fact, however, that subjects expressed their aggression in ways that clearly resembled the novel patterns exhibited by the models provides striking evidence for the occurrence of learning by imitation.

In the procedure employed by Miller and Dollard (1941) for establishing imitative behavior, adult or peer models performed discrimination responses following which they were consistently rewarded, and the subjects were similarly reinforced whenever they matched the leaders' choice responses. While these experiments have been widely accepted as demonstrations of learning by means of imitation, in fact, they simply involve a special case of discrimination learning in which the behavior of others serves as discriminative stimuli for responses that are already part of the subject's repertoire. Auditory or visual environmental cues could easily have been substituted for the social stimuli to facilitate the discrimination learning. In contrast, the process of imitation studied in the present experiment differed in several important respects from the one investigated by Miller and Dollard in that subjects learned to combine fractional responses into relatively complex novel patterns solely by observing the performance of social models without any opportunity to perform the models' behavior in the exposure setting, and without any reinforcers delivered either to the models or to the observers.

An adequate theory of the mechanisms underlying imitative learning is lacking. The explanations that have been offered (Logan, Olmsted, Rosner, Schwartz, & Stevens, 1955; Maccoby, 1959) assume that the imitator performs the model's responses covertly. If it can be assumed additionally that rewards and punishments are self-administered in conjunction with the covert responses, the process of imitative learning could be accounted for in terms of the same principles that govern instrumental trial-and-error learning. In the early stages of the developmental process, however, the range of component responses in the organism's repertoire is probably increased through a process of classical conditioning (Bandura & Huston, 1961; Mowrer, 1950).

The data provide some evidence that the male model influenced the subjects' behavior outside the exposure setting to a greater extent than was true for the female model. In the analyses of the Sex × Model interactions, for example, only the comparisons involving the male model yielded significant differences. Similarly, subjects exposed to the nonaggressive male model performed less aggressive behavior than the controls, whereas comparisons involving the female model were consistently nonsignificant.

In a study of learning by imitation, Rosenblith (1959) has likewise found male experimenters more effective than females in influencing children's behavior. Rosenblith advanced the tentative explanation that the school setting may involve some social deprivation in respect to adult males which, in turn, enhances the male's reward value.

The trends in the data yielded by the present study suggest an alternative explanation. In the case of a highly masculine-typed behavior such as physical aggression, there is a tendency for both male and female subjects to imitate the male model to a greater degree than the female model. On the other hand, in the case of verbal aggression, which is less clearly sex linked, the greatest amount of imitation occurs in relation to the same-sex model. These trends together with the finding that boys in relation to girls are in general more imitative of physical aggression but do not differ in imitation of verbal aggression, suggest that subjects may be differentially affected by the sex of the model but that predictions must take into account the degree to which the behavior in question is sex-typed.

The preceding discussion has assumed that maleness-femaleness rather than some other personal characteristics of the particular models involved, is the significant variable—an assumption that cannot be tested directly with the data at hand. It was clearly evident, however, particularly from boys' spontaneous remarks about the display of aggression by the female model, that some subjects at least were responding in terms of a sex discrimination and their prior learning about what is sex appropriate behavior (e.g., "Who is that lady? That's not the way for a lady to behave. Ladies are supposed to act like ladies. . . ." "You should have seen what that girl did in there. She was just acting like a man. I never saw a girl act like that before. She was punching and fighting but not swearing."). Aggression by the male model, on the other hand, was more likely to be seen as appropriate and approved by both the boys ("Al's a good socker, he beat up Bobo. I want to sock like Al.") and the girls ("That man is a strong fighter, he punched and punched and he could hit Bobo right down to the floor and if Bobo got up he said, 'Punch your nose.' He's a good fighter like Daddy.").

The finding that subjects exposed to the quiet models were more inhibited and unresponsive than subjects in the aggressive condition, together with the obtained difference on the aggression measures, suggests that exposure to inhibited models not only decreases the probability of occurrence of aggressive behavior but also generally restricts the range of behavior emitted by the subjects.

"Identification with aggressor" (Freud, 1946) or "defensive identification" (Mowrer, 1950), whereby a person presumably transforms himself from object to agent of aggression by adopting the attributes of an aggressive threatening model so as to allay anxiety, is widely accepted as an explanation of the imitative learning of aggression.

The development of aggressive modes of response by children of aggressively punitive adults, however, may simply reflect object displacement without involving any such mechanism of defensive identification. In studies of child training antecedents of aggressively antisocial adolescents (Bandura & Walters, 1959) and of young hyperaggressive boys (Bandura, 1960), the parents were found to be nonpermissive and punitive of aggression directed toward themselves. On the other hand, they actively encouraged and reinforced their sons' aggression toward persons outside the home. This pattern of differential reinforcement of aggressive behavior served to inhibit the boys' aggression toward the original instigators and fostered the displacement of aggression toward objects and situations eliciting much weaker inhibitory responses.

Moreover, the findings from an earlier study (Bandura & Huston, 1961), in which children imitated to an equal degree aggression exhibited by a nurturant and a nonnurturant model, together with the results of the present experiment in which subjects readily imitated aggressive models who were more or less neutral figures suggest that mere observation of aggression, regardless of the quality of the model-subject relationship, is a sufficient condition for producing imitative aggression in children. A comparative study of the subjects' imitation of aggressive models who are feared, who are liked and esteemed, or who are essentially neutral figures would throw some light on whether or not a more parsimonious theory than the one involved in "identification with the aggressor" can explain the modeling process.

SUMMARY

Twenty-four preschool children were assigned to each of three conditions. One experimental group observed aggressive adult models; a second observed inhibited nonaggressive models; while subjects in a control group had no prior exposure to the models. Half the subjects in the experimental conditions observed same-sex models and half viewed models of the opposite sex. Subjects were then tested for the amount of imitative as well as nonimitative aggression performed in a new situation in the absence of the models.

Comparison of the subjects' behavior in the generalization situation revealed that subjects exposed to aggressive models reproduced a good deal of aggression resembling that of the models, and that their mean scores differed markedly from those of subjects in the nonaggressive and control groups. Subjects in the aggressive condition also exhibited significantly more partially imitative and nonimitative aggressive behavior and were generally less inhibited in their behavior than subjects in the nonaggressive condition.

Imitation was found to be differentially influenced by the sex of the model with boys showing more aggression than girls following exposure to the male model, the difference being particularly marked on highly masculine-typed behavior.

Subjects who observed the nonaggressive models, especially the subdued male model, were generally less aggressive than their controls.

The implications of the findings based on this experiment and related studies for the psychoanalytic theory of identification with the aggressor were discussed.

REFERENCES

Bandura, A. Relationship of family patterns to child behavior disorders. Progress Report, 1960, Stanford University, Project No. M-1734, United States Public Health Service.

Bandura, A., & Huston, Aletha C. Identification as a process of incidental learning. *J. abnorm. soc. Psychol.,* 1961, *63,* 311–318.

Bandura, A., & Walters, R. H. *Adolescent aggression.* New York: Ronald, 1959.

Blake, R. R. The other person in the situation. In R. Tagiuri & L. Petrullo (Eds.), *Person perception and interpersonal behavior.* Stanford, Calif.: Stanford Univer. Press, 1958. Pp. 229–242.

Fauls, Lydia B., & Smith, W. D. Sex-role learning of five-year olds. *J. genet. Psychol.,* 1956, *89,* 105–117.

Freud, Anna. *The ego and the mechanisms of defense.* New York: International Univer. Press, 1946.

Grosser, D., Polansky, N., & Lippitt, R. A laboratory study of behavior contagion. *Hum. Relat.,* 1951, *4,* 115–142.

Lindquist, E. F. *Design and analysis of experiments.* Boston: Houghton Mifflin, 1956.

Logan, F., Olmsted, O. L., Rosner, B. S., Schwartz, R. D., & Stevens, C. M. *Behavior theory and social science.* New Haven: Yale Univer. Press, 1955.

Maccoby, Eleanor E. Role-taking in childhood and its consequences for social learning. *Child Develpm.,* 1959, *30,* 239–252.

Miller, N. E., & Dollard, J. *Social learning and imitation.* New Haven: Yale Univer. Press, 1941.

Mowrer, O. H. (Ed.) Identification: A link between learning theory and psychotherapy In, *Learning theory and personality dynamics.* New York: Ronald, 1950. Pp. 69–94.

Rosenbaum, M. E., & deCharms, R. Direct and vicarious reduction of hostility. *J. abnorm. soc. Psychol.,* 1960, *60,* 105–111.

Rosenblith, Judy F. Learning by imitation in kindergarten children. *Child Develpm.,* 1959, *30,* 69–80.

Schachter, S., & Hall, R. Group-derived restraints and audience persuasion. *Hum. Relat.,* 1952, *5,* 397–406.

Skinner, B. F. *Science and human behavior.* New York: Macmillan, 1953.

ENDNOTES

1. This investigation was supported by Research Grant M-4398 from the National Institute of Health, United States Public Health Service.

2. The authors wish to express their appreciation to Edith Dowley, Director, and Patricia Rowe, Head Teacher, Stanford University Nursery School for their assistance throughout this study.

CRITICAL THINKING QUESTIONS

1. Notice that the children's anger was aroused prior to their being placed in the situation where their aggression would be measured. Why was this done? What might have resulted had their anger not been aroused beforehand? Were there different effects, depending on whether the children experienced prior anger arousal? If so, then what are the implications for generalizing the results of this study to how violent television affects its young viewers? Explain your answers.

2. This study reported that the gender of the actor made a difference in how much physical aggression was imitated. It also mentioned that some of the children simply found it inappropriate for a female actor to act aggressively. Some 35 years have passed since publication of this study. Do you think children today would still see physical aggression by a female as inappropriate? Support your answer.

3. Analyze the content of television shows directed toward children (including cartoons) for aggression, examining the type of aggression (physical versus verbal) and the gender of the aggressive character. Relate the findings to question 2, above.

4. Examine research conducted over the last three decades that documents the impact of televised aggression on children's behavior. Given these findings, what should be done? Should laws be passed to regulate the amount of violence shown on television? Or should this form of censorship be avoided? Explain. What other alternatives might exist to reverse or prevent the potential harm of observing violence on television?

ADDITIONAL RELATED READINGS

Huessmann, L. R., & Guerra, G. (1997). Children's normative beliefs about aggression and aggressive behavior. *Journal of Personality and Social Psychology, 72,* 408–419.

van-Schie, E. G. M. (1997). Children and videogames: Leisure activities, aggression, social integration, and school performance. *Journal of Applied Social Psychology, 27,* 1175–1194.

ARTICLE 33 _____

An important area of research on aggression concerns its causes. Three general classes of theories have emerged: The first class, which can be called *instinct theories,* explains aggression as somehow rooted in biology. Thus, aggression stems from internally generated forces and is something that human beings are genetically programmed to do. A second type of theory, called *drive reduction,* essentially explains aggression as arising from forces outside the individual; for instance, experiencing frustration may produce readiness to engage in aggressive behavior. *Social learning* is the third theoretical explanation of aggression. Basically, this approach maintains that aggression, like many other behaviors, is learned. It is not instinctive nor is it simply a reaction to a specific external event. Rather, like other complex social behaviors, aggression is learned.

Each of these theoretical views attributes aggression to a different cause. It follows, then, that whichever theoretical explanation you adopt will influence how optimistic you are about the possible control of aggression. For example, if you believe that aggression is innate, a biological predisposition of sorts, then there is not much that can be done about it. It is simply human nature to be aggressive. However, if you believe that aggression is learned, then it is not inevitable that people be aggressive. After all, if aggressive behaviors can be learned, then nonaggressive behaviors can be learned, as well.

If aggressive behavior is somehow a biological predisposition, we might expect universal manifestations of its occurrence. For example, if males are more aggressive than females, then this pattern should be relatively constant in varying cultures around the world. If, on the other hand, aggression is mainly a matter of social learning, then how aggression is expressed should vary in different societies.

What do these cross-cultural studies show? Are males more aggressive than females? The answer is yes and no. Males are more aggressive with regard to physical aggression but not necessarily with other forms of aggression. The following article by Karin Österman, Kaj Björkqvist, Kirsti M. J. Lagerspetz, and associates examines the cross-cultural evidence of preadolescent and adolescent female indirect aggression among girls in four different countries. It seems that boys are not always more aggressive than girls, after all.

Cross-Cultural Evidence of
Female Indirect Aggression

■ Karin Österman, Kal Björkqvist, Kirsti M. J. Lagerspetz,
  with Ari Kauklainen, Simha F. Landau, Adam Fraczek, and Gian Vittorio Caprara

Three types of aggressive behavior (physical, verbal, and indirect) were investigated by help of peer estimations based on The Direct & Indirect Aggression Scales *(DIAS) (Finland Åbe Akademe University) [Björkqvist et al., 1992b]. Aggressive behavior of adolescents of three age groups (8, 11, and 15 years old), in Finland (Finnish*

Reprinted from "Cross-Cultural Evidence of Female Indirect Aggression," by Karin Österman et al., *Aggressive Behavior,* 1998, *24,* 1–8. Copyright © 1998 John Wiley & Sons, Inc. Reprinted by permission of Wiley-Liss, Inc., a division of John Wiley & Sons, Inc.

and Swedish speakers), Israel (secular and religious Israelis), Italy, and Poland were studied (n = 2094). Indirect aggression was, in proportional terms, the aggressive style mostly used by girls, across nations, ethnic groups, and age groups studied. Verbal aggression was their second most used style, and physical aggression was applied least often by girls. Among boys, indirect aggression was, in all ages, the least used aggressive style. Physical and verbal aggression was, by boys, used equally often at ages 8 and 11, while, at the age of 15, verbal action had surpassed physical aggression and was the most used style. Scores of victimization to other's aggression showed somewhat similar trends.

INTRODUCTION

Studies in Finland have reported that girls use indirect aggression significantly more than boys from age 11 onward [Lagerspetz et al., 1988; Björkqvist et al., 1992a, 1992c; Lagerspetz and Björkqvist, 1994]. Indirect aggression was defined as social manipulation, attacking the target in circuitous ways. These studies were all based on peer-estimated adolescent samples. Among adults, women have been found to use more indirect aggression, according to self estimations, than men, as a means of workplace aggression [Björkqvist et al., 1994]. Sex-related choice of aggressive style may or may not follow similar patterns in different cultural contexts.

Anthropological data suggests that adult females resort to indirect aggression in a number of cultures. Burbank [1987], in her review of studies on female aggression in 137 societies, describes several ways in which females are indirectly aggressive, although she does not use that particular term [c.f. Björkqvist, 1994]. Feshbach [1969] reported girls to exclude newcomers from a group (a kind of indirect aggression) more than boys did, in an observational study. Whitney and Smith [1993] found that girls in British schools exceeded boys in indirect bullying. These different studies suggest that a female preference for indirect aggression is valid in a variety of cultural contexts. So far, however, cross-cultural evidence of female indirect aggression based on the same methodology in different cultures has not been published.

The main purpose of the present study was to investigate whether the findings pertaining to female indirect aggression obtained among adolescents in Finland could be replicated in other cultures with the same methodology, the Direct & Indirect Aggression Scales [Björkqvist et al., 1992b]. The study was accordingly carried out in four countries, namely Finland, Israel, Italy, and Poland, and in adolescents of three age groups: 8-, 11-, and 15-years of age.

Peer Estimations

Norms of behavior vary between cultures, and a certain type of behavior regarded as being aggressive in one culture may not be considered hostile in another. By using a peer estimation technique in the present research, some of the problems involved in interpreting and comparing behavior in different cultures are avoided. Subjects are asked explicitly to assess to what extent their peers behave in particular ways when they are angry with, or in conflict with, other children. In that way, an outside observer from another culture does not impose his/her values and norms onto the process of measurement. Children in a class also make better raters of each others' behavior than any outside observer, since they know each other well and are better aware of whether the intention of a particular behavior is hostile or not. They are able to interpret social situations and to note subtle behaviors that will go unnoticed by the outside observer. The applied peer estimation measure allows the subjects to judge for themselves, and make their own interpretations of whether an act is carried out in anger and/or in a conflict situation.

Peer estimations are particularly useful as far as the measurement of indirect aggression is concerned. One central aspect of indirect aggression is that this type of hostile behavior is usually carried out in order to harm the opponent, while avoiding being identified as aggressive [Björkqvist, 1994]. Since indirect aggression is used in order to cover one's harmful intentions, self-reports are not likely to be honest. Self estimations are also likely to be less reliable than estimations made by others, due to the fact that aggression is socially undesirable. Self estimations of aggression have been found to be significantly lower than peer estimations [Österman et al., 1994]. The opposite has been found in the case of conflict resolution, a socially desirable behavior [Österman et al., 1997]. People tend to claim that they are less aggressive and better at solving conflicts than their peers think they are.

METHOD

Participants

Children from three age groups, 8-, 11-, and 15-years old, participated in the study. Two ethnic groups from Turku, Finland (Finnish and Swedish speakers), two ethnic groups from Jerusalem, Israel (secular and religious Israelis), samples from two cities in Poland (Warsaw and Morag) and one sample from Rome, Italy were studied. The total number of children in the study was 2094 (Table 1).

Procedure

The participants filled in questionnaires during school lessons. Subjects from the youngest age groups, the 8-year-old children, were individually interviewed by a native research assistant, who filled in the questionnaire on their behalf. A detailed description of the procedure of data collection is presented in Österman et al. [1994].

Direct & Indirect Aggression Scales (DIAS)

The DIAS inventory [Björkqvist et al., 1992b] facilitates the measurement of both direct (physical and verbal) and indirect (social manipulation) strategies of aggression among school children. The instrument may be applied in both peer and self estimations. In the present study, same-sex peer-estimated data was used, i.e., girls' ratings of girls, and boys' ratings of boys. DIAS comprises both an aggressor and a victim version; every item is listed in two forms, e.g. *hits/is hit, gossips/is gossiped about*. The scales measure direct physical aggression (5 items), direct verbal aggression (7 items), and indirect aggression (12 items). Ratings are made on a five-point scale, ranging from 0 (never) to 4 (very often). High levels of internal consistency (Cronbach's α), ranging from .80 to .94 were found in the case of most subsamples. The items are described in detail in Österman et al. [1994, p. 415].

Proportional Scores

The proportional usage of different styles of aggression was estimated. Each individual's scores of physical, verbal, and indirect aggression were added together to a total aggression score. The proportional distribution of each style was, in the case of each individual, calculated as percentages of his/her total aggression score.

RESULTS

Styles of Aggression in Proportion to Total Aggression

In order to investigate the response preference as determined by age and sex, i.e. how large proportions of the total aggression scores were formed by the three measured styles of aggression, a series of within-subject analyses of variance were conducted, separately for girls and boys, and for each age group.

When the extracted F-values confirmed the existence of significant differences in variance between the three measured aggressive styles, one-to-one differences between the three styles were identified by dependent (paired) t-tests, since it was a question of within-subject measurements. The results are presented in Figure 1 and Table 2.

TABLE 1 / Number of Peer Estimated Subjects from the Six Participating Ethnic Groups

	Girls	Boys
Finland, Turku		
Finnish-speaking	162	150
Swedish-speaking	126	118
Israel, Jerusalem		
Secular	163	172
Religious	139	156
Italy, Rome	122	157
Poland, Warsaw and Morag	313	316
Total	1025	1069

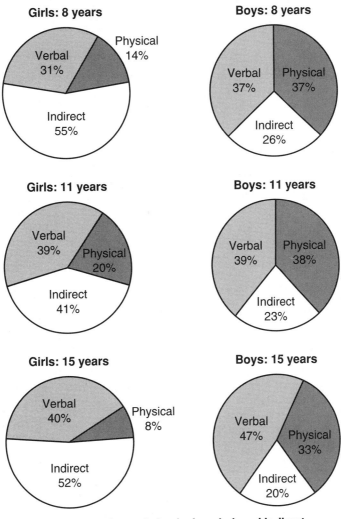

FIGURE 1 / Proportions of physical, verbal, and indirect aggression in percentage of total aggression scores. Peer-estimated data of girls (n = 1025), and boys (n = 1069), of three age groups from Finland, Israel, Italy and Poland, obtained with the Direct & Indirect Aggression Scales (DIAS) [Björkqvist, Lagerspetz & Österman, 1992].

Proportional Distributions of Three Types of Aggression Carried Out by Girls and Boys, According to Peer-Estimations

The within-subject analysis of variance (WSMANOVA) reveals (c.f. Table 2 and Figure 1) that indirect aggression was the style mostly used among girls in all age groups studied. Verbal aggression was the second most often applied, and physical aggression the style least used, the proportion of the latter diminishing by age.

Among boys, indirect aggression was the style least used, in all groups studied. There was no significant difference between the proportional shares of physical

TABLE 2 / F- and *p*-Values of Within-Subject Analyses of Variance (WSMANOVA) of Three Types of Aggression and Victimization (1025 Girls and 1070 Boys)

	n	F	df	p <	Sign. Differences According to Paired T-tests
Aggression, Girls					
8-years	294	188.80	2,586	.001	indirect > verbal > physical
11-years	353	235.09	2,704	.001	indirect > verbal > physical
15-years	378	486.64	2,754	.001	indirect > verbal > physical
Aggression, Boys					
8-years	345	31.21	2,688	.001	physical & verbal > indirect
11-years	369	267.11	2,736	.001	physical & verbal > indirect
15-years	356	188.72	2,710	.001	verbal > physical > indirect
Victimization, Girls					
8-years	294	.27	2,586	n.s.	n.s.
11-years	353	51.47	2,704	.001	verbal > indirect > physical
15-years	378	290.25	2,754	.001	indirect > verbal > physical
Victimization, Boys					
8-years	345	29.98	2,688	.001	verbal & physical > indirect
11-years	369	111.91	2,736	.001	verbal > physical > indirect
15-years	356	53.48	2,710	.001	verbal > physical > indirect

and verbal aggression during ages 8 and 11, while verbal aggression formed a greater part than physical at age 15 in the case of boys.

Victimization to Other's Aggression

Another series of within-subject analyses of variance was conducted, based on the scores of the Victim Version of DIAS. The purpose was to investigate the proportional share of the three different styles of aggression that victims were subjected to (c.f. Table 2 and Figure 2).

At the age of 8, girls were equally often victims of all three styles of aggression. At the age of 11, they were significantly more often victims of verbal than indirect aggression and more often victims of indirect than of physical aggression.

At age 15, girls were most often victims of indirect aggression and least often of physical aggression. That is, the proportion of physical aggression diminished consistently by age, while the proportional share of indirect aggression increased drastically from age 11–15.

In all age groups, boys were significantly less victimized by indirect than by physical or verbal aggression. At the age of 8, they were equally often victims of physical and verbal aggression, while at the age of 11 and 15, they were more often victims of verbal than of physical aggression. That is, the proportional share of victimization to verbal aggression increased by age among boys, especially during the period between ages 11 and 15.

DISCUSSION

The study presents cross-cultural evidence of the fact that indirect aggression is the most applied aggressive style among adolescent females in school settings. Boys use indirect less often than physical or verbal aggression.

The present study gives further indication of the importance of making distinctions between styles of aggression. Sex-specific variation will go unnoticed when such distinctions are neglected, and it is easy to

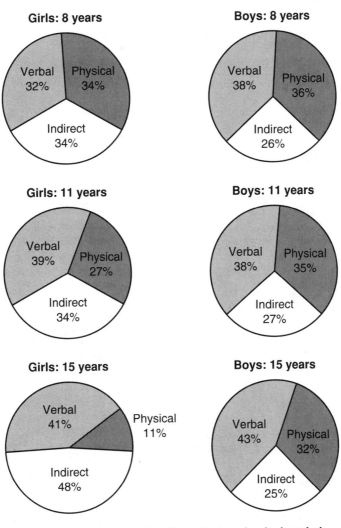

FIGURE 2 / Proportions of victimization to physical, verbal, and indirect aggression in percentage of total victimization scores. Peer-estimated data of girls (n = 1025), and boys (n = 1069), of three age groups from Finland, Israel, Italy and Poland, obtained with the Direct & Indirect Aggression Scales (DIAS) [Björkqvist, Lagerspetz & Österman, 1992].

be led astray. For example, in a textbook by Moghaddam et al. [1993] on cross-cultural social psychology, the authors discuss what they perceive as an "almost universal tendency" for males to be more aggressive than females (p. 129). Such oversimplifica-

tions may be made if physical violence exclusively is taken into consideration.

A developmental trend towards a decreasing usage of physical aggression could be noticed, especially among girls, but also among boys, who were less physically aggressive at the age of 15, as compared to ages 8 and 11. The proportion of verbal aggression increased slightly over age, faster among girls than among boys. It has been hypothesized that the development of cognitive capacities facilitates the use of nonphysical forms of aggression [see Björkqvist et al., 1992c].

The study by Björkqvist et al. [1992a], suggested that sex differences in indirect aggression are not clearly distinguishable until the age of 11. In that study, girls and boys were compared in a between-subjects analysis. When data are examined in proportional scores, in a within-subjects analysis, as in the present study, the preference for females to use indirect more than other forms of aggression is to be observed already at the early age of 8.

The proportion of indirect aggression varied between 41% and 55% for girls, in the different age groups studied. In the case of boys, the proportion of indirect aggression varied between 20% and 26%. Among boys, the most frequently used aggressive style, verbal, surpassed the other styles at the age of 15.

Victimization scores follow the same pattern as aggression scores in all age groups, in the case of boys. This is true also in the case of 15-year old girls. The 8- and 11-year old girls are exposed to more physical aggression than they apply themselves. This finding suggests that younger girls are exposed to aggression by boys to a larger extent than older girls are. Results pertaining to boys and 15-year old girls indicate that at least in these groups, aggression is indeed more common than between-sex aggression, as has been suggested [e.g., Björkqvist and Niemelä, 1992; Lagerspetz and Björkqvist, 1994].

To conclude, the present study shows that girls are not only indirectly more aggressive than boys, but they also use, in proportional terms, more indirect than other means of aggression in their conflicts with others. This finding seems cross-culturally valid, at least, in the four nations studied.

REFERENCES

Björkqvist K (1994): Sex differences in physical, verbal, and indirect aggression: A review of recent research. Sex Roles 30:177–188.

Björkqvist K, Niemelä P (1992): New trends in the study of female aggression. In Björkqvist K, Niemelä P (eds), "Of Mice and Women: Aspects of Female Aggression." San Diego, CA: Academic Press, pp 3–16.

Björkqvist K, Lagerspetz KMJ, Kaukiainen A (1992a): Do girls manipulate and boys fight? Developmental trends in regard to direct and indirect aggression. Aggressive Behavior 18: 117–127.

Björkqvist K, Lagerspetz KMJ, Österman K (1992b): "The Direct & Indirect Aggression Scales." Åbo Akademi University, Department of Social Sciences, Vasa, Finland.

Björkqvist K, Österman K, Kaukiainen A (1992c): The development of direct and indirect aggressive strategies in males and females. In Björkqvist K, Niemelä P (eds), "Of Mice and Women: Aspects of Female Aggression." San Diego, CA: Academic Press, pp 51–64.

Björkqvist K, Österman K, Lagerspetz KMJ (1994): Sex differences in covert aggression among adults. Aggressive Behavior 20: 27–33.

Burbank VK (1987): Female aggression in cross-cultural perspective. Behavioral Science Research 21: 70–100.

Feshbach ND (1969): Sex differences in children's modes of aggressive responses towards outsiders. Merrill-Palmer Quarterly 15:249–258.

Lagerspetz KMJ, Björkqvist K (1994): Indirect aggression in boys and girls. In Huesmann LR (ed), "Aggressive behavior: Current perspectives." New York: Plenum Publishing Corporation, pp 131–150.

Lagerspetz KMJ, Björkqvist K, Peltonen T (1988): Is indirect aggression typical of females? Gender differences in 11- to 12-year-old children. Aggressive Behavior 14:403–414.

Moghaddam FM, Taylor DM, Wright SC (1993): "Social Psychology in Cross-Cultural Perspective." New York: Freeman.

Österman K, Björkqvist K, Lagerspetz KMJ, Kaukiainen A, Huesmann LR, Fraczek A (1994): Peer and self-estimated aggression and victimization in 8-year-old children from five ethnic groups. Aggressive Behavior 20:411–428.

Österman K, Björkqvist K, Lagerspetz KMJ, Landau SF, Fraczek A, Pastorelli C (1997): Sex differences in styles of conflict resolution: A developmental and cross-cultural study with data from Finland, Israel, Italy, and Poland. In Fry DP, Björkqvist K (eds), "Cultural Variation in Conflict Resolution: Alternatives to Violence." New York: Lawrence Erlbaum, pp. 185–197.

Whitney I, Smith P (1993): A survey of the nature and extent of bullying in junior/middle and secondary schools. Educational Research, 35:3–25.

CRITICAL THINKING QUESTIONS

1. How do your own experiences with and observations of men's versus women's uses of indirect aggression compare to the results reported in this study? Are they comparable or different? Elaborate on your response.

2. Do the results of the present study suggest that the expression of aggression may be rooted in biology rather than in socialization? Why or why not? What else might explain the similarity of results obtained in the four countries studied?

3. Examine your own assumptions about aggression. Do you believe that it is part of human nature (i.e., genetically or biologically determined) or due to learning and experience? How do these personally held assumptions influence your view of the purpose of punishing criminals, in general, and the issue of capital punishment, in particular? Explain your answers.

4. How, exactly, would you operationally define *indirect aggression?* Is it the same as *passive-aggressive behavior?* Why or why not?

5. What do you think of the statement in the article that in giving self-reports, people underestimate how aggressive they are but overestimate how good they are at resolving conflicts? (Keep in mind that both these behaviors are socially desirable.) Design a study to determine if these self-reporting patterns indeed hold true in other situations.

Chapter Twelve

GROUPS AND INDIVIDUAL BEHAVIOR

How MUCH OF your life is spent interacting with people in some sort of group? If we use the simple definition of a *group* as "two or more individuals that have some unifying relationship," then most likely a significant amount of your time is spent in groups, whether informal (such as two friends trying to decide what to do on a Saturday night) or formal (a work group deciding on a course of action).

Research on group behavior has gone in many directions. The three articles selected for this chapter focus on some of the most commonly investigated topics. Article 34, "Groupthink," examines a set of circumstances found in certain types of groups that may lead them to make very poor decisions, even when they may be composed of very competent individuals. Since the conditions that may contribute to groupthink are not uncommon, the implications of the article for developing more effective groups are clearly important.

Article 35, "The Effect of Threat upon Interpersonal Bargaining," is a classic work. Think of these two possible situations: In the first situation, Party 1 has the potential to inflict harm on Party 2, but Party 2 cannot reciprocate. In the second situation, both parties have equal threat potential; that is, if Party 1 inflicts harm, Party 2 can reciprocate. Which situation would yield the best outcomes for *both* parties? As the article demonstrates, the answer is not what you might think.

Article 36 returns to the concept of groupthink by examining how it may have contributed to a decision that resulted in a well-known tragedy. "Group Decision Fiascoes Continue" applies the groupthink concept to the space shuttle *Challenger* disaster. The article also suggests how the concept should be revised to account for other variables that may be involved.

ARTICLE 34 _____

Let us suppose that you are in a position of authority. As such, you are called on to make some very important decisions. You want to make the best possible decisions, so you turn to other people for input. You assemble the best possible set of advisors—people distinguished by their abilities and knowledge. Before making a final decision, you meet with them to discuss the options.

Following such a procedure would seem to ensure that the decision you make will be a good one. After all, with your expert resources, how can you go wrong?

Actually, it is not very hard to imagine that the above procedure could go wrong. Working in a group, even when that group is composed of very competent individuals, does not guarantee quality decision making. To the contrary, as the following article by Irving L. Janis explains, groups may actually make some very poor decisions. The concept of *groupthink,* a term coined by Janis, explains how and why some groups come to make poor decisions, not only failing to recognize that they are poor decisions but actually convincing themselves more and more that they are good decisions. Considering the number of decisions that are made in groups, the process of groupthink, as well as the suggestions for how it can be minimized, are important indeed.

Groupthink

■ Irving L. Janis

The idea of "groupthink" occurred to me while reading Arthur M. Schlesinger's chapters on the Bay of Pigs in *A Thousand Days.* At first I was puzzled: How could bright men like John F. Kennedy and his advisers be taken in by such a stupid, patchwork plan as the one presented to them by the C.I.A. representatives? I began wondering if some psychological contagion of complacency might have interfered with their mental alertness.

I kept thinking about this notion until one day I found myself talking about it in a seminar I was conducting at Yale on the psychology of small groups. I suggested that the poor decision-making performance of those high officials might be akin to the lapses in judgment of ordinary citizens who become more concerned with retaining the approval of the fellow members of their work group than with coming up with good solutions to the tasks at hand.

When I re-read Schlesinger's account I was struck by many further observations that fit into exactly the pattern of concurrence-seeking that has impressed me in my research on other face-to-face groups when a "we" feeling of solidarity is running high. I concluded that a group process was subtly at work in Kennedy's team which prevented the members from debating the real issues posed by the C.I.A.'s plan and from carefully appraising its serious risks.

By now I was sufficiently fascinated by what I called the "groupthink" hypothesis to start looking into similar historic fiascoes. I selected for intensive analysis three that were made during the administrations of three other American presidents: Franklin D. Roosevelt (failure to be prepared for Pearl Harbor), Harry S. Truman (the invasion of North Korea) and Lyndon B. Johnson (escalation of the Vietnam war). Each decision was a group product, issuing from a series of meetings held by a small and cohesive group of government officials and advisers. In each case I found the same kind of detrimental group process that was at work in the Bay of Pigs decision.

Reprinted with permission from *Yale Alumni Magazine,* January 1973. Copyright 1973 by Yale Alumni Publications, Inc.

In my earlier research with ordinary citizens I had been impressed by the effects—both unfavorable and favorable—of the social pressures that develop in cohesive groups: in infantry platoons, air crews, therapy groups, seminars and self-study or encounter groups. Members tend to evolve informal objectives to preserve friendly intra-group relations, and this becomes part of the hidden agenda at their meetings. When conducting research on groups of heavy smokers, for example, at a clinic established to help people stop smoking, I noticed a seemingly irrational tendency for the members to exert pressure on each other to increase their smoking as the time for the final meeting approached. This appeared to be a collusive effort to display mutual dependence and resistance to the termination of the sessions.

Sometimes, even long before the final separation, pressures toward uniformity subverted the fundamental purpose. At the second meeting of one group of smokers, consisting of 12 middle-class American men and women, two of the most dominant members took the position that heavy smoking was an almost incurable addiction. Most of the others soon agreed that nobody could be expected to cut down drastically. One man took issue with this consensus, arguing that he had stopped smoking since joining the group and that everyone else could do the same. His declaration was followed by an angry discussion. Most of the others ganged up against the man who was deviating from the consensus.

At the next meeting the deviant announced that he had made an important decision. "When I joined," he said, "I agreed to follow the two main rules required by the clinic—to make a conscientious effort to stop smoking, and to attend every meeting. But I have learned that you can only follow one of the rules, not both. I will continue to attend every meeting but I have gone back to smoking two packs a day and I won't make any effort to stop again until after the last meeting." Whereupon the other members applauded, welcoming him back to the fold.

No one mentioned that the whole point of the meetings was to help each person to cut down as rapidly as possible. As a psychological consultant to the group, I tried to call this to the members' attention and so did my collaborator, Dr. Michael Kahn. But the members ignored our comments and reiterated their consensus that heavy smoking was an addiction from which no one would be cured except by cutting down gradually over a long period of time.

This episode—an extreme form of groupthink—was only one manifestation of a general pattern that the group displayed. At every meeting the members were amiable, reasserted their warm feelings of solidarity and sought concurrence on every important topic, with no reappearance of the unpleasant bickering that would spoil the cozy atmosphere. This tendency could be maintained, however, only at the expense of ignoring realistic challenges—like those posed by the psychologists.

The term "groupthink" is of the same order as the words in the "newspeak" vocabulary that George Orwell uses in *1984*—a vocabulary with terms such as "doublethink" and "crimethink." By putting "groupthink" with those Orwellian words, I realize that it takes on an invidious connotation. This is intentional: groupthink refers to a deterioration of mental efficiency, reality testing and moral judgment that results from in-group pressures.

When I investigated the Bay of Pigs invasion and other fiascoes, I found that there were at least six major defects in decision-making which contributed to failures to solve problems adequately.

First, the group's discussions were limited to a few alternatives (often only two) without a survey of the full range of alternatives. Second, the members failed to re-examine their initial decision from the standpoint of non-obvious drawbacks that had not been originally considered. Third, they neglected courses of action initially evaluated as unsatisfactory; they almost never discussed whether they had overlooked any nonobvious gains.

Fourth, members made little or no attempt to obtain information from experts who could supply sound estimates of losses and gains to be expected from alternative courses. Fifth, selective bias was shown in the way the members reacted to information and judgments from experts, the media and outside critics; they were only interested in facts and opinions that supported their preferred policy. Finally, they spent little time deliberating how the policy might be hindered by bureaucratic inertia, sabotaged by political opponents or derailed by the accidents that happen to the best of well-laid plans. Consequently, they failed to work out contingency plans to cope with foreseeable setbacks that could endanger their success.

I was surprised by the extent to which the groups involved in these fiascoes adhered to group norms and pressures toward uniformity, even when their policy was working badly and had unintended consequences that disturbed the conscience of the members. Members consider loyalty to the group the highest form of morality. That loyalty requires each member to avoid raising controversial issues, questioning weak arguments or calling a halt to soft-headed thinking.

Paradoxically, soft-headed groups are likely to be extremely hard-hearted toward out-groups and enemies. In dealing with a rival nation, policy-makers constituting an amiable group find it relatively easy to authorize dehumanizing solutions such as large-scale bombings. An affable group of government officials is unlikely to pursue the difficult issues that arise when alternatives to a harsh military solution come up for discussion. Nor are they inclined to raise ethical issues that imply that this "fine group of ours, with its humanitarianism and its high-minded principles, could adopt a course that is inhumane and immoral."

The greater the threat to the self-esteem of the members of a cohesive group, the greater will be their inclination to resort to concurrence-seeking at the expense of critical thinking. Symptoms of groupthink will therefore be found most often when a decision poses a moral dilemma, especially if the most advantageous course requires the policy-makers to violate their own standards of humanitarian behavior. Each member is likely to become more dependent than ever on the in-group for maintaining his self-image as a decent human being and will therefore be more strongly motivated to maintain group unity by striving for concurrence.

Although it is risky to make huge inferential leaps from theory to practice, we should not be inhibited from drawing tentative inferences from these fiascoes. Perhaps the worst mistakes can be prevented if we take steps to avoid the circumstances in which groupthink is most likely to flourish. But all the prescriptive hypotheses that follow must be validated by systematic research before they can be applied with any confidence.

The leader of a policy-forming group should, for example, assign the role of critical evaluator to each member, encouraging the group to give high priority to airing objections and doubts. He should also be impartial at the outset, instead of stating his own preferences and expectations. He should limit his briefings to unbiased statements about the scope of the problem and the limitations of available resources.

The organization should routinely establish several independent planning and evaluation groups to work on the same policy question, each carrying out its deliberations under a different leader.

One or more qualified colleagues within the organization who are not core members of the policy-making group should be invited to each meeting and encouraged to challenge the views of the core members.

At every meeting, at least one member should be assigned the role of devil's advocate, to function like a good lawyer in challenging the testimony of those who advocate the majority position.

Whenever the policy issue involves relations with a rival nation, a sizable block of time should be spent surveying all warning signals from the rivals and constructing alternative scenarios.

After reaching a preliminary consensus the policy-making group should hold a "second chance" meeting at which all the members are expected to express their residual doubts and to rethink the entire issue. They might take as their model a statement made by Alfred P. Sloan, a former chairman of General Motors, at a meeting of policy-makers:

"Gentlemen, I take it we are all in complete agreement on the decision here. Then I propose we postpone further discussion until our next meeting to give ourselves time to develop disagreement and perhaps gain some understanding of what the decision is all about."

It might not be a bad idea for the second-chance meeting to take place in a relaxed atmosphere far from the executive suite, perhaps over drinks. According to a report by Herodotus dating from about 450 B.C., whenever the ancient Persians made a decision following sober deliberations, they would always reconsider the matter under the influence of wine. Tacitus claimed that during Roman times the Germans also had a custom of arriving at each decision twice—once sober, once drunk.

Some institutionalized form of allowing second thoughts to be freely expressed might be remarkably effective for breaking down a false sense of unanimity and related illusions, without endangering anyone's reputation or liver.

PEARL HARBOR: GENIALITY AND SECURITY

On the night of Dec. 6, 1941—just 12 hours before the Japanese struck—Admiral Husband E. Kimmel (Commander in Chief of the Pacific Fleet) attended a dinner party given by his old crony, Rear Admiral H. Fairfax Leary, and his wife. Other members of the in-group of naval commanders and their wives were also present. Seated next to Admiral Kimmel was Fanny Halsey, wife of Admiral Halsey, who had left Hawaii to take his task force to the Far East. Mrs. Halsey said that she was certain the Japanese were going to attack. "She was a brilliant woman," according to Captain Joel Bunkley, who described the party, "but everybody thought she was crazy."

Admiral Leary, at a naval inquiry in 1944, summarized the complacency at that dinner party and at the daily conferences held by Admiral Kimmel during the preceding weeks. When asked whether any thought had been given to the possibility of a surprise attack by the Japanese, he said, "We all felt that the contingency was remote . . . and the feeling strongly existed that the Fleet would have adequate warning of any chance of an air attack." The same attitude was epitomized in testimony given by Captain J. B. Earle, chief of staff, Fourteenth Naval District. "Somehow or other," he said, "we always felt that 'it couldn't happen here.'"

From the consistent testimony given by Admiral Kimmel's advisers, they all acted on the basis of an "unwarranted feeling of immunity from attack," though they had been given a series of impressive warnings that they should be prepared for war with Japan.

Most illuminating of the norm-setting behavior that contributed to the complacency of Kimmel's in-group is a brief exchange between Admiral Kimmel and Lieutenant Commander Layton. Perturbed by the loss of radio contact with the Japanese aircraft carriers, Admiral Kimmel asked Layton on Dec. 1, 1941, to check with the Far East Command for additional information. The next day, discussing the lost carriers again with Layton, he remarked jokingly: "What, you don't know where the carriers are? Do you mean to say that they could be rounding Diamond Head [at Honolulu] and you wouldn't know it?" Layton said he hoped they would be sighted well before that.

This exchange implies an "atmosphere of geniality and security." Having relegated the Japanese threat to the category of laughing matters, the admiral was making it clear that he would be inclined to laugh derisively at anyone who thought otherwise. "I did not at any time suggest," Layton later acknowledged at a Congressional hearing, "that the Japanese carriers were under radio silence approaching Oahu. I wish I had."

But the admiral's foolish little joke may have induced Layton to remain silent about any vague, lingering doubts he may have had. Either man would risk the scornful laughter of the other—whether expressed to his face or behind his back—if he were to express second thoughts such as, "Seriously, though, shouldn't we do something about the slight possibility that those carriers might *really* be headed this way?" Because this ominous inference was never drawn, not a single reconnaissance plane was sent out to the north of the Hawaiian Islands, allowing the Japanese to win the incredible gamble they were taking in trying to send their aircraft carriers within bombing distance of Pearl Harbor without being detected.

That joking exchange was merely the visible part of a huge iceberg of solid faith in Pearl Harbor's invulnerability. If a few warm advocates of preparedness had been within the Navy group, steamed up by the accumulating warning signals, they might have been able to melt it. But they would certainly have had a cold reception. To urge a full alert would have required presenting unwelcome arguments that countered the myth of Pearl Harbor's impregnability. Anyone who was tempted to do so knew that he would be deviating from the group norm: the others were likely to consider him "crazy," just as the in-group regarded Mrs. Halsey at the dinner party on the eve of the disaster when she announced her deviant opinion that the Japanese would attack.

ESCALATION IN VIETNAM: HOW COULD IT HAPPEN?

A highly revealing episode occurred soon after Robert McNamara told a Senate committee some impressive facts about the ineffectiveness of the bombings. President Johnson made a number of bitter comments about McNamara's statement. "That military genius,

McNamara, has gone dovish on me," he complained to one Senator. To someone in his White House staff he spoke even more heatedly, accusing McNamara of playing into the hands of the enemy. He drew the analogy of "a man trying to sell his house while one of his sons went to the prospective buyer to point out that there were leaks in the basement."

This strongly suggests that Johnson regarded his in-group of policy advisers as a family and its leading dissident member as an irresponsible son who was sabotaging the family's interest. Underlying this revealing imagery are two implicit assumptions that epitomize groupthink: We are a good group, so any deceitful acts that we perpetrate are fully justified. Anyone who is unwilling to distort the truth to help us is disloyal.

This is only one of the many examples of how groupthink was manifested in Johnson's inner circle.

A PERFECT FIASCO: THE BAY OF PIGS

Why did President Kennedy's main advisers, whom he had selected as core members of his team, fail to pursue the issues sufficiently to discover the shaky ground on which the faulty assumptions of the Cuban invasion plan rested? Why didn't they pose a barrage of penetrating and embarrassing questions to the representatives of the C.I.A. and the Joint Chiefs of Staff? Why were they taken in by the incomplete and inconsistent answers they were given in response to the relatively few critical questions they raised?

Schlesinger says that "for all the utter irrationality with which retrospect endowed the project, it had a certain queer logic at the time as it emerged from the bowels of government." Why? What was the source of the "queer logic" with which the plan was endowed? If the available accounts describe the deliberations accurately, many typical symptoms of groupthink can be discerned among the members of the Kennedy team: an illusion of invulnerability, a collective effort to rationalize their decision, an unquestioned belief in the group's inherent morality, a stereotyped view of enemy leaders as too evil to warrant genuine attempts to negotiate, and the emergence of self-appointed mind-guards.

Robert Kennedy, for example, who had been constantly informed about the Cuban invasion plan, asked Schlesinger privately why he was opposed. The President's brother listened coldly and then said: "You may be right or you may be wrong, but the President has made his mind up. Don't push it any further. Now is the time for everyone to help him all they can."

Here is a symptom of groupthink, displayed by a highly intelligent man whose ethical code committed him to freedom of dissent.

Robert Kennedy was functioning in a self-appointed role that I call being a "mind-guard." Just as a bodyguard protects the President and other high officials from physical harm, a mindguard protects them from thoughts that might damage their confidence in the soundness of the policies which they are about to launch.

CRITICAL THINKING QUESTIONS
1. How common is groupthink? Do you think that the conditions that give rise to groupthink are relatively rare or relatively common? Explain your answers. Cite additional examples of decisions that may have been influenced by groupthink.
2. Have you ever been involved in a group that experienced some sort of groupthink process? Describe the situation, and discuss the process in terms of groupthink.
3. If groupthink is common, then it would be useful if people were made aware of how it works. Should the conditions of groupthink, as well as how it can be prevented, be taught to leaders and potential leaders? How could this be accomplished?
4. The article gave some suggestions as to how groupthink could be prevented or at least minimized. Would all leaders be equally open to following these suggestions? Or might individual characteristics influence how open various leaders might be? How so?

ARTICLE 35 _____

Whenever two or more individuals act as a group, a central part of the interaction may involve trying to reach some agreement about an issue or activity. When the group consists of individuals or nations, reaching agreement is often a major concern.

Bargaining is one form that such negotiations take. The bargaining may be about something small and be informal in style, such as a couple deciding on which movie to see, or it may be major and formal, such as two nations trying to reach an agreement on nuclear arms control. In either case, central to the bargaining is the belief by both parties that reaching a mutually agreed upon solution will possibly benefit both of them.

Two broad approaches to bargaining are cooperation and competition. In a *competitive* situation, individuals or groups view the situation in "win-lose" terms: I want to win, and it most likely will be at your expense. In a *cooperative* arrangement, the situation is more likely to be viewed as a "win-win" opportunity: We can both get something good out of this; neither one has to lose. Other things being equal, a cooperative strategy is more likely to ensure a good outcome for all concerned. But is that the strategy most likely to be used? Or do individuals and groups tend to use competitive strategies instead, even if it might not ultimately be in their best interest to do so?

The following classic contribution by Morton Deutsch and Robert M. Krauss examines the effect of threat on interpersonal bargaining. One major finding of the study is that the presence of threat, as well as whether only one or both parties are capable of threat, has a major impact on the outcome of the bargaining situation. Common sense might suggest that if my opponent has some threat that he or she can use against me, then I would be better off having the same level of threat to use against him or her, rather than having no threat to retaliate with. The findings of the study do not confirm this expectation, however, and may suggest a rethinking of the use of threat and power in real-world negotiations.

The Effect of Threat
upon Interpersonal Bargaining

■ Morton Deutsch and Robert M. Krauss

A bargain is defined in *Webster's Unabridged Dictionary* as "an agreement between parties settling what each shall give and receive in a transaction between them"; it is further specified that a bargain is "an agreement or compact viewed as advantageous or the reverse." When the term "agreement" is broadened to include tacit, informal agreements as well as explicit agreements, it is evident that bargains and the processes involved in arriving at bargains ("bargaining") are pervasive characteristics of social life.

The definition of bargain fits under sociological definitions of the term "social norm." In this light, the experimental study of the bargaining process and of bargaining outcomes provides a means for the laboratory study of the development of certain types of social norms. But unlike many other types of social situations, bargaining situations have certain distinctive features that make it relevant to consider the conditions that determine whether or not a social norm will develop as well as those that determine the

Reprinted from *Journal of Personality and Social Psychology,* 1960, *61,* 181–189.

nature of the social norm if it develops. Bargaining situations highlight the possibility that, even where cooperation would be mutually advantageous, shared purposes may not develop, agreement may not be reached, and interaction may be regulated antagonistically rather than normatively.

The essential features of a bargaining situation exist when:

1. Both parties perceive that there is the possibility of reaching an agreement in which each party would be better off, or no worse off, than if no agreement were reached.
2. Both parties perceive that there is more than one such agreement that could be reached.
3. Both parties perceive each other to have conflicting preferences or opposed interests with regard to the different agreements that might be reached.

Everyday examples of bargaining include such situations as: the buyer-seller relationship when the price is not fixed, the husband and wife who want to spend an evening out together but have conflicting preferences about where to go, union-management negotiations, drivers who meet at an intersection when there is no clear right of way, disarmament negotiations.

In terms of our prior conceptualization of cooperation and competition (Deutsch, 1949) bargaining is thus a situation in which the participants have mixed motives toward one another: on the one hand, each has interest in cooperating so that they reach an agreement; on the other hand, they have competitive interests concerning the nature of the agreement they reach. In effect, to reach agreement the cooperative interest of the bargainers must be strong enough to overcome their competitive interests. However, agreement is not only contingent upon the *motivational* balances of cooperative to competitive interests but also upon the situational and *cognitive* factors which facilitate or hinder the recognition or invention of a bargaining agreement that reduces the opposition of interest and enhances the mutuality of interest.[1]

These considerations lead to the formulation of two general, closely related propositions about the likelihood that a bargaining agreement will be reached.

1. Bargainers are more likely to reach an agreement, the stronger are their cooperative interests in comparison with their competitive interests.
2. Bargainers are more likely to reach an agreement, the more resources they have available for recognizing or inventing potential bargaining agreements and for communicating to one another once a potential agreement has been recognized or invented.

From these two basic propositions and additional hypotheses concerning conditions that determine the strengths of the cooperative and competitive interests and the amount of available resources, we believe it is possible to explain the ease or difficulty of arriving at a bargaining agreement. We shall not present a full statement of these hypotheses here but turn instead to a description of an experiment that relates to Proposition 1.

The experiment was concerned with the effect of the availability of threat upon bargaining in a two-person experimental bargaining game.[2] Threat is defined as the expression of an intention to do something detrimental to the interests of another. Our experiment was guided by two assumptions about threat:

1. If there is a conflict of interest and one person is able to threaten the other, he will tend to use the threat in an attempt to force the other person to yield. This tendency should be stronger, the more irreconcilable the conflict is perceived to be.
2. If a person uses threat in an attempt to intimidate another, the threatened person (if he considers himself to be of equal or superior status) would feel hostility toward the threatener and tend to respond with counterthreat and/or increased resistance to yielding. We qualify this assumption by stating that the tendency to resist should be greater, the greater the perceived probability and magnitude of detriment to the other and the less the perceived probability and magnitude of detriment to the potential resister from the anticipated resistance to yielding.

The second assumption is based upon the view that when resistance is not seen to be suicidal or useless, to allow oneself to be intimidated, particularly by someone who does not have the right to expect deferential behavior, is to suffer a loss of social face and, hence, of self-esteem: and that the culturally defined way of maintaining self-esteem in the face of attempted intimidation is to engage in a contest for supremacy vis-à-vis the power to intimidate or, minimally, to resist intimidation. Thus, in effect, the use of threat (and if it is available to be used, there will be a tendency to use it) should strengthen the competitive interests of the bargainers in relationship to one another by introducing or enhancing the competitive struggle for self-esteem. Hence, from Proposition 1, it follows that the availability of a means of threat should make it more difficult for the bargainers to reach agreement (providing that the threatened person has some means of resisting the threat). The preceding statement is relevant to the comparison of both of our experimental conditions of threat, bilateral and unilateral (described below), with our experimental condition of nonthreat. We hypothesize that a bargaining agreement is more likely to be achieved when neither party can threaten the other, than when one or both parties can threaten the other.

Consider now the situations of bilateral threat and unilateral threat. For several reasons, a situation of bilateral threat is probably less conducive to agreement than is a condition of unilateral threat. First, the sheer likelihood that a threat will be made is greater when two people rather than one have the means of making the threat. Secondly, once a threat is made in the bilateral case it is likely to evoke counterthreat. Withdrawal of threat in the face of counterthreat probably involves more loss of face (for reasons analogous to those discussed in relation to yielding to intimidation) than does withdrawal of threat in the face of resistance to threat. Finally, in the unilateral case, although the person without the threat potential can resist and not yield to the threat, his position vis-à-vis the other is not so strong as the position of the threatened person in the bilateral case. In the unilateral case, the threatened person may have a worse outcome than the other whether he resists or yields; while in the bilateral case, the threatened person is sure to have a worse outcome if he yields but he may insure that he does not have a worse outcome if he does not yield.

METHOD

Procedure

Subjects (*S*s) were asked to imagine that they were in charge of a trucking company, carrying merchandise over a road to a destination. For each trip completed they made $.60, minus their operating expenses. Operating expenses were calculated at the rate of one cent per second. So, for example, if it took 37 seconds to complete a particular trip, the player's profit would be $.60 – $.37 or a net profit of $.23 for that particular trip.

Each *S* was assigned a name, Acme or Bolt. As the "road map" (see Figure 1) indicates, both players start from separate points and go to separate destinations. At one point their paths cross. This is the section of road labeled "one lane road," which is only one lane wide, so that two trucks, heading in opposite directions, could not pass each other. If one backs up the other can go forward, or both can back up, or both can sit there head-on without moving.

There is another way for each *S* to reach the destination on the map, labeled the "alternate route." The two players' paths do not cross on this route, but the alternative is 56% longer than the main route. *S*s were told that they could expect to lose at least $.10 each time they used the alternate route.

At either end of the one-lane section there is a gate that is under the control of the player to whose starting point it is closest. By closing the gate, one player can prevent the other from traveling over that section of the main route. The use of the gate provides the threat potential in this game. In the bilateral threat potential condition (Two Gates) both players had gates under their control. In a second condition of unilateral threat (One Gate) Acme had control of a gate but Bolt did not. In a third condition (No Gates) neither player controlled a gate.

*S*s played the game seated in separate booths placed so that they could not see each other but could see the experimenter (*E*). Each *S* had a "control panel" mounted on a 12" x 18" x 12" sloping-front cabinet (see Figure 2). The apparatus consisted essentially of a reversible impulse computer that was pulsed by a recycling timer. When the *S* wanted to move her truck forward she threw a key that closed a circuit pulsing the "add" coil of the impulse counter mounted on her

FIGURE 1 / Subject's Road Map

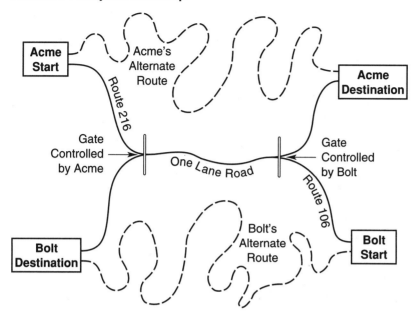

FIGURE 2 / Subject's Control Panel

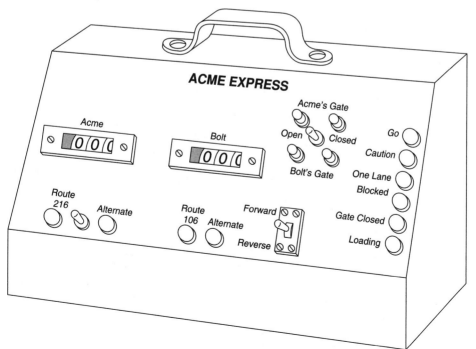

control panel. As the counter cumulated, *S* was able to determine her "position" by relating the number on her counter to reference numbers that had been written in on her road map. Similarly, when she wished to reverse, she would throw a switch that activated the "subtract" coil of her counter, thus subtracting from the total on the counter each time the timer cycled.

S's counter was connected in parallel to counters on the other *S*'s panel and on *E*'s panel. Thus each player had two counters on her panel, one representing her own position and the other representing the other player's. Provision was made in construction of the apparatus to permit cutting the other player's counter out of the circuit, so that each *S* knew only the position of her own truck. This was done in the present experiment. Experiments now in progress are studying the effects of knowledge of the other person's position and other aspects of interpersonal communication upon the bargaining process.

The only time one player definitely knew the other player's position was when they had met head-on on the one-way section of road. This was indicated by a traffic light mounted on the panel. When this light was on, neither player could move forward unless the other moved back. The gates were controlled by toggle switches and panel-mounted indicator lights showed, for both *Ss*, whether each gate was open or closed.

The following "rules of the game" were stated to the *Ss*:

1. A player who started out on one route and wished to switch to the other route could only do so after first reversing and going back to the start position. Direct transfer from one route to the other was not permitted except at the start position.
2. In the conditions where *Ss* had gates, they were permitted to close the gates no matter where they were on the main route, so long as they were on the main route (i.e., they were not permitted to close the gate while on the alternate route or after having reached their destinations). However, *Ss* were permitted to open their gates at any point in the game.

Ss were taken through a number of practice exercises to familiarize them with the game. In the first trial they were made to meet head-on on the one-lane path; Acme was then told to back up until she was just

off the one-lane path and Bolt was told to go forward. After Bolt had gone through the one-lane path, Acme was told to go forward. Each continued going forward until each arrived at her destination. The second practice trial was the same as the first except that Bolt rather than Acme backed up after meeting head-on. In the next practice trial, one of the players was made to wait just before the one-way path while the other traversed it and then was allowed to continue. In the next practice trial, one player was made to take the alternate route and the other was made to take the main route. Finally, in the bilateral and unilateral threat conditions the use of the gate was illustrated (by having the player get on the main route, close the gate, and then go back and take the alternate route). The *Ss* were told explicitly, with emphasis, that they did *not* have to use the gate. Before each trial in the game the gate or gates were in the open position.

The instructions stressed an individualistic motivation orientation. *Ss* were told to try to earn as much money for themselves as possible and to have no interest in whether the other player made money or lost money. They were given $4.00 in poker chips to represent their working capital and told that after each trial they would be given "money" if they made a profit or that "money" would be taken from them if they lost (i.e., took more than 60 seconds to complete their trip). The profit or loss of each *S* was announced so that both *Ss* could hear the announcement after each trial. Each pair of *Ss* played a total of 20 trials; on all trials, they started off together. In other words each trial presented a repetition of the same bargaining problem. In cases where *Ss* lost their working capital before the 20 trials were completed, additional chips were given them. *Ss* were aware that their monetary winnings and losses were to be imaginary and that no money would change hands as a result of the experiment.

Subjects

Sixteen pairs of *Ss* were used in each of the three experimental conditions. The *Ss* were female clerical and supervisory personnel of the New Jersey Bell Telephone Company who volunteered to participate during their working day.[3] Their ages ranged from 20 to 39, with a mean of 26.2. All were naive to the purpose of the experiment. By staggering the arrival times and choosing girls from different locations, we were able to insure that the *S*s did not know with whom they were playing.

Data Recorded

Several types of data were collected. We obtained a record of the profit or loss of each *S* on each trial. We also obtained a detailed recording of the actions taken by each *S* during the course of a trial. For this purpose, we used an Esterline-Angus model AW Operations Recorder which enabled us to obtain a "log" of each move each *S* made during the game (e.g., whether and when she took the main or alternate route; when she went forward, backward, or remained still; when she closed and opened the gate; when she arrived at her destination).

RESULTS[4]

The best single measure of the difficulty experienced by the bargainers in reaching an agreement is the sum of each pair's profits (or losses) on a given trial. The higher the sum of the payoffs to the two players on a given trial, the less time it took them to arrive at a procedure for sharing the one-lane path of the main route. (It was, of course, possible for one or both of the players to decide to take the alternate route so as to avoid a protracted stalemate during the process of bargaining. This, however, always results in at least a $.20 smaller joint payoff if only one player took the alternate route, than an optimally arrived at agreement concerning the use of the one-way path.) Figure 3 presents the medians of the summed payoffs (i.e., Acme's plus Bolt's) for all pairs in each of the three experimental conditions over the 20 trials.[5] These striking results indicate that agreement was least difficult to arrive at in the no threat condition, was more difficult to arrive at in the unilateral threat condition, and exceedingly difficult or impossible to arrive at in the bilateral threat condition (see also Table 1).

Examination of Figure 3 suggests that learning occurred during the 20 trials: the summed payoffs for pairs of *S*s tend to improve as the number of trials increases. This suggestion is confirmed by an analysis of variance of the slopes for the summed payoffs[6] over

the 20 trials for each of the 16 pairs in each of the 3 experimental treatments. The results of this analysis indicate that the slopes are significantly greater than zero for the unilateral threat ($p < .01$) and the no threat ($p < .02$) conditions; for the bilateral threat condition, the slope does not reach statistical significance ($.10 < p < .20$). The data indicate that the pairs in the no threat condition started off at a fairly high level but, even so, showed some improvement over the 20 trials; the pairs in the unilateral threat condition started off low and, having considerable opportunity for improvement, used their opportunity; the pairs in the bilateral threat condition, on the other hand, did not benefit markedly from repeated trials.

Figure 4 compares Acme's median profit in the three experimental conditions over the 20 trials; while Figure 5 compares Bolt's profit in the three conditions. (In the unilateral threat condition, it was Acme who controlled a gate and Bolt who did not.) Bolt's as well as Acme's outcome is somewhat better in the no threat condition than in the unilateral threat condition; Acme's, as well as Bolt's, outcome is clearly worst in the bilateral threat condition (see Table 1 also). However, Figure 6 reveals that Acme does somewhat better than Bolt in the unilateral condition. Thus, if threat-potential exists within a bargaining relationship it is better to possess it oneself than to have the other party possess it. However, it is even better for neither party to possess it. Moreover, Figure 5 shows that Bolt is better off not having than having a gate

FIGURE 3 / Median Joint Payoff (Acme + Bolt) over Trials

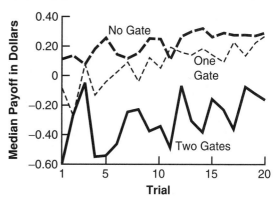

TABLE 1 / Mean Payoffs Summated over the Twenty Trials

Variable	Means			Statistical Comparisons: p values[a]			
	(1) No Threat	(2) Unilateral Threat	(3) Bilateral Threat	Overall	(1) vs. (2)	(1) vs. (3)	(2) vs. (3)
Summed Payoffs (Acme + Bolt)	203.31	−405.88	−875.12	.01	.01	.01	.05
Acme's Payoff	122.44	−118.56	−406.56	.01	.10	.01	.05
Bolt's Payoff	80.88	−287.31	−468.56	.01	.01	.01	.20
Absolute Differences in Payoff (A − B)	125.94	294.75	315.25	.05	.05	.01	*ns*

[a]Evaluation of the significance of overall variation between conditions is based on an F test with 2 and 45 *df*.
Comparisons between treatments are based on a two-tailed *t* test.

even when Acme has a gate: Bolt tends to do better in the unilateral threat condition than in the bilateral threat condition.

The size of the absolute discrepancy between the payoffs of the two players in each pair provides a measure of the confusion or difficulty in predicting what the other player was going to do. Thus, a large absolute discrepancy might indicate that after one player had gone through the one-way path and left it open, the other player continued to wait; or it might indicate that one player continued to wait at a closed gate hoping the other player would open it quickly but the other player did not; etc. Figure 7 indicates that the discrepancy between players in the no threat condition is initially small and remains small for the

20 trials. For the players in both the bilateral and unilateral threat conditions, the discrepancy is initially relatively larger; but it decreases more noticeably in the unilateral threat condition by the tenth trial and, therefore, is consistently smaller than in the bilateral condition.

By way of concrete illustration, we present a synopsis of the game for one pair in each of three experimental treatments.

No Threat Condition

Trial 1   The players met in the center of the one-way section. After some back-and-forth movement Bolt reversed to the end of the one-way section, allow-

FIGURE 4 / Acme's Median Payoff

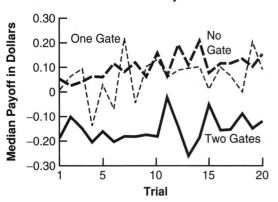

FIGURE 5 / Bolt's Median Payoff

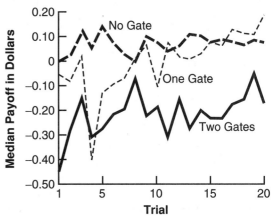

FIGURE 6 / Acme's and Bolt's Median Payoffs in Unilateral Threat Condition

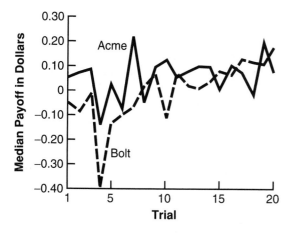

FIGURE 7 / Median Absolute Differences in Payoff

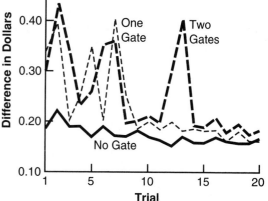

ing Acme to pass through, and then proceeded forward herself.

Trial 2 They again met at the center of the one-way path. This time, after moving back and forth deadlocked for some time, Bolt reversed to "start" and took the alternate route to her destination, thus leaving Acme free to go through on the main route.

Trial 3 The players again met at the center of the one-way path. This time, however, Acme reversed to the beginning of the path, allowing Bolt to go through to her destination. Then Acme was able to proceed forward on the main route.

Trial 5 Both players elected to take the alternate route to their destinations.

Trial 7 Both players took the main route and met in the center. They waited, deadlocked, for a considerable time. Then Acme reversed to the end of the one-way path allowing Bolt to go through, then proceeded through to her destination.

Trials 10–20 Acme and Bolt fall into a pattern of alternating who is to go first on the one-way section. There is no deviation from this pattern.

The only other pattern that emerges in this condition is one in which one player dominates the other.

That is, one player consistently goes first on the one-way section and the other player consistently yields.

Unilateral Threat Condition

Trial 1 Both players took the main route and met in the center of it. Acme immediately closed the gate, reversed to "start," and took the alternate route to her destination. Bolt waited for a few seconds, at the closed gate, then reversed and took the alternate route.

Trial 2 Both players took the main route and met in the center. After moving back and forth deadlocked for about 15 seconds, Bolt reversed to the beginning of the one-way path, allowed Acme to pass, and then proceeded forward to her destination.

Trial 3 Both players started out on the main route, meeting in the center. After moving back and forth deadlocked for a while, Acme closed her gate, reversed to "start," and took the alternate route. Bolt, meanwhile, waited at the closed gate. When Acme arrived at her destination she opened the gate, and Bolt went through to complete her trip.

Trial 5 Both players took the main route, meeting at the center of the one-way section. Acme immediately closed her gate, reversed, and took the alternate route. Bolt waited at the gate for about 10 seconds, then reversed and took the alternate route to her destination.

Trial 10 Both players took the main route and met in the center. Acme closed her gate, reversed, and took the alternate route. Bolt remained waiting at the closed gate. After Acme arrived at her destination, she opened the gate and Bolt completed her trip.

Trial 15 Acme took the main route to her destination and Bolt took the alternate route.

Trials 17–20 Both players took the main route and met in the center. Bolt waited a few seconds, then reversed to the end of the one-way section allowing Acme to go through. Then Bolt proceeded forward to her destination.

Other typical patterns that developed in this experimental condition included an alternating pattern similar to that described in the no threat condition, a dominating pattern in which Bolt would select the alternate route leaving Acme free to use the main route unobstructed, and a pattern in which Acme would close her gate and then take the alternate route, also forcing Bolt to take the alternate route.

Bilateral Threat Condition

Trial 1 Acme took the main route and Bolt took the alternate route.

Trial 2 Both players took the main route and met head-on. Bolt closed her gate. Acme waited a few seconds, then closed her gate, reversed to "start," then went forward again to the closed gate. Acme reversed and took the alternate route. Bolt again reversed, then started on the alternate route. Acme opened her gate and Bolt reversed to "start" and went to her destination on the main route.

Trial 3 Acme took the alternate route to her destination. Bolt took the main route and closed her gate before entering the one-way section.

Trial 5 Both players took the main route and met head-on. After about 10 seconds spent backing up

and going forward, Acme closed her gate, reversed, and took the alternate route. After waiting a few seconds, Bolt did the same.

Trials 8–10 Both players started out on the main route, immediately closed their gates, reversed to "start," and took the alternate route to their destinations.

Trial 15 Both players started out on the main route and met head-on. After some jockeying for position, Acme closed her gate, reversed, and took the alternate route to her destination. After waiting at the gate for a few seconds, Bolt reversed to "start" and took the alternate route to her destination.

Trials 19–20 Both players started out on the main route, immediately closed their gates, reversed to "start," and took the alternate routes to their destinations.

Other patterns that emerged in the bilateral threat condition included alternating first use of the one-way section, one player's dominating the other on first use of the one-way section, and another dominating pattern in which one player consistently took the main route while the other consistently took the alternate route.

DISCUSSION

From our view of bargaining as a situation in which both cooperative and competitive tendencies are present and acting upon the individual, it is relevant to inquire as to the conditions under which a stable agreement of any form develops. However, implicit in most economic models of bargaining (e.g., Stone, 1958; Zeuthen, 1930) is the assumption that the cooperative interests of the bargainers are sufficiently strong to insure that some form of mutually satisfactory agreement will be reached. For this reason, such models have focused upon the form of the agreement reached by the bargainers. Siegel and Fouraker (1960) report a series of bargaining experiments quite different in structure from ours in which only one of many pairs of *Ss* were unable to reach agreement. Siegel and Fouraker explain this rather startling result as follows:

Apparently the disruptive forces which lead to the rupture of some negotiations were at least partially controlled in our sessions. . . .

Some negotiations collapse when one party becomes incensed at the other, and henceforth strives to maximize his opponent's displeasure rather than his own satisfaction. . . . Since it is difficult to transmit insults by means of quantitative bids, such disequilibrating behavior was not induced in the present studies. If subjects were allowed more latitude in their communications and interactions, the possibility of an affront offense-punitive behavior sequence might be increased (p. 100).

In our experimental bargaining situation, the availability of threat clearly made it more difficult for bargainers to reach a mutually profitable agreement. These results, we believe, reflect psychological tendencies that are not confined to our bargaining situation: the tendency to use threat (if the means for threatening is available) in an attempt to force the other person to yield, when the other is seen as obstructing one's path; the tendency to respond with counterthreat or increased resistance to attempts at intimidation. How general are these tendencies? What conditions are likely to elicit them? Answers to these questions are necessary before our results can be generalized to other situations.

Dollard, Doob, Miller, Mowrer, and Sears (1939) have cited a variety of evidence to support the view that aggression (i.e., the use of threat) is a common reaction to a person who is seen as the agent of frustration. There seems to be little reason to doubt that the use of threat is a frequent reaction to interpersonal impasses. However, everyday observation indicates that threat does not inevitably occur when there is an interpersonal impasse. We would speculate that it is most likely to occur: when the threatener has no positive interest in the other person's welfare (he is either egocentrically or competitively related to the other); when the threatener believes that the other has no positive interest in his welfare; and when the threatener anticipates either that his threat will be effective or, if ineffective, will not worsen his situation because he expects the worst to happen if he does not use his threat. We suggest that these conditions were operative in our experiment; Ss were either egocentri-

cally or competitively oriented to one another[7] and they felt that they would not be worse off by the use of threat.

Everyday observation suggests that the tendency to respond with counterthreat or increased resistance to attempts at intimidation is also a common occurrence. We believe that introducing threat into a bargaining situation affects the meaning of yielding. Although we have no data to support this interpretation directly, we will attempt to justify it on the basis of some additional assumptions.

Goffman (1955) has pointed out the pervasive significance of "face" in the maintenance of the social order. In this view, self-esteem is a socially validated system that grows out of the acceptance by others of the claim for deference, prestige, and recognition that a person presents in his behavior toward others. Since the rejection of such a claim would be perceived (by the recipient) as directed against his self-esteem, he must react against it rather than accept it in order to maintain the integrity of his self-esteem system.

One may view the behavior of our Ss as an attempt to make claims upon the other, an attempt to develop a set of shared expectations as to what each was entitled to. Why then did the Ss' reactions differ so markedly as a function of the availability of threat? The explanation lies, we believe, in the cultural interpretation of yielding (to a peer or subordinate) under duress, as compared to giving in without duress. The former, we believe, is perceived as a negatively valued form of behavior, with negative implications for the self-image of the person who so behaves. At least partly, this is so because the locus of causality is perceived to be outside the person's voluntary control. No such evaluation, however, need be placed on the behavior of one who "gives in" in a situation where no threat or duress is a factor. Rather, we should expect the culturally defined evaluation of such a person's behavior to be one of "reasonableness" or "maturity," because the source of the individual's behavior is perceived to lie within his own control.

Our discussion so far has suggested that the psychological factors which operate in our experimental bargaining situation are to be found in many real-life bargaining situations. However, it is well to recognize some unique features of our experimental game. First, the bargainers had no opportunity to communicate verbally with one another. Prior research on the role of communication in trust (Deutsch, 1958, 1960; Loomis, 1959) suggests that the opportunity for communication would have made reaching an agreement easier for individualistically-oriented bargainers. This same research (Deutsch, 1960) indicates, however, that communication may not be effective between competitively oriented bargainers. This possibility was expressed spontaneously by a number of our *S*s in a post-game interview.

Another characteristic of our bargaining game is that the passage of time, without coming to an agreement, is costly to the players. There are, of course, bargaining situations in which lack of agreement may simply preserve the *status quo* without any worsening of the bargainers' respective situations. This is the case in the typical bilateral monopoly case, where the buyer and seller are unable to agree upon a price (e.g., see Siegel & Fouraker, 1960). In other sorts of bargaining situations, however, (e.g., labor-management negotiations during a strike, international negotiations during an expensive cold war) the passage of time may play an important role. In our experiment, we received the impression that the meaning of time changed as time passed without the bargainers reaching an agreement. Initially, the passage of time seemed to place the players under pressure to come to an agreement before their costs mounted sufficiently to destroy their profit. With the continued passage of time, however, their mounting losses strengthened their resolution not to yield to the other player. They comment: "I've lost so much, I'll be damned if I give in now. At least I'll have the satisfaction of doing better than she does." The mounting losses and continued deadlock seemed to change the game from a mixed motive into a predominantly competitive situation.

It is, of course, hazardous to generalize from a laboratory experiment to the complex problems of the real world. But our experiment and the theoretical ideas underlying it can perhaps serve to emphasize some notions which, otherwise, have an intrinsic plausibility. In brief, these are that there is more safety in cooperative than in competitive coexistence, that it is dangerous for bargainers to have weapons, and that it is possibly even more dangerous for a bargainer to have the capacity to retaliate in kind than not to have this capacity when the other bargainer has a weapon.

This last statement assumes that the one who yields has more of his values preserved by accepting the agreement preferred by the other than by extended conflict. Of course, in some bargaining situations in the real world, the loss incurred by yielding may exceed the losses due to extended conflict.

SUMMARY

The nature of bargaining situations was discussed. Two general propositions about the conditions affecting the likelihood of a bargaining agreement were presented. The effects of the availability of threat upon interpersonal bargaining were investigated experimentally in a two-person bargaining game. Three experimental conditions were employed: no threat (neither player could threaten the other), unilateral threat (only one of the players had a means of threat available to her), and bilateral threat (both players could threaten each other). The results indicated that the difficulty in reaching an agreement and the amount of (imaginary) money lost, individually as well as collectively, was greatest in the bilateral and next greatest in the unilateral threat condition. Only in the no threat condition did the players make an overall profit. In the unilateral threat condition, the player with the threat capability did better than the player without the threat capability. However, comparing the bilateral and unilateral threat conditions, the results also indicate that when facing a player who had threat capability one was better off *not* having than having the capacity to retaliate in kind.

REFERENCES

Deutsch, M. A theory of cooperation and competition. *Hum. Relat.,* 1949, *2,* 129–152.

Deutsch, M. Trust and suspicion. *J. conflict Resolut.,* 1958, *2,* 265–279.

Deutsch, M. The effect of motivational orientation upon trust and suspicion. *Hum. Relat.,* 1960, *13,* 123–140.

Dollard, J., Doob, L. W., Miller, N. E., Mowrer, O. H., & Sears, R. H. *Frustration and aggression.* New Haven: Yale Univer. Press, 1939.

Goffman, E. On face-work, *Psychiatry,* 1955, *18,* 213–231.

Loomis, J. L. Communication, the development of trust and cooperative behavior. *Hum. Relat.,* 1959, *12,* 305–315.

Schelling, T. C. Bargaining, communication and limited war. *J. conflict Resolut.*, 1957, *1*, 19–38.

Schelling, T. C. The strategy of conflict: Prospectus for the reorientation of game theory. *J. conflict Resolut.*, 1958, *2*, 203–264.

Siegel, S., & Fouraker, L. E. *Bargaining and group decision making.* New York: McGraw-Hill, 1960.

Stone, J. J. An experiment in bargaining games. *Econometrica*, 1958, *26*, 286–296.

Zeuthen, F. *Problems of monopoly and economic warfare.* London: Routledge, 1930.

NOTES

1. Schelling in a series of stimulating papers on bargaining (1957, 1958) has also stressed the "mixed motive" character of bargaining situations and has analyzed some of the cognitive factors which determine agreements.

2. The game was conceived and originated by M. Deutsch; R. M. Krauss designed and constructed the apparatus employed in the experiment.

3. We are indebted to the New Jersey Bell Telephone Company for their cooperation in providing Ss and facilities for the experiment.

4. We are indebted to M. J. R. Healy for suggestions concerning the statistical analysis of our data.

5. Medians are used in graphic presentation of our results because the wide variability of means makes inspection cumbersome.

6. A logarithmic transformation of the summed payoffs on each trial for each pair was made before computing the slopes for a given pair.

7. A post-experimental questionnaire indicated that, in all three experimental conditions, the Ss were most strongly motivated to win money, next most strongly motivated to do better than the other player, next most motivated to "have fun," and were very little or not at all motivated to help the other player.

CRITICAL THINKING QUESTIONS

1. For many years, the mutually assured destruction (MAD) policy defined U.S. nuclear strategy. That is, nuclear war was to be prevented by the threat of assured destruction of the aggressor nation. What might be the implications of this study for the nuclear policies of nations?

2. The best performance in this study was obtained in the no-threat condition; the unilateral threat condition in turn produced better results than the bilateral threat condition, which did the worst. To what extent are these findings generalizable to other situations? In some situations, might it be best to have bilateral threat instead of unilateral threat? What variables might be important in determining when each would be preferred? Explain.

3. In an area such as international relations, how can the existence of threat be reduced? What role may communication play in the process?

ADDITIONAL RELATED READINGS

Hyde, C. E. (1997). Bargaining and delay: The role of external justification. *Theory and Decision, 42*, 81–104.

Messick, D. M., Roore, D. A., & Bazerman, M. H. (1997). Ultimatum bargaining with a group: Underestimating the importance of the decision rule. *Organizational Behavior and Human Decision Processes, 69*, 87–101.

ARTICLE 36 _____

Article 34 in this chapter presented the concept known as *groupthink*. Since Irving L. Janis proposed this hypothesis over 20 years ago, he and others have continued to refine understanding of the antecedent conditions, symptoms, and consequences of groupthink. Since its introduction, groupthink has been widely studied and broadly incorporated into the literature and knowledge base, not only in the field of social psychology but also in areas such as management and organizational behavior.

Since the concept of groupthink provides the information necessary for identifying its causes as well as its symptoms, we would hope that the occurrence of groupthink would diminish. After all, the concept includes recommendations for decreasing the likelihood of its development. Unfortunately, that might not be the case.

The following article by Gregory Moorhead, Richard Ference, and Chris P. Neck applies the groupthink concept to the ill-fated decision to launch the space shuttle *Challenger* in 1986. The implication that the ensuing tragedy could have been prevented had groupthink not prevailed in the decision to launch is indeed sobering.

Group Decision Fiascoes Continue
Space Shuttle *Challenger* and a Revised Groupthink Framework

■ Gregory Moorhead, Richard Ference, and Chris P. Neck

This paper reviews the decision situation surrounding the decision to launch the space shuttle Challenger *in January 1986 in the light of the groupthink hypothesis. A revised framework is presented that proposes time and leadership style as moderators of the manner in which group characteristics lead to groupthink symptoms.*

INTRODUCTION

In 1972, a new dimension was added to our understanding of group decision making with the proposal of the groupthink hypothesis by Janis (1972). Janis coined the term "groupthink" to refer to "a mode of thinking that people engage in when they are deeply involved in a cohesive in-group, when the members' striving for unanimity override their motivation to realistically appraise alternative courses of action" (Janis, 1972, p. 8). The hypothesis was supported by his hindsight analysis of several political-military fiascoes and successes that are differentiated by the occurrence or non-occurrence of antecedent conditions, groupthink symptoms, and decision making defects.

In a subsequent volume, Janis further explicates the theory and adds an analysis of the Watergate transcripts and various published memoirs and accounts of principals involved, concluding that the Watergate cover-up decision also was a result of groupthink (Janis, 1983). Both volumes propose prescriptions for preventing the occurrence of groupthink, many of which have appeared in popular press, in books on executive decision making, and in management textbooks. Multiple advocacy decision-making procedures have been adopted at the executive levels in many organizations, including the executive branch of the government. One would think that by 1986, 13 years after the publication of a popular book, that its prescriptions might be well ingrained in our management and decision-making styles. Unfortunately, it has not happened.

Reprinted from G. Moorhead, R. Ference, and C. P. Neck, "Group Decision Fiascoes Continue," *Human Relations,* 1991, *44,* 539–549. Copyright © 1991, Plenum Publishing Corporation. Reprinted by permission.

On January 28,1986, the space shuttle *Challenger* was launched from Kennedy Space Center. The temperature that morning was in the mid-20's, well below the previous low temperatures at which the shuttle engines had been tested. Seventy-three seconds after launch, the *Challenger* exploded, killing all seven astronauts aboard, and becoming the worst disaster in space flight history. The catastrophe shocked the nation, crippled the American space program, and is destined to be remembered as the most tragic national event since the assassination of John F. Kennedy in 1963.

The Presidential Commission that investigated the accident pointed to a flawed decision-making process as a primary contributory cause. The decision was made the night before the launch in the Level I Flight Readiness Review meeting. Due to the work of the Presidential Commission, information concerning that meeting is available for analysis as a group decision possibly susceptible to groupthink.

In this paper, we report the results of our analysis of the Level I Flight Readiness Review meeting as a decision-making situation that displays evidence of groupthink. We review the antecedent conditions, the groupthink symptoms, and the possible decision-making defects, as suggested by Janis (1983). In addition, we take the next and more important step of going beyond the development of another example of groupthink to make recommendations for renewed inquiry into group decision-making processes.

THEORY AND EVIDENCE

The groupthink hypothesis has been presented in detail in numerous publications other than Janis' books (Flowers, 1977; Courtright, 1978; Leana, 1985; Moorhead, 1982; Moorhead & Montanari, 1986) and will not be repeated here. The major categories will be used as a framework for organizing the evidence from the meeting. Within each category the key elements will be presented along with meeting details that pertain to each.

The meeting(s) took place throughout the day and evening from 12:36 pm (EST), January 27, 1986 following the decision to not launch the *Challenger* due to high crosswinds at the launch site. Discussions continued through about 12:00 midnight (EST) via teleconferencing and Telefax systems connecting the Kennedy Space Center in Florida, Morton Thiokol (MTI) in Utah, Johnson Space Center in Houston, and the Marshall Space Flight Center. The Level I Flight Readiness Review is the highest level of review prior to launch. It comprises the highest level of management at the three space centers and at MTI, the private supplier of the solid rocket booster engines.

To briefly state the situation, the MTI engineers recommended not to launch if temperatures of the O-ring seals on the rocket were below 53 degrees Fahrenheit, which was the lowest temperature of any previous flight. Laurence B. Mulloy, manager of the Solid Rocket Booster Project at Marshall Space Flight Center, states:

> . . . The bottom line of that, though, initially was that Thiokol engineering, Bob Lund, who is the Vice President and Director of Engineering, who is here today, recommended that 51-L [the Challenger] not be launched if the O-ring temperatures predicted at launch time would be lower than any previous launch, and that was 53 degrees . . . (Report of the Presidential Commission on the Space Shuttle Accident, *1986, p. 91–92*)

This recommendation was made at 8:45 pm, January 27, 1986 (*Report of the Presidential Commission on the Space Shuttle Accident,* 1986). Through the ensuing discussions the decision to launch was made.

Antecedent Conditions

The three primary antecedent conditions for the development of groupthink are: a highly cohesive group, leader preference for a certain decision, and insulation of the group from qualified outside opinions. These conditions existed in this situation.

Cohesive Group   The people who made the decision to launch had worked together for many years. They were familiar with each other and had grown through the ranks of the space program. A high degree of *esprit de corps* existed between the members.

Leader Preference   Two top level managers actively promoted their pro-launch opinions in the face of opposition. The commission report states that several managers at space centers and MTI pushed for launch, regardless of the low temperatures.

Insulation from Experts   MTI engineers made their recommendations relatively early in the evening. The top level decision-making group knew of their objections but did not meet with them directly to review their data and concerns. As Roger Boisjoly, a Thiokol engineer, states in his remarks to the Presidential Commission:

> . . . and the bottom line was that the engineering people would not recommend a launch below 53 degrees Fahrenheit . . . From this point on, management formulated the points to base their decision on. There was never one comment in favor, as I have said, of launching by any engineer or other nonmanagement person. . . . I was not even asked to participate in giving any input to the final decision charts (Report of the Presidential Commission on the Space Shuttle Accident, *1986, p. 91–92)*

This testimonial indicates that the top decision-making team was insulated from the engineers who possessed the expertise regarding the functioning of the equipment.

Groupthink Symptoms

Janis identified eight symptoms of groupthink. They are presented here along with evidence from the *Report of the Presidential Commission on the Space Shuttle Accident* (1986).

Invulnerability   When groupthink occurs, most or all of the members of the decision-making group have an illusion of invulnerability that reassures them in the face of obvious dangers. This illusion leads the group to become overly optimistic and willing to take extraordinary risks. It may also cause them to ignore clear warnings of danger.

The solid rocket joint problem that destroyed *Challenger* was discussed often at flight readiness review meetings prior to flight. However, Commission member Richard Feynman concluded from the testimony that a mentality of overconfidence existed due to the extraordinary record of success of space flights. Every time we send one up it is successful. Involved

members may seem to think that on the next one we can lower our standards or take more risks because it always works (*Time*, 1986).

The invulnerability illusion may have built up over time as a result of NASA's own spectacular history. NASA had not lost an astronaut since 1967 when a flash fire in the capsule of Apollo 1 killed three. Since that time NASA had a string of 55 successful missions. They had put a man on the moon, built and launched Skylab and the shuttle, and retrieved defective satellites from orbit. In the minds of most Americans and apparently their own, they could do no wrong.

Rationalization   Victims of groupthink collectively construct rationalizations that discount warnings and other forms of negative feedback. If these signals were taken seriously when presented, the group members would be forced to reconsider their assumptions each time they re-commit themselves to their past decisions.

In the Level I flight readiness meeting when the *Challenger* was given final launch approval, MTI engineers presented evidence that the joint would fail. Their argument was based on the fact that in the coldest previous launch (air temperature 30 degrees) the joint in question experienced serious erosion and that no data existed as to how the joint would perform at colder temperatures. Flight center officials put forth numerous technical rationalizations faulting MTI's analysis. One of these rationalizations was that the engineer's data were inconclusive. As Mr. Boisjoly emphasized to the Commission:

> . . . I was asked, yes, at that point in time I was asked to quantify my concerns, and I said I couldn't. I couldn't quantify it. I had no data to quantify it, but I did say I knew that it was away from goodness in the current data base. Someone on the net commented that we had soot blow-by on SRM-22 [Flight 61-A, October, 1985] which was launched at 75 degrees. I don't remember who made the comment but that is where the first comment came in about the disparity between my conclusion and the observed data because SRM-22 [Flight 61-A, October 1985] had blow-by at essentially a room temperature launch. I then said that SRM-15 [Flight 51-C, January, 1985] had

much more blow-by indication and that it was indeed telling us that lower temperature was a factor. I was asked again for data to support my claim, and I said I have none other than what is being presented. (Report of the Presidential Commission on the Space Shuttle Accident, 1986, p. 89)

Discussions became twisted (compared to previous meetings) and no one detected it. Under normal conditions, MTI would have to prove the shuttle boosters readiness for launch, instead they found themselves being forced to prove that the boosters were unsafe. Boisjoly's testimony supports this description of the discussion:

. . . This was a meeting where the determination was to launch, and it was up to us to prove beyond a shadow of a doubt that it was not safe to do so. This is in total reverse to what the position usually is in a preflight conversation or a flight readiness review. It is usually exactly opposite of that . . . (Report of the Presidential Commission on the Space Shuttle Accident, 1986, p. 93)

Morality   Group members often believe, without question, in the inherent morality of their position. They tend to ignore the ethical or moral consequences of their decision.

In the *Challenger* case, this point was raised by a very high level MTI manager, Allan J. McDonald, who tried to stop the launch and said that he would not want to have to defend the decision to launch. He stated to the Commission:

. . . I made the statement that if we're wrong and something goes wrong on this flight, I wouldn't want to have to be the person to stand up in front of board in inquiry and say that I went ahead and told them to go ahead and fly this thing outside what the motor was qualified to . . . (Report of the Presidential Commission on the Space Shuttle Accident, 1986, p. 95)

Some members did not hear this statement because it occurred during a break. Three top officials who did hear it ignored it.

Stereotyped Views of Others   Victims of groupthink often have a stereotyped view of the opposition of

anyone with a competing opinion. They feel that the opposition is too stupid or too weak to understand or deal effectively with the problem.

Two of the top three NASA officials responsible for the launch displayed this attitude. They felt that they completely understood the nature of the joint problem and never seriously considered the objections raised by the MTI engineers. In fact they denigrated and badgered the opposition and their information and opinions.

Pressure on Dissent   Group members often apply direct pressure to anyone who questions the validity of the arguments supporting a decision or position favored by the majority. These same two officials pressured MTI to change its position after MTI originally recommended that the launch not take place. These two officials pressured MTI personnel to prove that it was not safe to launch, rather than to prove the opposite. As mentioned earlier, this was a total reversal of normal preflight procedures. It was this pressure that top MTI management was responding to when they overruled their engineering staff and recommended launch. As the Commission report states:

. . . At approximately 11 p.m. Eastern Standard Time, the Thiokol/NASA teleconference resumed, the Thiokol management stating that they had reassessed the problem, that the temperature effects were a concern, but that the data was admittedly inconclusive . . . (p. 96)

This seems to indicate that NASA's pressure on these Thiokol officials forced them to change their recommendation from delay to execution of the launch.

Self-Censorship   Group members tend to censor themselves when they have opinions or ideas that deviate from the apparent group consensus. Janis feels that this reflects each member's inclination to minimize to himself or herself the importance of his or her own doubts and counter-arguments.

The most obvious evidence of self-censorship occurred when a vice president of MTI, who had previously presented information against launch, bowed to pressure from NASA and accepted their rationalizations for launch. He then wrote these up and presented them to NASA as the reasons that MTI had changed its recommendation to launch.

Illusion of Unanimity   Group members falling victim to groupthink share an illusion of unanimity concerning judgments made by members speaking in favor of the majority view. This symptom is caused in part by the preceding one and is aided by the false assumption that any participant who remains silent is in agreement with the majority opinion. The group leader and other members support each other by playing up points of convergence in their thinking at the expense of fully exploring points of divergence that might reveal unsettling problems.

No participant from NASA ever openly agreed with or even took sides with MTI in the discussion. The silence from NASA was probably amplified by the fact that the meeting was a teleconference linking the participants at three different locations. Obviously, body language which might have been evidenced by dissenters was not visible to others who might also have held a dissenting opinion. Thus, silence meant agreement.

Mindguarding   Certain group members assume the role of guarding the minds of others in the group. They attempt to shield the group from adverse information that might destroy the majority view of the facts regarding the appropriateness of the decision.

The top management at Marshall knew that the rocket casings had been ordered redesigned to correct a flaw 5 months previous to this launch. This information and other technical details concerning the history of the joint problem was withheld at the meeting.

Decision-Making Defects

The result of the antecedent conditions and the symptoms of groupthink is a defective decision-making process. Janis discusses several defects in decision making that can result.

Few Alternatives   The group considers only a few alternatives, often only two. No initial survey of all possible alternatives occurs. The Flight Readiness Review team had a launch/no-launch decision to make.

These were the only two alternatives considered. Other possible alternatives might have been to delay the launch for further testing, or to delay until the temperatures reached an appropriate level.

No Re-Examination of Alternatives   The group fails to re-examine alternatives that may have been initially discarded based on early unfavorable information. Top NASA officials spent time and effort defending and strengthening their position, rather than examining the MTI position.

Rejecting Expert Opinions   Members make little or no attempt to seek outside experts opinions. NASA did not seek out other experts who might have some expertise in this area. They assumed that they had all the information.

Rejecting Negative Information   Members tend to focus on supportive information and ignore any data or information that might cast a negative light on their preferred alternative. MTI representatives repeatedly tried to point out errors in the rationale the NASA officials were using to justify the launch. Even after the decision was made, the argument continued until a NASA official told the MTI representative that it was no longer his concern.

No Contingency Plans   Members spend little time discussing the possible consequences of the decision and, therefore, fail to develop contingency plans. There is no documented evidence in the Rogers Commission Report of any discussion of the possible consequences of an incorrect decision.

Summary of the Evidence

The major categories and key elements of the groupthink hypothesis have been presented (albeit somewhat briefly) along with evidence from the discussions prior to the launching of the *Challenger,* as reported in the President's Commission to investigate the accident. The antecedent conditions were present in the decision-making group, even though the group was in several physical locations. The leaders had a preferred solution and engaged in behaviors designed to promote it rather than critically appraise alternatives. These behaviors were evidence of most of the symptoms leading to a defective decision-making process.

DISCUSSION

This situation provides another example of decision making in which the group fell victim to the groupthink syndrome, as have so many previous groups. It illustrates the situation characteristics, the symptoms of groupthink, and decision-making defects as described by Janis. This situation, however, also illustrates several other aspects of situations that are critical to the development of groupthink that need to be included in a revised formulation of the groupthink model. First, the element of time in influencing the development of groupthink has not received adequate attention. In the decision to launch the space shuttle *Challenger,* time was a crucial part of the decision-making process. The launch had been delayed once, and the window for another launch was fast closing. The leaders of the decision team were concerned about public and congressional perceptions of the entire space shuttle program and its continued funding and may have felt that further delays of the launch could seriously impact future funding. With the space window fast closing, the decision team was faced with a launch now or seriously damage the program decision. One top level manager's response to Thiokol's initial recommendation to postpone the launch indicates the presence of time pressure:

> With this LCC (Launch Commit Criteria), i.e., do not launch with a temperature greater [sic] than 53 degrees, we may not be able to launch until next April. We need to consider this carefully before we jump to any conclusions . . . (Report of the Presidential Commission on the Space Shuttle Accident, *1986, p. 96)*

Time pressure could have played a role in the group choosing to agree and to self-censor their comments. Therefore, time is a critical variable that needs to be highlighted in a revised groupthink framework. We propose that time is an important moderator between group characteristics and the development of the groupthink symptoms. That is, in certain situations

when there is pressure to make a decision quickly, the elements may combine to foster the development of groupthink.

The second revision needs to be in the role of the leadership of the decision-making group. In the space shuttle *Challenger* incident, the leadership of the group varied from a shared type of leadership to a very clear leader in the situation. This may indicate that the leadership role needs to be clearly defined and a style that demands open disclosure of information, points of opposition, complaints, and dissension. Inclusion of leadership in a more powerful role in the groupthink framework needs to be more explicit than in the Janis formulation in which leadership is one of several group characteristics that can lead to the development of the groupthink symptoms. We propose the leadership style is a crucial variable that moderates the relationship between the group characteristics and the development of the symptoms. Janis (1983) is a primary form of evidence to support the inclusion of leadership style in the enhanced model. His account of why the same group succumbed to groupthink in one decision (Bay of Pigs) and not in another (Cuban Missile Crisis) supports the depiction of leadership style as a moderator variable. In these decisions, the only condition that changed was the leadership style of the President. In other words, the element that seemed to distinguish why groupthink occurred in the Bay of Pigs decision and not in the Cuban Missile Crisis situation is the president's change in his behavior.

These two variables, time and leadership style, are proposed as moderators of the impact of the group characteristics on groupthink symptoms. This relationship is portrayed graphically in Fig. 1. In effect, we propose that the groupthink symptoms result from the group characteristics, as proposed by Janis, but only in the presence of the moderator variables of time and certain leadership styles.

Time, as an important element in the model, is relatively straightforward. When a decision must be made within a very short time frame, pressure on members to agree, to avoid time-consuming arguments and reports from outside experts, and to self-censor themselves may increase. These pressures inevitably cause group members to seek agreement. In Janis's original model, time was included indirectly as

FIGURE 1 / Revised Groupthink Framework

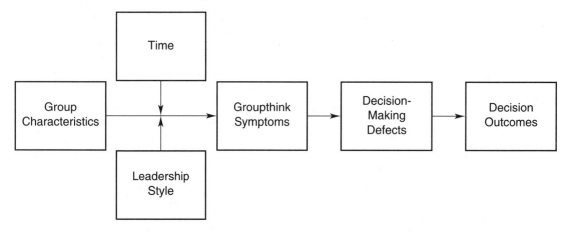

a function of the antecedent condition, group cohesion. Janis (1983) argued that time pressures can adversely affect decision quality in two ways. First, it affects the decision makers' mental efficiency and judgment, interfering with their ability to concentrate on complicated discussions, to absorb new information, and to use imagination to anticipate the future consequences of alternative courses of action. Second, time pressure is a source of stress that will have the effect of inducing a policy-making group to become more cohesive and more likely to engage in groupthink.

Leadership style is shown to be a moderator because of the importance it plays in either promoting or avoiding the development of the symptoms of the groupthink. The leader, even though she or he may not promote a preferred solution, may allow or even assist the group seeking agreement by not forcing the group to critically appraise all alternative courses of action. The focus of this leadership variable is on the degree to which the leader allows or promotes discussion and evaluation of alternatives. It is not a matter of simply not making known a preferred solution; the issue is one of stimulation of critical thinking among the group.

Impact on Prescriptions for Prevention

The revised model suggests that more specific prescriptions for prevention of groupthink can be made.

First, group members need to be aware of the impact that a short decision time frame has on decision processes. When a decision must be made quickly, there will be more pressure to agree, i.e., discouragement of dissent, self-censorship, avoidance of expert opinion, and assumptions about unanimity. The type of leadership suggested here is not one that sits back and simply does not make known her or his preferred solution. This type of leader must be one that requires all members to speak up with concerns, questions, and new information. The leader must know what some of these concerns are and which members are likely to have serious doubts so that the people with concerns can be called upon to voice them. This type of group leadership does not simply assign the role of devil's advocate and step out of the way. This leader actually plays the role or makes sure that others do. A leader with the required style to avoid groupthink is not a laissez faire leader or non-involved participative leader. This leader is active in directing the activities of the group but does not make known a preferred solution. The group still must develop and evaluate alternative courses of action, but under the direct influence of a strong, demanding leader who forces critical appraisal of all alternatives.

Finally, a combination of the two variables suggests that the leader needs to help members to avoid the problems created by the time element. For example, the leader may be able to alter an externally imposed time frame for the decision by negotiating an extension or even paying late fees, if necessary. If an extension is not possible, the leader may need to help the group eliminate the effects of time on the decision processes. This can be done by forcing attention to issues rather than time, encouraging dissension and confrontation, and scheduling special sessions to hear reports from outside experts that challenge prevailing views within the group.

Janis presents, in both editions of his book, several recommendations for preventing the occurrence of groupthink. These recommendations focus on the inclusion of outside experts in the decision-making process, all members taking the role of devil's advocate and critically appraising all alternative courses of action, and the leader not expressing a preferred solution. The revised groupthink framework suggests several new prescriptions that may be helpful in preventing further decision fiascoes similar to the decision to launch the space shuttle *Challenger*.

Much additional research is necessary to test the revised framework. First, laboratory research is needed to refine details of how time affects the development of groupthink. Second, the impact of various types of leadership style that may be appropriate for group decision-making situations needs to be investigated. Finally, research which tests the revised framework with real decision-making groups will be needed to refine new prescriptions for preventing groupthink.

CONCLUSION

This paper has reviewed the basic tenets of groupthink and examined the decision to launch the space shuttle *Challenger* in January 1986. The report of the Presidential Commission provided enough evidence of the antecedent conditions, the symptoms, and the decision-making defects to support a conclusion that the decision to launch can be classified as a groupthink situation. We have proposed, in addition, that other conditions may play important roles in the development of groupthink. These two variables, time and leadership style, are proposed as moderators of the relationship between group characteristics and groupthink symptoms. These two moderators lead to new prescriptions for the prevention of groupthink. Much additional research is needed to test the degree to which the revised framework can be used to guide prescriptions for prevention.

REFERENCES

Courtright, J. A. A laboratory investigation of groupthink. *Communications Monographs,* 1978, *45,* 229–246.

Flowers, M. L. A laboratory test of some implications of Janis's groupthink hypothesis. *Journal of Personality and Social Psychology,* 1977, *35,* 888–896.

Janis, I. L. *Victims of groupthink.* Boston: Houghton Mifflin, 1972.

Janis, I. L. *Groupthink* (2nd ed., revised). Boston: Houghton Mifflin, 1983.

Leana, C. R. A partial test of Janis's groupthink model: Effects of group cohesiveness and leader behavior on defective decision making. *Journal of Management,* 1985, *11,* 5–17.

Moorhead, G. Groupthink: Hypothesis in need of testing. *Group and Organization Studies,* 1982, *7,* 429–444.

Moorhead, G., & Montanari, J. R. Empirical analysis of the groupthink phenomenon. *Human Relations,* 1986, *39,* 399–410.

Report of the Presidential Commission on the Space Shuttle Accident. Washington, D.C.: July 1986.

Time. Fixing NASA. June 9, 1986.

CRITICAL THINKING QUESTIONS

1. Why do you think groupthink became a factor in the decision to launch the *Challenger?* In other words, why was no one involved in the decision able to recognize what was going on and thus do something about it? How commonly understood is the concept of groupthink in the real world? Is it important that leaders in all walks of life know about groupthink? How could the message be spread to them?

2. The article states that one of the two moderating variables that influence whether groupthink symptoms develop is leadership style. To what extent can leadership style be taught to people? On the other hand, to what extent is leadership style a product of

individual personality? Describe the personality characteristics of a leader who would *not* likely try to prevent the development of groupthink.

3. The second moderating variable discussed in the article is time. Design a laboratory study to investigate the impact of time on the development of groupthink.

4. Consult a social psychology textbook and read about different styles of leadership. Which styles might be most relevant to the development of groupthink? Design either a laboratory or a field study to examine the impact of leadership styles on the emergence of groupthink.

Chapter Thirteen

APPLYING
SOCIAL PSYCHOLOGY
Law and Business

Both OF THE last two chapters in this book of readings have *Applying Social Psychology* in their titles. This heading needs some explaining, however, since it otherwise might create the wrong impression for the reader.

Applying social psychology usually refers to the application of principles and findings generated by research in social psychology to real-world settings. In a sense, this is where social psychology is used to help solve practical problems. But by labeling these chapters *applied,* it might seem to suggest that the preceding 12 chapters were not applied and did not have real-world applications. If you already have read through the preceding chapters, you know that is not the case. Many of the studies in the earlier chapters have direct implications for real-world problems. Although the research may seem abstract and theoretical at times, we need only apply the principles to various social problems to yield applied forms of social psychology.

What distinguishes the research in Chapters 13 and 14 is that it was specifically designed and conducted to address significant real-world issues. Such research has been done in many, many areas. The issues presented here reflect some of the most common areas of concern, but they are by no means the only topics in the domain of applied social psychology.

This chapter addresses the contributions of social psychology to both the forensic (legal) and work arenas. In one form or another, you probably have had some contact with the legal system. Perhaps you (or someone you know) have been arrested and even tried for some offense. Maybe you have been asked to be a juror. More likely, you have watched televised trials or read about real or fictional trials in the media. Does the legal system, as it presently operates, guarantee an objective, unbiased outcome?

Social psychologists working in the forensic field have examined a number of factors that may influence the outcomes in legal settings. Two of the articles in this chapter look at jury trials, which clearly are a major element of the U.S. judicial system. Article 37, "Juries and Justice," examines the forces at work in the present legal system that make it difficult to assemble an impartial jury—for instance, extensive pretrial media publicity and the use of courtroom consultants to select specific jurors who will likely favor a certain side. The article tries to make the case that the current system may no longer work.

Article 38, "Beautiful but Dangerous," likewise examines jury trials. However, this article looks at the relationship between the attractiveness of an offender and the nature of the crime and how these two factors may influence the jury's judgment.

You may or may not ever have direct contact with the legal system, but it is very likely that a major part of your life will be spent at work. When you think of what type of work you are doing now or will be doing in the future, you may have many concerns; for instance, how much money will you make? But you also may be concerned about how much you will like the work you are doing. What, exactly, may influence your satisfaction with your work? Is it a sense of commitment to the organization? How you feel you are treated by the organization? In turn, how you feel about the work you are doing may influence how well you do it and how much "beyond the call of duty" you may be willing to give to the organization. Article 39, "The Influence of Job Satisfaction, Organizational Commitment, and Fairness Perceptions on Organizational Citizenship Behavior," examines which factors may influence the likelihood of workers doing more than is called for in their organizations.

ARTICLE 37 ⎯⎯⎯⎯⎯⎯⎯⎯⎯⎯⎯⎯⎯⎯⎯⎯⎯⎯⎯⎯⎯⎯⎯

One cornerstone of the U.S. legal system is the right to a jury trial by one's peers. Perhaps you have already served as a juror. If not, you may very well have that opportunity in the future. As a juror, you are expected to make a conscientious effort to determine a defendant's guilt or innocence based on the weight of the evidence presented in the trial. Your personal biases and beliefs should not come into play. Your decision is supposed to be made objectively.

But is that the way the legal system really works? Is it possible for people to somehow disconnect themselves from their own attitudes and biases and really judge a case objectively? A great deal of social psychological research conducted over the years suggests that achieving this objectivity may be easier said than done. For example, irrelevant factors such as a defendant's physical appearance, gender, and race been found to impact jurors' decisions.

In the last few years, a new set of factors has been imposed on the jury trial system that may further limit the objectivity of jurors. First is the amount of media coverage given to trials, especially in high-profile cases. Given the amount of pretrial publicity surrounding many cases, is it possible to find jurors who have not been influenced by what they may have heard or read outside the courtroom? Second, social psychology itself has entered into the jury selection process. Lawyers often employ courtroom consultants to help select jurors who will favor their side, which means that the jurors selected may not be a representative sample of the defendant's peers after all. Barbara Bradley explores these and other issues affecting contemporary jury trials and raises questions as to whether the trial-by-jury system really works anymore.

Juries and Justice
Is the System Obsolete?

■ Barbara Bradley

The murder trial of O. J. Simpson has gripped the country like no other in recent history. Broadcast live over cable's Court TV and recapped nightly on the evening news, it has been more popular than most made-for-TV movies—and the ratings prove it.

But as the trial nears its midpoint, a harsh and nagging question remains: Will the Simpson jury be able to deliver a fair verdict? Or have the months of testimony, the crowds of legal consultants, the confusing technical evidence and the pressure to reach a popular verdict so overwhelmed the jury that delivering justice may just be too much to ask?

"I think there will be skepticism and cynicism about this verdict no matter what happens," says Stephen Adler, a legal editor at the *Wall Street Journal* and author of *The Jury: Trial and Error in the American Courtroom,* one of several new books on the decline of the jury system. "There's a feeling that the system has gotten away from us, that it doesn't belong to the people any more—that lawyers are manipulative, jury consultants manipulate the process and that justice may not be the ultimate result."

The Simpson trial is only the latest in a series of high-profile cases that have contributed to the growing disillusionment. In the widely watched trials of Erik and Lyle Menendez, Lorena Bobbitt and the Los Angeles police officers who beat Rodney King, for example, no one disputed that the defendants actually committed the crimes of which they were accused—yet the juries found none of them guilty.

And the fault for these apparent miscarriages of justice, say many, lies with the jury system itself. "The jury as an institution is an anachronism," says Kate Stith, a criminal-law professor at the Yale Law School and former federal prosecutor in New York. "It's hard to believe that in the 20th century we'd come up with this system."

In fact, the right to a jury of one's peers dates back to 1791, when the Sixth Amendment was ratified. Jurors then were expected to be active participants in a trial, and since they were drawn from the local community, they often knew the defendant, the witnesses and the events surrounding the crime itself. But in the 19th century, jurors began to be seen as "blank slates," and the rules changed.

As modern technology and psychology transform the trial process, jurors today are forced to play by outdated rules. They can't ask questions in court, for example, and often they're barred from taking notes. They aren't allowed to discuss the case as it unfolds. They're selected specifically for their ignorance about the defendant and the crime itself and aren't allowed to gather any information on their own. They are kept from seeing critical evidence. As cases become longer, more complex and involve more technical evidence, jurors are finding they can't keep up. They have remained, in short, abacus users in the age of the computer.

During the last three decades, four seismic events have shaken the jury system to its core: the rise of media interest and courtroom cameras; the advent of racially diverse juries; the use of social psychology in the courtroom; and the increasing complexity of trials. These phenomena have reshaped the trial process, and the system has not made corresponding adjustments to help jurors cope. As a result, the fate of Simpson may have less to do with the evidence than with factors unrelated to his guilt or innocence.

Few, if any, argue that the jury system should be abandoned—and certainly not on the basis of cel-

ebrated trials such as Simpson's. Yet, the flaws of that case can be seen in other courtrooms across the country every day. True, few trials take place on prime-time television. But in the age of Court TV, more and more unknowns are candidates for national attention. (Whoever heard of Lorena Bobbitt before her famous slice?) Jury consultants and technical evidence are commonplace. And the race issue, considered to be the wild card in the Simpson trial, permeates trials in almost every part of the country.

Of all the new pressures on the system, the effect of the media is most visible. Shortly after the bodies of Nicole Brown Simpson and Ronald Goldman were found last June 13, the television cameras started filming—and haven't stopped. From the surreal chase of the white Bronco (covered live by helicopter) to the nationally broadcast 911 tape of Nicole Simpson screaming in fear, publicity made it almost impossible to find people who had not formed an opinion of the case. More than 100 candidates were rejected before 12 jurors and 12 alternates were picked.

The publicity of the trial will haunt even those seated, according to Thomas Hafemeister, senior staff attorney and psychoanalyst at the National Center for State Courts in Williamsburg, Va. "Jurors know the community is looking over their shoulders" in any high-publicity case, says Hafemeister, who is conducting a study on juror stress. "They have to face their family and friends, and they have to justify their verdicts."

Moreover, in high-publicity trials, jurors hear both more and less information than the public—which can create outrage with the system when the jury fails to arrive at the same verdict as the public. For example, when William Kennedy Smith was being tried for rape in 1991, the press widely reported Smith's history of aggressive sexual behavior. But the jury heard none of that and acquitted him—leaving many in the public furious.

The King trial demonstrated what can happen when the public has only partial information about a case. Viewers of the famous 81-second videotape had no trouble concluding that the four Los Angeles police officers had used excessive force with King. But many who actually saw the trial said the prosecution did not prove guilt beyond a reasonable doubt—a requirement of law, but not public opinion.

Perhaps more dramatically, says Professor Abraham Goldstein of the Yale Law School, the riots that followed the officers' acquittal raised the stakes for any future jury contemplating a socially unacceptable verdict. And because jurors routinely give interviews to journalists about the deliberations, every juror knows that he or she might become the target of public contempt. "Now jurors know that they will be pursued by the media, that many of their number will talk to the media and be unguarded in their comments," Goldstein tells *Insight.* "This has the potential to destroy the secrecy of the jury room and affect the freedom of the jury to deliberate."

Such concerns were on the mind of Hazel Thornton, a juror in the trial of Erik Menendez—who, with his brother Lyle, shot and killed their parents as they were eating ice cream in front of the television in 1989. During the five-month trial, another high-publicity trial in Los Angeles ended with a jury acquitting Damian Williams of all but one relatively minor charge in the beating of truck driver Reginald Denny during the Los Angeles riots. As in the King trial, the beating of Denny had been videotaped, and the verdict also was met with public dismay. Thornton says all she cared about was reaching the right verdict in the Menendez case—but she felt the pressure nonetheless.

"I wasn't allowed to pay that much attention to the news at that time, but I did know that the verdict was extremely unpopular," Thornton recalls. "What I did hear was the jurors being criticized as idiots, and I was afraid that we would be criticized in the same way when our verdict came out."

Clearly it would be constitutionally risky to muzzle either the news media or the jurors after a verdict is returned, although Goldstein advocates some limits. Still, he and others say, it's time to consider whether a jury operating under a media spotlight is capable of voting according to the facts, without second-guessing the reaction of the public.

Another hot-button issue in both the King and Simpson cases has been race. The very fact that the Simpson jury includes any members of minority groups at all underscores fundamental changes that have rewritten the book on courtroom dynamics. The Supreme Court outlawed discrimination on the basis of race in 1986 and last year extended the protection to gender. Still, race remains a factor: In the Simpson case, the Los Angeles District Attorney's office decided to try Simpson in central Los Angeles rather than the more predominantly white Brentwood area in which the murders took place, to avoid a predominantly white jury. Many court watchers believe that the prosecution is most worried about a hung jury, which they believe would be more likely if African-Americans were a minority in the jury room.

The strategy, of course, is a calculated risk; according to a recent Harris poll, 68 percent of African-Americans believe Simpson is innocent vs. 61 percent of whites who believe him guilty. And after the King beating, some believe that the resentment among many blacks toward the Los Angeles police could tip the scales. In a *Los Angeles Times* poll last fall, 70 percent of African-Americans in that city said they believed police officers commonly lie on the witness stand. That must give the prosecution pause: The star witness in the Simpson case, Mark Fuhrman, is a white detective; the defense is trying to portray him as a racist.

Another factor affecting juries has been the rise of professional trial consultants. About 20 years ago, attorneys began hiring social psychologists and market researchers to help them pick the most sympathetic jurors and tailor their arguments to specific juries. Author Stephen Adler says trial consultants have shaken the credibility of the jury system. "I think that one of the current crises of the jury system is this widening perception that, in fact, we don't have a true cross-section of the community—we have a manipulated, strategically placed jury that may not be there to do justice in the first place."

Jury consultants have been credited with snatching a victory—or a mistrial—from almost certain defeat. For example, in the case of the Menendez brothers, the Los Angeles prosecutors claimed the young men were after an early inheritance. The defense argued they were reacting to years of abuse—not an easy argument to sell, notes Lois Heaney, a trial consultant at the National Jury Project in Minneapolis, which was hired by the Menendez defense team.

"The idea that two young men would kill their parents is, for many, a phenomenon for which there can be no justification," she says. What was needed was a defense similar to battered woman syndrome, in which a wife kills her husband when he is, say, asleep on the couch, because she's afraid of the next beating. "You really need to have people who understand a psychological self-defense, an urgency to act."

To select a jury sympathetic to such a defense, Heaney focused on prospective jurors' attitudes toward psychologists and psychiatrists, who would be the keys to the young men's defense. When the jury for Erik Menendez was seated, it was evenly divided between men and women. Perhaps because women are more often the victims of domestic violence, the six women could accept a self-defense argument and wanted to convict for manslaughter. The six men held out for premeditated murder. "I realized we had a hung jury before we even deliberated," recalls juror Thornton.

Jurors also increasingly face long trials and complex evidence, as is the case with the Simpson trial. Will the jurors be able to remember all the instances in which Judge Lance Ito told them to disregard information, for example, and strike what they heard from their memories? "I say to my students, 'Okay, imagine you have to take a midterm exam,'" explains Valerie Hans, professor of criminal justice and psychology at the University of Delaware and author of *Judging the Jury*. "You have to sit there for several months. You are not allowed to take notes. You cannot ask any questions if you are confused—you have to allow other people to ask questions for you, and of course they may not ask the ones you were concerned about." Her students, she says, look terrified at the idea. "It really brings it home to them how antiquated this system is."

Some attorneys, critics say, use the faults of the system to their advantage by trying to pick the least-capable jurors they can find. "The whole nature of the game right now is to try to strike out people whose views, whose skills you're afraid of," says John Langbein, a legal historian at Yale Law School. "Particularly if you're defense counsel, what you're most concerned about is somebody who's smart enough to see your guy's guilty despite all the tricks you might be employing."

"When you see a lawyer trying to pick a smart jury," famed defense attorney F. Lee Bailey reportedly once said, "you know he's got a strong case. [Defense attorney] Percy Foreman and I once had an argument as to which of us had picked the most stupid jury."

Not surprisingly, the system tends to filter out educated jurors. According to a 1987 study by Joe Cecil at the Federal Judicial Center, the longer and more complex the trial, the less educated the jurors tended to be; while 32 percent of jurors in short cases had college degrees, that figure dropped to 22 percent in long and complex cases. "One thing we didn't do is figure out why the education level decreases," Cecil tells *Insight*. "Is it that attorneys are exercising more peremptories [to get smarter people off the jury]? Or is the judge excusing jurors who weren't able to serve for extended periods?"

Many judges will excuse candidates from a long trial if, for example they cannot take the time off work. What that often leaves, says William Jones, a trial attorney in Phoenix, is a jury pool heavily skewed toward unemployed and less-educated people. And that can have a direct impact on the verdict. Jones recalls one case in which he was defending the city of Phoenix in a personal-injury lawsuit. The issues were complicated, involving road design and questions of liability. The judge told the potential jurors that the trial probably would last eight weeks, and anyone who could not spare that much time could serve on another trial.

When the dust from the stampede settled, Jones was left with "largely unemployed people, people who didn't have any appreciation for what the value of a dollar really is," he says. "It had a horrible effect. There was a very large verdict for the plaintiff—$7 million, and we ultimately settled for $2 million—which didn't surprise me. They didn't understand one issue in the entire case."

Despite the flaws in the jury system, almost no one is suggesting abolishing the Sixth Amendment right to have one's "peers" decide one's fate. The alternative—placing that power solely in the hands of judges—runs counter to the democratic values that define this country.

"One of the most important things about the jury system is it brings credibility to the verdict, if it's working right," Adler concludes. "If you have a jury that's a true cross-section of community, I think the public is much more likely to accept the verdict if it comes from a jury than if it comes from a judge—even if it's unpopular."

The operative phrase, of course, is "if it's working right." With the memory of the Los Angeles riots still fresh and public faith in the system declining, legal experts say there must be some quick and fundamental reforms if justice is to be found in the courthouse and not on the streets.

A growing number of judges and legal scholars are trying to bring the system into the 21st century. Thomas Munsterman, director of the Center for Jury Studies at the National Center for State Courts in Arlington, Va., says that judges are going to profes-

---

DNA: 'Blood Evidence'

Generally, criminal trials are not as intellectually daunting as, say, patent or antitrust civil trials. But one area of criminal law that is perplexing jurors is central to the O. J. Simpson trial—DNA evidence.

"This is a case that really comes down to the blood evidence," says Erwin Chemerinsky, a law professor at the University of Southern California. "If the blood evidence is presented in an understandable, credible way, it could be a conviction. If the blood evidence is undermined by the defense, it could be an acquittal—and then obviously the jury could split all over the place."

Unfortunately, jurors are notoriously bad at understanding blood evidence—in particular the probabilities that there is a match between a blood sample and a defendant. Say that the blood type found on a crime scene is the blood type of 1 percent of the Los Angeles population. The "prosecutor's fallacy" would be that if that blood is the same type as that of the defendant, there's a 99 percent chance it came from that person; therefore, he or she is guilty. The "defense attorney's fallacy" implies innocence: It says that 1 percent of the population—thousands of people—could have committed the crime, so the evidence is worthless. According to DNA expert William Thompson of the University of California at Irvine, both arguments are wrong.

In a study of university students, who might be better-educated than the Simpson jury, Thompson found that the subjects fell into one of the two fallacies—that is, they misinterpreted the evidence 78 percent of the time. "We'd get some hilarious results," Thompson says. "You'd present them with one fallacy, and they'd say, 'Yeah, that sounds right.' And then you'd present them with the other fallacy, and they'd say, 'That sounds right too!'"

Thompson (who also is an adviser to the Simpson defense team) says his study does not indicate that jurors are stupid. Indeed, he found that only the most highly trained professionals, including statisticians and Ph.D. candidates, consistently figured out that both arguments were fallacies. But, he says, the inability of jurors to handle this kind of evidence presents ethical questions for attorneys. "It raises real concerns whether these problems can be dealt with effectively by arguments in front of the jury," he says, "because what it means is that an ethical lawyer who wants to argue for the truth is going to lose in face of these facile fallacies from the opposition. And it looks like the best way to fight one fallacy is with a contrary fallacy."

In the end, it may not matter, says Thomas Munsterman, director of the Center for Jury Studies at the National Center for State Courts. According to exit questionnaires, jurors generally ignore information that is confusing or conflicting. "If there is one expert who says yes and another expert that says no, the jurors basically tune out the experts. They say, if these two learned people, both being recognized by this court as experts, can't agree, what are we to do? Maybe we'll just base it on something else."   —*BB*

sional educators to ask them how people learn. "And they tell you, we permit them feedback, taking notes; every so often we'll stop and review where we've been," he says. "All of the things that we don't do in a jury trial."

According to B. Michael Dann, a superior court judge in Phoenix, several studies have shown that jurors do not understand 50 percent of the judge's instructions at the end of the trial—the equivalent of assembling all the ingredients of a cake but failing to follow the recipe. Dann says that to communicate with jurors, judges and attorneys should adjust their language to a level at which they might speak to sixth-graders because the legal jargon used in the courtroom often leaves jurors befuddled. This creates "frustration and anger" in the jury box, he says, "and it's danger-ous, because an angry, confused jury can distort the outcome, can distort the quality of their decision-making and make the jury more unpredictable than they otherwise are."

So, shortly after donning his robes in 1980, Dann began to experiment. He essentially ran his courtroom like a classroom. He allowed jurors to ask questions and take notes. He asked attorneys to give mini-summations throughout the trial. He also delivered his instructions to the jury at the beginning of the trial, not at the end, as most judges do. Therefore, jurors understood exactly what the prosecutor needed to show to prove manslaughter, for example.

"Most prosecutors don't like jury involvement—even less than defense attorneys," says Michael Kemp, a state prosecutor in Phoenix. "They're afraid the jury will come up with questions they don't want raised" and thus insert an element of doubt. But this situation has worked to his advantage. In a rape case a few years ago, a juror asked a question. "It was something like, 'Was the victim alone with the defendant at the time?'—very down-to-earth stuff, which lawyers al-ways overlook. And we just looked at each other and said, 'Wow, what were we thinking about?'" He won the case in part, he says, because of that question.

Dann's innovations sparked little controversy until last fall, when the Arizona Supreme Court proposed making them standard procedure in courtrooms across the state. The proposal raising the most hackles would allow jurors to discuss the case among them-selves as it goes along. Trial attorney Bill Jones, who supports most of the reforms, says this one will tip the scales toward the prosecution.

Jones says that educational research suggests people remember what they hear repeated most. Since the prosecution presents its case first, he says, jurors would be hearing and discussing the prosecution's evidence for perhaps several weeks before the defense began to tell its side of the story. "And you can instruct them until you're blue in the face not to arrive at any conclusions about what the facts are," Jones says, "but, inevitably, being human beings, they're going to arrive at those conclusions, and it's grossly unfair to the defense."

Despite objections, several states are looking at Arizona's proposals. In addition, New York recently expanded its jury pool to include more people from the welfare and unemployment rolls. California is considering allowing nonunanimous verdicts, as do Louisiana and Oregon. (A hung jury in the Simpson trial likely would give this reform some momentum.)

"I think we're kind of at a historic moment" in the process of jury reform, says Adler. In the last six months alone, he says he has been contacted by "prob-ably 20" state bar associations. "There's just a huge move in that direction."

Most agree that innovation won't come easily in the tradition-bound legal system. But when dealing with the Constitution, it's best to move carefully. "I think any reform has to be tinkering at the edges," says Yale's Stith. "If you tinker at the core, you abolish the jury system altogether."

CRITICAL THINKING QUESTIONS

1. What do you think of the idea expressed in the article that most trials "have a manipu-lated, strategically placed jury that may not be there to do justice in the first place"? What evidence can you find to support or refute this statement?
2. The article was written in 1995, prior to the verdict in the O. J. Simpson criminal trial. Find out what, if anything, has changed in the jury trial system since that time.

3. How can the concepts of social perception (Chapter 2) and social cognition (Chapter 3) be applied to the subjectivity that jurors seem prone to? Is there any way to minimize or eliminate any of these potential sources of bias? Explain.

4. How would you recommend improving the jury trial system? What problems and benefits may result from making such changes? Support your answers.

ARTICLE 38 _____

The previous reading (Article 37) examined some of the biases inherent in jury selection. But what happens after the jury has been formed and the trial has started? What factors may have an impact on determining the defendant's guilt or innocence? Jurors are asked to weigh the evidence presented during the trial. Hopefully, they will not permit irrelevant characteristics of the defendant—such as his or her physical appearance, race, or sex—to affect their judgment. But is it really possible to be totally objective in such situations? Or do irrelevant factors play a role in our beliefs about guilt or innocence?

The following article by Harold Sigall and Nancy Ostrove is a classic piece of research that investigated the impact of the defendant's physical attractiveness on the severity of sentences given to her. Earlier studies had indicated that physically attractive individuals often have great advantages over less attractive people in a variety of situations. This study not only examined the role of physical attractiveness in a trial-like setting but also how the nature of the crime and attractiveness interact to influence judgments about the defendant. The article also tests two different models that may explain why this particular effect occurs.

Beautiful but Dangerous
Effects of Offender Attractiveness and Nature of the Crime on Juridic Judgment

■ Harold Sigall and Nancy Ostrove

The physical attractiveness of a criminal defendant (attractive, unattractive, no information) and the nature of the crime (attractiveness-related, attractiveness-unrelated) were varied in a factorial design. After reading one of the case accounts, subjects sentenced the defendant to a term of imprisonment. An interaction was predicted: When the crime was unrelated to attractiveness (burglary), subjects would assign more lenient sentences to the attractive defendant than to the unattractive defendant; when the offense was attractiveness-related (swindle), the attractive defendant would receive harsher treatment. The results confirmed the predictions, thereby supporting a cognitive explanation for the relationship between the physical attractiveness of defendants and the nature of the judgments made against them.

Research investigating the interpersonal consequences of physical attractiveness has demonstrated clearly that good-looking people have tremendous advan-

tages over their unattractive counterparts in many ways. For example, a recent study by Miller (1970) provided evidence for the existence of a physical attractiveness stereotype with a rather favorable content. Dion, Berscheid, and Walster (1972) reported similar findings: Compared to unattractive people, better-looking people were viewed as more likely to possess a variety of socially desirable attributes. In addition, Dion et al.'s subjects predicted rosier futures for the beautiful stimulus persons—attractive people were expected to have happier and more successful lives in store for them. Thus, at least in the eyes of others, good looks imply greater potential.

Since physical attractiveness hardly seems to provide a basis for an *equitable* distribution of rewards, one might hope that the powerful effects of this variable would occur primarily when it is the only source of information available. Unfair or irrational consequences of differences in beauty observed in some

Reprinted from *Journal of Personality and Social Psychology*, 1975, *31*, 410–414. Copyright © 1975 by the American Psychological Association. Reprinted by permission.

situations would cause less uneasiness if, in other situations given other important data, respondents would tend to discount such "superficial" information. Unfortunately, for the vast majority of us who have not been blessed with a stunning appearance, the evidence does not permit such consolation. Consider, for example, a recent study by Dion (1972) in which adult subjects were presented with accounts of transgressions supposedly committed by children of varying physical attractiveness. When the transgression was severe the act was viewed less negatively when committed by a good-looking child, than when the offender was unattractive. Moreover, when the child was unattractive the offense was more likely to be seen as reflecting some enduring dispositional quality: Subjects believed that unattractive children were more likely to be involved in future transgressions. Dion's findings, which indicate that unattractive individuals are penalized when there is no apparent logical relationship between the transgression and the way they look, underscore the importance of appearance because one could reasonably suppose that information describing a severe transgression would "overwhelm the field," and that the physical attractiveness variable would not have any effect.

Can beautiful people get away with murder? Although Dion (1972) found no differences in the punishment recommended for offenders as a function of attractiveness, Monahan (1941) has suggested that beautiful women are convicted less often of crimes they are accused of, and Efran (1974) has recently demonstrated that subjects are much more generous when assigning punishment to good-looking as opposed to unattractive transgressors.

The previous findings which indicate a tendency toward leniency for an attractive offender can be accounted for in a number of ways. For example, one might explain such results with the help of a reinforcement-affect model of attraction (e.g., Byrne & Clore, 1970). Essentially, the argument here would be that beauty, having positive reinforcement value, would lead to relatively more positive affective responses toward a person who has it. Thus we like an attractive person more, and since other investigators have shown that liking for a defendant increases leniency (e.g., Landy & Aronson, 1969), we would expect good-looking (better liked) defendants to be

punished less than unattractive defendants. Implicit in this reasoning is that the nature of the affective response, which influences whether kind or harsh treatment is recommended, is determined by the stimulus features associated with the target person. Therefore, when other things are equal, benefit accrues to the physically attractive. A more cognitive approach might attempt to explain the relationship between physical appearance and reactions to transgressions by assuming that the subject has a "rational" basis for his responses. It is reasonable to deal harshly with a criminal if we think he is likely to commit further violations, and as Dion's (1972) study suggests, unattractive individuals are viewed as more likely to transgress again. In addition, inasmuch as attractive individuals are viewed as possessing desirable qualities and as having relatively great potential, it makes sense to treat them leniently. Presumably they can be successful in socially acceptable ways, and rehabilitation may result in relatively high payoffs for society.

There is at least one implication that follows from the cognitive orientation which would not flow readily from the reinforcement model. Suppose that situations do exist in which, because of his high attractiveness, a defendant is viewed as more likely to transgress in the future. The cognitive approach suggests that in such instances greater punishment would be assigned to the attractive offender. We might add that in addition to being more dangerous, when the crime is attractiveness related, a beautiful criminal may be viewed as taking advantage of a God-given gift. Such misappropriation of a blessing may incur animosity, which might contribute to severe judgments in attractiveness-related situations.

In the present investigation, the attractiveness of a defendant was varied along with the nature of the crime committed. It was reasoned that most offenses do not encourage the notion that a criminal's attractiveness increases the likelihood of similar transgressions in the future. Since attractive offenders are viewed as less prone to recidivism and as having greater potential worth, it was expected that under such circumstances an attractive defendant would receive less punishment than an unattractive defendant involved in an identical offense. When, however, the crime committed may be viewed as attractiveness-related, as in a confidence game, despite being seen as possessing more potential, the attractive defendant may be regarded as relatively more dangerous, and the effects of beauty could be expected to be cancelled out or reversed. The major hypothesis, then, called for an interaction: An attractive defendant would receive more lenient treatment than an unattractive defendant when the offense was unrelated to attractiveness; when the crime was related to attractiveness, the attractive defendant would receive relatively harsh treatment.

METHOD

Subjects and Overview

Subjects were 60 male and 60 female undergraduates. After being presented with an account of a criminal case, each subject sentenced the defendant to a term of imprisonment. One-third of the subjects were led to believe that the defendant was physically attractive, another third that she was unattractive, and the remainder received no information concerning appearance. Cross-cutting the attractiveness variable, half of the subjects were presented with a written account of an attractiveness-unrelated crime, a burglary, and the rest with an attractiveness-related crime, a swindle. Subjects were randomly assigned to condition, with the restriction that an equal number of males and females appeared in each of the six cells formed by the manipulated variables.

Procedure

Upon arrival, each subject was shown to an individual room and given a booklet which contained the stimulus materials. The top sheet informed subjects that they would read a criminal case account, that they would receive biographical information about the defendant, and that after considering the materials they would be asked to answer some questions.

The case account began on the second page. Clipped to this page was a 5 × 8 inch card which contained routine demographic information and was identical in all conditions.[1] In the attractive conditions, a photograph of a rather attractive woman was affixed to the upper right-hand corner of the card;

while in the unattractive conditions, a relatively unattractive photograph was affixed. No photograph was presented in the control conditions.

Subjects then read either the account of a burglary or a swindle. The burglary account described how the defendant, Barbara Helm, had moved into a high-rise building, obtained a pass key under false pretenses, and then illegally entered the apartment of one of her neighbors. After stealing $2,200 in cash and merchandise she left town. She was apprehended when she attempted to sell some of the stolen property and subsequently was charged with breaking and entering and grand larceny. The swindle account described how Barbara Helm had ingratiated herself to a middle-aged bachelor and induced him to invest $2,200 in a nonexistent corporation. She was charged with obtaining money under false pretenses and grand larceny. In both cases, the setting for the offense and the victim were described identically. The information presented left little doubt concerning the defendant's guilt.

The main dependent measure was collected on the last page of the booklet. Subjects were asked to complete the following statement by circling a number between 1 and 15: "I sentence the defendant, Barbara Helm, to _____ years of imprisonment." Subjects were asked to sentence the defendant, rather than to judge guilt versus innocence in order to provide a more sensitive dependent measure.

After sentencing had been completed, the experimenter provided a second form, which asked subjects to recall who the defendant was and to rate the seriousness of the crime. In addition, the defendant was rated on a series of 9-point bipolar adjective scales, including physically unattractive (1) to physically attractive (9), which constituted the check on the attractiveness manipulation. A post-experimental interview followed, during which subjects were debriefed.

RESULTS AND DISCUSSION

The physical attractiveness manipulation was successful: The attractive defendant received a mean rating of 7.53, while the mean for the unattractive defendant was 3.20, $F(1, 108) = 184.29$, $p < .001$. These ratings were not affected by the nature of the crime, nor was there an interaction.

The criminal cases were designed so as to meet two requirements. First, the swindle was assumed to be attractiveness-related, while the burglary was intended to be attractiveness-unrelated. No direct check on this assumption was made. However, indirect evidence is available: Since all subjects filled out the same forms, we obtained physical attractiveness ratings from control condition subjects who were not presented with a photograph. These subjects attributed greater beauty to the defendant in the swindle condition ($X = 6.65$) than in the burglary condition ($X = 5.65$), $F(1, 108) = 4.93, p < .05$. This finding offers some support for our contention that the swindle was viewed as attractiveness-related. Second, it was important that the two crimes be viewed as roughly comparable in seriousness. This was necessary to preclude alternative explanations in terms of differential seriousness. Subjects rated the seriousness of the crime on a 9-point scale extending from not at all serious (1) to extremely serious (9). The resulting responses indicated that the second requirement was met: In the swindle condition the mean seriousness rating was 5.02; in the burglary condition it was 5.07 ($F < 1$).

Table 1 presents the mean punishment assigned to the defendant, by condition. Since a preliminary analysis demonstrated there were no differences in responses between males and females, subject sex was ignored as a variable. It can be seen that our hypothesis was supported: When the offense was attractiveness-unrelated (burglary), the unattractive defendant was more severely punished than the attractive defendant; however, when the offense was attractiveness-related (swindle), the attractive defendant was treated more harshly. The overall Attractiveness × Offense interaction was statistically significant, $F(2, 108) = 4.55, p < .025$, and this interaction was significant, as well, when the control condition was excluded, $F(1,$

$108) = 7.02, p < .01$. Simple comparisons revealed that the unattractive burglar received significantly more punishment than the attractive burglar, $F(1, 108) = 6.60, p < .025$, while the difference in sentences assigned to the attractive and unattractive swindler was not statistically significant, $F(1, 108) = 1.39$. The attractive-swindle condition was compared with the unattractive-swindle and control-swindle conditions also, $F(1, 108) = 2.00, ns$. Thus, strictly speaking, we cannot say that for the swindle attractiveness was a great liability; there was a tendency in this direction but the conservative conclusion is that when the crime is attractiveness-related, the advantages otherwise held by good-looking defendants are lost.

Another feature of the data worth considering is that the sentences administered in the control condition are almost identical to those assigned in the unattractive condition. It appears that being unattractive did not produce discriminatory responses, per se. Rather, it seems that appearance had its effect through the attractive conditions: The beautiful burglar got off lightly, while the beautiful swindler paid somewhat, though not significantly, more. It can be recalled that in the unattractive conditions the stimulus person was seen as relatively unattractive and not merely average looking. Therefore, the absence of unattractive-control condition differences does not seem to be the result of a weak manipulation in the unattractive conditions.

Perhaps it is possible to derive a small bit of consolation from this outcome, if we speculate that only the very attractive receive special (favorable or unfavorable) treatment, and that others are treated similarly. That is a less frightening conclusion than one which would indicate that unattractiveness brings about active discrimination.

As indicated earlier, previous findings (Efran, 1974) that attractive offenders are treated leniently can be interpreted in a number of ways. The results of the present experiment support the cognitive explanation we offered. The notion that good-looking people usually tend to be treated generously because they are seen as less dangerous and more virtuous remains tenable. The argument that physical attractiveness is a positive trait and therefore has a unidirectionally favorable effect on judgments of those who have it, would have led to accurate predictions in the burglary

TABLE 1 / Mean Sentence Assigned, in Years (*n* = 20 per cell)

Offense	Defendant Condition		
	Attractive	Unattractive	Control
Swindle	5.45	4.35	4.35
Burglary	2.80	5.20	5.10

conditions. However, this position could not account for the observed interaction. The cognitive view makes precisely that prediction.

Finally, we feel compelled to note that our laboratory situation is quite different from actual courtroom situations. Most important, perhaps, our subjects made decisions which had no consequences for the defendant, and they made those decisions by themselves, rather than arriving at judgments after discussions with others exposed to the same information. Since the courtroom is not an appropriate laboratory, it is unlikely that actual experimental tests in the real situation would ever be conducted. However, simulations constitute legitimate avenues for investigating person perception and interpersonal judgment, and there is no obvious reason to believe that these processes would not have the effects in trial proceedings that they do elsewhere.

Whether a discussion with other jurors would affect judgment is an empirical, and researchable, question. Perhaps if even 1 of 12 jurors notes that some irrelevant factor may be affecting the jury's judgment, the others would see the light. Especially now when the prospect of reducing the size of juries is being entertained, it would be important to find out whether extralegal considerations are more likely to have greater influence as the number of jurors decreases.

REFERENCES

Byrne, D., & Clore, G. L. A reinforcement model of evaluative responses. *Personality: An International Journal,* 1970, *1,* 103–128.

Dion, K. Physical attractiveness and evaluation of children's transgressions. *Journal of Personality and Social Psychology,* 1972, *24,* 207–213.

Dion, K., Berscheid, E., & Walster, E. What is beautiful is good. *Journal of Personality and Social Psychology,* 1972, *24,* 285–290.

Efran, M. G. The effect of physical appearance on the judgment of guilt, interpersonal attraction, and severity of recommended punishment in a simulated jury task. *Journal of Research in Personality,* 1974, *8,* 45–54.

Landy, D., & Aronson, E. The influence of the character of the criminal and victim on the decisions of simulated jurors. *Journal of Experimental Social Psychology,* 1969, *5,* 141–152.

Miller, A. G. Role of physical attractiveness in impression formation. *Psychonomic Science,* 1970, *19,* 241–243.

Monahan, F. *Women in crime.* New York: Washburn, 1941.

ENDNOTE

1. This information as well as copies of the case accounts referred to below, can be obtained from the first author.

This study was supported by a grant from the University of Maryland General Research Board.

CRITICAL THINKING QUESTIONS

1. This article used pictures only of females to show defendants of varying attractiveness. Would the same results be obtained if male defendants were used? In other words, do you think that attractiveness stereotypes operate in the same way for females and males? Defend your answer.

2. As the authors of the article noted, the methodology of the study differed from real-life jury trials in several ways. For example, subjects made their decisions alone and were presented with a paper description of the person and deed, not a real-life person. Design a study that would investigate the same variables studied in the article in a more natural environment.

3. Would the results of this study be generalizable to situations other than jury trials? Think of a situation in which the attractiveness of a person making a request or performing a certain action may result in his or her being treated differentially as a result of his or her attractiveness. Explain your answer.

4. What implications do these findings have for the U.S. legal system? How could the effects of irrelevant factors such as attractiveness somehow be minimized in the real-world

courtroom? For example, would telling the jurors beforehand about the tendency to let attractiveness influence their judgments make any difference? Why or why not?

ADDITIONAL RELATED READINGS

Mazzella, R., & Feingold, A. (1994). The effects of physical attractiveness, race, socio-economic status, and gender of defendants and victims on judgments of mock jurors: A meta-analysis. *Journal of Applied Social Psychology, 24,* 1315–1344.

Popovich, P. M., Gehlauf, D. N., Jolton, J. A., & Everton, W. J. (1996). Physical attractiveness and sexual harassment: Does every picture tell a story or even draw a picture? *Journal of Applied Social Psychology, 26,* 520–542.

ARTICLE 39 _____

Why do people work? Do they do so just to earn a living (in some cases, a very good living), or do they have other reasons, too? If you look at the number of references in American culture to the *Monday morning blues* and *TGIF,* you might get the impression that people would rather *not* work. In fact, many people would consider it distinctly odd if someone looked forward to the prospect of returning to work on Monday morning. Do most workers feel that way?

The question of what motivates people to work has been of major interest to industrial/organizational psychologists for quite some time. Ultimately concerned with productivity and profits, business enterprises have an obvious interest in trying to discover ways to increase employee motivation, since increased motivation is often viewed as synonymous with increased output. But what exactly contributes to employee motivation? Is it people's satisfaction with the work they are doing? A sense of commitment to the organization? The feeling of being treated fairly?

The following article by Stephen P. Schappe examines how all these factors may contribute to a particular type of work activity: *organizational citizenship behavior.* This term refers to instances when people go beyond the requirements of their jobs or the scope of their responsibilities to help others in the organization do their jobs or to help the organization itself.

The Influence of Job Satisfaction, Organizational Commitment, and Fairness Perceptions on Organizational Citizenship Behavior

■ Stephen P. Schappe

ABSTRACT. *Previous research has indicated that job satisfaction, perceptions of procedural justice, and organizational commitment are all significant correlates of organizational citizenship behavior (OCB). Those variables were studied collectively to determine their relative effects on OCB. Hierarchical regression analyses indicated that when all three of the variables were considered concurrently, only organizational commitment accounted for a unique amount of variance in OCB.*

Recently, researchers have been investigating the nature, causes, and consequences of prosocial job behav-

ior. Specifically, *organizational citizenship behavior* (OCB) has been the subject of numerous recent studies (e.g., Becker & Vance, 1993; Moorman, 1991; Moorman, 1993; Niehoff & Moorman, 1993; Organ & Lingl, 1995; Organ & Ryan, 1995). Derived from Katz's (1964) category of extra-role behavior, OCB has been defined as "individual behavior that is discretionary, not directly or explicitly recognized by the formal reward system, and that in the aggregate promotes the effective functioning of the organization" (Organ, 1988, p. 4). Despite the proliferation of inquiry into this area, relatively little is

Reprinted from *The Journal of Psychology, 132,* 277–290, 1998. Reprinted with permission of the Helen Dwight Reid Educational Foundation. Published by Heldref Publications, 1319 Eighteenth St., N.W., Washington, D.C. 20036-1802. Copyright © 1998.

known about the relative effects of the antecedents of OCB.

The most frequently investigated correlate of OCB has been job satisfaction (e.g., Bateman & Organ, 1983; Moorman, 1993; Motowidlo, 1984; Organ & Lingl, 1995; Puffer, 1987; Williams & Anderson, 1991). Empirical support for the influence of procedural justice perceptions (the extent to which the processes or procedures used to make decisions are regarded as fair) on OCB exists, as well (Farh, Podsakoff, & Organ, 1990; Moorman, 1991; Niehoff & Moorman, 1993). In addition, links between organizational commitment and OCB have been suggested (Scholl, 1981; Weiner, 1982; Williams & Anderson, 1991). Organ and Ryan (1995) recently conducted a meta-analytic review of 55 studies that investigated attitudinal and dispositional predictors of OCB; their results indicated that satisfaction, fairness, and organizational commitment were the only correlates of single-factor measures of OCB in a sufficient number of studies to warrant inclusion in the meta-analysis.

Moreover, it has been suggested that the relationship between job satisfaction and OCB may be better described as one that reflects a relationship between perceptions of fairness and OCB (Moorman, 1991; Organ, 1988). Additionally, because job satisfaction and organizational commitment have been found to be highly correlated (e.g., Brooke, Russell, & Price, 1988), it has been suggested that they should be considered together to address their relative effects on OCB (Williams & Anderson, 1991). Because all three variables are associated with OCB, it is important that organizational researchers and managers better understand the relationship of each of these three variables to OCB with regard to the other two. Thus, although aspects of procedural justice and job satisfaction have been paired together to determine their relative influence on OCB (see, e.g., Farh et al., 1990; Moorman, 1991) and job satisfaction and organizational commitment have been paired together as predictors of OCB (Williams & Anderson, 1991), I considered the relationship of OCB to all three variables simultaneously in the present study. My purpose was to determine the relative contributions of job satisfaction, procedural justice, and organizational commitment to predicting OCB.

ANTECEDENTS OF ORGANIZATIONAL CITIZENSHIP BEHAVIOR

Job Satisfaction

There is substantial support for the relationship between job satisfaction and OCB. For example, in a survey of university employees, Bateman and Organ (1983) found a significant relationship between general measures of job satisfaction and supervisory ratings of citizenship behavior. Cross-lagged patterns of the relationships between OCB and specific facets of job satisfaction revealed essentially the same results as overall satisfaction. Smith, Organ, and Near (1983) identified two separate dimensions of OCB: altruism, behavior directly and intentionally aimed at helping specific people, and generalized compliance (later renamed conscientiousness by Organ, 1988), a more impersonal type of conscientious behavior that does not provide immediate aid to a particular individual but is indirectly helpful to other people in the organization. Using path analysis, Smith et al. (1983) found that job satisfaction, measured as a chronic mood state, showed a direct predictive path to altruism but not to generalized compliance.

In addition, Puffer (1987) surveyed employees of furniture stores and found a significant relationship between prosocial behavior and satisfaction with material rewards that paralleled the relationship between altruism and job satisfaction found by Smith et al. (1983). More recently, Williams and Anderson (1991) provided support for the job satisfaction–OCB relationship. They found the cognitive component (vs. an affective component) of job satisfaction to significantly predict what they labeled OCBI (i.e., altruism) and OCBO (i.e., generalized compliance). In a study yielding similar results, Moorman (1993) investigated whether the relationship between job satisfaction and citizenship could depend on the nature of the job-satisfaction measures used. He found support for the relative importance of cognitive job satisfaction (based on the rational evaluation of work conditions, opportunities, and outcomes) over affective job satisfaction (based on an overall positive emotional appraisal of the job) in the prediction of OCB. In addition, in a survey of U.S. and British manufacturing employees, Organ and Lingl (1995) found that overall job satisfaction yielded a significant increment in explained variance beyond that accounted for by personality factors in the OCB dimension of altruism, but not in the compliance dimension of OCB.

Procedural Justice

Procedural justice is concerned with the perceived fairness of the processes through which decisions are made (Thibaut & Walker, 1975). More recently, it has been suggested (e.g., Greenberg, 1990) that procedural justice consists of a structural dimension (i.e., the characteristics of the formal procedures themselves) and an interpersonal dimension (i.e., how one is treated during the enactment of procedures).

Several studies by Moorman and his colleagues provided support for the relationships between OCB and the structural and interpersonal dimensions of procedural justice. Using a structural-equations modeling approach (i.e., LISREL), Moorman (1991) found significant paths between interactive justice (i.e., the interpersonal dimension of procedural justice) and four of five OCB dimensions (i.e., paths to altruism, conscientiousness, courtesy, and sportsmanship were significant; the path to civic virtue was not). By contrast, no significant paths were found between formal procedures (i.e., the structural dimension of procedural justice) and any of the five dimensions of OCB.

Using similar analytic techniques, Niehoff and Moorman (1993) found contrasting results; OCB was best explained in terms of formal procedures, not interactional justice. Specifically, significant paths were found between formal procedures and three of five OCB dimensions (courtesy, sportsmanship, and conscientiousness), whereas the only significant path from interactional justice was to sportsmanship. Also using a structural-equations modeling approach, Moorman, Niehoff, and Organ (1993) found significant paths between perceptions of procedural justice (combining both the structural and interpersonal dimensions) and the OCB dimensions of courtesy, sportsmanship, and conscientiousness. Although the findings of these studies supported the ability of both dimensions of procedural justice to predict various dimensions of OCB, whether the structural or interpersonal dimension is the better predictor remains unclear.

A study by Farh et al. (1990) also provided support for the ability of procedural justice perceptions to predict OCB. Using a measure containing supportive and participative leader behaviors to represent forms of procedural justice, they found that leader fairness accounted for unique variance in the altruism dimension of OCB, but not with respect to the generalized compliance dimension. However, Farh et al. did not explicitly measure the structural and interpersonal dimensions of procedural justice. *Supportive* leader behavior reflected the extent to which subordinates believed that their supervisors considered their personal welfare, dignity, and suggestions for improvement. *Participative* leader behavior measured the degree to which subordinates perceived that their supervisors asked for their suggestions in decision-making processes. Moreover, the effects of the two sets of leader behaviors on OCB were not analyzed separately.

Organizational Commitment

In the present study, I considered organizational commitment to be "the relative strength of an individual's identification with and involvement in an organization" (Mowday, Steers, & Porter, 1979, p. 226). Models by Scholl (1981) and Weiner (1982) have provided theoretical support for a commitment–OCB relationship. Scholl suggested that because commitment maintains behavioral direction when there is little expectation of formal organizational rewards for performance, commitment is a likely determinant of OCB. Like Scholl's model, Weiner's suggests that commitment is responsible for behaviors that do not depend primarily on reinforcements or punishment. Prosocial behaviors that indicate a personal preoccupation with the organization or that reflect personal sacrifice made for the sake of the organization are also presumed to be affected by commitment.

Two studies conducted by O'Reilly and Chatman (1986) also provided empirical evidence for an organizational commitment–OCB relationship. In a study of university employees' psychological attachment to organizations, O'Reilly and Chatman found that identification (involvement based on a need for affiliation) was a significant predictor of self-reports of generalized compliance behaviors. In a second study, of undergraduates' and MBA students' attachments, they found identification and internalization (involvement based on the similarity between individual and organizational values) to be significant predictors of self-reports of extra-role compliance behaviors.

However, despite the generally strong support for a relationship between commitment and OCB, Tansky (1993) found no support for such a relationship. In a study of organizational supervisors and managers, she found no significant positive relationships between organizational commitment and five OCB dimensions (altruism, conscientiousness, sportsmanship, courtesy, and civic virtue). In addition, the meta-analysis conducted by Organ and Ryan (1995) revealed that affective organizational commitment (the emotional attachment one feels to an organization) was significantly related to both the altruism and compliance dimensions of OCB.

In virtually all of the studies in which job satisfaction or organizational commitment was found to significantly predict OCB, the researchers used one variable and excluded the other (for exceptions, see Moorman et al., 1993; Williams & Anderson, 1991). Because of the conceptual overlap between job satisfaction and commitment, it has been suggested that the significant relationships that have been found using only job satisfaction or organizational commitment to predict OCB are potentially spurious (Williams & Anderson, 1991). For that reason, the predictive abilities of those two variables should be studied concurrently. In addition, Organ (1988) suggested that the significant relationships found between job satisfaction and OCB likely reflect the influence of fairness perceptions. Indeed, Moorman (1991) measured both perceptions of fairness and job satisfaction and found that job satisfaction did not significantly influence OCB and fairness perceptions did significantly predict OCB.

On the one hand, some researchers suggest that fairness perceptions should be included when studying the effects of job satisfaction on OCB to better explain the relationships between those variables (Moorman, 1991; Organ, 1988). On the other hand, one could argue that organizational commitment should be included when studying the effects of job satisfaction on OCB, given the potentially spurious significant findings of previous research that has considered only one of the two variables (Williams & Anderson, 1991). In the present study, I responded to both of these suggestions by considering all three variables together to determine their relative effects on OCB. Specifically, I hypothesized that job satisfaction, procedural justice perceptions, and organizational commitment each explain unique variance in OCB.

METHOD

Sample and Data Collection

The participants, 150 employees of a mid-Atlantic insurance company, were given surveys to complete during regular working hours; 130 completed surveys were returned anonymously in sealed envelopes and deposited in a secure collection box located on the premises, yielding a response rate of 87%. The mean age of the participants was 35.0 years, and approximately two thirds of the respondents were women. The respondents had been employed by the organization an average of 6.0 years and had been in their current jobs an average of 3.7 years.

Measures

Procedural Justice Procedural justice was measured with a 19-item, 7-point Likert-type scale that asked respondents to express the extent of their disagreement or agreement with a series of statements regarding the structural dimension of procedural justice (e.g., "The procedures used to make decisions in your organization make sure that the decisions made are based on as much accurate information as possible") and an 8-item scale measuring the interpersonal dimension of procedural justice (e.g., "With regard to carrying out the procedures at your organization, your supervisor takes steps to deal with you in a truthful manner"). The scales included items adapted from scales used previously by Konovsky and Cropanzano (1991) and Moorman (1991). The reliability estimates (Cronbach's alphas) for the structural and interpersonal procedural justice scales were .92 and .97, respectively.

Job Satisfaction The short form of the Minnesota Satisfaction Questionnaire (MSQ; Weiss, Dawis,

England, & Lofquist, 1967) measured job satisfaction, broadly conceptualized by the scale's authors as the extent to which an individual's requirements are fulfilled by the work environment. On a 5-point Likert-type continuum, the respondents described the extent of their dissatisfaction or satisfaction on 20 statements that completed a sentence beginning with the phrase, "On my present job, this is how I feel about" (e.g., "the chance to do different things from time to time"). The scale's reliability estimate was .92.

Organizational Commitment   The short form of the Organizational Commitment Questionnaire (OCQ) developed by Mowday et al. (1979) measured organizational commitment, defined as "the relative strength of an individual's identification with and involvement in a particular organization" (Mowday et al., p. 226). The OCQ is regarded as a measure of affective, as opposed to normative or continuance, commitment. The participants marked on a 7-point Likert-type scale the degree to which they disagreed or agreed with nine statements about their feelings toward the organization (e.g., "I am willing to put in a great deal of effort beyond that normally expected in order to help this organization be successful") (α = .91).

OCB   As have other researchers in the majority of OCB studies, I used a variation of the citizenship-behavior scale developed by Smith et al. (1983). Three items each measured the altruism (e.g., "I help others who have heavy workloads") and generalized compliance (e.g., "I do not take unnecessary time off work") dimensions of OCB and combined to form a single 6-item scale. Respondents used a 5-point Likert-type scale to indicate the relative strength of their agreement or disagreement with responses ranging from 1 (representing strong disagreement) to 5 (strong agreement). The reliability estimate for this scale was .69.

Control Variables   The respondents also indicated their gender, age, job type (managerial or nonmanagerial), length of employment with the organization, and salary (within a given range) for the previous year. I gathered those data based on other researchers' (e.g., Hitt & Tyler, 1991) recommendations that those

types of variables be controlled because of their potential to affect the relationships among other organizational variables.

Analyses

I used a series of hierarchical regression analyses to test for the unique variance accounted for by procedural justice perceptions, job satisfaction, and organizational commitment. As recommended by Cohen and Cohen (1983), this procedure provides a unique partitioning of the total variance accounted for in a dependent variable by a set of predictors. The first equation included only the five control variables. At the next stage, both the structural and interpersonal measures of procedural justice were added to the equation. I added job satisfaction in the third equation and included organizational commitment in the fourth equation.

RESULTS

The means, standard deviations, alphas, and correlations are presented in Table 1. All scales except the OCB scale (α = .69) had reliabilities well above the .80 level recommended by Nunnally (1978). Preliminary results confirmed the significant correlations expected between job satisfaction and organizational commitment (r = .57, p < .001), as well as between job satisfaction and the structural dimension of procedural justice (r = .58, p < .001) and the interpersonal dimension of procedural justice (r = .68, p < .001). Contrary to expectations, however, organizational commitment was the only significant correlate of OCB (r = .21, p < .01). Neither age nor gender was significantly correlated with OCB. However, organization tenure, organization level (managerial or nonmanagerial), and salary were all significantly negatively correlated with OCB. A discussion of the regression analyses follows.

Hierarchical Regression Analyses

The initial equation regressed OCB on the five control variables (see Table 2 for the results of the hierarchical regression analyses). The addition of both the

TABLE 1 / Means, Standard Deviations, Scaled Variable Reliabilities, and Intercorrelations among Study Variables (N = 130)

Variable	M	SD	1	2	3	4	5	6	7	8	9	10
1. Structural procedural justice	4.79	.95	(.92)									
2. Interpersonal procedural justice	5.42	1.51	.65***	(.97)								
3. Job satisfaction	3.86	.62	.58***	.68***	(.92)							
4. Organizational commitment	5.93	.90	.36***	.30***	.57***	(.91)						
5. OCB	3.22	.43	−.02	−.03	−.06	.21**	(.69)					
6. Sex	1.66	.48	−.06	−.12	−.20*	−.11	.14	—				
7. Age	35.02	9.62	.04	−.06	−.11	.37***	.04	.05	—			
8. Organizational tenure	6.03	3.95	.04	.08	.26**	.21**	−.23**	.09	.51***	—		
9. Job type	1.21	.41	.08	.08	.19*	.26**	−.18*	−.36***	.36***	.21***	—	
10. Salary	2.62	1.45	.06	−.04	.14	.24**	−.27***	−.44***	.44***	.29***	.76***	—

Note: Values in parentheses are Cronbach's alphas.
*$p < .05$. **$p < .01$. ***$p < .001$.

structural and interpersonal dimensions of procedural justice in the second equation did not produce a significant change in R^2 (ΔR^2 = .000). Thus, the hypothesis that procedural justice perceptions account for unique variance in OCB was not supported. The addition of job satisfaction in the third equation also failed to yield a significant change in R^2 (ΔR^2 = .003), thus failing to support the hypothesis that job satisfaction accounts for unique variance in OCB. However, with the addition of organizational commitment to the fourth regression equation, I found a significant increment in R^2 (ΔR^2 = .071, p < .05), supporting the hypothesis that organizational commitment accounts for unique variance in OCB.

Of the four predictor variables, organizational commitment had the only significant relationship to OCB (β = .356, p < .001; see Table 3 for the standardized regression coefficients of the four predictor variables and the five control variables).

Exploratory Analyses

I attempted to address the unanticipated inability of perceptions of procedural justice and job satisfaction to predict OCB: I combined the altruism and generalized compliance (i.e., conscientiousness) dimensions of OCB into a single scale. However, given the support for the two-dimensional structure of the citizen-

TABLE 2 / Summary of Hierarchical Analyses, Including Controls (N = 130)

Step	Variable	OCB		
		R^2	ΔR^2	F
1	Controls	.183		5.546***
2	Interpersonal and structural procedural justice	.183	.000	3.899***
3	Job satisfaction	.186	.003	3.461***
4	Organizational commitment	.257	.071**	4.602***

**$p < 01$. ***$p < .001$.

TABLE 3 / Standardized Regression Coefficients for All Variables in Complete Regression Equation (*N* = 130)

	OCB	
Variable	β	t
Predictor Variables		
Structural procedural justice	−.051	−.465
Interpersonal procedural justice	.002	.017
Job satisfaction	−.129	−.952
Organizational commitment	.356	3.370***
Controls		
Sex	.009	.096
Age	.231	2.157*
Organizational tenure	−.287	−2.908**
Organizational level	.023	.188
Salary	−.371	−2.659**

Note: OCB = organizational citizenship behavior.
*$p < .05$. **$p < .01$. ***$p < .001$.

ship behavior scale of Smith et al. (1983) (e.g., Becker & Vance, 1993), I conducted a factor analysis on the OCB scale used in the present study to determine whether (a) the factor pattern loadings were consistent with a two-factor structure and (b) regressing the separate dimensions of OCB on the set of predictors would better explain the nature of these relationships.

I used principal-components analysis in a factor analysis of the OCB scale to determine which items should contribute to the separate scale scores; to allow for correlations among the factors, I also used analytic

oblique (oblimin) rotation. The analysis extracted three factors for the citizenship behaviors. The resulting pattern factor matrix of the rotated solution is presented in Table 4. With the exception of Item 3, all items loaded significantly on the factors hypothesized by Smith et al. (1983). I eliminated Item 3 and re-estimated the same series of regression equations, finding that the OCB dimensions of altruism and conscientiousness regressed separately on the set of predictors. I gained no insight from these analyses, because organizational commitment was still the only significant predictor of altruism (β = .333, $p < .01$) and conscientiousness (β = .196, $p < .10$) in the full regression equation (see Table 5).

DISCUSSION

One of the important contributions of the present study is that it clarifies the relative effects of three variables previously identified as antecedents of OCB. Because the effects of job satisfaction, perceptions of procedural justice, and organizational commitment on OCB were considered simultaneously, a clearer picture of the attitudinal influences on OCB has emerged. Contrary to findings from previous research that when considered alone, job satisfaction, procedural justice perceptions, and organizational commitment influence OCB, the present results indicate that when all three are considered together, only organizational commitment emerges as a significant predictor of OCB.

TABLE 4 / Factor Analysis of Organizational Citizenship Behavior (OCB) Scale (Pattern Matrix after Oblique Rotation)

Scale Item	Conscientiousness	Altruism	Factor 3
1. I help others who have heavy workloads.	−.06936	.89352	.03604
2. I help others who have been absent.	.07868	.87179	−.01643
3. I willingly give my time to help others who have work-related problems.	.01183	.02269	.98166
4. I take longer lunches or breaks.	.75948	.09270	−.18593
5. I take unnecessary time off work.	.80558	.11619	.14893
6. I take extra breaks.	.87647	−.18766	.05782
Eigenvalue (unrotated solution)	2.12	1.53	1.01
Percentage of variance explained	36	26	17
Cumulative variance explained	36	61	78

TABLE 5 / Results of Regression Analyses for OCB Subscales, with Controls (N = 130)

Variable	Altruism		Conscientiousness	
	β	t	β	t
Structural procedural justice	−.142	−1.25	.072	.614
Interpersonal procedural justice	.144	1.113	−.149	−1.118
Job satisfaction	−.083	−.593	−.110	−.764
Organizational commitment	.333	3.048**	.195	1.733†

†$p < .10$.
**$p < .01$. For altruism, $R^2 = .202$, $F = 3.381$ ($p < .001$). For conscientiousness, $R^2 = .153$, $F = 2.404$ ($p < .05$).

In contrast to many other researchers (e.g., Bateman & Organ, 1983; Smith et al., 1983; Williams & Anderson, 1991), I did not find job satisfaction to be a significant predictor of OCB. Given that job satisfaction was not even a significant correlate of OCB, it was not possible to replicate Moorman's (1991) finding that when fairness perceptions were controlled, job satisfaction did not influence OCB. In other words, Moorman (1991) and Organ (1988) implied that when considered alone, job satisfaction does influence OCB; it is when fairness perceptions are also considered that satisfaction no longer influences OCB (and perceived fairness will influence OCB).

Also contrary to earlier findings (e.g., Farh et al., 1990; Moorman, 1991; Moorman et al., 1993; Niehoff & Moorman, 1993), the present results indicate that neither dimension of procedural justice was a significant predictor of OCB. Moorman (1991) suggested that the relationship between job satisfaction and OCB may be better described as one reflecting a relationship between perceptions of fairness and OCB. Because of the inability of job satisfaction to predict OCB, it is perhaps the case that job satisfaction and perceptions of procedural fairness share a common antecedent not included in the present study, which has contaminated the relationships of these two variables with OCB. Future research should include measures of both perceived fairness and job satisfaction to clarify their relative effects on OCB.

In general, there exist several potential explanations for the inability of procedural justice and job satisfaction to predict OCB. First, the reliance in the present study on self-reports of OCB stands in contrast to the almost ubiquitous use of supervisory ratings of OCB (for exceptions, see O'Reilly & Chatman, 1986; Motowidlo, Packard, & Manning, 1986). However, significant relationships between supervisor and self-ratings of OCB have been found, indicating that self-ratings of OCB may not be that different from supervisory ratings (Becker & Vance, 1993). Another potentially limiting factor of the present study was the use of shorter versions of the scale developed by Smith et al. (1983). However, given the acceptable (although marginal) reliability of the scale and the generally consistent factor-loading pattern found in the present study, that does not appear to be a major limitation. Nonetheless, the restricted variance of the OCB scale ($SD = .43$) raises some concerns.

Within the context of managing organizational behavior, the results of the present study have a number of practical implications. The first of these implications is that managers should expand and diversify their view of desired job performance. Job performance has traditionally been measured by the extent to which an employee achieves a work-related quality or quantity goal. It is clear, however, that managers need to move beyond traditional conceptualizations of job performance and begin to incorporate the spontaneous and innovative behavior that is often critical to the effective functioning of organizations (Organ, 1988). Because citizenship behaviors are not mandated by job descriptions, they are rarely linked directly to the job or, more specifically, to job performance. OCB exists outside of the domain of traditional behavior that "gets the job done," yet citizenship behavior is still an important element of an employee's overall contribution to an organization (Organ).

Another important issue for managers is how to better manage and promote the relationship between meaningful organizational attitudes, such as commitment, and beneficial organizational behavior, such as OCB. Managers need to recognize that the feelings employees have for their organizations may manifest themselves in the form of prosocial job behaviors. Given the extra-role, as opposed to in-role, nature of OCB, it is not so much that employees are willing to go to great lengths to fulfill the requirements of their jobs as it is that they may engage in behaviors that are beneficial to co-workers, superiors, or the organization as a whole. Thus, managers' ability to motivate employees by relying on formal reward structures to reinforce specific role requirements is limited.

The present study has several limitations. First, it relied on cross-sectional, self-reported data. Therefore, my ability to make causal statements about the hypothesized relationships was constrained. Collecting longitudinal data would be a step toward making causal inferences about the relationships in the study. The exclusive use of self-reported data raises concerns about common method variance (Podsakoff & Organ, 1986). When all measures come from the same source, any deficiency in that source may contaminate all of the measures, resulting in erroneous correlations between measures. Using multiple measures for the variables would alleviate some of these concerns.

The major finding of this study is that despite the predictive abilities of job satisfaction, perceptions of procedural justice, and organizational commitment, when taken alone, only organizational commitment emerged as a significant predictor of OCB. Through a consideration of the simultaneous influence of those three variables on OCB, the nature of the relationships between variables has become clearer. Future OCB research should continue to explicate the relationship of employee attitudes to organizational citizenship behavior.

REFERENCES

Bateman, T. S., & Organ, D. W. (1983). Job satisfaction and the good soldier: The relationship between affect and employee citizenship. *Academy of Management Journal, 26,* 587–595.

Becker, T. E., & Vance, R. J. (1993). Construct validity of three types of organizational citizenship behavior: An illustration of the direct product model with refinements. *Journal of Management, 19,* 663–682.

Brooke, R., Russell, D., & Price, J. (1988). Discriminant validation of measures of job satisfaction, job involvement, and organizational commitment. *Journal of Applied Psychology, 73,* 139–145.

Cohen, J., & Cohen, P. (1983). *Applied multiple regression/correlation analysis for the behavioral sciences.* Hillsdale, NJ: Erlbaum.

Farh, J. L., Podsakoff, P. M., & Organ, D. W. (1990). Accounting for organizational citizenship behavior: Leader fairness and task scope versus satisfaction. *Journal of Management, 16,* 705–721.

Greenberg, J. (1990). Organizational justice: Yesterday, today, and tomorrow. *Journal of Management, 16,* 399–432.

Hitt, M. A., & Tyler, B. B. (1991). Strategic decision models: Integrating different perspectives. *Strategic Management Journal, 12,* 327–351.

Katz, D. (1964). The motivational basis of organizational behavior. *Behavioral Science, 9,* 131–133.

Konovsky, M. A., & Cropanzano, R. (1991). Perceived fairness of employee drug testing as a predictor of employee attitudes and job performance. *Journal of Applied Psychology, 76,* 698–707.

Moorman, R. H. (1991). Relationship between organizational justice and organizational citizenship behaviors: Do fairness perceptions influence employee citizenship? *Journal of Applied Psychology, 76,* 845–855.

Moorman, R. H. (1993). The influence of cognitive and affective based job satisfaction on the relationship between satisfaction and organizational citizenship behavior. *Human Relations, 46,* 759–776.

Moorman, R. H., Niehoff, B. P., & Organ, D. W. (1993). Treating employees fairly and organizational citizenship behavior: Sorting the effects of job satisfaction, organizational commitment, and procedural justice. *Employee Responsibilities and Rights Journal, 6,* 209–225.

Motowidlo, S. J. (1984). Does job satisfaction lead to consideration and personal sensitivity? *Academy of Management Journal, 27,* 910–915.

Motowidlo, S. J., Packard, J. S., & Manning, M. R. (1986). Occupational stress: Its causes and consequences for job performance. *Journal of Applied Psychology, 71,* 618–629.

Mowday, R. T., Steers, R. M., & Porter, L. W. (1979). The measurement of organizational commitment. *Journal of Vocational Behavior, 14,* 224–247.

Niehoff, B. P., & Moorman, R. H. (1993). Justice as a mediator of the relationships between methods of monitoring and organizational citizenship behavior. *Academy of Management Journal, 36,* 527–556.

Nunnally, J. C. (1978). *Psychometric theory.* New York: McGraw-Hill.

O'Reilly, C. A., III, & Chatman, J. (1986). Organizational commitment and psychological attachment: The effects of compliance, identification, and internalization on prosocial behavior. *Journal of Applied Psychology, 71,* 492–499.

Organ, D. W. (1988). *Organizational citizenship behavior: The good soldier syndrome.* Lexington, MA: Lexington Books.

Organ, D. W., & Konovsky, M. (1989). Cognitive versus affective determinants of organizational citizenship behavior. *Journal of Applied Psychology, 74,* 157–164.

Organ, D. W., & Lingl, A. (1995). Personality, satisfaction, and organizational citizenship behavior. *The Journal of Social Psychology, 135,* 339–350.

Organ, D. W., & Ryan, K. (1995). A meta-analytic review of attitudinal and dispositional predictors of organizational citizenship behavior. *Personnel Psychology, 48,* 775–802.

Podsakoff, P. M., & Organ, D. W. (1986). Self-reports in organizational research: Problems and prospects. *Journal of Management, 12,* 531–544.

Puffer, S. M. (1987). Prosocial behavior, noncompliant behavior, and work performance among commission salespeople. *Journal of Applied Psychology, 72,* 615–621.

Scholl, R. W. (1981). Differentiating organizational commitment from expectancy as a motivating force. *Academy of Management Review, 6,* 589–599.

Smith, C. A., Organ, D. W., & Near, J. P. (1983). Organizational citizenship behavior: Its nature and antecedents. *Journal of Applied Psychology, 68,* 653–663.

Tansky, J. W. (1993). Justice and organizational citizenship behavior: What is the relationship? *Employee Responsibilities and Rights Journal, 6,* 195–208.

Thibaut, J., & Walker, L. (1975). *Procedural justice: A psychological analysis.* Hillsdale, NJ: Erlbaum.

Weiner, Y. (1982). Commitment in organizations: A normative view. *Academy of Management Review, 7,* 418–428.

Weiss, D. J., Dawis, R. V., England, G. W., & Lofquist, L. H. (1967). *Manual for the Minnesota Satisfaction Questionnaire.* Minneapolis, MN: Industrial Relations Center, University of Minnesota.

Williams, L. J., & Anderson, S. E. (1991). Job satisfaction and organizational commitment as predictors of organizational citizenship and in-role behaviors. *Journal of Management, 17,* 601–617.

CRITICAL THINKING QUESTIONS

1. According to the article, organizational commitment seems to be the main determinant of organizational citizenship behavior (OCB). What steps can organizations take to enhance employees' sense of organizational commitment? Explain your answer.

2. Use the concepts from the article to explain organizational citizenship behavior in nonwork settings, such as in school or in a social group. Are all of these situations comparable, or are there distinct differences among the various types of settings? Explain.

3. The article concluded by saying that "future OCB research should continue to explicate the relationship of employee attitudes to organizational citizenship behavior." Based on your own experiences with work and various other groups, what might those attitudes be? How could they be tested?

4. The article noted that one limitation of the study is that it is correlational in nature, which means cause-and-effect links cannot be established. Outline a longitudinal study to test the cause-and-effect relationship between organizational commitment and organizational citizenship behavior.

Chapter Fourteen

APPLYING SOCIAL PSYCHOLOGY
Health and Environment

T HE FINAL CHAPTER in this book addresses the contributions of social psychology to both health and environmental issues.

When we think of *health,* often the first thing that comes to mind is the medical, biological component of illness. But what about the behaviors that are linked to illness? Obviously, we can do many things either to increase or decrease the likelihood of illness. Health psychology research examines issues such as personality factors that may be related to health—for instance, the underlying beliefs about health-related issues and how these beliefs can be changed.

Article 40 presents recent research on the topic of *resilience.* Until recently, psychology has tended to focus on adult negative behaviors as being rooted in early life experiences. For example, a child abuser would be viewed as someone who learned this behavior because he or she was abused as a child. And while many abused children do indeed grow up to be abusive parents, many do not. Likewise, many other individuals who experience different but equally traumatic childhoods are somehow able to transcend those experiences and turn out to be well-adjusted adults. "The Art of Overcoming" tries to answer the question of why some people overcome trauma while others do not. The article also addresses whether coping skills can be taught.

A second area addressed in this chapter is the environment. The ways in which people are influenced by the environments in which they live, as well as the ways in which people can modify their environments to suit their own desires and needs, is the focus of *environmental psychology.* Once considered an outgrowth of social psychological research, it is now regarded as a discipline in its own right. Article 41, "Territorial Defense and the Good Neighbor," examines the social environment. How people use and define personal space in public settings—and how they protect it from the intrusion of others—is the focus of this classic article.

Article 42, "Catastrophizing and Untimely Death," returns to the topic of health psychology by examining how patterns of thinking may be highly accurate predictors of early death. In fact, certain patterns of thinking may influence people's lifestyle choices, which, in turn, may result in their dying at an earlier than normal age.

ARTICLE 40 _____

You are no doubt familiar with the nature versus nurture debate. Specifically, the question centers around what most clearly determines behavior: biological influences, such as heredity, or environmental factors, such as early childhood experiences.

Consider one example of a behavior that begs the nature/nurture question: child abuse. Do you think that people who were abused as children grow up to be child abusers? If you do believe this (as most people do), you would be supporting the nurture side of the debate, arguing that early childhood experiences are what determined the subsequent abusive behavior. Yet as compelling as that argument sounds, the fact is that many people who were abused as children do not grow up to be child abusers. Moreover, many people who were abused go to great lengths not to inflict the same pain and harm on their children that their parents inflicted on them.

In the past, psychology tended to examine the negative patterns of recurring behavior. That is, the focus was on how adult problems (crime and abuse, for example) could be traced back to negative childhood experiences. Only recently has psychology begun to look at the other side of the picture: Namely, how do some people who have had awful childhoods transcend those experiences and grow up to be healthy, well-adjusted adults? The words *hardiness* and *resilience* often are used to describe those people who successfully have managed to overcome great obstacles in their lives.

The following article by Deborah Blum describes the fledgling research on how people overcome terrible traumas. In addition, it tries to answer the even more important question as to whether this ability can be taught.

The Art of Overcoming
The New Science of Resilience

■ Deborah Blum

For most of us, high-voltage transmission lines are blots on the landscape. They slice up the sky and emit a sinister little hum of energy that translates into "Stay back if you want to see tomorrow." So, for David Miller to like power lines so much—to see in them uplift and promise and future—well, you first have to understand the landscape of a child whose mother decided not to keep him.

He was born in 1960, in Reidsville, North Carolina, in a neighborhood of small, neat ranch houses—in the African-American-only part of town. This was,

after all, the deep South of almost forty years ago. He lived with his grandparents. His mother left him there; she couldn't do it, everyone knew that. She was 24, pregnant by mistake. "It's not that I didn't see my mother," Miller says, "but my grandparents raised me." Yet because his grandparents both worked—his grandfather at a dry cleaners, his grandmother as a laundry attendant—"I was a latchkey kid before the coin was termed."

And when they were home, they had little patience for a small boy's antics. "My grandmother would save

Reprinted from *Psychology Today,*1998 (May/June), *31,* 32–38, 66, 67, 69, 70, 72–73. Reprinted with permission from *Psychology Today* magazine. Copyright © 1998 (Sussex Publishers, Inc.).

up my spankings all week," says Miller. "Friday was judgment day." If the offense was grave enough, he ended up with welts across his back.

You might imagine that he was a child standing on a slippery hillside, his birth merely the first skidding step downward. In his spare time, though, he used to walk under the power lines. "It seemed like hours and miles," he recalls, "but I was pretty small." And he'd follow them with his feet and then his eyes until they disappeared into the clouded edges of the sky. And he'd think about where they went and wonder about the world beyond.

Miller is 37 now and an assistant professor of social work at Case Western Reserve University in Cleveland. He's chosen to study resilience—the ability, let's say, to stand steady on such treacherous hillsides, even to climb them—among other at-risk children, young African-Americans from the poor and drug-overrun neighborhoods of the inner city.

"I'm interested in strengths," he says. "What strengths allow you to deal with the violence, and the guns held to your head, and the fear of being molested? What is it that allows children to grow up in that and not be immobilized?" And when he talks to teenagers there, he remembers his own climb. "I do see myself as resilient. I always believed in my own abilities. I wasn't handcuffed by where I grew up. I'm happy with my life."

And when he travels to New York or Miami or into the power-line neighborhoods of Cleveland, where he lives, he still looks up and watches that unexpected flight of utility hardware to the horizon. And he thinks, "Oh, this is where they were taking me."

WHEN THE RED BALL BOUNCES

Could there be a research field more personal than that of resilience? When we all know that life, even for those who have had the best of childhoods, promises challenge after challenge, year after year? Who doesn't want to know where resilience comes from, how to transcend pain and grief, surmount obstacles and frustrations—to dream along the power lines, if you will?

I began thinking about it as a parent. There were days I hated: finding my son standing by a wall in the schoolyard, eyes filling with tears, unwanted by his playmates at that moment. I wanted, oh, I wanted revenge, although that was pure, lunatic fantasy. I wanted to bundle my son away in some cozy little world without hurt. An even greater fantasy.

Most of all, I wanted to know if I could teach him to bounce back. We all tumble. If we pick ourselves up, and learn from it, and go on with only superficial injury, well—I wanted to know if I could give my son that wonderful ability—that bounce.

I had a powerful visual image of the process. Not Miller's power lines, but the neat, clean, and quick bounce of a ball. The slap, the sting of being down, and then the easy rise, arching into a brighter air. It was a lovely image, really. It made me think of Paul Simon's old lyric about coming back from a failed love affair: "The morning sun is shining like a red rubber ball."

It was such a terrific thought. And this is what I wanted science to tell me: can resilience be deliberately acquired, or must we be born a David Miller, with some marvelous inner ability to see beyond where we stand?

It turns out to be a good time to ask those questions, because so many researchers are also asking them, in a professional capacity. Scientists now study resilience, it seems, in every possible niche: inner cities, tropical islands, families fleeing war or trying to live with it, children coping with the loss of a parent, entire families struggling with the loss of a home. It's part of what American Psychological Association President Martin Seligman, Ph.D., believes is a sea change in psychology, away from focusing on what damages people toward trying to understand what makes them strong.

---

7 Steps of Strength

- You have the *ability* right now
- *Faith*—in the future or in God—counts
- Recruit *others*
- Set *goals*
- *Believe* in yourself
- Recognize your *strengths*
- See yourself as a *strategist*

The first finding, to my chagrin, is that I'm going to have to tuck my red rubber ball image back into the lore of pop-rock. There's no: "Hey, the kid went down, but look, he bounced, he's fine" ending to this story. The ability to rebound is part of the process, sure, but it's not magically pain-free or instantaneous. Psychologists want that message out there. In fact, a professional alarm sounded last year when a national news magazine (okay, *U.S. News and World Report*) published a cover story about resilience research titled "Invincible Children."

"It is a primary example of what I have been calling the myth of the 'superkid,' who walks between raindrops, confronts any challenge and emerges unscarred and unscathed, never experiences a moment's pain," says Washington, D.C., psychologist Sybil Wolin, Ph.D., who, with husband and clinical psychiatrist, Steve Wolin, M.D., co-authored the popular book, *The Resilient Self.*

"The notion we try to put forth is that resilience embodies a paradox," she says. "We're talking about the capacity to rebound from experience, mixed with all the damage and problems that adversity can cause. It's not an either/or thing. And this 'media resilience' does kids who are struggling no good, does professionals no good in understanding them, has downright dangerous policy implications, and frankly, gives resilience research a bad name."

THE ROCKY CLIMB

Resilience research is often not bright and shiny at all. If you're going to study people climbing upward, you have to start at the very rocky bottom. "I decided to look at adults who'd had traumatic childhoods because I knew some very neat people who had come from that background," said John DeFrain, Ph.D., a professor of family studies at the University of Nebraska. "I thought it would be all warm and fuzzy-feeling. But these were people who were sometimes just barely hanging on. They were surviving as children, but just."

He found that it was in adulthood that people really began to transcend the difficulties of childhood and to rebuild. One man, beaten as a child by his father with belts, razor strops, and tree branches, reached a point in his mid-twenties, when he decided

to die. He wrote a suicide note, put the gun to his head, and then suddenly thought, "I'm not going to die because of what someone else did to me." That day, for the first time, he called a psychologist and went into counseling.

That dramatically emphasizes one of several key aspects of resilience research:

- *There is no timeline, no set period, for finding strength,* resilient behaviors and coping skills. People do best if they develop strong coping skills as children, and some researchers suggest the first ten years are optimum. But the ability to turn around is always there.

- *About one-third of poor, neglected, abused children are capably building better lives* by the time they are teenagers, according to all resilience studies. They are doing well in school, working toward careers, often helping to support their siblings.

- *Faith—be it in the future, the world at the end of the power lines, or in a higher power—is an essential ingredient.* Ability to perceive bad times as temporary times gets great emphasis from Seligman as an essential strength.

- *Most resilient people don't do it alone—in fact, they don't even try.* One of the standout findings of resilience research is that people who cope well with adversity, if they don't have a strong family support system, are able to ask for help or recruit others to help them. This is true for children and adults; resilient adults, for instance, are far more likely to talk to friends and even co-workers about events in their lives.

- *Setting goals and planning for the future is a strong factor* in dealing with adversity. In fact, as University of California–Davis psychologist Emmy Werner, Ph.D., points out, it may minimize the adversity itself. For instance, Werner found that when Hurricane Iniki battered Hawaii in 1993, islanders who were previously identified as resilient reported less property damage than others in the study. Why? They'd prepared more, boarded up windows, invested in good insurance.

- *Believing in oneself and recognizing one's strengths is important.* University of Alabama psychologist Ernestine Brown, Ph.D., discovered that when children of depressed, barely functioning mothers

Triumph Over Torture

I had never read a book as pitiless, terrifying, and inspiring in my life: a Tibetan woman's account of twenty-seven years of torture in labor camps for resisting China's occupation of her homeland. *Ama Adhe: The Voice That Remembers* (Wisdom Publications) is a memoir that describes—with unutterable calm—acts of unthinkable evil, and the unwavering spirit of the woman who withstood them. But meeting her was the true shock: when I sat with Adhe in my home, she took my hands in hers—strong, vital, calloused, caressing—and it was I, the baby boomer American journalist, who drew strength from her.

She was dressed in typical Tibetan garb—peasant style—and counted her prayer beads from time to time. Now in her sixties, Adhe lives in exile in India under the protection of the Dalai Lama. She has remarried, and speaks reverently of "waking each morning and realizing that I am in freedom, living in the same town that his Holiness the Dalai Lama lives in, and then I am very happy."

The facts: In 1954, when Adhe's son was just a year old, and she was pregnant with her second child, her husband was poisoned and died in front of her. Her husband's mother died soon afterward, of grief. In 1958, nine armed men came to Adhe's home, beat her in front of her children, and arrested her. Several months of physical torture followed, and finally she was brought before a large crowd and forced to watch as her brother-in-law was shot in front of her. "Pieces of his brain and his blood splashed on my dress," Adhe recalls. Her sister, his wife, lost her mind and died soon after.

Adhe, however, was not killed. "They said, 'We want you to suffer for the rest of your life. Now you see who has won.'" Almost three decades of imprisonment, forced labor, near starvation, and beatings followed. Moved from prison to prison, Adhe was not allowed to change or wash her only dress—known in Tibetan as a *chupa*—for years. When she menstruated, she let the blood dry and scraped it off. At one point she fainted while carrying stones; she was believed to be dead and was put in a hut that held the bodies of other dead prisoners. "The bodies looked like skeletons," says Adhe. "The eyes had blackened, the cheekbones were protruding. The sickening smell was overwhelming."

Over time, Adhe became something of a cause célèbre and was finally allowed to visit friends and family in 1979, twenty-one years after she was first imprisoned. She discovered that a friend had raised her daughter, but her son had gone insane after her arrest and one day fell into a river and drowned. "My surviving friends came to see me in the night," she says, "and told me of the fates of most of the women who had worked with me in the resistance. Now they were dead." That may have been Adhe's darkest moment: "There was nothing left. All these years I had been living for nothing, and now I didn't have to try anymore. A terrible restlessness came over me, and I began to wander around muttering to myself, totally unaware of my immediate surroundings."

How does one even use the word "resilience" in this context? It seems too small. There is a quality of indestructible strength and joy in Adhe that seems inborn. However, in her story, one does find the common traits of resilience that researchers have pointed out. For instance, perhaps the cardinal finding about the resilient is that they do not survive alone. Too weak to say her daily prayers (or even to remember them), Adhe sought the advice of an imprisoned monk who crafted her a shortened version of the prayer. Mourning the deaths of fellow women prisoners, Adhe began to make a quilt from their old dresses, and after a few years, it was large enough to sleep on. To this day she keeps the quilt: "My daughter used to beg me to get rid of it, saying, 'I can't stand it. Please throw it in the river.' But somehow I couldn't. It is with me even today."

Later, Adhe was sent food by her brother, and when prison officials wanted to take it away from her, a Chinese doctor at the labor camp who had taken an interest in Adhe's welfare intervened. "He said he would keep the food and give it to me slowly. 'If you overeat at this point, you will die.'" Adhe asked the doctor to use the food to prepare a special soup for all the prisoners. In her memoir, she recalls: "All the prisoners were so happy in getting their share that although it was still very hot, they drank it immediately. You could see their faces glowing red. Some licked the cups, then put in some water, shook the cup, and drank again. Some kissed my hand. They said, 'At least before we die, we are having our native food.'" One Tibetan, a man too weak to walk or stand, gave her his hat, in which a tiny portrait of the Dalai Lama was tied with thread. "After that,

I always wore the hat. This most precious gift gave me hope."

When asked how she survived, Adhe says it was through daily prayer. Today, she lives in two rooms with her husband, in Dharmshala, India. She wakes at dawn, makes an offering at her altar, and prays until noon. She then goes to meet and help new Tibetan refugees. She says that though the jailers, labor camps, and suffering of her fellow prisoners comes back to her constantly in dreams, every morning, as soon as she awakens, she is happy again.

The Chinese told her long ago, as they shot her brother-in-law to death in front of her, "Now you see who has won." Yes, now we see who has won.

---

took pride in helping take care of the family, they didn't feel as trapped. "You pick yourself up, give yourself value," Brown says. "If you can't change a bad situation, you can at least nurture yourself. Make yourself a place for intelligence and competence, surround yourself with things that help you stabilize, and remember what you're trying to do."

■ *And it's equally important to actually recognize one's own strengths.* Many people don't. Teaching them such self-recognition is a major part of the approach that the Wolins try when helping adults build a newly resilient approach to life. They are among a small group of professionals testing the idea that resilience can be taught, perhaps by training counselors and psychologists to focus on building strengths in their clients.

A WHOLE NEW VIEW OF STRENGTH

Steve Wolin tells a story about one of his clients, a woman whose father—if he felt threatened or challenged in any way—would batter the offender. The woman, who was whipped throughout her childhood, saw herself as helpless. But Wolin encouraged her to see it differently: she was smart; she had learned how to recognize and respond to her father's moods; she

was an accomplished strategist. "We encourage people to reframe the way they see themselves," he says. "We call this Survivor's Pride." Insight is only one of the abilities that he tries to persuade his clients to value. Others include humor, independence, initiative, creativity, and morality.

Edith Grotberg, who heads an international resilience project, tries to help people organize their strengths into three simple categories: I have (which includes strong relationships, structure and rules at home, role models); I am (a person who has hope and faith, cares about others, is proud of oneself); and I can (ability to communicate, solve problems, gauge the temperament of others, seek good relationships). She finds, by the way, that men tend to draw most confidence from the "I can" category and women from the "I am."

"But all people have the capacity for resilience," says Grotberg, Ph.D., from the University of Alabama, Birmingham. "We just have to learn to draw it out and to support them."

This is, without hyperbole, a breathtaking change from the approach of psychology just a few decades ago. Seligman describes the old approach—which he says took over after World War II—as victimology, an emphasis on psychological damage driven by the parallel emphasis of the same period on nurture over nature. Psychologists believed that people were shaped by environment—a harmful environment would inevitably result in a bent or skewed or non-functional person.

So powerful was this notion that when Norman Garmezy, Ph.D., of the University of Minnesota, studied children of severely depressed mothers and found that some of them seemed healthy and capable, his first response was that he had misdiagnosed the mothers. Michael Rutter, Ph.D., of the Institute of Psychiatry in London, tracked children of drug-addicted mothers, and reported the same, I-must-have-screwed-up reaction. But their findings—that at least one-fourth of the children seemed both confident and capable—wouldn't go away. Garmezy and Rutter re-focused on the coping skills of people in troubled families. Their work laid the foundation for today's entire generation of resilience researchers. This year's annual American Psychological Association meeting is focused on recognizing human strengths.

Garmezy gives credit to Emmy Werner for nurturing the field. "Mother Resilience" is his favorite nickname for her, and it makes her laugh. "Maybe at the age of 68, it needs to be changed to 'Grandmother Resilience,'" she jokes.

Her primary work for the last thirty years, a longitudinal study of native Hawaiians, does provide a terrific case study of resilience research in motion. Werner has followed the same group of islanders from late adolescence into middle age. She titled her last book about them *Overcoming the Odds.*

There are 505 people in Werner's study, born in 1955 on the small and beautiful island of Kauai. About half were born into poverty, mostly the children of sugar plantation workers. It should be noted, from the beginning, that this is almost a guarantee of poverty; the island sugarcane industry has been falling away almost since these children were born. Not surprisingly, many of them grew up in homes dominated by fears of even greater poverty, where alcoholism and anger and abuse were just the way of life.

As Werner says, victim-theory would have predicted that by the time those children reached their twenties, they would have simply sunk into a swamp of crime and unemployment. And most did. Yet there was still that startling number: one-third never seemed to sink at all; they did well in school, began

promising careers and—most important—defined themselves as capable and competent adults.

One woman profiled, Leilani, is a working mother of three sons; she is in her thirties, and put it like this: "I am proud of myself as a person now. I have received so much fulfillment in being a wife, mother, and worker. I feel I've finally grown up."

YOUR PAST IS NOT A PRISON

The ground breaking point in Werner's work—which Garmezy calls "the best single study" on resilience in children—is that one's upbringing does not build a lifelong prison. "The first, biggest surprise to me was that so many recovered," Werner said. And when she went back and looked at the islanders in their thirties and forties, she found that even more had determined not to repeat their parents' lives. More than half had fallen, as teenagers, into petty crime. Of that group, only 10 percent of the females and one-fourth of males still had criminal records in their thirties. The majority had struggled, but had moved on.

One of the unexpected spinoffs of resilience research, then, is that it has begun breaking down myths of failure—that having a bad beginning makes one a bad person; that abused children grow up to be abusers. In fact, the statistics are very comparable to Werner's resilience study. New studies show that a clear one-third of abused children grow up determined never to lay a hand on their children, and they don't.

And they can choose that even after childhoods that seem to hang on the dark edge of nightmare. John DeFrain and his colleagues—Nikki DeFrain, Linda Ernst, and Jean Jones—have compiled a horrific portrait of an abusive childhood, based on interviews with forty adults identified as growing up in traumatic family situations.

Consider a typical description from their study: "One time I remember sitting at the dinner table when I was six or seven. My sister was told to say grace and when she finished, my dad slapped her across the face. He told her she said it wrong and to do it over. She started again and he slapped her again. This went on and on, over and over, faster and faster, for what seemed like half an hour. I remember sitting there across from her, paralyzed. I just kept praying, 'Get it right.' The problem was, she was doing it right, just the way we learned it in Sunday School."

Or this one: "I learned to survive by letting myself go. I taught myself how to go numb, to have no feeling. I can feel myself floating out of my body and look down on a little girl screaming. A little dark-eyed girl sits in a big over-stuffed chair. She does not move or whimper, but prays that her mother will forget she is angry at her. 'I'm sorry, I'm sorry,' keeps playing in her ears, but she can't remember what for. 'I did my homework,' she reminds herself. 'I made my bed this morning and didn't forget to clean my room.' And then she loses herself in the cracks in the ceiling with the first blows to her head."

No one just bounces back in that type of situation, and DeFrain emphasizes this with great intensity: "I think if society comes to the conclusion that there are some magical little children out there who are somehow inoculated against savagery and violence, we will look the other way as children continue to be traumatized."

But as his work also emphasizes, if a family situation is insane, most people will build, within it, their own sanctuary and sanity.

They learn the tricks of mental distance, as did the little girl in the big chair. They escape: into music and books. Skills aren't only a way to build a better future, they are a safe house. "I took piano and sang in the church choir as well as the school choir," one woman said. "At home, I was quiet and stayed in my room most of the time. Away from home, I was cheerful and upbeat." Many braced themselves with religious faith; in DeFrain's study, people almost unanimously said that they had received little help from people in the church—56 percent said they had no one to talk to—but that they held to the idea of guardian angels or a God who, as one man puts it, "will always love me and forgive me."

DeFrain and his colleagues asked every person in their study if childhood still hurt. "If you're an eight-year-old girl and you're getting pounded every day, and all you have is a belief that there's a God out there who loves you, is that a wonderful story?" he asks. Not one person in his study said that they had left their childhood unscarred. Eleven percent said they considered themselves bare survivors, but an astonishing 83 percent said they had moved past, were transcending

their childhood, building an adult life they could be proud of.

Ann S. Masten, Ph.D., a professor of psychology at the University of Minnesota, reports a similar balancing of pain and determination in a study of Khmer-American teenagers in Minnesota, children of families who fled Cambodia.

"During the Pol Pot years, from 1975 to 1979," says Masten, "they were very young children, and most lived for many years afterwards under difficult conditions in Thai refugee camps. These children have lived through the unspeakable horrors of war. And most of them have witnessed torture and the death of family and friends from awful violence and starvation, or forced labor and other terribly traumatic events."

There's no arguing that many still suffer the consequences, Masten concedes. "They still have nightmares, periods when they are jumpy and cannot concentrate, or get depressed and anxious. For instance, when the Persian Gulf War was broadcast live on television, many Cambodians experienced an upsurge of the symptoms of trauma from their own wartime experiences."

"Yet these young people are living in Minnesota, getting on with their lives, worrying about what they are going to wear to the prom, or what college they are going to. They are absolute, living testimony to the human capacity for resilience."

RECRUITING HELP: THE MAGIC AND THE MYSTERY

Can one do that on their own, rise above the terrifying parent, the terrible neighborhood, or the trauma of living in a war zone? Resilience researchers find—anecdotally, at least—that there are individuals who possess an extraordinary will to transcend, to make their lives work. David Miller, who is studying African-American teenagers living in the drug-plagued neighborhoods of Cleveland, tells of one boy who made up his mind that he would not do drugs, not join a gang, not fall like his friends around him.

"They wanted him to, but he refused," says Miller. "He was threatened and he was beaten up and he steadfastly remained outside. He took the beatings, and he fought back. He said, 'I'm not doing this.'

Eventually, they left him alone. He's now a freshman in college."

Can you teach that kind of inner resolve? "No, I don't think so," Miller says. "You can teach people to understand consequences; you can teach them ways to go at life, so that when trauma strikes, they don't become overwhelmed. You can teach them ways to find strength. After all, it doesn't take strength to go the wrong way. It doesn't require any effort."

Miller—and, really, everyone in the field of resilience—emphasizes the importance of someone else's presence. Parents, first and best of all, who believe in you, and, if that fails, neighbors, friends, teachers. The foremost element in transcending trouble is not having to do it alone. Emmy Werner found that many islanders in her study group pulled their lives together when they married. There's an element of obvious common sense here—we all need love and hope and help. At an informational meeting for members of Congress in March 1996, Masten put it like this: "The most important message I have for you today is that there is no magic here."

But Steve Wolin points out that people who emerge successfully from tough times tend to be very good at recruiting people into a support system. He gives the example of a high school boy living in his girlfriend's basement. The boy's parents were drug addicts; his home life was awful, and the girl's mother, who liked him, had offered him a temporary home. He told Wolin that he courted the mother, studying the foods she liked best, bringing gifts like spaghetti sauce and loaves of French bread.

"I want people to see that this is not being manipulative," Wolin said. "This child was not a user. This is a strength." The boy was working after school to provide food for his younger brothers. He was also considering dropping out and taking a second job, to get them better clothes.

Peg Heinzer, who holds joint nursing appointments at LaSalle University in Pennsylvania and Albert Einstein School of Medicine in New York, studied the ways in which children cope with the death of a parent. Heinzer began by trying to help her own five children. Her husband, their father, died a decade ago of lymphoma. Her children ranged from eight to 17 at the time. One of her sons wrote a school paper on role models that began: "The person I most admire is no longer alive."

Determined to provide a strong and loving, single-parent home, she set out to explore whether love really made a difference. To her surprise, the child's attachment to the surviving parent did not directly predict a strong recovery. But children who came from supportive homes had a great ability to build extended networks; they were likable and considerate of others. "They were all delightful," she recalls. "I went into 89 homes and, in every case, the teenagers offered me something to drink or eat and made sure I was comfortable."

And that quality, she thinks, made them good at asking for help. "We need to be able to talk about the hard times," she says. "And I think we can teach people that it's okay to ask for help."

Miller can still remember the names of everyone on his grandparents' street: there was Mr. Sam and Miss Bertha and the Harrisons and the Watts. Those neighbors hired him to do chores, invited him to drop in for snacks, and urged him on to a better life. He recalls people constantly advising him on good manners, good grades. "It's as if you attract it. People see possibility in you. They would say to me, 'David, you be someone.' It's as if you just attract people who believe in you."

And if one is not a born recruiter, it turns out, organized programs can still make a remarkable difference. For example, a 1996 analysis of the Big Brother/Big Sister Program conducted by Public/Private Ventures, provided some remarkable statistics of success: The study looked at children from poor, single-parent homes where there was a high incidence of violence. Among children involved in the Big Brother/Big Sister program, first time drug use was 46 percent lower, school absenteeism was 52 percent lower, and violent behavior was 33 percent lower.

WHY SCHOOL COUNTS

Education remains one of the most important factors in resilience; its greatest side effect is the belief that one is building a roadway out of despair. One girl in Miller's study, the daughter of drug addicts, told him she felt completely isolated, except for school. There she felt competent. She is also now in college, he says. Werner found, in fact, that the ability to read at grade level by age ten was a startling predictor of whether or not poor children would engage in juvenile crime; at least 70 percent of youthful offenders were in need of remedial education by the fourth grade.

This has led some researchers to suggest that intelligence is a key factor in resilient behavior. But Werner argues that we should turn that around: if scholastic competence is important in rising above adversity, then, she says, that suggests we should put more effort into teaching children well in those early years. We don't have to fully understand resilience to concentrate on basics, such as fostering competence in school, learning to find help, learning to plan and set goals.

Peg Heinzer recalls that after her husband died—in a period when she felt that she might simply wash away in grief—she set tiny goals for herself. On her drive to graduate school, there was one particular intersection where she would begin to weep every day. She'd arrive in class with her lap drenched with tears. The first day that she made it through that intersection without weeping, she took as a measure of healing—that she was going to be all right.

"It's more than just surviving," she says now. "I built a new life. I raised five caring and close children. I'm proud of myself. I'm happy."

JOY: THE SILVER LINING

Actually, here is one place where we could let the red rubber ball back in. There can be a real joyfulness to the rebound. I've seen it in my son when he goes back to school the next day, plays with his friends again, and that day, partly by pure contrast, is just a wonderful day.

There's a triumph to overcoming the odds, one that doesn't come when you begin on high and stable ground. And many people, once they've made it through, have strong faith in themselves and their strengths, more so than those who have not been tried so hard. "The key person is me," one man told DeFrain. "In some ways I was fortunate to learn to rely on myself. I knew I had to make the change. No one else could do it for me."

DeFrain and his colleagues found that more than 80 percent of the people they talked to, while hating their childhoods, believed they'd become better people because of it: stronger, kinder, and quicker to care for and help others. People who've overcome adversity often try to make the world a better place. One of Steve Wolin's clients came breathlessly to a session after unhesitatingly jumping between an elderly woman and a group of muggers.

"We hear it all the time," Wolin says. "I've been tested and I've prevailed and I'm better for it. We think that kind of reaction fits right into Survivor's Pride, and that it's an antidote to the pain. And that's part of it too. These are people who have struggled mightily and who have wounds to show for it. No one's story is a clean one; we are all a checkerboard of strengths and scars."

Certainly, Miller sees himself that way. He recognizes how far determination has brought him: "I'll work and work to achieve something. I said that to a friend once, that there are people out there who are smarter than I am, but no one who will work harder." There are still things that come hard for Miller, though. His marriage failed; his wife and 13-year-old daughter live in another state. "Yes," he says, slowly, "there are things I wish I did better, that I work on still."

And his voice falls away from the pure confidence that it holds when he describes his work.

Resilience, as Werner points out, is many different things. It is multifaceted. We all respond differently to different challenges. And no one yet understands how the facets come together; no one can predict when we will be strong or when our strengths will fail us. On that point, there is rare unanimity among researchers: "We aren't there yet," says Peg Heinzer; "We need to evaluate," explains Emmy Werner; "We need more research," replies Ernestine Brown. "We don't want to think we're studying invincibility."

A child may dream along the power lines, if that's the only avenue. And the fact that the child follows the dreams? Does that come from an inner strength we don't understand or one that we do? Miller himself recognizes that his childhood led him, not simply to the town of Cleveland, but far beyond, to begin to map the power of the human soul.

CRITICAL THINKING QUESTIONS

1. According to the article, can the skills people need to overcome adversity be taught? If so, what skills might be best to teach and at what ages? Take one of the skills you listed and outline a plan for how long it could be taught at the age you think would be most suitable.

2. The article states that "the ability to turn around is always there." What are the implications of this statement for the availability of mental health services?

3. Edith Grotberg was cited in the article as saying that people can organize their strengths into three major categories: *I have, I am,* and *I can.* Furthermore, she asserts that men tend to draw most strength from *I can* statements, whereas women rely more on *I am* statements. Based on the research on gender differences, what might explain this difference in perspective? How might gender differences affect people's abilities to learn the skills you listed in Question 1?

4. What role might self-fulfilling prophecy play in the life of someone who has experienced trauma? In other words, if someone believes that being abused as a child necessitates his or her becoming an abuser as an adult, will that belief affect his or her behavioral choices? Explain your answers.

5. Some people see themselves as victims, rather than survivors, of past injustices. What do the findings presented in this article suggest about having a victim mentality?

ARTICLE 41 _____

Most people are aware that many species of animals claim and mark territory as belonging to them. Another animal, including a human, entering that territory may elicit defensive behaviors on the owner's part.

Humans also tend to claim territory as belonging to them. Some territories, such as our bedrooms, belong exclusively to us. If someone came into your bedroom and rearranged the furniture without your permission, you would most likely be unhappy, to say the least. In contrast with these private territories, we also lay claim, albeit temporarily, to semiprivate spaces. An example of this might be a seat in a classroom. You do not own it, and other people use it when you are not there, yet you most likely sit in the same seat every time you attend a particular class. If, after attending the class for a semester, you arrive one day to find someone else sitting in your seat, you might feel a little annoyed at whomever took your seat. Finally, there also are public spaces, which we use temporarily but over which we lay no claim other than when we actually occupy the space. Seats in a movie theater or in a restaurant are examples of this type of territory.

The following classic article by Robert Sommer and Franklin D. Becker concerns public spaces. When we occupy a public space, it sometimes becomes necessary to leave it for a short time. How can we effectively indicate that the space is already taken? Also, sometimes we want to protect our space from the presence of others. How can we keep people from sitting next to us if we want to be alone? These are but two of the questions addressed in a series of studies presented in the article.

Territorial Defense and the Good Neighbor

■ Robert Sommer and Franklin D. Becker[1]

A series of questionnaire and experimental studies was designed to explore how people mark out and defend space in public areas. The use of space is affected by instructions to defend actively the area or retreat, by room density, and by the location of walls, doors, and other physical barriers. Under light population pressure, most markers are capable of reserving space in a public area, but more personal markers have the greatest effect. As room density increases, the effect of the marker is seen in delaying occupancy of the area and in holding onto a smaller subarea within the larger space. Neighbors play an important part in legitimizing a system of space ownership.

The concept of human territoriality is receiving increased attention. In addition to the popular books by Ardrey (1961, 1966), a number of social scientists have become impressed with the utility of the concept (Altman & Haythorn, 1967; Esser et al., 1965; Hall, 1966; Lipman, 1967; Lyman & Scott, 1967). Hediger (1950) defined a territory as "an area which is first rendered distinctive by its owner in a particular way and, secondly, is defended by the owner." When the term is used by social scientists to refer to human behavior, there is no implication that the underlying mechanisms are identical to those described in animal research. The major components of Hediger's defini-

Reprinted from the *Journal of Personality and Social Psychology*, 1969, *11*, 85–92. Copyright 1969 by the American Psychological Association. Reprinted by permission.

tion are *personalization* and *defense*. Roos (1968) uses the term *range* as the total area an individual traverses, *territory* as the area he defends, *core area* as the area he preponderantly occupies and *home* as the area in which he sleeps. Goffman (1963) makes the further distinction between a territory and a jurisdiction, such as that exercised by a janitor sweeping the floor of an office and keeping other people away. Territories are defended on two grounds, "you keep off" and "this space is mine." Jurisdictions are controlled only on the former ground; no claim of ownership, no matter how transitory, is made.

In a previous study, the reactions to staged spatial invasions were investigated (Felipe & Sommer, 1966). There was no single reaction to a person coming too close; some people averted their heads and placed an elbow between themselves and the intruder, others treated him as a nonperson, while still others left the area when he came too close. The range of defensive gestures, postures, and acts suggested that a systematic study of defensive procedures would contribute materially to our knowledge of human spatial behavior. Following the tradition of ecological research, the studies would be undertaken in naturally occurring environments.

QUESTIONNAIRE STUDIES

During previous observations of library study halls Sommer (1967) was impressed by the heavy concentration of readers at the side-end chairs. Interviewing made it clear that students believed that it was polite to sit at an end chair. Someone who sat, for example, at a center chair of an empty six-chair table (three chairs on each side) was considered to be "hogging the table." There appeared to be two styles by which students gained privacy in the library areas. One method was avoidance, to sit as far away from other people as one could. The other method was offensive ownership of the entire area. To study the two methods of gaining privacy, a brief questionnaire was constructed which presented the student with table diagrams containing 6, 8, and 10 chairs, respectively (Sommer, 1967). Two forms to the questionnaire were distributed randomly within a class of 45 students. Twenty-four students received avoidance instructions: "If you wanted to be as far as possible from

the distraction of other people, where would you sit at the table?" Twenty-one other students in the same class were shown the same diagrams and given the offensive display instructions: "If you wanted to have the table to yourself where would you sit to discourage anyone else from occupying it?" Even though both sets of instructions were aimed at insuring privacy, the two tactics produced a striking difference in seats chosen. Those students who wanted to sit by themselves as far as possible from other people overwhelmingly chose the *end* chairs at the table, while those students who wanted to keep other people away from the table almost unanimously chose the *middle* chair.

When the findings were discussed with architect James Marston Fitch, his first question concerned the location of the door in regards to the table. This seemed a good question, since the preferred location for retreat or active defense should be guided by the path the invaders would take or by the most accessible escape route. The previous diagrams had depicted only a table and chairs, so it seemed necessary to undertake another study in which the entrance to the room was indicated. This conception of the study suggested that additional information could be obtained on the ecology of retreat and active defense by varying the location of walls and aisles and the table size.

Method

The present study involved four diagrams, each one drawn on a separate 8 1/2 × 11-inch sheet.

> *Form G* showed eight rectangular six-chair tables, with a large aisle down the center and two smaller aisles along the walls. (See Figure 1.)
> *Form H* was the same as Form G, only the tables were set against the wall and the center aisle was wider.
> *Form J* was a hybrid of G and H, with the right row of tables against the wall and the left row of tables away from the wall.
> *Form I* contained one row of four-chair tables and one row of eight-chair tables, with aisles in the center and along both walls.

Four different sets of instructions were used with the forms (two defense styles and two densities), but

FIGURE 1 / Arrangement of Tables and Chairs in Form G

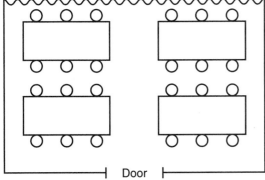

Door

any single subject received only one set. One form asked the subject where he would sit if he wanted to be by himself and away from other people—the retreat instructions. The other form asked where he would sit if he wanted to keep other people away from the table—the active defense instructions. In each case, the prospective room density was also indicated. On half the questionnaires, it was stated that room density was likely to be low throughout the day and very few people would be using the room, while remaining subjects were told that room density was likely to be high and many people would be using the room. All the instructions described the room as a study hall such as that already existing in the campus library, and the respondent was informed that he was the first occupant in the room, so he could take any seat he wanted. Booklets containing some combination of instructional set (Defense Style × Room Density) and two diagrams in random order were passed out randomly among 280 students in introductory psychology classes.

Results

Hypothesis 1 stated that during the retreat condition people gravitate to the end chair closest to the wall. During the active defense condition they make greater use of the center and aisle chairs. Hypothesis 1 was confirmed beyond the .01 level. During the retreat conditions 76% of the subjects occupied a wall chair

compared to 48% during the active defense condition.

Hypothesis 2 stated that with the retreat instructions the subjects face away from the door, while they face towards the door with the active defense instructions. The data disclose a preference in all conditions for a subject to sit with his back to the door—60% of the subjects faced away from the door compared to 40% who faced towards it. However, the results were still in the predicted direction since 44% of the subjects in the active defense condition faced the door compared to 36% in the retreat condition ($p < .05$).

Although the authors had imagined that the use of different-sized tables and the variation in wall placement would influence seating patterns, specific hypotheses had not been formulated. In all conditions there was a marked preference for chairs towards the rear of the room. Overall, 79% selected chairs in the rear half of the room. However, occupancy of the rear was significantly higher with the retreat instructions under high room density than in any of the other conditions ($p < .05$). There was also a highly significant preference for the four-chair tables when they were paired with the eight-chair tables, with 73% selecting a small table compared with 27% selecting a large table. There was a slight trend in the active defense condition to make greater use of the small tables, but this was not statistically significant.

When tables against the wall were paired with tables with aisles on both sides, 62% of the subjects selected a table against the wall compared to 38% who chose a table with aisles on both sides ($p < .001$). As an independent variable, description of the projected room density as high or low made very little difference in where people sat. However, density interacted with the defense instructions on several of the tabulations. With high density *and* retreat instructions, there was significantly greater use of (a) the rear half of the room, (b) a wall compared to an aisle table, and (c) the chair closest to the wall. In essence, the attribution of high room density increased the degree of physical retreat. It had no observable effects on the active defense conditions.

The results make it clear that room dimension and the location of barriers must be considered if we are to understand the ecology of spatial defense. In a library reading room, the best chair for retreat is at the rear, facing away from the door, next to a wall, and at a small table if one is available. Distance from the door protects the person against people simply walking by as well as lazy intruders who are more likely to sit in the first available chair; facing away from the door tends to minimize distraction and also displays an antipathy toward social intercourse; a wall table protects a person's entire left (or right) side; and a small table reduces the number of invaders in close proximity. At this point the authors felt they had derived many useful hypotheses from the questionnaire data which they wanted to extend using an experimental approach under natural conditions. The first experimental studies took place in two soda fountains, and the remainder took place in library areas.

EXPERIMENTAL STUDIES

Most territories are marked and bounded in some clear way. In the animal kingdom, markers may be auditory (bird song), olfactory (glandular secretions by deer), or visual (bear-claw marks on a tree). Since humans rely almost exclusively on visual markers, the authors decided to test the strength of various markers ranging from the physical presence of a person to impersonal artifacts.

Study 1

The first study took place in a popular soda fountain on campus. The soda fountain was located in a converted office building which still contained a number of small rooms. Patrons would obtain their refreshments at a central counter and then repair to one of the smaller rooms to eat and chat informally. Prior to the study, the authors had been struck by the sight of students walking up and down the corridor looking for an empty room. One of the small rooms which contained three square tables, each surrounded by four chairs, was used for the study. A 20-year-old girl who appeared to be studying stationed herself at a table facing the door. On other occasions during the same hours she stationed herself down the hall so she could observe who entered the experimental room. A session took place only when the room was unoccupied at the outset.

If an all-or-none criterion of room occupancy is applied, the experimenter's defense was not very successful. During only 1 of the 10 experimental sessions was she able to keep the entire room to herself. The average length of time before the room was occupied during the experimental sessions was 5.8 minutes compared to 2.6 minutes during the control sessions, but the difference was not statistically reliable. Although the experimenter was unable to keep the room to herself, she was able to protect the table at which she studied. The remaining three seats were occupied only once during the experimental sessions compared to 13 occupancies during the control sessions ($p < .01$). It seems clear that territorial defense in a public area is not an all-or-none affair. The defender's presence may be seen in a delay in occupancy rather than an absence of invaders and in the avoidance of a subarea within the larger area.

Study 2

The next study took place in a more traditional open-plan soda fountain and, instead of the physical presence of the experimenter, three sorts of objects were used as territorial markers—a sandwich wrapped in cellophane, a sweater draped over a chair, and two paperback books stacked on the table. In each case the experimenter located two adjacent empty tables and arbitrarily placed a marker on one with the other as a control. Seating himself some distance away, he was able to record the duration of time before each table was occupied. The sessions all took place at moderate room density. There were 8 sessions with a sandwich marker, 13 with a sweater, and 20 with the books.

The authors were interested in whether a marker would reserve an entire table as well as the marked chair. The answer for all of the markers was affirmed. The unmarked control tables were occupied significantly sooner than were the marked tables, and the difference was significant for each of the three markers. In fact, in all 41 sessions the control table was occupied sooner or at the same time as the marked table. In only three of the sessions did anyone sit at the marked *chair*. All three were occupied by males, a finding whose significance will be discussed later. It is also interesting to examine the occupancy patterns at the two sorts of tables. The marked tables were eventually occupied by 34 lone individuals and 4 groups of 2 persons, while the unmarked tables were occupied by 18 lone individuals and 20 groups. It can be noted that a group of 2 or 3 could easily be accommodated at a marked table even assuming that the marker represented one person, yet virtually all the groups sat at unmarked tables. It is clear that the markers were able to (a) protect the particular chair almost totally, (b) delay occupancy of the entire table, and (c) divert groups away from the table.

Study 3

A similar study using books and newspapers as markers was undertaken in a dormitory study hall at a time of very light room density. Virtually all the markers proved effective in reserving the marked chair. The only exceptions were two sessions when the school paper which had been used as a marker was treated as litter and pushed aside. After more than 30 individual sessions where virtually all the markers were respected, the authors decided to move the experiments to the main university library where room density was much heavier. It seemed clear that at low densities almost any marker is effective. One qualification is that the object must be perceived as a marker and not as something discarded and unwanted by its former owner. Certain forms of litter such as old newspapers or magazines may, indeed, attract people to a given location.

The locus of study was switched to the periodical room in the university library where room density was high and pressure for seats was great. This room contained rectangular six-chair tables, three chairs to a side. The experimenter arrived at one of the six seats at a designated table at 6:50 P.M., deposited a marker, and then departed to another table at 7:00 P.M. to view any occupancy at the marked position by a student seeking space. During each session, a similarly situated empty chair which was unmarked was used as the control. There were 25 experimental sessions, each lasting 2 hours. The markers included two notebooks and a textbook, four library journals piled in a neat stack, four library journals randomly scattered on the table, a sports jacket draped over the chair, and a sports jacket draped over the chair in addition to the notebooks on the table.

If one compares the average time before occupancy of the marked and the control chairs, it is apparent that all markers were effective. Seventeen of the 25 marked chairs remained vacant the entire 2-hour period, while *all* control chairs were occupied. The average interval before the control chairs were occupied was 20 minutes. Some of the markers were more potent than others. Only one student occupied a chair that was marked either by a sports jacket or a notebook-and-text. Chairs marked by the neatly-piled journals were occupied three of the five sessions, while chairs marked by the randomly placed journals were occupied all five sessions, even though the interval in each case exceeded that of the control chairs. It is clear that the personal markers, such as the sports jacket and notebooks, were able to keep away intruders entirely, while the impersonal library-owned markers (journals) could only delay occupancy of the marked chairs.

An interesting sidelight is that eight of the nine students who sat down despite the markers were males. Since there were more females than males in the control chairs at the same time, the high incidence of males is quite significant. It may be recalled in the previous study that the only three individuals who pushed aside the marker and sat at a marked chair were also males. It is likely that some sort of dominance or risk-taking factor is at work in the decision to disregard a territorial marker. The relationship between personality characteristics and the likelihood of invading someone else's space seems an exciting topic for further investigation.

Another serendipitous finding concerns the role of the neighbor, the person sitting alongside the marked chair, in defending the marked space. In all five trials with the scattered journals, the potential invader questioned the person sitting alongside the marked chair (the neighbor) as to whether the space was vacant. Early in the 2-hour session, the neighbor unknowingly served as the protector of the space. He informed all inquisitive intruders that the space was taken, since he believed the experimenter would return in view of the marker left on the table. As time passed, the neighbor's belief that the experimenter would return to the chair began to wane. At this point he would impart his new conception of the situation to potential invaders, "Yes, somebody was sitting there, but that was over an hour ago. Maybe he's not coming back."

Study 4

Since the role of the neighbor seemed an important aspect of a property-ownership system, the authors decided to investigate it experimentally. The first of such studies involved two experimenters and a person sitting alongside an empty chair. One experimenter seated himself next to a stranger (the neighbor) for 15 minutes and then departed, leaving behind an open book and an open notebook upon the table as territorial markers. After a fixed interval, the second experimenter, in the role of a student looking for a chair, came and inquired about the marked space nonverbally. The nonverbal questioning was a pantomime which included catching the neighbor's eye, pulling out the chair slightly, hesitating, looking at the place markers and at the neighbor, and then back at the markers. The authors had very little experience with such nonverbal cues, but expected that the neighbor's reactions might include verbal defenses ("That seat is taken") and nonverbal defenses (moving the books to reinforce the marker). The independent variable was the length of time between the departure of the first experimenter and the arrival of the second—which was either a 5- or a 20-minute interval. Some sessions had to be terminated when the neighbor departed before the second experimenter arrived on the scene.

Overall the results were discouraging. In only 6 of the 55 trials did the neighbor respond to the nonverbal gestures of the second experimenter in what could be described as a space-defending manner, such as a statement that the seat was taken. Five of the six defensive acts occurred when the experimenter had been away 5 minutes, compared to only one defensive act when he had been away 20 minutes, but considering that there were 55 trials the difference was unimpressive.

Study 5

The authors decided to make another attempt to see if the neighbor could be involved in property defense on a spontaneous basis—that is, if he would defend marked space without being questioned directly. Un-

like in the preceding study, the "owner" attempted to establish a relationship with the neighbor prior to the "owner's" departure. There were two phases of the study; when it seemed that the first approach was not leading anywhere, another approach was used. The markers were a neat stack of three paperback books left on the table in front of a chair. The sessions took place at six-chair tables where there was at least 1 empty seat between the marker and the neighbor. The first experimenter entered the room and found the location meeting the experimental requirements (a person sitting at the end chair of a six-person table with two empty chairs alongside him—O-O-S). The experimenter (a girl) sat down on the same side of the table but one seat away (E-O-S). There were 13 trials in each of the following conditions: (a) The experimenter sat 5 minutes and then departed from the table, leaving her books neatly stacked on the table. During this time she did not interact with her neighbor. (b) Similar to Condition *a*, the experimenter sat for 5 minutes except that during the 5-minute wait, the experimenter asked the neighbor "Excuse me, could you tell me what time it is?" (c) Similar to Condition *a*, the experimenter sat for 5 minutes except that during the 5-minute wait the experimenter engaged the neighbor in conversation four times and, while leaving and placing the stack of three paperback books on the table, declared, "See you later." Fifteen minutes later, the second experimenter (a male) entered the room, walked directly to the marked chair, pushed the books directly ahead of him, and sat down at the table.

The results were again discouraging. In none of the 39 trials involving Conditions *a*, *b*, and *c* did the neighbor inform the intruder that the seat was taken. The authors therefore decided to strengthen the conditions by having the "owner" return and directly confront the intruder. Seven of such trials were added to Condition *a*, 6 to Condition *b*, and 6 to Condition *c*, making 19 trials in all when the "owner" came back and told the intruder "You are sitting in my chair." Each time she hesitated about 30 seconds to see if the neighbor would intervene, and then she picked up her books and departed. There was no verbal response from the neighbor in any of the 19 sessions. The most that occurred would be a frown or a look of surprise on the part of the neighbor, or some nonverbal communication with someone else at the table. Stated simply, despite a flagrant usurpation of a marked space, all neighbors chose to remain uninvolved. It became clear that if one wanted to study the neighbor's role in such an informal regulatory system one would have to question him directly as to whether the seat was occupied.

Study 6

The next study employed two experimenters, a male and a female, and the same three paperback books as markers. Two different girls were used as experimenters, and the sessions occurred in two different, nearby college libraries. The experimental situation involved six-chair tables where the first experimenter (female) sat down at the same side of a table with a subject, leaving an empty chair between them (E-O-S). The goal of the study was to learn whether a greater amount of interaction between the former occupant and the neighbor would increase the neighbor's likelihood of defending the chair. Unlike in the previous study, the neighbor was questioned directly as to whether the seat was taken. There were three different instructional sets, and these took place according to a prearranged random order. In 14 trials, the first experimenter sat at the chair for 5 minutes without saying anything, deposited the marker (three paperback books), and left. Fourteen other sessions were similar except that at some time during her 5-minute stay, the first experimenter asked the neighbor for the time. Ten other sessions were similar except that the experimenter engaged the neighbor in conversation as to where to get a coke, what was happening on campus, and other minor matters. Fifteen minutes after the first experimenter departed, the second experimenter (a male) entered the room, walked over to the marked chair, and asked the neighbor "Excuse me, is there anyone sitting here ?"

The results differ markedly from those in the previous study. A total of 22 out of the 38 neighbors defended the seat when questioned directly on the matter. The typical defense response was "Yes, there is" or "There is a girl who left those books."[2] However, the amount of contact between the first experimenter and the neighbor made little difference in defensive behavior. When there had been no contact,

or minimal contact, between the first experimenter and neighbor the seat was protected 58% of the time, while the use of several items of conversation between the experimenter and her neighbor raised the percentage of defensive responses only to 66%. The difference between conditions is small and statistically unreliable; what is impressive is the great increase in defensive behavior when the neighbor was questioned directly. Two other parameters of the situation are (a) the time that the first experimenter remained in the seat before depositing her marker, and (b) the length of time that the first experimenter was out of room before the second experimenter approached the marked chair.

Study 7

The final study employed two experimenters, both males, and the same three paperback books. The sessions took place at six-chair tables in the library, where the first experimenter again sat down on the same side of the table with a subject, leaving an empty chair between them (E-O-S). He remained either 5 minutes or 20 minutes, depending upon the experimental condition, and then departed, leaving on the table a neat stack of three paperback books. After a designated interval of either 15 or 60 minutes, the second experimenter entered the room and asked the neighbor whether the (marked) chair was taken. The second experimenter recorded the neighbor's reply verbatim just as soon as he was able to sit down somewhere. Since both experimenters were males, it was decided to use only male neighbors in the experiment.

The independent variables were (a) the length of time the first experimenter had been seated before he left his marker and departed and (b) the length of time the first experimenter was absent before the neighbor was questioned by the second experimenter. Some sessions were unusable since the neighbor departed before the designated time and could not be interviewed. Most of the unusable sessions occurred when the experimenter had been absent for 60 minutes. The sessions took place at times of light-to-moderate room density.

Although the design had not called for comparison of marked and unmarked chairs, it is noteworthy that the markers were effective in keeping people away.

Not one of the 64 marked chairs was ever occupied. Regarding the inclination of the neighbor to defend the marked space when questioned by the second experimenter, a content analysis of the neighbor's responses to the query "Is this seat taken?" into defense and nondefense categories revealed that 44 neighbors defended the marked space by indicating that it was taken, while 20 failed to do so either by pleading ignorance or by stating that the chair was empty. The response to a direct question stands in contrast to the lack of involvement when neighbors were approached nonverbally. The length of time that the first experimenter had originally occupied the chair (his tenure period) had no effect on the willingness of the neighbor to defend the chair. However, the length of time that the previous owner was away—either 15 or 60 minutes—had a significant effect. When the former owner had been absent 15 minutes, 80% of the neighbors defended the space compared to 54% defending it when the former owner had been away a full hour ($p < .05$).

Several aspects of the results require elaboration. It is possible that initial tenure periods of 5 and 20 minutes were not sufficiently different. Yet it seems noteworthy that even with a rather impersonal marker, more than two-thirds of the neighbors defended the marked chair upon direct questioning. Most of those who didn't defend it simply pleaded ignorance ("I don't know if it's taken") rather than indicating that the seat was vacant.

After the experiments had been completed, 15 additional students in the library were interviewed on the question of how personal belongings could reserve space. Each student was asked how he would react if he saw someone intrude into a marked space, particularly if the original owner came back and claimed the space (i.e., the actual experimental situation was described to him). The replies were at variance with what the authors had actually found in such a situation. Most of the respondents maintained that they would indeed protect a marked space, although some of them added qualifications that they would defend the space only if the person were away a short time. Typical responses were: "I would protect the person's books and state (to the intruder) that the place was obviously taken by the presence of the books," and "Yes, I would mention that someone was sitting there." Although the majority mentioned specifically that they would protect a marked chair, in the actual situation no one had done so unless approached directly. The ethic regarding space ownership in the library exists, but is paid lip service, probably because institutional means of enforcement do not exist.

DISCUSSION

The present article represents a small beginning toward understanding how markers reserve space and receive their legitimacy from people in the area (neighbors) and potential intruders. Psychologists have paid little attention to boundary markers in social interaction, perhaps because such markers were regarded as physical objects relegated to the cultural system (the province of the anthropologist) rather than an interpersonal system which is the true province of the social psychologist. Generally it is the geographers and lawyers who are most concerned with boundaries and markers. Since the present studies took place in public spaces, we are dealing more with norms and customs than with legal statutes. Stated another way, the situations involve an interpersonal system where sanctions are enforced by the individuals immediately present. Goffman (1963) labels the situations the authors used in the experiments *temporary territories.* It is clear that a person placing his coat over the back of a chair desires to reserve the space, and most people in the immediate vicinity will support his claim if questioned (although they will remain uninvolved if they can); such behavior meets Hediger's (1950) definition of territory presented previously as well as the more simple one provided by Noble (1939) that a territory represents "any defended area." The phenomena the present authors have studied do not belong under other available rubrics of spatial behavior, such as home range, biotope, niche, or life space. The major differences between the experimental situations and more enduring territories is that the latter are meshed with a legal-cultural framework and supported in the end by laws, police, and armies. The marked spaces in the present authors' experiments have no legal status and are supported only by the immediate social system. Occasionally it became necessary to articulate the structure of the system by "requiring" neighbors to enter the situation.

People are now spending an increasing portion of their time in public or institutional spaces, including theaters, airport lobbies, buses, schools, and hospitals, where the use of personal belongings to mark out temporary territories is a common phenomenon. The study of territories, temporary as well as enduring ones, deserves study by psychologists. There is some danger that such work will lose much of its force if some semantic clarity is not obtained. While the ethologist's definition of a territory as "any defended area" has considerable heuristic value, there is no need to assume that the mechanisms underlying human and animal behavior are identical. The paucity of data about human territorial behavior makes it most reasonable to assume that the mechanisms are analogous rather than homologous.

In conclusion, the present series of studies suggests that further investigation of spatial markers is feasible and warranted. The physical environment has for too long been considered the background variable in psychological research. The time is past when we can have theories of man that do not take into account his surroundings. Boundary markers not only define what belongs to a person and what belongs to his neighbor, but also who he is and what it means to be a neighbor in a complex society.

REFERENCES

Altman, I., & Haythorn, W. W. The ecology of isolated groups. *Behavioral Science,* 1967, *12,* 169–182.

Ardrey, R. *African genesis.* London: Collins, 1961.

Ardrey, S. *The territorial imperative.* New York: Atheneum, 1966.

Esser, A. H. et al. Territoriality of patients on a research ward. In J. Wortis (Ed.). *Recent advances in biological psychiatry.* Vol. 8. New York Plenum Press, 1965.

Felipe, N., & Sommer. R. Invasions of personal space. *Social Problems,* 1966, *14,* 206–214.

Goffman, E. *Behavior in public places.* New York: Free Press of Glencoe, 1963.

Hall, E. T. *The hidden dimension.* Garden City: Doubleday, 1966.

Hediger, H. *Wild animals in captivity.* London: Butterworths, 1950.

Lipman, A. Old peoples homes: Siting and neighborhood integration. *The Sociological Review,* 1967, *15,* 323–338.

Lyman, S. M., & Scott, M. B. Territoriality: A neglected sociological dimension. *Social Problems,* 1967, *15,* 236–249.

Noble, G. K. The role of dominance in the social life of birds. *Auk,* 1939, 263–273.

Roos, P. D. Jurisdiction: An ecological concept. *Human Relations,* 1968, *21,* 75–84.

Sommer, R. Sociofugal space. *American Journal of Sociology,* 1967, *72,* 654–660.

ENDNOTES

1. The authors are grateful to Harriet Becker, Martha Connell, Ann Gibbs, Lee Mohr, Tighe O'Hanrahan, Pamela Pearce, Ralph Requa, Sally Robison, and Nancy Russo for their assistance.

2. The neighbors' replies to the intruder's question were scored separately by two coders as indicating defense of the space ("Yes, that seat is taken") or nondefense ("No, it isn't taken" or "I don't know"). There was 100% agreement between the two raters in scoring the replies into defense or nondefense categories.

CRITICAL THINKING QUESTIONS

1. The study noted that, in several instances, males were much more likely to ignore territorial markers than were females. Why do you think this was the case? Design a study to determine why males treat territorial markers differently than females do.

2. This article studied various territorial markers in several different settings. What other public spaces might be interesting to study in terms of territorial defense? Besides the markers used in the article, what other ones might be examined?

3. Following the presentation of Study 7, the authors mentioned that they interviewed additional subjects on the question of how personal belongings could reserve space. These subjects' responses differed from what was found in the research. What does this

suggest about the relationship between what people do and say? Does it imply that how people respond to a questionnaire also may differ from how they really act? Explain.

ADDITIONAL RELATED READINGS

Ruback, R. B., & Juieng, D. (1997). Territorial defense in parking lots: Retaliation against waiting drivers. *Journal of Applied Social Psychology, 27,* 821–834.

Wollman, N., Kelly, B. M., & Bordens, K. S. (1994). Environmental and intrapersonal predictors of reactions to potential territorial intrusions in the workplace. *Environment and Behavior, 26,* 179–194.

ARTICLE 42 _____

It is an unfortunate fact of life that bad things happen to people. Whether it is a major loss, such as a divorce or the death of a loved one, or a more minor setback, such as failing an exam or getting turned down for a date, each of us, at one time or another, has to deal with difficult outcomes and situations. The question is: *How* do we deal with them? For example, do you tend to dwell on the negative events and losses in your life, or do you bounce back relatively quickly from such setbacks? As it turns out, people differ considerably as to how they handle adversity. More importantly, how people view these negative events may have serious implications not only for their mental health but also their physical well-being.

More than two decades ago, Martin Seligman proposed a concept known as *learned helplessness*. Basically, the original concept maintained that people who are exposed repeatedly to uncontrollable, aversive events eventually stop trying to control things. In a sense, they just give up because they have learned that nothing they do really matters. Not surprisingly, having this approach to life is often a factor in depression.

A more recent reformulation of the concept of learned helplessness maintains that it is how someone explains the cause of a negative event that determines whether the outcome will be depressive. Specifically, when you are confronted with a negative event, you can try to explain it along three dimensions: First, you can view the event as *stable versus unstable*. In other words, will this event go on and on, or is it only temporary? Second, you can consider whether the event is *global versus specific*. Does it affect many different aspects of your life, or is it specific and limited to a given situation? Finally, you can attribute the event to *internal versus external* factors. Was it due to your own personal characteristics and behaviors, or was it due to outside factors? In sum, these three dimensions comprise your *attributional* or *explanatory style*.

As noted in the following article by Christopher Peterson, Martin E. P. Seligman, Karen H. Yurko, Leslie R. Martin, and Howard S. Friedman, attributional or explanatory style has been studied mainly as a predisposition for depression. These authors take a different approach by examining how attributional or explanatory style may be related to early death.

Catastrophizing and Untimely Death

■ Christopher Peterson, Martin E. P. Seligman, Karen H. Yurko,
Leslie R. Martin, and Howard S. Friedman

Abstract—Participants in the Terman Life-Cycle Study completed open-ended questionnaires in 1936 and 1940, and these responses were blindly scored for explanatory style by content analysis. Catastrophizing (attributing bad events to global causes) predicted mortality as of 1991, especially among males, and predicted accidental or violent deaths especially well. These results are the first to show that a dimension of explanatory style is a risk factor for mortality in a large sample of initially healthy individuals, and they imply that one of the mechanisms linking explanatory style and death involves lifestyle.

Explanatory style is a cognitive personality variable that reflects how people habitually explain the causes

Reprinted from *Psychological Science*, 1998, *9*, 127–130. Copyright © 1998 by Blackwell Publishers. Reprinted with permission.

of bad events (Peterson & Seligman, 1984). Among the dimensions of explanatory style are

- internality ("it's me") versus externality
- stability ("it's going to last forever") versus instability
- globality ("it's going to undermine everything") versus specificity

These dimensions capture tendencies toward self-blame, fatalism, and catastrophizing, respectively. Explanatory style was introduced in the attributional reformulation of helplessness theory to explain individual differences in response to bad events (Abramson, Seligman, & Teasdale, 1978). Individuals who entertain internal, stable, and global explanations for bad events show emotional, motivational, and cognitive disturbances in their wake.

Explanatory style has been examined mainly with regard to depression, and all three dimensions are consistent correlates of depressive symptoms (Sweeney, Anderson, & Bailey, 1986). More recent studies have looked at other outcomes (notably, physical well-being), and researchers have also begun to examine the dimensions separately. Stability and globality—but not internality—predict poor health (Peterson & Bossio, 1991). This is an intriguing finding, but questions remain.

First, do these correlations mean that explanatory styles are risk factors for early death? Previous studies are equivocal either because of small samples or because research participants were already seriously ill.

Second, is the link between explanatory style and health the same or different for males versus females? Again, previous studies are equivocal because they often included only male or only female research participants.

Third, what mediates the link between ways of explaining bad events and poor health? The path is probably overdetermined, but one can ask if fatalism and catastrophizing predict differentially to particular illnesses. These explanatory styles, as cognates of hopelessness, may place one at special risk for cancer, implying an immunological pathway (Eysenck, 1988). Alternatively, these explanatory tendencies, because of their link with stress, may place one at special risk for heart disease, suggesting a cardiovascular pathway (Dykema, Bergbower, & Peterson, 1995). Or perhaps fatalism and catastrophizing predispose one to accidents and injuries and thus point to an incautious lifestyle as a mediator. Once again, previous studies are equivocal either because illness was deliberately operationalized in nonspecific terms or because only one type of illness was studied.

We attempted to answer these questions by investigating explanatory style and mortality among participants in the Terman Life-Cycle Study (Terman & Oden, 1947). The original sample of more than 1,500 preadolescents has been followed from the 1920s to the present, with attrition (except by death) of less than 10% (Friedman et al., 1995). For most of those who have died (about 50% of males and 35% of females as of 1991), year of death and cause of death are known. In 1936 and 1940, the participants completed open-ended questionnaires about difficult life events, which we content-analyzed for explanatory style. We determined the associations between dimensions of explanatory style on the one hand and time of death and cause of death on the other.

METHOD

Sample

The Terman Life-Cycle Study began in 1921–1922, when most of the 1,528 participants were in public school. Terman's original objective was to obtain a reasonably representative sample of bright California children (IQs of 135 or greater) and to examine their lives. Almost every public school in the San Francisco and Los Angeles areas was searched for intelligent children. The average birth date for children in the sample was 1910 (*SD* = 4 years). Most of the children were preadolescents when first studied; those still living are now in their 80s. Data were collected prospectively, without any knowledge of eventual health or longevity.

In young adulthood, the participants were generally healthy and successful. In middle age, they were productive citizens, but none was identifiable as a genius. The sample is homogeneous on dimensions of intelligence (above average), race (mostly white), and social class (little poverty).

Content Analysis of Causal Explanations

We scored explanatory style of the responses to the 1936 and 1940 questionnaires using the CAVE (content analysis of verbatim explanations) technique (Peterson, Schulman, Castellon, & Seligman, 1992). A single researcher read through all responses in which bad events were described. Examples of questions that elicited such responses include

(from 1936): Have any disappointments, failures, bereavements, uncongenial relationships with others, etc., exerted a prolonged influence upon you?

(from 1940): What do you regard as your most serious fault of personality or character?

When a bad event was accompanied by a causal explanation, the event and the attribution were written down. These events, each with its accompanying attribution, were then presented in a nonsystematic order to eight judges who blindly and independently rated each explanation on a 7-point scale according to its stability, its globality, and its internality. The researchers (supervised by Peterson) who identified and rated attributions were independent of the researchers (supervised by Friedman) who collected and coded mortality information (see the next section).

A total of 3,394 attributions was obtained from 1,182 different individuals, an average of 2.87 attributions per person, with a range of 1 to 13. Each of these attributions was rated by each of the eight judges along the three attributional dimensions. We estimated coding reliability by treating the judges as "items" and calculating Cronbach's (1951) alpha for each dimension; alphas were satisfactory: .82, .73, and .94, for stability, globality, and internality, respectively. Ratings were averaged across raters and across different attributions for the same participant. These scores were intercorrelated (mean $r = .52$), as previous research has typically found (Peterson et al., 1982). The means (and standard deviations) were 4.52 (0.86) for stability, 4.46 (0.64) for globality, and 4.49 (1.29) for internality.

Cause of Death

Death certificates for deceased participants were obtained from the relevant state bureaus and coded for underlying cause of death by a physician-supervised certified nosologist using the criteria of the ninth edition of the International Classification of Diseases (U.S. Department of Health and Human Services, 1980) to distinguish among deaths by cancer, cardiovascular disease, accidents or violence, and other causes. For approximately 20% of the deceased, death certificates were unavailable; whenever possible, cause of death was assigned from information provided by next of kin. Among the 1,182 participants for whom explanatory style scores were available, mortality information was known for 1,179. The numbers of deaths as of 1991 were 148 from cancer (85 men, 63 women), 159 from cardiovascular disease (109 men, 50 women), 57 from accidents or violence (40 men, 17 women), 87 from other (known) causes (50 men, 37 women), and 38 from unknown causes (24 men, 14 women).

RESULTS

Explanatory Styles and Mortality

To investigate the association between explanatory styles and mortality (through 1991), we used Cox Proportional Hazards regressions and checked them with logistic regressions. The Cox approach is nonparametric and assumes that the ratio of hazard functions for individuals with differing values of the covariates (stability, globality, and internality) is invariant over time. We used Tuma's (1980) RATE program for the Cox models, and LOGIST of SAS for the logistic regressions. When all three attributional dimensions were examined simultaneously for the entire sample, only globality was associated with mortality, with a risk hazard *(rh)* of 1.26 *(p < .01)*. Results from the logistic regression analyses (predicting to a dichotomous variable of survival to at least age 65 vs. not) were consistent with this finding; only the odds ratio associated with globality was significant *(rh = 1.25, p < .05)*.

Figure 1 depicts the probability of a 20-year-old in this sample dying by a given age as a function of sex and globality (top vs. bottom quartiles of scores). The point at which each curve crosses the .50 probability line represents the "average" age of death of individuals in the group. As can be seen, males with a global

FIGURE 1 / Probability of a 20-Year-Old Dying by a Given Age as a Function of Sex and Globality (Upper vs. Lower Quartiles)

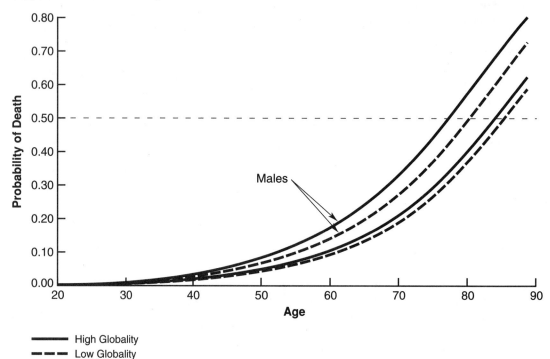

explanatory style were at the highest risk for early death.

To test whether the effects of globality were due to individuals being seriously ill or suicidal at the time of assessment, we conducted additional survival analyses that excluded individuals who died before 1945. The effects of globality remained for males.

Globality of Explanatory Style and Cause of Death

Next we investigated whether globality was differentially related to causes of death (cancer, cardiovascular disease, accidents or violence, other, and unknown) by comparing Gompertz models (see Table 1). When comparing a model with both sex and globality as predictors but constraining the effects of globality to predict equally across all causes of death (Model 2) with an unconstrained model in which globality was allowed to predict differentially to separate causes of death (Model 3), we found that the unconstrained

model fit the data better than did the constrained model. This finding was also obtained when participants who did not survive until at least 1945 were excluded, $\Delta\chi^2(4, N = 1,157) = 13.29, p < .01$.

Globality best predicted deaths by accident or violence ($rh = 1.98, p < .01$) and deaths from unknown causes ($rh = 2.08, p < .01$). The risk ratios associated with other causes were 1.03 for cardiovascular disease (n.s.), 1.18 for cancer (n.s.), and 1.22 for other (known) causes (n.s.).

Finally, we computed a Cox model for prediction from globality specifically to suicide (which had been included in the accident-violence group). The result was marginally significant ($rh = 1.84, p < .06$), but only 25 individuals in the sample with globality scores available were known to have committed suicide. When these 25 individuals were excluded, along with individuals who died of accidents (some of which may have been suicides), and the analyses already described were repeated, the same results were obtained:

TABLE 1 / Goodness of Fit for Gompertz Models Predicting (Age-Adjusted) Cause of Death from Sex and Globality of Explanatory Style (*n* = 1,179)

Model	$\Delta\chi^2$	*df*
Model 1: predicting mortality from sex	705.44**	10
Model 2: predicting mortality from sex and globality, constraining the effect of globality to be equal across all causes of death	715.83**	11
Model 3: predicting mortality from sex and globality, not constraining the effects of globality to be equal across all causes of death	726.62**	15
Model 2 vs. Model 1	10.39**	1
Model 3 vs. Model 1	21.18**	5
Model 3 vs. Model 2	10.79*	4

*$p < .05$. **$p < .001$.

Globality predicted mortality for the entire sample (rh = 1.20, $p < .05$), especially for males (rh = 1.31, $p < .05$).

Additional Analyses

How might we explain the finding that globality of explanatory style predicted untimely death? In terms of simple correlations, men who had years earlier made global attributions experienced more mental health problems in 1950 ($r = .14, p < .001$), had lower levels of adjustment at this time ($r = -.11, p < .02$), and reported that they drank slightly more ($r = .07, p < .08$) than men who had made more specific attributions (see Martin et al., 1995). We examined other variables such as education, risky hobbies, and physical activity from 1940 through 1977, but none of the simple associations with globality was significant. The subsample of individuals for whom we had smoking data available was substantially smaller than the original sample because these data were collected in 1990–1991: however, within this group, no associations with globality were found.

Additional survival analyses were conducted, controlling for mental health and psychological adjustment. In these analyses, the association between globality and mortality risk remained stable and significant. When mental health was controlled, the relative hazard associated with globality was 1.27 ($p < .05$). When level of adjustment was controlled, the relative hazard was 1.29 ($p < .01$). A final model controlling for both mental health and adjustment resulted in a relative hazard of 1.24 ($p < .05$). Globality, although related to these aspects of psychological well-being, was distinct, and its association with mortality was not substantially mediated by these other factors.

Finally, globality of explanatory style was inversely related to a measure of neuroticism constructed from 1940 data ($r = -.15, p < .001$) (Martin, 1996). This finding seems to rule out confounding of our measures by response sets involving complaints or exaggeration.

DISCUSSION

The present results extend past investigations of explanatory style and physical well-being. They represent the first evidence from a large sample of initially healthy individuals that a dimension of explanatory style—globality—is a risk factor for early death, especially among males. Because globality scores were the least reliably coded of the three attributional dimensions and had the most restricted range, the present results may underestimate the actual association between globality and mortality. In any event, our findings were not due to confounding by neuroticism, suicide, or psychological maladjustment. Stability per se did not predict mortality, perhaps because it involves a belief that is circumscribed, that is, relevant in certain situations but not others.

In contrast, globality taps a pervasive style of catastrophizing about bad events, expecting them to occur across diverse situations. Such a style can be hazardous because of its link with poor problem solving, social estrangement, and risky decision making across diverse settings (Peterson, Maier, & Seligman, 1993). Supporting this interpretation is the link between globality and deaths due to accident or violence. Deaths like these are often not random. "Being in the wrong place at the wrong time" may be the result of a pessimistic lifestyle, one more likely among males than females. Perhaps deaths due to causes classified as unknown may similarly reflect an incautious lifestyle.

Explanatory style, at least as measured in this study, showed no specific link to death by cancer or cardiovascular disease. Speculation concerning explanatory style and poor health has often centered on physiological mechanisms, but behavioral and lifestyle mechanisms are probably more typical and more robust. We were unable to identify a single behavioral mediator, however, which implies that there is no simple set of health mediators set into operation by globality.

Previous reports on the health of the Terman Life-Cycle Study participants found that childhood personality variables predicted mortality (Friedman et al., 1993). Specifically, a variable identified as "cheerfulness" was inversely related to longevity. Its components involved parental judgments of a participant's "optimism" and "sense of humor." Because a hopeless explanatory style is sometimes described as pessimistic and its converse as optimistic, these previous reports appear to contradict the present results. However, in this sample, cheerfulness in childhood was unrelated to explanatory style in adulthood. If cheerfulness and explanatory style tap the same sense of optimism, then this characteristic is discontinuous from childhood to adulthood. It is also possible, perhaps likely, that these two variables measure different things: An optimistic explanatory style is infused with agency: the belief that the future will be pleasant because one can control important outcomes.

In summary, a cognitive style in which people catastrophize about bad events, projecting them across many realms of their lives, foreshadows untimely death decades later. We suggest that a lifestyle in which an individual is less likely to avoid or escape potentially hazardous situations is one route leading from pessimism to an untimely death.

Acknowledgments—This research was supported by Research Grants AG-05590 and AG-08825 from the National Institute on Aging, by Research Grant MH-19604 from the U.S. Public Health Service, and by the Health and Behavior Network of the MacArthur Foundation. Some of these data were made available from the Terman Life-Cycle Study, begun by Lewis Terman. Further assistance was provided by Eleanor Walker, Albert Hastorf, and Robert Sears at Stanford University. Help in identifying, transcribing, and rating causal attributions was provided by Laura Brauninger, Julie Brody, Debbie Dormont, Rikki Feinstein, Eric Franz, Elissa Gartenberg, Denise Glenn, Karen Kantor, Margot Morrison, Madhuri Nannapaneni, Elysa Saldrigas. Kristin Shook, and Lynn (Hannah) Smitterberg at the University of Michigan.

REFERENCES

Abramson, L. Y., Seligman, M. E. P., & Teasdale, J. D. (1978). Learned helplessness in humans: Critique and reformulation. *Journal of Abnormal Psychology, 87,* 49–74.

Cronbach, L. J. (1951). Coefficient alpha and the internal structure of tests. *Psychometrika, 16,* 297–334.

Dykema, J., Bergbower, K., & Peterson, C. (1995). Pessimistic explanatory style, stress, and illness. *Journal of Social and Clinical Psychology, 14,* 357–371.

Eysenck, H. J. (1988). Personality and stress as causal factors in cancer and heart disease. In M. P. Janisse (Ed.), *Individual differences, stress, and health psychology* (pp. 129–145). New York: Springer-Verlag.

Friedman, H. S., Tucker, J. S., Schwartz, J. E., Tomlinson-Keasey, C., Martin, L. R., Wingard, D. L., & Criqui, M.H. (1995). Psychosocial and behavioral predictors of longevity: The aging and death of the "Termites." *American Pychologist, 50,* 69–78.

Friedman, H. S., Tucker, J. S., Tomlinson-Keasey, C., Schwartz, J. E., Wingard, D. L., & Criqui, M. H. (1993). Does childhood personality predict longevity? *Journal of Personality and Social Psychology, 65,* 176–185.

Martin, L. R. (1996). *Consonance of archival and contemporary data: A comparison of personality scales constructed from the Terman data set with modern personality scales.* Unpublished doctoral dissertation, University of California, Riverside.

Martin, L. R., Friedman, H. S., Tucker, J. S., Schwartz, J. E., Criqui, M. H., Wingard, D. L., & Tomlinson-Keasey, C. (1995). An archival prospective study of mental health and longevity. *Health Psychology, 14,* 381–387.

Peterson, C., & Bossio, L. M. (1991). *Health and optimism.* New York: Free Press.

Peterson, C., Maier, S. F., & Seligman, M. E. P. (1993).

Learned helplessness: A theory for the age of personal control. New York: Oxford University Press.

Peterson, C., Schulman, P., Castellon, C., & Seligman, M. E. P. (1992). CAVE: Content analysis of verbatim explanations. In C. P. Smith (Ed.), *Motivation and personality: Handbook of thematic content analysis* (pp. 383–392). New York: Cambridge University Press.

Peterson, C., & Seligman, M. E. P. (1984). Causal explanations as a risk factor for depression: Theory and evidence. *Psychological Review, 91,* 347–374.

Peterson, C., Semmel, A., von Baeyer, C., Abramson, L. Y., Metalsky, G. I., & Seligman, M. E. P. (1982). The Attributional Style Questionnaire. *Cognitive Therapy and Research, 6,* 287–299.

Sweeney, P. D., Anderson, K., & Bailey, S. (1986). Attributional style in depression: A meta-analytic review. *Journal of Personality and Social Psychology, 50,* 974–991.

Terman, L. M., & Oden, M. H. (1947). *Genetic studies of genius: IV. The gifted child grows up: Twenty-five years follow-up of a superior group.* Stanford, CA: Stanford University Press.

Tuma, N. (1980). *Invoking RATE.* Unpublished manuscript, Stanford University, Stanford, CA.

U.S. Department of Health and Human Services. (1980). *International classification of diseases* (9th revision, clinical modification, 2nd ed., DHHS Publication No. PHS 80-1260). Washington, DC: U.S. Government Printing Office.

This article is one of a series developed from a large-scale, multiyear, multidisciplinary project on psychosocial predictors of health and longevity. The data are derived from thousands of variables in the 70-year Terman Life-Cycle Study archives or follow-ups. Relevant findings are included to the extent feasible in each report, but multiple publication is necessitated because of the complexity and scope of the project. Care should be taken not to include overlapping findings in meta-analyses or other reviews.

CRITICAL THINKING QUESTIONS

1. Examine a social psychology textbook to learn more about the topics of *social perception* and *social cognition* (also see Chapters 2 and 3, respectively, of this book). How do these topics relate to the findings of this article?

2. This study used a longitudinal method, which is correlational by nature. As you know, a correlation does not show cause and effect, only that two events are somehow associated. Is there some way to test the conclusions of this study *experimentally?* If so, how? What difficulties and limitations would be involved in such an investigation?

3. According to the article, an "optimistic explanatory style" is associated with longevity. Given this, could people (especially children) be taught to develop such an outlook? Or is explanatory style a personality variable that would not be influenced by such interventions? Explain your answers.

4. If lifestyle and behavior choices are an underlying mechanism that can be responsible for early death, what, if anything, can be done to help people who may be at risk due to their pessimistic attributional style? Explain.

5. Review the contemporary literature on learned helplessness. What is the current status of the concept?

Author Index

Subject Index